SECOND EDITION

# HUMAN ANTIQUITY

## An Introduction to Physical Anthropology and Archaeology

KENNETH L. FEDER
MICHAEL ALAN PARK

CENTRAL CONNECTICUT STATE UNIVERSITY

MAYFIELD PUBLISHING COMPANY
MOUNTAIN VIEW, CALIFORNIA
LONDON • TORONTO

*To my parents, who ignited my sense of wonder*
*To Melissa, whose love makes life wonderful*
*To our son, Josh, who is a wonder*

*To Joyce, Gabby, and Stanley*
*who kept me company and provided a*
*sometimes humbling perspective*
*on the human species.*
*And to Jan*
*who knows why.*

*This is the story of how we begin to remember.*
—Paul Simon

Copyright © 1993, 1989 by Mayfield Publishing Company
All rights reserved. No portion of this book may be reproduced in any form or by any means without written permission of the publisher.

Library of Congress Cataloging-in-Publication Data

Feder, Kenneth L.
    Human antiquity: an introduction to physical anthropology and archaeology/Kenneth L. Feder, Michael Alan Park.—2nd ed.
        p.   cm.
    Includes bibliographical references and index.
    ISBN 1-55934-169-6
    1. Physical anthropology.   2. Archaeology.   3. Man, Prehistoric.
I. Park, Michael Alan.   II. Title.
GN60.F43   1992                                                92-26574
573—dc20                                                            CIP

Manufactured in the United States of America
10   9   8   7   6   5   4   3

Mayfield Publishing Company
1240 Villa Street
Mountain View, California 94041

Sponsoring editor, Janet M. Beatty; managing editor, Linda Toy; manuscript editor, Betty Duncan; art director, Jeanne M. Schreiber; text and cover designer, Anna George; illustrator, Joan Carol; cover photograph, O. Louis Mazzatenta, © 1984 National Geographic Society; manufacturing manager, Martha Branch. The text was set in 10½/12 Berkeley by York Graphic Services, Inc. and printed on 50# Mead Pub Matte by Arcata Graphics.

# TO THE INSTRUCTOR

Physical anthropology and archaeology, often treated separately, are, in reality, merely two starting points on the road to a common goal—the understanding of our past.

The two subfields, however, are seen in this integrated way too rarely and so are not often presented as such. This may be somewhat understandable. The authors' specialties, for example, seem at first quite distinct: Feder is an archaeologist who conducts research aimed at understanding the native inhabitants of southern New England. Park is a physical anthropologist interested in the application of evolutionary theory to the biological history of our species. But a full understanding of the human past is simply not possible without the kinds of research *both* of us do. Our approach to the study of human antiquity in this book, then, is to truly combine the ideas, methods, and knowledge of these two subfields into the unified effort they really are. This unified approach is, we believe, an important contribution of this textbook.

We begin in **Part One: Thinking About the Past** with some examples of mythological explanations of the past and a discussion of how these explanations differ from those offered by science. We then give a brief account of some early scientific attempts to study and explain the human past. The section ends with a narrative overview of what we now understand about evolutionary history to help give readers a sense of time and events.

**Part Two: The Study of the Past** describes the theories and methodologies of our present day study of human antiquity. We include here, in separate chapters, a discussion of genetics, the evolution of the primates, the use of animal behavior in developing models of the behavior of our evolutionary ancestors, and the methodology of archaeology and paleoanthropology. In a sense, the chapters that constitute Part Two focus on the intellectual tools we apply to our study of the human past.

**Part Three: The Story of the Human Past** chronicles what we have learned so far about human antiquity. We begin with the origins of the human family and trace our evolutionary journey into the modern era.

Finally, we conclude with an **Afterword** in which we hope to show how this knowledge may be applied to improving our present state and, perhaps, to ensuring that our species' tenure on this planet lasts a little longer.

## WHAT'S NEW IN THE SECOND EDITION

The most immediately obvious change is our use of color in many of the photographs and artwork. We wanted to bring alive the places, things, and species that comprise the human past, and we wanted to make the diagrams and charts graphically clearer and easier to understand.

The anthropology of the past changes at an almost frustrating rate. We have made every effort to bring the book up to date by adding new material on many topics, including: a comparison of science and myth; the nature of the early primates; ethnoarchaeology and remote sensing; relationships among the australopithecines; the evolutionary status of the Neandertals; the origin of anatomically modern humans; mitochrondial DNA and the "Eve" hypothesis; origins of speech and its anatomical correlates in fossils; human biological variation; ideas about the origins of agriculture; and the origins of European civilization.

Based largely on suggestions from users of the first edition, we have changed the order and content of some of the chapters. **Chapter 1: Frameworks** now includes a discussion of science and the scientific method to contrast with the use of mythology in explaining the nature of the world. We have replaced the discussion of Asmat myth with that of the ancient Maya to give a broader range of culture types discussed. **Chapter 3: Evolution: An Overview** has been moved to the end of **Part One.** Before proceeding with "**The Study of the Past,**" it is helpful to have some perspective on just how long the past is and what happened when.

**Part Two: The Study of the Past** has been expanded. A primer in population genetics has been added to **Chapter 4: Understanding Change: Modern Evolutionary Theory,** and the discussions on natural selection and punctuated equilibrium have been revised for clarity. The chapter on taxonomy, the primates, and early primate evolution, **Chapter 5: Learning About the Past: The Primates,** now appears in this section because these topics are indeed tools for our understanding of our past. Another tool is the study of the behavior of nonhuman primates and of contemporary human groups, particularly foragers. This is the topic of a new chapter, **Chapter 6: Learning About the Past: Behavioral Models for Human Evolution.**

**Part Three** remains much the same except for updating and for the placement of **Chapter 13: Human Variation: The Tip of the Twig** at the end of the series of chapters on the fossil record and before the chapters on agriculture, civilization, and historic archaeology.

To make the book more pedagogically useful, we've added a concise summary and a list of **Key Terms** at the end of each chapter; we've introduced a running glossary of the key terms where they first appear, in boldface. All terms are defined within the text, in the running glossary, and in the main **Glossary of Terms.** These three definitions may vary in length and wording; our intention is to help readers truly understand the term rather than memorize the text's definition. We have retained the **Glossary of Human and Nonhuman Primates.** Names included in this glossary appear in the text in boldface italics. Although by convention only genus, species, and subspecies names are italicized, we have bypassed this convention in favor of clearly signaling the reader as to which glossary the term can be found in.

Many of the illustrations have been improved, and many are new. Of particular note is a series of comparative drawings of fossil crania in Chapters 9 through 12 representing *A. africanus, H. habilis, H. erectus, H. sapiens* (archaic), *H. sapiens* (Neandertal), and *H. sapiens* (anatomically modern). As each new species is introduced, its cranium is added to the hominid lineup in the text margin. Students can watch the record unfold.

Finally, we have added new **Contemporary Issue** sections on the Human Genome Project, the consequences of the hypothetical survival of another hominid species, the "Eve" hypothesis, and the impact of agriculture on human history.

As before, references appear in the text in parentheses with full citations in the **Bibliography,** to which many items have been added in this edition. We think this book can thus serve as a useful resource.

This is a book written with the student in mind. We have attempted to at least touch on all relevant topics within this broad subject and to discuss all reasonable points of view around individual issues, giving the pros and cons of each and indicating our leaning, and the reasons for it, where we have one. Some things, naturally, will be left out or will not be covered as completely as some might wish. We can only say that our goal here is to help our readers, particularly anthropology students, to understand what we know about the human past and, just as important, *how* we have come to know it.

## SUPPLEMENTARY MATERIAL

Available with *Human Antiquity* is a complete package of supplementary materials to enhance both teaching and learning.

The *Instructor's Manual* includes a test bank of over 500 multiple-choice and essay questions, chapter summaries, learning goals, suggested activities, and lists of key terms.

The *Computerized Test Bank* is a powerful, easy-to-use test generation system that provides all test items on computer disk for IBM-compatible, Apple, and Macintosh computers. Instructors can select, add, or edit questions, randomize them, and print tests appropriate for their individual classes. The system also includes a convenient "gradebook" that enables the instructor to keep detailed performance records for individual students and for the entire class; maintain student averages; graph each student's progress; and set the desirable grade distribution, maximum score, and weight for every test.

## ACKNOWLEDGMENTS

We wish particularly to thank those of you who responded on the comment cards supplied with the first edition. Many colleagues were generous, both with praise and criticism, and we genuinely appreciate these responses and value the wise counsel contained therein. We would also like to thank those colleagues who went even further and wrote to us with suggestions and reprints that might help us in subsequent editions of the book. In particular, we thank Clifton Amesbury, Jonathan Kent, Patricia Rice, and Ann Paterson. Your suggestions, comments, and criticisms have resulted, we hope and trust, in a much improved second edition.

Thanks again to all those who supplied photographs and artwork. They are acknowledged with their contributions.

Once again, all the people at Mayfield Publishing Company have done a marvelous job in helping make our idea a reality. In particular, we thank Jan Beatty, sponsoring editor, who has been with this book through two incarnations and has been a true partner in our work. Special thanks also to Linda Toy, project editor, Pamela Trainer, permissions editor, Debby Horowitz, marketing manager, Betty Duncan, copyeditor, Jeanne Schreiber, art director and Anna George, designer.

We would also like to thank those colleagues who reviewed the manuscript and provided specific advice and criticism for this edition: Marie Geise, State University of New York at Buffalo; Barbara Hornum, Drexel University; Don Lenkeit, Modesto Junior College; Leanne T. Nash, Arizona State University; and Gail E. Wagner, University of South Carolina.

# TO THE READER

Very simply, this book tells what we now know about the most basic questions we can ask regarding our species: where we came from, why we behave as we do, why we look like we do, what is our place in nature, and what exactly has happened to us during our 5 or 6 million years on earth. And, just as important, we tell *how* we have arrived at our answers to these questions.

Obviously, many academic disciplines focus on aspects of our long tenure on this planet. Our approach is that of *anthropology*—a field that broadly studies the entire human species, and that looks for the connections between our past and our present, one culture and another, and human cultural behavior and biological endowments.

The two areas of anthropology most concerned with the human past are physical anthropology, whose starting point is the biological nature of human beings, and archaeology, whose focus is the human cultural past. Often treated as separate fields, these two anthropological sub-fields are clearly interrelated. One cannot fully understand the history of human culture without understanding how we were *before* we had culture, and how the biological nature of our complex brains made our cultural behavior possible. Similarly, one cannot understand how and why our biology changed over time without understanding how our behavior, especially our cultural behavior, helped us adapt to the various environments we have encountered during our 6-million-year evolution.

The study of *both* human biology and human culture is achieved by

integrating the methods, the data, and the conclusions of physical anthropology and archaeology, and it is the approach we use in this book
to answer the questions posed earlier.

## STUDY HELPS

We have tried to make this book readable and easy to use. All references
within the text are in parentheses, giving the author's last name and the
date of publication, and page numbers where applicable. Details of these
references may then be looked up at your convenience in the **Bibliography**. For each chapter, a **Summary** is provided where the key concepts
and ideas of the chapter are briefly discussed. Each chapter ends with a
section called **For More Information** where we list some additional
works we think would be helpful should you wish to do further reading
on a particular topic. Full references to these works are also in the
**Bibliography**.

Important terms are in **boldface** in the text and are listed under **Key
Terms** at the end of each chapter. These terms are defined in three
places: in the text itself, in a running glossary found in the margins, and
in the main **Glossary of Terms** at the back of the book. Although the
wording of the definitions of a term may differ in these three places,
they all carry the same meaning; we hope that defining a term in several
slightly different ways will help you more fully grasp its meaning.

Scientific names of living and extinct primates are in ***boldface italics***
in the text and are defined (with a pronunciation key) in a second
glossary, the **Glossary of Human and Nonhuman Primates**. It is technically correct to italicize only genus, species, and subspecies names, but
we have chosen to bypass this convention in order to signal you as to
which glossary to use.

Many of our chapters contain a **Contemporary Issue** section. Here,
we have applied the perspective gained in our study of the human past
to some modern problem. The data of human antiquity are not merely
interesting bits of information—fascinating, but esoteric and essentially
useless. The perspective gained from understanding our roots is
uniquely important to our full comprehension of ourselves, past and
present.

# CONTENTS

## PART TWO   THE STUDY OF THE PAST

## PART THREE  THE STORY OF THE HUMAN PAST

# 1

# FRAMEWORKS

*"Where do I come from?"*

This is a question most of us, as children, ask our parents. Eventually, we come to understand that we haven't always been here; we had a beginning, we developed and changed, and we will continue to do so. Finally—and the hardest concept to comprehend—we realize that we will not always exist.

Human groups also are curious about their origins, their development, and their fates. "Where do *we* come from?" we ask as conscious, intelligent, curious beings.

**Figure 1.1** *The Yąnomamö live in villages that consist of a large circular building, surrounded by a log palisade and covered around the edges by a thatched roof, seen here in the background. The people in the picture are visitors to this village, waiting to be welcomed by their hosts for a ritual feast aimed at promoting political alliance and trade relations between villages.*

(Napoleon Chagnon/Anthro-Photo)

# HUMAN ORIGINS: THE FRAMEWORK OF MYTH

For much of the history of our species we have addressed this question with **myths** and stories involving magic and gods. For a long time these supernatural accounts, taken on faith, provided satisfying answers to this most profound of queries.

Virtually every culture has had its own myth explaining the creation of the earth, of plants and animals, and of human beings. **Science**, through a different process, attempts to explain the same things. To better understand the process of the scientific investigation of human origins and development and to comprehend how it differs from the methodology of myth, we will look at three origin tales, one of which you likely know. We will begin with the creation story of the Yąnomamö, Native Americans living in Venezuela and Brazil (Figure 1.1).

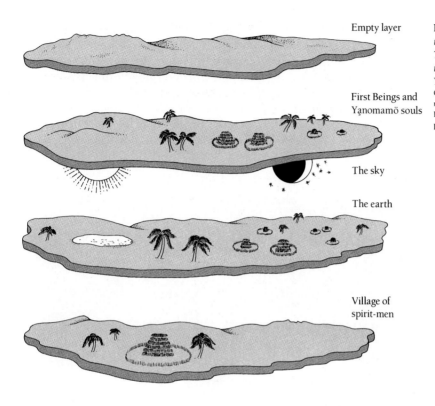

Empty layer

First Beings and
Yąnomamö souls

The sky

The earth

Village of
spirit-men

**Figure 1.2** *A schematic diagram of the Yąnomamö image of the cosmos. The layers resemble the layers of the rain forest canopy in which the Yąnomamö live.* (Redrawn from Verdun P. Chagnon in Napoleon A. Chagnon, *Yąnomamö: The Fierce People,* 2nd ed., New York: Holt, Rinehart and Winston, 1977, p. 27. Reproduced by permission of the publisher.)

## The Yąnomamö

The Yąnomamö hunt and farm in the jungles of the Orinoco River. They tell of their past this way (Chagnon 1977):

In the beginning, they say, the cosmos was made of four layers (Figure 1.2). The top layer once had a function, but now it is empty. The undersurface of the next layer is the visible sky. The layer below that is the earth, a huge jungle dotted with countless Yąnomamö villages. Even foreigners, who degenerated from the Yąnomamö, live in such villages. The bottom layer contains a single village inhabited by spirit people who sometimes travel up to earth to capture and eat the souls of children and so must be constantly guarded against.

The "First Beings"—the Yąnomamö gods—originated along with the layers of the cosmos. Each Being is credited with a specific function, usually the creation of something useful in Yąnomamö life—important plants, tools, fire, animals, knowledge of farming.

The Yąnomamö themselves were created when one of the First Beings, Periboriwä, came to earth to eat the souls of children. Two other Beings shot at him with arrows as he ascended to the second layer. One

**myth:** A story, usually invoking the supernatural, to account for a society's origin and early history.

**science:** The method of inquiry that requires the testing and subsequent acceptance or rejection of hypotheses.

arrow found its mark, and Periboriwä was wounded. The wound bled, and each drop of blood that hit the earth became a Yąnomamö man. Because they were originally created of blood, all Yąnomamö men are, to this day, fierce warriors. One of the men created in this way became pregnant in his legs, and from his legs were born other men and a new type of being, woman. Unlike the men created from blood, these new Yąnomamö people were timid and docile. Later, all the First Beings became spirits and now dwell, along with the souls of departed Yąnomamö, on the second layer, a replica of the "real-world" third layer.

**Figure 1.3** *Renaissance engraving of the expulsion of Adam and Eve from the Garden of Eden, a key event in the Judeo-Christian creation myth.* (Albrect Dürer, Nuremberg, Germany (1471–1528), engraving, 252 × 195 mm. Centennial Gift of Landon T. Clay. 68.187. Courtesy Museum of Fine Arts, Boston)

## The Ancient Hebrews

The ancient Hebrews told two different versions of their creation story. One told of an all-powerful Being who brought order to a chaotic world of water. Over six days he created, in succession, light, land, plants, seasons and days and years, aquatic animals, flying creatures, land animals, and finally, in his own image, man and woman. This Being, God, told the man and woman that all his other creations were for their use, instructing them to "be fruitful and multiply" and to "fill the earth and subdue it."

The second version of the Hebrew creation story concerns both the origin of humans and the early history of the Hebrew people. In this story, a fallible, humanlike god creates water on a dry world and produces a man out of clay. He plants a garden for the man to care for and eat from. Feeling the man needs a partner, God begins creating all sorts of beasts and fowl, which the man names, but none proves to be a suitable companion and helper. So God puts the man to sleep and makes a woman from one of his ribs.

All is well in the garden until one day God, walking there, discovers that his two human creations have eaten from the forbidden tree of knowledge. Now they are too much like gods themselves. Angry, God curses them, condemning them to the "sorrow" of bearing children, to the rule of man over woman, and to the hard labor of farming the land to acquire food. He expels them from the garden (Figure 1.3). Generations pass, during which their descendants become increasingly sinful. God realizes he has erred and produces a catastrophic flood that destroys all his creations except one human family and a few representatives of each other kind of living thing. The story then describes in great detail how these survivors produced all the generations that became the Hebrews and related peoples.

## The Maya

The Maya are indigenous to Central America. More than 2000 years ago, they developed a complex civilization with magnificent pyramids, a sophisticated calendar, and far-reaching trade networks. The Maya also developed a writing system, and it is from one of their books, the *Popol Vuh,* that we can learn about their creation story (Saravia 1965).

Before creation, according to the *Popol Vuh,* there were no people, animals, birds, fish, crabs, trees, or stones. There was only the calm sea. The creators, K'ucumatz and Tepew (Figure 1.4), first made the earth with its mountains, plains, and rivers and then made animals like deer, jaguars, and snakes. The creators assigned each animal its own place to live in the newly created world.

**Figure 1.4** *In the Maya creation story in the* Popol Vuh, *the creators, K'ucumatz and Tepew, first made the earth and its mountains, plains, and rivers.*

**Figure 1.5** *Here, from the* Popol Vuh, *the parrot tells one of the creator beings about the yellow and white corn. The creator then uses the corn meal to make the flesh and blood of the first true people.*

The creators next ordered the animals to speak so that they might praise the creators for their work; the animals, however, could not speak. The creators then decided to make creatures that could; these would be people. The first people, made of mud, could speak, but they had no minds and merely dissolved in the water. Then the creators made people out of wood. These people multiplied and spread across the earth. They could speak but lacked blood and minds, and they did not remember the creators who made them. K'ucumatz and Tepew ordered that they be destroyed; birds plucked out their eyes, and jaguars devoured their woody flesh. Some of these wooden men, nevertheless, managed to escape into the jungle where all that remains of them today are the monkeys. According to the Maya, this is why monkeys are similar to human beings.

Finally, the fox, the coyote, the parrot, and the crow told the creators about the yellow and white corn that grew on the earth (Figure 1.5). The creators ground and mixed the yellow and white corn; from this corn meal, they made the flesh and blood of the first true people. These people had blood and minds, and they worshiped the gods who created them and the world in which they lived.

## Creation Myths

These stories are what we call **creation myths**. Every culture has one or more of them. A creation myth performs several functions. It provides an account of the origin of the world. It tells the story of a people's beginnings and their early history. It lays out the society's world view and belief system. It explains the origin and meaning of a people's rules of social behavior. In having these functions, creation myths ultimately serve to codify, rationalize, justify, and stabilize a given social system—generally under the auspices of some supernatural power.

Consequently, a creation story reflects the history and cultural system of the society that tells it. The mythical layers of the Yąnomamö cosmos, for example, resemble the ecological layers of the rain forest canopy in which they live. Yąnomamö men see themselves as—and indeed they are—fierce warriors who regularly wage war on neighboring villages and generally lead lives centered around violent conflict. Such wars and conflicts have, of course, perfectly concrete explanations. But the Yąnomamö explanation—the abstract justification that maintains this behavior—is found in their creation story of men formed from drops of blood. The subservient position of women in Yąnomamö society and, presumably, the presence of a few men who are not fierce warriors are nicely accounted for by the story of the creation of the timid, docile Yąnomamö from the pregnant legs of one of the first men born from drops of blood.

**creation myth**: A myth that specifically addresses the origin of the world and its inhabitants.

Similarly, the Maya creation story includes animals that were important inhabitants of their world and accounts for the vital role played by corn farming in their culture.

The same sort of analysis, of course, can be applied to the creation myths of the ancient Hebrews. We have come to know these stories well, and they have exerted a great deal of influence on Western culture. They were written down and make up the book of Genesis—the first book in the Jewish Torah (the Old Testament) and the Christian Bible (the Old and New Testaments). Parts of these stories have been traced to the creation myths of the Babylonians and Sumerians, other peoples living in the Middle East at about the same time. But the specific details of the Genesis stories, and even the fact that they were written down, are direct results of the environment and history of the Hebrew people at specific times.

For example, Biblical scholars now think that the Hebrew creation story was first put into writing about 3000 years ago, by a man or men we know only as $J^1$, as a political protest against King David's having moved the seat of government to a new location (Asimov 1969; Buttrick 1952). $J^1$'s reasoning was that such a document would reinforce in the Jewish people the ideas of their common bond, heritage, and commitments to God. About 100 years later, in response to a subsequent political split between northern and southern Hebrew groups, a man or men we call $J^2$ added the details of the second creation story—the one about the humanlike god, the garden, and the flood. Like $J^1$, he was trying to demonstrate the common heritage of his people in order to reunite them.

This attempt failed, and the Jews were divided and conquered by the Assyrians and the Babylonians. When the Babylonian captivity ended in the sixth century B.C., the Jews needed to establish their uniqueness and identity and to formalize their history and cultural heritage. To help accomplish this goal, a group of priests we now call P edited the old writing of $J^1$, $J^2$, and others. They took out some internal contradictions and added some of the history that had taken place since. They also wrote a type of "preface" to the story of the garden and the flood: the account of the six-day creation by an all-powerful god, taken largely from a then-popular Babylonian myth called the *Enuma Elish*.

It is this Hebrew creation myth that is of direct concern to us here. As the very beginning of the basic document of Judeo-Christian tradition, it has had an important impact on many aspects of the development of Western civilization—including the ways in which people asked and answered questions about the history of their physical world and its inhabitants. Our own creation myth, in other words, has deeply affected the way in which Western peoples have studied the past.

## HUMAN ORIGINS:
## THE FRAMEWORK OF SCIENCE

In this book, we focus on human **evolution**, the *scientific* study of the origin and development of our species. The specific science that focuses on humanity, including its biology, behavior, culture, and history, is **anthropology**. Anthropologists study humanity, investigating our origins and subsequent biological and cultural development—in essence, our evolution. In simplest terms, our focus is the past, present, and future of the human species.

A scientific investigation of humanity differs fundamentally from mythic constructs of human origins of the sort just outlined. Paleoanthropologist Misia Landau (1991) justifiably asserts that scientific narratives of human evolution—the "stories" scientists devise for how they think human evolution transpired—are similar in their configuration to traditional folktales. For us, however, their structure is not as important as how they develop, how they are used, and their intent. There are, after all, clearly distinctive differences between science and myth.

For instance, the methodology of mythmaking is highly variable and idiosyncratic; it may or may not be based on observation of the real world. The point of mythmaking is essentially the construction of satisfying stories aimed at explaining some aspect of reality and reinforcing or maintaining a social or political order. The creation myths of the Yanomamö, the ancient Hebrews, and the Maya are just this—tales that, although performing valuable functions, have no necessary grounding in fact.

In contrast to this, the **scientific method** is always predicated on observation of the world and generalization from those observations. In formal logical terms, creating general explanations of how things work based on observation is called **induction**. The general explanations, the "educated guesses" at the rules that govern the way things work, are called **hypotheses**.

But scientists do not stop here with seemingly plausible explanations for how things like volcanoes, the weather, or human behavior operate or how things like stars, planets, plants, animals, or people came into being. Science goes beyond its own reasonable, credible guesses to rigorous testing of these guesses or hypotheses. In science we always ask the question: *If* our hypothesis, constructed from the building blocks of concrete observation, is valid, *if* it accurately describes or explains how some part of reality functions, *then* we should be able to predict what new, specific data will be found by further study. This process of suggesting what *specific* data should be found *if* our *general* explanation is to be supported, is called **deduction**.

**evolution:** A systematic change, through time, of organisms or social systems.

**anthropology:** A scientific study of the human species.

**scientific method:** The method of inquiry that requires the generation, testing, and subsequent acceptance or rejection of hypotheses.

**induction:** Developing a general explanation from specific observations.

**hypothesis:** A testable explanation of a natural phenomenon.

**deduction:** Suggesting specific data that would be found if a hypothesis is true.

By way of comparison, consider the story told in the nineteenth century by the Mpongwe people of Gabon in coastal Africa concerning chimpanzees and gorillas. Just as the Maya perceived similarities between monkeys and people and explained this in the context of their creation myth, the Mpongwe recognized the physical and behavioral similarities between apes and human beings, and they attempted to explain it through their myths. They viewed chimps as being the physical incarnation of the departed souls of highly intelligent and peaceable people; in other words, they thought of chimps as reincarnated Mpongwe. On the other hand, they perceived gorillas as being the embodiment of the souls of less intelligent but fiercer forest peoples. Thus, a curious similarity between people and apes was explained within the context of a belief system that included the mobility of the soul while accounting for a feeling of intellectual superiority.

On the other hand, scientists *hypothesize* that chimpanzees, gorillas, and human beings are so similar because we share a relatively recent common ancestor; in other words, we are evolutionarily closely connected in time. That sounds reasonable, but we don't stop there. *If* our hypothesis is correct that humans and these apes are indeed biologically closely related, *then* our genetic codes—our **DNA** (see Chapter 4)—should be quite similar, and chronologies constructed by DNA comparisons should show our recent divergence. In addition, the fossil record should bear witness to increasing similarity between human ancestors and the African apes as we go back in time (see Chapter 5), and behavioral studies of these apes and humans should show detailed and specific similarities (see Chapter 6). As you will see in subsequent chapters, this is precisely what is found. Thus, we are not content merely to suggest what seems like a reasonable, pleasing, or congenial explanation for the perceived similarity. We predict what *must* be true if our hypothesis of biological affinity is valid, then we go about the task of seeing if those predictions pan out.

In the scientific method, if new data are found through experiment or if further data collection contradicts the predictions derived from our hypothesis, we reject that "plausible" guess and try to come up with a better explanation. If our predictions are supported, we keep the hypothesis (technically, we can never absolutely "prove" it), unless and until something better comes along—that is, an explanation that is superior at predicting, explaining, or encompassing new data. Such constant testing and refining are the hallmarks of science and distinguish science, absolutely, from myth.

Eventually, a hypothesis that holds up under rigorous testing is elevated to a status of a **theory**. Scientists have developed many such theories; the theory of gravity and atomic theory are two developed by physics. As you will see, evolution, as an explanation of how life developed and proceeds on this planet, is a scientific theory from the field of biology. It is a hypothesis that has held up so well and for so long under scientific scrutiny—we are so certain of its validity in a general sense—we view it as virtual fact.

Although evolution is a general theory of life, many specific hypotheses that seek to explain particular aspects of how evolution transpired are still being tested. Much of this book presents the data and arguments that have been generated in the extensive testing of the many specific hypotheses concerning how human evolution proceeded.

Because the general theory of evolution and some specific hypotheses concerning how it may have happened were generated within a cultural framework where the Judeo-Christian creation myth was paramount, we will outline in the next chapter how the theory of evolution itself evolved within that context.

## SUMMARY

People use two basic frameworks for explaining the past. Myths are stories, not necessarily either factual or fictional, created to explain some aspect of the world as a group of people sees it at a given time. Myths satisfy the need to place events in chronological order and in a sequence of causality, and they address the basic questions of how, what, who, when, and why. Many myths, like the three described, specifically attempt to account for a people's origins, for their early history, and for their present lifestyle.

Science also seeks to answer these questions but with a methodology that requires skepticism, testing, and continual reexamination. Science uses observations of real-world data to generate hypotheses. It then tests these hypotheses in an attempt to derive theories—generalizations based on factual data—about the hows, whats, whos, whens, and whys of the world in which we live, including our origin and our past.

What follows in this book is an account of what the scientific method has told us so far about the origin and early history of our species.

## KEY TERMS

myth
science
creation myth
evolution

anthropology
scientific method
induction
hypothesis

deduction
DNA
theory

**DNA**: The molecule that contains the genetic code.

**theory**: A hypothesis that has been well supported by evidence and experimental testing.

## FOR MORE INFORMATION

The best book on the Yąnomamö remains Napoleon A. Chagnon's *Yąnomamö: The Fierce People*.

A useful summary of the archaeology and history of the Maya is *A Forest of Kings: The Untold Story of the Ancient Maya* by Linda Schele and David Freidel.

There are many Biblical interpretations. A standard is G. A. Buttrick, ed., *Interpreter's Bible*. See also Isaac Asimov's *Asimov's Guide to the Bible* and John Romer's *Testament: The Bible and History*.

For a useful discussion of scientific methodology, see *Science and Unreason* by Daisie Radner and Michael Radner.

# 2

# EDEN QUESTIONED: HISTORICAL PERSPECTIVES

So much of what we now know about the past was not known just a few hundred years ago. For most Europeans in the centuries before ours, the biblical framework of history (including the Judeo-Christian creation myth) was the only acceptable way of looking at the past. The stories of the six-day creation, the Garden of Eden, Adam and Eve, and Noah's flood were all regarded as genuine history. These stories clearly defined and limited Western understanding of the past.

In the same way the Maya and the Yąnomamö looked to their myths and legends for information about their worlds, Europeans invoked the Bible as the ultimate source of knowledge, even concerning specific questions of earth history. Many, for example, were curious about the actual age of the world. Over the years, numerous attempts had been made to find an answer, but the most famous—and infamous—was that of Archbishop James Ussher, an Irish cleric. In 1650, through reference to biblical detail and historical records, the archbishop determined that the world was created in the year 4004 B.C. at noon on Sunday, October 23. By his reckoning, the earth and indeed the entire universe were less than 6000 years old. Ussher's calculation was widely accepted, and this date was printed in the margins of many Bibles.

Although we now know that Ussher was wrong, he was perhaps not as foolish as some modern writers would have us believe. After all, he arrived at his figure by careful calculation. There was no claim of divine revelation; it was simple math and historical analysis although based in part on literal interpretations of the Bible.

There were, however, some Europeans and Americans of the seventeenth, eighteenth, and nineteenth centuries who, though still believing in God, began to seek enlightenment about the world around them from a source other than the Bible—that is, from nature itself (Greene 1959). Calling themselves "natural scientists" or "natural philosophers," they began a vigorous exploration of various natural sources of information about the earth and the heavens. The natural sciences that we now know as biology, astronomy, and geology gradually emerged as distinct disciplines. Eden was being questioned.

## UNIFORMITARIANISM: THE CONTRIBUTION FROM GEOLOGY

Some of these early natural scientists still accepted Ussher's claim of a recent divine creation, but when they looked directly at nature they saw mounting evidence for both a greater age than Ussher had calculated and for physical change in the earth itself. The new science of geology described natural features that clearly indicated the earth had undergone vast amounts of change in its appearance. How, then, to reconcile this evidence with the accepted biblical interpretation that the earth was created in its then-present form less than 6000 years before?

The answer for some thinkers was to view the earth's appearance as the result of a series of catastrophes. Noah's flood was seen as the latest—and maybe the most catastrophic—of these occurrences, but not the only one. Perhaps a number of other divine creations had occurred before the one described in the Bible. For reasons beyond the understanding of mortals, God had seen these prior creations as imperfect and

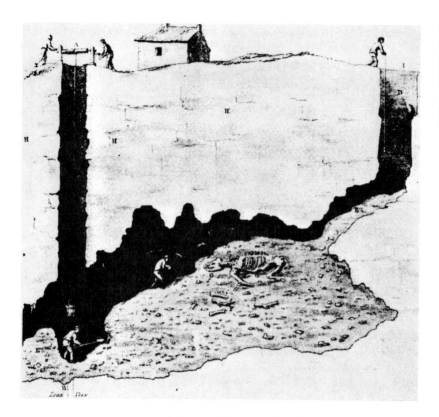

**Figure 2.1** *Early depiction of fossil hunters recovering ancient animal remains in a cave. The seventeenth-century natural scientist Robert Hooke was one of the first to recognize that fossils were the remains of extinct plants and animals.* (From Buckland 1823)

had "erased" them by means of great catastrophic events. Some natural scientists believed these catastrophes—floods, earthquakes, and the like—accounted for the diverse layers of rock and other evidence of substantial change that they had observed. Others, leaning toward a more "natural" explanation, described the catastrophes without reference to divine intervention, but all who adhered to this general interpretation were called, appropriately enough, **catastrophists**.

There were, however, opponents to this view. The Reverend Thomas Burnet, writing in 1681, suggested that the condition of the earth could best be explained and its age determined by reference to ordinary, slow-acting, noncatastrophic natural processes of erosion by ice, wind, and water. Still, he concluded, the world was very young. He argued that if the earth had been ancient, processes of erosion would *already* have worn away even the tallest mountains. Burnet was unaware that mountain building was still taking place, but he was on the right track by looking strictly at natural phenomena even if his conclusion of a young earth was incorrect.

Robert Hooke, another seventeenth-century English scientist, was fascinated by fossils (Figure 2.1). Whereas others contended that fossils

**catastrophist:** An adherent of the idea that the world was produced through a series of catastrophic events.

were mere tricks of nature, Hooke correctly interpreted them as the remains of animals and plants that no longer existed. He contended that organisms became extinct because the earth was always changing. These changes were only partially a result, he said, of the flood of Noah; they were also caused by long-term phenomena—ordinary occurrences like erosion that went on all the time in nature.

It turns out that Hooke was more correct than he knew. We now understand that the geological and biological records are indeed the results of slow, ordinary, long-term phenomena *and* catastrophic events. For example, the extinction of the dinosaurs 65 million years ago appears to have been initiated by the impact of an asteroid with the earth, an impact that radically altered the planet's climate. The differences between our modern understanding of such events and the catastrophism of the seventeenth and eighteenth centuries lie in the divine origin of the catastrophes assumed by early thinkers, and in the idea that all of the earth's features were the results of some regular *series* of catastrophic events.

Like Burnet, however, Hooke also believed that the earth was quite young. He was confused by the fact that ancient histories, such as those of Egypt and China, did not contain descriptions of fossilization actually taking place. He failed to realize that even the most ancient of human histories were far too recent to have borne witness to that process.

By the late eighteenth century, however, we begin to see some scientists doing more than simply looking to nature for confirmation of the creation myth as presented in Genesis. They began doing what had heretofore been inconceivable—they were actually calling into question the historical accuracy of Genesis. In 1774, the first volume of *A Natural History,* by the French scholar Georges Buffon, was published. In this work, for perhaps the first time, a perspective called **uniformitarianism** was articulated. In essence, Buffon stated that in trying to explain the present appearance of the earth and to determine its age,

> We ought not to be affected by causes which seldom act and whose action is always sudden and violent. These have no place in the ordinary course of nature. But operations *uniformly* repeated, motions which succeed one another without interruption, are the causes which alone ought to be the foundation of our reasoning [emphasis ours]. (Greene 1959:55)

What Buffon was saying was simple and straightforward: We can learn about the earth by actually studying the earth. Our world looks the way it does because of known, natural, observable processes—*not* because of catastrophic events that no one has ever witnessed. Rivers cut channels, wind and rain wear away mountains, and waves bite into the shore. These simple, everyday processes can be observed all around us. Given enough time—far more time than Ussher, Burnet, or Hooke had reckoned—rivers could eventually create vast canyons, tall mountains could be worn away leaving flat plains, and coasts could be entirely redrawn.

The implications of Buffon's work were not entirely lost on those who still maintained that the world, exactly as it presently appeared, was the very recent creation of God. In fact, as pressure mounted on Buffon, by the fourth volume of *A Natural History* he felt obliged to retract just about everything he had said about the age of the earth in the first three volumes. Twenty-five years later, however, in *Epochs of Nature,* Buffon tried to accommodate the biblical story of Genesis with his uniformitarian perspective. He suggested that the world was indeed ancient and that earth history could be divided into six distinct epochs. Although he estimated the duration of each of these epochs in thousands of years, it was also clear that the six epochs were meant to correspond to the six days of creation that appear in the Bible.

Perhaps the most important eighteenth-century work on the uniformitarian approach was that of the Englishman James Hutton. In *Theory of the Earth* (1788), Hutton explicitly advanced the notion that by studying natural, slowly working, repetitive processes—that is, *uniform* processes—we could explain the earth's geology and geography. Again, the key element was time. Given enough time—counted in at least hundreds of thousands, not merely thousands of years—the present appearance of the earth could be understood and explained.

According to Hutton, God had created the earth as a self-regulating system. The slow erosion of mountains produced the soil in which plants could grow, which, in turn, could feed animals and humans, for whom it was all created (Figure 2.2). The pressure of this soil on the surface of the earth would, over a long period of time, push up more mountains, ultimately providing new sources of soil on which more plants could grow, and so on. Hutton presented uniformitarianism in a way that made it appear even further to glorify the creator who had produced such a clever, self-sustaining system for the benefit of his crown of creation, man. For such a system to work, however, a 6000-year time span was simply insufficient, which is why Hutton suggested that the earth was at least hundreds of thousands of years old. Even this radical suggestion, however, greatly underestimated the actual age of the earth.

The English geologist Charles Lyell was, perhaps, the most important nineteenth-century advocate for the uniformitarian perspective. It was Lyell who uttered the memorable statement, "The present is the key to the past." In other words, the key to understanding the past rests in our study of those geological processes we can observe in the present. By examining geological data, Lyell was able to estimate the age of specific features of the earth. For example, because the present rate of deposition at the mouth of the Mississippi River (Figure 2.3) can be measured

**uniformitarianism:** The concept that biological and geological processes that affected the earth in the past are still in operation today.

**Figure 2.2** *Bryce Canyon in southern Utah reflects some of the processes of erosion that eighteenth-century natural scientist James Hutton recognized.* (Kenneth Feder)

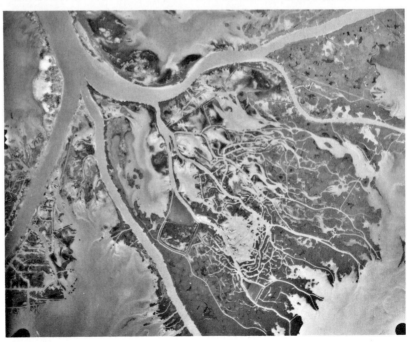

**Figure 2.3** *Aerial view of the Mississippi Delta. By estimating the amount of material deposited in the delta, nineteenth-century geologist Charles Lyell concluded that the Delta was 100,000 years old.*
(U.S. Geological Survey)

and because the total size of the existing deposit in the Mississippi Delta can be estimated, the amount of time required for the delta to be formed can be approximated, assuming a uniform rate of deposition. Lyell's figure was about 100,000 years (1873:44–47).

Many were shocked at the time span proposed by Hutton and Lyell. Their work was attacked, partially on scientific grounds, but largely on the basis that it contradicted the accepted interpretation of Genesis. But when a respected English cleric, Reverend Thomas Chalmers, accepted Hutton's work and the principle of uniformitarianism, proclaiming, "The writings of Moses do not fix the antiquity of the globe" (Howard 1975:69), many others followed. Eventually, almost all scientists viewed the hypothesis of an ancient earth as contradicting only Archbishop Ussher, not the Bible itself. At the very least, the work of Buffon and especially Hutton and Lyell had opened the door for the concept of an old earth—an earth that had existed long enough for the slow erosion of mountains, the cutting of great canyons, the change of animal species, and even, perhaps, the evolution of humanity.

## NATURAL SELECTION: THE CONTRIBUTION FROM BIOLOGY

It was shocking enough for people of the late eighteenth and early nineteenth centuries to realize that the earth on which they lived had undergone significant change. At the same time, they learned that the earth was far older than 6000 years and that the vast changes recorded in the geological record were the results not of a series of supernatural catastrophes but of mostly rather mundane, everyday processes. What may have been most shocking, however, was the further implication of these ideas: That *life* on earth, including human life, may also have undergone change.

Despite the mounting geological evidence for a changing earth, there were still biologists who denied the possibility of biological change. Like some geologists, however, many were willing to go beyond the Bible into nature to seek support for divine creation. They sought to glorify creation by *studying* it. Perhaps the most famous was the Swedish botanist, Karl von Linné (1707–1778), better known to us by his Latinized name, Carolus Linnaeus.

Linnaeus was a **creationist** in that he believed the world and all its inhabitants had been divinely created all at once and had undergone no change (or perhaps only limited change) since that point. But he also observed that living things resembled or differed from one another to varying degrees. A bear and a deer, for example, have far more features in common than either has with an earthworm. There was, Linnaeus felt, a system to God's creative works, and he set out to describe it scientifically.

**creationist:** One who believes that a supernatural power was responsible for the origin of the universe, the earth, and living things.

**Figure 2.4** *The discovery of the fossils of extinct animals, like these dinosaur bones from Dinosaur National Monument on the Utah–Colorado border, showed natural scientists of the seventeenth and eighteenth centuries that life on earth was not static but changing.*
(Kenneth Feder)

Linnaeus looked at the varying degrees of similarity and difference among organisms, a process we call today **comparative biology**. Based on these comparisons, he devised a system of categories and names that identified living things and indicated their physical similarities as he felt God had planned it. Linnaeus's system of classification—we call it a **taxonomy**—was published in final form in 1758. We still use his system today and we'll show you how it works in Chapter 5.

Although Linnaeus thought he was describing a static, unchanging world of living things, he was actually setting the stage for a more complex interpretation. The similarities and differences Linnaeus recorded might just possibly reflect not some divine plan but a series of biological relationships. That is, the *reason* bears and deer are similar in certain ways (they are warm-blooded, bear live young, suckle their young) is that they are biologically related, having once had an ancestor in common—much the same way that you and your cousin are related in that you both have the same set of grandparents as common ancestors. In other words, one could infer from Linnaeus's descriptions that

**Figure 2.5** *The stratigraphic layers exposed by the Green River in Dinosaur National Monument represent millions of years of deposition and erosion.* (Kenneth Feder)

life on earth had indeed undergone change—and many people were beginning to infer just that.

It was the hard evidence of the fossil record that finally made the study of living things completely "natural." Robert Hooke and others had recognized that some fossils (those of dinosaurs, for example) represented the remains of creatures that no longer existed (Figure 2.4). Clearly, this showed that life in general was anything but static. Other fossils (like those of extinct forms of elephants) showed that particular kinds of creatures had undergone change over time.

Moreover, fossils were often found in identifiable layers of rock and soil. We call these layers **strata** (sing. **stratum**) and their study **stratigraphy**. The strata indicate a *sequence* of geological events, the deeper strata representing older events and those closer to the surface representing more recent events (Figure 2.5). Thus, the fossils embedded within the strata represent a sequence of events in the history of living things.

As with geological change, the rapidly mounting evidence for biological change quickly became irrefutable, and by the late 1700s the idea

**comparative biology:** The study of the similarities and differences among plants and animals.

**taxonomy:** A classification based on similarities and differences.

**strata** (sing. **stratum**): Layers of different rock and soil types.

**stratigraphy:** The study of the earth's strata.

had been fairly well accepted within the scientific community and by much of the educated public. The big question, as the 1800s began, was not *if* but *how* change had occurred.

It is interesting to note that even in their attempts to answer this question, some investigators still tried to include an aspect of stability. If living things themselves could not be stable and unchanging, then, they thought, at least the process that brought change about could be stable, dependable, and predictable. And so, one of the first popular proposals of a regular mechanism for biological change was that of Jean-Baptiste de Lamarck (1744–1829).

Lamarck, who we can thank for the very term *biology*, was a French naturalist. In the early years of the nineteenth century, he proposed an explanation for how and why plants and animals had changed—in modern terms, how they had evolved. One part of his idea was absolutely correct; the other two parts were wrong. The correct part was his recognition that organisms and their environments have an intimate and dynamic relationship: Plants and animals are **adapted** to their environments, that is, they possess physical characteristics and patterns of behavior that help them survive under a given set of natural circumstances. When environments change (as the geological record shows they continually do), organisms must alter their adaptive characteristics if they are to survive.

Where Lamarck went astray was in his overall concept of the direction of evolution and in the specific mechanism he proposed for it. He believed that evolution was **progressive**, causing organisms to become increasingly complex. It followed from this that no organisms would become extinct; creatures represented only by fossils were simply creatures that had undergone so much change they existed in unrecognizably different forms today. Of course, if all organisms were evolving to become more complex, you might logically ask why very simple organisms still exist. Lamarck would have answered by saying—against a great deal of evidence to the contrary—that new, and therefore simple, living things were always being "spontaneously generated" (naturally created).

Progressive evolution is really the heart of Lamarck's idea, but it is not what he is remembered for. His name has come to represent the second erroneous part of his evolutionary concept, his mechanism for change. Lamarck supported an idea that had been around for some time, namely, the **inheritance of acquired characteristics**. His own words in *Philosophie Zoologique* (1809) describe this theory best:

> When the will guides an animal to any action, the organs which have to carry out that action are immediately stimulated to it by the influx of subtle fluids. . . . Hence it follows that numerous repetitions of these organised activities strengthen, stretch, develop and even create the organs necessary to them. . . . Now every change that is wrought in an organ through habit of

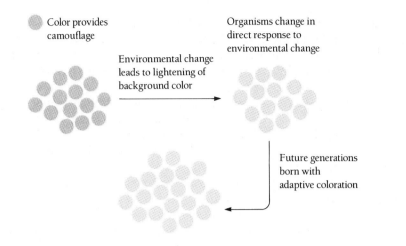

Color provides camouflage

Environmental change leads to lightening of background color

Organisms change in direct response to environmental change

Future generations born with adaptive coloration

**Figure 2.6** *Schematic diagram of Lamarckian evolution.*

(Compare with Figure 4.6)

frequently using it, is subsequently preserved by reproduction. . . . Such a change is thus handed on to all succeeding individuals in the same environment, without their having to acquire it in the same way that it was actually created. (Harris 1981:116–17)

When the environment changes, said Lamarck, organisms perceive the change and use, cease using, or even create the organs necessary to alter their adaptation. The effects of this use or disuse, or the new organ, are automatically passed on to succeeding generations (Figure 2.6).

Lamarck's scheme doesn't work, of course. Traits acquired during one's lifetime cannot be inherited by one's offspring. A bodybuilder's children will not be born with bulging muscles. Furthermore, how can simple creatures or plants have some sort of "will" that allows them to know which organs to use and which not to use, or even to create new organs? How can a butterfly will itself to change color? How can a sightless creature sense the need for eyes and then develop them? These were the very sorts of objections many people voiced during Lamarck's time.

The hypothesis, though, maintained some popularity. First, nobody had come up with anything better. Second, it was a comfortable idea that if organisms were going to change, at least they were changing progressively and had some direct control over the process. Indeed, the effects of use and disuse and the "inheritance of acquired characteristics" seem to keep popping up in the history of evolutionary thought.

The scientific objections remained, however, and so the search was still on to explain why and how living things had evolved. Enter Englishmen Charles Darwin and Alfred Russel Wallace. The story of these two scientists is fascinating in itself. (Consult the sources at the end of

**adapted**:  Adjusted to a particular set of environmental conditions.

**progressive**:  In a particular direction; in this case, toward increasing complexity.

**inheritance of acquired characteristics**:  The incorrect idea that traits acquired during an organism's lifetime could be passed to its offspring.

the chapter for a fuller recounting.) For our purposes, suffice it to say that Darwin (1809–1882) and Wallace (1823–1913), as a result of separate worldwide travels and observations and influenced by previous thinkers, independently became aware of two important facts that had seemingly been overlooked by their predecessors.

First, both noticed that **species** of organisms exhibit variation. Not every member of a species looks like every other member. Just look around your classroom. If Lamarck's idea were correct, you would expect very little variation because all members of a species would have used, not used, or created the same characteristics.

Second, both men expanded the inference from Linnaeus that similarities and differences among organisms represent biological relationships resulting from their descent from previous organisms. Species, they concluded, descend from other species, like members of your family descend from earlier members. Darwin and Wallace pictured life on earth as a gigantic and complex family tree.

Given these assumptions, how did Darwin and Wallace think evolution actually worked? We know their theory, developed independently by each man, by the name Darwin gave it: **natural selection**. Like Lamarck's concept, natural selection is based on the premise that organisms are adapted to their environments and undergo adaptive change when the environments change. But the theory differs from Lamarck's in its explanation of the nature and source of variation.

The theory of inheritance of acquired characteristics requires variation to arise *when it is needed*. The theory of natural selection, on the other hand, requires that variation *already* exists (Figure 2.7). Neither Darwin nor Wallace understood why variation existed within species because the nature of the genetic code had yet to be discovered, but they realized that this variation was important. From the existing variation within a species, nature "selects" by allowing those individuals to survive who, by chance, are best adapted. These are the most reproductively successful and so pass on their adaptive traits to more offspring. The most adaptive traits of a species tend to increase in frequency; the less adaptive traits tend to decrease.

It follows that evolution has no particular direction. Organisms do not all evolve into more complex forms, as Lamarck had suggested, or bigger or smarter ones. Rather, populations of organisms are evolving to become better adapted, or at least to stay adapted, to their environments. There is no overriding principle of progression. The variation from which selection selects is random, not "willed" by the organism.

Furthermore, it follows that if populations from one species are geographically separated, the separate populations, in their different environments, will face different selective pressures. As changes are selected for and accumulate through time, the populations may eventually become so different that they constitute separate species—that is, they

**Figure 2.7** *Variation within a population represents the raw material for natural selection. The tiger swallowtail butterflies* (upper right *and* bottom) *are members of the same species. The dark one is a mimic of the pipe-vine butterfly* (left) *that is protected from predation by its foul taste.* (National Geographic Society/Robert F. Sisson)

will not be able to interbreed and produce fertile offspring. Thus, not only can a single species change through time as a result of environmental change, but it can also generate several new species. Indeed, the title of Darwin's most famous book, published in 1859, is *On the Origin of Species by Means of Natural Selection.*

Finally, it must be understood that such a process, using random variation as its raw material, can't always assure species adaptation. Sometimes there is simply no variation available that is adapted to a particularly extensive or rapid environmental change. In such a case, the species becomes extinct. This, in fact, is the norm. Perhaps more than nine-tenths of all species that have ever existed are now extinct.

Wallace, younger and brasher than Darwin, was willing to go public with his new idea right away. But Darwin, who actually thought of natural selection some twenty years before Wallace, kept the idea a secret from all but his closest colleagues; even his wife didn't know about it. Darwin was finally talked into publishing by his friends only

**species:** A closed genetic population.

**natural selection:** Evolution based on relative reproductive success within a species.

after Wallace made his version known. Why had he kept quiet about it for so long?

Darwin's delay was not—as popular opinion has it—because he feared public reaction to his support of the *idea* of evolution. That concept had been accepted for some time. Rather, Darwin was afraid that his *mechanism* for evolution, as confident as he was about it, was everything that Lamarck's was not and so would not be well received. Natural selection was not progressive. It did not involve the organism's conscious control, and it freely acknowledged extinction. And Darwin, a reclusive hypochondriac who feared any sort of unpleasantness or controversy, may have been wise to delay. The world may not have accepted natural selection when he first came up with the theory, around 1836.

As the second half of the century began, however—a period marked by rapid and extensive social, political, technological, and economic change—the Western world was ready. Darwin's book sold out in a single day and was, for the most part, hailed as a major scientific breakthrough. One scientist of the time is said to have remarked, "How stupid of me not to have thought of that!"

In this way, the scientific revolution brought about by the work of the geologists and biologists, put together so well by Charles Darwin, altered forever our view of the past. The past was now seen as a series of events, often caused initially by random change, that were linked to each other through time and linked to the present by uniformitarian processes. This new concept even changed our view of our own behavior.

## CULTURAL EVOLUTION:
## THE CONTRIBUTION FROM ANTHROPOLOGY

### The Discovery of "New" People

Darwin and Wallace focused on variation in plants and animals, but what about variation in people and their cultures—a concept we take for granted today? We read about or see television shows about foreign peoples. We are aware that some live in industrialized, technologically complex societies, while others live in societies of farmers who plow their fields with oxen. Still others (at least until fairly recently) rely on hunting animals and gathering wild plants for their subsistence. Most of us realize that different cultures representing different ways of life— some simple, some complex—coexist in the modern world.

Before the Renaissance and the Age of Exploration, however, Europeans were unaware of the diversity of the world's cultures. They knew only a very few cultures beyond their own—the Arabs to the south, for

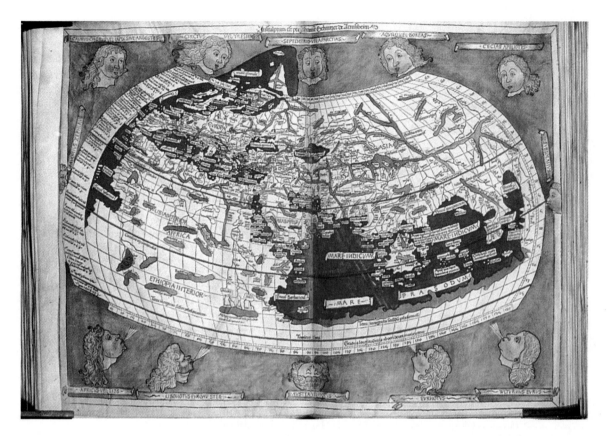

**Figure 2.8** *Fifteenth-century map of the world, based on the work of the second-century geographer Ptolemy, from the* Ulm Atlas of 1482. *Much of Africa is labeled* terra incognita, *literally "unknown land."* (British Library, London)

example, and the Mongols to the east whom Marco Polo described in the thirteenth century. Most of Africa and Asia and the peoples living there were unknown to Europeans. On maps before the sixteenth century, these areas are labeled *terra incognita*—literally, "unknown land" (Figure 2.8). The Americas remained largely unexplored until the sixteenth, seventeenth, and eighteenth centuries.

Europeans looked to the Bible to explain the existence of those other cultures of which they were aware. Remember, the Judeo-Christian creation myth was accepted as a factual account of human history. Adam and Eve were the first people and, therefore, the ultimate ancestors of all human beings. After their eviction from the Garden of Eden, the direct descendants of the first couple spread across the land. They were simple, hard-working farmers, but eventually they strayed from the righteous life and were destroyed by God in a great flood. Only Noah, his family, and the animals aboard the ark were saved from destruction. Some time after Noah's flood, the story goes, God became angry at a group of people attempting to build a great tower, the Tower of Babel, up to heaven. He caused them all to speak in different languages, ruining their plans by destroying their ability to communicate.

This is how the Bible accounts for the origin of language differences and, by inference, the origin of separate cultures. The European interpretation of subsequent history is derived from this biblical framework. The Egyptians, the Greeks, and others were each seen as having originated at Babel. Within this framework, human history was fairly neat and simple; it conformed to the Bible and could be contained in a 6000-year-old universe.

Imagine the surprise of the Europeans, then, when early explorers brought home stories of previously unknown peoples—peoples not mentioned in the Bible. They didn't look like Europeans, and some lived very differently from them; in some cases, they were not as technologically advanced. These new peoples and their cultures simply did not fit, at least not neatly, into the accepted, biblically based chronology of human societies. For example, the Portuguese patron, Prince Henry the Navigator, financed exploration of the coast of Africa where societies of dark-skinned people were encountered who knew nothing of the Bible or Jesus. Looking for a route to the Indies, Christopher Columbus sailed west and instead came upon an unknown world with unimagined cultures, none of which were described in the Bible (Figure 2.9).

Many European thinkers were perplexed by these discoveries. Initially, they assumed that the newly encountered peoples of Asia and Africa were the descendants of Noah's sons Shem and Ham. (Europeans, it was asserted, were the descendants of the third—and, of course, wisest—son, Japheth.) The "simpler" cultures of Africans and Asians were explained as the result of intellectual degeneration of the descendants of Noah's less worthy offspring.

**Figure 2.9** *A seventeenth-century Spanish version of a 1594 engraving (de Bry) depicting Columbus's first contact with natives of the New World.* (Granger Collection)

Unfortunately, this neat arrangement left no ancestor for the American Indians, a circumstance that gave rise to a tremendous amount of speculation about who, exactly, the Indians were and how they fit into the biblical chronology. Practically every European and Asian culture was proposed, at one time or another, as having given rise to Native Americans (Huddleston 1967). One idea was that a group of sailors or fishermen—perhaps Greeks, maybe "Hindoos," even Norwegians— may have long ago been lost at sea. They fortuitously washed up on the American shore and established a population. Over the years their appearance changed, they forgot their religion, and they became the Indians Columbus encountered. For a while it was also popular to believe that American Indians were actually the "Lost Tribes of Israel"—groups of biblical Hebrews historically unaccounted for. Even the so-called lost continent of Atlantis was suggested as a source of American Indian culture. Europeans were indeed having a hard time trying to make an ever-expanding world fit within their creation myth.

## The Discovery of Mysterious Artifacts

While some Europeans were exploring unknown lands and encountering unknown cultures, others were exploring the soil beneath their own feet and discovering some rather strange objects. These fragments of chipped stone, many of which were symmetrical and finely, even artistically, worked, appeared to some to be the result of human manufacture (Figure 2.10).

Most, however, denied the possibility that these artifacts represented human craftsmanship, and their initial interpretation was firmly rooted in biblical literalism. The Bible did not mention the existence of a primitive stage of development, certainly not one in which people made tools of stone and knew nothing of metal. Therefore, it was presumed that the tool-like objects were tricks of nature. (Remember that fossils were also explained this way by those seeking to deny the earth's antiquity.) It was thought the stone objects were the result of lightning striking the ground, hence the name "thunderstones." Others presumed they were the work of mischievous spirits and called them "fairy stones." Still others did accept these objects as made by humans; they believed, however, that the makers of such simple stone tools must have been some degraded form of humanity that existed just before Noah's flood.

## The Evolutionary Explanation

Just as not everyone accepted a strict biblical interpretation of geology and biology, similarly not everyone saw non-European cultures as degenerate offshoots of Noah's family, and not all saw stone tools as the

**Figure 2.10** *Woodcut of handaxe, from Charles Lyell's* The Geological Evidences of the Antiquity of Man. (John Murray, 1863)

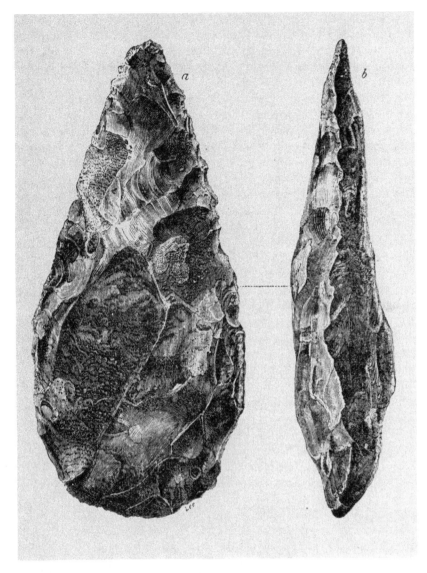

artifacts of recent people fallen from the grace of God. Instead, some interpreted these artifacts and the people who made them as reflecting cultures that represented more primitive and more ancient ways of life—stages, in fact, of human **cultural evolution** through which all people, including Europeans, had passed.

Anthropologist Edward Burnett Tylor, in his book *Primitive Culture* (1871), argued that the existence of primitive—that is, less complex—societies could be explained in one of two ways: Either culture was created more or less as is and primitive societies represent degeneration, or modern civilization developed over a very long period of time from an initial state of "barbarism." For the former theory, Tylor concluded that there was absolutely no evidence. He championed the latter and became one of the first cultural evolutionists.

Lewis Henry Morgan, an American anthropologist and cultural evolutionist, followed Tylor's idea and suggested, in *Ancient Society* (1877), that all cultures change through time, evolving through stages of *savagery, barbarism,* and *civilization.* Cultures could get "stuck" at a particular level if certain key inventions and advances were not made—the bow and arrow, domestication of plants and animals, the smelting of iron. Modern primitives, then, were societies frozen at a particular level of development, a stage through which all other more advanced societies had already passed.

We no longer accept Tylor's and Morgan's simplistic schemes of cultural evolution. But they did show that human beings and their cultures have undergone great change just like plants and animals. They showed that cultures have evolved and that there are processes of cultural change that we can identify and understand.

Direct physical evidence for such change was found in those enigmatic stone objects being excavated throughout Europe. The French naturalists Issac de la Peyrère in the seventeenth century, John Frere in the eighteenth century, and Jacques Boucher de Perthes in the nineteenth century each suggested that these stone objects represented the remains of tools produced by ancient people. They proposed that such tools were direct evidence of a previous primitive stage of human development—a *stone age.*

In *The Geological Evidences of the Antiquity of Man,* first published in 1863, Charles Lyell, the ardent uniformitarianist we met earlier, presented detailed evidence for the association of some of these tools with the fossilized bones of extinct animals and even humans. This supported his contention for human antiquity:

> For the last half-century, the occasional occurrence, in various parts of Europe, of the bones of Man or the work of his hands, in cave-breccias and stalagmites, associated with the remains of the extinct hyaena, bear, elephant, or rhinoceros, has given rise to a suspicion that the date of Man must be carried further back than we had heretofore imagined." (1873:1–2)

Evidence was mounting in the newly developing field of *anthropology,* literally, the study of people. As with geology and biology, the interpretation of the anthropological evidence virtually required that both the earth itself and the human race were ancient and always changing. Science was supplying enormous amounts of new data about human history and the world around us. And these data simply could no longer be contained within a 6000-year-old, static universe.

**cultural evolution:** Changes in cultural patterns through time.

# CONTEMPORARY ISSUE

## Scientific Creationism: An Old Idea in a New Form

The belief that the universe and everything in it were created by a divine being did not die out when the theories of uniformitarianism and natural selection were developed. These theories took many years to gain acceptance, and even today many people continue to have faith that their god or gods had some hand in designing the world we see around us.

For most Westerners, no conflict exists between such a belief and the actual processes of earth history and evolution that have been so laboriously learned and described by science. Many Jews and Christians, for example, simply feel that God created those processes along with everything else. But a sizable minority still holds that the Judeo-Christian creation myth is factual and true. Like most Europeans in previous centuries, they take the stories in Genesis literally.

To the majority of people who hold them, religious beliefs usually fall into a category of knowledge that also includes ethical precepts, moral values, and philosophical tenets. There is no inherent conflict between this kind of knowledge and the kind we label "science." Indeed, the two usually live in harmony with each other.

Scientific knowledge involves a rational, logical attempt to understand the physical world in which we live. It is based on the scientific method described in the last chapter. In honest science, this method of inquiry is continuous; no idea is ever accepted as proven for all time. Rather, it is tested, retested, refined, and changed as new evidence and new ideas accumulate. As the evolutionary scientist John Maynard Smith puts it, science tells us "what is possible" (1984:24). Or, in the words of Pope John Paul II, the function of science is to instruct us "how heaven is."

The other type of human knowledge consists of "belief systems," and these are not open to testing and experimentation. They are taken on faith, accepted as "given." A belief in God, for instance, or, for that matter, a disbelief in God,

simply cannot be subjected to the scientific method. What is the concrete evidence? How is it tested? What person, believing in a supreme deity, is going to change his or her mind in light of some scientifically derived theory about the physical world? What sort of rational thinking would convince someone that human life is not sacred? Rather than serving to describe the physical world, belief systems function to tell us about our behavior toward one another and toward that world. They also serve to define for us the meaning of life and of our existence. They tell us, says John Maynard Smith, "what is desirable" (1984:24),and instruct us, says Pope John Paul II, "how to get to heaven."

In fact, rather than being eternally in conflict with each other—as we all too often tend to see them—these two spheres of knowledge must interact harmoniously for any society to thrive and prosper. People require scientific knowledge, based on the scientific method, to tell them how to hunt animals, grow plants, make tools, and program computers. We also require rules of behavior, taken on faith, to ensure unity, cooperation, and harmony within our societies. It is perhaps part of the human condition to wonder why we are here, and belief systems also help answer this sort of question. Again, science tells us what is possible; belief systems tell us what is desirable.

Sometimes, however, the harmonious interaction of these spheres of knowledge is broken when they are forced into conflict with one another—when science attempts to challenge a belief system or when a belief system claims its tenets are scientifically valid. The latter occurred in Tennessee in 1925, when a bill was passed in the state legislature that declared it illegal to teach, in a state-supported school, any theory that denied the biblical creation story and claimed humans were descended from some "lower order of animals." Initially, the bill was not taken seriously (except by its sponsor, of course), but the governor signed it as a demonstration of Christian faith. No one thought it would be enforced.

In Dayton, Tennessee, however, teacher John T. Scopes and some of the town leaders thought that Scopes's violation of this act would "put their town on the map." While substituting in a biology class, Scopes assigned a text section dealing with evolution and so was arrested and charged. And then things got out of hand. People came from all over the country to watch the trial, not so much because of the issue but because the attorney for the prosecution was William Jennings Bryan, fundamentalist speaker and failed presidential candidate, and for the defense, Clarence Darrow, perhaps the best-known and most successful lawyer of his time.

The town of Dayton took on a circus atmosphere, though the trial itself turned out to be rather unspectacular and boring. Convicted and fined $100, Scopes later had his conviction overturned on a technicality. But the trial did feature a memorable and now-famous confrontation between Bryan and Darrow—which did not become part of the formal record. In an unprecedented move, Darrow put prosecutor Bryan on the stand and questioned him about his views on the literal truth of the Bible. During this exchange, which demonstrated the wit and oratorical skills of both men, the separate natures of science and religion became clear as Bryan was unable to support his interpretation of creation with anything other than faith. Here is a brief excerpt (as quoted in Appleman 1970:543–44):

DARROW: [asking about the accepted date of 4004 B.C.] Don't you know that the ancient civilizations of China are 6,000 or 7,000 years old, at the very least?

BRYAN: No; but they would not run back beyond the creation according to the Bible, 6,000 years.

DARROW: You don't know how old they are, is that right?

BRYAN: I don't know how old they are, but probably you do. I think you would give preference to anybody who opposed the Bible, and I give the preference to the Bible.

As this exchange became part of American folklore, the common interpretation was that science had "won." In fact, both science and religion suffered. One result of the trial was to draw attention to a conflict that didn't necessarily exist. Shortly after the trial, the topic of evolution began to disappear from textbooks, where previously it had occupied a prominent place. It only reappeared after 1957, when the Soviet launching of Sputnik prompted the United States to reexamine the quality of its science education.

We might see the story of this trial (called the "monkey trial" because of the implications of Darwin's theory for our ancestry) as an amusing little bit of Americana but for its larger implication and present-day echoes. The issue the trial brought to the public's attention has lingered, and recently creationism has returned—in a particularly complex and dangerous form.

Called "scientific creationism," this latter-day notion has as its basic tenets (1) that real scientific evidence exists to support the biblical creation story and (2) that no evidence exists to support evolutionary theory. The Bible, according to this view, is thus a scientific and historical document as well as a religious one. Moreover, it posits, if evolution can be shown to be false, then scientific creationism *must* be true.

As we have outlined briefly and will discuss in detail later, an enormous quantity of evidence exists to support the ideas of geological, biological, and cultural evolution. That is why these topics are part of mainstream science. There is not one shred of scientific evidence to support

*(cont'd)*

*William Jennings Bryan (right) and Clarence Darrow at the Scopes trial.* (Wide World Photos)

"scientific" creationism. But the scientific creationism movement cannot be ignored.

One of the corollary ideas of the scientific creationists is that, as a science, creationism should be given equal time in schools alongside the evolution model as an equally viable scientific hypothesis. It is this argument that has gained some support here and in other countries. With our very basic belief in religious freedom and tolerance, we are reluctant to deny people access to an idea with religious (especially Judeo-Christian) connections.

The fact is, though, that "equal time" is for equal things, and creationism is *not* the equivalent of evolution. Scientific creationism is no less than one group's interpretation of the content and message of the Bible. It is a belief system and thus is not even open to scientific investigation. But it is more. In its attempt to attribute scientific and historical accuracy to the Bible, scientific creationism becomes a clever and insidi-

ous device for injecting a partisan religious view into public education.

Teaching the two models side-by-side in science classes would contradict the principle of religious freedom, for it would mean that one group's religious ideas were being taught, *as scientific theory,* to individuals who hold other religious views or no religious views at all. Furthermore, it would undermine the whole idea of free scientific inquiry and intellectual honesty.

We will be describing a great many hypotheses and theories throughout this book. We have no vested interest in whether any specific idea proves to be true or false. As scientists, we believe that our only vested interest is in seeking and understanding the nature of the world— *whatever* that may be. The strides made by science toward that goal and the benefits to our species that have resulted are only possible in an atmosphere of free inquiry and harmonious interaction between science and belief systems.

## SUMMARY

Until a few hundred years ago, most European thinkers sought to interpret the nature of the world in the context of biblical history. The more they looked into nature itself, however, the more the biblical framework became supplanted by the scientific method—the inductive development of hypotheses to account for observed data and the deductive testing of these hypotheses to generate theories.

Science thus altered the European view of the world. Where the earth was seen previously as young and unchanging, by the eighteenth century Europeans confronted an ancient earth undergoing virtually continual change. The work of natural scientists like James Hutton and Charles Lyell and their principle of uniformitarianism provided evidence for this ancient and changing earth. Where living things had been seen as the unaltered creations of a supreme being, species were now viewed as the ever-changing products of natural processes. The work of Alfred Wallace and Charles Darwin in the nineteenth century explained the mechanisms for these processes of change. Even humans themselves came to be seen as a topic for scientific investigation and as a species whose history stretched far into antiquity.

## KEY TERMS

catastrophist
uniformitarianism
creationist
comparative biology
taxonomy
strata (sing.
    stratum)
stratigraphy

adapted
progressive
inheritance of
    acquired
        characteristics
species
natural selection
cultural evolution

## FOR MORE INFORMATION

Perhaps the most famous book on the history of evolution, and one that still holds up over thirty years later, is John C. Greene's *The Death of Adam: Evolution and Its Impact on Thought*. Another treatment of the same subject, using excerpts from original writings, is *Evolution: Genesis and Revelations*, edited and with comments by C. Leon Harris.

A collection of writings by Charles Darwin and many of his contemporaries, predecessors, and successors is *Darwin,* edited by Philip Appleman. Finally, paleontologist and science historian Stephen Jay Gould has written a number of essays on the history of evolutionary thought, many aimed at reexamining old ideas on the subject. They can be found in his books *Ever Since Darwin, The Panda's Thumb, Hen's Teeth and Horse's Toes, The Flamingo's Smile,* and *Bully for Brontosaurus.*

# 3
# EVOLUTION: AN OVERVIEW

In the remainder of this book, we'll be painting a picture of human antiquity. Our palette will be the methods of inquiry and investigation we call science; some of these methods were described in Chapter 1. Our paints will be the hypotheses, theories, and facts about our subject that science has provided us. The canvas we paint on will be the dimension of time.

Time can often be a problem for those of us who seek to learn about the past, for we are dealing with vast quantities of it. It is easy to conceive of a day, a week, a month, even a year. By stretching our imagination, we can get a feel for the chunk of time that makes up our individual lives. But it becomes increasingly difficult to imagine the time involved in the last few generations, or in the history of the United States, or the period of time since the ancient Egyptians built the pyramids more than 4000 years ago (ya).

It gets even more difficult when we think about the time since the invention of writing, since the beginnings of modern humans, since the dawn of our evolutionary line. And it becomes a monumental task to conceive of the span of time back to the dinosaurs, to the first land animals, to the beginning of life on earth, and on to the very origin of the universe.

But it's vital for someone interested in human antiquity to acquire a concept of the time involved in our tenure on earth, and for just where that time fits into the broader scheme of events that makes up earth history. In the chapters that follow, we'll be presenting many details about human evolution. But it's difficult, we think, to develop a concept of time working from the specific to the general; so, in this chapter we'll give you a brief narrative outline of evolutionary history, focusing on human evolution. Then, as you read about the detailed evidence and ideas, you'll have a context—of time and basic events—in which to place those details. We think it will make more sense that way.

## BIG BANG TO BIG DINOSAURS

There are a number of hypotheses attempting to account for the origin of the universe. But according to the majority of scientists, in the beginning—the very beginning—all the energy, space, and matter of the known universe were condensed into a dense, inconceivably tiny speck of pure energy. The laws of physics as we now understand them can't account for the existence of this speck, so science has yet to answer the question of where it came from. Some people turn to religion for an answer; some simply believe the universe has always been here, cycling through eternity; others wait, assuming science will one day be able to provide an explanation.

We accept that science cannot yet determine where the universe came from or why it is here. But science can account for most of the history of the universe by using the established fact that the universe is rapidly expanding. To this fact we apply the current laws of physics and astronomy and work backward, rather like running a movie of an explosion in reverse. We hypothetically "shrink" the universe and determine what would happen to all its matter and energy under conditions of

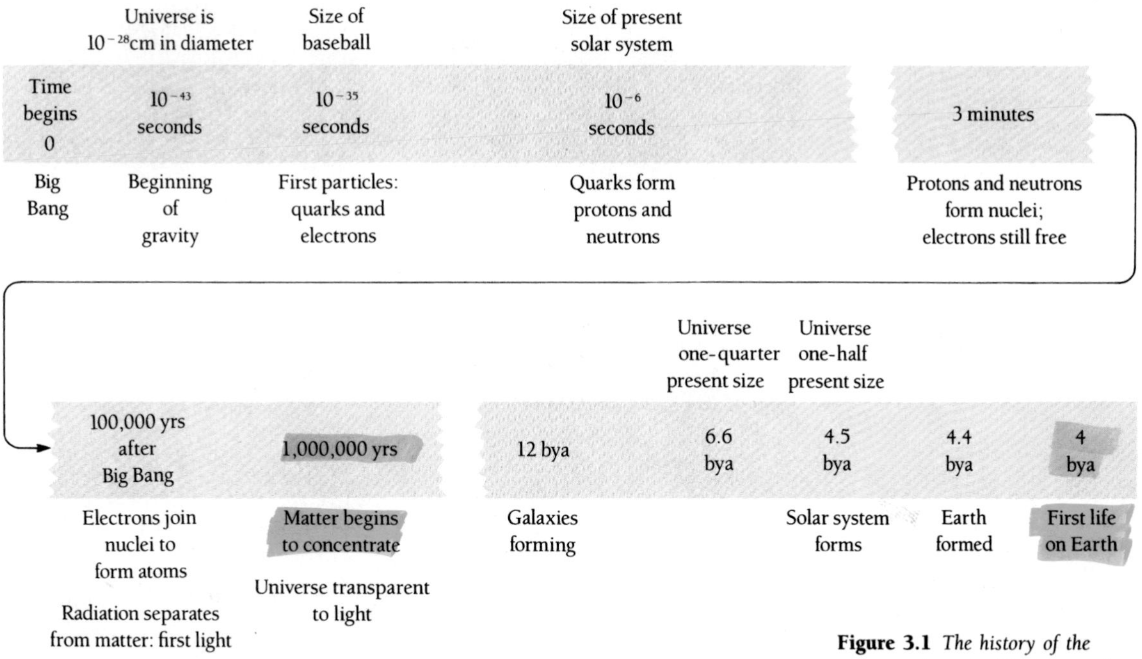

| Universe is $10^{-28}$cm in diameter | Size of baseball | | Size of present solar system | |
|---|---|---|---|---|
| $10^{-43}$ seconds | $10^{-35}$ seconds | | $10^{-6}$ seconds | 3 minutes |
| Time begins 0 | | | | |
| Big Bang | Beginning of gravity | First particles: quarks and electrons | Quarks form protons and neutrons | Protons and neutrons form nuclei; electrons still free |

| | | | Universe one-quarter present size | Universe one-half present size | | |
|---|---|---|---|---|---|---|
| 100,000 yrs after Big Bang | 1,000,000 yrs | 12 bya | 6.6 bya | 4.5 bya | 4.4 bya | 4 bya |
| Electrons join nuclei to form atoms | Matter begins to concentrate | Galaxies forming | | Solar system forms | Earth formed | First life on Earth |
| Radiation separates from matter: first light | Universe transparent to light | | | | | |

**Figure 3.1** *The history of the universe, from the Big Bang to the origin of life on earth. The scale of the time line changes because some events are condensed into incredibly small periods and others are stretched over unimaginable spans.*

decreasing size and increasing density and heat. We also devise a time frame for the events involved.

Through this procedure, we trace the chronology of a long series of events and processes set in motion somewhere around 15 billion years ago (bya) (Figure 3.1). (Estimates for the age of the universe vary greatly, but 15 billion is an average. For more detail on the evolution of the universe and life, see Attenborough 1979, Calder 1983, Lewin 1982, and Sagan 1980.) It was then that the tiny speck began to expand. We call this event the "Big Bang" although it wasn't really an explosion. It was more like a balloon being rapidly inflated, a balloon that contained both energy and space.

A fraction of a second after the expansion began, the space–energy speck, now the size of a baseball, began cooling off, and matter began to condense from energy. The first matter was in the form of the smallest subatomic particles, but as the infant universe continued to grow and cool, increasingly larger particles formed. By three minutes after the Big Bang, there were atomic nuclei, but it took another 100,000 years to form the first atoms. They were atoms of hydrogen, the element with the simplest atomic structure.

To make a *very* long story short, expansion continued; and the cooling universe eventually saw the condensation, from simple elements, of galaxies and their stars. The first stars were made mainly of hydrogen,

**Figure 3.2** *The crab nebula, remnant of a supernova explosion like those that produced the elements that make up our planet and even our own bodies.* (National Optical Astronomy Observatories)

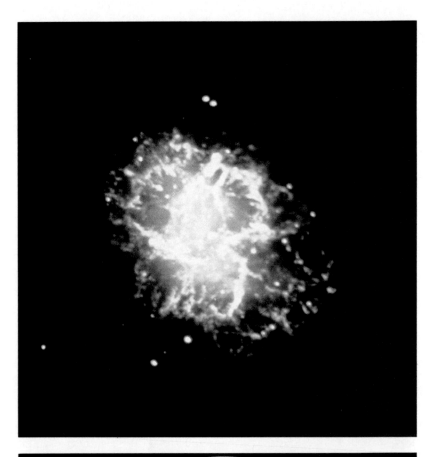

**Figure 3.3** *The whole earth from space.* (NASA)

but in the nuclear furnaces of these stars heavier elements with larger, more complex atoms were formed. When these early stars died in tremendous explosions called supernovas, their new elements were shot out into the universe, ultimately contributing to the formation of more galaxies, stars, and planets (Figure 3.2). On one planet at least, the atoms formed inside stars provided the raw material that eventually evolved into living creatures. When astronomer Carl Sagan (1980) says we are "star stuff," he is being literal.

By a little over 4.5 bya, the universe was about half its present size. At about this time, our star, the sun, was formed, and our earth took shape shortly thereafter (Figure 3.3). The early earth contained only inorganic (nonliving) molecules, but about 4 bya some of these were rearranged and formed organic molecules, those that make up living organisms. Figure 3.4 summarizes what we know about the time of important events in the evolution of life on earth.

Although creating living molecules out of nonliving ones may sound like some sort of magic, it's not. Scientists have been producing a simple version of this reaction in laboratories for over thirty years; all they do is add water to the chemicals that made up the early earth atmosphere and subject the mixture to a source of energy like electricity. Among the molecules that result are amino acids, the raw materials from which genes form proteins. These are the building blocks of all known life.

An amino acid, though, is still a long way from a living organism, and another 500 million years were required for these and other organic chemicals to react in just the right ways to form living, reproducing creatures. We know these reactions occurred because we have fossils of bacteria-like cells—among the simplest of living things—from 3.5 billion-year-old strata, now exposed by various geological processes in Greenland, southern Africa, and Australia (Figure 3.5).

The earth's first creatures were all asexual—that is, they reproduced by splitting or budding, making copies of themselves. Change was very slow because it relied solely on mutations, but it still took place. By 2.7 bya and perhaps earlier, we have evidence of the first single-celled organisms that could photosynthesize—make nutrients from water, sunlight, and carbon dioxide. This is what modern green plants do. A waste product of photosynthesis is oxygen. Originally, no free oxygen was present in the earth's atmosphere, but as a result of photosynthesis it appeared by 1.8 bya. Shortly thereafter came the evolution of organisms that could use it. A new branch of the evolutionary tree had begun.

Evidence from the stratigraphic record shows us that by 1.5 bya cells that were more complex than bacteria had evolved. These cells had a nucleus and functionally differentiated internal parts. And around 1 bya, they "invented" something new: sex. With sexual reproduction came more possibilities for change because the genes of two parents

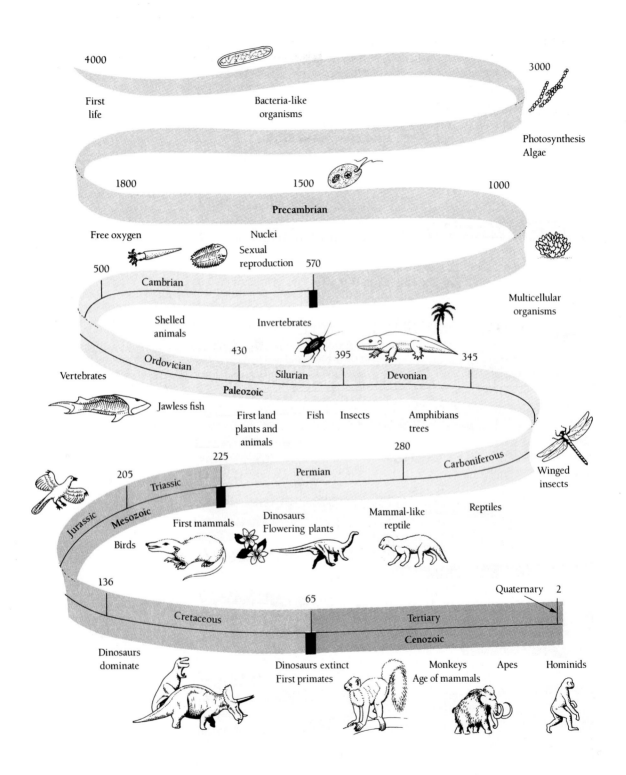

4000

3000

First
life

Bacteria-like
organisms

Photosynthesis
Algae

1800          1500          1000

**Precambrian**

Free oxygen          Nuclei

Sexual
reproduction          570

500

**Cambrian**

Multicellular
organisms

Shelled
animals          Invertebrates

430                    395                    345

**Ordovician**          **Silurian**          **Devonian**

Vertebrates

**Paleozoic**

Jawless fish          First land          Fish     Insects          Amphibians
                      plants and                                     trees
                      animals
                                                                     280

225

205                                                                  Carboniferous

**Triassic**          **Permian**

**Jurassic**     **Mesozoic**          Winged
                                        insects
First mammals          Dinosaurs          Mammal-like
                       Flowering plants   reptile          Reptiles

Birds

136                                      2
                                         Quaternary

65

**Cretaceous**          **Tertiary**

                        **Cenozoic**

Dinosaurs
dominate          Dinosaurs extinct          Monkeys     Apes     Hominids
                  First primates             Age of mammals

◄ **Figure 3.4** *Time line showing the major events in the history of life on earth. The placement of sample organisms is approximate, and some are stylized representatives. Time is in millions of years; the last 570 million years are drawn to scale.*

were now recombined in the production of offspring. Natural selection had more variation from which to choose and evolution accelerated.

By the beginning of the Cambrian period, 570 million years ago (mya), we find a wealth of fossils representing many new and different kinds of creatures—complex multicellular animals such as jellyfish and worms. This relatively sudden appearance has been called the Cambrian Explosion. By 530 mya there were animals with hard outer coverings, forerunners of clams and lobsters, and 510 mya saw the first vertebrates, creatures with internal skeletons. We, of course, are vertebrates.

*CAMBRIAN EXPLOSION*

**Figure 3.5** *Stromatolites in Australia, formed when mats of blue-green algae are covered with sand, silt, and mud, which the algae cement down and then grow over. Blue-green algae represent one of the oldest known forms of life and fossil stromatolites date to 3.5 bya.*
(©Rick Smolen/Lifetime Productions)

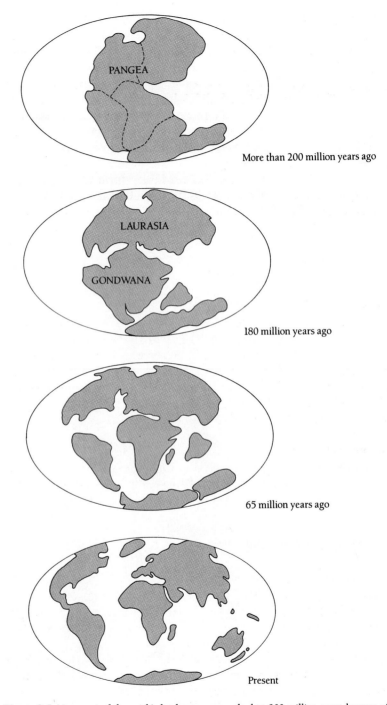

More than 200 million years ago

180 million years ago

65 million years ago

Present

**Figure 3.6** *Movement of the earth's land masses over the last 200 million years because of continental drift.*

The pace of change continued to accelerate. Around 425 mya, fish evolved, and plants and simple animals began to colonize the land. Insects appeared 395 mya and evolved winged forms 330 mya. Reptiles first showed up 313 mya, and the form of reptile that would give rise to mammals appeared about 256 mya.

During all this time, the earth didn't look as it does now. The continents that seem so permanent to us aren't. They move or, in the term used by geology, "drift." This process, called **plate tectonics**, is complex, but basically the hard outer shell of the earth, the crust, is made up of a number of plates that fit together like a jigsaw puzzle. The continents are the portions of these plates that protrude above the oceans. The plates are in constant interaction with the inside of the earth, which is made up of liquid rock continually in motion. As this liquid moves, it adds solid rock to some parts of the crust and melts away solid rock from other parts, causing the plates with their continents to drift slowly but constantly around the surface of the planet (Figure 3.6). Where the plates meet, they grind against one another, producing the tremendous forces that are largely responsible for great geological events like volcanoes, earthquakes, and mountain building.

About the time the dinosaurs and the flowering plants were evolving, around 235 mya, land masses that are part of all the present continents were drifting together to form a single "supercontinent." We call it **Pangea** (literally, "all lands"). This supercontinent was fully formed by 210 mya. We find similar fossils of early dinosaurs and other organisms in such diverse places as the Gobi Desert in China, the Badlands of South Dakota, and Antarctica because these were all part of one unbroken land mass.

Mammals first appeared around 220 mya, and about 150 mya a small upright dinosaur with feathers heralded the beginning of the birds (see Figure 4.11). By this time, however, Pangea was breaking up, and it is here that the story of the human evolutionary line really starts.

## GRASPING HANDS AND BIG BRAINS

Pangea broke up into six land masses that are approximately the present-day continents, although not in the same locations as today. As these new lands began to drift over the globe, a greater variety of separate environments was produced, offering a greater opportunity for the evolution of new types of living things.

One new evolutionary line began around 65 mya on a large northern land mass called **Laurasia**, made up of parts of modern North America and Eurasia. It consisted of a group of mammals whose fossilized skeletons are reminiscent of rodents. But their multipurpose teeth, the beginning of grasping hands and feet, and other details of their anatomy

**plate tectonics:** The theory that the earth's surface consists of a number of moving plates.

**Pangea:** The supercontinent that included parts of all present-day land masses.

**Laurasia:** The former land mass made up of present-day North America and Eurasia.

**Figure 3.7** *Humans are not typical primates. These rhesus monkeys from Nepal are probably as close as any species to being an "average" primate.* (©Fred Whitehead/Animals, Animals)

**Figure 3.8** *Of all living species, this Asian tree shrew, though not a primate, most closely resembles what we think the first primates looked like.* (Zoological Society of San Diego/F. D. Schmidt)

were not rodentlike. They were more like the features of the primates, the group of mammals that today includes monkeys, apes, and us (Figure 3.7).

Like the other mammals at the time, the early primates were sort of evolutionary "second-class citizens"—mostly small, inconspicuous, nocturnal creatures (Figure 3.8). This was largely because the dinosaurs, one of evolution's most successful groups, had occupied and dominated the world's major environments. Add the fact that many dinosaurs were carnivores who certainly included mammals on their menu, and it is understandable why mammalian evolution was slow at first.

But about 65 mya, something happened that we can probably thank for our very existence: The dinosaurs became extinct. We don't know for certain what caused this, but clearly some major and rapid environmental change took place to which the dinosaurs were unable to adapt, and so they disappeared (Figure 3.9). The only direct living descendants of the dinosaurs are the birds; snakes, lizards, and other living reptiles had a separate evolution.

The extinction of this major and widespread group opened the world up for the evolution of some of the "minor" organisms, especially the mammals. No longer having to compete with the dinosaurs, the mammals flourished. Shortly after the extinction of the dinosaurs, we find fossils of most major kinds of mammals—creatures as diverse as bats, whales, and primates. The mammals began to spread rapidly, filling in the ecological gaps left by the dinosaurs.

By 45 mya, North America and Eurasia drifted apart, and the Western and Eastern Hemispheres were formed. This split the populations of living things that once inhabited Laurasia and set the groups in each hemisphere off on their own separate evolutionary courses. The New World primates of the Americas and the Old World primates of Europe, Africa, and Asia have been separate ever since, or at least until the human primate entered the New World from Asia about 15,000 ya.

North America and Eurasia drifted northward toward their present locations, and their climates began to get cooler and increasingly inhospitable to many of their tropical adapted inhabitants. South America and Africa, then farther south than today, were also drifting northward and by 30 mya had joined their respective northern partners. Now warm-climate animals like the early primates, the prosimians, had somewhere to go. As they moved into the southern land masses, they underwent further evolution, adapting to the new niches they found there. One result was a new, more arboreal (tree-living), larger-brained, leaf-eating group of primates—the monkeys. The monkeys were successful and began to spread and diversify. In the New World, they completely outcompeted the prosimians, leaving only monkeys to be found now in Central and South America. In the Old World, the early primates

**primate:** A large-brained arboreal mammal with stereoscopic, color vision and grasping hands.

**prosimians:** The most primitive primates.

**arboreal:** Adapted to life in the trees.

**Figure 3.9** *The dinosaurs once dominated the earth but became extinct fairly rapidly about 65 mya. Many now believe that the cause of the extinction was an enormous asteroid that crashed into the earth, causing a stupendous explosion. The resulting cloud of dust would have blocked out the sun for a time, causing a rapid cooling of the earth and leading to the demise of the dinosaurs and perhaps 75 percent of marine species.* (Peabody Museum of Natural History, Yale University. Painted by Rudolph F. Zallinger)

**Figure 3.10** *A ring-tailed lemur, one of the living prosimians from Madagascar.* (Zoological Society of San Diego)

were pushed into isolated areas and nocturnal ways of life. Most living species of prosimians, representing the earliest types of primates, now inhabit the island of Madagascar (Figure 3.10).

Continental drift and climatic change continued, and more new niches were produced. The primates responded to these, and around 25 mya another new group evolved. They were larger than the monkeys, had bigger brains, were tailless, spent more time on the ground, and were adapted to a more varied diet that included some seasonal foods like nuts and fruits and maybe even some meat. These were the first apes, smaller, more monkeylike forerunners of our present-day chimpanzees, gorillas, and orangutans.

Between 23 and 14 mya, various species of apes flourished across Europe, Africa, and Asia, by this time in about their present-day positions. Ape species from that time ranged in size from that of a large monkey to a giant grain eater from India and China, possibly larger than modern gorillas. But the heyday of the apes began to end about 12 mya. Many ape species became extinct. Populations of an ape that survived in the forests of Africa gave rise to modern-day chimps and gorillas. Another group, probably living where forest and **savanna** met, changed in a different direction and became adapted to life on the vast and dangerous open plains (Figure 3.11). These were our ancestors.

**Figure 3.11** *The savannas (open plains) of present-day Africa are sufficiently similar to those of 6 mya to give us a glimpse into what life was like at that time for the living creatures, including our earliest ancestors, that inhabited them.* (Rob Blumenschine)

Data are scarce at present, but we can make an educated guess about when our evolutionary line split from that of the apes. Based on existing fossil and geological evidence and on the genetic similarities between humans and chimpanzees, we think the human ancestor diverged from the ape line about 6 mya. By the time the fossil record starts to provide us with more substantial evidence, nearly 4 mya, we have before us a

**savanna:** Tropical grasslands.

**Figure 3.12** *The importance of bipedal locomotion for our species can be seen in the drive of infants to master upright walking.* (Michael Park)

creature with the face and brain size of an ape, but with an added feature that sets it off from all other primates that had ever existed: It walked upright (Figure 3.12).

It seems as if the most important and earliest human adaptive response to life on the African plains was upright, or **bipedal**, locomotion. This adaptation, seen in rudimentary form in modern apes, allowed our earliest ancestors to move efficiently over great distances and to carry things at the same time. On the savannas, where food sources were more widely scattered and less varied than in the forests and where numerous creatures lurked who were ready to make meals out of small mammals, this ability was particularly important. It was a successful adaptation, for we find fossil evidence of these early humans all over eastern and southern Africa. In broad evolutionary perspective then, bipedalism is our most distinguishing feature because it was first. In Chapter 8, we'll explore some ideas about just how and why this adaptation took place.

We refer to our earliest ancestors, the topic of Chapter 9, as australopithecines. The term means, literally, "southern ape," a holdover from the fact that the man who first identified one of their fossils and named them, in 1925, recognized but wasn't quite ready formally to admit they were **hominids**, part of the human lineage. But they were.

About 3 mya, another evolutionary event took place. The australopithecines diverged. Two branches, which we continue to call australopithecine, seem to have evolved toward an increasingly vegetarian diet. These branches became extinct about 1 mya.

A third branch evolved a different adaptation. These hominids had bigger brains, smaller, more modern-looking teeth and chewing muscles, and a new and important behavior: They made stone tools. We call them by the scientific name *Homo habilis*, "the skillful people." *Homo habilis* began to be a major factor in the savanna environment. With their big brains and more complex intellect, and with the tools that resulted, they could exploit savanna food sources more efficiently than other hominids. They even, if one interpretation of the evidence is correct, built crude shelters. We'll examine this in detail in Chapter 9.

*HOMO HABILIS*

By this time, bipedal locomotion was established as a major adaptation. Now the big brain became the adaptive focus. By 1.75 mya, the brains of our African ancestors had reached a point where their size approached the lower limit of modern humans. Their heads and faces were notably different from ours today, but from the neck down their skeletons were, in many ways, of modern form. We call this stage of our evolution *Homo erectus*, the topic of Chapter 10. This name, which means "the people who stand upright," is a holdover from the time when these fossils were thought to be the oldest humans and thus the first bipeds. It's only recently that we've realized we were walking erect at least 2 million years before *H. erectus* appeared.

*HOMO ERECTUS*

Their bigger brains allowed *H. erectus* to improve on toolmaking and probably on the ability to devise schemes for social organization and cooperation. Their populations increased, and they began to spread. By a little under 1 mya, we find *H. erectus* fossils throughout Africa and in Europe, Southeast Asia, and northern China. Their adaptations, originally geared for life on the savannas of Africa, turned out to be good all over the world.

For the next 750,000 years, human evolution can be said to have stabilized. To be sure, various populations of *H. erectus* devised different sorts of tools and other cultural adaptations specifically geared to the environments in which they lived—everywhere from the savannas of Africa to the forests to Southeast Asia to the Ice Age glaciers of Europe and China (which we'll also tell you about in Chapter 10). But so successful were their basic adaptations—shelters, clothing, fire, and perhaps organized hunting—that, despite the unstable climate, we see relatively little biological or cultural change until after 400,000 ya.

At that time, there was another "burst" of change in human evolution: an increase in average brain size to that of modern people. We're not sure what caused this development, but it may have been that the advances and retreats of the glaciers became more rapid and severe, making adaptation to the changing climate a more difficult task. Natural selection, operating with the trend already begun and proven successful, may have promoted the reproductive success of those humans with

**bipedal:** The ability to walk on two feet.

**hominid:** The bipedal primate; humans and their ancestors.

*Homo Sapiens*

still bigger, more complex brains. These people may have had a slightly better ability to think up answers to the problems of survival. This point, at any rate, we mark as the beginning of *Homo sapiens* ("the wise people"), the species to which all living humans belong. In Chapter 11, we will describe the beginnings of our species.

After this turning point, it becomes harder to generalize about our evolutionary history. The adaptation of culture, made possible by our big brain, allowed for great diversity in our behaviors. We spread all over the Old World, fitting our tools and our social organizations to the specific problems the various environments posed. But we were to some extent still at the mercy of the climatic fluctuations of the ice ages, and environment still had some effect on our biology.

Evidence for this effect can be seen in a striking set of physical features possessed by one variety of fossil hominid, the Neandertals. Appearing in the fossil record from before 100,000 ya to 35,000 ya, they displayed some unique traits that distinguish them from other hominids living at the same time who were more probably ancestral to modern humans. The Neandertals were, however, responsible for a number of innovative and important inventions—activities like burial of the dead. The exact relationship between the Neandertals and modern people remains controversial, and we will also examine this controversy and the story of the Neandertals in Chapter 11.

New evidence indicates that the earliest fully modern humans can be traced back to at least 100,000 ya. In Chapter 12, we will discuss the continued success of our species as we entered new habitats and populated new worlds. Around 40,000 ya, humans entered Australia. Perhaps that long ago, and certainly soon after 15,000 ya, humans entered the Americas, crossing over a broad land connection between Siberia and Alaska. *Homo sapiens* now inhabited nearly the entire globe, and it was at this point that we began to evolve the physical variation that characterizes our species today (and that seems to present us with so many social problems). We will discuss this topic in Chapter 13.

Culture change continued to accelerate; people increased their populations and adapted to new and increasingly specific ecological niches. Sometime after 12,000 ya, some populations found it necessary to use their vast knowledge of their environments to gain more control over their food resources. They invented farming and animal domestication (Chapter 14). With this came even more cultural diversity and a whole host of new cultural adaptations: cities, metallurgy, warfare, complex political and economic organization, and writing—the beginning of the historical record (Chapter 15). Our story does not end here. We can trace the human saga into the modern period (Chapter 16).

Thus, the canvas of time on which we will paint the picture of human antiquity begins with the very first primates and continues to the recent past.

**Figure 3.13** *All that our species has achieved—from observing the universe to its actual exploration, from the efficient transmission of knowledge to the drive of children to understand and participate in their world—all can be traced back to the Big Bang some 15 bya.* (telescope, National Optical Astronomy Observatories; astronaut, courtesy of NASA; computer kids, ©Edward Schullery; boy, Kenneth Feder)

## SUMMARY

We hope this brief narrative will provide you with a basic context into which all the details of the next chapters can be easily fit. We also hope it has demonstrated two other general ideas. First, you should see that the story of human evolution, as complex as it is, takes up only the smallest fraction of time in the whole history of the universe; it is just the latest tick of the evolutionary clock. We find that a rather humbling thought (Figure 3.13).

Second, though we use terms like *beginning* and *origin*, notice that the whole story contains only one *real* origin: that tiny, dense speck of energy and space that started the whole thing. Since then, nothing brand new has really entered the picture. There have only been *rearrangements* of what already existed: matter condensing from cooling energy; large particles formed from combinations of smaller ones; stars and planets coming together from cosmic dust; inorganic molecules shuffling their parts and producing the molecules of life; the genes of living things recombining in a nearly infinite variety of ways to evolve the wondrous array of creatures that have inhabited the earth. Indeed, "uniformitarianism" has a broader meaning than James Hutton and Charles Lyell could have imagined. We are all truly "star stuff."

## KEY TERMS

| | | |
|---|---|---|
| plate tectonics | primate | savanna |
| Pangea | prosimian | bipedal |
| Laurasia | arboreal | hominid |

## FOR MORE INFORMATION

The evolution of the universe is one of the themes of Carl Sagan's *Cosmos.* The evolution of life on earth is described in *Life on Earth,* by David Attenborough. Both these books accompany public television series of the same names. The evolution of life is also covered and nicely illustrated in Roger Lewin's *Thread of Life: The Smithsonian Looks at Evolution.*

A detailed outline of the history of the universe, with many helpful diagrams and charts, is found in Nigel Calder's *Timescale.*

# 4

# UNDERSTANDING CHANGE: MODERN EVOLUTIONARY THEORY

Chapter 2 ended with a discussion of scientific creationism and evolution. We said that the theory of evolution, unlike creationism, is supported by a massive amount of interrelated evidence gathered and interpreted according to the scientific method.

What is the evidence for evolution as we understand it today? How does evolution work? What does it have to do with human beings?

## GENETICS

As we noted neither Charles Darwin nor Alfred Wallace understood the biological variation that was so crucial to their theory of natural selection. They knew variation existed, but, as Darwin admitted, such variations "seem to us in our ignorance to arise spontaneously" (1898:239).

Why did Darwin fail to understand this principle? The answer is that he was operating without knowledge of **genetics**. Adhering to the notion current in his day, he thought inheritance worked through some sort of "blending"—a mixing of parental substances in the offspring. There seemed to be ample evidence for this idea from plant and animal breeding, where offspring often exhibited traits that appeared to be 50 : 50 mixtures of their parents' traits—pink flowers from a cross of red-flowered with white-flowered parents, for instance.

Plenty of traits, of course, aren't inherited in this way. Organisms inherit their sex from their parents and, with few exceptions, are not 50 : 50 blends but are simply either male or female. Traits that seem to blend, though, like flower color, appear to have been more influential in early thinking about the mechanism of inheritance.

Ironically, at about the same time Darwin was writing *On the Origin of Species,* a monk named Gregor Mendel (1822–1884), working in a monastery in what is now Czechoslovakia, established that inheritance did not operate by blending but rather was **particulate**. By conducting breeding experiments with the pea plants in the monastery garden (the culmination of many years of experimentation with plants and mice),

**Figure 4.1** *What genes are and how they work. The portion of a DNA molecule at left shows four codons. The DNA unwinds, and mRNA reads the code and moves out of the cell nucleus where it acts as a template along which tRNA, carrying specific amino acids, lines up. The strand of amino acids, in their proper order, is one of the proteins responsible for some structure or function in the cell. In reality, no protein is only four amino acids long, but the process works exactly as shown.*

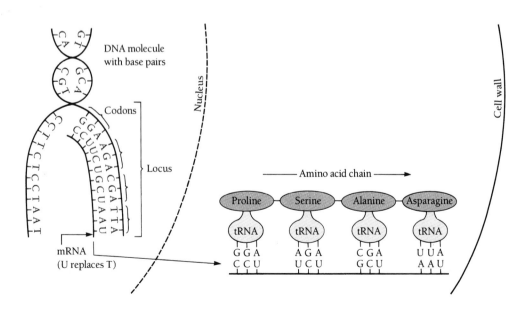

Mendel showed that an organism's individual traits are passed from generation to generation by individual particles or "factors"—what we now call **genes**.

As a further irony, it seems Mendel's work, which was not widely disseminated (Darwin never knew of it), was not fully appreciated by those who did know about it. They failed to see any implications beyond some interesting facts about pea plants. After Mendel's death, his work fell into obscurity, and it was not until 1900 that it was rediscovered. By then the implications of his experiments were clear, and so the stage was set for the series of discoveries that led to our modern understanding of genetics.

We now understand that a gene is actually a chemical code for the production of a **protein**. Proteins make up the basic structure of the cells of living things and, in the form of **enzymes**, are responsible for the cells' functions. Because organisms are made up of cells, it's safe to say that, in a sense, living things *are* proteins.

Figure 4.1 illustrates our current understanding of the process by which proteins are manufactured according to the genetic code, a process known as **protein synthesis**. The code is made up of a variable sequence of bases (a family of chemicals) that are part of a long chemical strand called **deoxyribonucleic acid (DNA)**. The individual strands of DNA are themselves arranged in longer strands called **chromosomes**, found in the nuclei of all cells. Four bases are involved in the code: adenine (A), thymine (T), cytosine (C), and guanine (G). Chemical bonds between these bases hold the DNA molecule together, but the bases are only bonded in A-T or T-A and C-G or G-C pairs.

The first function of this pairing is to enable the DNA molecule to make copies of itself during cell division (Figure 4.2). The DNA molecule, normally shaped like a double helix, unwinds, and each strand, with its now unpaired bases, picks up the proper complementary bases, which are in solution in the cell. This is called *replication*. Thus, when the whole cell divides, each new, or daughter, cell has a complete set of DNA.

The sequence of these DNA bases is divided into groups of three; these are called **codons**. Think of them as three-letter words. Each codon "word" is the code for a particular **amino acid**, and a sequence of words—a genetic "sentence"—puts together a chain of amino acids. A chain of amino acids is a protein or enzyme—one of the chemicals that make up and run the body's cells. To complete the analogy, some codons also act as capitalization and punctuation, beginning and ending the sentences.

A gene can thus be thought of as that portion of the DNA molecule that carries the codon sentence for a particular protein. We call that portion a **locus** (pl. **loci**), a term more specific than, and so preferable to, *gene*.

**genetics**: The study of the mechanism of inheritance.

**particulate**: The idea that biological traits are controlled by individual factors rather than by a single hereditary agent.

**gene**: The portion of the DNA molecule that codes for a specific trait.

**protein**: The family of molecules that makes cells and carries out cellular functions.

**enzyme**: A protein that controls chemical processes.

**protein synthesis**: The process by which the genetic code puts together proteins in the cell.

**deoxyribonucleic acid (DNA)**: The molecule that carries the genetic code.

**chromosome**: A strand of DNA in the nucleus of cells.

**codon**: A section of DNA that codes for a particular amino acid.

**amino acid**: The chief component of proteins.

**locus** (pl. **loci**): A location on the chromosome of the genetic code for a specific trait.

**Figure 4.2** *Cell division occurs in two ways. Mitosis produces exact copies of the parent cell and is the most common form of cell division. Meiosis results in four daughter cells, each with one-half the genetic content of the parent cell, and is the process by which the sex cells (sperm and egg) are manufactured. Meiosis assures that when fertilization occurs, the new individual has a complete set of genes, one-half from each parent.*

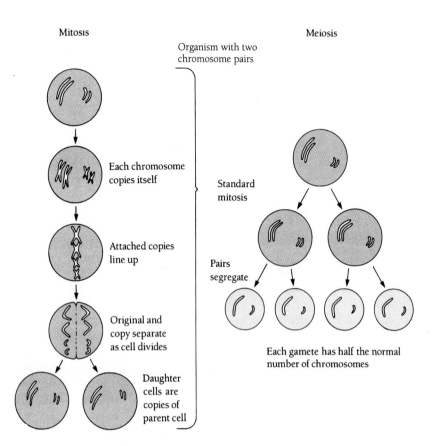

Mitosis

Meiosis

Organism with two chromosome pairs

Each chromosome copies itself

Standard mitosis

Attached copies line up

Pairs segregate

Original and copy separate as cell divides

Each gamete has half the normal number of chromosomes

Daughter cells are copies of parent cell

The genetic code is "read" by **messenger ribonucleic acid (mRNA)**. The DNA unwinds, as it does during replication, exposing the bases of the strand that carries the code. The mRNA, with uracil (U) replacing thymine (T), transcribes the code, its bases matching up with their complements on the DNA molecule. The mRNA then moves out of the cell's nucleus where it acts as a template for the translation of the code into a protein. **Transfer ribonucleic acid (tRNA)** molecules, carrying bases in the original code words, pick up the proper free-floating amino acids (from about twenty different ones) and line them up along the mRNA, the bases paired up as in the original DNA molecule. The amino acids bond, and a protein, which can then serve its specific function in the cell, is synthesized. The cell can now serve its specific roles in the structure and function of the organism.

Traits—the measurable, observable chemical or physical features of an organism—are the results of the actions of proteins that have been manufactured by the cells according to genetic instructions. Some traits, such as the blood component hemoglobin, are chemically simple. Hemoglobin is a protein made up of two paired amino acid chains and thus is determined by two loci. Skin color is made up of many proteins and is thus coded for by many loci.

Each species has a characteristic number of chromosomes. Humans, for example, have forty-six; chimpanzees, forty-eight; and wheat, forty-two. Bacteria have a single chromosome. Obviously, no necessary relationship exists between chromosome number and organism complexity.

In sexually reproducing species, chromosomes come in pairs. An organism inherits one chromosome from each parent and thus gets half its genetic material from each parent. It follows that the genetic loci also come in pairs, so each organism has two of every locus.

The catch is that a genetic locus can have variants, called **alleles**, each with a slightly different set of codons. The alleles of a locus influence the same trait but may produce different expressions of that trait. For example, whether you have blood type A, B, AB, or O depends on your particular pair of the three possible alleles of the locus that codes for the amino acid chain determining blood type. Each allele codes for a version of the chain with a different specific sequence of amino acids. Your allele pair is your **genotype** for that locus.

An organism can have two of the same allele, a condition called **homozygous**, when both its parents have contributed the same allele of that genetic locus. Or, it may have two different alleles, called **heterozygous**, when the loci contributed by the parents carry different codes. Alleles are products of **mutations**, genetic mistakes—in this case at the level of the individual genetic locus—that alter the exact "spelling" of the code and thus transform one allele into another.

The expression of a genotype—the trait that results from the genetic code—is called the **phenotype**. In homozygotes both alleles are the same, so the trait they code for is expressed; there is no alternative. In many heterozygotes, the influence of *both* alleles is expressed in the phenotype. This is what gives rise to the appearance of blending.

On occasion the expression of one allele in heterozygotes may be hidden. Such alleles are said to be **recessive**. The other member of the pair, the one expressed, is **dominant**. The words *dominant* and *recessive* carry no implications of value, no significance for adaptation. Dominant alleles are not necessarily better than recessive alleles.

When an organism reproduces, it obviously cannot pass on *both* alleles of each pair to its offspring. If this were the case, the offspring would end up with twice the proper number of genetic loci. Instead, organisms produce cells for reproduction that are different from those that make up the rest of the organism. These are the sex cells, or **gametes** (sperm and eggs, for instance). Gametes are produced through a process that splits the chromosome pairs and thus the allele pairs so that each gamete only has one of each locus (see Figure 4.2). Mendel called this effect **segregation**.

**messenger ribonucleic acid (mRNA):** The molecule that carries the genetic code out of the nucleus for translation into proteins.

**transfer ribonucleic acid (tRNA):** RNA that lines up amino acids along mRNA to make proteins.

**allele:** A variant of a genetic locus.

**genotype:** The alleles possessed by an organism.

**homozygous:** Having two of the same allele.

**heterozygous:** Having two different alleles in a pair.

**mutation:** A change in an organism's genetic material.

**phenotype:** The chemical or physical results of the genetic code.

**recessive:** An allele of a pair that is not expressed.

**dominant:** An allele of a pair that is expressed.

**gamete:** The cell of reproduction.

**segregation:** The breaking up of allele pairs during gamete production.

**Figure 4.3** *Normal red blood cells (right) and those showing the abnormal shapes that result from the presence of hemoglobin with one incorrect amino acid (left). Such cells fail to transport oxygen properly to the body's tissues.* (AP Wide World Photos)

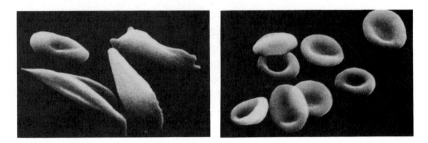

When a sperm from the male parent fertilizes an egg from the female, the resultant **zygote** once again has a pair of each genetic locus. But because the members of each pair have two different sources, the combination of loci in each pair may well be different from that of either parent. This effect is called **recombination** and produces genetic variation among individuals of the same species and, in fact, among offspring of the same parent.

These principles can be demonstrated in a concrete example. Sickle cell anemia is a genetic disease of the blood often erroneously associated only with black people. This is not because the disease is found only in blacks but because it is found in its highest frequencies in a band across central Africa, a region from which most American blacks trace their ancestry. It is also found in southern Europe, the Middle East, and India.

Sickle cell anemia is the result of a mutation affecting hemoglobin, the protein on the red blood cells that carries oxygen from the lungs to the body's tissues. Hemoglobin is made up of two paired amino acid chains, an alpha chain of 141 amino acids and a beta chain 146 amino acids long. If, through a mutation, an incorrect amino acid is substituted for the correct one at position 6 on the beta chain, the disease results. In terms of the genetic code, this means that the mutation is one wrong "word"—a mistake in one codon—in a sentence of 146 words.

When the abnormal hemoglobin is present and stress, high altitude, or illness lowers an individual's oxygen supply, the red blood cells take on peculiar shapes. Some resemble sickles (Figure 4.3). In this condition they cannot carry sufficient oxygen to nourish the body's cells. The result is fatigue, retarded physical development in children, increased susceptibility to infection, miscarriage in pregnant women, fever, and severe pain. People with sickle cell anemia frequently die before their twenties; even if they live longer, they have a very low reproductive rate. In terms of evolutionary success, sickle cell anemia may be considered nearly 100 percent fatal.

The abnormal allele for sickle cell acts like a recessive. A person must have the homozygous genotype to be afflicted with the disease, but heterozygotes still carry the sickle cell allele. When two individuals carrying one allele each for sickle cell mate, they have a one-quarter chance of producing an offspring with the sickle cell anemia phenotype. A device called a Punnett square shows how this process works (Figure 4.4).

Sickle cell anemia also demonstrates some of the complexity of genetics and its intricate relationship to the environment and to evolution. The sickle cell allele is not completely recessive. Heterozygotes possess about 40 percent abnormal hemoglobin, and, under extreme conditions of low oxygen, they experience sickle cell symptoms, although not as severely as homozygotes. Indeed, complete dominance and complete recessiveness are the exception; the alleles of most loci are both expressed to some degree. A heterozygote may be somehow intermediate between either homozygote, or it may show the phenotypes of both alleles. This is called **codominance**.

The general rule is that in most cases the phenotype is not a clear-cut indication of the genotype. Besides various relationships among alleles, most phenotypic traits are simply not coded for by a single genetic locus (**monogenic**) but by many loci (**polygenic**). This effect should be obvious in complex traits like stature or skin color, where numerous individual cellular and chemical actions operate together to make up those phenotypes.

Moreover, not all loci are always in operation. Some are switched on by other loci in response to environmental changes or to some internal "timing." In other words, not all genetic loci are equally influential or direct in producing phenotypic traits. In addition, many loci can influence several seemingly unrelated traits. Think of the many symptoms of sickle cell anemia—highly variable specific expressions all resulting from a one-codon or **point mutation**.

Finally, the relationship between genotype and phenotype can be influenced by environmental factors, that is, any factor outside the codon-to-trait process just outlined. Your skin color, for example, though coded for in your DNA, can change noticeably depending on your health, how much sun you get, and even your emotional state. All these factors can be considered *environmental* in the broadest sense of the word. Heterozygotes for sickle cell anemia, who all have the same genotype, nonetheless vary greatly in the degree to which they exhibit the symptoms of the disease and in how easily those symptoms are triggered. This variation occurs because of a complex interaction of numerous features that affects the genotype–phenotype relationship.

With the rediscovery of Mendel's work in 1900, an understanding of the mechanism of inheritance and of the basic source of variation was added to Darwin's framework for a theory of evolution. From this synthesis, over the next three-quarters of a century, our current knowledge both of genetics, as outlined here, and of the processes of evolution, has developed.

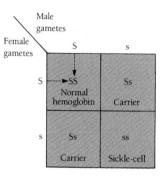

**Figure 4.4** *Punnett square showing sickle cell inheritance. (S is the normal allele; s is the sickle cell allele.) Two individuals, each heterozygous for the hemoglobin locus, produce gametes with normal and abnormal alleles in about equal numbers. When they mate, they have a one-quarter chance of producing a child with normal hemoglobin, a one-half chance of producing a heterozygote like themselves, and a one-quarter chance of producing a child who will almost certainly die from sickle cell anemia.*

**zygote:** A fertilized egg before cell division begins.

**recombination:** The reconstitution of allele pairs at fertilization.

**codominance:** The expression of both alleles of a gene pair.

**monogenic:** A trait coded by a single locus.

**polygenic:** A trait coded by more than one locus.

**point mutation:** A mutation of a single codon.

## THE GENETICS OF POPULATIONS

The physical evidence for evolution is change in the phenotypic features of organisms through time. If evolution manifests itself as phenotypic change and if the genetic code is responsible for determining phenotypic traits, then evolution may be accurately regarded as genetic change through time. Because the genetic makeup of an individual doesn't change (except for mutations), individuals don't evolve. The unit of evolution is the **population**, defined generally as a group within which mates are normally found. Technically, a whole species could be treated as a genetic population because members of a species, by definition, can only mate within that species. But most species are unevenly distributed within their range and so contain subunits of interbreeding individuals, often further defined by a particular locality and perhaps even particular adaptations and physical characteristics. These groups are called **breeding populations**, or **demes**. The evolution of the species can be seen as the collective evolution of the demes within that species, as they change independently and as they interact among themselves by exchanging genetic material.

We genetically characterize the breeding population by identifying how often a certain allele appears in the population relative to the other alleles of that locus. This is called **allele frequency**. Thus, the essential definition of evolution is *change in allele frequency over time*. The processes of evolution, then, are all those factors that bring about changes in allele frequency.

To understand how this concept can help us study and explain the nature and operation of evolutionary processes, let's use sickle cell anemia in a hypothetical breeding population. In a population of 152 individuals under study, the following numbers were found:

| Phenotype | Genotype | Number |
|---|---|---|
| Normal | SS | 71 |
| Heterozygote | Ss | 71 |
| Sickle cell | ss | 10 |
| | | 152 |

Because individuals with normal hemoglobin have genotype *SS*, there are twice as many *S* alleles as there are "normal" individuals. In addition, all heterozygotes possess one *S* allele, so this must be added to the total *S* allele count. Thus,

Number of *S* alleles = (71 × 2) + 71 = 213

Similarly, for the *s* allele,

Number of $s$ alleles = $(10 \times 2) + 71 = \dfrac{91}{304}$

Now, to calculate the frequency (that is, the percentage) of occurrence of each allele, divide the number of each allele by the total number of alleles in the population. For the $S$ allele,

$$\frac{213}{304} = 0.70$$

and for the $s$ allele,

$$\frac{91}{304} = 0.30$$

In a population of 152 individuals with 304 loci of the hemoglobin gene, the allele for normal hemoglobin occurs 70 percent of the time, and the allele for sickle cell occurs 30 percent of the time. These are the allele frequencies for that population.

Given those allele frequencies, we can now calculate the expected *genotype* and *phenotype* frequencies under ideal conditions, that is, under conditions where none of the processes of evolution are in operation. This device is called a *null hypothesis*. If you can state the condition under which nothing occurs, you can then compare it to situations where something *does* occur, observe the nature and direction of the difference, and possibly discern factors that are responsible. With reference to the genetics of populations, the null hypothesis is specifically known as the **Hardy–Weinberg equilibrium**.

Using our two alleles, $S$ and $s$, we designate the frequency of $S$ as $p$ and the frequency of $s$ as $q$. The probability of creating each of the possible genotypes is the product (the result of multiplication) of the frequencies of the alleles of that genotype. Thus,

| Genotype | Product of Frequencies |
|----------|------------------------|
| $SS$ | $p \times p = p^2$ |
| $Ss$ | $p \times q = pq$ |
| $sS$ | $q \times p = qp = 2pq$ |
| $ss$ | $q \times q = q^2$ |

Because all genotypes are now accounted for,

$$p^2 + 2pq + q^2 = 1$$

(that is, 100 percent of the genotypes).

We can now return to our hypothetical population and see what its genotype frequencies would be if they were based solely on the frequencies of the alleles, if, in the terminology of population genetics, the population were in Hardy–Weinberg equilibrium.

**population:**  A reproductive unit.

**breeding population:**  A population with some degree of genetic isolation from other populations of the species.

**deme:**  Generally, the same as a breeding population.

**allele frequency:**  The number of times (in percentage) that a particular allele appears in a population.

**Hardy–Weinberg equilibrium:** The formula that shows genotype percentages under hypothetical conditions of no evolutionary change.

| Genotype | Expected Frequency | Expected Number | Observed Number |
|----------|-------------------|-----------------|-----------------|
| SS | $p^2 = .7^2 = .49$ | $.49 \times 152 = 74$ | 71 |
| Ss | $2pq = .7 \times .3 \times 2$ $= .42$ | $.42 \times 152 = 64$ | 71 |
| ss | $q^2 = .3^2 = .09$ | $.09 \times 152 = 14$ | 10 |

Although close, the observed numbers are not in equilibrium. The allele frequencies have changed relative to the null hypothesis situation. Evolution, by definition, is taking place: There are fewer "normal" individuals than expected, more heterozygotes, and fewer sickle cell victims. An evolutionary trend seems to favor heterozygotes; given what we know about sickle cell anemia (to be discussed in the next section), this could make perfect sense depending on the population in question. Indeed, data like the above hinted at the nature of the disease and led to our understanding of it.

**Figure 4.5** *Where trees are light in color, the light form of the peppered moth has a selective advantage over the dark form* (left). *Where trees are blackened by soot, the dark form has the advantage* (right). *As pollution increased in England, the dark peppered moth became more common.* (M. W. F. Tweedie/Photo Researchers, Inc.)

What processes, then, can bring about allele-frequency change in populations and thus alter the phenotypic nature of the group?

## THE PROCESSES OF EVOLUTION

### Natural Selection

As Darwin explained, from the physical and behavioral variation within a species, nature selects the best adapted characteristics. The measure of nature's selection is the relative reproductive success of the individual organisms that possess those characteristics. This is called **differential reproduction**. Individuals with the most adaptive traits will tend to produce more offspring on the average, passing on relatively more often the alleles that code for their advantageous traits. In this manner the better adapted traits accumulate over time, and the poorly adapted ones become less frequent and may even disappear if their possessors fail to reproduce at all. The result is that the species as a whole stays adapted to its environmental **niche**—the particular set of environmental circumstances with which it comes in contact and to which it must adjust.

The traits that make an individual better adapted will, of course, vary with the species in question and with that species' particular niche. Bigger size, smaller size, bright colors, dull colors, speed, stealth, intelligence, reliance on built-in instincts—each of these can be adaptive depending on the species.

In addition, in some species selection of mating partners takes place. Males may directly compete with one another for access to females. The famous head-clashing "duels" of bighorn sheep are an example. In other cases females choose mates based on things like the establishment of a nesting site or colorful feather displays as in the peacock (although the adaptive benefit of this is still not fully understood). This form of selection is called **sexual selection**, and, as we'll see, it may have played a part in early human evolution.

Thus, by assuring that the more advantageous traits are passed to more offspring, natural selection maintains a species' adaptation to its environment. But, as we have seen, environments change. When this happens, traits that were once adaptively neutral or even poorly adapted may actually be better adapted. These traits will begin to occur in higher frequencies because their possessors are becoming increasingly reproductively successful. At the same time, once-normal traits may become increasingly rare and perhaps even eventually nonexistent. Even under new environmental conditions then, the species can remain viable and adapted, though its adaptive features may be different.

A classic example of differential reproduction in changing environments is the peppered moth (Figure 4.5). When first described in En-

**differential reproduction:** The differing reproductive success of individuals within a population.

**niche:** The environment of an organism and its adaptive response to that environment.

**sexual selection:** The active, rather than random, selection of mating partners chosen by individuals within a population.

**Figure 4.6** *Schematic diagram of Darwinian natural selection. As in the case of the peppered moth, an environmental change makes the darker individuals more reproductively successful, and they become the most common representative of their species. Compare with Figure 2.6, Lamarck's concept of evolutionary change.*

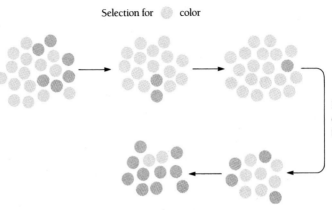

Selection for ⬤ color

Environmental change—selection for darker color

gland before the Industrial Revolution, most members of this species were multicolored. This coloration provided them with camouflage when they landed on lichen-covered trees and made them less easily seen by birds. Some uniformly dark moths appeared each generation, however, the results of a different allele (or alleles) for coloration. These members of the species were rare because they were highly visible and thus far less successful at staying alive to reproduce. In the nineteenth century, when pollution, largely from coal burning, killed off the sensitive lichens and blackened tree trunks, the once-rare dark moths had an adaptive advantage. They—and thus the alleles causing their coloration—became more frequent, and the multicolored moths occurred less frequently. More recently, with less coal burning and better pollution control, the multicolored moths are once again becoming the most frequent type.

Note that in this case, as in any example of natural selection, the variation that proved useful under changed circumstances was *already present*. It did not appear when it was needed or because it was needed. This is the essential difference between Lamarck's inheritance of acquired characteristics and Darwin's natural selection (Figure 4.6).

A more complex example comes once again from sickle cell anemia. Despite the fact that it is so disadvantageous, sickle cell anemia is found in high frequencies in certain areas of the world. One would expect a lethal allele to disappear quickly, or in other words, to be "selected out." But in some parts of West Africa, sickle cell is found in at least one in every sixty-four people. There's clearly more to the persistence of this disease than first meets the eye.

The reason is that besides not usually having severe symptoms of sickle cell anemia, heterozygotes, with one allele for normal hemoglobin and one for the abnormal form, also have a resistance to malaria, a potentially fatal disease caused by a parasitic single-celled organism and transmitted by mosquitoes. This resistance comes about because red blood cells with abnormal hemoglobin (heterozygotes have 40 percent abnormal hemoglobin) take on abnormal shapes when infected by the malaria parasite and die; thus, they fail to transport the parasite through the system. Sickle cell is found in highest frequencies where malaria is found in highest frequencies. In no environment is there any advantage in being homozygous recessive. In malarial environments, however, heterozygotes do have an advantage, and—as you saw in the Punnett square—when two heterozygotes mate, they have a one-quarter chance of producing a homozygous recessive child who will probably die at an early age from sickle cell. They also have a one-half chance of producing more heterozygotes who carry the defective mutation.

Adaptive fitness, then, is relative to particular environmental conditions. What is adaptive in one environment may not be adaptive in another. What is adaptive at one time may not be at another. A lethal allele may actually be adaptive in certain genotypic combinations within certain environments. The gene–environment relationship is a complex one.

This is something to keep in mind as we discuss the various phenotypic evolutionary changes our species has undergone. Few evolutionary events are as simple as they first seem. When we discuss the evolution of our upright posture or our large brains, you should appreciate the complex genetic changes that must have occurred, as well as the complex interactions between genotype and phenotype and between phenotype and environment.

It is also important to remember that because it operates on variation already present in existing traits, natural selection is not always successful in maintaining the viability of a species. When some environmental change is too severe or too rapid, there may simply not be any variation within a species that enables some of its members to reproduce in quantities sufficient to perpetuate the species. Extinction is the result and has been the fate of perhaps 90 percent of all species that have ever existed.

For example, dinosaur species occupied a great diversity of niches and were around in some form for over 100 million years. Yet a rapid environmental change occurred to which none of the dinosaurs (or too few to matter) had sufficiently adapted traits. The dinosaurs died out in a fairly short period of time. Human activity also constitutes a form of environmental change and can bring about the same kinds of results. Overhunting of passenger pigeons in North America, coupled with the felling of forests, resulted in the extinction, by 1914, of a species that once numbered in the billions.

Natural selection is not magic, nor is it the only process that changes allele frequency and thus contributes to evolution. Whereas natural selection produces change in the direction of better adaptation, other processes are said to be random, that is, with no predictable adaptive direction. Because they cause allele-frequency change through time, however, they are considered evolutionary processes (Figure 4.7).

**Figure 4.7** *The processes of evolution. Each acts in different ways at different levels, but they all bring about change within species by altering allele frequency over time.*

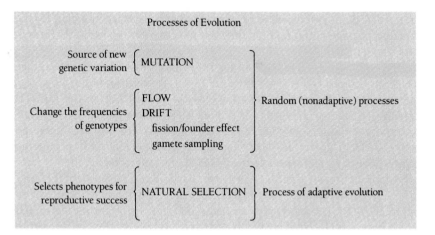

## Mutation

Mutations are random—that is, unpredictable—changes in the material of inheritance. Mutations may affect individual genetic loci as in the case of sickle cell anemia, the result of 1 wrong codon in a sequence of 146. Or they may affect a whole, or a portion of a, chromosome and therefore many loci. Mutations may occur spontaneously as a result of mechanical errors during the processes by which the genetic code copies itself during cell division or is translated into working proteins. Mutations may also be the results of certain outside stimuli like cosmic or nuclear radiation, various chemical pollutants, and some insecticides.

Mutations are frequent. Some have occurred in cells somewhere in your body since you started reading this page. The only ones that matter to evolution, though, are those that occur in the sex cells or the cells that produce the sex cells. These are the mutations that can be passed on and can thus change the allele frequencies of the population.

Because mutations are sudden, random changes, they may logically be considered mistakes. As mistakes, many have deleterious effects. Such mutations tend to disappear because individuals having them may be less reproductively successful. In other words, they are selected *against*. Other mutations may produce alleles that are neutral in terms of adaptation—that is, at the time they occur they are neither more nor less adaptive than the original allele. And some mutations may even be more adaptive than other variations. In this case, natural selection is provided with new raw material.

Mutation, then, is a source of variation upon which natural selection can act. It is also itself a process of evolutionary change because it alters the hereditary material of a species. The effect of a mutation on the species as a whole depends, of course, on just what traits are affected and the importance of those traits to the relative reproductive success of the individual. A small, inconsequential mutation has little or no effect on the individual and so may or may not be passed to a proportionately large number of offspring; *that* depends on the success of the individual based on what other traits it possesses. A large mutation, or a small one with extensive effects (like the sickle cell allele), will be passed on to *no one* if it is deleterious, but it may spread rapidly through the species in subsequent generations if it confers a distinct advantage on those who carry it.

Mutations affect the hereditary material itself. Natural selection operates on the physical manifestations of the hereditary material. Two other processes of evolution, **gene flow** and **genetic drift**, work at a level between selection and mutation. These processes change allele frequency by altering the frequencies of genotypes, that is, allele combinations. They work, however, *without regard* to their specific adaptive characteristics. They are thus, like mutation, referred to as random processes.

## Gene Flow

Members of a species interbreed with one another. But species tend to be divided into breeding populations or demes, that are delimited by geographic distance, specific environmental range and niche, and social organization. Populations within a species may undergo natural selection to their particular environmental situations and may therefore exhibit minor differences among one another (a topic we'll take up in more detail in Chapter 13). So when members of several populations do interbreed—when the genes of one "flow" into the **gene pool** of another—new genetic combinations result in the offspring. New physical manifestations appear in the mixed population and provide even more raw material for natural selection on the species level.

When flow is extensive among populations within a species, it has the effect of reducing the genetic variation among those populations. This is the case, for example, in our own species, where our mobility and tendency to interbreed have blurred physical distinctions among our individual populations (see Chapter 13).

## Genetic Drift

Several distinct processes fall under the heading of genetic drift. **Fission** is the opposite process from gene flow. When a population within a species splits, the new subpopulations will differ from one another and from the original population in the average expression of their physical

**gene flow:** The exchange of genes among populations through interbreeding.

**genetic drift:** The change in gene frequency by random fluctuations.

**gene pool:** All the genes of a population.

**fission:** The splitting up of a population to form new populations.

**Figure 4.8** *Diagram of founder effect where a population split produces new populations with potentially distinct gene pools. (Gene flow can be pictured by reversing the arrows, producing one population from two.)*

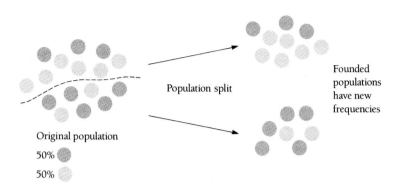

Population split

Founded populations have new frequencies

Original population

50%

50%

traits and in the combinations of the genetic loci that code for those traits. This may not seem obvious at first, but suppose you calculate the average stature of members of your anthropology class to be 5′9″ with a range from 5′1″ to 6′7″. If you divide the class into two groups without considering height, do you think the average stature and range for each new group will be the same as the original? Unless the class is extremely large—say, thousands of people—the laws of probability are heavily against it. It works the same with genes in natural populations. Any population split—a common enough occurrence—will provide evolutionary change as well as new gene pools for selection to operate on (Figure 4.8).

This effect is enhanced when the split is uneven—when, for example, 10 percent of a population splits from the original and founds a new population. It is virtually impossible for that 10 percent to possess the same average physical traits, gene combinations, and allele frequencies as the original. This is known as the **founder effect**. It and fission are usually considered one form of genetic drift.

The other form of genetic drift is **gamete sampling**. When fertilization takes place in sexually reproducing species, the genetic material from two parents is mixed. The potential number of new genetic combinations in the offspring is enormous. You may resemble your parents, but you are not a "carbon copy" of either, and your specific genetic makeup is absolutely unique to you (unless you have an identical twin). This means there will be change every generation, based solely on the laws of probability applied to the recombination of parental genes in the new offspring. This change is not related to the adaptive fitness of the traits involved because it is produced at the time of fertilization, before the environment has a chance to act on the physical traits.

Recombination affects only the offspring of one set of parents, but the combined effects of this process at the population level, in many sets of parents and offspring, can bring about a great deal of change from one generation to the next. Especially if the trait expressions coded for by the new genetic combinations are adaptively unimportant, the specific expressions may change at random across generations, "drifting" in whatever direction chance takes them—hence the name of the process.

Suppose, for instance, two parents are both heterozygous for a certain locus, say, *Aa*. A Punnett square would reveal that they stand a one-quarter chance of producing an *AA* offspring, a one-half chance of producing an *Aa* offspring, and a one-quarter chance of producing an *aa* offspring. These figures, however, are probabilities, not certainties. Each fertilization is an event independent of all previous fertilizations. They may, for example, produce nothing but *AA* offspring. In that case, all their *a* alleles are lost. In a large population, there is a good chance that two other parents of genotype *Aa* will produce only *aa* offspring, and it will all balance out. But in a small population, under 100, the chance of such a balance is very small. All forms of drift have greater effects in small populations. In this way some alleles may ultimately be lost, and others may reach a frequency of 100 percent, all with no necessary relation to adaptation.

As with the other processes, drift produces evolutionary change as well as new population variation on which natural selection may then operate. It may not, however, always be a positive process. A further threat to species already on the brink of extinction because of low population size is the fact that what little genetic variation they have left may be depleted more by the drifting of some alleles to high frequencies and others to low frequencies. The less genetic variation, the less chance a species has of containing enough individuals well enough adapted to reproduce in sufficient numbers. This is part of the current plight of cheetahs, gorillas, condors, and other endangered species.

## THE ORIGINS OF SPECIES

Although natural selection was the cornerstone of Darwin's theory of evolution, it was not the phenomenon he ultimately sought to explain. What interested Darwin, and Wallace, was the question of where all the species of plants and animals had come from in the first place. Natural selection was the mechanism they proposed as the answer. Darwin, in fact, felt it was *the* answer. Natural selection, he said, brought about "the accumulation of innumerable slight variations, each good for the individual possessor" (1898:267). He added,

> What limit can be put to this power, acting during long ages and rigidly scrutinizing the whole constitution, structure, and habits of each creature,— favoring the good and rejecting the bad? I can see no limit to this power, in slowly and beautifully adapting each form to the most complex relations of life. (1898:267)

**founder effect:** Differences in populations caused by genetic differences in the individuals who establish the populations.

**gamete sampling:** The genetic change caused when genes are passed to new generations in frequencies unlike the parental population.

**Figure 4.9** *The various species of Darwin's finches evolved when small groups from an original single species underwent adaptation to the specific environmental conditions of the Galapagos Islands. Because the islands are relatively isolated, they often provide clear examples of speciation.* (Eric Mose from "Darwin's Finches" by D. Lack, *Scientific American*, April 1953, p. 66)

So, according to Darwin's view, new species arise simply as a result of constant adaptive change within an existing species. Eventually, the species changes so much it evolves into a new species. In addition, such constant selection, Darwin said, will produce variation among populations within a species in response to slight differences in the environments. He referred to these populations as "varieties." Eventually, selection brings about such marked distinctions that new species are produced from the old one. Species, said Darwin, "are only well-marked varieties, of which the characters have become in a high degree permanent" (1898:285). Thus, one species gradually but inexorably gives rise to new species, forming in the process "an interminable number of intermediate forms . . . linking together all the species in each group by [fine] gradations" (1898:271–72).

Darwin, then, saw natural selection as more than a mechanism for the origin of species. To him it was the driving force, constantly choosing from among innumerable small variations those best suited to an environment, and in the end turning one species into another or producing first new varieties within species and finally new species. Evolution, according to Darwin, is a long string of small adaptive changes through time.

For example, fourteen species (some authorities recognize thirteen) of related finches inhabit the Galapagos Islands in the Pacific. These are collectively known as "Darwin's finches" because he first described them, although he surprisingly did not realize they provided a classic example of **speciation** (Gould 1985b). Later it was realized that all fourteen species were descended from a single South American species. Over a long span of time, individuals from this original population were blown out to sea from the mainland and a few managed to end up on the fourteen or so Galapagos Islands and gradually adapted to the varying ecological conditions on the islands. Natural selection to those conditions, along with the relative isolation of the islands and long periods of time, allowed the finch populations to diverge to such a degree that they are now separate species, characterized by such features as differences in size and beaks specifically shaped to aid in acquiring whatever sort of food each environment provides. Subsequent invasions have resulted in a dispersal of the various species among the islands. Some of the larger and more ecologically varied islands of the group support as many as ten of the finch species (Figure 4.9).

Darwin was challenged, however, on one aspect of his idea about speciation. Where, some of his contemporaries asked, were all those "intermediate forms" in the fossil record? Darwin's answer was that the fossil record was "imperfect," that more time and study would reveal all the transitions. He was wrong.

Although the last 100 years have brought to light fossils representing the transitions between major forms of life (reptiles to birds and reptiles

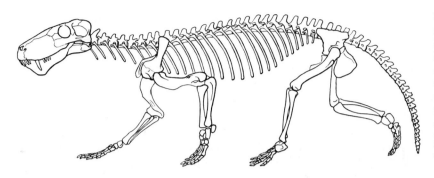

**Figure 4.10** Lycaenops, *a mammal-like reptile from 240 mya. Its legs were long and under its body, allowing it to keep its body continually off the ground, like mammals and unlike earlier reptiles. Lycaenops also had long canine teeth like mammals, though its other teeth were reptilian.* (Neg. #2A3387. Courtesy Department of Library Services, American Museum of Natural History)

to mammals, for example), transitional forms between individual species have, for the most part, failed to appear (Figure 4.10). The concrete evidence does not support the theory. Moreover, Darwin's **gradualism** itself presents a theoretical problem. If each small variation selected for is "good for the individual possessor," then we must account for the adaptive benefit of each small step toward the development of some completed characteristic. Does one-tenth of a wing, or one-hundredth of an eye, convey to its possessor a reproductive advantage over the members of its species that lack this trait?

It seems more likely that new forms of a trait, or whole new traits, arise fairly rapidly in more complete form, the results of mutations of large numbers of loci or of loci that code for important phenotypic traits. The adaptive value of the new or radically changed characteristic is then acted on by natural selection. Selection will eliminate it if it is not adaptive, ignore it if it is neutral, or keep it if it is adaptively advantageous. According to this view, the origin of a new species involves not a series of small steps but an initial big step.

This idea was first seriously proposed in the 1940s, but no genetic mechanism was generally accepted that could account for such large changes so rapidly. Mutations were thought to involve only slight alterations. Now, however, we recognize that not all genetic loci are of equal importance and that a mutation of an important locus, or of a large number of important loci, can produce a major change in the offspring of the organism that passes it on. There are, for example, genes influencing developmental changes that act on the individual at an early age but may have important consequences for the structure and function of the adult organism. There appears to have been one such change, more than 140 million years ago, that altered the development of reptilian scales to produce featherlike structures, thus beginning the evolution of the birds (Figure 4.11). Differences of this sort appear to be responsible for distinguishing us from chimpanzees, a topic we'll take up in Chapter 8.

**speciation:** The evolution of new species.

**gradualism:** The view that evolution is slow and steady with cumulative change.

With this new genetic information providing a theoretical basis, the "sudden change" idea about the origin of species could reemerge. It did so in 1972, proposed by paleontologists Niles Eldredge and Stephen Jay Gould (1972), who called it **punctuated equilibrium**. The new reformulation says that the evolutionary history of a species is marked by equilibrium—long periods of little change—with natural selection acting conservatively to maintain the species' adaptation to its environment, mostly by selecting against maladaptive variations.

This equilibrium, however, is "punctuated" by bursts of change. These occur when a mutation with important results—a **macromutation**—takes place, producing a variation of a trait or maybe a whole new feature. If it is particularly adaptive, the character can increase in frequency as new generations are produced, rapidly spreading through the species by means of differential reproduction. In other cases the new character may arise in small populations that are isolated at the edge of a species' range. A new adaptive trait will spread very rapidly through such a group and will set that group off on a new adaptive mode of life.

After a new trait appears, it will itself begin to exhibit variation that natural selection can then use to "fine-tune" the new adaptive feature to the specific environment. In time, a new species may be evolved. This is

**Figure 4.11** *The fossil remains of Archeopteryx ("ancient bird"), actually a small, bipedal dinosaur with feathers. The feathers, modifications of reptilian scales, are an example of a punctuation, a sudden but fairly sizable alteration in a species' genetic makeup, eventually giving rise to a whole new group of organisms.* (Neg. #319836. Courtesy Department of Library Services, American Museum of Natural History)

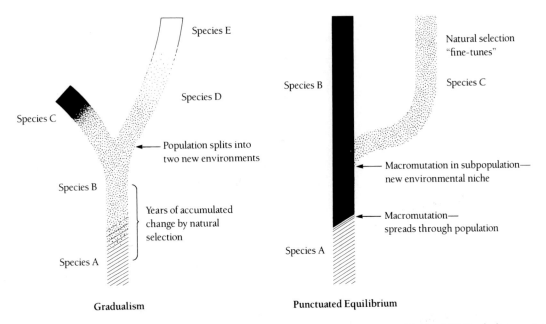

Species E

Species D

Species C

Species B

Species A

Population splits into
two new environments

Years of accumulated
change by natural
selection

**Gradualism**

Natural selection
"fine-tunes"

Species C

Species B

Macromutation in subpopulation—
new environmental niche

Macromutation—
spreads through population

Species A

**Punctuated Equilibrium**

**Figure 4.12** *Gradualism compared with punctuated equilibrium. It is likely that both processes have been responsible for the evolution of new species, but it appears as if punctuated equilibrium accounts for the general picture of the evolution of life on earth.*

not an instant process; it may take thousands of years. But it is not a gradual evolution marked by a long series of small transitional steps, as Darwin had proposed. It begins with a big step—a "jump," some call it—providing natural selection with something brand new and very different to work with (Figure 4.12).

With this theory in mind, the fossil record makes more sense. For instance, we don't find a long, gradual series of stages in the evolution of birds from dinosaurian reptiles. The first evidence of birds, from about 140 million years ago, is in the form of a small, bipedal dinosaur with feathers (see Figure 4.11). These are not one-tenth feathers, but feathers nearly like those of modern birds. Even bigger changes, such as the evolution of mammals from early reptiles—although this took a long time to accomplish—still show a number of jumps rather than a long accumulation of minor changes.

Almost certainly, Darwinian gradualism has accounted for the beginnings of some species like the populations of Darwin's finches responding to the different environments of the islands of the Galapagos. Natural selection is always in operation and might well respond, as Darwin suggested, to a situation where a species' environmental range is large, variable, and constantly changing. For the most part, though, it would now seem as if the general record of evolution—the origin of all those species Darwin wondered about—is best explained by punctuated equilibrium.

**punctuated equilibrium:** The view that species tend to remain stable, with evolutionary change arising fairly suddenly.

**macromutation:** Mutation with extensive physical results.

## CONTEMPORARY ISSUE

### The 3 Billion Names of Man

In Arthur C. Clarke's haunting short story "The Nine Billion Names of God," a group of Tibetan monks purchase a supercomputer to speed their task of compiling the 9 billion names of the Supreme Being. Once accomplished, they believe, God's purpose will be achieved, and the world will end.

In 1986 the U.S. Department of Energy (DOE) initiated, with the cooperation of a number of other agencies and institutions, an ambitious project to develop a "complete description of the human genome at the molecular level [the genome being the total genetic endowment of the species]" (Woodhead and Barnhart 1988:v), ideally by the year 2000. This project, known officially as the Human Genome Initiative, is mapping the locations of the 100,000 to 300,000 human genes and will ultimately determine the exact sequence of the 3 billion bases that make up our genetic code. This "library" will then act as a tool to allow researchers to understand just how the genetic code functions to generate our various phenotypic traits. We may then be able to apply this knowledge to matters of human health, to the understanding of the diversity within our species and our evolutionary relationships to other species, and to the improvement of domesticated plants and animals.

So far about 35 million bases have been sequenced, and the participating agencies are trying to improve computer and biotechnology to greatly increase the number of bases that can be sequenced each year. Indeed, some researchers talk of achieving a rate of 5000 bases per person per *day* in order to reach their goal in the projected time.

It all sounds ominously like Clarke's monks, and some people are fearful of what might happen when the project is finished and we possess such intimate knowledge about just who and what we are. Are such fears warranted?

It should be clear that knowledge itself is not the problem; what we *do* with our knowledge is what should concern us. For starters it must be noted that sponsorship of the project by the DOE is explained as "a logical extension of its long term commitment to investigating genetic damage from exposures to radiations and energy-related chemicals" (Woodhead and Barnhart 1988:v). One has to wonder just what the DOE's practical motivation is and exactly how it will affect us in the future. Moreover, one participant in a conference on the project noted (not negatively) that there were financial benefits involved: "The first group or institution to achieve access to data contained in the human genome will be in a position to dominate the biotechnology and pharmaceutical industries for years" (McConnell 1988:2).

Other worries have been expressed as well. Might such detailed knowledge of the genetic differences between individuals and among various populations only serve to fuel the problems of racism and bigotry that we still have not solved?

## SUMMARY

To fully account for the evolution of species, an understanding of the workings of genes is vital. Genes code for the traits that make up the physical organism by giving instructions for the synthesis of proteins. Proteins make cells and control their functions, and cells, in turn, make up the tissues that make up the organism.

The gene pool of a species changes over time because of four processes that change the frequencies with which the alleles of genes ap-

Could employers deny people jobs or insurance companies deny coverage because of the presence of potentially harmful genetic codes? Will human dignity suffer when we have to acknowledge that we are the result of a bunch of chemical sentences that we can now read and manipulate?

All these could happen, but it would not be the fault of the information. Rather, the responsible party would be us and the social and ethical environment in which we put this information to use. It is this we need to work on because the potential benefits of the human genome project far outweigh these preventable deleterious results.

Through our understanding of genetics to date, we have been able to diagnose and treat a number of genetic illnesses and to identify persons who may fall victim to a genetic disease or may pass it on to offspring. We can use techniques commonly called genetic engineering—the human manipulation of the genetic process—to do such things as "trick" bacteria into producing real (rather than artificial) human insulin for the treatment of diabetes. Human growth hormone and interferon, a chemical that is part of the body's immune system, have also been manufactured in this way. We have designed plants that are resistant to certain diseases or that can grow in climates to which they were not originally adapted. We have even created bacteria that can "eat" oil spills.

More detailed knowledge of the genome of humans and other organisms can lead to even more progress in these areas. We have, for example, already discovered the base sequence for the AIDS virus. Although we have yet to cure or even treat this disease, a complete understanding of the organism that causes it is obviously essential and can guide new and specific experiments.

Understanding completely our genetic code can help us individualize medical care. Although many diseases have a single cause, many, like heart attacks, strokes, and cancers, are caused by multiple factors. Being able to read and understand the human genome will help us in dealing with these on an individual basis, allowing us to find genetic markers that may indicate a greater susceptibility to a particular ailment.

At the end of Clarke's story, the monks, with the aid of the new computer, complete their task in a few months and, indeed, as the American computer technicians are leaving Tibet, they look up to see the stars going out. Will that happen when we have decoded the genetic code? Hardly. For one thing, even after we know all 3 billion bases, we will still have to figure out exactly how the protein products of our genes operate to produce all our traits and behaviors. Knowledge is never finished; there's always more to learn. But mostly it's clear that, if used ethically and with care and caution, the knowledge gained through the Human Genome Initiative will greatly benefit human health and general welfare.

pear. Mutations produce new alleles or, on the chromosomal level, new sequences or combinations of alleles. Gene flow shuffles the alleles of populations within a species to produce new genotypic frequencies. Genetic drift tells us that new genotypic frequencies occur each time a population splits and each time a new generation is produced. And natural selection affects allele frequencies via the differential reproduction of the carriers of adaptive phenotypes.

A great enough degree of this change, under the right circumstances, can evolve new species out of existing ones. Charles Darwin thought

*[handwritten margin note: eventually can all lead to evolving or adapting the species into new ones]*

this occurred as a result of the gradual yet inexorable force of selection changing each species every generation. We now understand that natural selection is more a conservative force than a creative one and largely acts to maintain the adaptation of a species to its environment. Speciation seems most often to occur when a sudden change, via a large or important mutation, provides natural selection with a new and important choice. If the new choice is adaptively advantageous, it can give a "head start" to the evolution of a new species.

## KEY TERMS

genetics
gene
particulate
protein
enzyme
protein synthesis
deoxyribonucleic
    acid (DNA)
chromosome
codon
amino acid
locus (pl. loci)
messenger
    ribonucleic acid
    (mRNA)
transfer RNA
    (tRNA)
allele

genotype
homozygous
heterozygous
mutation
phenotype
recessive
dominant
gamete
segregation
zygote
recombination
codominance
monogenic
polygenic
point mutation
population
breeding population
deme

allele frequency
Hardy–Weinberg
    equilibrium
differential
    reproduction
niche
sexual selection
gene flow
genetic drift
gene pool
fission
founder effect
gamete sampling
speciation
gradualism
punctuated
    equilibrium
macromutation

## FOR MORE INFORMATION

Many excellent books on evolution and evolutionary processes are available. We recommend G. Ledyard Stebbins, *Darwin to DNA: Molecules to Humanity.*

A "must" for anyone interested in genetics—or, for that matter, the nature of scientific inquiry in general—is *The Double Helix* by James D. Watson. It's about the race to discover the nature of the genetic code and thereby win the Nobel Prize. The author was one of the winners.

Also on genetics, try Daniel L. Hartl's *Our Uncertain Heritage: Genetics and Human Diversity* for a good general text. *Genetics: Readings from Scientific American,* edited by Cedric F. Davern, provides a wealth of original important articles including some of historical interest (even one by Mendel).

For information on genetic engineering, see "Changing Life's Genetic Blueprint," by Robert F. Weaver, in *National Geographic* (December 1984).

# 5

# LEARNING ABOUT THE PAST: THE PRIMATES

"What is man, that thou art mindful of him?" asks David in the biblical psalm. It is a question we must ask as well, but in a broader form: "What is a human being?" Before we embark on our journey through human evolution, we must understand modern humans, the species with which our journey ultimately ends.

Two problems are encountered in addressing this question. First, all modern human beings belong to just one species. Try describing any animal without referring to other organisms: "Well, a spider has body segments and jointed legs like an insect, only it has eight legs instead of six. . . ." Second, we are members of the very species we're describing. It's difficult to step back and see ourselves from an objective perspective. We have a tendency to focus on things that are important to us in a certain cultural setting at a certain time. For example, Carolus Linnaeus, the great eighteenth-century Swedish naturalist we discussed before, listed as the distinguishing characteristics of *Homo sapiens* "diurnal [active during the day]; varying by education and situation." He then described five subspecies of humans using a combination of physical features and subjective European attitudes. Of the Native American, for instance, he said: "Hair black, straight, thick; nostrils wide, face harsh; beard scanty; obstinate, content free. Paints himself with fine red lines. Regulated by customs" (Kennedy 1976:25).

Clearly, we need to look at ourselves not from cultural perspectives like Linnaeus's but in terms of how we compare with other living organisms. Demosthenes, a fourth-century B.C. Greek orator, described us as "featherless bipeds"; twentieth-century biologist Desmond Morris dubbed us the "naked ape." These are better definitions because they are free from cultural values and recognize both our similarities to other organisms and our distinctive differences.

But despite his obvious ethnocentric biases, it was Linnaeus who first recognized the importance of describing living organisms in comparison with each other. His **taxonomy**, or system of classification, placed living things in categories based on their similarities to and differences from other living things. The system uses a hierarchical set of nested categories: a few general categories, each containing a number of more specific ones, each of those with more specific ones, and so on down to the most specific, the species or individual interbreeding group of organisms (Table 5.1).

Humans, for example, fall into the group *Animalia* within the largest category kingdom. We are animals because we ingest our nutrients, move about, and have sense organs. We are clearly not members of any of the other four kingdoms: simple single-celled organisms, complex single-celled organisms, fungi, or plants.

Within each kingdom are a number of phyla (sing. phylum). Among the animals, for example, are some thirty phyla—such groups as sponges, jellyfish, flatworms, roundworms, molluscs, insects, and chordates. We have backbones, a fairly distinctive feature in the animal kingdom, so we are members of phylum *Chordata*—animals with a **notochord**, a long cartilagenous structure running down the back for support—and subphylum *Vertebrata*—chordates whose notochord is replaced by a bony spine.

**Table 5.1** *Taxonomies of Four Familiar Mammals with Basic Features for Each Category*

|  | Jaguar | Mountain Lion | Chimpanzee | Human |
|---|---|---|---|---|
| **Kingdom** | *Animalia*<br>Ingestion<br>Movement<br>Sense organs | *Animalia* | *Animalia* | *Animalia* |
| **Phylum** | *Chordata*<br>Notochord | *Chordata* | *Chordata* | *Chordata* |
| **Class** | *Mammalia*<br>Hair<br>Warm-blooded<br>Live birth<br>Mammary glands<br>Active and intelligent | *Mammalia* | *Mammalia* | *Mammalia* |
| **Order** | *Carnivora*<br>Meat eaters | *Carnivora* | *Primates*<br>Arboreal<br>Developed vision<br>Grasping hands<br>Large brains | *Primates* |
| **Family** | *Felidae*<br>Retractable claws<br>Furred feet<br>Sharp vision | *Felidae* | *Pongidae*<br>Large<br>Tailless<br>Brachiators | *Hominidae*<br>Habitual bipeds |
| **Genus** | *Panthera*<br>Larger roaring cats | *Felis*<br>Smaller purring cats | *Pan*<br>Smaller of African<br>  apes<br>Open forest | *Homo*<br>Tool-making<br>Omnivore |
| **Species** | *onca*<br>Largest New World cat<br>Only roaring cat<br>Spotted | *concolor*<br>Largest N. American<br>  purring cat<br>Solid color | *troglodytes*<br>Larger of two *Pan*<br>  species | *sapiens*<br>Brain size<br>  1000–2000 ml |

**taxonomy:** A classification based on similarities and differences.

**notochord:** The evolutionary precursor of the vertebral column.

There are seven classes within the vertebrates: the jawless fishes, the cartilagenous fishes (sharks and their kin), the bony fishes, amphibians, reptiles, birds, and mammals. We are obviously members of class *Mammalia*—vertebrates with constant body temperature, hair, live births, mammary glands for nursing young, and relatively large, complex brains.

We've narrowed things down quite a bit, but there are still over 4000 species of mammals, everything from kangaroos to blue whales to bats. Where do we focus our comparison? The key is to remember that the mechanism of natural selection is adaptation. What characterizes a group of organisms—not in our minds, but in nature—is their adaptive behavior. Physical features are important, but the reason they are important is that they make possible a set of behaviors that allows a creature to survive in a certain way under a specific set of environmental circumstances.

Looked at this way, the taxonomic categories become statements about adaptation, with each level more specifically focused. Mammals, for example, are animals that adapt through active lifestyles, relying more than other creatures on learned behavior and thus requiring more care and nurturing of the young as well as a protected constant body temperature to maintain their activity level.

But mammals have many different ways of using this general adaptation, and the next category, order, focuses to a great extent on these more specific adaptive strategies. Among the mammalian orders are the flying bats, the aquatic whales and dolphins, the meat eaters, the insect eaters, the pouched marsupials, and a group of large-brained tree dwellers called the primates. This last group is our own, and our physical and behavioral features can only be understood as expressions of the basic primate adaptive pattern.

## THE PRIMATES

The essential primate environment is arboreal, or tree-dwelling. The fact that the human species is obviously built for locomotion on the ground—and clearly not for moving around in the trees—should not be misinterpreted. Among the primates, we humans are exceptional for our mode of locomotion. The vast majority of primates spend their time in the trees and, indeed, our own bodies and behaviors still reflect that arboreal theme.

There are, of course, many other arboreal creatures. Squirrels, birds, many insects, and even a few snakes all have adaptations for a tree-dwelling way of life. Primates don't have a monopoly on that environment, but they do adapt to it in a way none of these others do. It has obviously been a successful adaptation. For even now, with all the

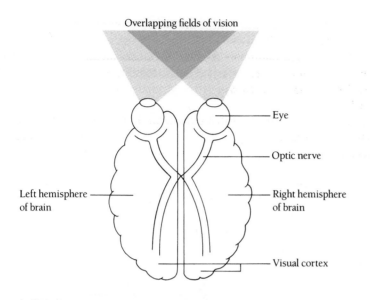

Overlapping fields of vision

Eye

Optic nerve

Left hemisphere
of brain

Right hemisphere
of brain

Visual cortex

**Figure 5.1** *Stereoscopic vision. The fields of vision overlap, and the optic nerve from each eye travels to both hemispheres of the brain. The result is true depth perception.*

changes and disruptions of the natural environment brought about by the human primate, there are still about 200 species of primates spread pretty much worldwide—in Central and South America, Africa, Asia (including northern Japan), and Europe (on Gibraltar).

To examine the characteristics that make possible this arboreal adaptation, we'll use categories that reflect an organism's relation to its environment: (1) the senses, (2) locomotion, (3) reproduction, (4) intelligence, and (5) behavior patterns.

## The Senses

The world in which an organism lives is to a great extent determined by its senses. All the information a creature takes in about its environment comes through the sense organs, which send signals to the brain for interpretation and (if possible) storage. The predominance of one sense over the others can make an enormous difference. Sound rules the sensory world of a dolphin or a bat; smell predominates for dogs. The primate's world is a visual one.

Unlike most mammals, the majority of primates see in color. Primate eyes face forward instead of out to the sides so they see just about the same scene from slightly different angles. When the signals from such eyes are interpreted by the brain, the result is a world of three dimensions. Primates are said to have true depth perception or **stereoscopic vision** (Figure 5.1). To protect their delicate muscles and nerves, primate eyes are enclosed in a bony socket.

**stereoscopic vision:** Three-dimensional vision; depth perception.

This emphasis on the visual sense in primates seems connected to a reduction in the sensitivity of the other senses, at least as compared with many other mammals. Primates have neither the olfactory (smell) nor auditory (hearing) acuity of such familiar animals as dogs, cats, cattle, and horses. The areas of the primate brain that interpret these data are reduced in comparison with those of other mammals, and primates tend to have flat faces, reducing the nasal receptor area within the nose. But no living creature, except possibly birds of prey, see as well as we primates do.

## Locomotion

Most mammals are **quadrupedal;** they walk on all fours. With the notable exception of humans, so do primates, but how they use their four limbs differs from other mammals. Whereas the limbs and feet of mammals in general are built for firm, solid contact with the ground (via hooves or paws with pads), primate limbs are highly flexible; the hands and, in many primates, the feet have the ability to grasp objects. This ability is referred to as **prehensile** (Figure 5.2). Moreover, the hands of most primates have some degree of **opposability**—the ability to touch the other fingers with the thumb, enabling them to pick up objects. Finally, primates have nails instead of claws on the ends of their fingers and toes. Nails lend support to the sensitive tactile receptors of the

**Figure 5.2** *An orangutan holding the hand of its trainer demonstrates the prehensile grasp of the primates, both human and nonhuman.* (Courtesy Marine World/Africa USA and Darryl W. Bush)

fingertips, and they don't get in the way as claws would when the hand is closed.

## Reproduction

In contrast to many other mammals that bear litters or to fish and reptiles that may produce dozens of offspring at a time, nearly all primates have only a single offspring at a time. A small number of primate species normally give birth to twins. As mammals the primates take direct care of their young, protecting, nursing, showing affection, and (even if indirectly) teaching. Particularly because of their large, complex brains, primates take the longest time to mature. This time is related to size, so a mouse lemur (which you could hold in the palm of your hand) grows up faster than a gorilla or a human. Relative to size, however, the primates have the longest period of **postnatal dependency** of all mammals.

*postnatal/infant dependency*

## Intelligence

By **intelligence** we mean the relative ability of an organism's brain to acquire, store, and process information. To a great extent, these abilities are related to brain size. A bigger brain simply has more room for the neural connections that make it all work. But intelligence is also related to the complexity of the brain—how many parts it has—and to its size relative to the organism's body. No primate has a brain the size of a whale's or an elephant's; compared to body size, however, primates have the largest and most complex brains of all mammals.

The relatively large and absolutely more complex brains of primates allow them to take in, store, and process more information in more complicated ways than other mammals. The primates are smart.

*smart cookies (largest) brain size : body ratio*

## Behavior Patterns

*social-dominance hierarchy*

Primates are social creatures. Most live in social groups, but even solitary primates interact with other species members in ways far more complex than would be found among, say, a herd of antelope. The difference is that primates recognize individuals, and individuals each hold a certain status within a primate group (usually called a troop). Some primates—baboons, for example—exhibit a form of **dominance hierarchy** where individuals have differential social power and influence, and, perhaps, access to mates. Nearly all primates recognize a special status for females with infants. Chimpanzees have varying atti-

**quadrupedal:** The ability to walk on four legs.

**prehensile:** The ability to grasp.

**opposability:** The ability to touch thumb to tips of other digits.

**postnatal dependency:** The period, after birth, of dependency on adults.

**intelligence:** The ability to take in, store, process, and use information.

**dominance hierarchy:** The individual differences in power, influence, and access to resources and mating.

tudes about members of their troop that can only be described by our human term *friendship.*

Much of the reason for this social structure stems from the long dependency period of the young. Born helpless and with much to learn about their world, using large brains that take a long time to grow, primate babies need protection. The close bond between mother and infant common to all primates supplies most of this. But especially in dangerous areas like the open plains of Africa, the presence of a troop adds greatly to the chance of successfully rearing offspring to become functioning members of the species' next generation. Care of offspring thus becomes another distinguishing feature of the primate behavior pattern.

**Figure 5.3** *Grooming, which serves to strengthen social bonds, begins early, as seen in these chimpanzees.* (© Halpern/Animals, Animals)

Primate social systems are maintained through communication. Among the primates only humans have a complex symbolic language. Most primates, however, do have a large repertoire of signs and signals with specific meanings. These take the form of facial expressions, body movements, and vocalizations. Touch, usually through mutual **grooming** to remove dirt and parasites, is another form of communication common to most primates and seems to serve as a source of reassurance to maintain group harmony and unity (Figure 5.3).

Given this set of mutually reinforcing traits, the primates may be generally defined as arboreal mammals with well-developed visual senses who, by virtue of a large, complex brain, complex social organization, and a long period of infant dependency with extensive and direct care of the young, adapt to life in the trees. They learn about, move with agility through, and manipulate this environment, with the last two abilities made possible by grasping and dexterous hands and feet.

## A PRIMATE PORTFOLIO

For groups with numerous species and a variety of geographical locations and environmental niches, we find it necessary to add to the basic seven Linnaean taxonomic categories.

The order *Primates* (Figure 5.4) is divided into two major groups, suborder *Prosimii* and suborder *Anthropoidea.* Prosimians represent the most primitive primate types. Biologically, the term *primitive* implies no value judgment but merely refers to age. Thus, prosimians are said to be primitive because they most closely resemble the earliest primates. As newer, more adaptively flexible primates evolved, the early prosimians were pushed into isolated, protected areas. Prosimians do live in mainland Africa and India but most inhabit the isolated islands of Southeast Asia and Madagascar.

As a group, prosimians show some differences from the general primate pattern outlined in the last section (Figure 5.5). Most prosimians are nocturnal, probably a holdover from the days when early mammals tended to be active at night because the dinosaurs were active during the day. As nocturnal creatures, prosimians have a better sense of smell than most primates. To aid this sense, they have a protruding snout with a large olfactory receptor area and a moist, naked nose (like a dog or cat) to help pick up molecules that provide the olfactory signal.

Like nocturnal creatures everywhere, prosimians have large eyes to gather more light. But they have virtually no color vision because it's not as useful at night. They do, however, have stereoscopic vision because, like all primates, they need to judge distances in bushes and trees; many use this ability to catch insect prey.

**grooming:** The cleaning of fur of another animal; promotes social cohesion.

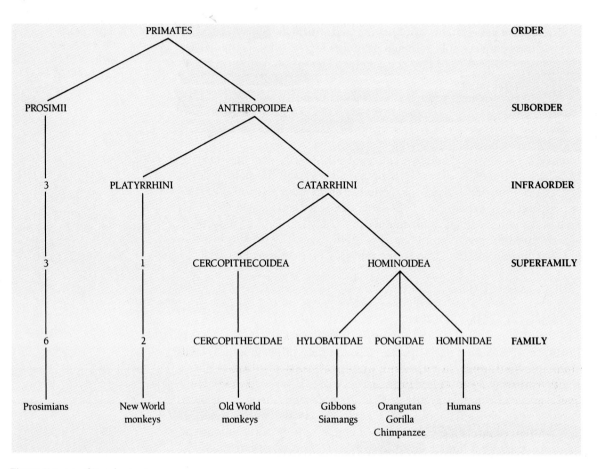

**Figure 5.4** *A traditional primate taxonomy. Numbers refer to living groups in that category.*

Prosimians have prehensile hands and feet, but their opposability is different from the other primates. Rather than being able to touch the thumb to the other fingers individually, the four other digits of prosimians (or three, as some prosimians lack an index finger) move together. In addition, some prosimians have claws on a couple of fingers or toes known as *grooming claws,* which are used for cleaning fur.

Prosimians spend most of their time in the trees or, if they are small, in bushes. Their form of locomotion depends, of course, on their ability to grasp with hands and feet the trunks and branches on which they are moving. The characteristic way many move about has been called "vertical clinging and leaping" because they jump from branch to branch in a rather upright position, pushing off with their legs and landing with both arms and legs. This trait differs from the behavior of other primates, who "walk" one limb at a time through the trees, or **brachiate**, swinging arm over arm.

**Figure 5.5** *A young loris from Southeast Asia, a prosimian. Note the large eyes and moist, naked nose.* (©Paul Freed/Animals, Animals)

A few of the Madagascar primates, the lemurs (see Figure 3.10), give birth to twins or even triplets on a regular basis. Transporting them seems to pose no problem because a male or an older sibling often helps the mother take care of the babies.

A particularly interesting prosimian is the tarsier (Figure 5.6) of Southeast Asia, a small (4 or 5 ounces) primate noted for its powerful hindlimbs for leaping, enlarged fingertips and toetips for friction, and ability to turn its head 180 degrees like an owl and for its almost exclusively insect diet. Although classed as a prosimian, some authorities think it may be evolutionarily more closely related to anthropoids.

Suborder *Anthropoidea* (meaning "humanlike") includes the monkeys, the apes, and humans. It is divided into two infraorders, ***Platyrrhini*** and ***Catarrhini***. This division is based on a geographical separation, a result of continental drift, that early in primate evolution split the primates into a Western Hemisphere, or New World, group and an Eastern Hemisphere, or Old World, group. All the New World, or platyrrhine, primates are monkeys and have several physical characteristics that distinguish them from the Old World, or catarrhine, primates (Figure 5.7).

One distinguishing feature is the nose. *Platyrrhine* means "flat nose," and the noses of the New World monkeys have widely spaced nostrils separated by a broad septum. Compare this with your own catarrhine nose. We are considered Old World primates because that is where humans first evolved. In addition, platyrrhine New World primates have more teeth than the catarrhines—twelve premolars or bicuspids compared to the Old World primates' eight. Because most New World monkeys are almost completely arboreal, they have evolved long limbs and long curved nails; a few even have prehensile tails capable of grasping things and supporting their weight. No Old World primate has this kind of tail. Finally, one group of platyrrhines, the marmosets, normally gives birth to twins.

*premolars*

---

**brachiate:** The ability to swing through the trees, using arms and hands.

**Figure 5.6** *The tarsier of Southeast Asia (approximately life size). Note the enlarged fingertips and toetips and powerful hindlimb.* (Zoological Society of San Diego)

Referring to Figure 5.4, we see that the Old World primates are divided into two superfamilies. The monkeys of Europe, Africa, and Asia make up superfamily *Cercopithecoidea* and family *Cercopithecidae*. The apes and humans are superfamily *Hominoidea*.

Within the cercopithecids are two subfamilies and about a dozen genera with numerous individual species. These monkeys have the nasal shape and tooth number of all Old World primates, and most have tails, though none are prehensile. Males tend to be larger than females, unlike the New World species, which show little sexual dimorphism. The cercopithecids have fully opposable thumbs (also unlike the platyrrhines). In general, the monkeys of the Eastern Hemisphere seem more adaptively flexible. One large genus, *Macaca*, has representative species all the way from North Africa to India to the mountains of northern Japan, where they are called "snow monkeys" (Figure 5.8).

Another genus, *Papio*, is of particular interest to us because it contains most of the baboons, the large, long-snouted monkeys of the African savannas (Figure 5.9). This is the environment in which our lineage developed. The savannas are nearly the same today as they were when

**Figure 5.7** *The wooley spider monkey, or* muriqui, *of Brazil. Note the widely separated nostrils and the prehensile tail.* (Andrew L. Young, © 1987 National Geographic Society)

the first humans lived on them. By observing the adaptations of another primate to the same environment, we may get some idea of how our ancestors survived. We'll discuss this topic in detail in Chapter 6.

Superfamily *Hominoidea,* the large, tailless primates, is made up of three families. Family **Hylobatidae** includes the gibbons and siamangs of Southeast Asia and Malaysia, sometimes referred to as the "lesser apes." These species are especially noted for their form of locomotion, called brachiation—arm-over-arm swinging from branch to branch (Figure 5.10). To aid in this movement, the arms of gibbons and siamangs are much longer and more powerful than their legs and end in hands with short thumbs and long, hooklike fingers. The hylobatids have, for the primates, an unusual social group: A male and female are monogamous and their offspring stay together and establish and defend a territory.

Family *Pongidae* are the "great apes," of which there are four living species: the orangutan of Southeast Asia, two species of chimpanzee, and the gorilla of Africa (Figure 5.11). These are the most robust primates, heavy-boned with large, powerful jaws and chewing muscles they use in eating a wide range of fruits and vegetables and, in the case

**Figure 5.9** *Family of olive baboons, focused on the oldest female, far right.* (Shirley C. Strum, © 1987 National Geographic Society)

of the chimpanzee, meat. The apes are essentially quadrupeds. The chimps and gorillas spend a large portion of their time on the ground, whereas the orangutan spends almost all of its time in the trees. In fact, the orangutan is so well adapted to arboreal locomotion that its feet look and function like two additional hands. All the great apes are built like brachiators with large and powerful shoulder girdles and arms, but they are too large to do much traveling in this fashion. Despite their build and quadrupedal moving, though, the apes can and do walk upright on occasion, usually when they want to look around or carry something.

Orangutans are solitary, but chimps and gorillas live in social units marked by a changing group membership, loose organization, and some degree of dominance recognition. Because the apes don't live in areas that present the dangers faced by savanna primates, dominance and its recognition may be even looser and more flexible than among baboons.

Apes have large brains, some having been measured at more than three-quarters the size of the smallest modern human brains. Many features of the anatomy of pongid brains are also similar to those of humans. Apes are intelligent. They have, for example, a vast knowledge of a great number of food sources. Because many of these foods are

◄ **Figure 5.8** *Japanese macaques, the "snow monkey," well adapted to life in cold, mountainous areas, even to the point of warming themselves in volcanic hot springs.* (Steven Kaufman/Peter Arnold, Inc.)

**Figure 5.10** *A gibbon brachiating.*
(Kenneth Feder)

**Figure 5.11** *The great apes: orangutan, chimpanzee, and gorilla.*

(Orangutan, Ron Garrison/Zoological Society of San Diego; chimpanzee, Nancy Nicolson/ Anthro Photo; gorilla, © Michael A. Nichols/ Magnum)

fruits, they need to be aware of seasonal changes so they can be at the right place when the fruits ripen, a cognitive behavior found also in some monkeys.

Chimpanzees can even make simple tools. Their most famous are the "fishing sticks" they make from twigs and blades of grass. They stick these down termite holes, wiggle them around, and draw out a meal of termites that have attacked the "invader" by clinging to it with their powerful pinchers. By nearly anyone's criteria, this is a cultural behavior: It is learned. It involves abstract concepts because the chimps must visualize the tool within the bush or grass as well as the behavior of the unseen termites. It involves an artifact—a natural object specifically modified for a specific purpose. This tool-using behavior also differs from individual to individual, with each chimp having her (usually only females perform this activity) favorite raw material, and from troop to troop. Most chimp troops don't do it at all, a sure sign that the behavior is learned rather than genetic. Humans are clearly not the sole possessors of culture.

Chimps are also known to hunt small mammals, including young baboons. Often just one chimp, nearly always a male, does the hunting and killing, but at times it is a cooperative venture appearing to have some sort of group strategy. The meat acquired is the one food that chimps share with one another.

Like all primates, apes use vocalizations, facial expressions, and body language to communicate. They have nothing like a human language, but they do have brains capable of learning the rudiments of human language. Chimps, gorillas, and orangutans have been taught to use various symbolic representations of language, most notably American Sign Language for the hearing impaired (AMESLAN). It is said that with this device they can communicate at about the level of a 4- or 5-year-old human.

The other family within the hominoids, *Hominidae*, includes living humans, all of whom belong to the same genus and species, *Homo sapiens*. Humans of the past, when at times several genera and species existed, also belong to family *Hominidae,* the hominids.

## THE HUMAN PRIMATE

It should now be clear that we humans are primates. We share with some 200 other species a common set of basic physical and behavioral traits. Each primate species, though, has its own unique expression of the primate adaptation. Humans are no exception. In fact, our expression of the primate adaptation involves not being arboreal at all. Let's go over the five categories from before and see how we compare.

1. *The senses.* Our sensory organs are basically the same as those of the anthropoid monkeys and apes. Smell seems exactly the same. Monkeys can hear higher sound frequencies than we can, but we are more sensitive to changes in pitch and intensity. Color vision is the same in humans, apes, and monkeys, except that humans may be more sensitive to slight differences in colors than are monkeys. It is possible, though, that this may be because we have assigned cultural names to slightly different shades of color and so recognize them because we have learned them. It has also been suggested that we can distinguish many colors because we can concentrate harder on such tasks (Passingham 1982). In general, humans, apes, and monkeys perceive the same world.

2. *Locomotion.* The most striking physical difference between us and the other primates is the way we move about. We are the only primate that is habitually bipedal, walking on two feet. The bones of our back, pelvis, legs, and feet are all structured to balance and hold us erect. Our musculature has evolved to serve the same purpose. Even the rather spherical shape of our head, as opposed to the more elongated heads of other primates, may have evolved in part to be more balanced atop a vertical spine. Because our legs are the limbs of locomotion, they are longer and more muscular than our arms—just the opposite of apes. Completely freed from locomotor functions, our hands have become organs of manipulation. We have the most precise opposability of the primates, facilitated by the longest and relatively strongest primate thumb.

3. *Reproduction.* Like nearly all primates, we normally have one offspring at a time. Though we are not the largest primate (gorillas are), we have the longest period of dependency and maturation. Chimps, for example, reach sexual maturity in about nine years and physical maturity in about twelve years. For us, the averages are thirteen years and twenty-one years. Not only do we grow up more slowly, we are born relatively more immature and helpless than other primates, so we get off to a late start.

4. *Intelligence.* We are clearly the most intelligent primate because we can store and process more information in more complex ways than the others. Our cultural behavior—our languages, societies, abstract belief systems, scientific knowledge—attests to these abilities. Our intellect is made possible by our big brain, the result of and reason for the extended period of growth after our immature births. Otherwise, our brains are built on the basic primate pattern, with the same proportions of various parts as most primates. In fact, some primates have larger brains, relative to the size of their bodies, than ours. In absolute terms, however, our brains are larger and more complex. Especially large is our **neocortex**, the outer layer of the brain where abstract thought, problem solving, and attentiveness take place.

**neocortex:** The part of the brain responsible for memory and thought.

5. *Behavior patterns*. Like most primates, humans live in social groups. The difference is that our groups are structured and maintained by cultural values—ideas, rules, and behavioral norms we have created and share through complex communication systems. Moreover, we respond not only to a social system in its entirety but also to individual people within the society. A human social system is the result of the collective conscious responses of a group of individuals.

This is not to say that the social systems of nonhuman primates are entirely based on instinctive behaviors. The other primates can be quite flexible, adapting their actions to the specific situation at hand. But other primates' basic model of social organization is less flexible and more stable than ours.

Our big brains have allowed us to move well beyond purely biological evolutionary processes. Certainly, natural selection brought about the evolution of our big brains in the first place, but the way in which this organ functioned permitted us to think up answers to the problems of our survival. As human societies moved around and encountered varying environmental situations and other human groups, these answers became so complex that strikingly different social systems evolved. In a sense, culture *became* our environment to which we responded with still newer cultural ideas, systems, and artifacts.

Chimps may exhibit some cultural behaviors, may be able to learn to use the basic features of human language, and may differ from us genetically by only about 1 percent of their genes, but our behavior—the extent to which we use and indeed rely on culture—is very different from that of the other primates.

## THE EVOLUTION OF THE PRIMATES

To say that the fossil record of the early primates is confusing is to understate the case. There are a large number of fossil specimens of primates, but, as one authority notes, 65 percent of extinct primate species are based on fossils that are "extremely fragmentary," mostly pieces of jaw or sometimes just teeth (Martin 1990:39). Although one extinct species may be represented by many specimens, fossils of its contemporaries are lacking, giving us no basis for comparison. For certain periods of primate evolution, all fossils are found in one or two locations, even though we know that primates were widely dispersed. Still, we have been able to piece together the basic picture of the primate evolutionary story (Figure 5.12).

Very little exists to tell us about the beginnings of the primates. There are a few primatelike teeth from Montana dated at 65 million years ago (mya), and some bones from Wyoming, from 60 mya, that show primatelike anatomical features related to climbing. There is a whole

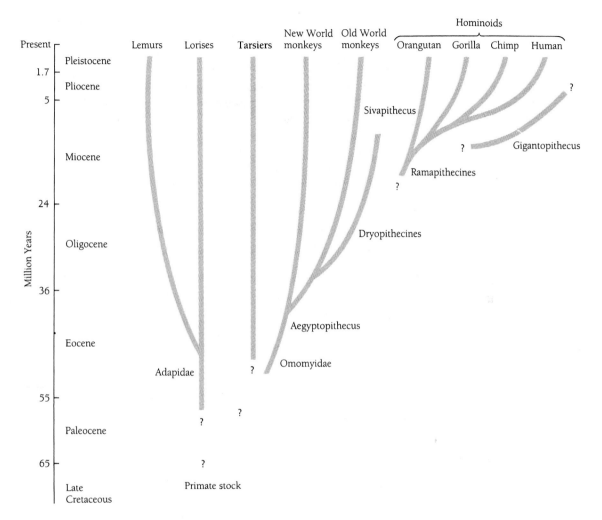

**Figure 5.12** *Generalized time line for primate evolution, including major geological periods and dates. Question marks indicate insufficient data to establish evolutionary relationships.*

group of species from North America and Europe, the plesiadapiforms, once thought to have linked the very early primates to more modern forms. New evidence, however, suggests they are actually related to the Southeast Asian colugo, a gliding mammal.

It is not until about 55 mya that undisputed primates are found. They are often referred to as "primates of modern aspect" and are classed as **prosimians**. The fossils seem to come in two groups, both from North America and Europe, still connected at the time. One group, the lemur-like *Adapidae* (Figure 5.13), is thought to be ancestral to modern lemurs and lorises. The other group, the tarsier-like *Omomyidae*, which may date back to 60 mya, gave rise to modern tarisers (Figure 5.14). It is thought to either have also given rise to the anthropoids or to represent the tarsier-like primates that just split from the ancestors of the anthropoids.

**prosimian:** The most primitive primate.

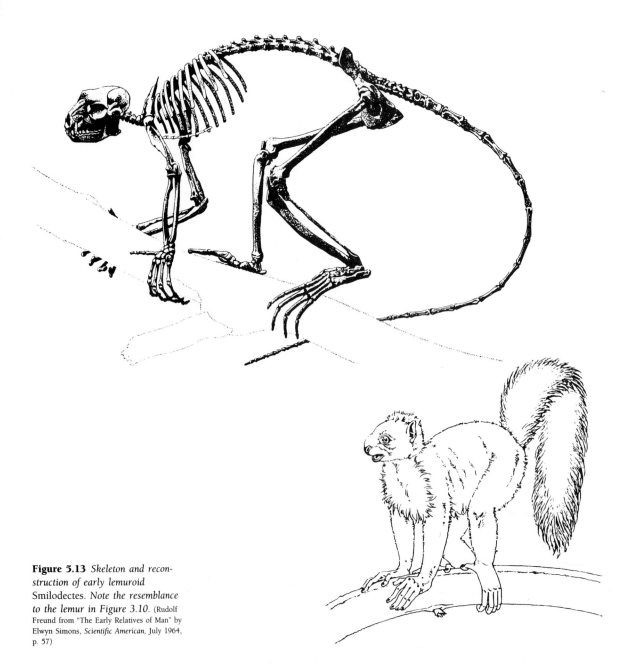

**Figure 5.13** *Skeleton and reconstruction of early lemuroid* Smilodectes. *Note the resemblance to the lemur in Figure 3.10.* (Rudolf Freund from "The Early Relatives of Man" by Elwyn Simons, *Scientific American*, July 1964, p. 57)

By the time the omomyids were moving into Asia, the Eastern and Western Hemispheres were separate. The New World has so far offered virtually no fossil evidence to tell us what happened next. It may be that the prosimian forms that ended up in the New World moved into South America once it joined North America and evolved into the present-day

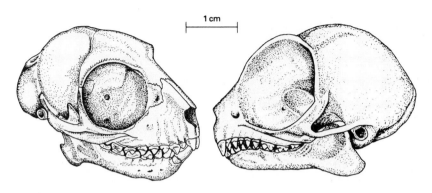

**Figure 5.14** *Comparison of fossil omomyid* Necrolemur *(left) with modern tarsier.* (From R. D. Martin, *Primate Origins and Evolution: A Phylogenetic Reconstruction*, Princeton, N.J.: Princeton University Press, 1990, p. 61)

platyrrhine monkeys. A second view is that prosimian evolution got no farther in the Western Hemisphere and that early monkeys from the Old World "rafted" over to South America, floating on logs and branches, or crossed over on a chain of volcanic islands when South America and Africa were still fairly close together. The degree of physical similarity among all modern anthropoids suggests a single origin and so argues for the second scenario.

The early evolutionary history of the Old World monkeys themselves is known largely from a single site, though it has yielded a large number of fossils. This site is a desert depression, an ancient lake, southwest of Cairo, Egypt, called the Fayum.

From the Fayum come a number of monkeylike forms dated 40 to 25 mya, perhaps the most important of which is *Aegyptopithecus* (Figure 5.15). From its postcranial skeletal remains, this anthropoid of 10

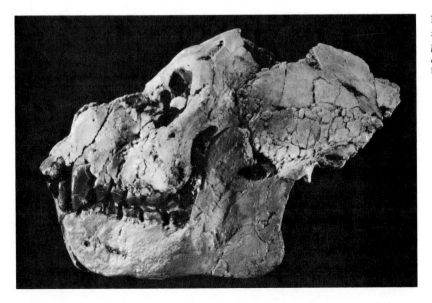

**Figure 5.15** Aegyptopithecus, *possible ancestor to the hominoids and perhaps to the Old World monkeys as well.* (Courtesy of Peabody Museum of Natural History, Yale University)

## CONTEMPORARY ISSUE

### Why Save the Primates?

Two days after Christmas, 1985, American biologist Dian Fossey was murdered—hacked to death with machetes—at her camp in the mountains of Rwanda, central Africa. Fossey had spent the last eighteen years studying and trying to save from extinction the endangered mountain gorilla, one subgroup of that ape. There are now only a few hundred mountain gorillas left in the wild. The other group, the lowland gorilla, is more numerous, but not by much.

Fossey is alleged to have been killed because of her campaign against poachers who regularly murder gorillas for their hands and heads, which bring high prices as "souvenirs," and because the park in which she was working is wanted for farmland. It is clear that the answer to the question "Why save the primates?" cannot be because they are so similar to us—look what we can do to members of our own species. Rather, the answer must come from broader, less anthropocentric scientific and ethical considerations.

The problem is severe. Besides the gorilla, over 60 species of primates are classed as endangered (on the verge of extinction) or as vulnerable or rare. These include the golden lion tamarin, the uakari, and the woolly monkey of South America, and the proboscis monkey, the pileated gibbon, and many lemurs of the Old World.

The endangered status of these primates, and of many other animals and plants, is largely the result of human actions—destroying natural habitats, hunting (usually for trophies rather than for food), and capture for zoos and various medical experiments and tests, many of questionable value.

The world changes, and as it does species become extinct. That has been, as we pointed out, the normal trend of evolution. By accelerating the extinction rate, however, we could be doing irreparable damage. We are really just beginning to appreciate the great complexity of ecological relationships. We do know that sometimes the loss of one species can bring about change in those species with which it had some ecological connection. Take away a source of food, for example, and the creatures that depended on it might disappear as well. Destroy the world's rain forests

pounds or more seems to have been an arboreal quadruped. It shows a number of features of the teeth, brain, and skull that resemble those of the later hominoids, the apes and humans. *Aegyptopithecus* may be an early ancestor of the hominoids, although it is still primitive enough to be ancestral to the modern Old World monkeys as well.

Definite apes appear beginning about 23 mya and became more numerous over the next 10 to 15 million years. We refer to these as "dental apes" because their teeth have the characteristics of modern apes. Their bodies, though, are distinctly different. Do not get the impression that modern-looking chimpanzees were running around in these very ancient times. The early apes seem to come in two groups: an arboreal forest-dwelling form from Africa and Europe called dryopithecines and a later, open-country, more ground-living form called ramapithecines

by cutting them down and the ocean's plankton by pollution, and we decrease the amount of breathable oxygen produced by those plants.

In addition, by speeding the extinction of so many species, we are losing valuable knowledge about the world and—especially in the case of the primates—about ourselves. As we have seen, new scientific techniques and ideas arise all the time, but without the raw data from nature they remain abstract and unproven.

But there are also ethical reasons for saving species. Ethical precepts are, of course, belief systems, and therefore not scientific. And yet what we have learned about the world through science, we believe, can support certain ethical ideas on this crucial matter. We have seen that no matter how different the human species is from other organisms, we still arose and evolved through the actions of the very same processes that bring about the evolution of all living things. We are variations on the theme we call "life," sharing with every other living creature the same genetic code, amino acid building blocks, and metabolic processes. The very cells that make up our bodies evolved billions of years ago from the joining of different simple organisms that worked together in what is called a symbiotic relationship.

When the matter is seen in this light, one has to ask whether we have any right to tamper with the welfare of other species. That the random changes of evolution have endowed us with big brains and thus with the ability to manipulate the environment hardly makes us any "better" than our fellow creatures. Indeed, we think it gives us a *responsibility* to use these evolutionary gifts for the betterment of the world—not, as has been the case so often, for its selfish destruction.

Primates are smart, they're cute, they're a lot like us. The argument is often convincing when applied to them. But what good are less humanlike creatures such as the California condor, the spotted owl, or other species that are facing extinction? Well, what good was that little insect-eating mammal who, some 65 mya, started clambering about in the trees?

from Eurasia. Their names derive from genus names given to some of the first-discovered members of each group, *Dryopithecus* and *Ramapithecus*. The classification of these primates as apes is based on a number of physical features, the most important of which is a trait of the molar teeth found only in modern hominoids and no other primate— the Y-5 cusp pattern (Figure 5.16).

*Y-5 cusp.*

The dryopithecines show a great deal of physical variation and wide geographical distribution, but all seem to be arboreal (forest-living) and fruit-eating. Although classed as apes, none shows a great resemblance to any of the modern ape species. The fossil record of these forms ends about 12 mya, just about the time that of the ramapithecines begins.

Ramapithecine fossils have been found in Africa, India, Pakistan, Turkey, Hungary, and Greece. The earliest specimens are teeth and partial jaws. On the strength of one interpretation of these remains, the ramapithecines were claimed to be the earliest hominids, the first members of the human lineage. This conjecture coincided nicely with what was then thought to be the 12- to 15-million-year separation of humans from apes.

In the 1960s, however, new chemical and genetic techniques (see Chapter 8) showed that humans and the African apes were much more closely related than had previously been thought. Put simply, humans and chimpanzees differ in only about 1 percent of their genes. The implication for evolution is that we could not possibly have been evolving along separate lines for 12 million years. The new evidence pointed to a divergence of our lineages only 5 or 6 mya.

Recently, additional and more complete fossils of the ramapithecines have supported this idea. The ramapithecines are clearly apes. In fact, the form from India, Pakistan, and Turkey, called *Sivapithecus* (Figure 5.17), is, according to anthropologist David Pilbeam, an ancestor of the orangutan. *Sivapithecus* and the modern orangutan share detailed features of the face and teeth as well as a similar relative size and structure of the arms.

Another interesting fossil form in this general group is a giant ape from China and northern India called *Gigantopithecus*. So far, only its massive jaws and teeth have been found, but estimates from these indi-

**Figure 5.16** *Chewing surfaces of primate molars, showing four-cusp pattern of monkey (bottom) and Y-5 pattern of hominoid.*

**Figure 5.17** *Artist's reconstruction of* Sivapithecus, *probable ancestor to the modern orangutan.* (Enid Kotschnig, *Scientific American,* March 1984, cover)

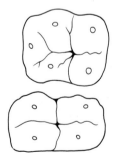

cate that it may have been 10 to 12 feet tall when standing upright and weighed from 700 to 1200 pounds. Evidence from its teeth indicate that, like the gorilla, it was a vegetarian, and certain features of the teeth link it to the ramapithecine group.

Taking into account physical features and dates for the half-dozen or so forms of ramapithecines, Pilbeam (1986) suggests the following sequence: The large apes evolved in Africa about 20 mya and split from there into a number of distinct evolutionary lines. Gradually, though, these decreased, leaving relatively few forms to evolve into modern hominoids. One of these is the Asian *Sivapithecus*–orangutan line. A form remaining in Africa first gave rise to gorillas and, about 5 or 6 mya, split into two further lineages that would become chimpanzees and humans.

There is virtually no fossil evidence in Africa that shows us just where, when, and how this branching took place. The record stops about 8 mya with ramapithecine apes and picks up a little under 4 mya with a group of bipedal hominids. For now, we can only take the fossil evidence at both ends of that gap, add to it what we know about climatic changes and ecological conditions as well as the differences between us and the modern apes, and make some informed guesses about what happened to start our evolutionary line. That is the subject of Chapter 8.

## SUMMARY

One important tool for learning about the past is to understand the results of all events that made up the past. By determining our place in nature and our relationships with other primates, we can see what the present-day products are of the 65 million years of primate evolution. This gives us a road map for journeying into the past and looking at the other tool, the fossil record.

Humans are 1 of some 200 species of living primates. In many ways we are typical of this group with our three-dimensional color vision, our prehensile, opposable hands, our emphasis on social groups, the long period of dependency of our single-birth offspring, and the intelligence and flexibility of our brains in dealing with our world.

In other ways, however, we are atypical primates. We are not arboreal. Our feet are not prehensile but are built to support the entire weight of our upright locomotion. We have especially dexterous hands with long, strong opposable thumbs. We take the longest time of any primate to mature, and we have the largest, most complex brains. Finally, we rely for our very survival on one of the products of those brains: our culture.

The primate fossil record is a complex one that stretches back to the time of the last dinosaurs. Much remains to be explained, especially about the early stages. We do know that our group, the hominids, is a late arrival on the primate scene, splitting off from the African apes a mere 5 or 6 mya.

## KEY TERMS

| | | |
|---|---|---|
| taxonomy | opposability | grooming |
| notochord | postnatal | brachiate |
| stereoscopic vision | dependency | neocortex |
| quadrupedal | intelligence | prosimian |
| prehensile | dominance hierarchy | |

## FOR MORE INFORMATION

An excellent book that examines humans as an animal species is Richard Passingham's *The Human Primate.*

Perhaps the major reference work on the nonhuman primates is *A Handbook of Living Primates* by J. R. and P. H. Napier.

On the evolution of the primates up to the hominids, see Frederick S. Szalay and Eric Delson, *Evolutionary History of the Primates,* and R. D. Martin, *Primate Origins and Evolution.*

# 6

# LEARNING ABOUT THE PAST: BEHAVIORAL MODELS FOR HUMAN EVOLUTION

In reconstructing the human past, our focus is the concrete evidence from the fossil and archaeological records. Neither fossil bones nor artifacts alone, however, tell us who our ancestors were in the most profound biological sense—in terms of how they were adapted to their environments, how they lived, in short, *how they behaved.*

Were the early hominids social? If so, how were their societies organized? Were group members social equals, or were there leaders and followers? How did they communicate? What did they eat, and how did they acquire their food? Were there family units within the group? Did they care for the sick or the aged? Did they share food? Were they self-sufficient, or did they divide their labors? Did groups recognize a territory, and did they defend it?

Fossils and artifacts alone cannot normally be used to answer these questions directly. Another source of information is living animals who serve as models for prehistoric hominid behavior. The rationale for such studies is this: Although living animals do not represent "fossils" of ancient human behavior, they can provide us with insight concerning the behavior of those ancient humans, folks we know only from their bones and their material artifacts.

## BEHAVIOR, ADAPTATION, AND EVOLUTION

The idea of using behavioral models is based on the same premise as is our use of physical comparisons with other primates: We share a common heritage with the other primates and so have inherited our shared features from the same source, a common ancestor. It is not a coincidence, for example, that all primates have prehensile hands. Rather, our common prehensile ability comes from the same ancient ancestor and, in this case, serves the same basic function. Such traits, shared by multiple species through inheritance from a common ancestor, are called **homologies**. Thus, we gain some perspective on our prehensile hands by fully examining the prehensile appendages of species with whom we share an ancestor from whom we all derived the trait.

Homologous traits need not share a common function. Your arms and the wings of a bat, although they are used for different things, are homologues. They are similar by virtue of having evolved from the same source, an early mammal.

The wings of a bat and the wings of an insect, however, although they share a similar function, have evolved independently and are not at all similar in structure. These functional but evolutionarily unrelated similarities are known as **analogies**. We can certainly learn something about the physics of flight by comparing these wings; however, we can get only a limited amount of information about the wings of *bats* by studying the wings of *insects* because they evolved quite separately from one another to facilitate very different adaptive systems.

Just as organisms pass on anatomical and physiological features in their genes, they also pass on behavioral characteristics. In some groups—ants, for example—whole behaviors are passed on. Ants completely rely on built-in instinct; they don't really think or, in fact, have much of anything to think *with*. So, even though ants live in highly complex societies and act in elaborate ways, all their behaviors are coded for in their genes, to be triggered by outside stimuli but with little or no flexibility or variation in the response (Figure 6.1).

Other organisms, with larger and more complex brains, can vary their behavior as needed to cope with specific situations. They have behavioral potentials or "themes" carried in their genetic codes. They

**Figure 6.1** *Weaver ants build nests by pulling edges of leaves together. While some of the ants hold the leaves in this position, others gently carry larvae along the "seam," stimulating them to excrete silk, which "sews" the leaves together.* (Animals/Animals)

respond to their environments by building onto these potentials—taking in information from the outside, remembering it, and using stored information in appropriate circumstances. In other words, they think.

The nature of the in-born behavioral potentials in complex organisms is still a matter of debate, especially when humans are the topic. Some argue that we are born as "blank slates," or, in a more modern image, as computers with internal hardware but nothing programmed. Others hold the extreme opposite view: Our brains come equipped with *specific* behaviors that are only modified to a degree by outside stimuli—like a computer with some basic programs already in the system.

The truth is no doubt somewhere in the middle. Certainly, we come into this world with some basic, built-in behavioral responses. Facial expressions like smiling, nursing behavior among infants, the bond between a mother and her offspring, and the drives to walk upright and learn language are all recognized as universal in our species and as being preprogrammed in our biology. But just as certainly—in light of

**homology:** A trait shared by two or more species through inheritance from a common ancestor.

**analogy:** A trait similar in function but unrelated evolutionarily.

the highly complex structures of our brains and the great variability in our psychologies, intellects, and personal and cultural behaviors—we are not programmed for particular ways of expressing these and other behaviors. Language ability, for example, may be instinctive, but the specific language you speak is learned within a specific cultural context.

At any rate, if it is the case that at least behavioral themes can be inherited, then we can shed light on our behaviors by looking into the behaviors of other creatures. In doing so, however, we need to take into account the concepts of homology and analogy. In comparing the behaviors of humans and chimpanzees, it is highly likely that a behavior is shared because it is the *same* behavior, derived by both species from our common ancestor of 5 or 6 million years ago. Understanding the nature and function of that behavior in chimpanzees is likely to provide insight into the origin of the behavior in humans because the behavior in question is homologous.

A behavior similar in humans and baboons is more likely to be analogous. Our two species have evolved independently for about 36 million years, so there is a greater chance that the behaviors evolved separately, under separate environmental circumstances, for different adaptive reasons. Still, they may be variations on some general behavior pattern common to the primates and inherited from an early common ancestor.

The chance of two behaviors being analogous increases as we compare species that are less and less closely related. Some investigators

**Figure 6.2** *A wolf cub begs for food from its mother. She will shortly regurgitate a partly digested meal for the cub.* (Jim Brandenburg/ Minden Pictures)

have compared the behavior of humans with that of social carnivores like lions, wolves, and African wild dogs. There are strikingly "human" behaviors in these species. All three hunt cooperatively. Wolves and wild dogs have complex social relationships, use vocal and gestural signs to maintain them, and both actively feed their young (Figure 6.2). Wolves are territorial.

These collections of similarities, however, are probably not derived from a common ancestor but have, at most, evolved independently from some general mammalian traits of social interaction, care of young, and relatively large complex brains allowing for flexibility of behavior. What we do learn from the **ethology** of such species is that one possible route to adaptive success for mammals is through complex social behavior and that it is common in species that include meat in their diet, especially meat from large animals. But it is only one route; other carnivores—the fox and the leopard, for example—are solitary hunters. Lions, although they hunt cooperatively, never share food with their young.

Comparing analogous behaviors, then, can be informative and can point out possible clusters of adaptive traits. But analogies must be used with the understanding that the more evolutionarily distant the species, the less useful is the comparison. Ants live in highly complex societies to which investigators often apply human names (slave, caste, queen, nurse, soldier), but studying the social behavior of ants probably tells us nothing directly about our own societies.

We can now look at the behavior of some other species that have, to varying degrees, been used as models for the origin and evolution of our behavior. For years, nearly all our information about other species came from studies of their behavior in the artificial environments of zoos and laboratories. Only when the science of ethology started to study creatures in the wild, under natural conditions, could we see how they were *really* adapted. And only then did we begin to learn some of the truly remarkable adaptations that our fellow species possess.

## BABOONS

The five species of genus *Papio* have long been of interest to anthropologists because of the obvious complexity of the baboon's social organization and because among baboon habitats are the savannas of East and South Africa—the very habitat of our early hominid ancestors.

Our common notion of baboon behavior, handed down since the 1950s, once provided us with what seemed like a reasonable model for the behavior of our hominid ancestors, for baboon societies appeared to share a number of features we saw as characteristic of our own social systems. Baboon troops were seen as centered around and held together

**ethology:** The study of the natural behavior of organisms under natural conditions.

by a dominance hierarchy. Male baboons, often twice as large as females and equipped with long, sharp canine teeth, were thought to vie with one another from youth for social position. The baboon who was the largest, strongest, most aggressive, and smartest became the dominant member, a position recognized and acknowledged by the whole troop. The dominant male was the leader and decision maker. He had first rights to food and females. He produced the most offspring, perpetuating those traits that made him dominant.

According to this view, female baboons had a loose hierarchy among themselves but always ranked below males within the troop. A female's social position was often determined by that of the male she mated with during her **estrus** (fertile) period. The female's main function was thus to bear and raise offspring, and her identity was essentially based on this function.

Such a system, the thinking ran, was an obvious aid to surviving the rigors of savanna life. The vulnerable troop members—females and young—were an undifferentiated group found in the middle of the troop and surrounded by males, who held individually defined and recognized positions in the hierarchy. The males were thought to be organized in an almost military fashion to protect and defend the females and to pass on their genes through them.

The short duration of early studies, combined with the expectations (and perhaps wishful thinking) of some (almost always male) researchers to observe a hierarchical, male-oriented society, led to an overemphasis on the aggressive, decision-making, mate-choosing role of the males. This perception made it hard, in turn, to see the females as

**Figure 6.3** *A male baboon shows his long canine teeth and flashes his white eyelids in a "threat gesture," probably directed toward a less dominant male.* (Irven DeVore/Antro-Photo)

possessing differentiated identities and roles. The logical conclusion was the prime importance of males and their competition for dominance.

This interpretation of baboon social organization has recently been questioned, if not put to rest (Fedigan and Fedigan 1988; Smuts 1985). Studies over the last decade have verified that male baboons do have individual identities and differential social power and influence and that they do protect and defend the troop from members of other troops and from predators (Figure 6.3). But a formal, tightly structured dominance hierarchy among males does not exist. Rather, the structure of the troop is based on "a network of social alliances" (Fedigan and Fedigan 1988:14), including friendships between females and between females and males (see Figures 5.3 and 5.9). These friendships may be so strong that a male will aid his female friend's infants even though he is not their father. Such friendships, rather than the social position of the males, may be what determines who mates with whom.

Differential social positions exist, but they are based not on those "masculine" traits listed before but on an individual's (male or female) "experience, skill, and . . . ability to manipulate others [and] mobilize allies" (Fedigan and Fedigan 1988:15). If there is any subgroup that is central to a troop and that ties generations together, it is that made up of related females, the males being more mobile and less a stable part of the troop than was previously supposed. In fact, the competition that may be most important to the troop is not that among males but among females competing with one another "over access to the resources necessary to sustain them and their offspring" (Fedigan and Fedigan 1988:5). Finally, it appears that mate choice is more a female prerogative. Males make overtures toward females, but it is the females who decide with whom they will mate.

The earlier version of baboon social organization indicated that to survive on the savannas a primate needed a tightly organized, male-oriented and -dominated, almost militaristic society (the use of the term *troop* is not arbitrary). The obvious conclusion (then) was that the early hominid savanna dwellers probably had a similar set of behaviors and that our modern social systems are, to one extent or another, variations on this theme. Many found this a satisfying idea.

But, again, we must remember that we can share with baboons only the most general primate homologous traits. Similarities between us and baboons exist because we have evolved variations of the same behavioral themes. Our specific expressions of those themes, however, are the results of separate and independent evolutionary histories.

Those separate histories, however, have produced results that are similar in baboons, humans, and, as we will see, chimpanzees: the adaptive focus of a social structure built around a family unit, friendships, mutual aid within the group, defense of the group, and recognition of

**estrus:** The period during which a female is fertile; the signals indicating this condition.

individuals. This at least tells us that such a focus is one possible adaptive path among primates; thus, it is conceivable to assume that something like it was the key to the survival of the early hominids. Given that our closest relative, the chimpanzee, exhibits this cluster of traits, it seems an even more reasonable assumption.

## CHIMPANZEES

Some of the most remarkable results of ethological observations have come from three landmark studies of the great apes, all initiated by paleoanthropologist Louis Leakey: Jane Goodall's study of the chimpanzee, Dian Fossey's study of the gorilla, and Biruté Galdikas's study of the orangutan. Each study is interesting in its own right and tells us something of the variations possible on the basic primate pattern of social organization. The species most relevant to our present subject, however, is the chimpanzee.

The orangutan is an Asian ape and, as we have seen, is separated from us by 12 million years or more. The gorilla, although according to some is as close to us genetically as the chimp and although exhibiting many of the same basic social behaviors, is a rather specialized ape. Unlike the chimpanzee the gorilla spends nearly all its time on the ground, and its almost exclusively vegetarian diet is largely of ground plants. It makes its sleeping nests on the ground. It is not known to make or use tools. The gorilla's huge size (males in the wild average 400 pounds) means that it has no enemies (except us), and this, along with its easily obtained plant diet, makes its life fairly "laid-back." Gorilla groups are headed by a dominant male, but on the whole the groups are unified and peaceful (Figure 6.4), without the tension over social position that is more characteristic of baboon and chimp societies. As zoologist and writer David Attenborough puts it, the gorilla has "no need [to] be particularly nimble in either body or mind" (1979:291). Although perhaps overstated—gorillas, like chimps, can be taught to communicate through sign language, for example—this statement seems an accurate impression of the nature of gorilla adaptation.

In contrast the chimpanzee is "both agile and inquisitive" (Attenborough 1979:291). Most of what we know of the ethology of the chimp comes from the more than thirty years of research at Gombe Stream National Park in Tanzania led by Jane Goodall (1971, 1986, 1990). Goodall's studies have shown that, besides physical and physiological traits, we share with chimps a number of behavioral characteristics. These are centered around aspects of social interaction, and this is instructive for our understanding of our own behavior (Figure 6.5).

A herd of antelopes on the savannas of Africa is a social group, but the group itself is the focus. Antelopes interact with one another but do

so largely as anonymous members of the herd. Chimpanzees, however, live in groups, and the members interact with one another as *individuals*. The chimp group is the sum of all the relationships among the individuals that make it up at any given time. It is also defined by the relationships between its members and members of other groups. Although there are "norms" of social behavior in chimps, these are highly flexible and vary depending on the specific individuals and the specific situation.

The bond between mother and infant is strong in chimps, as it is in most mammals. These apes, though, have large, complex brains and have much to learn about their world before they can become functioning adults. Thus, the mother–infant bond is particularly long-lived and important, and the nature of that interaction can have a lasting effect on the rest of a chimp's life. Poor treatment by its mother, for example, often makes a chimp a poor mother herself when she bears young. Chimps have been seen to help their mothers with younger siblings,

**Figure 6.4** *A group of mountain gorillas peacefully resting on a sunny slope.* (© Michael A. Nichols/ Magnum Photos Inc)

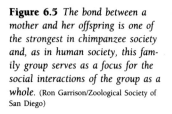

**Figure 6.5** *The bond between a mother and her offspring is one of the strongest in chimpanzee society and, as in human society, this family group serves as a focus for the social interactions of the group as a whole.* (Ron Garrison/Zoological Society of San Diego)

and siblings often remain close into adulthood. Chimps, in other words, don't just give birth to an offspring that is then cast out on its own. Rather, chimps *raise* their young, and the family bonds that result may last a lifetime.

The chimps in a group are arranged in a dominance hierarchy. Males are generally dominant over all females, but within females a loose hierarchy exists. Males actually compete with one another in an attempt to achieve the highest position possible. The rewards are access to feeding places and females. Social position, although attained in males through violent but seldom injurious actions, is maintained via a series of expressions, gestures, and vocalizations. One of the most important is grooming, which maintains social cohesion and on occasion is a sign of dominance when a subordinate male grooms his superior. Other expressions of social interaction include kissing, hugging, bowing, ex-

**Figure 6.6** *A chimpanzee exhibiting a* low open grin *indicating he is moderately frightened or excited.* (© Joe McDonald/Animals, Animals)

tending the hand, sexual gestures, grinning, and various vocalizing (Figure 6.6); we can freely use these terms because the meanings of these actions in chimp society seem to be precisely what they are in human society.

But a chimp society is in no way some sort of dictatorship. Instead, it is marked by cooperation and mutual concern. This is seen mostly within the family unit of mother and offspring (because chimps are sexually promiscuous, the father is unknown) who, throughout their lives, will protect and care for one another, especially during illness and injury. Males have even been known to help brothers in their competition for dominance.

But care also extends outside the family unit. When chimps hunt, for example, portions of the kill are often shared, sometimes proportionately depending on the degree of friendship between the hunter and the

chimp begging for food. Offspring are important to the group as a whole, and unrelated adults will come to the aid or protection of a youngster threatened with some harm, even risking their own welfare. Once, an adolescent male adopted an unrelated youngster who had been orphaned (Goodall 1990: 202).

Group membership is somewhat fluid. Chimps, for various reasons, will leave a group, and outsiders will occasionally enter it. Despite this, there is a sense of group identity and territory. Small bands of males will sometimes patrol the boundaries of their group's range, and, when members of other groups are encountered, they are reacted to and treated differently. In one chilling series of events, males from Goodall's main study group attacked and killed a female and all the males of a group that had broken away to establish its own territory. Goodall thinks the motivation may have been to reclaim the area.

The vast majority of our information about this species comes from Goodall's research, but work on other chimp groups amply bears out her observations and conclusions and lends support to the idea that chimp behavior is flexible, adaptable, and the result of a degree of intelligence and reasoning. For example, a chimp group in the forests on the west coast of Africa uses hammerstones to crack open nuts, something the Goodall chimps never did. They also have different hunting techniques, relying more on cooperation between hunting males than did the Gombe chimps (Boesch and Boesch-Achermann 1991).

Recently, even more intriguing information has come to light about the other species of chimpanzee: the "pygmy" chimp, or bonobo (Kano 1990). The bonobo lives in the lowland forests of Zaire and has been estimated by molecular studies to have been separate from the common chimp for 1.5 million years. Not really pygmies at all, these chimps are as large as the common chimps, although more slender with smaller heads and shoulders. They walk upright more often than the common chimps (Figure 6.7). But there are more striking differences.    *bonobo*

The bonobos are more peaceful and gregarious than the common chimps. They have a hierarchy, but it is looser than the common chimp and much less male-oriented. They more readily share food with one another, and the food shared is not limited to luxury items like meat. They have never been observed to kill another of their kind, and they appear to bind their group together with sex.

A group of bonobos, especially when feeding, constantly posture toward one another, rubbing rumps or "presenting" themselves as if initiating sexual activity. When sex does follow, it is usually face-to-face, a position common in humans but notably uncommon in non-human primates. Sexual activity is not limited to opposite-sex partners. Females commonly rub genitalia with other females, and males will mount each other.

Moreover, the signs of fertility, the estrus signals (or "heat" in popular terminology), seem nearly always present in bonobo females. In all chimps, the fertile and therefore sexual period is marked by a swelling and coloration of the skin of the genital area. This stimulates sexual interest on the part of the males. In common chimps, the swelling only occurs when the female has ovulated and is fertile. In bonobos, however, there is some swelling almost all the time, and, indeed, bonobos seem almost constantly sexually receptive. Sexual activity in this species has become separate from purely reproductive activity and is responded to on a conscious level. The motivation for sex may be as much psychological and social as it is reproductive.

The function of all this seems to be the same as some of the expressions and gestures among the common chimp: to prevent violence; to ease tension, especially while feeding; as a greeting, a sign of reconciliation, or to reassure another group member. Sex or some form of sexual activity, heterosexual or homosexual, has even been seen to precede food sharing.

Now, if all the behaviors of the chimp species sound more than vaguely human, the reason may be simple. We share certain behavioral patterns because we inherited them from a common ancestor. To be sure, our line and that of the chimps have been going their separate and independent ways for 5 or 6 million years, and even shared features have had the chance to become modified by all the processes of evolution—to be changed, eliminated, enhanced, and differently adapted to our species' different niches. Chimps are not "living fossils," stuck in some 5-million-year-old rut, while our ancestors continued to evolve. But the fact that our common ancestor is relatively recent and the striking similarity of our bodies and behaviors argue for our shared behaviors being homologous.

This does not mean that we humans have specific genes for friendship, food sharing, territoriality, or continual sexuality. These are complex behaviors, and the chimps and we are complex species. The lesson is that, like the chimps, the focus of the human adaptation—the thing that adapted our earliest hominid ancestors and that has been the adaptive theme of our line—is social interaction based on individual recognition, a strong bond centered around family relationships (generally, mothers and their offspring), long-term friendships, sexual consciousness, mutual care within the group, and recognition and defense of the group. These are some of the possible answers to the questions that are listed at the beginning of the chapter. It seems reasonable to assume that our hominid ancestors—represented by the fossils to be discussed in Chapters 8 through 12—behaved in similar ways. As Goodall says,

> . . . The concept of early humans poking for insects with twigs and wiping themselves with leaves seems entirely sensible. The thought of those ancestors greeting and reassuring one another with kisses or embraces, cooperating in protecting their territory or in hunting, and sharing food with each other, is appealing. The idea of close affectionate ties within the Stone Age family, of brothers helping one another, of teenage sons hastening to the protection of their old mothers, and of teenage daughters minding the babies, for me brings the fossilized relics of their physical selves dramatically to life. (1990:207)

## ETHNOGRAPHIC ANALOGY

One more area of behavior has been used to try to open a window into our behavioral past. Modern human societies vary greatly in their cultural systems, including their degree of technological complexity and the extent to which they manipulate their environments to extract needed resources. Perhaps by examining the least technologically complex societies, those that live "close to the land," we can see ways of life that may parallel in some aspects the lives of our ancestors. Such groups are collectively called **hunter-gatherers**, or **foragers**.

Foragers are peoples who rely on naturally occurring resources for their subsistence. They *collect* food rather than *produce* it, by hunting wild animals and gathering wild plants. They don't farm, and they don't have domesticated animals (except for dogs). This is how all our ancestors lived until only about 12,000 years ago (see Chapter 14). Thus, by observing modern foragers we are observing the real "human condition," the lifestyle of most humans throughout most of human history.

It is probably safe to say that no true foragers are left in the world. But until recently, there have been groups whose adaptive focus was on this pattern of subsistence, and they have been observed and studied. Examples include a number of Native American cultures, most notably the Eskimo, the native populations of Australia, some societies from the Philippines, and, perhaps the most studied, the !Kung San from the Kalahari Desert of southern Africa, sometimes referred to as Bushmen (Figure 6.8). (The ! represents a click sound in the !Kung language.) The !Kung have always seemed the best model because they inhabit dry, open areas of Africa, environments with much the same potential sources of plant and animal food as was available to early hominids.

The specific cultural systems of foraging peoples show a great deal of variation, but we can make some generalizations. Foraging bands are usually small collections of related family units, each known as a **nuclear family**—a mother, her offspring, and, unlike the chimps and baboons, a father. Band sizes vary according to particular environmental circumstances, but around twenty-five people seem to be the average number supported by this form of subsistence. Foragers often have a home range within which they are mobile as they follow the travels of the animals they hunt and the seasonal cycles of the plants they gather.

Foraging societies tend to be **egalitarian**—that is, they don't have formalized social or economic hierarchies. Not everyone, of course, can do an equal amount of labor or fend completely for themselves. Thus, sharing is an important feature of such groups, to ensure that everyone benefits equally from the labors of the group as a whole. There is no division of labor as we think of it—no occupations. But tasks do tend to be associated with one gender or the other. Generally, men hunt, and

**hunter-gatherer:** A society that relies on naturally occurring sources of food.

**forager:** A synonym for hunter-gatherer.

**nuclear family:** The family unit made up of parents and their offspring.

**egalitarian:** A type of a society that does not recognize differences in social position or wealth.

**Figure 6.8** *A !Kung campsite in the Kalahari. The huts, usually built by the women, serve mostly as windscreens and for storage; the !Kung themselves spend most of the day, and may even sleep, outside. This camp is in a grove of mongongo trees that supply a highly nutritious nut.* (Richard Lee/Anthro-Photo)

women gather. This, of course, makes practical sense in that hunting is more strenuous, more dangerous, and more time-consuming and often takes hunters far from home. Participating in hunting is probably seen as normally too much of a burden on the gender that produces, nurtures, and socializes the society's future generations.

When women gather, they may do so in groups, but each woman normally works by and for herself and her immediate family. Plant foods, which may comprise up to 75 percent of a foraging group's subsistence, are usually a more reliable source than meat. Hunting, on the other hand, especially if large game is the target, requires cooperation among the men; the meat acquired, usually much more scarce and less dependable than plant foods, is shared, sometimes via elaborate, ritualized series of exchanges to symbolize group unity.

Although foraging societies are egalitarian with regard to politics and economics, the people themselves still have differential relationships with one another. As in any group, there are friends of varying degrees and individuals who are not so friendly. Indeed, irreconcilable conflicts are one of the things that contribute to the flexibility of foraging-band membership. People come and go in these groups for various reasons—from personal choice to economic necessity, as when a scarcity of resources causes a band to split apart.

Striking similarities exist between many of the general traits of foraging societies and the societies of chimpanzees and baboons. Because we humans have been foragers for most of our time on earth, it seems a reasonable assumption that a similar set of behavioral features characterized the earliest humans. This assumption, however, must be made with caution. It is important to remember that modern foraging peoples are just that—modern. Though "primitive" perhaps by the **ethnocentric** standards of the industrial world, they are decidedly *not* humans arrested at some previous stage of evolution. They possess fully modern human intellectual capabilities, and these have given them cultural assets unknown to any humans until recently. The !Kung, for example, use the bow and arrow, which is only about 10,000 years old.

In addition, evidence indicates that modern foraging groups are not as pristine as we had thought or hoped. The most infamous example is the Tasaday, discovered in the jungles of the Philippines in 1971. This group of twenty-five people were thought to be hunter-gatherers (if catching frogs can be considered hunting) who used very simple stone tools and had been completely isolated for 2000 years. This was a glimpse into the past if ever there was one! But it turns out that at the very least the Tasaday were part of or had traded with a larger agricultural group, and they may even have been a publicity hoax (Berreman 1991). Indeed, it can fairly be said that all societies today have been influenced and changed by contact with other groups and so probably none accurately represents our species' previous way of life.

Moreover, like all humans, foraging peoples are culture-bearing. They consciously create and modify cultural systems to fit their environments and the basic ways they cope with those environments. So, rather than reflecting some lifestyle inherited from our ancient past, the social systems of foragers must be seen as the collective cultural responses of groups of people to the worlds they know and have to deal with.

Still, the behavioral themes running through this discussion cannot be ignored. What the foraging cultures may show us is that, despite our cultural ability to vary our specific behaviors over an incredible range, this variation may be based on certain general patterns of behavior established in our prehominid past. And so, when we look at baboons or, especially, chimpanzees, we are not necessarily seeing ourselves in the past, but we are seeing the patterns of behavior from which ours has evolved.

## SUMMARY

As we noted in Chapter 5, one way to guide us as we look into our past is to understand the results of the events that made up that past. This approach works for behavior as well as for physical adaptations. We can compare the behavior of various modern human groups to that of species with whom we share general traits or environmental conditions.

**ethnocentric:** Judging another society's values in terms of one's own social values.

We search for trends or tendencies that may indicate how our ancestors might have adapted to similar circumstances. The importance of a well-defined organization among social African carnivores like the lion and wild dog and as seen in another savanna primate, the baboon, is a good hint that an analogous behavior was a key to the survival of early savanna hominids.

More useful is the behavior of close evolutionary relatives, especially the chimpanzee. Chimp behavior differs in specifics from ours and has been evolving separately from ours for 5 or 6 million years, helping that species adapt to its particular niche. The basic patterns for the behavior of our two species, however, are homologous. They are the same because we inherited them from a common ancestor. It is highly likely, then, that our remote hominid ancestors also used some manifestation of these patterns.

What such studies indicate to us is that the early hominids of the plains of Africa may very well have been highly social creatures and that their social organization was built around differing interpersonal relationships, a family unit, conscious sexuality, recognition of group membership and territory, and mutual care at both the individual and the group level.

## KEY TERMS

| | | |
|---|---|---|
| homology | estrus | nuclear family |
| analogy | hunter-gatherer | egalitarian |
| ethology | forager | ethnocentric |

## FOR MORE INFORMATION

The latest thinking on baboon behavior can be found in Shirley Strum's *Almost Human* and in Barbara Smuts's *Sex and Friendship in Baboons.*

Dian Fossey recounts her study of gorillas in *Gorillas in the Mist;* her own story in turn, including her murder, is told by Farley Mowat in *Woman in the Mists* and in the 1988 movie *Gorillas in the Mist.*

Biruté Galdikas tells about orangutans in "Living with the Great Orange Apes: Indonesia's Orangutans" in the June 1980 issue of *National Geographic.*

Jane Goodall's latest work on the chimps and her experiences studying them is *Through a Window: My Thirty Years with the Chimpanzees of Gombe.*

Some basic information about foragers can be found in *Man the Hunter,* by Richard Lee and Irven DeVore, and, for the other half of the population, *Woman the Gatherer,* edited by F. Dahlberg.

# 7

# LEARNING ABOUT THE PAST: THE MATERIAL RECORD

How do we learn about the past? How do we collect and analyze data about the antiquity of our species?

Our approach in this book to understanding our past will be through the field of anthropology, defined previously as the study of humanity. If you think about it, though, nearly all the courses you're now taking deal in some fashion with people or their works. What makes anthropology different?

## ANTHROPOLOGY: STUDYING OURSELVES

To use an analogy, we might say that anthropology studies humans much the way a branch of biology, such as zoology, studies its subjects. Anthropologists mostly study a single species—the human species. We try to make generalizations about the entire group of organisms. We look for connections between the present condition and past history of

**Figure 7.1** *Raymond Hames using a battery-powered computer and printer gathers data from Yano-mamö about the history of their settlement patterns.* (Raymond Hames)

the organism. Anthropology assumes that all facets of the organism's anatomy, physiology, behavior, environment, and evolution are interrelated and can only be fully understood in terms of those interrelationships. Thus described, we can define anthropology as *the* holistic study *of people.* Anthropology studies the whole species and all its features in interaction with one another.

Such a broad subject is necessarily subdivided into a number of specialties, or subfields. Perhaps the most characteristic feature of our species is our cultural behavior, with all its various manifestations. The specialty of **cultural anthropology** focuses on this behavior, seeking to understand the nature of culture. In its most general definition, culture is the sum total of those things people have invented or developed and passed down.

Culture is often defined by anthropologists as the *extrasomatic* (nonphysical, literally "beyond the body") means of adaptation. Whereas most other animal species rely on very specific physical adaptations or adjustments to their environment, people, through culture, produce their own means of survival. In other words, culture is viewed as constituting all aspects of the human strategy for survival that we, as a result of our great intelligence, have been able to think up. Cultural anthropology attempts to describe various cultural systems and to explain the variations these systems exhibit (Figure 7.1). It also searches for processes that account for change in culture through time. Cultural anthropologists characteristically study living societies.

Because language is unique to human beings and such an important part of what makes us different from other animals, some anthropologists focus on linguistics, the nature and structure of human language. **Anthropological linguistics** focuses on issues like the evolution of speech, the historical connections between the many and various human language systems, and the ways in which language affects our perception of the world.

But cultural systems also have a past. **Archaeology** is the branch of anthropology that studies this past (Figure 7.2). Much of the evidence to be presented in this book has been obtained through the study of our cultural past.

Finally, we are, of course, living organisms, subject to the same biological processes that affect all other organisms. The study of how these processes apply to us is the subject of **physical**, or **biological anthropology** (Figure 7.3). Some specialists in this subfield gather biological data from living human populations. Others focus on groups of the past, represented by fossil remains; the latter we sometimes call **paleoanthropologists**.

Our subject in this book is human antiquity. Thus, in terms of the field of anthropology, this book focuses on the data and methods of archaeology and paleoanthropology—the "anthropology of the past."

**holistic:** Viewing culture as an interconnected whole.

**cultural anthropology:** The branch of anthropology that focuses on cultural behavior.

**culture:** The nongenetic means of adaptation; those things people invent and pass down.

**anthropological linguistics:** The branch of anthropology that focuses on language and languages.

**archaeology:** The branch of anthropology that focuses on cultural evolution through the study of material remains.

**physical anthropology:** The branch of anthropology that focuses on humans as a biological species.

**biological anthropology:** Synonym for physical anthropology.

**paleoanthropologist:** A physical anthropologist specializing in the study of human fossil remains.

**Figure 7.2** *Ken Feder* (right) *map-ping an archaeological site. Careful record keeping is a vital aspect of archaeological fieldwork.* (B. Calogero)

**Figure 7.2** *Ken Feder* (right) *mapping an archaeological site. Careful record keeping is a vital aspect of archaeological fieldwork.* (B. Calogero)

Remember, though, that in a real sense the subfield designations in anthropology have limited meaning. They refer not to separate disciplines but to starting points or foci in the general process of trying to understand the human species. Our subject—people—does not divide itself neatly into discrete categories such as present, past, cultural, and biological. Neither does the discipline that studies that subject. All branches of anthropology work together toward a common goal: understanding the human species.

## THE ANTHROPOLOGY OF THE PAST

**Figure 7.3** *Michael Park examining a prehistoric human skull. The nature of individuals, species, and their evolutionary histories can be discerned by examining skeletal remains.*

Many people have some very strange ideas about what archaeology and physical anthropology are and what scientists in these fields do. Some people think we study dinosaurs. (They have seen too many episodes of "The Flintstones.") In reality, the dinosaurs became extinct more than 50 million years before even our earliest human ancestors appeared on the scene. Others think that archaeologists are tough, globe-trotting vagabonds who loot sites for treasure. Physical anthropologists are often stereotyped as those who identify the skeletal remains of dead people.

Actually, archaeology is simply that branch of anthropology focusing on the human cultural past. Whereas other anthropologists may study a people by actually living among them, archaeologists must study a people through analysis of what they left behind. Archaeology exists out of the necessity born of one simple fact: The only way we can learn *directly* about people in the past, especially those who lived before the invention of writing, is by studying the things they made and used. So archaeologists have, as their primary data, the material consequences of human behavior—the tools, edifices, art, and even garbage a society leaves behind. From potsherds to pyramids, from arrowheads to Stonehenge, these are the archaeologist's raw materials.

Because the materials archaeologists deal with can be so interesting in and of themselves, it is easy to lose track of why we are studying pyramids, cave paintings, pots, and the like. Just remember that archaeologists are anthropologists; they are interested in the same sorts of things that all anthropologists are. Our aim is to understand how ancient people lived, not simply to collect interesting antiques.

Similarly, whereas some physical anthropologists collect data from living individuals, paleoanthropologists deal with the skeletal remains of people, and even then usually not with the complete skeleton. Nevertheless, they also seek to learn about the biology of the people who made the tools and pots and paintings. What did they look like? What diseases did they suffer from, and what sorts of injuries caused their deaths? What were the sex ratios and average ages of their populations? Moreover, paleoanthropologists are interested in how and why human biology changed over the 4 million years or so we and our upright-walking ancestors have been around. In other words, how do the processes of evolution apply to our species? The physical anthropologist also addresses these matters. The answers to such questions round out our understanding of ancient people.

We can break down the goals of the anthropology of the past into a series of general questions we wish to "ask" of the data:

1. *Where* did people live?
2. *What* materials did they leave behind?
3. *When* was an area occupied, and when did certain human activities occur?
4. *How* did people in a given region or time period live?
5. *Who* were the people, biologically?
6. *Why* did they live the life they did?

It is through asking and attempting to answer these questions that we can illuminate the story of human physical and cultural evolution. In the rest of this chapter, we will briefly describe how the anthropologists who study the past go about this task.

## Where?

To know where prehistoric people settled, where they lived out their lives, and where they died, you must find the material traces of their existence. You must, in other words, find archaeological **sites**—locations where humans once lived or worked and where their traces, in

**site:** A place that contains evidence of a human presence.

the form of **artifacts** and **features**, were left behind and have been preserved. For nonarchaeologists, this ability to find sites may seem almost magical. It would probably not be giving away any trade secrets to tell you that, in reality, the discovery of archaeological sites does not depend on intuition, "psychic power," or magic. Instead, archaeological sites are discovered through a scientific process demanding hard work and, often, a bit of luck.

Archaeological site survey, the actual process of finding sites, includes a set of basic, commonsense techniques. Among these we can include previous research, local history, local collectors, environmental factors, and field survey.

**Previous Research.** Previous research refers to other archaeological work done in the region. Here, archaeologists can simply take advantage of previous study. In years past, an archaeologist may have located a site that he or she did not have the time to examine further. Perhaps now it can be excavated.

**Local History.** The local history of an area may provide clues concerning the location of sites. During construction projects—road building, for example—workers digging into the ground may have unearthed artifacts, and this discovery may have been recorded in old newspaper accounts. Children exploring an area may have located a now-forgotten cave, an event that may also have been recorded. These sorts of locations, long since covered over or forgotten, can be examined by the archaeologist to see if anything still remains for investigation.

**Local Collectors.** Local artifact collectors may have valuable information for the archaeologist. Collecting Indian artifacts has become a popular pastime in the United States. Elsewhere in the world, people similarly become involved in "amateur archaeology." Some have enormous collections. It must be said that some collectors have little interest in the scientific study of the past. They collect to sell the artifacts or simply to possess them, and in so doing they destroy sites and much of the information they contain. Many amateur artifact collectors, however, are responsible individuals who appreciate the importance of careful archaeology. They keep accurate records of where individual specimens came from. They rarely *dig* for artifacts, content with recovering those items that have come to the surface through some sort of disturbance. They are more than happy to share their knowledge with professionals.

Even people who do not go out consciously looking for artifacts or sites sometimes have valuable information for archaeologists. Farmers plowing their fields, homeowners building an addition to their house, workers constructing a highway, gardeners planting their tomatoes, all disturb the soil and may encounter the remains of buried artifacts.

Many of the important archaeological sites mentioned in this book were found accidentally by people engaged in nonarchaeological pursuits.

**Environmental Factors.**    An important part of archaeological site survey is environmental analysis. Whether they are prehistoric hunters, primitive farmers, or twentieth-century Americans, all people depend, ultimately, on nature's bounty. We can use that fact to help find archaeological sites.

For example, all people need a source of fresh water, and no one is likely to live too far from one. Hunters will tend to concentrate their settlements in areas where animals are likely to be found. Farmers may prefer extensive areas of fertile flatland to make a living. People with nasty neighbors may choose to settle in protected areas. Pottery-making people may want to live close to a source of clay. The archaeologist must consider a constellation of environmental variables just to isolate the kinds of areas where sites are most likely to be found. In this endeavor, there are clearly no guarantees, only probabilities.

**Field Survey.**    Both surface and subsurface investigation of an area are ordinarily included in **field survey**. Before applying procedures in which the soil is actually turned over in search of archaeological evidence, archaeologists can apply techniques of **remote sensing**. Such methods are non invasive, like a medical CAT scan. Photographs taken from a unique perspective (as from an airplane or satellite), radar images, analysis of magnetic anomalies in the ground, and variations in subsurface resistance to an electrical current can provide the archaeologist with data concerning the presence of archaeological materials unavailable by simple inspection and without having to dig holes in the ground. The results of remote-sensing procedures cannot ordinarily replace excavation, but they certainly are valuable in helping the archaeologist decide where to investigate further by surface inspection and subsurface investigation.

Where prehistoric people have left above-ground structures of relatively resilient material (as in the case of the ancient Egyptians or the Pueblo Indians of the American Southwest), an above-ground investigation can locate sites. At present, throughout the world, most sites visible on the surface have been inventoried, but the discovery of unknown surface sites in less populated areas is still a very real possibility.

An above-ground inspection is also valuable when nature itself has conducted its own kind of excavation through erosion. A river eroding its bank or a gulley being cut by a flash flood may expose previously unknown archaeological material. In many instances, the fossil remains of human ancestors have been found in places where ancient soil levels have been exposed by natural processes. Olduvai Gorge, in Africa, is a famous example of this effect (see Figure 9.8). Searching for and sur-

**artifact**:  Any object made by humans.

**feature**:  An element of a site, composed of artifacts; for example, a grave or fireplace.

**field survey**:  The process of discovering archaeological sites.

**remote sensing**:  Noninvasive examination of sites where no soil is removed.

**Figure 7.4** *Excavators digging a line of test pits along the floodplain of the Farmington River in Avon, Connecticut (top). Test pits are dug with shovels, and all soil is passed through ⅛-inch mesh hardware cloth (bottom). Systematic subsurface sampling is an important component of archaeological field survey.*

veying areas where such ancient deposits have been exposed by natural erosion is an important part of the search for the vestiges of prehistoric humanity.

Most prehistoric archaeological sites, however, have been buried by natural processes of deposition. Rivers deposit soil when they flood, sand gets blown about by winds, volcanoes erupt and spew out lava and ash, mountains erode, and cave roofs collapse. All these processes can result in the burial of the remains of a town, camp, or cemetery. To find sites subjected to thousands and even millions of years of these natural processes of deposition, we must dig.

**Test borings**, or **test pits**—simply, small holes in the ground—are part of most archaeological surveys. Their purpose is to establish, without a full-scale excavation, the presence or absence of a site. Based on local history, the reports of amateur archaeologists, an assessment of the local environment, or simply the desire to cover a given area, test pits are placed according to a number of different sampling strategies. They may be placed every 10 meters along a straight line or **transect** (Figure 7.4). They may be placed in a square grid or checkerboard pattern. Thousands of these shovel-dug holes may be excavated without finding much of anything. It may seem like looking for the proverbial needle in a haystack—and it is. There are no shortcuts to finding archaeological remains and thus answering the question, "Where did the ancient people live?" If the archaeologist has done his or her homework, however, by the time test pits are excavated the most likely areas have been isolated, and there is a good chance of finding something.

## What?

All scientists are faced with the problem of data collection. Astronomers need telescopes and microbiologists need microscopes to collect the information they must have to answer questions in their fields. Archaeologists are faced with the problem that what they are interested in is the stuff people made, used, and threw away. Most of it ends up in the ground and, through the processes mentioned, gets buried. Once sites have been discovered through site survey, our main tools of data collection are items to help us remove the soil from around the artifacts.

Not everybody recognizes the difficulty in accomplishing this task while preserving the *information* a site contains. For example, a local developer uncovered some 10,000-year-old woolly mammoth bones and invited us to take a look and dig them up; perhaps the mammoth had been killed by prehistoric people. We arrived with our dental picks and trowels, ready to spend days or even weeks removing the handful of bones from the ground. The developer, however, assured us that he could accomplish the same task with his backhoe in a few minutes, swearing he would be "real careful"!

The material archaeologists ordinarily study has been lying in the ground for hundreds, thousands, even millions of years. It would be a terrible irony if, in our attempt to recover these objects that have been preserved for so long, we were to destroy them instead. Consequently, archaeologists need to be meticulous and exacting in excavation. Using only the most delicate of tools, including masons' trowels for careful scraping of the soil, dental picks, artists' brushes, and whisk brooms, archaeologists remove the soil from around the pieces of the prehistoric puzzle.

**test boring:** A small excavation to establish the presence or absence of a site.

**test pit:** Synonym for test boring.

**transect:** A line or grid of systematically located test borings.

Not only do we want to preserve the items themselves, but we also want to preserve their spatial contexts. Knowing *where* an arrow was left or placed thousands of years ago can tell us as much about what it was used for as the arrow itself. We want to know if the arrow was found in an isolated spot with no other objects nearby (a weapon lost, perhaps, during a hunt). Or was it found with a cluster of arrows inside the remains of a hut (perhaps a hunter's storage area)? Maybe the arrow was found in a fireplace (having fallen out of the animal it killed), or even in a human grave (a tool to accompany the deceased to the after-life). In each case, the tool itself would look exactly the same. But where it was found (its **provenience**) and what was found with it (its **associations**) tell us quite a bit about what the people who used it were up to. A backhoe would make short work of this wealth of valuable evidence associated with the artifact itself.

So archaeological sites are excavated in an extremely orderly and logical fashion (Figure 7.5). Ordinarily, a site is segmented into grids or squares, usually 1 or 2 meters on a side, although this practice varies.

**Figure 7.5** *Sites are excavated in a regular, orderly fashion to preserve the spatial contexts of the material uncovered. The archaeological site at Non Nok Tha in Thailand shows the application of this procedure.* (Courtesy William G. Solheim II)

The squares are excavated individually or in clusters, with the soil scraped back very carefully in regular increments, only a few centimeters at a time—like peeling back the layers of an onion. The soil is then sifted through screens with $\frac{1}{4}$-inch, $\frac{1}{8}$-inch, or even smaller mesh to catch anything that may have escaped the watchful eye of the archaeologist.

When possible, artifacts encountered in excavation are left in place (*in situ*) so they can be viewed in their spatial contexts, as they were placed and last seen by the ancient inhabitants of the site. Maps are made, and photographs are taken, all in an attempt to create a permanent record of the spatial contexts. In digging a site and in taking its materials to the laboratory or museum, of course, we do destroy it. We destroy the site systematically, however, to be able to study it. The careful recording of all information is crucial if we hope to reconstruct what took place at the site from the often meager remains left behind.

## When?

How old is a site? When were specific cultural advances made in human prehistory? When did people begin walking on two feet? When was agriculture invented? How old is a given artifact or the pieces of a skeleton? When did certain environmental changes occur? There are a number of techniques for answering these questions. We will describe the most important ones here.

**Stratigraphy.**    The term applied to the layering of the earth's soil is stratigraphy. You saw earlier how the recognition of this basic fact of geology was an important step in the development of uniformitarianism and the modern concept of biological evolution.

Geologists recognize that the history of the earth is written in its rock. Rock and soil (which may later harden into rock) are deposited by flooding rivers, eroding mountains, erupting volcanoes—the same processes that bury archaeological sites. Soil is often deposited in distinguishable layers or may develop them later. The layering may result from different sources, or **parent materials**. For example, in the same spot one layer of soil may be from a river flood, another from a dust storm, and another still from a rock slide. Layering may also result from different conditions of deposition. For example, some layers may have been deposited underwater, others under dry conditions. Different weather conditions after deposition may cause layering because soil texture is altered by temperature. Plants growing on the soil may also have an impact, and layering develops as a result of the specific chemical and biological action of various plants extracting nutrients from the soil. Soil layers are superimposed, one on top of another, through time. Thus, successively older layers are encountered as you dig deeper. Ar-

**spatial context:**  Where and with what an artifact is found in a site.

**provenience:**  The precise location of an artifact.

**association:**  The spatial relationships of artifacts, one to another.

**stratigraphy:**  The study of the earth's strata.

**parent material:**  The source material for a particular soil.

chaeologists, paleoanthropologists, and geologists use this **law of super-position** to help them place their sites in what is known as a **relative chronological sequence**.

Many of the objects people make and use eventually become incorporated into the soil beneath their feet through a number of cultural processes—loss, discard, storage, and abandonment. After the people are gone, soil may be deposited over their artifacts. Sometime later, another group may move in and their objects become a part of the stratigraphic record—at a level *above* that of the previous group (Figure 7.6).

Let us imagine that many years later you have a picnic on the very spot where these prehistoric people lived. During the course of your picnic, some change falls out of your pocket. You leave, unaware of your loss. Next spring a nearby river floods, depositing a fine layer of silt over your "artifacts." Now your personal detritus too has been incorporated

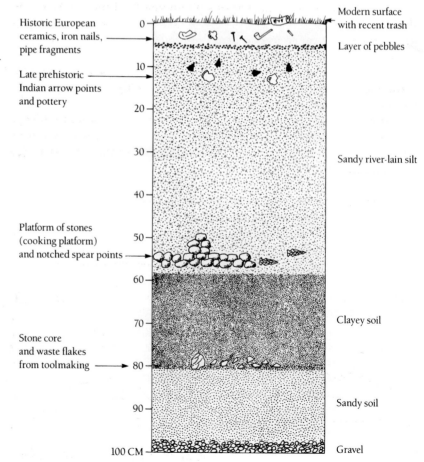

**Figure 7.6** *Stratigraphic section from the Old Farms Brook Site in Avon, Connecticut, showing a sequence of three prehistoric occupations and one historic occupation of the same location.*

Historic European ceramics, iron nails, pipe fragments

Late prehistoric Indian arrow points and pottery

Platform of stones (cooking platform) and notched spear points

Stone core and waste flakes from toolmaking

Modern surface with recent trash
Layer of pebbles

Sandy river-lain silt

Clayey soil

Sandy soil

Gravel

0
10
20
30
40
50
60
70
80
90
100 CM

into the stratigraphic record of this site. Not only is the history of the earth written in the soil, so is the history of humanity.

**Absolute Techniques.**   Stratigraphy can provide us with only a relative chronology. We can know the order in which a series of different cultures inhabited a spot, but we cannot know *when* those cultures existed— we cannot determine an age in years simply from the layering of soil. We do, however, have techniques that enable us to derive actual dates from material. We call these procedures **absolute dating** techniques.

Absolute dates can be expressed in a number of ways: B.C.E. (before the common era) or B.C. (before the birth of Christ), A.D. (after the birth of Christ), or B.P. (before present). B.P. has the "present" fixed at 1950. Virtually all sites we will be discussing are far too old and the dating techniques too imprecise for it to make a difference; but technically, if the "present" in B.P. were not set at some fixed point, all dates expressed in this way would need to be changed each year.

One set of absolute methods is called **radiometric dating**. This means that the dating procedure is based on the decay of a **radioactive isotope** of a particular element. Radioactive isotopes decay by a variety of natural processes. We can measure the rate of decay of most radioactive isotopes—that is, how fast they change from an unstable to a stable form. We can also measure how much of the radioactive isotope is left in a given archaeological, biological, or geological specimen. If we then can estimate how much of the isotope must have been present initially, we can determine how old the object is—how long it must have taken for the initial quantity of the radioactive isotope to decrease to whatever the level is today.

There are many radioactive isotopes in nature, all with measurable decay rates. Most are useless to archaeologists and paleoanthropologists, though, because the elements are so rare that it would be unlikely to find any of them in cultural or biological specimens. Many are useless because their decay rates are so fast that even fairly recent specimens are unlikely to have any of the radioactive isotope left to be measured. Other radioactive elements have such slow rates of decay that even the oldest of anthropological specimens have not been around long enough for any measurable decay to have taken place; thus, no age can be derived.

A few elements, however, are abundant and have decay rates that make them useful for the dating of sites. Radioactive carbon is one of those. It provides the raw material for the **carbon dating technique**.

Carbon is found in the atmosphere, linked to oxygen, in the form of carbon dioxide and it is found in all living things. Most carbon atoms are called $^{12}C$ for the twelve particles in their nuclei (six protons and six neutrons). Some carbon atoms, however, have two additional neutrons in their nuclei. These are called $^{14}C$, an unstable isotope of carbon.

**law of superposition:**   The stratigraphic law stating that the more recent layers are superimposed over the older.

**relative chronological sequence:** A sequence arranged in an older-to-younger relationship.

**absolute dating:**   A dating technique assigning a specific age.

**radiometric dating:**   A dating technique using the decay rate of a radioactive substance.

**radioactive isotope:**   An unstable form of an element that decays to a stable form by giving off particles, or rays.

**carbon dating:**   A radiometric technique using the decay rate of a radioactive isotope of carbon found in organic remains.

The rate at which $^{14}C$ decays is a constant called a **half-life.** $^{14}C$'s half-life is about 5730 years. In that amount of time, about half of the $^{14}C$ in a dead organism decays to nitrogen. In another 5730 years, half of what was left after the first half-life has decayed, leaving one-quarter of what was there initially, and so on. By knowing the rate of decay, how much $^{14}C$ was present initially, and how much is left now, we can tell how old the item is. It's like knowing how much sand there is in an hourglass, how fast it flows to the bottom, and how much has flowed out of the top. From that, you know how much time has elapsed since the hourglass was overturned. From the measure of $^{14}C$, we can know how many years have elapsed since the death of a living thing.

This technique has a few constraints. If something is only a few hundred years old, not enough decay has taken place to be measurable. Although new procedures have extended the temporal range of carbon dating, if something is much more than 60,000 years old, not enough $^{14}C$ is usually left for the technique to work. Also, we now know that the $^{12}C : {}^{14}C$ ratio in the atmosphere has changed during the last several thousand years, which creates a built-in error factor. Nevertheless, if an organic remain was part of an archaeological site, we can obtain a fairly good idea of how old the site is using the radiocarbon technique.

Another important radiometric technique is **potassium/argon, or K/Ar, dating.** Many of the fossil human sites we will be discussing have been dated with this technique, which measures the age of volcanic rocks. The presence of the element argon in volcanic rock is primarily the result of the decay of a radioactive isotope of potassium ($^{40}K$). A measurement is made of the amount of argon gas that has built up in the rock. Because we know the half-life of $^{40}K$ (1.31 billion years), we can determine how old the rock is—when it last solidified—by measuring how much argon has accumulated. Because of the very long half-life, there is virtually no upper limit to the technique—nothing is too old to be dated. On the other hand, although it is technically feasible to date rock that is only 10,000 years old, the long half-life generally renders the technique inaccurate for anything less than a few hundred thousand years old.

Potassium/argon dating tells us the age of the rock, how long ago it came out of a volcano. It is not, therefore, a direct measure of the date of a site. We can, however, combine K/Ar dating with stratigraphic analysis. For example, if artifacts or bones are found in a stratigraphic layer *above* a volcanic flow that is dated to 3.8 mya (million years ago) and *below* a subsequent flow dated to 3.2 mya, then we are reasonably certain that the occupation of the site is not more than 3.8 million and not less than 3.2 million years old (Figure 7.7).

Still another series of radiometric techniques is based on calibrations of the decay rate of uranium isotopes to their various daughter isotopes and elements. For example, $^{234}U$ decays to thorium, and $^{235}U$ decays to protactinium. Rather than disappearing entirely, these isotopes decay

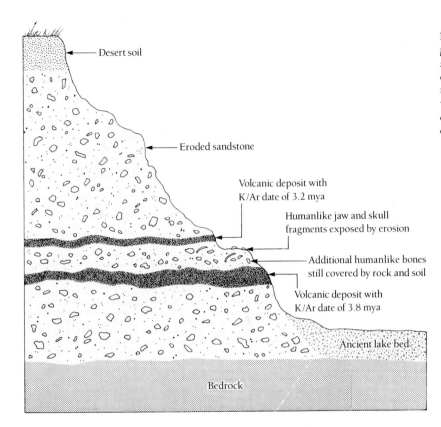

Desert soil

Eroded sandstone

Volcanic deposit with
K/Ar date of 3.2 mya

Humanlike jaw and skull
fragments exposed by erosion

Additional humanlike bones
still covered by rock and soil

Volcanic deposit with
K/Ar date of 3.8 mya

Ancient lake bed

Bedrock

**Figure 7.7** *Hypothetical geological profile showing human remains stratigraphically between two layers of volcanic rock. The archaeological material must be younger than the volcanic deposit below it (3.8 mya) and older than the volcanic deposit above it (3.2 mya).*

at a known rate to an equilibrium level with their daughter isotopes. When a carbonate or phosphate has been deposited at the time of site occupation, typically as in a cave deposit called travertine, the site can be dated. Encrustations found on bones have also been dated using this technique. The decay to thorium is extremely useful because the half-life of $^{234}$U is about 250,000 years and that of thorium, 75,000 years. As a result, sites too old to date with radiocarbon but too young to apply K/Ar dating to can sometimes be dated by means of uranium series.

**Dendrochronology**, or tree-ring dating, is an extremely accurate technique but very limited in its application. It depends on four conditions:

1. Trees add one growth ring for each year they are alive.
2. The size of a ring in a given year varies according to some environmental condition or set of conditions like rainfall or temperature.
3. Any sequence of varying tree-ring widths over a long period of time will be unique.
4. All trees in a given area reflect the same changes in tree-ring width.

**half-life:** The amount of time needed for half of a radioactive isotope to decay to a stable one.

**potassium/argon (K/Ar) dating:** A radiometric technique using the decay rate of radioactive potassium, found in volcanic rock, into stable argon.

**dendrochronology:** A dating technique using tree-ring sequences.

1970

1960

1950

1940

1930

1920

1910

1900

**Figure 7.9** *Styles of artifacts change over time as technology and taste change. Automobiles are one example.* (Archaeology: Discovering Our Past, Sharer and Ashmore, 1987, Mayfield Publishing)

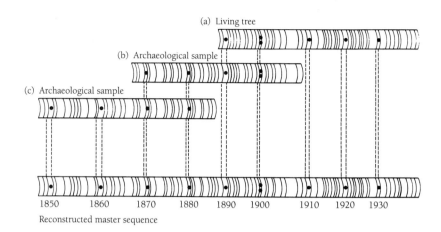

Reconstructed master sequence

**Figure 7.8** *Cross section of tree rings from a living tree (a) overlaps the ring sequence from an archaeological sample (b) which, in turn, overlaps part of the sequence of another archaeological sample (c). The overlapping of many samples allows for the construction of a "master sequence" of three-ring patterns (d).* (Archaeology: Discovering Our Past, Sharer and Ashmore, 1987:354, Mayfield Publishing)

By overlapping ring sequences of living trees with those of old dead trees, a master sequence of tree-ring width variation over many years can be developed. A sequence of over 2000 years has been produced for the American Southwest. When an archaeological site is located that contains wood or even entire logs, the unique sequence of thick and thin rings in the ancient specimens can be compared to the master sequence (Figure 7.8). By seeing in what year these archaeological specimens were cut down, an exact date can be associated with the site.

**Cultural Techniques.**    The final techniques we will discuss here are perhaps not the most accurate but are valuable nonetheless. These are known as **cultural techniques**.

Imagine you are walking down the street and a car drives by. It is large with sharp tailfins and built low to the ground. You can tell almost immediately that this car is a 1950s model. Or I hand you a photograph of a young woman. She has a pony tail, saddle shoes, knee socks, a frilly blouse, and a pleated skirt with a picture of a poodle sewn onto it. Again, the 1950s. But how do we know this?

We know because we are aware of certain style changes that have taken place in our own culture (Figure 7.9). Archaeologists are performing almost the same kind of identification when they determine the age of a site based on the style of the architecture or artifacts found there. You knew the automobile and the girl were from the 1950s because you are familiar with our own recent history. Archaeologists can pick up a piece of pottery or a stone tool and provide an estimate for its

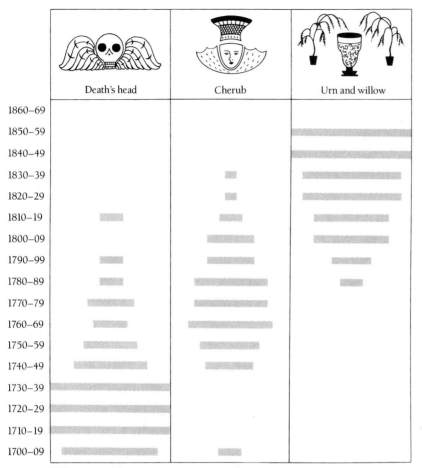

| | Death's head | Cherub | Urn and willow |
|---|---|---|---|

1860–69

1850–59

1840–49

1830–39

1820–29

1810–19

1800–09

1790–99

1780–89

1770–79

1760–69

1750–59

1740–49

1730–39

1720–29

1710–19

1700–09

▨ = 10% of the stones in a ten-year period

**Figure 7.10** *Seriation graph of tombstone design 1700 to 1860 in central Connecticut cemeteries. Here, as elsewhere in New England, the so-called Death's Head, or skull design, was replaced by the Cherub, or smiling angel face, which was, in turn, replaced by the urn and willow tree design.*

age because they are familiar with style changes in the ancient past. We can apply actual dates to these items because we know that at other sites, where absolute dates have been obtained, the styles were identical.

We can also measure the rates of change and gauge how quickly styles replace each other by a process called **seriation**. Here, we assume that styles of certain artifacts, like pottery, change in fairly regular patterns. When a new way of doing something—making arrowheads, designing gravestones, opening soft drink cans—is introduced in a culture, it starts off slowly, gains in acceptance until it reaches a peak, and then is slowly replaced by another, newer way of doing the same thing (Figure 7.10). We can use the predictable pattern of this process as a relative dating technique by placing sites in the most logical chronological order based on these changes in style.

**cultural technique:** A dating technique using cultural comparisons.

**seriation:** Establishing a relative chronological sequence using the pattern of replacement of artifact styles.

**Table 7.1** *Other Dating Methods*

| Dating Method | Age Range | Material Dated | Basis |
|---|---|---|---|
| Thermoluminescence | No effective limits | Fired clay, pottery, bricks, burned rock | Measure of amount of energy captured in material from decay of radioactive elements in surrounding soil; amount of energy captured is proportional to age |
| Paleomagnetism | 2000 B.P.–present | Material with magnetic minerals | Movement of earth's magnetic pole and known dates of the position of the pole |
| Amino (aspartic) acid racemization | 1,000,000–2000 B.P. | Bone | Shift in polarity of amino acids |
| Obsidian hydration | 800,000 B.P.–present | Obsidian (volcanic glass) | Regular build up of "hydration layer" caused by chemical reaction of obsidian with water over time |
| Fission track dating | 1,000,000–100,000 B.P. | Volcanic rock | Radioactive decay leaves microscopic damage "tracks" in rock at regular rate |
| Electron spin resonance | | Cave deposits, bone | Electrons produced by natural radiation become trapped in crystalline materials at a regular rate |

Overview of time range, application, and basis of dating methods not discussed in the text.

Many other dating techniques are available to the archaeologist. Table 7.1 presents a list and some details of their applicability.

## How?

How did the people at a given archaeological site get by? What did they eat, how did they make their tools, how did they bury their dead? How did agriculture develop? How did the first cities evolve? Our major problem in answering these questions is, of course, that the people we study are dead. We cannot ask them about their relations with their neighbors. We cannot observe their religious ceremonies. We cannot interview them about their reasons for adopting agriculture.

One way around this is through the approach of **ethnoarchaeology**. Here, archaeologists examine living groups in the same manner as ethnographers, but they focus on how human behavior becomes translated into the archaeological record. This is an important approach when analyzing the general processes by which sites are produced. But when it comes to attempting to reconstruct a particular culture, generally, all we have are their physical remains, the hardware they left behind, the stuff they made and used. Much of our methodology concerns itself with this task: How do we go from a bunch of broken pots, pieces of bone, arrowheads, and ruins to a picture of a once vibrant, now departed culture? Anthropologists who live with a people to understand their way of life are performing what we call **ethnography** (literally, "cultural description"). Archaeologists trying to understand an ancient way of life can be said to perform **paleoethnography**.

We can break down the task of paleoethnography into a series of general categories of cultural inquiry: technology, environment, diet, social systems, trade, and ideology. Certainly, society's activities could be categorized other ways, but these should encompass most of the major questions an anthropologist might ask.

**Technology.**   The study of prehistoric technology involves figuring out how the people made the things they used and how they used them. This can include everything from a simple stone spear point to an enormous pyramid. Technology is one of the areas of ancient life an archaeologist can study most directly. After all, most of what we find is a direct product of a given technology. We can figure out how a stone tool was made by studying it directly. We can analyze how an ancient canal was built by examining the remains of the canal, and so on.

This is not, however, quite as simple a task as it sounds. How can you tell how an object was made simply by looking at it? Actually, of course, you can't. But archaeologists can use information from a number of sources to give them clues about how the things we dig up were actually made by prehistoric people.

**ethnoarchaeology:**   Observing living peoples to understand how archaeological records are produced.

**ethnography:**   The intensive study and description of a particular culture.

**paleoethnography:**   Reconstructing a past cultural system through archaeological analysis.

The historical record is one source of data. For example, the early Spanish settlers in Mexico described in their writings how the Aztecs manufactured artifacts of silver and gold. We know how the longhouses of the Iroquois Indians of New York State were made because the early Jesuit missionaries wrote extensively about Iroquois lifestyles—at the same time that they were trying to change them. The archaeologist simply attempts to extend the historical record back into the prehistoric past.

Another way to study prehistoric technology is by experimentation. The archaeologist attempts, through a process of trial and error, to replicate objects that have been recovered (Figure 7.11). If you wish to know how a certain variety of prehistoric stone tool was made, you try to make one exactly like it—same raw material, same size, same proportions.

To determine how a tool was used, experiments can be performed to identify the **wear patterns** that result from particular modes of use. In one such experiment, a series of sharp-edged stone tools were made by an experimental archaeologist (Keeley 1980). They were then used for different functions (cutting, scraping, chopping, engraving, piercing) on different raw materials (bone, wood, meat, leather, antler). The resulting wear patterns were different for each kind of use and included polish, chipping, scratching, and dulling of the edge used (Figure 7.12).

Another researcher in this experiment was not told how the experimental tools were used or on what raw materials. Nevertheless, he was

**Figure 7.11** *Experimental archaeologist Terry del Bene produces replicas of stone tools with stone and antler hammers. By replicating stone tools, the archaeologist can gain some insight into how the prehistoric specimens were made and used.* (Courtesy Terry del Bene: photographed by Margaret Jodry-Stanford)

**Figure 7.12** *Microphotograph of characteristic scratches (area indicated by arrow)* on a prehistoric gouge. *Wear pattern analysis can provide information concerning how a particular tool was used.*

able to deduce very accurately how these experimental tools had been used. The fact that wear patterns come in many varieties and are often diagnostic of specific forms of use gives us some degree of confidence in our ability to examine a prehistoric tool and suggest how it was most probably used.

Archaeological experiments can range from trying to replicate a single artifact type—say, prehistoric axes from France—to an entire way of life. The latter may involve actually renouncing the twentieth century, at least for a time, and trying to live, as completely as possible, according to an ancient pattern. Just such an experiment was carried out in Denmark by a group of people who lived for about four months in a dwelling patterned on the remains of Danish **Bronze Age** structures. They worked and slept in the house in an isolated part of Denmark. They grew their own food, kept animals, and made tools. They immersed themselves in what we think life was like in the Bronze Age, based on what we have found archaeologically. By actually attempting to live our reconstructions, we can get a pretty good idea of where we are right—and where we are wrong.

**Environment.**    A number of techniques are available for ancient environmental reconstruction. Dendrochronology, mentioned previously for dating, can be used to reconstruct general rainfall patterns in some areas.

Changes in worldwide climate can be recognized through an analysis of the ratio of two isotopes of oxygen, $^{16}$O and $^{18}$O, in seawater. This ratio varies through time as a function of changes in the earth's climate. Simply stated, water bearing $^{16}$O, the lighter isotope, evaporates at a higher rate than does water containing $^{18}$O. In generally warm periods, this has little impact on the $^{16}$O : $^{18}$O ratio in the ocean because most of

**wear pattern:**  A mark indicative of certain uses, left on a stone tool (or teeth).

**Bronze Age:**  The period of European history when bronze toolmaking began.

the seawater that evaporates falls as rain and returns to the sea. When the planet as a whole is colder, however, large quantities of seawater evaporate, fall as snow in northern latitudes and high elevations, and do not melt off. This effectively depletes the ocean of some of its $^{16}$O, changing the ratio of the two isotopes.

How can we measure the $^{16}$O : $^{18}$O ratio in sediments hundreds of thousands of years old? We can't, directly. Fortunately, however, we can measure the $^{16}$O : $^{18}$O ratio in the skeletons of small marine organisms called **foraminifera**. These organisms incorporate oxygen into their skeletons, reflecting the $^{16}$O : $^{18}$O ratio in the surrounding seawater.

Stratigraphic columns of suboceanic deposits have been dated by assuming a constant rate of deposition and by reference to a 180-degree shift in the earth's magnetic field recently dated with a new, more precise version of the K/Ar technique to 780,000 years ago (Montastersky 1992). A chronological sequence of changes in the $^{16}$O : $^{18}$O ratio has

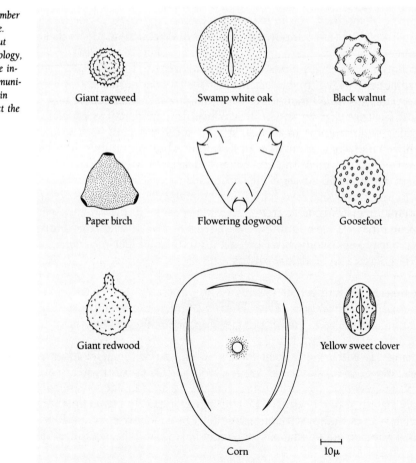

**Figure 7.13** *Pollen from a number of plant species, drawn to scale. (The grains are magnified about 5000 times actual size.) Palynology, the study of pollen, can provide information about the plant communities growing in an area. This, in turn, can be used to reconstruct the environment.*

Giant ragweed

Swamp white oak

Black walnut

Paper birch

Flowering dogwood

Goosefoot

Giant redwood

Yellow sweet clover

Corn            10μ

been constructed by Nicholas Shackleton and Neil Opdyke (1973; see Figure 10.3). Currently, the $^{16}O : ^{18}O$ ratio is also being analyzed a bit more directly in ancient ice brought up in cores taken from deep in the Greenland ice sheet. It is hoped that the cores will cover 200,000 years of weather history (Montastersky 1991).

A widely applicable procedure for environmental reconstruction is **palynology**—the study of pollen. The pollen from each species of plant is unique in its appearance (Figure 7.13). Every year great quantities of pollen are produced, and much of it ends up in the soil, where it preserves quite well under the right conditions. Palynologists can recover prehistoric pollen, identify the species represented, and date the pollen by reference to stratigraphy or by carbon-dating organic remains associated with the pollen. (Usually pollen itself is not dated because there is too little of it by weight.) Because individual plant communities thrive under varying environmental conditions, knowing which plants grew in an area in given periods provides insight into what the climate was like. Knowing what grew there, and when, gives us an idea of what the people who lived in that area may have subsisted on.

**Diet.**   One of the most important pieces of information about a prehistoric people is the nature of their diet. This is especially true when we are trying to answer questions related to the origins of agriculture. This is a topic archaeologists can approach in a number of ways.

Diet can be studied indirectly: We can figure out what people might have eaten based on what was available in their natural environment. For example, we know that deer, moose, raccoon, duck, turkey, and fish have been available in New England for about 7000 years. A hunting and gathering people in this area are likely to have used such resources at one time or another. The modern environment, however, may be quite different from the prehistoric one.

On the other hand, archaeologists can approach the question of diet a bit more directly if there has been good preservation. In many instances, the food remains themselves are still present in archaeological sites. Archaeologists can find features: the fireplaces, hearths, and garbage heaps of the people who lived at a site (Figure 7.14). From these we may recover food material if it has preserved.

But such remains as bone, seeds, or nuts are often fragile and fragmentary. This makes it difficult to get them out of the ground and back to the lab for identification and analysis. In many cases, an archaeologist will take the entire feature, including all soil, back to the laboratory, instead of attempting the often impossible task of separating the dry soil matrix from the fragile archaeological remains in the field. In the lab, through a number of different procedures collectively called flotation, the archaeologist takes advantage of the fact that soil and rock will not float in some liquids, whereas organic remains will. Liquid does the delicate job of separation for us.

**foraminifera**:   Microscopic marine organisms whose exoskeletons are used in oxygen isotope analysis.

**palynology**:   The identification of plants through their preserved pollen remains.

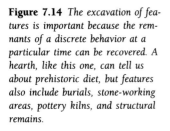

**Figure 7.14** *The excavation of features is important because the remnants of a discrete behavior at a particular time can be recovered. A hearth, like this one, can tell us about prehistoric diet, but features also include burials, stone-working areas, pottery kilns, and structural remains.*

The next task in the reconstruction of a prehistoric diet is the precise identification of the species of plant or animal represented by the remains. This can be difficult because of the fragmentary nature of such remains. In some cases, no precise identification can be made—the piece of bone is too small or the seed too broken up to tell with any degree of confidence. But by using a **comparative collection**—a sort of "library" of bones, nuts, and seeds—we can often identify many of the dietary remains found at a site.

Examining the animal remains of a site is called **faunal analysis**. Here the species represented, their sex, ages at death, health, and physical characteristics are identified. Knowing the species of the remains as well as their age, sex, and health status can provide insight into the hunting practices of prehistoric people. Were they able to kill large animals in their prime, or only the very young, very old, or sick? Also, because many animals give birth to their young during restricted periods, knowing the age of death of a juvenile allows you to determine the season of the hunt. For example, the North American white-tailed deer usually bears its young in May or June. If the bones of a deer found at an archaeological site indicate, for example, an age of 9 months, the site was most probably occupied in February or March.

A new line of research indicates that blood traces can be preserved on the edges of stone tools used to kill animals or process animal products. When this occurs, the blood can be analyzed, and the animal species identified. For example, Australian archaeologist Tom Loy was able to identify blood residues on a stone artifact recovered at a 9000-year-old archaeological site in Turkey, as belonging to sheep, humans, and an extinct form of cattle (Bower 1989a).

An important factor that must be taken into account in using faunal analysis to reconstruct prehistoric diet is taphonomy. **Taphonomy** involves the analysis of how bones (animal or human) become part of the archaeological or paleontological record. How did the animal die? Was it killed by animals or by people? What happened to the bones of the animal after its death? Was it scavenged or immediately buried, say, in a flood? How were the bones deposited? Were they moved from the kill site by scavengers or some other process?

Taphonomy is a crucial consideration when we are trying to generate and test hypotheses concerning the behavior of an ancient people. Were they the hunters—or the hunted? Did they engage in organized communal hunts, or did they merely scavenge the remains of creatures killed by carnivorous animals? Were they ritualistic cannibals, or were their bones simply picked over by scavengers?

Imprecision in taphonomic details has led in the past to what Lewis Binford calls "modern myths" about the ancient past (1981:1). Before we can conclude that an animal was hunted, killed, and eaten by humans, we need to be able to distinguish between the marks left on animal bones by stone tools and the traces left by animal teeth on those bones. Before we can make inferences about hunting practices from a pile of bones in a cave, we need to be able to distinguish between an assemblage of bones left by people and one left by carnivorous animals.

Detailed analyses of how carnivores and scavengers kill, dismember, and deposit bones (Binford 1978, 1981; Read-Martin and Read 1975) and microscopic analysis of cut and tooth marks on bones (Shipman and Rose 1983) are contributing to our understanding of taphonomy and, ultimately, to the nature of the diet of our prehistoric ancestors.

Another important method used in dietary reconstruction is usually only applicable in very dry areas of the world where the level of organic preservation is high. This technique, called **coprology**, is based on the simple fact that most animals, including human beings, do not completely digest everything they eat. In other words, some of what goes in very often comes out in recognizable form.

The data of the coprologist are **coprolites**, the fossilized remains of prehistoric feces. In coprolites we find undigested particles of food that survived an organism's digestive system. Although you may not be motivated to rush out and become a coprologist, you must admit that, short of actually being there and seeing what people were eating, there are few better ways of reconstructing a person's diet than by examining what passes through his or her system.

Finally, examination of the preserved bones and teeth of an ancient people can provide clues about diet. We'll tell you about this in the section titled "Who?"

**comparative collection:** A "library" of animal bones for comparison with archaeological specimens.

**faunal analysis:** An examination of animal remains from archaeological sites.

**taphonomy:** The study of how organisms become part of the archaeological or paleontological records.

**coprology:** The study of preserved fecal remains.

**coprolite:** Preserved fecal remains.

**Social Systems.**   We now know the various ways in which the archaeologist can study prehistoric technology and diet. These may be difficult tasks, but at least tools and food remains are often preserved, allowing archaeologists to study these aspects of culture directly. But now we come to reconstructing something that leaves little in the way of material remains: social systems, or the interrelationships of people. Who do people marry, and with whom do they live? Who do they consider to be family, and who is not family? To whom do they owe their allegiance, and who can they depend on in time of trouble? All these ties are crucial to human survival, but direct remains are few.

Reconstruction of social systems is possible because the objects that people make and use—the material remains we find at archaeological sites—were made, used, and discarded within a *social context*. The very careful analysis of sometimes minute details of artifact manufacture and design can inform us about the social system of the people we are studying. Social information is *encoded* into the things that people make.

A good example of this phenomenon is found in archaeologist James Deetz's classic study of Arikara Indian ceramics (Deetz 1965). According to the historical record, the Arikara, who lived in Nebraska, were a **matrilocal** society. This means that after marriage a young woman stays in her home village and her husband, usually someone living in another village, moves in with her. At any given time therefore, a village is composed of grandmothers, daughters, and granddaughters, all of whom grew up in the same village, and their husbands, who have moved in from different villages.

Deetz was able to show that in matrilocal Arikara villages the pottery, which was made by the women, was homogeneous. In other words, because all the women were related and learned their craft from women who were related, their styles were highly similar. Different villages, then, each had their own unique style.

When the matrilocal pattern broke down after European contact, however, women no longer stayed in one place. Women from villages with differing pottery styles moved into their husbands' villages when the postmarital residence pattern became **patrilocal**. The pottery in any one village was now heterogeneous, having been made by women from different villages with their different styles. Deetz could trace these changes in pottery-style patterning as the social system changed through time. The material objects—the pots—reflected changes in the social context in which they were made.

In another example, at the 11,000-year-old Lindenmeier site in Colorado, there were two major concentrations of artifacts of a particular kind of spear point used in killing big-game animals (Wilmsen 1974). Careful analysis of the points in the two concentrations showed subtle differences in the style of the points, a fact that led the researcher, Edwin Wilmsen, to conclude that two separate bands of hunters had inhabited Lindenmeier at the same time. The points were probably made by men living in two different patrilocal bands. Like the Arikara women making pottery in their matrilocal groups, men learned spear making from their fathers and brothers, all of whom stayed in the band when they got married. Thus, each patrilocal band developed its own unique style of point making.

**Trade.**   Archaeologists are also interested in the relationships among the inhabitants of different ancient societies. Many prehistoric people, even those living at great distances from one another, engaged in trade. Obsidian (natural volcanic glass) from Turkey is found at sites in Syria, hundreds of miles from its source. Copper from Michigan is found in New York State. Turquoise from the American Southwest is found in Mexico. Shells from the Pacific Ocean are found in highland New Guinea. By using techniques of trace element analysis, the precise source of raw materials can be ascertained, and maps showing the movement of such materials can be drawn.

We can sometimes determine the precise raw-material sources by *macroscopic* (naked eye) inspection. Often, however, it is not so easy, and much more sophisticated techniques are needed. One example is a set of procedures called **trace element analysis**. These techniques measure the quantities of so-called trace elements in materials. For example, whereas obsidian, wherever it comes from, is made up largely of silica, there are also tiny amounts (traces) of other elements—impurities like arsenic and copper. The precise proportions of these trace elements are generally unique to the area where the raw material originated and thus can serve as a sort of "fingerprint" for a raw-material source. Archaeologists can determine the trace elements in the raw material of an artifact and then match up that "fingerprint" to a source with the same trace element chemistry.

In the Lindenmeier example just discussed, the researcher performed trace element analysis on the obsidian tools from the two different concentrations. In one of the concentrations, obsidian from northeastern Wyoming was found; in the other area, obsidian from central New Mexico was identified. The hypothesis of two separate hunting bands was supported. Two distinct bands, making tools in their own styles and traveling in different territories, came together at Lindenmeier. That we can know this 11,000 years after the fact is a testament to anthropology of the past.

**Ideology.**   It might not seem that ideology, philosophy, or religion are topics an archaeologist could readily deal with. After all, archaeologists study physical or material remains. Ideology, by its very nature, is a nonmaterial, abstract aspect of human existence. We can, however, make the same argument here that we did for the archaeologist's ability

**matrilocal:**   A type of society where a married couple lives with the wife's family.

**patrilocal:**   A type of society where a married couple lives with the husband's family.

**trace element analysis:** Determining the source of a material through identifying small (trace) amounts of impurities.

to reconstruct social systems. Everything we do takes place within the context of a specific social system, and, by inference, what we make bears some imprint of that system. Similarly, what we do also takes place within the context of an ideological system. In a general sense, all our artifacts are made within the context of an ideology and should reflect certain aspects of that ideology.

For example, to the Inca of South America, gold was the "tears of the gods." We know this from the reports of the Spanish who invaded Inca territory in the sixteenth century. It was therefore their ideological belief that only people close to the gods—priests and rulers—should possess gold objects. This is precisely what we find at pre-Contact, prehistoric Incan sites. Gold artifacts are found only in what we can conclude, based on other artifacts found there, were temples and homes of the religious and political elite.

It is also necessary to point out that, although we can break culture down into categories such as social systems and ideology, human beings do not really compartmentalize their lives. Culture is not simply a bundle of vaguely connected parts; it is an integrated approach to survival. Very often artifacts or features simultaneously reflect several of the separate aspects that we define as making up a culture. One example of this expression of multiple cultural features is burials.

The manner in which a human being is buried reflects a number of abstract concepts. Think in terms of our own culture. Our tombstones—and tombstones are certainly very important "artifacts" in our culture—often record the accomplishments of individuals and their family lives as well as reflecting their religious beliefs (Figure 7.15). If some future archaeologist were to walk into a twentieth-century graveyard, he or she would almost certainly be provided with some insight into our perspective on life, social system, religion, and, of course, death.

In prehistoric archaeology, we do not uncover tombstones to read. However, in burying their dead, prehistoric people were making as much of a statement about their ideological beliefs as we do. Instead of using a written language, these people wrote their "epitaphs" in the language of artifacts. Tools and food were often placed in graves to accompany the deceased to the afterlife. Sometimes animals, or even other people, were killed and buried, apparently to serve the needs of the departed. Precious objects manufactured from valuable raw materials were placed in some graves; other burials contain no artifacts. In some instances, huge pyramids were raised over the remains of the dead; other bodies were thrown away in the trash heap. Information about social status, trade, religion, and even economics is contained in burials. (You need an economic system with many "extra" people to build a pyramid every time a ruler dies.) This is why archaeologists are often so anxious to excavate grave sites. They provide valuable data not otherwise available to anthropologists who study the past. In addition,

**Figure 7.15** *The tombstone* (left) *from colonial America and the sarcophagus lid* (right) *from the Maya site of Palenque can be interpreted as artifacts reflecting the religious, social, economic, and political systems of the people who produced them.* (K. Feder(l); Merle Green and Lee Hocker, © National Geographic Society(r))

of course, the physical remains of the people themselves provide us with a great deal of information about just who they were.

## Who?

We are all aware, from newspaper accounts, television, and movies, just how much information can be derived from examining the remains, through autopsies, of recently deceased humans. Even though anthropologists studying the past cannot usually identify individual personalities, we also are interested in the study of the deceased, for we want to

**Figure 7.16** *The human skeleton with the major bones identified. Adult humans actually have a total of 206 bones, many of which are the result of fusing of the nearly 270 bones a human has at birth. Each bone has features that characterize it as belonging to a member of our species.*

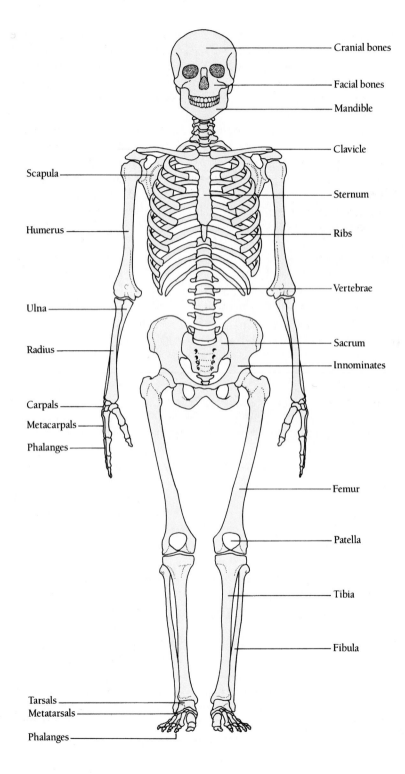

know, in a general sense, who the people were whose lifestyle we are trying to reconstruct. Moreover, we are interested in ourselves as a biological species, and the study of human remains addresses certain biological and evolutionary questions. We are also concerned with issues such as cause of death, for they tell us something important about the lives of our subjects.

The problem anthropologists face is that the remains they study are almost always in the form of bones. The further back in time one goes, the more fragmentary those skeletal remains become. So just what can we hope to discover from the biological data of human antiquity?

When skeletal remains are unearthed, often in connection with an archaeological excavation, perhaps the most basic task is identifying the species to which the bones belong. How do we know if the bones we find are human? A survey of **comparative osteology** (the study of bones of different species) is far beyond the scope of this book. Suffice it to say, though, that the anthropologist interested in this area of study is intimately familiar with the 206 bones of the adult human and is generally able to identify a recovered bone. To help in this endeavor, most universities maintain comparative bone collections so that a bone that cannot be readily identified can be compared with similar ones from many species until a match is found (Figure 7.16).

**Sex.**    Once a skeleton or, more usually, a portion of one is identified as human, the next detail to be discerned is usually its sex. This is fairly easy to determine: A skull alone can be "sexed" with over 90 percent accuracy; a skull and pelvis provide about 98 percent accuracy.

The general rule is that males on the average are larger and more heavily muscled than females. In fact, this generalization applies to many of the primates, especially our closest relatives, the great apes. Thus, one looks at a skull for overall size and for the size and presence of certain features on the bones related to muscle attachment: The bigger the muscles, the more prominent the attachment area.

Similarly, the pelvis of a male tends to be larger and more rugged than that of a female. But the human female pelvis must be adapted to the process of giving birth to very large-headed babies. So the pelves of females are generally wider in their openings and angles than those of males. Where the sex of a skull may be ambiguous, the pelvis is usually a dead giveaway (Figure 7.17).

Other bones of the body can also aid in sexing. The same criteria of size and muscle attachment features can be used with the long bones of the arms and legs.

These rules, of course, represent *averages*. Averages can vary from group to group; similarly, an individual may not conform to the average and can be misidentified. For this reason, it is preferable, as in any kind of skeletal analysis, to deal with a large sample of skeletons, which

**comparative osteology:** Comparing bones of different species.

**Figure 7.17** *Male and female pelves. In general the female pelvis is broader with wider openings, an adaptation to childbirth.*

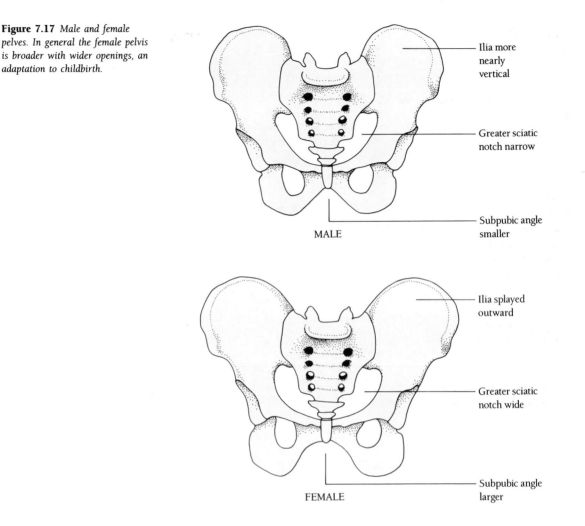

Ilia more
nearly
vertical

Greater sciatic
notch narrow

Subpubic angle
smaller

MALE

Ilia splayed
outward

Greater sciatic
notch wide

Subpubic angle
larger

FEMALE

allows comparisons to be made. In the case of sex identification, many females are larger than the average male, and many males are smaller than the average female. No absolute criteria can be applied to sexing a skeleton or, for that matter, most other forms of skeletal analysis. It is a skill that takes practice, a great deal of observation of bones of known sex, and a good helping of intuition. With all this, though, we can sex most human skeletal remains with acceptable accuracy.

But what about the remains of premodern humans? What happens when we have a skeleton from 30,000, or 300,000, or 3 million years ago? We really have little choice but to begin with the assumption that the same criteria apply. After all, these are members of the same basic evolutionary line, and they are primates. One of the earliest sets of human remains, from 3.5 mya, was determined to be that of a female, using just such reasoning. (We call her "Lucy," and we'll tell you about her in Chapter 8.)

This approach, though, has its limitations because we don't know for sure if the sexual dimorphism—the differences in appearance between the two sexes—was always the same in the past. In Lucy's case, more representatives of her stage of evolution were found, and the assessments of sex were substantiated—in other words, here we had not just an individual but a sample of a population. In other cases, lack of evidence can be misleading. One authority proposed that two sets of human fossils from Africa, dated around 2 to 3 million years old, represented male and female of the same species. It seemed reasonable because one form was large and big boned, and the other was smaller and more graceful. With the accumulation of more data, however, it turned out that these two forms were more likely the early and late stages of a single human evolutionary line that eventually became extinct.

**Age.**    What about a person's age at death? How old was he when he met his end? The body goes through many physical changes as it develops, matures, and grows old. Many of these changes, as well as many others you don't see, are reflected in the skeleton. We know at what times in a human's life certain skeletal changes take place. By determining which changes have already occurred and which have yet to occur in a given set of remains, we can get an approximate figure for a person's age at death.

Perhaps the best known method for "aging" a skeleton is the use of dental eruption dates (Figure 7.18). Like many mammals, humans have two sets of teeth: deciduous, or "baby," teeth, and adult teeth. Each tooth in both sets "erupts" through the gum line at a certain average age. When we find dental remains (among the most common because the outer layer of the teeth, the enamel, is the hardest substance the body produces), we determine which tooth was the last to erupt and which unerupted tooth would have erupted next. The dates of eruption of those two teeth determine the minimum and maximum probable age at which that person died. Once all the adult teeth have erupted, of course, this method is no longer applicable.

Another aging technique makes use of the skull. You are no doubt familiar with the *fontanelles*, or "soft spots," on a baby's head. These are actually spaces between the bones of the skull. The bones develop separately, in part to allow for flexibility of our large heads during the birth process. Shortly after birth, these bones grow and fit together like a jigsaw puzzle. Later still, additional bone is added to the lines of attachment called **sutures**, eventually forming a single cranial bone late in life. Because the sutures close at a fairly regular rate, by determining the latest closure that has occurred and the next closure that would have

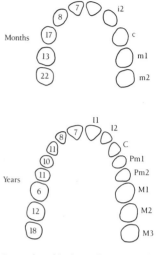

*Eruption dates of deciduous and permanent teeth.*

| I, i | incisors |
| C, c | canines |
| Pm | premolars |
| M, m | molars |

(lowercase letters stand for deciduous teeth)

**Figure 7.18** *Average ages of eruption of the deciduous ("baby") teeth (top) in months and permanent teeth in years. Individuals may deviate from these dates for some teeth, but most people display this basic pattern.*

**sexual dimorphism:** The distinguishing anatomical features between the sexes of a species.

**suture:** A line of contact between the bones of the skull.

**Figure 7.19** *Patterns of cranial suture closure. A great deal of individual variation is seen in the shapes of the sutures as well as in their closure dates. This aging technique was more popular in the past.*

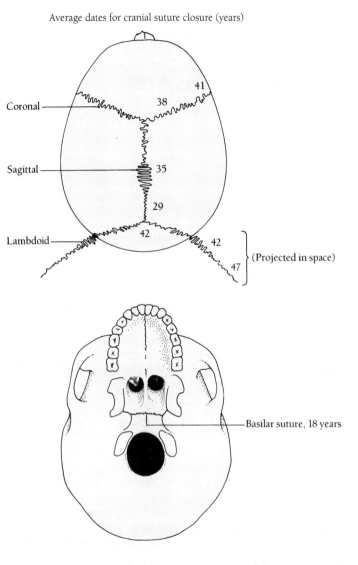

Average dates for cranial suture closure (years)

Coronal

Sagittal

Lambdoid

41

38

35

29

42   42

47

(Projected in space)

Basilar suture, 18 years

occurred, a range may be derived for age at death (Figure 7.19). This method, which can be used from about age 18 to 50 and even beyond, is now seen as fairly unreliable. It may, however, be the only method available if just a skull is recovered.

A third popular aging technique makes use of the bones of the arms, legs, hands, and feet. These bones all grow in three sections: a shaft, or **diaphysis**, and two caps, or **epiphyses**. When growth is complete, the cartilagenous disks between caps and shaft become ossified (turn to bone), and a single long bone, finger bone, or toe bone is produced. Ages for **epiphyseal union** are known, and the same logic outlined before is used to determine age at death (Figure 7.20).

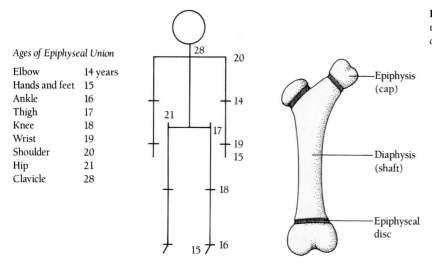

*Ages of Epiphyseal Union*

| | |
|---|---|
| Elbow | 14 years |
| Hands and feet | 15 |
| Ankle | 16 |
| Thigh | 17 |
| Knee | 18 |
| Wrist | 19 |
| Shoulder | 20 |
| Hip | 21 |
| Clavicle | 28 |

**Figure 7.20** *Pattern of epiphyseal union, one of the most reliable indications of skeletal age.*

The final aging method uses the inner surface of the area where the two halves of the pelvis meet in front. This is called the *pubic symphysis*. Between the ages of 18 and 50+, the appearance of this surface undergoes characteristic changes. By assessing the phase to which a specimen belongs, approximate age at death may be determined.

As with sexing, methods for aging rely on averages. No two humans are identical, and not everyone's growth pattern and rate follow the rules. Thus, the more data one can gather from a skeleton, the more accurate the determination will be. As with sexing, we must assume similar growth patterns and rates for our early ancestors, at least until we have a large enough number of fossils to establish separate criteria for different stages of human evolution.

We are now beginning to be able to go beyond appearance and determine certain chemical characteristics of ancient bone. Presently, for some bones preserved under the right conditions, we can determine blood type in the ABO system. This not only tells us something about an individual, but if a large enough sample of skeletal material is found at one site, it may also give us some genetic information about an entire population.

**Health.**    The anthropologist of the past, like a medical examiner, plays detective and tries, where possible, to determine presence of illness and injury as well as cause of death. This area of study is called **paleopathology**. What people suffer and die from can tell a great deal about the nature of their environments, their diets, and their relations with other humans. Many diseases leave characteristic marks on the human skeleton. These include such ailments as certain forms of arthritis, tumors and other cancers, tuberculosis, leprosy, some anemias, syphilis, osteoporosis, and various infections such as dental abscesses (Figure 7.21).

**diaphysis:** The shaft of a long bone.

**epiphysis:** The end, or cap, of a long bone.

**epiphyseal union:** The fusion of the ends of long bones with the shafts.

**paleopathology:** The study of ancient disease.

Nutritional deficiencies may show up as porous bones or abnormal bone growth. Two specific deficiencies, those of vitamin D (rickets) and vitamin C (scurvy), leave characteristic signs on the skeleton. Any developmental anomalies, such as curvature of the spine or other deformations, will, of course, be clearly evident on the bones.

People also die from wounds and accidents. Bones have revealed that people of the past suffered as we do today from fractures, dislocations, and accidental amputations. Deaths from arrow, spear, knife, and gunshot wounds have also been seen. Scalping (usually done after death) shows up as a characteristic set of cut marks on top of the skull, and large holes cut into the skull show us that **trephining**, a form of prehistoric skull surgery, was not always successful, although healing around some holes indicates that many obviously survived the operation (Figure 7.22).

**Appearance.**   The skeleton acts as a framework for the body as a whole; thus the size and shape of the bones can reveal something of the appearance of the entire living person. We know, for example, from the sheer size and ruggedness of their bones, that a group of humans from ancient Europe (the "Neandertals"; see Chapter 11) were big, brawny, and extremely strong. We can obtain a more exact idea of size, especially stature, by using a series of mathematical formulas. By measuring, say, a femur, we can calculate the height of the individual who once owned it.

We have already mentioned that there is a direct relationship between bone and muscle because muscles attach to bones. This relationship has led a number of investigators to attempt to reconstruct the faces of our ancestors from the shapes of their skulls and facial skeletons. Using their knowledge of human anatomy, they artistically add missing bones, eyes, fatty tissue, cartilage, muscle, and skin to ancient

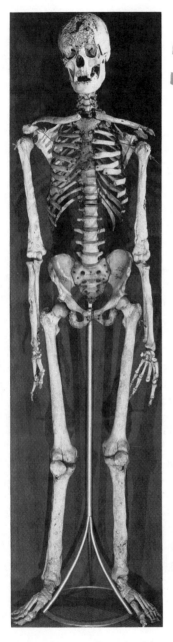

**Figure 7.21** *The effects of syphilis on the human skeleton. Note the extensive lesions of the skull and the ends of the humeri and tibias.* (Identification of Pathological Conditions in Human Skeletal Remains, Ortner and Putschar, 1985:195, Smithsonian Institution Press)

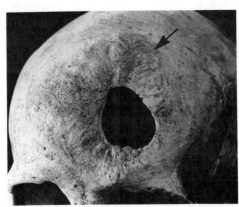

**Figure 7.22** *A trephined skull from Peru. The arrow shows the outer margin of the wound. The edge of the hole indicates healing has taken place.* (Identification of Pathological Conditions in Human Skeletal Remains, Ortner and Putschar, 1985:98, Smithsonian Institution Press)

skulls, literally "fleshing out" our picture of early humans. As before, of course, we are assuming that present anatomical relationships also held true in the past. We have yet to find an entire ancient face preserved as a fossil. (The same procedure is used also in law enforcement to try to identify skeletal remains and match them with missing persons.)

The relationship between bone and soft tissue also provides a basis for determining geographical location or origin. In living humans, a number of physical and chemical characteristics show variation on a geographical scale. Such traits as skin color, eye shape, nose shape, hair color and texture, blood type, and other genetic features are all variable in our species, and all show some geographical regularity.

Similarly, just as living people "look" as if they come from a particular area of the world, so too some skulls look as if they come from a certain place or belong to a certain general population (we will discuss this phenomenon in more detail in Chapter 13). Such analysis is, to be sure, rather subjective and intuitive, but with enough examples and enough practice, one can get a feel for guessing the general population from which a skull came. Some numerical generalizations can also accomplish the same task. Average head length, relative length of arms and legs, and other measurements tend to differ geographically. Last, some very specific traits can be found most often in certain populations. "Shovel-shaped incisors"—upper front teeth with an appearance rather like a shovel—are not exclusive to, but are very common among, Asian groups. This trait, in fact, can help distinguish Native American skeletal remains from those of Europeans (Native Americans, of course, being originally of Asian origin).

**Behavior.** Finally, the skeleton can be a source of information about behavior. In evolutionary perspective, the first distinguishing feature of human anatomy was upright posture and locomotion. We know when this feature first evolved because the skeleton directly reflects it: The nature of the bones of the pelvis and the femur along with the position of the hole in the base of the skull are clear indications of locomotor posture. It is obvious from such evidence that humans have walked upright for over 3.5 million years.

Diet, too, can be discerned from skeletal evidence. In mammals the nature of the dentition is a clue to overall food sources. Carnivores like your dog or cat, for example, have slicing teeth adapted to meat eating. Humans have a more generalized dentition, built for chewing a varied diet. More specifically, certain wear patterns on the teeth, examined microscopically, reveal whether the diet was made up of soft foods like fruits or more abrasive, gritty foods like roots and tubers. We can even examine the chemical content of ancient bones for their proportion of strontium and calcium to determine whether plants or meat made up the bulk of the diet of certain populations.

**trephining:** Cutting a hole in the skull to treat an illness.

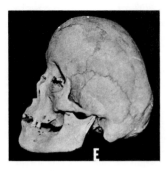

**Figure 7.23** *An example of cradleboard deformation from ancient Illinois. The board flattened the forehead and, especially, the back of the skull, but probably had no ill effect.* (Illinois State Museum, Reproduction by Written Permission Only)

**Figure 7.24** *Small arrow embedded in the base of the skull of an ancient Illinois Indian, no doubt causing this individual's death.* (Illinois State Museum, Reproduction by Written Permission Only)

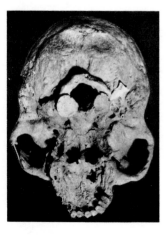

Previously, we discussed carbon dating and the fact that one isotope of carbon, $^{14}$C, was unstable and its decay could be used to assess the age of an object. Along with $^{12}$C, the most abundant isotope of carbon, there also is another stable variety, $^{13}$C. About 1 in 100 carbon atoms are $^{13}$C. It turns out that different varieties of plants use the $^{12}$C and $^{13}$C isotopes differentially in what are called their photosynthesis pathways. There are two major pathways, and the differences in $^{12}$C and $^{13}$C absorption is detectable not only in the plants themselves but also in the tissues of the animals that eat them. Thus, under certain circumstances, human bones can be analyzed for their $^{12}$C : $^{13}$C ratio and a determination can be made concerning which kinds of plants were abundant in the diet. This approach has been applied in the examination of the domestication of maize (corn), which uses a photosynthesis pathway different from most of the wild plants that grow in the same area in Central America (Farnsworth et al. 1985; and see Chapter 14).

Sometimes skulls are found deformed in uniform ways, although the individuals themselves seem otherwise normal. Such artificial deformation was sometimes performed to reflect standards of beauty. We know this because we have historic records—from ancient Egypt, for example—of the practice. The famous Queen Nefertiti had cranial deformation of this sort. Sometimes, however, the deformation was accidental, caused by pressure from a cradleboard, a device used in many parts of the world that served to hold an infant's head (and thus the infant itself) steady and secure while the parents were otherwise occupied (Figure 7.23).

Finally, evidence of wounds from arrows, spears, and guns indicates another kind of human behavior (Figure 7.24). Such evidence tells us something about the relations of a group of people with its neighbors.

So, we can tell a great deal about the people of the past from their physical remains. We know for example that the skeleton on the cover, found at the site of Herculaneum, an ancient Roman town (see Chapter 15), belonged to a tall woman of about 45. Her bones show none of the effects of poor nutrition, which, along with the gold rings and bracelets, indicate that she belonged to the upper class. Her teeth had no cavities or abscesses, but she did suffer from periodontal (gum) disease.

While we are studying these remains, however, we should keep in mind an ethical consideration. In the case of recent remains, our data are the bodies of people whose living descendants belong to an identified group. This is true for many Native American populations, whose ancestral burial areas have long been sources of human skeletal remains for the anthropologist. The scientific value of such studies cannot be denied and is certainly valid. But the rights and values of the people involved should also be respected. Remains ought not to be treated as curiosities.

**Why?**

Over 3.5 mya, the first humans stood upright. Why?

About 80,000 years ago (ya), our human ancestors began the practice of burying their dead. Why?

About 32,000 ya, the "Neandertals" disappeared. Why?

Soon after 12,000 ya, in Southeast Asia and the Middle East, we find evidence that human beings were raising their own crops and domesticating animals, instead of simply hunting and gathering what nature provided. Why?

About 5000 ya, in the Middle East, and soon after in India, China, Mesoamerica, and South America, people began to live in cities and build enormous monumental works like pyramids and temples. Why?

Why, indeed! The final question the anthropologist studying the past confronts is perhaps the most difficult of all. We can locate sites, figure out how old they are, describe the people themselves, and to a large extent reconstruct what went on. But answering the many "whys" poses the greatest challenge.

It is indeed difficult to be able to suggest why a given people 3 million, 10,000, or even 500 ya made a certain decision or changed their culture in a way that affected the cultural evolution of our species. As difficult as it is, however, we must remember that the answers to certain crucial "why" questions about humanity in general can only be pursued by the application of anthropological data. Many of the important questions about ourselves we want to answer have roots extending far back into the mists of antiquity. We can only hope to penetrate these puzzles by applying the types of biological and cultural analyses we have described.

Imagine a book 400 pages long. Imagine further that each page represents a period of time in the development of humanity. The very first sentence on the first page represents the first time a human ancestor stood upright on the African savanna. The very last sentence on page 400 is today. The amount of space in the book devoted to certain time periods is proportional to their actual length.

There's just one hitch; we can only read that part of the book corresponding to the period after human beings invented writing some 6000 ya. The pages in the book before the invention of writing are blank.

Can you guess where the writing would begin? On the last half of the final page! Imagine reading a 400-page book with writing only on the last half of the last page and then being asked to explain what happened. If the book were a detective novel, you might know that "the butler did it," but it is unlikely you would know what he did, when, to whom, or, most importantly, why.

So the first $399\frac{1}{2}$ pages of the book about our human story are blank, at least as far as writing is concerned—for these $399\frac{1}{2}$ pages are filled

# CONTEMPORARY ISSUE

## Preserving the Past

*Looters dug more than 450 holes in this Kentucky field in search of Native American artifacts. Archaeologists have gathered evidence in the criminal case against the looters while at the same time recovering what archaeological data remains.* (Steve Wall, © 1989 National Geographic Society)

We have tried to impart to you the importance of anthropological research in our quest to understand human physical and cultural evolution. Unfortunately, however, the raw data of archaeology and paleoanthropology are in great danger. Many agricultural practices, mining techniques, and construction projects, along with general greed and indifference, contribute jointly to the destruction of important sites all over the world each year. Farmers in some countries practice land-leveling techniques that result in the destruction of buried sites. Strip mining in some places causes terrific destruction of archaeological resources. In developed and developing nations alike, the building of roads and the construction of water projects contribute to the destruction of the fragile prehistoric record. In some countries, including our own, sites are looted for their more aesthetically pleasing artifacts, which are then sold to the highest bidder.

No more ancient sites are being made. They are, in a sense, nonrenewable resources like coal and oil. Some nations have recognized the impor-

not with words but with spears and pots, burials and monuments, bones and seeds. In the story of our species, the first 99.99 percent of our existence on this planet is prehistoric and therefore the purview of archaeologists and paleoanthropologists. To ask who we are and why we are is to be almost by definition an anthropologist studying the past.

## SUMMARY

Our approach to the study of human antiquity includes the methodologies of the archaeologist and the physical anthropologist. In our research, we attempt to answer these general questions: where, what, when, how, who, and why. To investigate the human past, we must determine *where* the physical evidence of ancient people can be found.

tance of protecting these fragile remnants of the past. A series of federal, state, and even town laws in this country serve to afford at least some protection to archaeological sites. Other countries have patrimony laws that make it illegal to export the artifacts of their ancestors (usually to be sold to the wealthy of other nations for their amusement). Many countries and some U.S. states have laws against the disturbance of ancient human burials.

Laws are very important, but people's attitudes are perhaps most important of all. If people would only recognize the importance of understanding the past, site destruction would become unthinkable. Ancient sites would be preserved for future study, money would be made available for archaeological research, and the market for antiquities would dry up. It would be a terrible tragedy and irony indeed if, just as our study of the past is becoming a sophisticated scientific enterprise, the raw data of the past were to become as extinct as the cultures we are attempting to understand.

*Construction related development often poses the greatest threat to archaelogical resources. Here an archaeological excavation is conducted in the shadow of highway expansion in Southbury, Connecticut.* (Kenneth Feder)

We have developed techniques to locate and recover the physical remains of these people—*what* they left behind, the artifacts and features clustered in the sites where they once lived. We apply techniques from various disciplines to determine the age of the remains we study, to establish *when* the people lived. Acting as ethnographers, we analyze the remains of the human past to establish *how* these people survived— how they made their tools, the nature of their physical environment, and their diet, social systems, trading networks, and ideology. We study the physical remains of the people themselves—their bones—to understand *who* they were as individuals and as populations. Finally, we attempt to discern and reveal *why* they lived the lives they did. Through the application of the procedures outlined in this chapter, anthropologists studying the human past attempt through science to illuminate the story of our species.

## KEY TERMS

holistic
cultural
  anthropology
culture
anthropological
  linguistics
archaeology
physical
  anthropology
biological
  anthropology
paleoanthropologist
site
artifact
feature
field survey
remote sensing
test boring
test pit
transect
spatial context
provenience

association
stratigraphy
parent material
law of superposition
relative
  chronological
  sequence
absolute dating
radiometric dating
radioactive isotope
carbon dating
half-life
potassium/argon
  (K/Ar) dating
dendrochronology
cultural technique
seriation
ethnoarchaeology
ethnography
paleoethnography
wear pattern
Bronze Age

foraminifera
palynology
comparative
  collection
faunal analysis
taphonomy
coprology
coprolite
matrilocal
patrilocal
trace element
  analysis
comparative
  osteology
sexual dimorphism
suture
diaphysis
epiphysis
epiphyseal union
paleopathology
trephining

## FOR MORE INFORMATION

Although we have been able to devote only a chapter to the techniques of learning about the human past, there are many fine texts dealing with the methodology of archaeology and physical anthropology. A few of the best are *Archaeology: Discovering Our Past*, by Robert Sharer and Wendy Ashmore; *In the Beginning: An Introduction to Archaeology*, by Brian Fagan; and *Archaeology*, by David Hurst Thomas.

For more detailed discussions of analysis of the human skeleton, *Human Osteology: A Laboratory and Field Manual of the Human Skeleton*, by William Bass, and *Handbook of Forensic Archaeology and Anthropology*, by Dan Morse, Jack Duncan, and James Stoutamire, are excellent. Especially good is the volume *Human Osteology* by Tim White and Pieter Folkens.

*Ancient Disease in the Midwest*, by Dan Morse, is a good source for information on paleopathology.

# 8

# THE EMERGENCE OF THE HUMAN LINEAGE

In 1912 amateur scientist Charles Dawson announced the recovery, from a gravel pit in Piltdown, England, of perhaps the most famous and controversial bones in the history of anthropology. The find consisted of a mandible and several cranial bones in association with some primitive stone tools. The cranial bones were clearly those of a large-brained human, but the mandible was indistinguishable from that of an ape. This combination of traits was precisely what many scientists of the time expected of the evolutionary "missing link" between ape and human.

The remains were named *Eoanthropus*, the "dawn man" (Figure 8.1). For nearly forty years, many scientists, especially in Britain, accepted "Piltdown Man" as the earliest human. In other countries, however, opinion ranged from withheld judgment to downright skepticism. Many felt the combination of the apelike jaw and human brain case was too good to be true. Furthermore, during those forty years no similar fossils were found that could provide supporting evidence for *Eoanthropus*.

The skeptics were proven correct. In the early 1950s, in a classic example of the self-correcting nature of science, Piltdown was unmasked as a fraud—literally, the cranium of a modern human and the jaw of a modern orangutan, filed, painted, and otherwise modified to appear ancient. With that revelation, other early remains suddenly took their rightful place as the (then) earliest human fossils.

To this day, incidentally, no one knows who perpetrated the fraud. Piltdown remains one of the great mysteries of science. For accounts of the story, see J. S. Weiner (1955), Stephen Jay Gould (1983), Charles Blinderman (1986), Kenneth Feder (1990), and Frank Spencer (1990).

What accounts, then, for the popularity and acceptance of so obvious a fake as Piltdown for so long a time? Despite a great deal of skepticism, the Piltdown find did appear in most books on human evolution during those forty years. The answer, in part, is nationalism. No important fossil human had yet been found on British soil, so the possibility that the "dawn man" might be British had obvious appeal. More important, however, Piltdown fulfilled expectations of what the earliest human *should* look like. At that time, the most important difference between human and ape was believed to be our big brain. The "missing link" should therefore be essentially an ape with a big head.

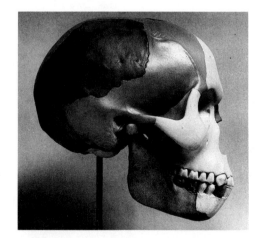

**Figure 8.1** *Reconstruction of the skull of the Piltdown fraud. This modern human braincase was found with an orangutan jaw, planted in the same site and assumed by the discoverers to belong together. The result was exactly what science at that time expected of the first human.* (Courtesy Department of Library Services, American Museum of Natural History, neg. no. 36240A, photo: A. E. Anderson).

In this expectation, scientists were committing one of the classic errors in the study of evolution: the mistake of thinking that a modern situation represents the original situation—in this case, that the most characteristic feature of modern humans would also have been the first feature of our lineage. This is part of the reason why the evolutionary position of the **australopithecines**, whose remains first came to light in 1925, remained enigmatic for so long. Their bipedal posture but ape-sized brains did not fit the expected model of what the earliest humans should look like.

From all our modern evidence, it is now clear, and really has been clear for nearly forty years, that the large brains of humans are an evolutionary afterthought. Our heads achieved their modern size 250,000 years ago at the earliest, whereas the feature that first distinguished us from the apes—our bipedalism—is over 3 million years old. So the first question in our discussion of the emergence of the human lineage is not how and why we evolved big brains, but rather how and why we stood up.

## THE FOSSIL EVIDENCE

By far the most striking and convincing concrete evidence for the time and nature of our evolutionary split from the apes are the remains of a diminutive female who lived and died in northeast Africa over 3 million years ago (Figure 8.2). She is called Lucy (after a character in a Beatles song), and she was found in Ethiopia in 1974 by paleoanthropologist Donald Johanson (Johanson and Edey 1981). Lucy was indeed small, only about 3′ 8″ and 65 pounds. Her face was protruding and apelike, and her brain was only about one-third the size of the modern human average. But she is remarkable and important for several reasons.

First, at the time of her discovery Lucy was the oldest hominid fossil known. Potassium/argon dating placed the soil in which she was found at a little over 3 million years old. For her age, she was remarkably complete. Most human remains more than 1 million years old are fragmentary and usually represent teeth and portions of the head, with bits and pieces from the rest of the body. Lucy's skeleton is 40 percent complete, with every area of the body well enough represented to give us an accurate picture of what she looked like. The picture that emerges from the analysis of Lucy's bones shows us without doubt that over 3 mya—while we still had the face and the brain size of an ape—we walked upright. Lucy was an habitual biped. She may not have had the graceful stride of later humans, and her long arms and curved fingers and toes may indicate that she was a better tree climber than we are

**australopithecine**: A small-brained hominid from 4 to 1 mya that represents the ancestor of all hominids and several extinct hominid branches.

**Figure 8.2** *The remains of Lucy, over 3 million years old, consist of bones representing enough of the body to give us a very accurate image of Lucy's size, appearance, and upright posture.* (The Cleveland Museum of Natural History)

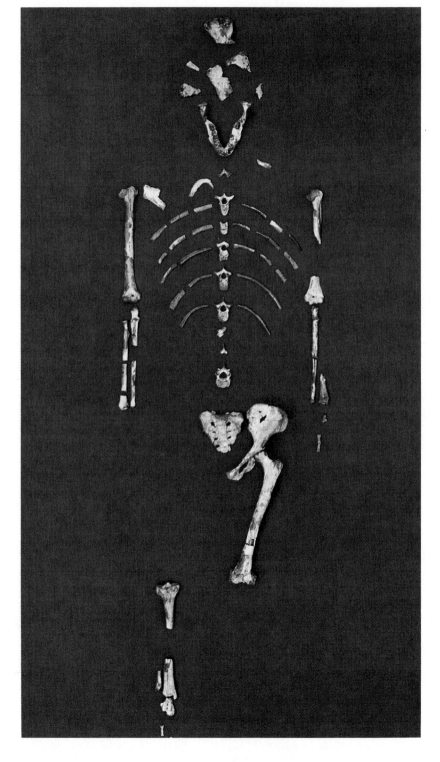

today. On the ground, she moved not as an ape, however, but as a hominid.

Because of Lucy's basic resemblance to the australopithecines, Johanson placed her in that genus. Because she was more primitive than the later members of that group in certain features of brain size, teeth, hands, and feet, he placed her in a new species. Lucy technically became *Australopithecus afarensis* (after the Afar region in Ethiopia, where she was found).

There is always a danger in drawing too many conclusions from a single piece of evidence, no matter how compelling. Lucy was a single individual. Did she truly represent a new and ancient type of early human?

The answer came the following year. Near where Lucy had been found, Johanson's team recovered about 200 hominid teeth and bone fragments. When sorted and analyzed, they were seen to represent at least thirteen individuals—males and females, adults and children—who seem to have died together. These remains were dubbed "The First Family." Not only were they from the same time period as Lucy, but they also had the same features. It appears that, indeed, a new type of early hominid had been discovered and that support existed for their designation as a separate species, *afarensis*.

Even at this point, some differences of opinion existed about just how bipedal these early hominids were. Estimates were based on inference from the structure of the bones; no one had actually *seen* them walking around. In 1976, however, the next best thing was unearthed. A group led by Mary Leakey uncovered a set of footprints in a layer of ancient volcanic ash at the site of Laetoli in Tanzania (Figure 8.3). These clear prints were obviously those of two bipedal hominids. The nature of the prints and their orientation to each other show no difference from footprints made by people today. But these were made in volcanic ash that was 3.7 million years old.

In the last decade, more fossils have appeared from Ethiopia—jaws, skull fragments, and parts of leg bones—that match the basic *A. afarensis* pattern and are dated at nearly 4 million years. It seems clear that between 3 and 4 mya there existed in northeast Africa a hominid with the cranial capacity of a chimpanzee or gorilla and the basic posture of a human. Because of their posture—perhaps the most unique feature of the hominids—we consider *afarensis* a hominid. If we insist, however, on calling something a "missing link," so far *afarensis* is it—the closest thing that we have to our last common ancestor with the chimpanzees.

The exact place of *A. afarensis* in human evolution is still being debated. Johanson thinks that this form was ancestral to all later hominids and that shortly after Lucy's time the human evolutionary line split in two. One line—in a way, the main branch—continued australopithecine evolution to its eventual extinction about 1 mya. The second

**Figure 8.3** *The Laetoli footprints, left in volcanic ash 3.7 mya prove the antiquity of our bipedalism.* (Photo by Peter Jones. Courtesy Tim White)

branch—the offshoot—involved a still newer kind of hominid that would evolve eventually into all modern humans.

Other authorities, such as Richard Leakey (Leakey and Walker 1980), while accepting this basic two branch arrangement, contend that *A. afarensis* is insufficiently different from later australopithecines to warrant a separate species name. The split, he thinks, came before, rather than after, Lucy and her kin, and therefore the common ancestor of the hominids has yet to be found and identified. As of now, the jury is still out. (There may also have been a short-lived third branch of hominids, but we'll examine the whole australopithecine period more closely in the next chapter.)

The inferences drawn from all these fossils and footprints, however, seem fairly clear. First, it is now beyond question that bipedalism was the first human trait to evolve. To explain why we emerged, we must try to account for the evolution and adaptive significance of this trait.

Second, *A. afarensis* is, in a sense, a "bipedal ape." Its posture is its one clearly human trait. Other features of the teeth, cranium, and limbs either merely hint at hominid status or carry clear remnants of a pongid ancestry. Thus, unless *afarensis* had possessed that combination of features for many millions of years—that is, unless evolution had pretty much stabilized for a long period—the split between ape and human could not have occurred much before 4 mya. We are probably, on a geological time scale, the "new kids on the block." And another form of evidence bears this estimate out in a most striking way.

## THE GENETIC EVIDENCE

Physical features are controlled by a complex interaction of genetic loci, evolutionary processes, and environmental factors. Trying to work out evolutionary relationships based solely on physical traits can lead us astray. A trait may look the same in two organisms, but the expressions of the trait may be based on very different genetic and developmental processes, and the traits themselves may differ in their adaptive significance. A famous example (Gould 1980) is the "thumb" of the panda, a bear. It looks very much like the thumb of many primates, but its use is specialized—it enables the panda to handle and strip the leaves off bamboo stalks. And it's not a finger at all but an elongated wrist bone.

Would it not be more accurate, then, some investigators asked, to look at the genes themselves—or at least at the immediate products of the genes? Two organisms with similar genes must certainly be closely related evolutionarily.

In the 1960s, Vincent Sarich and Allan Wilson of the University of California at Berkeley pioneered research along just such lines (Sarich

1971). They compared the blood proteins of a number of organisms, with the goal of quantifying similarities and differences. Blood proteins such as albumin are large, easy to work with, and are made up of amino acids, which are the immediate products of the genetic loci.

Sarich and Wilson indicated the degree of similarity between proteins by an "index" number. The proteins of an organism compared with themselves are represented by a figure of 1 unit since they are identical. Human protein compared with that of a cow gives a figure of 20 units; with an Old World monkey, a figure of 2.38. Human protein with chimpanzee protein gives the startlingly low figure of 1.17 units. The blood proteins of our two species are almost identical.

There was an even more startling inference from this research. Sarich and Wilson wondered if their figures might provide a relative idea not only of evolutionary distance but also of evolutionary divergence. Because evolution involves the accumulation of mutations, the differences between two species in a genetic product like albumin might act as a "clock" if the mutations causing those differences take place at a fairly constant rate and if we can then figure out how many of those mutations take place over a certain period of time.

Comparing species whose time of divergence was well established from the fossil record, Sarich and Wilson concluded that the 1.17-unit difference between chimps and humans corresponded to an evolutionary separation of only 5 million years. At the time, the accepted date stood between 12 and 15 million, with *Ramapithecus* as the earliest hominid. Based on the "protein clock," Sarich said that *Ramapithecus* couldn't be a hominid no matter what it looked like. He was right.

But the protein clock theory was not universally accepted, largely because of two limitations. First, the mutations used must be neutral. If they are adaptively important, natural selection will bring about either their accumulation through generations or their disappearance. The genetic differences that actually appear between two species will thus reflect not simply how many mutations occurred but also how selectively advantageous they were. There is also some disagreement about whether any mutation *can* be adaptively neutral in the first place.

Second, different species have different generation times. The more frequently a species reproduces, the more chances mutations have to pass to a succeeding generation. Thus, even if mutations occur at a standard rate—an idea that is still open to question—they may differ in rate of accumulation depending on the generation time of the species in question.

Even so, the protein clock idea does seem to agree with the fossil evidence on the divergence time of some species, including chimps and humans. At the very least, the clock provides us with a rough estimate. In addition, four other types of genetic tests support a recent date of divergence for our two species.

**Figure 8.4** *Banding patterns on the X (female sex) chromosomes of human, chimpanzee, gorilla, and orangutan. The patterns are essentially identical.* (Redrawn from Dorothy A. Miller, "Evolution of primate chromosomes." *Science,* 198:1116–1124, 1977, American Association for the Advancement of Science)

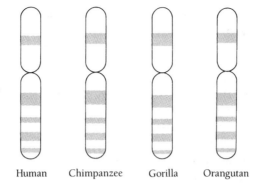

Human     Chimpanzee     Gorilla     Orangutan

The second type of genetic evidence comes from the examination of the amino acid sequences in certain proteins, especially some of the shorter proteins like hemoglobin and other blood system components. Amino acids, you recall, are the direct products of the genetic code. Different amino acids may undergo mutations of their genetic loci at different rates. But averages for the results of amino acid sequence comparisons between primates match remarkably well with the blood protein tests. Humans and Old World monkeys show a difference of 3.9 percent for amino acid sequences in the proteins examined. A 2.8 percent difference was found between humans and orangutans, and, again, the amazingly low figures of 0.6 percent for humans compared with gorillas and 0.3 percent for humans compared with chimpanzees. Certainly not much time can have elapsed since our evolutionary branch diverged from that of the African apes.

A third method, called **DNA hybridization**, is very important because it compares actual genetic material. The strands of the DNA double helix, with their pairs of loci, can be broken apart with heat. Because the loci are paired, the strands will attempt to bond again. A measure of species similarity can be made by seeing how well a strand from one species will bond with a strand from another. The tightness of the new bond is determined by measuring how much heat is necessary to break it. Again, the results coincide with those of the other genetic tests. The difference between humans and Old World monkeys is expressed as 9; between humans and orangutans, 4.5; humans and gorillas, 2.5; and humans and chimps, 2.4. The derivation of the numbers is complicated, but, simply put, the lower the number, the more heat is needed, thus the tighter the bond and more similar the species.

The fourth method involves comparison of the patterns of bands appearing on chromosomes treated with certain dyes (Figure 8.4). The exact meaning of the patterns is unclear, but the patterns are unique for each chromosome within a species. There is evidence that when species are compared, similar banding patterns are an indication that the chro-

**DNA hybridization:** A method for comparing species based on relative ability of strands of DNA from each species to bond to one another.

mosomes carry similar genetic loci. There is approximately 98 percent similarity in the 500 bands observed in humans, chimps, gorillas, and orangutans. Twelve chromosomes of humans and chimps have virtually identical patterns. For certain important specific regions on some chromosomes, humans show a greater affinity with gorillas.

The chromosome-banding studies show something else interesting. A major difference in the chromosomes of humans and the great apes is the fact that apes have more—48 as opposed to our 46. But when banding patterns are observed, it appears that one of our chromosomes may have been derived from two of the apes'. The difference in chromosome number may not indicate all that much difference in evolutionary relationship.

The final method uses **mitochondrial DNA**, found not in the nucleus of the cell but in **organelles** outside the nucleus. This topic will be described in detail in Chapter 12. For now, suffice to say that this test, too, indicates a close relationship among humans and the African great apes.

Taken together, this genetic evidence points to the chimpanzee as our closest living relative, but some specific tests within these four types give somewhat ambiguous results regarding the precise relationship among chimps, humans, and gorillas. Some indicate we have a closer affinity with gorillas; others seem to show that our three species are equally related. The exact nature of our evolutionary kinship is, according to one authority, "a close call" (Marks 1991).

We are left, however, with two undeniable conclusions: that we diverged from our closest relatives, the African apes, in the recent past, maybe as recently as 5 or 6 mya, and that our initial distinction was our bipedal method of locomotion. But this evidence must be put into two contexts. It must make sense adaptively—that is, we must be able to explain *why* this happened in terms of a reasonable primate response to a certain set of environmental conditions. Furthermore, it must make sense in terms of genetic and evolutionary theory. *How* could bipedalism have emerged and evolved in such an apparently short time?

## WHY WE STOOD UP

If you give it some thought, you might consider bipedalism a fairly awkward method of getting around. Not many creatures use this means of locomotion, which balances the weight of a whole body vertically on top of two small points of contact with the ground. In humans, the body's center of gravity is several feet up. When a biped walks, it throws that center of gravity forward, pushing off with one leg, then tries to get the other leg out in front in time to keep itself from falling flat on its face. Then it starts the whole process over again. Bipeds can't run very

**Figure 8.5** *Chimpanzee walking bipedally while carrying bananas. Carrying may have been one of the functions that promoted the evolution of bipedalism in early hominids.* (A. Kortlandt)

fast, and they aren't very stable on rough or slippery terrain. Compare the ease with which a dog walks over slippery ground in winter with the comical manner in which we must cautiously make our way. There must be a very good reason why this posture evolved in our earliest ancestors.

New phenotypic traits don't just arise out of thin air. They have to be based on a characteristic already present in some form, even if rudimentary. An obvious question is whether any of the nonhuman primates use bipedal locomotion and, if so, under what circumstances and why?

We find that nearly all the primates, from time to time, stand upright. Some prosimian vertical clinger-leapers, built with humanlike limb proportions, can't walk quadrupedally at all on those rare instances when they come to the ground, so they hop bipedally. It looks comical to us, but it works. Gibbons, with their extremely long arms, must also use a bipedal posture on the ground, balancing with their arms like a tightrope walker uses a pole. Monkeys and apes often stand upright to be able to look around and see farther, and chimps and gorillas in particular can and often do walk upright when they need to free their arms and hands from their usual locomotor functions in order to carry something (Figure 8.5).

**mitochondrial DNA:** DNA from the mitochondria of cells rather than from the nucleus.

**organelle:** A structure in the cytoplasm of cells that performs various functions for the cell.

What sorts of things do these primates carry? Chimps have been observed carrying sticks that they wave around to frighten off another chimp or perhaps some potential predator. Mother chimps sometimes walk upright while carrying their babies. Apes often walk bipedally when they have food to carry. Can we, by analogy, hypothesize that our form of locomotion was originally selected for to facilitate carrying and walking at the same time?

As we said, it's an error automatically to assume an original situation from a current one—in this case, the original function of bipedalism from what we see to be current functions. But it seems reasonable that this adaptation—the ability to stand and walk bipedally for a short time—has the same use for modern apes as it did for their ancestors of several million years ago, who are similar enough to be classified as apes, too. Moreover, the biological closeness of apes and humans, and the fact that we evolved from a common ancestor, makes it fairly safe to assume that our habitual bipedalism evolved because the occasional bipedalism of our apelike ancestors was selected for as its use became more important for survival. The behavior, in other words, is homologous.

But what happened in Africa that made this trend adaptive? Chimps can walk bipedally, but they don't do it all the time, perhaps because their food is usually plentiful and the forests fairly safe, so food can be eaten where it is found. But we know now that a major climatic change on a worldwide scale occurred just about 6 mya, the time when we think our story starts. Called the "Terminal Miocene Event," it was a cooling trend that, among other effects, caused increasing aridity in many parts of the world, including Africa.

From a continent that was once almost entirely forest, Africa became a continent with forests in the central highlands and most of the rest open woodland and vast stretches of savanna with patches of forest (Figure 8.6). This is obviously important because so far fossils of early hominids have been found largely in areas that are or were savanna. (The great deserts of North Africa are relatively recent.) Of course, our ancestors may also have lived in the woodlands, an environment not conducive to fossilization. But the decrease in forest area and the accompanying dominance of the savannas would still have affected our evolution, even if we were not strictly savanna dwellers at first.

For a primate, the savannas, or even the open woodlands, are a very different environment from the forests. The variety and availability of food are not as great. Fewer species of edible plants grow on the open grasslands. The plant life is not as concentrated, so an animal has to range over a wider area in search of food. All life on the savannas is more directly affected by seasonal changes, particularly in rainfall. There are, on the open plains, abundant sources of meat, but it must be caught and killed, taken away from predators, or scavenged after the

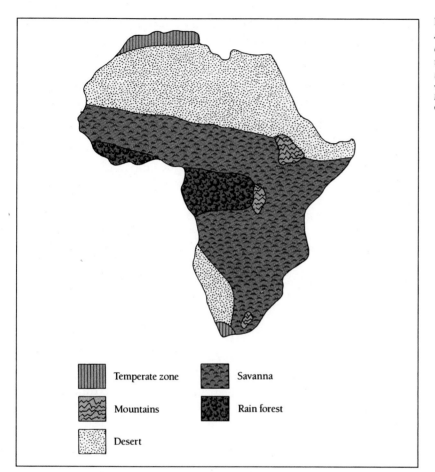

**Figure 8.6** *The climatic zones of Africa today, except for the large deserts in the north and south, are nearly the same as when our evolutionary story began 6 mya.* (Redrawn with permission from: Bernard Campbell, *Human Ecology* (New York: Aldine de Gruyter) © 1983 by Bernard Campbell)

Temperate zone

Mountains

Desert

Savanna

Rain forest

predators are done. Then there's the direct danger from the predators themselves. Lions, leopards, cheetahs, wild dogs, and a host of other meat eaters are ever-present threats.

So how could bipedalism have helped solve the problems our ancestors faced as they moved out onto the savannas? There are a number of current hypotheses. The "carrying things" idea certainly makes some sense. With food sources in open, dangerous areas, it might have been beneficial to be able to carry the food one had found back to some safer refuge—a grove of trees, perhaps, or a rock shelter. Children could be carried while mothers searched for food. We know that modern foragers do this. Maybe sticks or rocks could be carried or even thrown to scare predators or other scavengers away from a carcass.

But attributing such an important change to a single cause violates a basic idea of adaptive evolution: that an organism is a *system* of traits and behaviors that have evolved in response to a dynamic complex of environmental circumstances. The evolution of habitual bipedal loco-

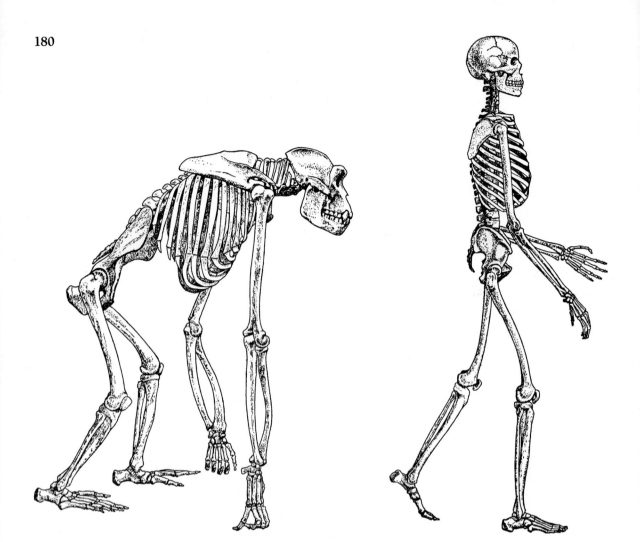

**Figure 8.7** *The skeletons of a gorilla* (left) *and a modern human. Note especially the differences in shape and orientation of the pelvis, the relative lengths of arms and legs, and shape of the feet.*
*The size and shape of the muscles of posture and locomotion would also reflect the difference between quadrupedalism and bipedalism.*

motion, although grounded in the rudimentary ability of apes, nonetheless involved major realignments of the bones and muscles of most of the body as well as much of the nervous system (Figure 8.7). Moreover, these changes most probably did not occur all at once. If bipedalism were a simple response to a single adaptive need, one might expect other primates—especially the savanna baboons—to possess this ability to a greater degree than they do. There must have been other, related benefits to our ancestors that promoted selection for this important adaptive change.

Biologist Pat Shipman (1984, 1986b) suggests that our early ancestors acquired meat on the savannas by scavenging rather than by hunting, as has traditionally been thought. She arrived at this conclusion through her taphonomic analysis of carnivore tooth marks and hominid tool-cut marks on the bones of ancient savanna animals (see Chapter 7).

Many bones show both kinds of marks, and some even display the cut marks *over* the tooth marks, indicating the order in which the marks were made.

The implication, according to Shipman, is that our ancestors located animals already killed by some predator, chased the predator off if need be, and took off—or cut off—what usable parts of the kill were left. Such an activity requires endurance because large areas have to be covered to locate kills, although the fact that the "prey" is already dead means scavengers can move more slowly than if tracking and killing live game. Scavenging also requires a means to help locate the kill and avoid getting killed oneself. For example, hyenas, another savanna scavenger, have a well-developed sense of smell to locate carrion as well as other carnivores. Vultures use aerial location, both efficient and safe.

Bipedalism, Shipman offers, might have been useful in adapting to these problems. Bipedalism is not a very energy-efficient posture for running and is therefore not a particularly good adaptation for hunting, which often requires running. But bipedal walking is highly energy-efficient and so would be useful for scavenging, which requires long periods of walking in search of food. Bipedalism also elevates the head, aiding in seeing potential food or potential danger from a distance. Finally, this adaptive change would allow early hominids to carry the pieces of meat they managed to get off the carcass and, at a later time, the tools they used to help them do this.

For Shipman's idea to work, however, very early hominids would have to have depended on scavenging to such a degree that selection for habitual bipedalism was important. At this point, we simply cannot say to what extent scavenging for meat was part of our earliest ancestors' diet. Moreover, even if Shipman's cut mark analysis is accurate, were earlier hominids—those around before stone tools—also relying on scavenging? Bipedalism evolved over a million years before the first evidence of stone tool manufacture.

Anthropologist C. Owen Lovejoy proposes a somewhat different basis for the adaptive advantage of bipedalism. He suggests that the focus was "the provisioning of sexually faithful females and their young by reliable mates" (1984:28). When the African climate changed and the forests declined, one population of apes—those that would become our ancestors—experienced greater than normal loss of offspring. Apes have offspring up to five or six years apart but act to assure their successful maturation by lavishing extensive care upon them. A drastic decrease in food supply would affect offspring first and would be especially devastating to a species that spaced births so widely. Any variation that would aid in more successful reproduction would have been selected for.

Lovejoy suggests that males who provisioned (found food and brought it back to) females and offspring provided a reproductive advantage by supplying females with more food and allowing them more time to care for their young. Males who did this, and females who selected such males as mates, had greater than average success at passing on their genes. Provisioning behavior and a permanent bond between such males and females would thus have been selected for. Provisioning, in turn, requires travel in search of food and transport of the food back to the female and offspring. Bipedalism, Lovejoy claims, was the adaptive response to this requirement because it "enhanced the carrying of provisions" (1984:28).

As with Shipman's hypothesis, there are objections to Lovejoy's. His idea would only work if the females were loyal to the provisioning males. The behavior could not be selected for if the provisioned female's offspring were not conceived by the provisioning male. Lovejoy assumes that the females remained "faithful" while the males were off looking for food. Indeed, he claims that this situation was the origin of the human traits of continuous (rather than periodic) sexual receptivity and monogamy. But human monogamy is a cultural, not necessarily a biological, trait. Over one-half of human societies are polygamous— that is, they allow or even encourage plural marriages. And continual receptivity is not advantageous if the male happens to be away searching for food when the female is ovulating and capable of conceiving.

Lovejoy's idea is also male-oriented. As Nancy Tanner (1981) and Adrienne Zihlman (1979) point out, gathering foods and caring for children were no doubt *at least* as important to the survival of the group as male food-collecting activities. In the same ways that bipedalism would have aided males in gathering, scavenging, and carrying, it would have aided the ability of the females to efficiently and safely locate, collect, and carry food *and* their offspring.

It is perhaps impossible to conclude once and for all just why bipedalism was selected for and became our species' first distinguishing feature. We will never be able to watch our ancestors scavenging or provisioning or living in a family unit. But by applying the methods of science, we can generate a reasonable working hypothesis. We have already used this process to evaluate the various individual ideas about the adaptive significance of bipedalism, testing each by seeing if it makes sense in terms of what we know of evolutionary theory, the fossil record, and the nature of primate anatomy and behavior.

So what sort of picture can we put together of the nature of the ancestor for whom bipedalism played so vital a role? Integrating the ideas of Shipman, Lovejoy, Tanner, Zilhman, and others (see, for example, Cartmill 1983), we can envision small groups of early hominids living in open forest and savanna areas, moving about in search of plant foods augmented by scavenging and perhaps some hunting of small animals. The group itself was recognized as a unit and possibly defended, but it was made up of and held together by a series of differential personal relationships, centered around the family of mother and offspring. Whether a "father" was recognized is unknown, but the group was likely promiscuous rather than strictly monogamous, with sexual consciousness acting as an additional incentive for social cohesion.

In such a situation, bipedalism may have conferred an adaptive advantage, allowing for more energy-efficient and safer mobility and for the ability to move and carry food, offspring, and perhaps some tools. If this advantage was consciously recognized, there may have been sexual selection for individuals more proficient at the activities facilitated by bipedalism. This type of mobility would have been all the more important if the success of the group as a whole depended on the sharing of the collected food.

We may conduct one more test of this portrait by looking back to the description of chimpanzee behavior in Chapter 6 to see if the picture is a reasonable one. In other words, could such a group have evolved from an apelike ancestor? In asking this, we must keep clearly in mind that chimps are modern apes, not holdovers from the past, and that we are using them as a model only for the behavior of a common ancestor.

Recalling the behavior of chimps, we see all the general features of our portrait of early hominids: personal recognition, sharing of food, the family unit, tool use, hunting, occasional bipedalism (especially in bonobos), sexual consciousness (again, especially in bonobos) with anything but monogamy, and—although only one case has been observed—even scavenging of kills made by leopards and left in trees (Byrne and Byrne 1988; Cavallo 1990). In the face of an environmental change, such as an increase in open forest and savanna, it is quite conceivable that an adaptive system like the chimps' could have been maintained through selection for some existing trait—in this case, the ability to walk bipedally.

But what sorts of genetic changes could have been involved in the evolutionary trend of bipedalism and, later, of big brains?

## HOW WE EMERGED

Because we now differ from our closest relations, the chimps, in only about 1 percent of our genetic material, it seems obvious that a relatively small number of genetic mutations must have taken place to bring about the divergence of our evolutionary line from theirs. Given, furthermore, the distinct morphological difference between our two species, it also seems reasonable that these mutations were macromutations—mutations of genes that code for important processes or features with far-reaching phenotypic effects.

Mutations of genes for developmental rates are important examples of macromutations, for even a slight change in the timing of development of certain features can make a great difference in an organism's final appearance and function. There can be, after all, an incredible distinction between forms of organisms at different stages of their life cycles. Consider tadpoles and frogs, for instance, or caterpillars and butterflies. The different stages could easily be mistaken for separate species. It seems possible, then, that the overall difference between humans and chimpanzees lies in the rate at which certain important traits develop.

A theory exists to support this idea. It is called **neoteny** (literally, "holding onto youth") and refers to the fact that adult members of some species possess characteristics of young, even fetal, members of related species. Such a phenomenon could be the result of a mutation of one or more developmental genes that slow or "retard" the growth rates of those features. There are many examples in nature, perhaps the most famous being the Mexican axolotl. The axolotl is a salamander that never grows up. Although a reproducing adult, it retains the totally aquatic life of a salamander larva, including the larva's external gills. This occurs because the axolotl fails to secrete a growth hormone, a condition caused by a single genetic locus. As amazing as it may seem at first, similar phenomena may have led to the evolution of our species from that of the African apes.

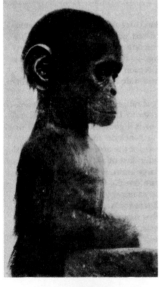

*Figure 8.8 Young chimpanzee compared to adult, showing the striking resemblance of the young chimp to a modern human, an example of neoteny.*

Many of the most notable features of adult humans are possessed by fetal or newborn chimpanzees (Figure 8.8). These include

1. *Lack of body hair.* Actually, it's not that we have no body hair, it just hasn't developed into the thick fur of the apes.
2. *Rounded cranium and flat face.* Newborn chimps have heads remarkably like ours and only later develop a protruding face, heavy jaws, and sloping forehead.
3. *Position of the foramen magnum underneath the skull.* As the chimp grows, the position of this feature shifts toward the rear of the skull, a characteristic of quadrupeds.
4. *Nonopposable big toe,* not widely separated from the other toes. The grasping foot of the chimp develops later.
5. *The late closure of cranial sutures.* By the time a chimp is born, the sutures have fused to form a single bone; in humans they remain separate for about a year and don't fully fuse for decades. Ossification occurs more slowly at other sites in humans than it does in apes.
6. *Prolonged growth of the brain.* The brains of apes grow very rapidly shortly before, and just after, birth. The brain of a chimp is 40 percent fully developed at birth and 70 percent by age 1 year. Our brains, on the other hand, spread the growth period out over a much longer time. At birth our brains are only 25 percent com-

plete and don't achieve 70 percent until age 3 years. Full size is not reached in humans until about age 10 years, compared to half that time in chimps. This growth rate, as well as the fact that our brains are still larger than a chimp's at birth, accounts for the prolonged suture closure.

Neoteny, then, may help account for two of our most distinguishing features. To be sure, the shift to habitual bipedalism required a great many anatomical and neurological changes. But a retention of the skull-to-spine orientation of newborn apes along with the rounded crania and nonopposable big toe may have given bipedalism a head start by endowing those individuals who were more neotenous with an adaptive advantage pronounced enough for selection to act on.

Second, our big brains seem very nicely accounted for by a mutation that caused our ancestors to retain the period of rapid brain growth. Although the difference between quadrupedalism and bipedalism is profound, the difference between the brain of a chimp and that of a human may not be so profound. Certainly, the human brain is capable of more complex functions than that of a chimp, but the basic structure does not seem fundamentally different. Our brains are larger, more complex versions of chimpanzee brains. This difference can be compared to two computers: One may be bigger and capable of performing functions the other can't, but the only structural difference between them is in size and complexity of the same basic parts. Our big brains might actually be less of an evolutionary accomplishment than our upright posture.

This hypothesis has been criticized (B. T. Shea 1989, for example) on two grounds: (1) These supposed neotenous features may be superficial similarities in shape caused by processes other than the actual retention of fetal or newborn characteristics, and (2) a single cause is being posited for two changes—bipedalism and an increase in brain size—that took place several million years apart. Still, the list of juvenile features does lend support to the general idea that our features are variations on those of our nearest evolutionary relative.

Thus, the emergence of the human lineage as we've described it seems to fit not only the fossil evidence but evolutionary theory and modern knowledge of genetics and behavior as well. If all the foregoing is correct, macromutations of genetic loci involved with developmental timing occurred among a group of apes living on the boundary of the drying forests and widening savannas. These mutations provided for the initial variation that gave rise to the basic adaptive responses selected for and enhanced during our evolution. The human lineage emerged as a punctuation, a burst of change, a new side branch off the evolutionary line of the African apes.

**neoteny:** The retention in one species of juvenile traits of a related species.

## CONTEMPORARY ISSUE

### Our Cousin, the Chimp?

It is clear that humans and chimps are members of different species: We are reproductively isolated from each other. Humans and chimps cannot produce offspring. (At the very least, this is because the chromosome numbers are different, so that at fertilization the chromosome pairs can't match up.) But it is also clear that we are very closely related species. In broader perspective, however, how close *are* we, compared with other organisms? Are we distant cousins? First cousins? Siblings?

The classic way of answering this question is to place species into taxonomic relationships based on their degrees of similarity and difference. This was the approach adopted by Linnaeus. By this method, although we are closer genetically to chimps and gorillas than to orangutans, humans and those other three species are classed in different taxonomic families. *They* are all apes because of the features they share with one another that they do not share with us.

There is now a new way of looking at evolutionary relationships, called the cladistic or "branching," method, which uses the pattern of evolutionary branching to determine classification. If two or more species are derived from a common ancestor and no other line branched from that ancestor, those species are said to be a *sister group* regardless of how similar or different they look today. Phrased another way, species that share homologous traits derived from a common ancestor and found in no other lineage are classed together.

Applied to our topic, the cladistic method works like this. The latest evolutionary divergence among the hominoids is between the common chimp and the bonobo. These two species share a great many homologous traits with relatively minor differences. They form a sister group. The hominid line, according to anatomical, behavioral, and most genetic evidence, was the next to branch, going back in time. Thus, hominids, chimps, and bonobos form the next, larger sister group. Then comes the sister group that includes hominids, chimps, bonobos, and gorillas, and so on.

Viewed *this* way, our traditional taxonomic categories may no longer be valid. Under the cladistic scheme, there is no such thing as an ape (traditional family Pongidae) because there is no sister group that includes the four great apes and excludes the hominids. Adherents to cladistics have thus proposed new taxonomies to better capture this idea. One places only the orangutan in family Pongidae and lumps the gorilla, the two chimps, and humans under family Hominidae

## SUMMARY

To understand the place of our species in the broad evolutionary scheme of things requires an understanding of the adaptive significance of bipedalism—the first of the characteristic hominid traits to appear. The evidence from the fossil record shows that habitual bipedalism was already established by nearly 4 mya. Genetic comparisons with our "cousins" indicate that the African great apes and hominids split only shortly earlier. It's clear, then, that bipedalism was the initial hominid

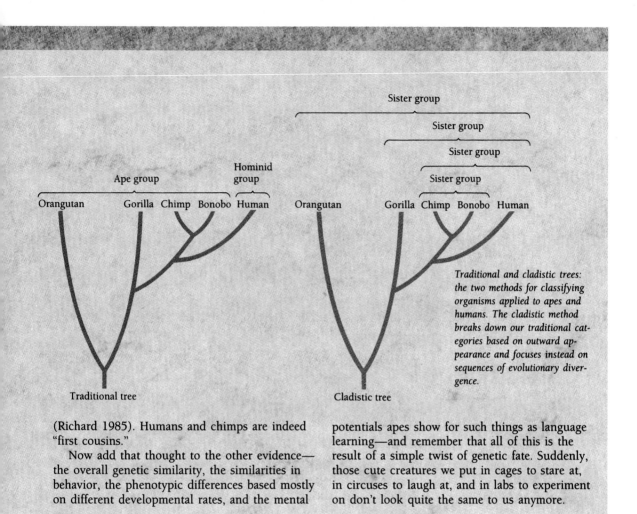

*Traditional and cladistic trees: the two methods for classifying organisms applied to apes and humans. The cladistic method breaks down our traditional categories based on outward appearance and focuses instead on sequences of evolutionary divergence.*

(Richard 1985). Humans and chimps are indeed "first cousins."

Now add that thought to the other evidence—the overall genetic similarity, the similarities in behavior, the phenotypic differences based mostly on different developmental rates, and the mental potentials apes show for such things as language learning—and remember that all of this is the result of a simple twist of genetic fate. Suddenly, those cute creatures we put in cages to stare at, in circuses to laugh at, and in labs to experiment on don't look quite the same to us anymore.

trait and that it was relatively rapidly selected for within a population of the common ancestor of us and the chimpanzees.

Analysis of the fossil record and of the ethology of modern chimps allows us to imagine the situation in which bipedalism might have been adaptively advantageous. The picture that emerges is of small groups living in open areas, gathering, scavenging, and perhaps hunting small animals, organized around some sort of family unit and with interpersonal bonds often supported by conscious sexuality, sharing important resources, and defending the group members and territory.

## KEY TERMS

australopithecine
DNA hybridization
mitochondrial DNA
organelle
neoteny

## FOR MORE INFORMATION

For more on the Piltdown controversy, see Kenneth Feder, *Frauds, Myth, and Mysteries: Science and Pseudoscience in Archaeology.*

See Donald Johanson and Maitland Edey's *Lucy: The Beginnings of Humankind,* for the story of the early hominid fossils. The book also contains more about Piltdown as well as a detailed explanation of Owen Lovejoy's theory of bipedalism. Many good pictures and diagrams too. The story of Johanson's work continues in *Lucy's Child* by Johanson and James Shreeve. For a lively recounting of the personalities involved in the major fossil finds, see Roger Lewin's *Bones of Contention: Controversies in the Search for Human Origins.* For great pictures and diagrams and the most up-to-date summary of the latest thinking about human evolution, try the November 1985 issue of *National Geographic,* which is devoted to that subject.

See Stephen Jay Gould *Ever Since Darwin* and *The Panda's Thumb* for more on neoteny; and, in the latter, an article titled "The Telltale Wishbone" about the cladistic method.

# 9

# THE HUMAN LINEAGE
# ESTABLISHED

In 1999, according to current projections, the 6 billionth living human will be born. Six *billion* of us, in various shapes, sizes, colors, and cultures. And yet we recognize and acknowledge that we all belong to the same species, *Homo sapiens*. Our ability to produce fertile offspring, no matter how different the parents' biological and cultural backgrounds, proves it.

The present-day biological unity of humankind makes it hard for us to imagine that a single hominid species inhabiting the earth was not always the case. For a large part of hominid history—perhaps as much as half—there were at least two evolutionary lineages of bipedal primates, that is, two species of hominids. Clearly, only one of those survived to the present, but we must not think that line was somehow *destined* to survive or that the lines that became extinct were mere side branches.

Evolution, even human evolution, is not a simple ladder or even a mighty tree trunk with smaller branches extending from it. It is not the record of uninterrupted progress toward perfection. Rather, evolution is, to use Stephen Jay Gould's metaphor (1987a,b,c), a bush, with countless, endlessly branching twigs representing individual species—evolution's experiments.

In fact, Gould says it is "life's little joke" that the oversimplified view of evolution as a ladder of progress can be forced on the data only when there is just one living species to represent a family of organisms—in other words, when the lineage has, as a whole, been relatively unsuccessful. Only our twig remains on the bush of hominid evolution, so we can easily get the impression that evolution has been leading toward us all along.

Indeed, primate evolution as a whole is typical of the bush model. It is, as Gould (1987a:25) puts it, "a formerly luxuriant bush" now reduced to a relatively few surviving twigs. And the human primate is "a fragile little twig of recent origin" although of "unparalleled subsequent success" (1987c:19). It is this perspective on ourselves that we need to keep in mind as we continue.

## THE AUSTRALOPITHECINES

When South African anatomist Raymond Dart described the first known specimen of this twig of evolution in 1925, he used the genus name *Australopithecus*, which literally means "southern ape." Although he seems to have been fully appreciative of its rounded forehead, hominid dental features, and indications of upright posture, neither he nor the times were ready to acknowledge its membership in family Hominidae. As more specimens came to light over the next decades and with the fall of Piltdown and its brain-centered view of human evolution in the 1950s, the australopithecines were fully accepted as the earliest known representatives of our portion of life's "evolutionary bush."

The story of the discovery and interpretation of the australopithecines is full of twists and turns, flashes of insight and changes of direction with almost every new fossil discovery. A fascinating story that is far from over, it is nicely summarized in Donald Johanson and Maitland Edey (1981) and in Roger Lewin (1987c).

This period of hominid evolution is complex indeed. At least a half-dozen different family trees have been proposed to show hypothesized relationships among the australopithecines and the beginnings of genus *Homo* (Boaz 1988; Grine 1988a; Kimbel et al. 1988), each with evidence in its support as well as arguments against it. The differences are often based on highly technical data—a difference or similarity between two fossils in a small anatomical detail, for instance. Getting deeply into these arguments is, as paleoanthropologist David Pilbeam puts it (1984, 1986), like "peering" too closely at a pointillist painting or a newspaper photograph; they become a bunch of "meaningless dots." Here, we will indicate some of the disagreements over placement of the fossils, but we will basically, as Pilbeam advises, view the australopithecines "from a distance," trying to see the dots come together to present a general picture. Table 9.1 presents an overview of hominid species from this period that are generally agreed on, and Figure 9.1 shows the major fossil sites. Use these for reference as we proceed.

Genus *Australopithecus* begins clearly with Lucy and the other specimens of *A. afarensis* from Ethiopia and Tanzania 3 to 4 million years ago (mya). There are fragmentary fossils from Kenya and Ethiopia, dating back as far as 5.5 mya, that many attribute to *afarensis*, but their affiliations are still debatable (Hill and Ward 1988). Johanson (Johanson and Edey 1981), along with a majority of specialists in the field, contend that *afarensis* was the common ancestor of all future hominids. Richard Leakey and colleagues (Leakey and Walker 1980), on the other hand, believe that the yet unknown common ancestor was in the more remote past, maybe 6 mya, and that Lucy, the First Family, and the Laetoli footprints come after the split between the australopithecines and the line leading to modern humans (Figure 9.2).

We think Leakey's scheme, although it may turn out to be right, does not provide the best working hypothesis at the present time. Rather than arranging the evidence that is *known* into a set of evolutionary relationships, Leakey's idea requires the acceptance of a common ancestor whose very existence is hypothetical. If there were some indication that *A. afarensis* might not be the common ancestor of all later hominids, then the use of some undiscovered form would be justified. But *afarensis* makes a perfectly good candidate for common ancestor, and nothing as yet argues persuasively against this interpretation. It's complicated enough just dealing with the known evidence, much less confounding it with unnecessary evidence yet to be found. (This idea, that the best working hypothesis is the simplest one, is in fact a tenet of modern science known as Occam's Razor.) For now, we'll adopt Johanson's model as our working hypothesis.

**Table 9.1** *An Overview of Fossil Hominids*

|  | A. afarensis | A. africanus | A. robustus | A. boisei | H. habilis |
|---|---|---|---|---|---|
| Dates | 4–3 mya | 3–2.3 mya | 2.2–1.5 mya (?) | 2.2–1 mya (excludes "Black Skull") | 2.2–1.6 mya |
| Sites (see Fig. 9.1) | Hadar Omo Laetoli | Taung Sterkfontein Makapansgat Lake Turkana (?) Omo (?) | Kromdraai Swartkrans | Olduvai Lake Turkana Omo | Olduvai Lake Turkana Omo Sterkfontein (?) Swartkrans (?) |
| Cranial capacity (in ml) | 380–500 $\bar{x}$ = 440 | 435–530 $\bar{x}$ = 450 | 520 (based on one specimen) | 500–530 $\bar{x}$ = 515 | 500–800 $\bar{x}$ = 680 |
| Size (average, in lb.) | 110 | 100 | 105 | 101 | 89 |
| Skull | Very prognathous Receding chin Large teeth Pointed canine with gap Arcade between ape and human Hint of crest | Less prognathous than *afarensis* Jaw more rounded Large back teeth Canines smaller than *robustus*, larger than *afarensis* No crest | Heavy jaws Small canines and front teeth Large back teeth Definite crest | Very large jaws Very large back teeth Large crest | Flatter face Less sloping forehead Teeth similar to *africanus* No crest |
| Postcranial Skeleton | Long arms Short thumb Curved fingers and toes Bipedal | ←————— | Hands and feet more like modern humans Retention of long arms | —————→ | Limited evidence Retention of long arms Maybe retention of primitive features of hand and foot |

As we noted in Chapter 8, *A. afarensis* might be described as a bipedal ape (Figure 9.3). Its average brain size is about 440 ml (milliliters), a little bigger than a chimpanzee's, but with the same maximum of about 500 ml. It has the jutting face (**prognathism**) of an ape and the remnants of pointed canine teeth, an ape feature. Small gaps in the tooth row accommodate long canine teeth when the mouth is closed; this is also an ape characteristic. There is a hint of a sagittal crest, a ridge of bone along the top of the skull for the attachment of the temporalis

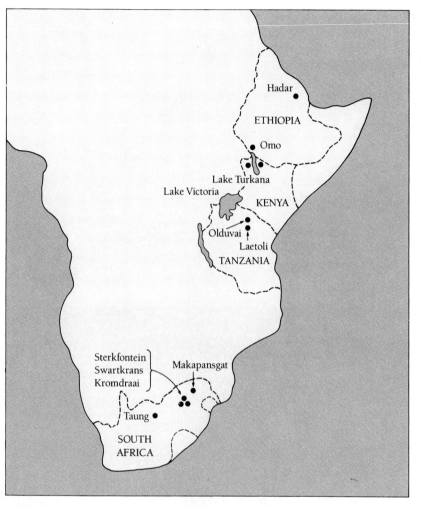

**Figure 9.1** *Location of major australopithecine and early* Homo *sites in Africa. See Table 9.1 for species found at each site.*

muscles, major chewing muscles. Gorillas have such crests (Figure 9.4); our temporalis muscles are attached at the sides of our skulls. The long arms and slightly curved fingers and toes are apelike as well and may indicate that, though bipedal, *afarensis* was still a good tree climber.

The ancestral hominids represented by Lucy and the First Family are dated from between 4 and 3 mya. Then, around 3 mya, the hominid branch split into *at least* two lines: the line that evolved into modern humans and the line that became the extinct hominid forms.

The reasoning behind this assessment is fairly simple. Most authorities agree that, prior to 3 mya, hominid remains are all similar enough to warrant placing them in the same species, *A. afarensis*. But by 2 mya,

**prognathism:** Protrusion of the lower portion of the face.

**Figure 9.2** *Comparison of Richard Leakey's and Donald Johanson's views on the place of Lucy in hominid evolution and on the timing of the split between the australopithecines and the Homo line. Most authorities favor Johanson's model.*

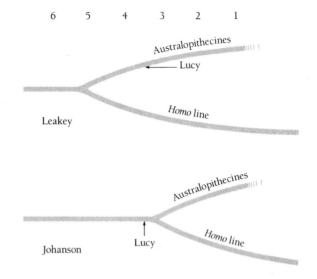

**Figure 9.3** *Reconstruction by Dr. T.D. White and W.H. Kimbel of* Australopithecus afarensis, *using parts from several individuals.* (Institute of Human Origins)

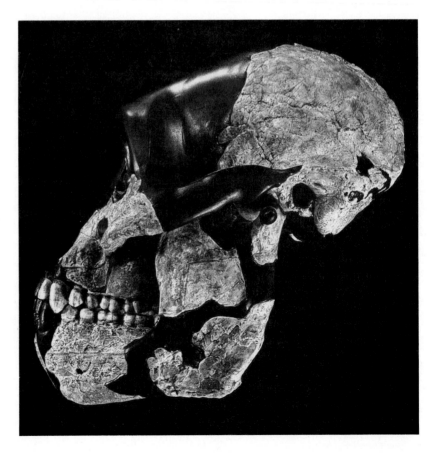

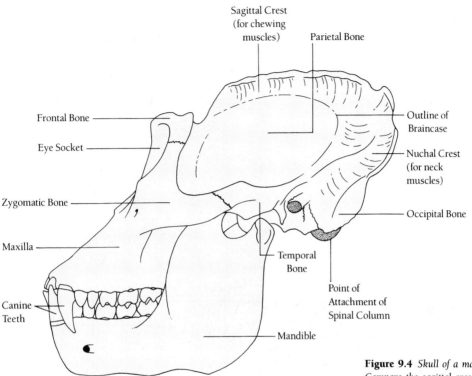

**Figure 9.4** *Skull of a male gorilla. Compare the sagittal crest with those of* Australopithecus robustus *(Figure 9.7) and* Australopithecus boisei *(Figures 9.9, 9.10).*

two general types of hominids can be described from the fossils. One possesses features that lead us to consider it the first member of our genus, *Homo*. The other type retained important features of *afarensis*. Based on what we know about the degree of species difference among living primates, we conclude that these fossils represent distinct hominid lineages.

Even though little changed from *A. afarensis*, the next fossils in the australopithecine line get a new species name. They are called **Australopithecus africanus**, the "southern ape of Africa." These southern African specimens were the first australopithecines to be discovered, beginning in 1925. The rules of scientific nomenclature dictate that we keep the name even though we now recognize its inaccuracy.

*A. africanus* (Figure 9.5), whose remains may also have been found in Kenya and Ethiopia, is essentially the same as *A. afarensis* in body size and shape as well as cranial capacity (average size 450 ml). Some authorities (Leakey and Walker 1980; Tobias 1980), in fact, feel that *afarensis* should be included within species *africanus*. There are, however, some changes apparent in the fossils designated *africanus*. The face

**Figure 9.5** *Skull of* Australopithecus africanus *(female?) from Sterkfontein, South Africa. Note the general similarity to* Australopithecus afarensis. (Transvaal Museum, D. C. Panagos)

of *africanus* is less prognathous than that of *afarensis*. It lacks a sagittal crest. The canine teeth are smaller than *afarensis*, and the dental arcade is somewhat more rounded, that is, more humanlike than apelike. There are no gaps in the tooth row (Figure 9.6).

Most of the south African *A. africanus* specimens come from limestone caves, which present serious problems for dating. Dating through faunal analysis, though, has indicated that specimens of the *africanus* type are found from 3 mya to 2.3 mya. There is disagreement about the relationships between *africanus* and the two main hominid lines that appear after *A. afarensis*. Some see *africanus* as a member of the line that led to *Homo* (Skelton et al. 1986; Susman 1988). Others see it as part of the line that retained australopithecine characteristics (Johanson and White 1979; Walker and Leakey 1978). Arguments exist for several versions of both viewpoints, with none "unambiguously favored" (Kimbel et al. 1988:265).

About 2.2 mya, we find a new set of australopithecine features has replaced those of *A. africanus*. These fossils, also from southern Africa, represent more robust australopithecines, hence their scientific name ***Australopithecus robustus*** (Figure 9.7). Cranial capacity has increased to an average of about 520 ml, but body size remains virtually unchanged (McHenry 1988).

The major difference, however, and the reason for the species name, seems to have been in dietary emphasis. The jaws of *A. robustus* are much heavier than those of *A. africanus*. The incisors and canine teeth

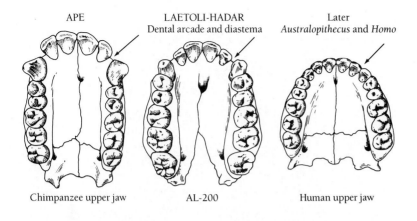

APE

LAETOLI-HADAR
Dental arcade and diastema

Later
*Australopithecus* and *Homo*

Chimpanzee upper jaw

AL-200

Human upper jaw

**Figure 9.6** *Shape of the dental arcade, size of the canines, and presence or absence of a gap (diastema) are important diagnostic features for establishing hominid status.* (Adapted from drawings by Luba Dmytryk Gudz from *Lucy: The Beginnings of Humankind,* © 1981 Donald C. Johanson and Maitland A. Edey)

are smaller, but the back teeth are much larger. There is also a definite indication of a sagittal crest. Large back teeth indicate an emphasis on a grinding motion for chewing food. In support of this interpretation, the placement of the sagittal crest points to an orientation toward supplying power to the back teeth. In gorillas the crest and the temporalis muscles act on the front teeth. The implication is that *robustus* was adapted to a diet of large amounts of vegetable material, perhaps small tough items like seeds that would require grinding. Although the back teeth of *afri-*

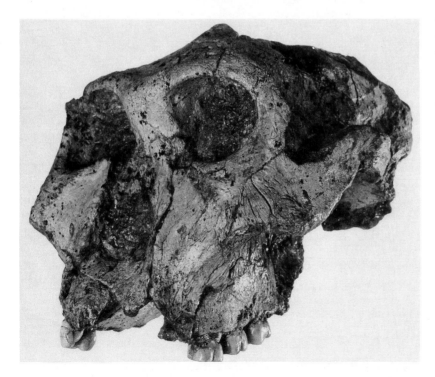

**Figure 9.7** *Skull of* Australopithecus robustus *from Swartkrans, South Africa. Note the increase in robusticity over* Australopithecus africanus *and, especially, the remnant of a sagittal crest.* (Transvaal Museum, D.C. Panagos)

**Figure 9.8** *Erosion of the sort that exposed the strata of Olduvai Gorge, Tanzania, has made the Gorge one of the most productive sites in the world for paleontologists.* (Tim D. White)

*canus* are still relatively larger than in modern humans, they are not as large as those of *robustus*, implying that *africanus* was more of an omnivore. These important differences have led some to propose placing the "robust" australopithecines into their own genus, **Paranthropus** ("almost human"). This idea is still under debate (see Grine 1988b:509–20); so, for simplicity, we will continue to lump them within genus *Australopithecus*, which seems at the moment to remain the majority viewpoint.

The last robust fossil from southern Africa dates from about 1.5 mya. In the meantime, a group of fossils from Ethiopia, Kenya, and Tanzania have taken the robust theme to the extreme. These remains date from over 2 mya to nearly 1 mya and are classified as **Australopithecus boisei**. The first find, made by Louis and Mary Leakey at Olduvai Gorge in Tanzania in 1959, was the famous "Zinjanthropus" (literally, "East African Man"; Figures 9.8, 9.9).

Zinjanthropus was dubbed "Nutcracker Man" because of the extremely large size of its jaws and back teeth, both larger than in

*A. robustus.* Also much larger was the size of the sagittal crest. In all other respects, *A. boisei* is a variation of the robust australopithecine theme. Its maximum body size is like that of the southern African remains, and its cranial capacity averages about 515 ml, again about the same as *robustus.*

The evolutionary relationship between the southern African robust form and the East African "hyperrobust" form is unclear, but a recent find may suggest a solution.

In 1985, near Lake Turkana, Kenya, a skull was discovered that possessed an intriguing combination of traits (Walker et al. 1986). It has been called the "Black Skull" because of its dark coloration, the result of minerals in the ground in which it has lain (Figure 9.10). No official taxonomic name has been applied to this fossil as yet. It is usually known by its specimen designation, KMN-WT 17000, although some have proposed naming it *Australopithecus aethiopicus* (Kimbel et al. 1988). It resembles *A. boisei* in its robusticity and, in fact, exceeds *boisei* in the size of its sagittal crest, which is the largest ever seen in a hominid. Its molar teeth also are among the largest hominid molars ever found—four or five times the size of a modern human's. At the same

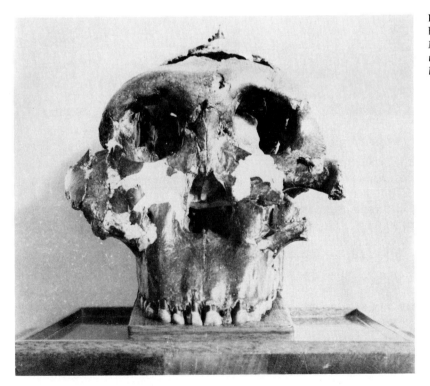

**Figure 9.9** Australopithecus boisei, *"Zinjanthropus" specimen. Note the extremely large teeth and the remnants of what was a very large sagittal crest.* (© Bob Campbell)

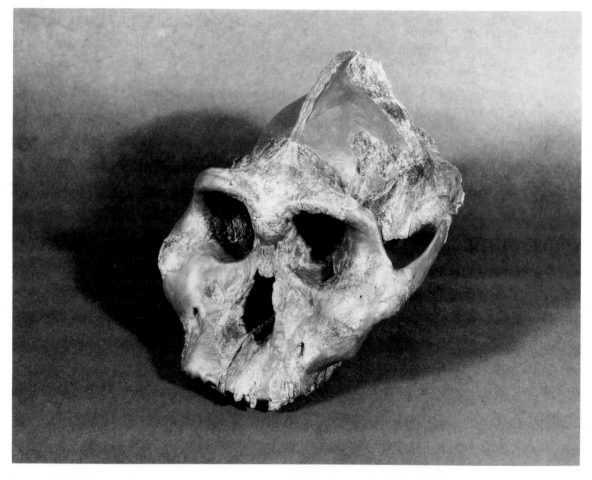

**Figure 9.10** *The Black Skull, possibly an ancestor of Zinjanthropus, showing a great degree of prognathism and the largest hominid sagittal crest.* (Alan Walker, © 1986 National Geographic Society)

time, the cranial capacity of the Black Skull is a mere 410 ml, smaller than the average for *A. afarensis*. Of course, we must be cautious in making generalizations from one specimen, which might not be typical of its population.

Supposing, however, that it is typical—that is, representative of a population with that set of traits—then we might have expected the Black Skull to be either older than *A. afarensis* because of its smaller brain or younger than *A. boisei* because of its extreme robusticity, the trend among the australopithecines seeming to have been toward increasing cranial and dental robustness. In fact, however, it is dated at 2.5 mya—a contemporary of late *A. africanus* and slightly before the first *A. robustus*.

So, can we put together *any* picture, even tentative, of the evolutionary relationships among the fossils from this period? Combining the

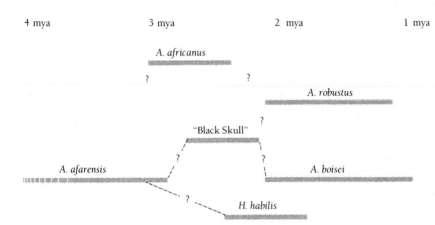

**Figure 9.11** *A generalized evolutionary bush of the early hominids. Question marks indicate lack of current consensus about relationships and times of divergence.*

known anatomical and geographical data, and following the principle of Occam's Razor to keep things simple, we see two lineages of australopithecines (small-brained bipedal primates) splitting from a common ancestor, *A. afarensis*. In southern Africa, there was evolution toward increasing cranial and dental robusticity, an adaptation to a tough vegetable diet. This is seen in the fossils of *A. robustus*. In eastern Africa, the robust theme is found in a more exaggerated form in *A. boisei*. The Black Skull, with its similarities to both the robust forms and to *afarensis*, may be considered a link between the earliest known hominids and the later robust australopithecines, at least the east African species. *A. africanus* presents a problem. There is no consensus about its place in hominid evolution. In light of its geographical location in southern Africa, however, it may most easily be considered as somehow related to the *afarensis–robustus* line. The *Homo* line (the larger-brained bipedal primates), which we'll discuss next, can, pending new evidence, most simply be seen as also branching from the common hominid ancestor, *afarensis*. Figure 9.11 diagrams what seems to be, at present, a reasonable *generalized* view of the first 3 million years of hominid evolution.

## THE BEGINNING OF THE GENUS *HOMO*

When the Leakeys found the fossil of Zinjanthropus in 1959, they also found simple stone tools in the same stratum. It seemed logical at first that "Zinj" was the toolmaker. Yet it began to bother them that so primitive a hominid could have been adept enough to make even such rudimentary items. Chimpanzees are known to make simple tools of branches, grass stems, and leaves, but the shapes of those natural resources may be thought of as suggesting the final tool and thus of mak-

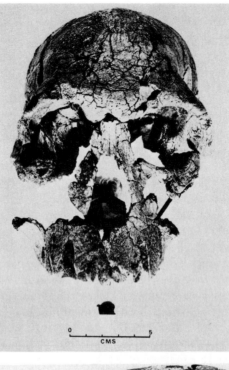

**Figure 9.12** *Front and side views of* Homo habilis *from Lake Turkana, Kenya. Note the flat face, smooth contours, lack of sagittal crest, and rounded braincase.* (National Museum of Kenya)

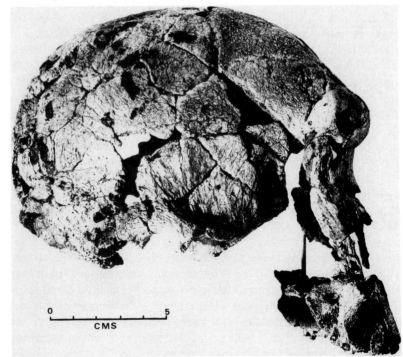

ing fairly obvious the modifications needed to get it. There is really nothing in a stone that immediately suggests either the tools that can be made from it or the method of manufacture. Chipping a stone tool requires the toolmaker to have a mental image of the tool within the stone and a concept about what process will produce the desired result. That is why the emergence of stone tools is so important.

The problem was apparently solved in 1961 when the Leakeys identified remains of still another type of hominid from over 2 mya. In fact, fragmentary fossils of this form had been uncovered back in 1959 but went unrecognized. It was different from *Australopithecus boisei*, and the differences indicated that it was not only a more likely candidate for toolmaker but also for the first member of genus *Homo*.

Remains classified as **Homo habilis** ("handy man") have been recovered from Tanzania, Kenya, Ethiopia, and perhaps southern Africa, dated from at least 2.2 mya to 1.5 mya (Figure 9.12). Although the face of *H. habilis* is smaller and a little less prognathous, in many respects *habilis* still resembles the australopithecines. The back teeth are large, although not as proportionately large as in *Australopithecus robustus*. In dentition, *H. habilis* more closely resembles *africanus*.

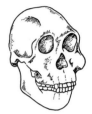

**Figure 9.13** *Comparison of cranial features of* Australopithecus *(top) with* Homo habilis.

Recently, the first postcranial remains that can definitely be associated with *H. habilis* were found (Johanson et al. 1987). They reveal the retention of the long arms of the australopithecines and the small body size of *Australopithecus afarensis*. Indeed, the partial skeleton of an adult *habilis* from Olduvai Gorge, dated 1.85 mya, is "as small as, or smaller than, any known fossil hominid" (Johanson et al. 1987:208).

Such similarities support those who consider *A. africanus* as a direct ancestor to *H. habilis*. There are even some who suggest that *habilis* is merely an "advanced" *africanus*. Still others, noting variation in cranial size of the *habilis* specimens, suggest that they represent more than one species. The arguments are complex, and the problem has yet to be resolved; but it seems clear (Johanson et al. 1987:209; Miller 1991) that at least most of the remains designated *habilis* are indeed members of a variable group that legitimately warrants a separate species category. The evidence for inclusion in genus *Homo* is brain size and the association with stone tool manufacture.

*H. habilis* has an average brain size of 680 ml, with a possible maximum of 800 ml. This is significantly larger than the brains of previous hominids and of other hominid lines living at the same time. Because from the neck down *habilis* was still like the australopithecines, it would appear as if a jump in brain size, rather than some overall evolutionary change, is what began our genus (Figure 9.13).

It would also appear that *H. habilis* was using those bigger brains for some behaviors that fall under our definition of culture. What can we discern, from the fossil and archaeological evidence, about the behavior of the hominids of this stage of our evolution?

**Table 9.2** *Archaeological Periods*

| Age | Division | Tool Types | Time Frame |
|---|---|---|---|
| Neolithic | | Ground stone | Begins ~12,000 ya |
| Paleolithic | Upper | Aurignacian | Begins 30,000 ya |
| | | Mousterian | Begins 130,000 ya |
| | Middle | Acheulean | Begins 1.5 mya |
| | Lower | Oldowan | Begins 2 mya |

## Lifestyles of the Short and Prognathous

It is easy to get lost in the maze of data about brain sizes, sagittal crests, and chewing muscles and to forget that the goal of paleoanthropology is to put together a picture of what our ancestors were like—what they looked like, how they behaved, what they did to survive.

Such a picture is really just beginning to emerge and, even now, there is no clear consensus, no single picture on which everyone agrees. We do, however, agree on some of the specific pieces of evidence, and the various interpretations seem to be narrowing down to provide us with at least a shadowy image of our remote ancestors.

We know, for example, that they made tools of stone. It seems reasonable that, before the manufacture of stone tools, the australopithecines were using wood and maybe bone and unmodified stone for tools. Many species *use* such natural objects as tools. Chimpanzees even *make* tools by modifying natural objects. Sea otters open abalone by hitting the shells against rocks, and Egyptian vultures drop rocks on ostrich eggs they otherwise could not crack.

But around 2.5 mya, some hominids began to modify stone and, as we noted, this seems to indicate a leap in conceptual ability—the imagining of a tool within the stone and of the means needed to make it.

Stone tools are so important to our understanding and reconstruction of human evolution that our evolutionary history has traditionally been divided into periods based on the types of stone tool technology found. These periods are summarized in Table 9.2. Although still used as general indicators of time periods and adaptive focuses, these terms were coined with reference to the prehistory of Europe and, by themselves, fail to capture the variation in times of appearance, in rates of change, in order of events, and in combinations of technologies, all of which typify human culture history.

The earliest stone tools are known as **Oldowan**, named after Olduvai Gorge. The Leakeys first identified Oldowan tools in the same stratum as Zinjanthropus at about 1.8 mya but later decided that *Homo habilis* was the toolmaker. This decision was based largely on the bigger brains

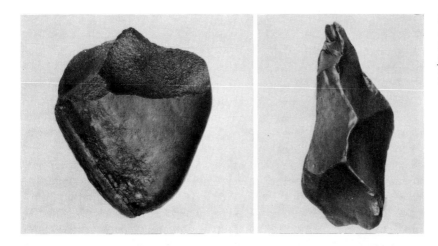

**Figure 9.14** *Oldowan tools:* (left) *a chopper with one face flaked;* (right) *side view of a bifacially flaked chopper.* (Courtesy F. E. Grine, SUNY, Stony Brook. Photograph by Chester Tarka)

of *H. habilis*; if one of the Olduvai hominids was the manufacturer, it seemed logical that it would be the one with the most developed brain. The inclusion of those fossils in *Homo* and their species name are based on this assumption, which, for all its circularity, does seem reasonable. No clear tools of any sort have been associated with the australopithecines. There are, however, Oldowan tools from Ethiopia dated at 2.5 mya, before any existing *habilis* remains. Some tools from southern Africa, dated at 1.8 mya, are claimed by some researchers to have possibly been made by *Australopithecus robustus*, whose finger bones have recently been interpreted as more modern than previously thought and thus more dexterous (Bower 1988b). The case of just who made the Oldowan tools is still open.

The most characteristic Oldowan tools are commonly called "pebble tools" or, Mary Leakey's term, "choppers," although they were doubtless used for numerous functions. These are water-smoothed cobbles, up to 3 or 4 inches across, that have been modified by knocking a few chips off one or two faces to make a sharp edge (Figure 9.14). The chips are called **flakes**, and the remaining tool a **core**. The flakes are taken off the core with an unmodified **hammerstone**.

Chopper tools may not appear at first much different from stones that have been broken naturally. Indeed, it is often difficult to tell naturally broken stones from those modified by humans. But even a tool as simple as a chopper shows a regularity in the flakes taken off that would not be found in nature—specifically, in the sharp angle created to make an edge. Moreover, when numerous such stones are found in the same location along with flakes and broken animal bones, it can be safely assumed that they are of human origin.

More common in the Oldowan "industry" than choppers are the flakes that resulted from their manufacture. These may themselves have been used as tools for finer work such as scraping skin off a carcass or

**Neolithic:** The "New Stone Age," characterized by domestic plants and animals.

**Paleolithic:** The "Old Stone Age," starting approximately 2 mya and ending when a society acquires domestication.

**Oldowan:** Tool technology associated with *Homo habilis*.

**flake:** A stone fragment removed from a core.

**core:** A stone that is shaped into a tool or serves as a source of flakes.

**hammerstone:** A stone used to strike a core to shape it or to remove flakes.

removing small portions of meat from a bone. They may even have been further modified to give them sharper cutting edges. There are also hammerstones, used in making the choppers and probably for other hammerlike tasks such as breaking open bones to extract protein-rich marrow. We know these unmodified stones are tools because they are found in places other than where they naturally occur. They were purposely carried from their place of origin and are thus referred to as **manuports**.

Even more intriguing than the Oldowan tools themselves is the fact that they are often found concentrated in an area in association with animal bones and numerous useless flakes left over from their manufacture. Such archaeological sites, called **living floors** or **occupation floors**, have long been thought to be places where early hominids gathered, made tools, butchered hunted animals, ate, and slept. In other words, they were presumed to have been home bases. Ten such sites have been identified at Olduvai Gorge from the *Homo habilis* period.

In support of the home-base interpretation is a 14-foot diameter ring of stones described at one of the Olduvai sites from 1.8 mya. Tools, flakes, and bones were found within the circle and even more were found outside it, including the remains of some large game animals. The inference has been that the stones served to support branches, which were somehow tied together and covered to produce a crude shelter (Leakey 1971).

The home-base interpretation implies a way of life for our ancestors similar to that of hunter–gatherer groups who have lived recently enough to be observed and described. Such people—the !Kung of the Kalahari, for example—set up true home bases that function as primary sites for social activity, tool manufacture, and the butchering and eating of hunted animals. Was *Homo habilis*, assuming they were the Oldowan toolmakers, behaving in a way analogous to modern peoples? Does the presence of big brains and stone tools with animal bones indicate that by 2 mya our ancestors were organized hunters with stable social relations and true living sites?

This was, until fairly recently, the accepted picture: "man the hunter," using an upright posture, a big brain, and a new-found technology to become a major force on the savannas of Africa. The hunter–gatherer way of life was thus seen as extending back to the very beginnings of our genus. As romantic as this image may be (especially to males), it appears to be incorrect.

Recent analysis (Binford 1985; Potts 1984; Shipman 1986b) has indicated that the Olduvai living floors were probably *not* home bases. They would have been dangerous places to stay for long periods, sleeping and caring for young, especially with parts of animal carcasses around. There are numerous predators and scavengers on the savannas even now, and there were even more during the time in question. More probably, suggests Richard Potts (1984), these were "stone cache" sites, where hominids left supplies of stones in order to have a choice of nearby places to take recently obtained animals for quick and fairly safe processing and maybe eating. Evidence seems to show that these sites were indeed used repeatedly for short periods rather than a few times for longer durations. The evidence for shelters, such as the stone ring, says Potts, probably represents the results of natural processes.

Analysis of the taphonomy of these sites shows that, far from hunting for the large animals they obtained, our ancestors were, as we discussed in the last chapter, scavenging for them—using the remains of game that died naturally or were killed by other predators. Lewis Binford (1985) has analyzed the types of bones found at Olduvai. They are predominantly lower leg bones of antelope-type creatures, bones that carry little meat and that, along with the skull, are about the only parts left after a large predator is finished feeding (Blumenschine 1986). Such bones, though, are rich in marrow, and that may explain the hammerstones and choppers; these tools were used to cut off what meat remained and to break open bones for marrow.

Pat Shipman's microscopic studies of cut marks supports this (1984, 1986b). She found that the tool-cut marks were not near joints, as they would be if a hunter had an entire carcass to disarticulate, but were on the shafts of bones, as they would be if pieces of meat were cut off. The majority of bones bearing such marks were bones that contain little meat but much marrow. As we discussed before, the hominid tool marks sometimes overlie carnivore tooth marks, indicating the carnivores were there first. Finally, microscopic observation of wear patterns on teeth (Shipman 1986b) shows that fruit made up a large portion of the diet of *Homo habilis*. It is the mark of a scavenger that alternate food sources are important for times when meat is unavailable.

It would seem, then, that we cannot envision even *Homo habilis* living like recent hunting and gathering peoples with semipermanent hunting camps, relying on meat hunted by the men and plants gathered by the women. Rather, we must picture small groups of hominids, eating largely fruits and other plants, who on occasion managed to obtain portions of big-game animals that died naturally or were leftovers from the meal of a carnivore. They took what pieces remained back to safe areas where they had made and stashed some tools, quickly processed and ate marrow and a little meat, and then continued their search for food or sought refuge, possibly—considering the evidence for the retention of long arms—in the trees. Indeed, Binford (1985) suggests that this was our way of life until we moved into temperate zones, where seasonal differences in the availability of plants may have promoted hunting, a more active method of obtaining protein.

Once again, we have an example of the error of assuming that a current situation can be extrapolated back in time to explain a past

**manuport**:  An object, usually stone, removed from its source by humans.

**living floor**:  A surface occupied by inhabitants of a site.

**occupation floor**:  Synonym for living floor.

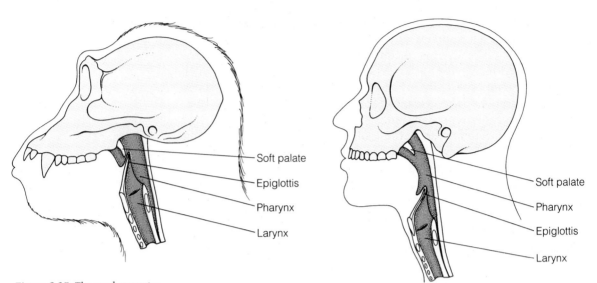

**Figure 9.15** *The vocal apparatus of a chimp* (left) *compared to a modern human's, showing features discussed in text.* (Redrawn and reprinted by permission of the Smithsonian Institution Press from Roger Lewin; *In the Age of Mankind: A Smithsonian Book of Human Evolution,* 1989: 181, Smithsonian Institution Press

condition. The presence of accumulations of stone tools and animal bones at Olduvai does not automatically indicate hunting, home bases, and complex social interaction, as it would for more recent humans. At the establishment of our lineage, its earliest members lived a very different lifestyle from any we previously imagined.

## The Question of Language

The chimpanzees we described in Chapter 6 support their lifestyle with a fairly complex communication system made up of a large number of calls, facial expressions, and body gestures. It is legitimate to ask whether our hominid ancestors had an even more complex system to support a more complex lifestyle with its inclusion of scavenging and the manufacture and use of stone tools.

This is a difficult question to answer. After all, speech itself is not like stone tools or animal bones. It is ephemeral; once spoken, it is gone, leaving no material evidence of its existence. Beyond this, virtually all anatomical features of an organism that relate to the ability to communicate orally are soft parts that do not preserve in the paleontological record.

So it would seem that we are only able to speculate on the origin and evolution of this basic, definitive human ability. Luckily, however, this is not quite the case. Those soft anatomical parts related to the human ability to speak—most notably the pharynx and larynx—are connected to hard parts that do preserve (Figure 9.15). The most important of these are the bones of the base of the skull, the **basicranium**. The form and positioning of the basicranium enable us to reconstruct, to a degree, the form and positioning of the soft parts. This, in turn, provides an indirect indication of whether a particular hominid species possessed a human ability to speak.

The question of the origin and evolution of speech has been the focus of several scientists (Crelin 1987; Laitman and Heimbach 1984; Leiberman 1984). Although there is some argument over details, they all agree on a number of fundamental points. Virtually all terrestrial mammals exhibit a flat skull base. Such a base accommodates a straight pharynx and a larynx positioned high up in the throat. Such positioning is advantageous in one sense; animals with such a configuration can breath and swallow at the same time, greatly diminishing the possibility of choking to death while eating or drinking. Human infants up to about 18 months of age possess this configuration and the attendant ability to nurse and breath simultaneously. This positioning of the pharynx and larynx, however, also diminishes the ability to produce sounds.

In the modern human adult, the basicranium is uniquely flexed. The rear of the skull base is, in comparison to a chimpanzee, for example, bent forward, in, and down. This produces a bend in the pharynx and pushes the larynx farther down in the throat. Computer models show that it is this anatomical conformation that enables the broad range of sounds and great speed that characterize human speech (Leiberman 1984).

Unfortunately, not enough remains of the basiacrania of *Homo habilis* specimens to allow for vocal tract reconstruction. The fossil evidence for *Australopithecus*, however, is clear in this regard. The cranial bases of australopithecine fossils are quite flat and indistinguishable, in fact, from the cranial bases of apes. This seems to indicate that *Australopithecus* could communicate through sound, but such sounds were likely more similar to the hoots and howls of chimps than the spoken language of human beings.

There is some evidence, on the other hand, that *H. habilis* possessed the capacity for spoken human language, if not the ability to produce all the sounds of modern languages. According to Phillip Tobias (1987), endocasts of *habilis* skulls show impressions of certain features of the brain that have, in modern humans, been associated with language production and comprehension. Selection in *habilis* for the beginnings of language of a modern type may have been underway as a response to that species' more complex adaptive behavior. We will return to the topic of language evolution in the following chapters.

**basicranium:** The bones of the base of the skull.

### The Environmental Factor

Two questions remain about the beginning of our lineage: Why did the common ancestor of all hominids (presumably *Australopithecus afarensis*) split into three separate lineages? Why did two of those lineages become extinct, somewhere around 1 mya?

You recall that a drying trend in Africa, caused by a drop in world temperature, is thought to be the initial impetus for the evolution of the hominids in the first place. About 5 mya, the earth warmed up for a while, but temperatures dropped once more around 2.5 mya (Vrba 1988). Once again the African forests declined, giving way to still larger areas of open woodland and arid savanna. The results of this climatic change are seen in the geological record and in the extinction of some species and the appearance of others. The hominids branched somewhere around this time, perhaps as a response to this environmental change. Separate populations of early hominids underwent different adaptive changes. The robust australopithecines became increasingly specialized to a diet of tough vegetables typical of open, arid regions. *Homo*, on the other hand, became more generalized, undergoing selection for an increase in brain size and the behavioral flexibility that accompanies it.

The same phenomenon may also help explain the extinction of the australopithecine lineages. Each hominid line represents an adaptive experiment, in this case three somewhat different approaches to survival in the open woodlands and savannas of eastern and southern Africa. Two of the experiments ultimately failed, not so much because they weren't as good as the other, but more because there simply wasn't enough room in that ecological niche for three upright, intelligent hominids. In this case, the one with the more generalized and flexible adaptive abilities—as evidenced by a larger brain and the presence of stone tools—prevailed by increasing its population and, in so doing, pushed its hominid relations into marginal areas to which their adaptations were insufficient. Direct and violent confrontation makes an intriguing image but probably had little to do with it. Ecological competition is enough to account for what happened. There is also evidence (Vrba, 1988) for still another temperature drop around 900,000 ya that may have been a contributing factor.

One more mystery surrounds the earliest recognized members of *Homo*: They were only around for a little over half a million years. Their appearance at 2.2 mya represents one evolutionary jump in brain size, but still another was to follow at 1.8 mya. These may represent two punctuations—two sudden changes given the chance to survive because of the rapidly changing conditions on the African plains. Or, future evidence may show a more gradual transition. At any rate, the fairly short-lived *Homo habilis* provides us with a preview of the long-lived, successful humans that were to come next.


## SUMMARY

The changing environment of Africa, which produced the hominid branch in the first place, nurtured a number of individual hominid twigs during the first three-quarters of our evolutionary history. These twigs can be divided into two general types. The australopithecines were small, upright primates who retained the brain size and, perhaps, some of the arboreal abilities of our pongid ancestors. They represent the common ancestor of all later hominids as well as at least two line-ages of specialized savanna vegetarians characterized by robust crania and teeth. These twigs were extinct by about 1 mya.

The second type was also small and, at first, also retained the long arms of the apes and early australopithecines. But this twig, the genus *Homo*, is defined by a new adaptive trend—an increase in brain size, which, as it turns out, afforded it an advantage in the ever-changing environs of the African plains. Although the first members of our genus still had brains only about half the size of the average modern human's, they were large and complex enough to allow their possessors, *Homo habilis*, to manufacture stone tools, an imaginative and technological leap in adaptive behavior. This set the stage for the next million years.


## KEY TERMS

| | |
|---|---|
| prognathism | hammerstone |
| Paleolithic | manuport |
| Neolithic | living floor |
| Oldowan | occupation floors |
| flake | basicranium |
| core | |


## FOR MORE INFORMATION

Donald Johanson and Maitland Edey's *Lucy*, Johanson and James Shreeve's *Lucy's Child*, the November 1985 issue of *National Geographic*, and Roger Lew-in's *Bones of Contention* are all good sources for information about this and other stages of human evolution. They also tell more about the story of the discoveries and the controversies.

For more on the "bushes vs. ladders" matter, see "Bushes and Ladders in Human Evolution" in Stephen Jay Gould's *Ever Since Darwin* and Gould's columns in the April, May, and June 1987 issues of *Natural History*.

On the evolution of language, see John McCrone's *The Ape That Spoke: Language and the Evolution of the Human Mind*.

# 10
# THE HUMAN LINEAGE EVOLVES

A swirling white powder cascades past the streetlights as a heavy snowfall blankets the campus in the third major storm of an exceptionally cold winter in southern New England. The weather forecast calls for continued snowfall into tomorrow with accumulations of more than a foot. This follows a period of about ten days when the temperature during the day did not exceed 10° Fahrenheit and commonly fell to more than −10° at night. Though by no means the coldest or snowiest part of the nation, winters in southern New England can be long and fierce. Winter is long but not unending. But it hasn't always been this way.

## THE COMING OF ICE: THE PLEISTOCENE

Beginning more than 1.5 million years ago (mya) and ending perhaps 10,000 years ago (ya), the earth was, at times, substantially colder than it is today. For reasons that are still debated, the cycle of seasons was disrupted, and large areas of our planet's surface were covered with ice. We call this period of time the **Pleistocene Epoch**.

It may have come about as a result of a decrease in heat put out by the sun. It may have been precipitated by interplanetary dust blocking out a portion of the sun's radiation to all the planets. It could have been caused by a substantial increase in volcanic activity here on earth, with

**Figure 10.1** *Hubbard Glacier in Alaska meets the sea at Disenchantment Bay* (right). *Note the person at lower left for scale.* (Jan Roletto)

material spewed out by volcanoes blocking the warming rays of the sun. It may have been initiated by a change in the geometry of the earth's orbit, resulting not in a change in the total amount of solar heat reaching our planet but merely its distribution. The ultimate reasons have never been determined.

Though initially regarded as an "Ice Age," the Pleistocene was actually a climatologically complex period with several extremely cold episodes separated by a number of phases with average temperatures as warm or even warmer than today. Geologists and **paleoclimatologists** have established that eight or nine distinct cold periods separated by warmer spells occurred during the last 780,000 years of the Pleistocene (Shackleton and Opdyke 1973). An additional ten cold phases separated by warmer periods may have characterized world climate between 780,000 ya and 1.6 mya (Bowen 1979).

During these cold phases, some of them lasting tens of thousands of years, worldwide temperature dropped, and ice and snow accumulated in higher elevations and northern latitudes. As these ice fields grew in size—hundreds of meters to several kilometers in thickness—internal pressures forced the ice to move in frozen rivers and great ice sheets called **glaciers** (Figure 10.1). These glaciers covered many higher elevations in the world, much of Canada and the northern United States, Europe, and part of Asia (Bradley 1985; Flint 1971; Figure 10.2). Nonglaciated parts of the world, the tropics and subtropics, also underwent climate changes, experiencing generally cooler summers and wetter winters. The coasts of the continents were redrawn as sea level dropped as much as 125 meters, a result of the tying up of so much of the planet's water in land-based glaciers.

The periods during which world ice cover expanded are called **glacials** or **glacial periods**. The times between the glacials, when the glaciers receded and temperature warmed up, are called **interglacials**. The glacials themselves were made up of shorter, colder periods called **stadials** and warmer periods called **interstadials**. Although some paleoclimatologists contend that the cycle of glacials and interglacials, stadials and interstadials ended about 10,000 ya, others are not so sure. It is believed by many that we are merely in an interglacial remission, with another glacial period certain to follow.

The precise sequence of glacials and interglacials is difficult to study on land because ice advances are discontinuous events and each subsequent movement of ice obliterates much, if not all, of the evidence of previous glacial expansions. The stratigraphy of the ocean floor, however, provides a more or less continuous column of sediment for the entire Pleistocene. We cannot directly study glacial deposits underwater, but we can examine an indirect effect of ice expansion and meltoff— the ratio of two isotopes of oxygen, $^{16}O$ and $^{18}O$, in seawater. The oxygen isotope curve derived by Nicholas Shackleton and Neil Opdyke (1973)

**Pleistocene Epoch:** The geological time period, from 1.5 mya to 10,000 ya characterized by a series of glacial advances and retreats.

**paleoclimatologist:** A specialist in ancient climatic conditions.

**glacier:** A massive body of ice that can move and expand.

**glacials:** Synonym for glacial periods.

**glacial periods:** Phases of Pleistocene glacial expansion.

**interglacial:** A period between glacial advances.

**stadial:** A short period of rapid glacial advance and extreme cold.

**interstadial:** A short period of glacial retreat during a longer phase of glacial advance.

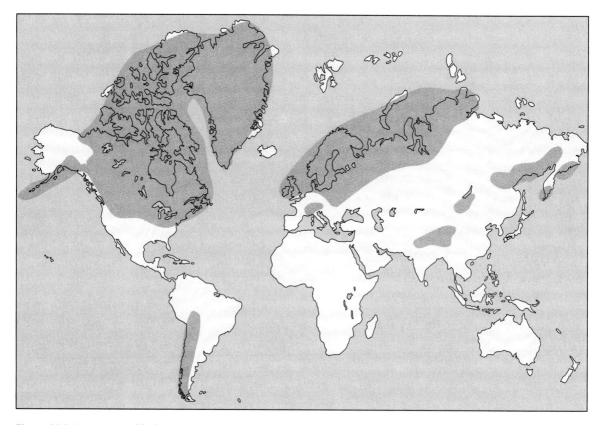

**Figure 10.2** *Maximum worldwide glacial expansion during the Pleistocene. The Antarctic ice cover, not shown here, also expanded during this epoch.* (Data compiled from Bowen 1978; Bradley 1985; and Flint 1971)

and discussed in Chapter 7 provides us with a sequence that can be interpreted as representing changes in the quantity of water evaporating from the oceans and then either returning or being concentrated on land in ice fields. This, in turn, can be construed as a chronology of glacial expansion on land—the greater the relative concentration of $^{18}O$ in seawater, the colder the worldwide temperature and the greater the extent of ice cover. The resulting curve gives a fairly detailed picture of climate change during at least the last 780,000 years of the Pleistocene (Figure 10.3).

Beyond this, the Pleistocene is commonly divided into three sections. The beginning of the Pleistocene, about 1.5 mya to 780,000 ya, when the earth's magnetic field shifted, is called the **Lower Pleistocene** (this used to be dated at 730,000 B. P., but recent redating of the shift using a more precise dating method has resulted in the new date)(Montastersky 1992); 780,000 to 200,000 ya, the **Middle Pleistocene**; and 200,000 to 10,000 ya, the **Upper Pleistocene**.

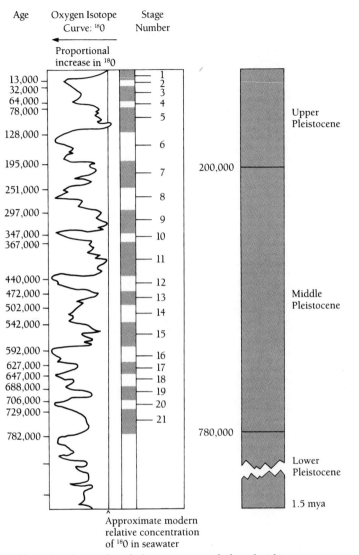

Age | Oxygen Isotope Curve: ¹⁸O | Stage Number

**Figure 10.3** *Pleistocene glacial chronology based on the oxygen isotope ratio in seawater as derived from foraminifera in Pacific core V28-238.* (Data compiled from Shackleton and Opdyke 1973).

Odd numbered stages (in color) = warmer periods, less glacial ice cover
Even-numbered stages = colder periods, more glacial ice cover

## HOMINIDS OF THE PLEISTOCENE

A little before the time we designate as the beginning of the Pleistocene Epoch, a hominid species more modern in appearance than *Homo habilis* emerged in Africa (Figure 10.4). We call this species *Homo erectus*. Although there are many continuities between *H. habilis* and *H. erectus*,

**Lower Pleistocene:** Part of the Pleistocene from 1.5 mya to 780,000 ya.

**Middle Pleistocene:** Part of the Pleistocene from 780,000 ya to 200,000 ya.

**Upper Pleistocene:** Part of the Pleistocene from 200,000 ya to 10,000 ya.

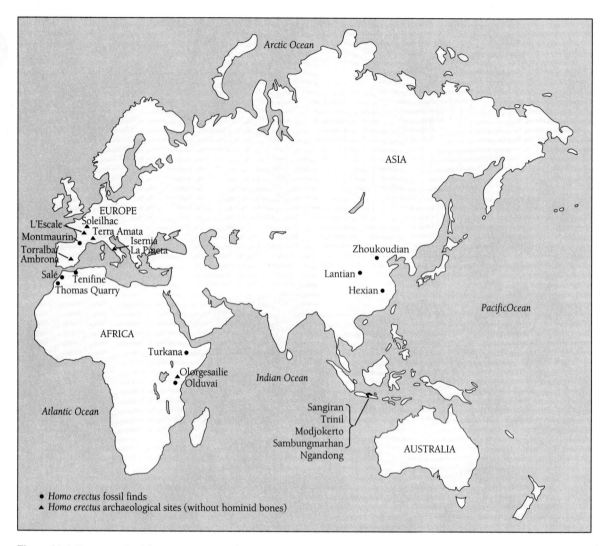

**Figure 10.4** H. erectus *fossil localities and archaeological sites.*

this new species (Figure 10.5) was distinctly different (Rightmire 1990; Wood 1984).

The typical *H. erectus* skull is long and low, with large brow ridges, a sharply angled **occipital** with a marked **torus**, a robust, prognathic face, and a sagittal keel—a long ridge of bone running the length of the top of the skull from front to back. At a shade under 1000 ml (two-thirds of the modern human mean of 1450 ml), the mean cranial capacity of *erectus* is significantly greater than that of *H. habilis*, calculated at 680 ml. Larger specimens fall within the lower limit of modern human crania. The range for *erectus* cranial capacity falls between 750 and 1250 ml (Table 10.1).

It is important to point out that the *H. erectus* skull was not just a larger version of that of *H. habilis*. After all, *erectus* was a larger creature than *habilis*, and at least part of the increase in skull size—and, therefore brain size—can be attributed simply to an increase in body size. The *erectus* skull, however, is differently proportioned, reflecting the differential growth of specific parts of the brain, especially the frontal and posterior portions (Wolpoff 1980a). The front of the *erectus* skull is higher and the back more rounded than *habilis*. The brain of *erectus*, then, was not just an enlarged *habilis* brain but qualitatively different and more similar to the modern form. The implication is that the intelligence of *erectus* was also more evolved.

Differences in the architecture of the *H. erectus* skull when compared with that of *H. habilis* are also significant. These changes reflect evolutionary alterations in areas of muscle attachment and may reflect the response to selective pressures resulting from behavioral changes. Specifically, areas of muscle attachment at the base and back (occiput) of the skull are significantly larger in *erectus*, with a bone ridge (the nuchal torus) being prominent. These changes imply a great increase in neck muscle size and strength over that of *habilis*. This development has been attributed to selection for stronger necks and jaws as a result of increased use of the mouth as a "third hand" in tool use (Wolpoff 1980a:178).

Even the *H. erectus* nose, as indicated by the preserved nasal bones, was more modern in appearance than that of *H. habilis*. *H. erectus* was our first hominid ancestor with the typically human projecting nose, an adaptation, apparently, for moisture conservation in arid environments (Franciscus and Trinkaus 1988).

Below the neck, the *H. erectus* skeleton is, in many ways, quite modern in appearance. On the whole, they appear to have been relatively short, stocky, and powerfully built, although more recent discoveries may indicate regional differences in body build. The bones of the arms and legs, the pelvis and vertebrae, and the hands and feet are similar to those of modern humans, with a few exceptions. For example, their femurs have quite thick shaft walls and are flattened, characteristics that indicate muscularity and great strength. Despite the differences, however, we can infer that their ability to walk upright and manipulate objects with their hands was virtually indistinguishable from that of modern humans.

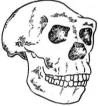

**Figure 10.5** *Comparison of cranial features of* Australopithecus (top) *with* Homo habilis (middle) *and* Homo erectus (bottom).

## Africa

The oldest known *Homo erectus* fossil is a nearly complete cranium found by Richard Leakey in 1975 on the east shore of Lake Turkana in Kenya (Leakey and Walker 1985a; Figure 10.6). The skull, designated

**occipital:** The rear portion of the skull.

**torus:** A continuous ridge of bone.

**Table 10.1** *Overview of* Homo erectus *Fossils*

| Country | Locality | Fossils | Crania | Age | Brain Size (ml) |
|---|---|---|---|---|---|
| Java | Trinil | Skull cap, femur | "Java Man" | <1 million years | 940 |
| | Sangiran | Cranial and post- | S-2 | <1 million years | 800 |
| | | cranial fragments | S-4 | <1 million years | 900 |
| | | from about 40 individuals | S-10 | <1 million years | 850 |
| | | | S-12 | <1 million years | 1050 |
| | | | S-17 | <1 million years | 1000 |
| | Ngandong | Cranial and post- | N-1 | <1 million years | 1170 |
| | | cranial fragments | N-6 | <1 million years | 1250 |
| | | from more than a dozen | N-11 | <1 million years | 1230 |
| | | individuals | N-12 | <1 million years | 1090 |
| | Sambungmachan | Cranial fragment | Sambungmachan | <1 million years | 1000 |
| | Modjokerto | Fragmentary remains of a child | | | |
| China | Zhoukoudian | Cranial and post- | II | <.5 million years | 1030 |
| | | cranial remains of | III | <5 million years | 915 |
| | | more than 40 individuals | VI | <.5 million years | 850 |
| | | | X | <.5 million years | 1225 |
| | | | XI | <.5 million years | 1015 |
| | | | XII | <.5 million years | 1030 |
| | Hexian (Lontandong) | Partial skull | "Hexian Man" | <.5 million years | 1000 |
| | Lantian (Gongwangling) | Cranial fragments, Mandible | "Lantian Man" | .7–.8 million years | 800 |
| Tanzania | Olduvai | Cranial and post- | OH 9 | 1.25 million years | 1060 |
| | | cranial fragments including mandibles and pelvis and long-bone fragments | OH 12 | .6–.8 million years | 700–800 |
| Kenya | East Turkana | Cranial and post- | KNM-ER 3733 | 1.78 million years | 850 |
| | | cranial fragments including mandibles and pelvis and long-bone fragments | KNM-ER 3883 | 1.57 million years | 800 |
| | West Turkana | Nearly complete juvenile individual | KNM-WT 15000 | 1.6 million years | 900 |
| Algeria | Ternifine | Three mandibles and a skull fragment | | .5–.7 million years | |
| Morocco | Thomas Quarries | Mandible and skull fragments | | .5 million years | |
| | Sidi Abderrahman | Two mandible fragments | | | |
| | Salé | Skull fragments | Salé | .4 million | 880 |
| | | | | *Mean* | 984.79 |
| | | | | *Standard Deviation* | 138.05 |

Data from Day (1988); Feibel et al. (1989); Holloway (1980, 1981); Rightmire (1990).

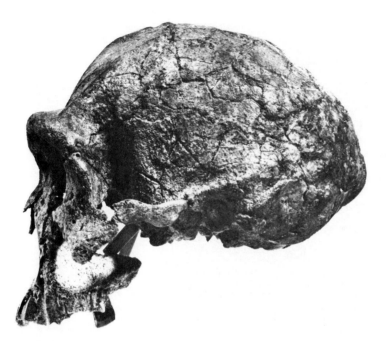

**Figure 10.6** *The skull of fossil ER 3733 from the area around Lake Turkana, Kenya, appears to be that of a female. Its cranial capacity is estimated to have been about 850 ml.* (National Museums of Kenya)

ER 3733, with its jutting brow ridges, distinct sagittal keel, small face, and 850-ml cranial volume, is now estimated to be 1.78 million years old (Feibel et al. 1989). A similar but less complete skull (ER 3883), dating to 1.57 mya, was also found by the Leakey team on the east shore of the lake. Although its cranial capacity is about the same as that of ER 3733, it appears to be more ruggedly constructed. It has been suggested that ER 3883 is a male and 3733 is a female.

Several other cranial fragments that reflect the morphology of *H. erectus* have been found on the east shore of the lake. Also found here and dating to the same period have been a few fragmentary mandibles and bits of leg and pelvic bones (Day 1971).

On the west side of Lake Turkana, the Leakey team found a remarkably complete specimen (KNM-WT-15000; Figure 10.7) that included most of the skull, the jaw, some ribs, most of the vertebrae, the right shoulder blade and forearm, the complete pelvis, and elements of both legs (Leakey and Walker 1985b). The skeleton was found on a volcanic deposit dated 1.6 mya; it is believed that this fossil is probably also about that old.

The fossil is that of a 12-year-old boy, as determined by tooth eruption and the shape of the pelvis. The skeleton is essentially modern in appearance from the neck down, but the proportions of the upper part of the femur or thigh bone are slightly unlike that of either modern or more ancient hominids. The exact significance of this difference is unclear, although it seems not to imply any major difference between his ability to walk and that of modern humans (Lewin 1984).

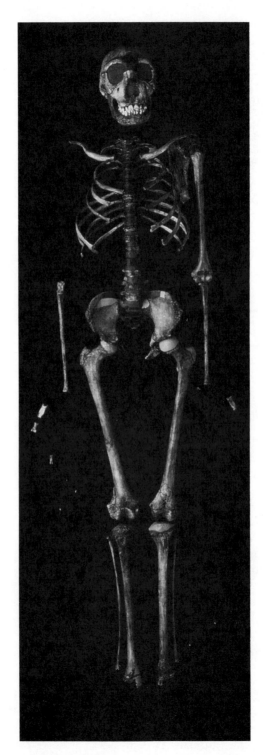

**Figure 10.7** *The skeleton of the 12-year-old boy from the west shore of Lake Turkana in Kenya (fossil KNM-WT 15000) is the most complete specimen of* Homo erectus *yet discovered.* (David L. Brill, © National Geographic Society, National Museums of Kenya)

Although we commonly picture previous hominid species as smaller than modern humans, this boy was already close to $5\frac{1}{2}$ feet tall and might have attained a height of 6 feet had he survived to adulthood. Although we cannot be certain of the growth curve for *H. erectus*, the appearance of the skeleton is that of a physically immature, still growing individual. None of his epiphyses had yet fused, the cranial sutures were also all unfused, and his teeth were those of a modern human 12-year-old (Brown et al. 1985).

The fact that this individual was 12 years old and still growing has significant evolutionary implications. We humans begin life at a rather immature stage of fetal development. This may have resulted from the evolution of our larger brains and anatomical changes in the shape of the pelvis necessitated by the evolution of upright walking. If we were born at the more advanced level of development of some of the other primates, our heads would be too large to pass through our mothers' birth canals, which are restricted in size as a result of the evolution of bipedalism. It is estimated that, in a sense, we are born three months "prematurely" when compared with the level of development of the great apes (Trinkaus 1983a).

Beyond this, even after birth, we develop slowly. In most other animal species, a 12-year-old individual would be a fully grown, physically mature adult. Yet we know that this is certainly not the case for modern humans, and it seems not to have been so for *H. erectus*, either.

Why do we have such a long period of immaturity, and what are the implications of a similarly long developmental phase for *H. erectus*? Although it is difficult to point to any one cause for this phenomenon, it is clear that a long physical maturation period—in other words, a long childhood—provides more time for young individuals to learn what they need to know to become successful adults. Remember, the major adaptational strategies of our species are cultural, and culture must be learned. The more complex the knowledge that needs to be mastered, the longer the period needed for such learning. The physical immaturity of KNM-WT-15000 may be evidence of selection for a longer period of development to allow for the mastery of sophisticated cultural skills. Moreover, a longer period of dependence contributes to a stronger social bond between offspring and their parents than that seen in other species. We can speculate that *H. erectus* may have shared this characteristic with modern humans.

A few younger *H. erectus* fossils have been found in Olduvai Gorge in Tanzania (Rightmire 1979a). Dating to about 1.25 mya, OH 9 is a partially preserved brain case with an estimated cranial capacity of more than 1000 ml (Figure 10.8). OH 9, although larger, is similar in its anatomical details to ER 3733. OH 12, found nearby and estimated to be between 600,000 to 800,000 years old, consists of several cranial fragments. Although quite small and less complete, it is clear that OH

**Figure 10.8** *The OH 9 cranium, thought to be more than 1.1 million years old, is similar in appearance to ER 3733 but has a somewhat larger cranial capacity (1000 ml).*
(Courtesy G. P. Rightmire)

12 is another *erectus*, with an estimated cranial capacity of between 700 to 800 ml. OH 28 consists of a pelvic fragment and part of a femur. Although slightly different from the modern human configuration, together they reinforce the notion that *erectus* was completely bipedal (Day 1988).

Even more recent are the skull fragments and three mandibles from Ternifine, Algeria, and the mandible and skull fragments from Thomas Quarry, the two mandible fragments from Sidi Abderrahman, and the braincase from Salé, all from Morocco. The Ternifine material is dated to more than 500,000 ya and as much as 700,000 ya. The fossils from Thomas Quarry are probably a bit younger. The fossils from Salé and Sidi Abderrahman have not been reliably dated.

## Out of Africa: Hominid Radiation

All the fossil hominids discussed up to this point were discovered in Africa, for an obvious reason: Africa was home to the species that gave rise to the hominid line. Apparently, for a few million years after the ape–hominid split, our ancestors did not expand beyond that continent. The first hominids and the species from whom they developed were physically adapted to life in the warm climate of Africa. The first evolutionary steps of our hominid ancestors were taken in Africa. The evolution of our pattern of upright walking, the initial expansion of our brain case, the beginnings of tool use and manufacture all took place on that continent. All the australopithecines as well as *Homo habilis* were African species. And, as we have just shown, the earliest examples of the next hominid, *Homo erectus*, are all found in Africa.

Remember, however, that humans are culture-bearing animals. Our culture more than our biology is our means of adaptation. And as hominids evolved and their cultures became more complex, their ability to adapt to new environments and circumstances also grew. It is members

**Figure 10.9** *The "Java Man" skull-cap was the first known specimen of what we now call* Homo erectus. *It was discovered by a Dutch physician, Eugene Dubois, near the town of Trinil on the island of Java.* (Rijks Museum of Natural History, Leiden)

of the species *H. erectus* who, for the first time in the history of hominid evolution, were able to expand beyond the confines of the African continent to populate Europe and Asia. Whether a result of population increase, climate change, or merely the search for food, we call this geographic expansion **hominid radiation**.

### Homo Erectus in Asia and Europe

**Java**   The first recognized discovery of what we now call *Homo erectus* was made by a Dutch physician, Eugene Dubois. Serving in the military in the Dutch colony of Java, Dubois set out to unearth the story of human evolution. There, in 1891, along the Solo River near the village of Trinil, workmen found the top of a skull at a depth of close to 50 feet. The skull was small by modern standards, flat, with large brow ridges (Figure 10.9). Some distance away, a completely modern-looking diseased human femur was found. Dubois felt certain that the skull and femur belonged together and represented a link in evolution between apes and humans. He called the specimen *Pithecanthropus erectus*—the upright ape-man.

The skull from Trinil has an estimated cranial capacity of about 900 ml and shows the array of typical *H. erectus* features. The femur allegedly belonging to "Java Man" has had its association with the skull disputed, although at this point such a connection is not crucial because we have femurs of other *erectus* fossils and they are largely modern in appearance. Absolute dating of volcanic material from the area has been confusing. At this point, it is safe to say only that all of the *erectus* fossils on Java are less than 1 million years old (Rightmire 1990:14) and some may be much less (Bartstra et al. 1987).

Since 1937 a number of *H. erectus* fossils have been recovered 40 miles west of Trinil. The site at Sangiran has yielded the cranial remains of about forty individuals. Those crania that can be reconstructed with

**hominid radiation:**   The expansion of the hominids out of Africa, beginning about 1 mya.

**Figure 10.10** *The Sangiran 17 cranium is the best preserved of several* Homo erectus *specimens discovered about 40 miles west of Trinil on the island of Java.* (R. Holloway)

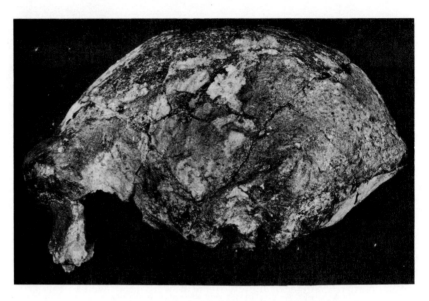

some degree of confidence (Sangiran 2, 4, 10, 12, and 17) clearly belong to *erectus* (Holloway 1981). The most complete skull, Sangiran 17, has thick, arching brow ridges; a sharply angled occiput; a distinct sagittal keel; and a long, low vault (Figure 10.10). In most of its characteristics, Sangiran 17 and the others are similar to the African and other Asian specimens. Their cranial capacities range from about 800 to 1000 ml. The fossils are probably 700,000 to 800,000 years old.

Northeast of Trinil, on the Solo River, is the locality of Ngandong where the crania of about a dozen individuals were found in the 1930s. With a mean of about 1185 ml, their cranial volumes fall at the upper range for *H. erectus*, leading some to suggest that they might represent a later hominid line (Wolpoff et al. 1984). Beyond this, dating the material excavated more than sixty years ago has been a problem. (Bartstra et al. 1987). Nevertheless, cranial **endocasts** (Holloway 1980) and a recent, detailed analysis (Rightmire 1990) show that, despite their great size, the proportions as well as the anatomical details of the Ngandong crania place them firmly in the species *erectus*. Other Javanese sites where more evidence of the presence of *erectus* has been found include Sambungmachan (a skull) and Modjokerto (the fragmentary remains of a child).

**China.** Beginning in the 1920s, a large sample of *Homo erectus* fossils representing as many as forty individuals was unearthed in a cave at Zhoukoudian, outside of Beijing, China (Shapiro 1974). Interestingly, the cave was seen initially as a good place to verify the discovery at Piltdown, and some of the scientists present there were also involved in the Zhoukoudian excavations.

Sadly, the spectacular collection of the so-called "Peking Man" fossils was lost during World War II when U. S. marines, attempting to take the fossils out of China, were captured by Japanese troops. The entire assemblage of fossils may very well have been destroyed, although stories have occasionally surfaced that all or some of the fossils are in the possession of the Japanese government, museums on Taiwan, or even widows of the captured marines. A long, sustained effort to track down the fossils, including the offer of a substantial reward and the promise of immunity from prosecution, has resulted in a few interesting leads but little of substance (Janus 1975).

Although the fossils themselves were lost, they were in the possession of scientists long enough for the most important measurements to be taken and casts to have been made. The fossil assemblage consisted of 6 nearly complete skulls, 12 other skull fragments, 15 pieces of lower jaws, 157 teeth and a few fragments of the postcranial skeleton (pieces of femur, humerus, tibia, ulna, and lunate, a bone in the wrist; Wu and Lin 1983).

Although the number of postcranial bones was small, we can summarize that H. erectus at Zhoukoudian was short and stockily built, with males averaging just over 5 feet in height and females a few inches shorter. Their arms were relatively longer than in modern humans, and their shoulders were broad. The average capacity of the Zhoukoudian crania is just under 1100 ml. Their faces were broad, their brow ridges thick, and their skulls displayed the sagittal keeling so common in their species (Figure 10.11). Recent uranium series dating of the fossil-bearing strata in the cave indicates that it was first occupied by erectus 460,000 ya, with subsequent use of the cave until about 230,000 ya (Wu and Lin 1983).

Just as with some of the Homo habilis sites in Africa, the Zhoukoudian site was interpreted for many years as a home-base habitation for wandering hunters. It was even suggested that these hominids practiced ritual cannibalism; the bases and faces of most of the skulls recovered at Zhoukoudian were broken as if shattered to provide access to the brains.

This view has recently been questioned (Binford and Chuan 1985; Binford and Stone 1986). The skulls of Zhoukoudian H. erectus were indeed broken into, but in a manner that is now understood to be typical of carnivorous animals. Closer examination of the faunal assemblage shows tool marks on relatively few of the animal bones and plenty of evidence of carnivore tooth marks on both the animal and hominid remains. One of the species showing the greatest proportion of tool-cut marks was the horse, but even here only 11 percent of the horse bones

**endocast:** A natural or artificial cast of the interior of a skull.

**Figure 10.11** *A replica of one of the famous "Peking Man" skulls lost during World War II.* (Courtesy Department Library Services, American Museum of Natural History, neg. no. 315446, photo: Charles H. Coles)

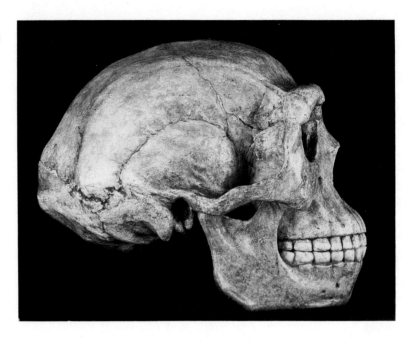

show evidence of butchering with stone tools (Binford and Stone 1986:468). Many of the horse mandibles show tool-cut marks, and this seems to be best explained as the scavenging by hominids of undesirable anatomical parts left by carnivores. In a very small sample of animal bones (four), tool marks overlay teeth marks, clearly indicating that meat-eating animals got at the meat first.

The presence of stone tools is indisputable evidence that *H. erectus* used the cave at Zhoukoudian. It is likely, however, that most of the hominid and animal remains were brought into the cave by carnivores returning to their lairs with prey. Those bones that display hominid activity indicate scavenging, not hunting. Although Zhoukoudian should still be considered an enormously significant hominid fossil locality, it appears not to represent a long-term Middle Pleistocene village site.

The sites of Lantian (Gongwangling) and Hexian (Lontandong) have also yielded significant remains of *H. erectus* in China. The Lantian specimen consists of the top of a skull, including the brow ridges, and fragments of the upper and lower jaw. The cranial capacity has been estimated at 800 ml. The skull is probably about 700,000 to 800,000 years old (Woo 1966). The Hexian fossils (at least two individuals are represented) are probably younger, perhaps 250,000 to 500,000 years old and therefore generally contemporary with the Zhoukoudian fossils. The skulls are, as are all other *erectus* crania, low-vaulted, flat, angled to the rear, and possessed of enormous brow ridges. Cranial capacity has been estimated at 1000 ml (Wu 1985).

Outside of Africa and Asia, no indisputable *H. erectus* fossil remains are known; in fact, there are no European hominid remains dating to before the Middle Pleistocene (Cook et al. 1982).

There are, however, some Middle Pleistocene age sites in Europe where artifacts have been found. One of the oldest of these sites is Isernia La Pineta in central Italy. Here a stone tool industry of limestone choppers and unmodified flint flakes was found in association with the remains of bison, deer, elephant, rhinoceros, and hippopotamus (Coltorti et al. 1982). The site was found under a volcanic deposit K/Ar-dated to 730,000 ya. At Soleilhac in France, possibly the oldest site in Europe, artifacts and faunal remains have been dated to 800,000 ya (Weaver 1985). At present, however, there does not appear to have been a substantial *H. erectus* presence in Europe.

## THE BRAIN OF *HOMO ERECTUS*

Although the brains of ancient hominids have not been preserved, the containers that held them sometimes have. The inside surfaces of skulls often bear evidence of the external appearance of the brains they housed. The skull is not a dead, inert vessel but a living part of an organism. It is made of living bone that reacts with the material it is in contact with, whether that be muscle, arteries, or brain tissue.

In the case of some fossil crania, endocasts have been created naturally when fine sediments filled in the skull as the brain decayed. These sediments then fossilized, leaving a model in stone of the prehistoric brain. Where natural endocasts did not form, they can still be made artificially by pouring or painting liquid latex into the interior of the skull, producing a general model of the inside surface and therefore a model of at least the major features of the exterior surface of the ancient brain.

Ralph Holloway (1980, 1981) has produced a series of endocasts for the Ngandong and Sangiran *Homo erectus* fossil skulls from Java and compared them with endocasts made from the skulls of gorillas, chimpanzees, orangutans, and forty prehistoric hominid fossil crania, including australopithecines and, *Homo habilis, erectus,* and *sapiens* (Figure 10.12).

Holloway notes some interesting similarities between the endocasts of the brains of *H. erectus* and modern *H. sapiens.* The *erectus* endocasts show that the brains of this species were asymmetrical. Although some asymmetry is present in the brains of apes, the human brain is asymmetrical to a much greater degree. This asymmetry is caused by the hemispheric specialization of our brains; because the two halves of our

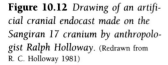

**Figure 10.12** *Drawing of an artificial cranial endocast made on the Sangiran 17 cranium by anthropologist Ralph Holloway.* (Redrawn from R. C. Holloway 1981)

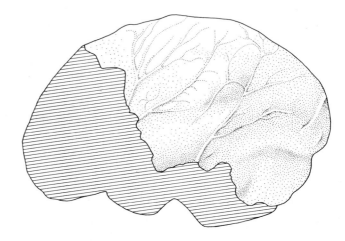

brains perform different functions, they look a bit different. For example, in general our left hemispheres house our abilities for language and symbol utilization, whereas our right hemispheres control spatial-visual manipulation, as in hand–eye coordination.

The same kinds and degree of asymmetry of the brain seen in modern humans and visible in endocasts made from modern human skulls is apparent in the endocasts made from the Sangiran and Ngandong crania as well as the African skulls labeled ER 3733, ER 3883, and OH 9. From this evidence, we can directly infer that *H. erectus* possessed a level of hemispheric specialization of the brain similar to that of modern humans. The fascinating though indirect inference that Holloway makes is that linguistic skills and the ability to manipulate symbols, along with a level of hand–eye coordination similar to, or at least approaching, that of modern humans, were present more than 1.7 mya in *erectus*. Although the scientific jury is still out on this suggestion, Holloway's is an extremely interesting approach that will probably make a major contribution to our understanding of the intellectual abilities of extinct hominids. At the least, we can be certain that the brain of *erectus* resembled ours in some very specific ways.

Although Holloway's approach hints at the ability of speech, *H. erectus* cranial anatomy lends further support for this interesting hypothesis. As mentioned previously (Chapter 9), **basicranial** anatomy can be used to reconstruct the vocal tracts of prehistoric hominids. Australopithecine basicrania, as mentioned, are quite similar in their architecture to those of modern apes, and, therefore, they likely could not speak. The extant fossil record indicates that *erectus* basicranial anatomy, on the other hand, was quite different, far more like the modern form (Laitman and Heimbach 1984). Researcher Jeffrey Laitman (as quoted in Bower 1989c:25) compares *erectus* basicrania—and, by inference, their vocal tract anatomy and their ability to produce humanlike speech—to that of a 6-year-old human child. Anyone who has listened to a group of first-graders knows the range—as well as the volume and rapidity—of the speech of which they are capable. Although some of the anatomical details certainly were different, such research indicates that *erectus* may have been capable of some level of humanlike speech.

## BEHAVIORAL INNOVATIONS OF *HOMO ERECTUS*

The greater intellect of *Homo erectus* certainly allowed for the elaboration of culture and innovations in behavior. There is a good deal of debate, however, on how this is reflected in the archaeological record. We will look at four important areas of such possible innovation: tool manufacture, the controlled use of fire, construction of dwellings, and cooperative hunting.

### Stone Tools

The essentials of the stone tool tradition practiced by the precursors of *Homo erectus* were continued by them. Simple chopping tools created by the removal of a relatively small number of flakes from a stone cobble are present at many *H. erectus* sites. A new, more sophisticated toolmaking tradition, however, was developed by *erectus*. Called **Acheulian** after the site of St. Acheul in France where it was first identified (though the tradition is actually older in Africa), it involved an elaboration upon the removal of a few flakes. The end result is called a **hand axe**: a symmetrical, edged, pointed tool, flaked on both sides or faces (Figure 10.13). Hand axes were probably all-purpose tools for piercing animal flesh, butchering, hide scraping, wood cutting, root digging—a sort of Swiss Army rock of the Middle Pleistocene. They may even have served as projectiles, thrown like a discus (O'Brien 1984).

Experimental archaeologist Mark Newcomer (1971) has made replicas of Acheulian hand axes in an attempt to understand the processes by which they were made. In one attempt, he was able to produce a hand axe weighing 230 grams from a stone nodule of around 3 kilograms. In the production of this one hand axe, 51 large and potentially usable flakes were also produced, as were more than 4500 smaller waste pieces.

From this and other experiments, Newcomer concluded that the manufacture of a hand axe probably progressed in three stages: First, a rough form was produced from a nodule of stone by striking it directly with a stone hammer. Next, the rough blank was thinned and shaped by percussion with a softer tool, perhaps an antler. Finally, the tool would

**basicranial**: Referring to the base of the skull.

**Acheulian**: The toolmaking tradition of *H. erectus,* including hand axes, cleavers, and flake tools.

**hand axe**: A bifacial, symmetrical all-purpose tool first produced by *H. erectus.*

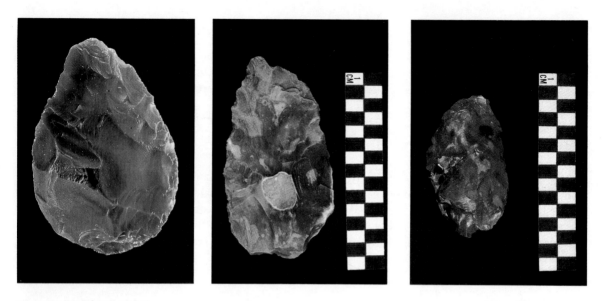

**Figure 10.13** *Bifacially flaked symmetrical hand axes, produced by* Homo erectus *beginning 1.5 mya, represent an advance in stone tool technology over the Oldowan tradition. This popular tool has been found in a variety of sizes and showing varying degrees of quality.*

have been finished, again with a soft hammer, straightening the edge of the axe and producing the final, symmetrical shape.

The hand axe certainly shows more forethought, greater skill, and more utility in its design and manufacture than the Oldowan chopper. It is a more sophisticated tool and represents a great technological advance over the ability of previous hominids. That the Acheulian tradition of toolmaking evolved from the Oldowan, however, seems clear. Oldowan choppers from Sterkfontein in Africa were well enough made to resemble crude hand axes.

*H. erectus* also made cleavers with a straight, sharp edge. (The hand axe, in contrast, had a point.) Along with these core tools—both hand axes and cleavers were shaped cores of stone—*erectus* also used flake tools (Figure 10.14). Stone flakes removed from a core in the process of making hand axes or cleavers were often used, without further modification, for cutting, scraping, or piercing animal flesh as well as for cutting or scraping plant material, including wood. Some flakes were themselves worked to produce a desired shape or cutting edge.

The hand axe tradition began in Africa about 1.5 mya and continued for all of the Middle Pleistocene and lasted even into the Upper Pleistocene. It spread into Europe after its invention in Africa.

Hand axes are often absent from *H. erectus* sites in East Asia like Zhoukoudian or Sangiran. When they are found at East Asian sites, they never dominate the stone tool assemblage. Instead, in Asia there is a tradition of making choppers from stone nodules by removing flakes from one side and chopping tools with flakes removed from both sides of the stone core.

CHOPPER

SCRAPERS

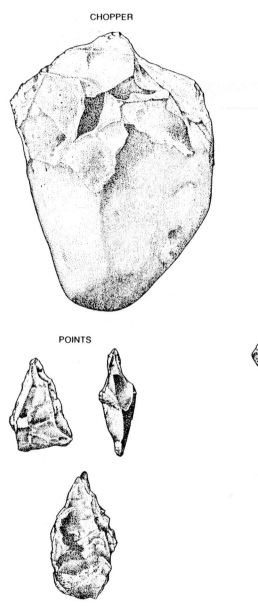

POINTS

BURIN

**Figure 10.14** *Flake tools associated with* Homo erectus *from the cave at Zhoukoudian.* (Drawings by Patricia J. Wynne from Wu Rukang and Lin Shenglong, "Peking Man" *Scientific American,* June, 1983:92)

## Quest for Fire

We have seen that the end of the Lower and the beginning of the Middle Pleistocene marks the period of hominid expansion beyond the African homeland. The presence of *Homo erectus* outside of Africa was made possible not by any change in the physical adaptations of our ancestors but through cultural innovation. Among the most significant of these innovations may have been the controlled use of fire. Although there is some possible evidence for the controlled use of fire by *H. erectus* perhaps as much as 1.5 mya in Africa (James 1989; Sillen and Brain 1990) and 750,000 ya at the French cave of L'Éscale, the earliest confirmation of the control of fire comes from Zhoukoudian in China and is dated to after 500,000 B.P. (Binford and Chuan 1985; Binford and Stone 1986).

The ability to control fire is extremely significant. Fire provides heat, which may have helped our tropically adapted ancestors to survive in the inhospitably cold climate of Pleistocene Europe and Asia. Fire can provide protection from animals, and it can be used in cooking, which makes more of the nutrition present in meat available to our digestive systems.

Perhaps just as significantly, says science writer John Pfeiffer (1969), fire extends the day. We are—and our ancestors were—a visually oriented species. *H. erectus*, like us, depended on vision for most sensory input, yet like us did not see very well in the dark. The light produced by the fires of *erectus* allowed for an increase in the number of hours during which they could interact and create.

Residues of million- or half-million-year-old fireplaces, however, are not so easy to distinguish from other, natural phenomena. Even the evidence for fire at Zhoukoudian, long thought to be definitive, has been questioned at least in part by Lewis Binford and Kun Ho Chuan (1985) and Binford and Nancy Stone (1986), who remind researchers that indisputable hearths have not been found in the cave. Instead, large deposits of supposed ash have been interpreted as the result of hominid-controlled fires. Binford and Chuan point out, however, that these so-called ash deposits are not generally found in the same strata as the tools and hominid remains. Some of the animal bones found in the ash deposits appear to have been mineralized, not burned. Finally, they have reidentified much of the so-called ash as more likely to have been owl (or other bird) droppings. Though Binford and Stone agree that fire belonged in the cultural repertoire of *H. erectus*, they maintain that the evidence, at least in Zhoukoudian, occurs late in the sequence.

We can only conclude that *H. erectus* almost certainly used fire as part of an adaptation to the colder regions of the earth, but that much more research needs to be conducted to determine with any certainty how long ago and where this occurred.

### Construction of Dwellings

The geology of Terra Amata in southern France indicates that the site was occupied perhaps as much as 400,000 and certainly before 200,000 ya. Here, it is asserted, a population of hominids built what are some of the oldest known shelters in the world (de Lumley 1969, 1975).

Based on the presence of a few fireplaces, presumed decayed wooden posts, and the distribution of artifacts and organic debris, it was suggested by the excavator Henri de Lumley that the *Homo erectus* inhabitants of Terra Amata built oval structures measuring between 7 to 15 meters in length by 4 to 6 meters in width. It was suggested that a number of saplings or branches a few inches in diameter were driven into the ground, bent together on top, and somehow connected. In this reconstruction, stones were placed around these stakes to help support the walls; and larger wooden poles were erected inside, probably to serve as roof supports. This is much like the original and now discounted interpretation for the stone ring at Olduvai.

On the floors of all of the supposed huts discovered at Terra Amata were the remains of hearths with stone windscreens around them. Littering the floors of the huts were tools, stone flakes resulting from the manufacture of tools, and the bones of the animals perhaps eaten by the inhabitants, including those of an extinct species of elephant, wild boar, stag, ibex, wild ox, and rhinoceros. Although meat was apparently a significant part of the diet of the inhabitants of the site, they also collected shellfish and fished in the nearby Mediterranean. Again, we have the image of a home-base village, this time with actual structures, where people returned again and again.

This scenario, however, depends on the archaeological "integrity" of the site. The assumption is that natural processes have not acted to disturb the spatial contexts of the archaeological material over a period of more than 200,000 years and perhaps twice that long. Recent research by archaeologist Paola Villa (1982), however, calls into question how intact the site really was and renders questionable the suggestion of a Middle Pleistocene village of huts on the Mediterranean.

Villa shows that there has been substantial postdepositional movement of artifacts at Terra Amata. Fragments of stone that could be put together again, particularly cores and the flakes from those cores, were recovered from what were defined by the excavators as different stratigraphic layers. In fact, 40 percent of the pieces that could be joined back together were found in different levels. In one case, four flakes and the core they all were derived from had been vertically separated by as much as 40 centimeters. On this basis, Villa characterizes detailed reconstruction of prehistoric life at Terra Amata as being "largely speculative" (1982:285). The reality of huts at Terra Amata is therefore questionable, as is the image of a *H. erectus* home-base village on the Mediterranean.

**Cooperative Hunters or Opportunistic Scavengers?**

The sites of Torralba and Ambrona in Spain, Olorgesailie in Kenya, and Olduvai BK II in Tanzania, dating perhaps to at least 400,000 ya, are associated with the artifacts of *Homo erectus*. They have been interpreted by some as seasonal camps where groups of related individuals came together perhaps on a yearly basis to hunt, socialize, and exchange information. At these sites, according to some, we see the earliest evidence of cooperative hunting associated with our hominid ancestors.

Torralba and Ambrona are two hills flanking a major pass in the Guadarama Mountains of Spain and a natural migration route for people and animals. The remains of at least fifty prehistoric elephants, twenty-six horses, twenty-five deer, ten wild cattle, and six rhinoceros have been excavated. It has been suggested that they represent perhaps as many as ten separate cooperative *H. erectus* hunts (Butzer 1971, 1982; Howell 1966). The animals may have been stampeded into swampy, boggy traps where, mired, they could be killed and butchered by *erectus* hunters. There is even the suggestion that the animals were stampeded and directed to the wetlands by the use of fire.

At the BK II locality at Olduvai Gorge, groups of wild cattle were also thought to have been driven into a swamp, where they were then killed and butchered by *H. erectus*.

Olorgesailie is a site in Kenya where baboons may have been cooperatively hunted by a *H. erectus* population living west of a large lake (Isaac 1977). Recent K/Ar dating of the site indicates that it may be more than 700,000 and as much as 900,000 years old (Bower 1987b). More than sixty individuals of a now-extinct baboon species have been discovered. All around the bones were large, unmodified, round cobbles that Isaac believes were used as weapons thrown by the hominids. Other stone tools, used in butchering the animals, were also found. In Isaac's reconstruction, the hominids surrounded the baboons in their tree roosts, forced them to flee by throwing rocks at them, and clubbed them to death as they attempted to escape. Next, the animals would have been butchered and their bones cracked open to extract the nutrient-rich marrow inside. A more recent excavation at the same site has revealed possible evidence of an elephant kill. The bones of a now-extinct elephant species were discovered surrounded by hand axes, and there appear to be tool marks on some of the bones (Bower 1987a).

If the interpretation of hunting provided here is correct, we can infer a high level of knowledge, cooperation, and coordination among hominids living several hundred thousand years ago. The *H. erectus* hunters of the Middle Pleistocene would have had to possess a sophisticated understanding of animal behavior, they would have had to know migration and herding schedules and patterns, and they would have needed to be familiar with different animal reactions to a threat. The level of cooperation and coordination of activity necessary for such hunts at Torralba and Ambrona, Olduvai BK II, and Olorgesailie implies an ability to communicate, delegate responsibilities, divide labor, and possibly even distribute results of a successful hunt.

Based on our discussion of the possible similarity of the brain of *H. erectus* to ours, such a reconstruction, though remarkable, is cer-

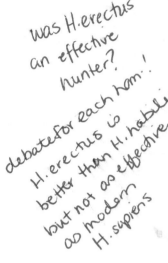
was H. erectus an effective hunter? debate for each hom. H. erectus is better than H. habilis but not as effective as modern H. sapiens

tainly not out of the question. Recent careful investigation of the **taphonomy** of these alleged *erectus* kill sites, however, has called the cooperative hunting scenario into serious question (Binford 1981; Shipman and Rose 1983). In the case of Torralba and Ambrona, for example, it must be stated that the animal bones were found in an area where carnivorous animals were likely to have been active. Very few indisputable tools were found in association with the bones.

One way of determining human activity at these sites involves the search for cut marks on animal bones. The question here is, "Are there marks made by stone tools present on animal bones found at these sites?"

In an analysis of approximately 3000 bones from Torralba and Ambrona, Pat Shipman and Jennie Rose (1983) determined that over 95 percent of the specimens were so heavily damaged they could not be used in the search for cut marks. In fact, they maintain that the great majority of marks on the Torralba and Ambrona bones previously identified as cut marks are merely the scratches left by soil abrasion and root growth. Of the 55 specimens intact enough for analysis, a scanning electron microscope revealed only sixteen stone tool cut marks on 14 bones (1983:467), and these show no pattern that could be interpreted as systematic butchering (Figure 10.15). Shipman and Rose also found very little evidence of animal tooth marks, indicating that carnivores,

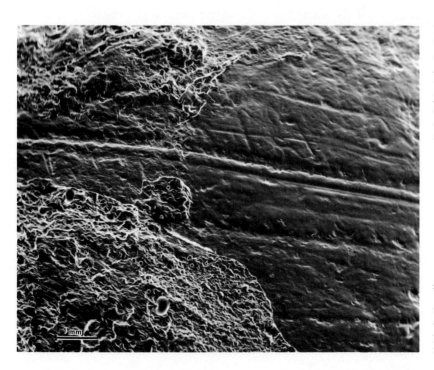

**Figure 10.15** *Scanning electron microscope photograph of cut marks on an elephant bone recovered at Ambrona, Spain. These longitudinal marks made by stone tools 400,000 ya are some of the few bits of evidence that indicate the butchering of animals by Homo erectus at this site.* (Pat Shipman and Academic Press)

**taphonomy:** The study of how organisms become part of the paleontological or archaeological record.

including scavengers, also cannot be shown to have played a major role in producing the assemblage.

Although it is impossible to determine whether the rest of the bones had been cut with stone tools, it would seem at best that *H. erectus* was present at Torralba and Ambrona and cut some meat off of animal carcasses there. The site, however, cannot be used to support a hypothesis of big-game hunting for *erectus*.

Our understanding of the cultural capabilities and achievements of *H. erectus* is in flux. As with *Homo habilis*, projecting modern hunting—gatherer analogues into the past to explain *erectus* settlement and subsistence, though once popular, now seems to be unwarranted. The evidence can no longer be interpreted as supporting their construction of dwellings at home bases or cooperative hunting—though it should also be said that the evidence does not necessarily disprove that this group of hominids possessed these adaptations, either. They almost certainly scavenged animal meat where they could. They may have hunted, although probably not big game and not habitually. They probably gathered wild plant foods where they could. They used fire, and they may have built shelters.

Whatever the case, *H. erectus* was an enormously successful hominid. Simply the fact that *erectus* was able to expand into Asia and Europe shows the ability of this group of hominids. They lasted as a species for more than 1 million years. That their adaptations do not mirror those of modern humans is to be expected. Only more research will enable us to understand the nature of those adaptations more completely.

## CONTINUITY AND CHANGE IN *HOMO ERECTUS*

Although it would be an exaggeration to say that if you've seen one *Homo erectus* you've seen them all, there is, nevertheless, a fair degree of homogeneity in these fossils across both space and time. *H. erectus* fossils in Africa, Asia, and Europe, though certainly exhibiting some degree of regional variation, are quite similar. As G. Philip Rightmire (1990) shows, comparisons of *erectus* specimens widely separate in time and space denote a great degree of similarity—for example, OH 9 from Tanzania and Sangiran 17 from Java, or KNM-ER 3733 from Kenya and Sangiran 2 from Java. Beyond this, the oldest specimens from Africa dating to more than 1.7 mya do not look so different from Asian examples dated to more than 1 million years later. As Rightmire maintains in his synthesis of the *erectus* evidence, although the fossils come from an enormously broad geographical as well as temporal range, all are "built on a common plan" (1990:190). The evolutionary bush of our lineage, with several twigs sticking out previously, seems to have been pruned back to a single, stable branch during this period.

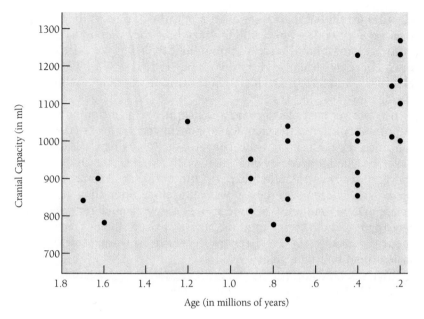

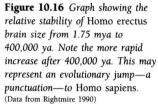

**Figure 10.16** *Graph showing the relative stability of* Homo erectus *brain size from 1.75 mya to 400,000 ya. Note the more rapid increase after 400,000 ya. This may represent an evolutionary jump—a punctuation—to* Homo sapiens. (Data from Rightmire 1990)

Regular anatomical change through time appears to be relatively minor in *H. erectus*. The posterior teeth decrease in size, and there is a similar decrease in the size of the structures of the face and lower jaw, which supported the muscles needed to use those back teeth (Wolpoff 1980b). At the same time, the incisors of *erectus* increase in size through time. Many other features such as bone thickness in the skull and limbs remain constant, however, and the size, position, and proportions of the sagittal keel, nuchal torus, and supraorbital torus as well as the size and proportions of the limbs remain fairly constant through time or at least show no consistent pattern of change.

Even as important a feature as brain size seems to exhibit relative temporal stability. Rightmire (1985) has shown that there is a measurable but surprisingly weak pattern of increase in *H. erectus* brain size from their initial appearance in the Lower Pleistocene right through the entire Middle Pleistocene (Figure 10.16). He estimates this weak pattern of growth at about 180 ml per 1 million years (1990:196). As Rightmire quickly points out, however, the sample size in this analysis is quite small—just twenty-six crania—and in some cases the precise dating of crania is uncertain. For example, the very large Ngandong crania confound this analysis because they cannot be firmly dated. If you eliminate these five crania, the overall cranial growth rate drops substantially to only about 120 ml per 1 million years—a figure that is not statistically significant. If the Ngandong specimens are quite recent—younger than 500,000 years—they indeed serve to verify a general and significant trend of increasing brain size through time. If they are relatively ancient—closer to 1 million years old—they support a deduction of no pattern of brain increase throughout the tenure of *erectus*. Other researchers, in particular Milford Wolpoff (1980b, 1984), J. E. Cronin et al. (1981), and Steven Leigh (1992) argue for the former, Rightmire for the latter.

It is not yet possible to come to a definitive conclusion on this very important point, but the technical argument concerning "statistical significance" is, perhaps, not the crucial issue for us here. However the data are manipulated, even if the exhibited increase in brain size through time was an authentic trend and not just an artifact of incomplete data, its tempo, certainly, was quite slow. After all, a 180-ml increase over a 1-million-year time span is not very much (an 18 percent increment). The increase from the *Homo habilis* to the *H. erectus* mean capacity was about 300 ml (a 44 percent increase)—and this occurred in less than half that time.

The *H. erectus* toolkit also seems to exhibit temporal stability. Hand axes vary little over the course of more than 1 million years. Flake tools also exhibit stability. In their reexamination of the Zhoukoudian material, Binford and Chuan see little change over more than 200,000 years of use of the cave. In fact, they state: "We can see no evidence that the form and composition of the tool assemblage is changing at any greater rate than the anatomy of the hominids themselves" (1985:429).

On the other hand, it should be added that the toolkit is not entirely static, and hand axes become more symmetrical and their edges straighter in later specimens. Similarly, there appear to be a greater number of distinct flake tool forms at later *H. erectus* sites. Nonetheless, here too, although change clearly took place, the overall impression is one of stability.

In contrast to this, as Rightmire points out, beginning about, or shortly after, 400,000 ya, fossil hominids in Africa and Europe exhibit a noticeable increase in cranial capacity. This brain size expansion after 400,000 ya might be interpreted as representing a punctuation in hominid evolution after a long period of equilibrium. Again, however, the sample size is quite small.

Such a hypothesis would be supported if features other than brain size exhibited this same jump toward a more modern appearance. The fossil hominid record is rarely simple, however. As we will see, other anatomical characteristics of these new hominids, such as cranial bone thickness, brow ridge size, occipital form, postcranial robustness, and even the shape of their skulls are highly variable, and many show no great leap toward modern forms. Some characteristics of some of the skulls seem no more modern than those of many *H. erectus* specimens, others seem to be intermediate in form, and still others seem even to be more primitive—that is, less modern—than the same features in *erec-*

*tus.* Such complexities, though frustrating, make the story all the more intriguing.

Regardless of other features found in the hominids that followed *H. erectus,* the apparently rapid increase in cranial capacity, based on our admittedly small sample of fossil crania that date to this period, has led to the hypothesis that at least some of the post–400,000-year-old fossil hominids represent a new species. At least in terms of their brain size, they are so much closer to us than *Homo erectus* that we call the new species *Homo sapiens.*

## SUMMARY

In Africa, beginning sometime about 1.8 mya, a hominid appeared with a more modern cranial architecture than *Homo habilis* and a cranial capacity about 44 percent larger; at a bit under 1000 ml, it approaches two-thirds of the modern human mean brain size (1450 ml). The species exhibiting this rapid increase in cranial capacity is called *Homo erectus.*

From East Africa, there are a number of well-preserved crania and the nearly complete skeleton of a young boy, all dating to the period between 1.78 and 1.57 mya. The skeleton of the boy shows that he was physically immature at his death at around 12 years of age. This is evidence for the beginning of the typically human pattern of delayed maturation of children, beginning with the birth of large-brained, relatively undeveloped babies, and providing for the time necessary for imparting the cultural adaptation.

*H. erectus* was the first of our ancestors to have expanded its range beyond Africa. Fossils exhibiting typical *erectus* morphology have been found in Indonesia on the island of Java, dating to after 1 mya and China after 800,000 ya. The famous site of Zhoukoudian is located near the modern city of Beijing and dates to after 500,000 ya. Forty or more individuals were found in the cave, located in an area with a climate very different from the tropical and subtropical home of the species. Evidence at Zhoukoudian and elsewhere indicates that it was culture—including the use of fire, at least toward the end of its existence—that enabled *erectus* to survive in areas with cold climates.

Over its tenure of more than 1 million years, *H. erectus* seems to have been a remarkably stable species with only a very weak pattern of cranial capacity increase. Other features of *erectus* anatomy are also quite stable, exhibiting a very modern human appearance from their first occurrence in the archaeological record more than 1.7 mya. It is not until about 400,000 ya that brain size appears to surge again, and *erectus* is replaced by a more modern-appearing fossil form: archaic *Homo sapiens.*

## KEY TERMS

| | | |
|---|---|---|
| Pleistocene Epoch | interstadial | hominid radiation |
| paleoclimatologist | Lower Pleistocene | endocast |
| glacier | Middle Pleistocene | basicranial |
| glacials | Upper Pleistocene | Acheulian |
| glacial periods | occipital | hand axe |
| interglacial | torus | taphonomy |
| stadial | | |

## FOR MORE INFORMATION

The November 1985 issue of *National Geographic* provides information on some of the more recent *Homo erectus* discoveries (Weaver 1985). An informative although somewhat dated presentation of the *H. erectus* evidence is provided in the volume *The First Men* in the Time-Life series, *The Emergence of Man*; the artwork is appealing (The Editors of Time-Life 1973). The most thorough and recent synthesis of *erectus* can be found in G. Philip Rightmire's *The Evolution of Homo erectus: Comparative Anatomical Studies of an Extinct Human Species*. The discussion is detailed and enormously informative.

# 11
# ON THE ORIGIN OF OUR SPECIES

We have journeyed a great distance in our story of human antiquity. Beginning with a creature that appears to have been little more than an ape that walked on two feet (*Austra-lopithecus*), we have traced the human saga through a species with an expanded braincase and the ability to make and manipulate stone tools (*Homo habilis*). They were not apes, but they certainly were not *us* either. We then continued the tale with the discussion of a creature (*Homo erectus*) with a braincase expanded to two-thirds of the modern human mean and whose reliance on culture, a product of its increased intelligence, allowed it to expand beyond Africa for the first time. We can easily recognize, in its appearance as well as its abilities, the developing humanity of *Homo erectus*. Yet here too, its "otherness"—its alienness—is apparent. *Homo erectus*, like *Homo habilis* before it, is familiar to us, but, again, it is not us.

Finally, in this chapter, we confront the "man in the mirror." To be sure, it is not an exact match, for we do not see our precise image. Nevertheless, the face looking back at us is so familiar we can call this creature by the human name: genus *Homo*, species *sapiens*.

## "ARCHAIC" *HOMO SAPIENS*

**Figure 11.1** *Fignal localities of archaic* Homo sapiens. *(excluding Neandertals).*

We saw in the last chapter that the evolutionary bush had been pruned from at least three, highly variable twigs—*Australopithecus africanus/ robustus, Australopithecus boisei,* and *Homo habilis*—to a single, rather homogeneous species, *Homo erectus*. About 400,000 years ago (ya),

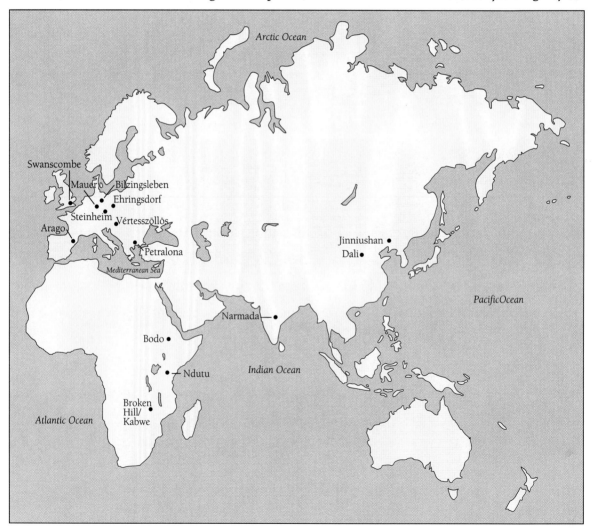

however, our evolutionary bush branched again after a punctuational event. In other words, the single twig of *H. erectus* seems to have sprouted a new twig. We call the fossils who made up this twig on the evolutionary bush *Homo sapiens* (Figure 11.1). As mentioned, although they are classified as belonging to the same species as all modern human beings, they were not exactly like us. To distinguish them from anatomically modern humans, many characterize them as **archaic *Homo sapiens***, whereas some assign them to various nonmodern subspecies. One of the later populations of these archaic humans, the Neandertals, are probably the best known and have generated the greatest amount of controversy.

Remember our discussion of biological nomenclature in Chapter 5: Calling a fossil species *Homo sapiens* is not an arbitrary act. It means we believe the species was so similar to our own that it shares all our biological designations—it lived, in other words, at practically the same evolutionary address as we do. Technically, modern people are *Homo sapiens sapiens*—the second *sapiens* designating our subspecies. Subspecies designations are based on even finer distinctions than the species label. There is only one recognized human subspecies today and, as we will see in Chapter 13, all people belong in it. The archaics, on the other hand, are thought to represent an ancient and extinct subspecies—or several subspecies—of the human species. According to the rules of biological nomenclature, all the different groups of people alive today, no matter how different their appearances, are more similar to each other than any of us are to these extinct members of our species.

As mentioned at the end of the last chapter, the one consistent difference between the archaics and *H. erectus* in general is the larger cranial capacities and, therefore, bigger brains of the archaics. The mean cranial capacity of a small sample (nine) of preserved braincases of archaic *H. sapiens* (not including the Neandertals, to be discussed separately) is just over 1220 ml (Rightmire 1985; Table 11.1). Compare that to the mean for *erectus*, about 1000 ml—a 22 percent increase over a very short period. Just as in the comparison between the skulls of *H. habilis* and *erectus*, however, the brains of the archaic *sapiens* were not just larger than those of previous hominids, but they appear to reflect a different arrangement, with greater similarity to modern humans.

Continuing the same trend seen in the comparison of *H. habilis* and *H. erectus* cranial morphology, the brains of the archaics were differently proportioned than those of earlier hominids, with a greater emphasis on the front or forebrain, and a resulting higher forehead, although the latter is not nearly as steep as in modern humans. The size of the face, relative to the rest of the head, is reduced; and the overall degree of prognathism is less than in *erectus*. The bones that make up their skulls, at least in some of the archaics, are thinner than in older fossils and more similar to modern humans with our quite thin cranial bones. In some specimens, the brow ridges, although still spectacular by

**Table 11.1** Archaic *Homo Sapiens* in the Late Middle Pleistocene

| Country | Locality | Fossils | Age | Brain Size (in ml) |
|---------|----------|---------|-----|--------------------|
| Germany | Steinheim<br>Bilzinsleben<br>Ehringsdorf<br>Mauer | Cranium<br>Cranial fragments<br>Cranial fragment<br>Mandible | 200,000–240,000<br>228,000<br>225,000<br><450,000 | 1200 |
| England | Swanscombe | Occipital cranium | 225,000 | 1300 |
| Greece | Petralona | Cranium | 160,000–240,000 | 1230 |
| France | Arago | Cranium and fragmentary remains of seven individuals | 250,000 | 1200 |
| Hungary | Vértesszölös | Occipital fragment | 200,000 | 1250 |
| Zambia | Kabwe (Broken Hill) | Cranium, additional cranial, and post-cranial remains of several individuals | 125,000 | 1280 |
| Tanzania | Ndutu (Olduvai) | Cranium | >200,000 | 1100 |
| Ethiopia | Bodo | Cranium | 200,000–400,000 | |
| South Africa | Elandsfontein | Cranium | | |
| India | Nardama | Cranium | | 1300 |
| China | Yingkou | Nearly complete skeleton | 250,000 | |
| | Dali | Cranium | 250,000 | 1200 |
| | | | Mean | 1222.86 |
| Data from Day (1988) and Rightmire (1990). | | | Standard Deviation | 66.01 |

modern standards and as clearly defined as in *erectus*, do not dominate the face to the degree seen in earlier hominids. The **postorbital constriction**, so prominent in *erectus*, is greatly diminished. This is a result of the expansion of the front of the braincase to accommodate the increasing size of the frontal part of the brain (Figure 11.2).

The archaic members of our species are a varied lot. They share in common a brain larger than that of *H. erectus*, and within the normal human range. Beyond that there seems to be quite a bit more variation than that seen in *erectus*. Several famous fossils show these contrasts clearly.

## Steinheim

In 1933 the cranium of an archaic *Homo sapiens* was found in a gravel pit adjacent to the Murr River, in the town of Steinheim, just north of Stuttgart, Germany (Howell 1960; Figure 11.3). The skull was found along with the fossil remains of several extinct species, including straight-tusked elephant, wild ox, cave bear, and cave lion. The gravel bed in which the hominid skull was found was probably laid down at the end of an interglacial or the beginning of a glacial stage. We know that the straight-tusked elephant was adapted to life in woodlands. This suggests an interglacial or relatively mild early glacial rather than a full-blown glacial period. Although dating of the skull has been problematic, a recent electron spin resonance date indicates that it is probably between 200,000 and 240,000 years old (Ikeya 1982). No artifacts were found with the hominid remains.

The skull is long and relatively narrow. Although the brow ridges are substantial, they are smaller than in most *Homo erectus* specimens. The face is flat and rather small, as in modern humans. There is no occipital torus, giving the rear of the skull a modern appearance. The bone of the skull is thinner than in *H. erectus* but thicker than in modern humans. The cranial capacity has been estimated at just below 1200 ml, toward the small end of the modern human range but large for *erectus*.

## Swanscombe

Another probable example of archaic *Homo sapiens* was found in Swanscombe, England, in 1935 (Howell 1960; Ovey 1964). The Swanscombe find includes three major skull fragments: the back (**occipital**) and both sides (**parietals**). Remarkably, the three fragments that fit together so perfectly were found over a period of more than twenty years and were located as much as 50 feet away from each other.

The base of the skull as well as the face was missing, so it is difficult, if not impossible, to judge brow ridge size or the degree of prognathism. What was recovered of the skull, however, is informative. The bone itself is quite thick, as in older specimens. Additionally, in a detailed analysis of seventeen cranial measurements (Weiner and Campbell 1964), it was concluded that in many respects the skull is quite similar to *Homo erectus*.

A few of the characteristics of the Swanscombe skull, though, are more modern. As in Steinheim, the occiput shows little sign of a torus.

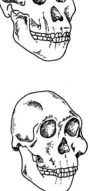

**Figure 11.2** *Comparison of cranial features of* Australopithecus *(top) with* Homo habilis, Homo erectus, *and archaic* Homo sapiens.

**postorbital constriction:** A narrowing of the skull behind the eyes as viewed from above.

**occipital:** The rear of the skull.

**parietals:** The bones of the sides and top of the skull.

**Figure 11.3** *The nearly intact cranium of an archaic* Homo sapiens *from Steinheim, Germany. Note the more rounded appearance of the skull and the higher forehead than in* Homo erectus. *However, also note the large brow ridges.* (State Museum for Nature, Stuttgart, Germany)

Beyond this, the skull is quite large, with an estimated cranial capacity of over 1300 ml. This places the brain size of "Swanscombe Man" well within the modern human range, though, it must be said, its general appearance is a mosaic of primitive and modern traits.

The skull fragments were found in a gravel deposit along with the fossilized remains of wolf, lion, straight-tusked elephant, horse, ox, deer, and rhinoceros. A radiometric date (uranium series) for this associated material was calculated at 326,000 B.P. (Szabo and Collins 1975). The margin of error for this date, however, is large, and the skull could be 100,000 years older or 50,000 years younger. Flint tools, including hand axes and flakes, were found in the same deposit.

## Petralona

A cavern at Petralona, southeast of Thessalonika, Greece, was investigated in 1959. Initially, only fossilized animal bones were discovered, but in 1960 an ancient-looking and very well-preserved hominid skull was found encased in a stalagmite deposit (Poulianos 1971–72).

The Petralona skull possesses very large brow ridges, but it is rounder and the face is flatter than in *Homo erectus* (Figure 11.4). The cranial capacity is judged to have surpassed 1200 ml.

A detailed statistical analysis (Stringer 1974a) of fifty cranial measurements comparing Petralona to a large number of other fossil hominids including Steinheim, *H. erectus*, and the Neandertals unfortunately shows that the Petralona skull cannot be easily categorized. Although its

**Figure 11.4** *The Petralona skull from Greece is clearly that of an archaic* Homo sapiens. *Discovered in a cave near Thessalonika, the rest of the skeleton was, apparently, lost.* (Christopher B. Stringer)

cranial vault is similar to that of the later Neandertals, some of its cranial measurements are reminiscent of *erectus* from Zhoukoudian. To complicate matters further, its face is more like Steinheim, with the upper part being relatively flat and the lower jutting out. Christopher Stringer concluded from his analysis that Petralona represents an early form of *Homo sapiens*, even though it possesses a mixture of traits.

Animal bones found in the cave included cave bear, lion, several kinds of deer, wolf, and rhinoceros. The mix of animals indicates a possible contemporaneity with the Steinheim skull, suggesting an interglacial date corresponding to stage 7 on the oxygen isotope curve (see Figure 10.3). The skull, however, could be much older or much younger because it may have washed into the cave from somewhere else. Electron spin resonance performed on an encrustation on the skull resulted in a date of between 160,000 and 240,000 ya (Henning et al. 1981).

## Other European Archaics

Several other examples of archaic *Homo sapiens* have come from Europe. Material associated with a small occipital fragment found in Vértesszöllös, Hungary, has produced a uranium series date of between 250,000 and 475,000 ya (Gamble 1986). The bone is rather thick, and there is an indication of an occipital torus, but the extrapolated cranial capacity is larger than in *Homo erectus*. At Arago, near the village of Tautavel, France, the fragmentary remains of at least four adult and three juvenile hominids were found (Cook et al. 1982). The best preserved of these is a distorted face with large, thick brow ridges (Figure 11.5). The Arago fossils appear to represent archaic *H. sapiens* dating to more than 250,000 ya (Gamble 1986).

In Germany the Bilzingsleben site produced two occipitals, two frontal bones, and a molar. These were found together with about 60,000 flint flakes reflecting a range of scraping tools, awls, points, and chopping tools (Gamble 1986). A minimum age of 228,000 B.P. has been calculated (Harmon et al. 1980). An adult skull fragment was also found in Ehringsdorf, Germany, and dated to 225,000 B.P. (Cook et al. 1982). Bifacially worked points and scrapers were also found at this site. The "Mauer Mandible" from Heidelberg, Germany, is a robust lower jaw found in 1907. Although sometimes identified as one of the only European *H. erectus* specimens, it is more likely a representative of early *H. sapiens*.

**Figure 11.5** *The postdepositionally deformed Arago skull from France shows the typical array of archaic characteristics. Note the very large brow ridges.* (The Institute of Human Paleontology, Paris. H. deLumley)

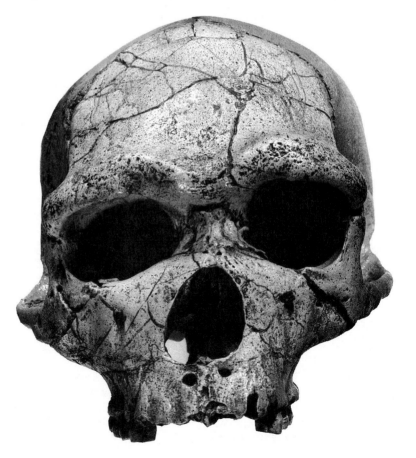

## African and Asian Archaics

Outside Europe a growing number of specimens has been found that, based on cranial capacity, seems to fit in the archaic *Homo sapiens* category (Brauer 1984; Rightmire 1984). The Broken Hill, or Kabwe, site in Zambia produced an ancient skull with brow ridges larger than many of the *Homo erectus* specimens. Its cranial capacity (just under 1300 ml), however, and the roundness of the skull are similar to archaic *H. sapiens*. Unfortunately, dating the fossil has been a problem; estimates ranging from 250,000 to 40,000 years have been suggested. It is probably about 125,000 years old.

In East Africa, the Ndutu skull has a cranial capacity of over 1100 ml and is more rounded in profile than in *H. erectus*. Also from East Africa, the Bodo fossil probably fits into the archaic human category. Ndutu and Bodo are both likely to be more than 200,000 years old; the latter may be as much as 400,000 years old. Interestingly, it has recently been suggested that the Bodo cranium shows evidence of cannibalism, or at least defleshing for some unknown purpose. Paleoanthropologist Tim White (1986) identified thirteen areas on the skull where scanning electron microphotographs show clusters of what appear to be cut marks made by stone tools. White is currently examining a series of other fossil hominid bones to assess evidence for similar behavior.

The Dali cranium with a cranial capacity of just under 1200 ml and an estimated age of 250,000 years and the nearly complete skeleton found at the site of Yingkou ["Jinniushan Man": Lu (1987) and Pope (1988), but no detailed publication is yet available on this fascinating specimen] and dated to after 200,000 B.P., represent Asian examples of archaic *H. sapiens*. The Narmada cranium found in central India is another early representative of our species. The dating of the specimen is not entirely clear, and its analysts recognize some affinities with the Ngandong crania (Kennedy et al. 1991:492). Nevertheless, its estimated cranial capacity of about 1300 ml, and a range of anatomical traits comparable to those seen in the fossils from Petralona, Bilzingsleben, Kabwe, Dali, Steinheim, and Swanscombe supports its identification as an early *Homo sapiens* (Kennedy et al. 1991).

## ARCHAIC HUMAN CULTURE

Having introduced you to a sample of archaic *Homo sapiens*, it must be admitted that, beyond knowing what they looked like, we are certain about little else. Several of the discoveries were accidental and made by nonscientists with no training in proper techniques of excavation. We have little in the way of habitation remains dating to the period 400,000 to 100,000 ya that could enlighten us about their culture.

One aspect of their culture, however, is fairly well represented, and that is stone tool technology. It is clear that many aspects of earlier Middle Pleistocene technology continued among these hominids. They continued making Acheulian hand axes and using the larger flakes that resulted from the hand axe–manufacturing process.

About 200,000 ya, however, these archaic *H. sapiens* were responsible for a great advance in toolmaking. They invented a technique of preparing stone cores according to a regular pattern that ensured a certain degree of consistency in the proportions of the stone flakes to be removed. In other words, they did not simply rely on accidentally well-shaped flakes to make tools but developed a technique for controlling the shape of the flakes. The new technique is called **Levallois** after the French suburb where it initially was recognized.

Before Levallois, stone tools were either core tools like the Oldowan choppers of *Homo habilis* or the Acheulian hand axes of *Homo erectus* or else were made on flakes that came off cores and happened to meet the needs of the toolmaker; undoubtedly, a certain amount of luck was involved in this process. With Levallois, in contrast, we see a great deal of forethought in the preparation of the stone core to ensure that a

**Figure 11.6** *The Levallois technique has been described by experimental archaeologist Bradley (as quoted in Gamble 1986:19) as involving a series of steps including: (a) producing a margin along the edge of the core, (b) shaping the surface of the core, (c,d) preparing the surface to be struck (the striking platform), (e) removing the flake, and either returning to step b for additional flake removal or, if the core had become too small, discarding the core.* (After Bordaz 1970)

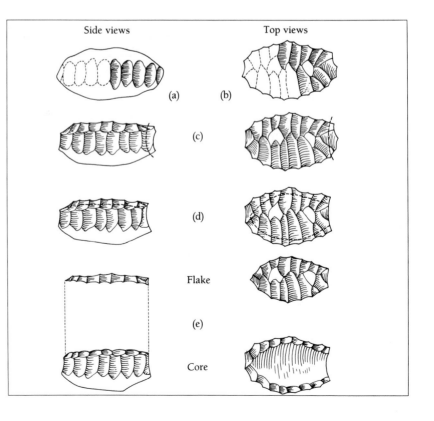

number of flakes of the desired shape would ultimately be produced (Figure 11.6). The core reduction process involves more work in the beginning but results in better flake "blanks," which can then be made into specific cutting, scraping, or piercing tools. The technique was also more efficient, getting more sharp edge for the amount of stone started with.

In an archaeological experiment designed to analyze the Levallois technique, B. Bradley (1977, as cited in Gamble 1986) produced twenty Levallois cores on flint blocks. He found that he could usually strike off four or five similarly shaped flakes from a core before the core became too small to use. Preshaping the core was the key to controlling and standardizing the shape of the flakes. The Levallois technique was clearly a more complex way of producing stone flake blanks for tools and also more effective and efficient than any previously used method.

Beyond their stone tool technology, we see little else in the way of cultural innovation among the archaics. This is perplexing considering the increase in their brain size compared to *H. erectus*. But perhaps we can suggest something else about these earliest members of our species. In Europe they managed to survive during a period of great climate change, with the ending of an interglacial (isotope stage 7) and the beginning of a glacial (isotope stage 6). In all likelihood, glacial periods came on slowly relative to the length of a human generation. The ability of a *culture* to change over several generations, however, reflects a flexibility that is diagnostic of humanity.

Archaic humans were faced with substantial changes in their environment. Animal species on which they relied became extinct or migrated. Plants on which they depended for food, fuel, and construction materials changed in response to the fluctuations in climate. Seasonal duration and intensity shifted, with longer, deeper winters and shorter, cooler springs and summers. Scheduling of subsistence activities would also have necessarily been shifted to meet the demands of nature's shift in seasons.

Whereas other species, biologically adapted to specific environments, were forced to move or die, archaic humans with their *cultural* adaptations were able to change their way of life. This flexibility allowed for their continued existence under new, drastically different circumstances.

## THE NEANDERTALS: A SPECIAL CASE

Neandertal. The name itself has entered our language as an insult. People use the term to describe someone who is stupid, violent, brutish. Yet what we now know about so-called Neandertal Man and his culture shows that he bore little similarity to this caricature.

**Levallois:** A tool technology involving striking flakes from a prepared core.

**Figure 11.7** *The skullcap found in the Neander River Valley in Germany in 1856. This is the find that gave the name "Neandertal" to all similar specimens in Europe. The cranial vault held a very large brain, but the brow ridges betray obvious differences with modern humans.* (Rheinisches Landesmuseum, Bonn, Germany)

The fossil that gives us the name was discovered by workmen in the Neander Valley in the Rhine Province of Germany in 1856 (Figure 11.7). Only the top of the skull was recovered, but this fragment was enough to make the Neandertal fossil an enigma. It was a relatively large skull, with a probable cranial capacity even larger than the modern average, but flattened and with enormous, thick brow ridges. These characteristics gave the skull a primitive look. It was not at all what people in the nineteenth century expected a human ancestor to look like. People were just getting used to the general notion of biological evolution and its specific application to our own species. The Neandertal skull looked simply too primitive for most to accord it a place in the human lineage.

Those who accepted the notion of human evolution had expected the discovery of a "missing link," a creature part ape, part human, like Piltdown. As mentioned in Chapter 8, because what most clearly distinguishes us from other animals is our intelligence, the assumption was that the brain had evolved first. Those looking for a missing link expected it to be primitive from the neck down but to have an advanced, almost modern head. The Neandertal skull did not meet that expectation.

Though a few similar-looking skulls had already been discovered in Europe, these had not generated great interest. In comparison the find in the Neander Valley produced a large amount of publicity and public attention (Kennedy 1975). Scientists pondered the significance of the skull in terms of human evolution. Many decided that it could not have been a human ancestor but was, instead, a pathological oddity—a relatively recent, deformed individual. One well-known anatomist, Rudolf Virchow, even suggested that the large brow ridges were the result of blows to the head.

As more Neandertals (what all similar fossils were called in Europe) were found, however, it became impossible to ignore their evolutionary significance. Many specimens were discovered, especially in caves. Geological and paleontological evidence indicated that they inhabited Europe during the latter part of the Pleistocene, from about 130,000 to after 40,000 ya. Nevertheless, even with its acceptance as an ancient, primitive variety of human, biases and preconceptions (and, as it turns out, misconceptions) colored scientific interpretations of Neandertal's place in the human family.

In 1913 the French anthropologist Marcellin Boule produced one of the most important and influential reconstructions of Neandertal Man (Boule and Vallois 1923; Figure 11.8). Unfortunately, his model was riddled with errors. Most of the mistakes stemmed from Boule's preconception that the Neandertals did not fit into the human evolutionary mainstream. Having already decided that they were very primitive, he

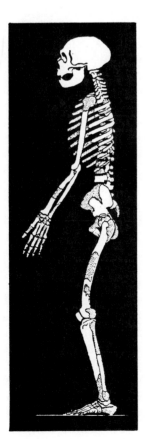
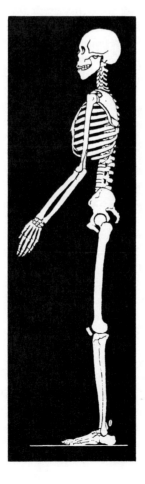

**Figure 11.8** *Marcellin Boule's reconstruction of the skeleton of the so-called Old Man of La Chapelle-aux-Saints* (left) *compared to that of a modern human. Boule regarded the Neandertals as primitive and reconstructed this skeleton in a way that made it appear to be apelike with bowed legs and head thrust forward.* (From *Fossil Men* by Marcellin Boule and Henri Vallois, Dryden Press (CBS Educational and Professional Publishing))

exaggerated their differences from modern humans and ignored their points of similarity. His reconstruction had the Neandertals barely upright, with their heads so far forward they could hardly stand, shoulders hunched, and knees bent. He even gave the Neandertals an opposable big toe similar to that of the apes.

It has been thought that Boule's reconstruction of a stooped-over individual resulted from the fact that the skeleton with which he was working, from the French cave of La Chapelle-aux-Saints, was actually an aged man crippled by arthritis. We now know that this was not the case and Boule did not make an accurate reconstruction that was based on a pathological specimen (Trinkaus 1985). Although the individual did suffer from degenerative bone disease, those areas of the skeleton most directly involved would not have affected his ability to walk to any great degree. Beyond this, Boule had two other perfectly normal Neandertal specimens (La Ferrassie 1 and 2) in his lab at the time and also used them in his reconstruction. It is much more likely that Boule simply reconstructed the "typical" Neandertal as apelike because that is how he expected it to look. After Boule, even reconstruction of facial characteristics emphasized the primitive; in most of these, Neandertal has a vacuous and rather stupid expression on his face—an open mouth and dazed look contribute to this impression. Certainly none of this was indicated by the actual fossil skulls.

**Neandertals: Not Brutes, but Not Us**

When we examine the evolution of the Neandertals, we cannot help also considering the evolution of our thinking about them. Since Boule's time, researchers have drastically revised their opinions of the Neandertals to the point where recently these archaics were considered to be quite advanced and, in fact, virtually modern in appearance and behavior (Figure 11.9 and see, for example, *The Neandertals* (Constable 1973) in the Time-Life series, *The Emergence of Man*). Their physical appearance was reassessed and reconstructions of the face became much more humanlike. Often, merely choosing to depict the Neandertal face as shaven and clean did wonders for its appearance (see, for example, the artwork in the article by Boyce Rensberger in the October issue of *Science 81*). The opinion had shifted so far that until recently the Neandertals have been considered by just about all researchers to be an archaic subspecies of *Homo sapiens*, specifically, ***Homo sapiens neanderthalensis***. In fact, by 1957, W. L. Straus and A. J. E. Cave could generate little disagreement when they said: "If he could be reincarnated and placed in a New York subway—provided that he were bathed, shaved, and dressed in modern clothing—it is doubtful whether he would attract any more attention than some of its other denizens" (1957:359). In a recently published *Newsweek* article, referring to Nean-

**Figure 11.9** *In the last few decades, reconstructions of Neandertal physical features and cultural practices have emphasized similarities to modern humans. Here, a painting by Rudolph Zallinger depicts Neandertals conducting a ceremony, much in the same manner of modern human hunters.* (Courtesy of R. F. Zallinger and Life Magazine)

dertal, Sharon Begley and Fiona Gleizes maintain, "With a decent shave he would be hard to distinguish from the linebacker at the next table" (1989:70).

We now know that just as Boule and other researchers at the turn of the century exaggerated alleged primitive features of the Neandertals, some more recent scientists and writers have exaggerated the degree of similarity these archaics show to modern humans. In fact, although they were by no means primitive brutes, the Neandertals did differ in some important ways from modern humans in their cranial as well as postcranial characteristics (Trinkaus 1988).

Some of these differences have been ascribed to Neandertal physical adaptation to the cold climate maximum of the last glacial stage. For

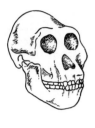

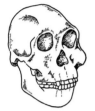

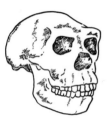

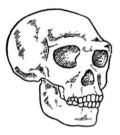

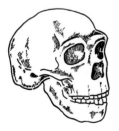

**Figure 11.10** *Comparison of cranial features of* Australopithecus (top) *with* Homo habilis, Homo erectus, *archaic* Homo sapiens, *and* Neandertal.

example, Neandertal bodily proportions, with relatively short distal limb segments (that is, the lower arms and lower legs), were probably adaptive (Trinkaus 1983a). Such a configuration is common in cold-adapted mammals because body heat loss increases with the surface area of the organism and limbs expose a proportionally large amount of surface to the elements. Among modern people, those living nearest the Arctic have proportionally the shortest lower limbs, and those living nearest the equator have the longest.

On the other hand, there are some much more basic differences between the skeletons of the Neandertals and those of modern people. For example, Neandertal skulls are immediately recognizable as different from those of modern humans. Although their cranial capacity ranged from about 1300 ml to 1640 ml, well within the modern span, the front part of their skulls was rather flat, so the Neandertals had little or no forehead. The back of their skulls was broad, and the sides were bulging. Their brow ridges were not straight, as in earlier *H. sapiens*, but were rounded over each eye orbit. The ridges were thick, long, and protruding, although not as large as in some of the earlier archaics. The Neandertal face was large and prognathous, with broad cheeks, a wide nose, and widely set eyes. The mandible showed little development of a chin, unique to modern humans. So their heads and faces are clearly distinguishable from those of modern people (Figure 11.10).

Below the neck, Neandertals exhibit a consistent pattern of significant differences from modern humans. Certainly, they were fully bipedal, and we need not resurrect Boule's image. On close inspection, however, almost all of the bones of Neandertal show a robustness and enlargement of the areas of muscle attachment that are either at the limit or outside the range of modern human variation (Trinkaus 1983a).

For example, their ribs display a thickness and heaviness that reflect the great size and strength of shoulder and back muscles. Neandertal shoulder blades (**scapulae**) similarly display the enormous power of Neandertal musculature in comparison with modern humans (Churchill and Trinkaus 1990). In a comparative analysis of Neandertal upper-arm bones (**humeri**) and fossil, as well as recent modern humans, researchers found a clear pattern of greater strength and weight in the Neandertal specimens (Ben-Itzhak et al. 1988). The authors of the study suggest that these differences are likely genetically based for several reasons. First, the differences are simply very striking. Second, they are seen not only between the Neandertals and present-day humans (with our relatively easy lifestyle), but also between Neandertals and ancient modern humans, who lived lives probably not all that different from the Neandertals (Ben-Itzhak et al. 1988:241).

Neandertal leg bones show this same pattern of size and strength. When C. Owen Lovejoy and Erik Trinkaus (1980) subjected three Neandertal tibia and a sample of modern American Indian and European tibia to a test of twisting and bending strength, they found the Neandertal bones to be twice as strong as the modern human examples. Neandertal stamina for walking must have been impressive.

Even in the hands, the Neandertal bones display evidence of enormous strength and power. In an extremely detailed comparative analysis of the finger bones (**phalanges**) of Neandertals and modern human beings, Eric Trinkaus and Isabelle Villemeur (1991) have shown that the relative proportions of the bones in the Neandertal thumb provided them with a grip far more powerful than that exhibited by modern human beings. Neandertal stone toolmakers may have been able to perform actions that both earlier and subsequent hominids could not.

The pattern is quite clear and consistent; when Neandertal bones are compared with their counterparts in anatomically modern human beings (both fossil and contemporary), the Neandertals always come out on top when it comes to features of strength and power. Simply put, Neandertals were strong, powerful creatures, exhibiting anatomical features of the skeleton related to muscle size, power, and strength that fall beyond the range of modern human beings. While those cited earlier seem to believe that all Neandertal would have needed was a shower and a shave to pass muster on the cover of *Gentlemen's Quarterly*, it is clear that scientist and writer Jared Diamond is closer to the truth when he states, "While a Neandertal in a business suit would attract your attention, one in shorts or a bikini would be even more startling" (1989:54).

Recent analysis of Neandertal pelves also shows significant differences from modern humans. Whereas the Neandertal pelvis is, in many respects, just like ours in those features related to locomotion, it is different in the length and configuration of the pubic bones, possibly indicating a larger birth canal. It has been estimated by Trinkaus (1983a, 1984b), in an analysis of the preserved pubic portions of seven fossils, that the Neandertal pelvic outlet could have accommodated the birth of a baby's head of up to 25 percent greater volume than what can pass through the birth canals of modern human females (1984b:510). This suggests to Trinkaus that Neandertal gestation length might have been up to or even more than twelve months, implying that their newborns would have been more physically developed than ours. Compare a 3-month-old baby to one just born, and you can see what an enormous difference that would have made.

There is some disagreement on this issue. Trinkaus was dealing with a small sample of fragmentary pelves. Recently, a nearly complete 60,000-year-old Neandertal pelvis was excavated in Kebara Cave on Mt. Carmel, Israel, by Yoel Rak and Baruch Arensberg (1987; Rak 1990). They identified this specimen as belonging to a male, a not unimportant fact when you consider the sexual dimorphism in pelvic outlet shape among modern humans. These researchers maintain that the pelvic out-

**scapula** (pl. **scapulae**): The shoulder blade.

**humerus** (pl. **humeri**): The bone of the upper arm.

**phalange** (pl. **phalanges**): A finger bone.

let in this specimen was differently shaped but not larger than it is in modern humans.

Rak (1990) compared the Neandertal Kebara pelvis to the fossil pelvis of an anatomically modern human being found just 35 kilometers away (from the site of Qafzeh; see Chapter 12). His study reinforces the assertion that the Neandertal pelvic inlet was not larger than that of modern human beings, but that the configuration of the Neandertal pelvis was significantly different from the modern human mode. The differences, Rak maintains, are therefore not the result of "obstetric demands" but differences of posture and locomotion.

On a related issue, M. C. Dean, Christopher Stringer, and T. G. Bromage (1986) analyzed the cranial remains of a Neandertal child from Gibraltar. They concluded that the child died at the age of 3 and that his cranial development was advanced when compared to a modern human's of the same age. They suggest that Neandertal gestation was the same length as in modern humans. They believe instead that Neandertal children were probably more developed at birth than are modern humans and that Neandertals developed more quickly after birth.

If Trinkaus is correct, then there might have been some selective advantage to a shorter gestation period in the evolution of modern humans. He suggests that it might allow for a greater number of births during a female's reproductive years because less time is spent gestating each child. This might be advantageous, particularly when infant mortality is high. Also, being exposed to the world at an earlier stage in brain development might have hastened neurological development, up to a point. Whatever the case, this possibility would mark a significant difference between Neandertals and modern humans.

If, on the other hand, Rak and Arensberg are correct, there was no significant difference between the Neandertal and modern human gestation length. Their analysis suggests, however, that there were significant differences between the Neandertals and modern humans in the biomechanics of their locomotion.

If Dean, Stringer, and Bromage are correct, then Neandertal gestation length was the same as ours, but Neandertal children were more fully developed at birth and matured more quickly than we do.

Whoever is right here (and they all might be, in part), we can conclude that the Neandertals and modern humans were, in some important ways, physically quite different from each other. Reconstruction of Neandertals as virtually identical to modern humans turns out to be almost as much a caricature as Boule's image of the primitive brute. As a result of the now-recognized differences between the Neandertals and modern humans (and other extinct archaics), the idea has been resurrected that the Neandertals do not belong in the species *sapiens* at all, but deserve the status of a separate species, *Homo neanderthalensis* (Gould 1988). The irony here is that this is what Boule suggested more than seventy years ago. Although he had the wrong reasons, he may have been right about Neandertal's place in human evolution after all.

## The Neandertal Fossils

In many Neandertal sites, we can determine age more precisely than for *Homo erectus* and even the earlier archaic *Homo sapiens*. In some cases, we can assign a fossil to an individual stage of the oxygen isotope chronology derived from sea cores (see Figure 10.3). For example, we can state with some confidence that hominids with Neandertal-like skulls first begin to turn up in the archaeological record at the juncture of isotope stages 5 and 6 of the Upper Pleistocene, about 130,000 ya (Figure 11.11). Among the 400 or so Neandertals thus far cataloged (Table

**Figure 11.11** *Neandertal fossil localities. This distribution shows quite clearly that the Neandertals were essentially a European-Southwest Asian population.*

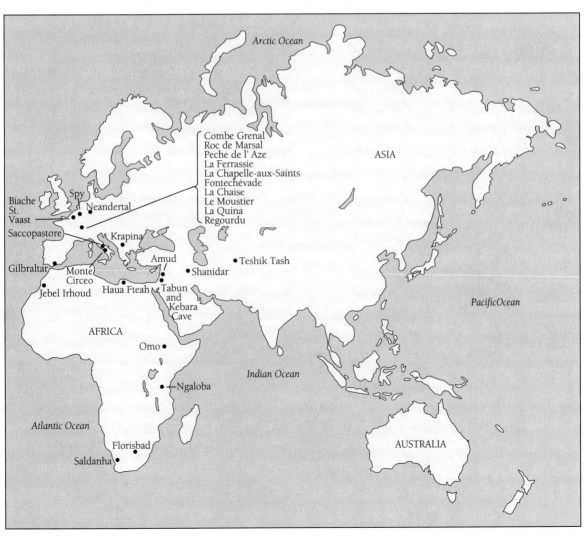

**Table 11.2** *Neandertal*

| Country | Locality | Fossils | Crania | Age | Brain Size (in ml) |
|---|---|---|---|---|---|
| Germany | Neandertal | Skullcap | | | 1250 |
| France | La Chappelle | Skeleton | "Old Man" | | 1620 |
| | Fontéchevade | Cranial fragments of several individuals | | 100,000 | 1500 |
| | La Ferrassie | Eight skeletons | LF-1 | >38,000 | 1680 |
| | La Chaise | Cranium | | 126,000 | |
| | Biache St. Vast | | | | |
| | Saint Césaire | Skeleton | | <34,000 | |
| Yugoslavia | Krapina | Cranial and post-cranial fragments of more than forty-five individuals | | Isotope stage 5 | 1300 |
| Morocco | Jebel Irhoud | Two crania, mandible | | Isotope stage 5 | 1400 |
| Ethiopia | Omo | Numerous cranial and postcranial fragments | OMO2 | 130,000 | 1435 |
| Tanzania | Ngaloba | | | Isotope stage 5 | |
| South Africa | Florisbad | Cranium | | 40,000 | |
| Israel | Tabun | Skeleton, mandible, and postcranial fragments | T-1 | 60,000 | 1270 |
| | Amud | Skeleton | A-1 | 70,000 | 1740 |
| | Kebara | Postcranial skeleton | | | |
| Iraq | Shanidar | Nine partial skeletons | S-1 | 70,000 | 1600 |
| | | | | *Mean* | 1505.00 |
| | | | | Standard Deviation | 166.32 |

Data from Day 1988.

11.2), for example, the Neandertal from La Chaise, France, has been associated with a thermoluminescence date of 126,000 B.P. (Cook et al. 1982). Another isotope stage 6 Neandertal-like hominid from France comes from Biache Saint-Vaast.

The Fontechévade skull fragments also are possible early Neandertals dating to this period. Found in a cave in France, they were recovered under a stalagmite layer and may be more than 100,000 years old (Gamble 1986). Although the remains are fragmentary, cranial capacity has been estimated at just under 1500 ml.

The Krapina finds in Yugoslavia consist of the fragmentary remains of at least forty-five and as many as sixty-five individuals (Trinkaus and Thompson 1987). Although very broken up, they appear to have large brow ridges and fairly rugged occiputs; cranial capacity estimates range from 1200 ml to 1450 ml. They appear to reflect an isotope stage 5 date.

A number of rather more modern-looking specimens from Africa exhibiting a mixture of Neandertal-like and modern traits probably date to the early part of isotope stage 5 (Brauer 1984; Rightmire 1984). Among these we can include the fossils from Jebel Irhoud (see Figure 12.8) in Morocco (although the dating is uncertain), Florisbad in southern Africa, and Ngaloba from Tanzania.

Also in Africa, two skulls found about 1 kilometer apart near the Omo River in Ethiopia are important. The layer in which the Omo 1 skull was recovered has been radiometrically dated to about 130,000 B.P. Omo 2 was found some distance away and may be from the same stratigraphic level, but it cannot be dated with certainty. The Omo skulls have cranial capacities of about 1400 ml but are quite different in appearance. Omo 2 exhibits a mixture of primitive and modern characteristics and, in fact, seems to be intermediate between Neandertal and modern. Omo 1 is surprisingly modern-looking and is discussed in Chapter 12.

It was isotope stage 4, however, in Europe and Southwest Asia that witnessed an apparent flowering of Neandertal population and culture (Trinkaus 1986). Neandertal sites dating to between 80,000 and 40,000 ya are abundant in these areas. Sites include Le Moustier, La Chapelle-aux-Saints, La Qunia, Regourdu, La Ferrassie, Pech de l'Aze, Roc de Marsal, and Combe Grenal, all in France; Monte Circeo and Saccopastore in Italy; Spy in Belgium; Gibraltar on the southern tip of the Iberian Peninsula; and Neandertal Valley in Germany (Figure 11.12). Outside Europe, examples of fossils similar to the European or "Classic" Neandertals have been recovered in Shanidar in Iraq, Teshik-Tash in the Soviet Union, Haua Fteah in Libya, Saldanha in southern Africa, and Amud and Tabun in Israel (Figure 11.13). An additional group of even more modern-looking fossils that still exhibit some Neandertal traits is known from the Middle East. This last group will be discussed in more detail in Chapter 12.

**Figure 11.12** *A Neandertal skull from La Ferrassie, France, exhibits many of the typical Neandertal features. The skull also shows the degree of variation among Neandertals because it is relatively rounded, with a high forehead.* (Courtesy Museum of Man, Paris)

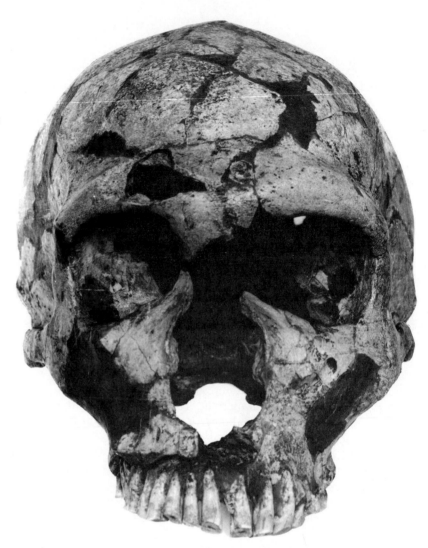

## NEANDERTAL CULTURE

Just as our reconstruction of the physical appearance of the Neandertals has drastically changed, so too has their behavior been rehabilitated. Here again, we see a pattern of the initial verdict of brutishness and savagery replaced by the other extreme, seeing them as kind and gentle souls. Neither of these views accurately describes Neandertal behavior.

The European Neandertals were certainly highly intelligent and adaptive hominids who faced the extreme climate of a glacial maximum. During such extended cold periods, large portions of the forested land of central Europe were transformed into arcticlike **tundra**—virtually treeless expanses covered by ground-hugging bushes, mosses, and lichens (Figure 11.14). Those trees that survived in this climate were all

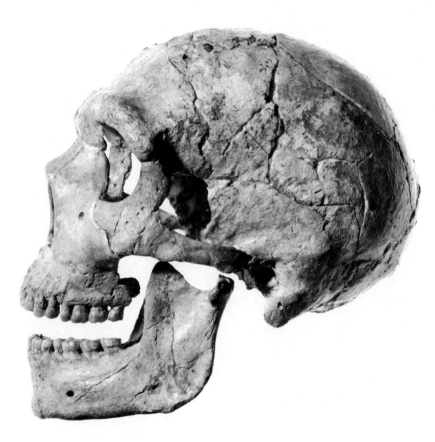

**Figure 11.13** *The Amud Neandertal cranium from Israel is quite similar to those from Europe, indicating, at least in part, the geographic range of this variety of archaic* Homo sapiens. (Department of Antiquities and Museums, Jerusalem)

cold-loving conifers, grouped in bunches, few and far between. Into this environment moved great numbers of woolly rhinoceros and mammoth, bison, horse, reindeer, and musk ox (Kurtén 1968).

The Neandertals of glacial Europe flourished in this seemingly forbidding climate. They became supremely adapted to life on the windswept tundra, scavenging and perhaps hunting large game animals, collecting what vegetable foods they could in season, and controlling fire. Although these Neandertals may have possessed some physical adaption to the cold, it was truly their culture that enabled them to survive in the freezing world of Europe during the last glacial period.

## Tool Technology

The Neandertals continued the Levallois technique of flake removal observed in earlier archaics and elaborated on it. The stone tool tradition of the Neandertals, called **Mousterian** after the French site of Le Moustier, is technically characterized as a retouched flake technology. This means that the Neandertals removed flakes from cores that they then proceeded to sharpen and/or shape by precise additional flaking, usually on a single face or side of the flake but occasionally on both

**tundra:** A treeless expanse with low-growing vegetation and permanently frozen ground.

**Mousterian:** The culture associated with European Neandertals.

**Figure 11.14** *Modern Alaskan tundra resembles parts of Europe as they appeared during glacial stages of the Pleistocene.* (M. Banks)

**Figure 11.15** *Unifacially retouched Mousterian flint flakes from sites in France.*

faces. Using this method, the Neandertals produced cutting, scraping, and piercing tools (Figure 11.15). They also continued the tradition of making bifacially flaked hand axes in some areas.

The Mousterian industry exhibits a much greater level of variation than did the earlier Acheulian. One of Europe's preeminent prehistorians, François Bordes, identified sixty-three tool types and twenty-one hand axe forms in a detailed analysis of the Mousterian (Bordes 1972). He notes that these different tool categories do not all co-occur at all sites. Instead, Bordes maintains that at least five different groupings of the sixty-three categories can be recognized in Europe. He interprets these as representing the toolmaking traditions of five and possibly more distinct Mousterian cultures who "co-existed in the same territory but influenced each other very little" (1972:146).

A contrasting view of this situation has been offered by Lewis and Sally Binford (Binford and Binford 1966; S. Binford 1968). Using a statistical approach called factor analysis, they found that there were indeed five discernable groupings of the sixty-three artifact types Bordes defined, but that these could be explained on functional grounds. They suggest that the groupings do not reflect the different traditions of coexisting, noninteracting Mousterian people. Instead, they believe that these clusters reflect different toolkits used for different functions like hunting, bone and antler tool manufacture, and plant processing, by the same people in different places.

Archaeologist Harold Dibble has suggested a third possibility for one of the tool categories (1987): that different types of scraping tools defined by Bordes reflect different stages in the use histories of these tools. According to Dibble, single-edged, double-edged, and converging-edged scrapers do not reflect different styles of separate groups of people, nor do they represent different functions. He proposes that when scrapers with a single edge got dull, a second edge was sharpened; as more edge was sharpened, the edges converged.

A recent analysis of Neandertal tool function was conducted by archaeologist John Shea (1989). Focusing on **wear patterns** (see Chapter 7) on tools recovered from Kebara Cave in Israel, Shea noted patterns of wear on the stone tools diagnostic of various activities: animal butchering, woodworking, bone and antler carving, and hideworking. Among the 448 artifacts on which he found wear, Shea identified 50 triangular flakes with wear on their bases, of the sort typically produced by the friction of a stone spear point in its wooden shaft. These 50 flakes also exhibited small breaks on their pointed tips. Shea suggests that such breaks may have been made when the points were thrust into the bodies of hunted animals. Such evidence may indicate that at least here, in a site dated to between 50,000 and 100,000 ya, Neandertals were hunting game animals.

**wear pattern:** A mark left on tools as a result of their use.

## Subsistence

The precise meaning of the different Mousterian tool types is still a point of contention among European prehistorians. In any event, with such tools the Neandertals developed a way of life dependent on the animals that flourished in Europe during the height of the final glacial stage, including reindeer, ibex, horse, woolly rhinoceros, bison, bear, and elk.

There is no question that Neandertal existence was largely dependent upon animal resources; Europe during glacial maxima offered little else. But were the Neandertals great hunters, as is sometimes suggested? Binford examined the faunal assemblages of a number of Neandertal sites and concluded that there is little evidence to support such a claim.

Binford conducted an ethnoarchaeological study among the Nunamiut Eskimo of Alaska, focusing on their hunting, butchering, and disposal practices (1978). He compared his findings among these living people with archaeological evidence from the French Mousterian site of Combe Grenal (Binford 1981). Binford found a patterned distribution of cut marks on the bones from France that were similar in some ways to those he saw in the ethnographic sample. For example, characteristic marks on aurochs (wild ox), horse, and reindeer mandibles from Combe Grenal matched those the Nunamiut made on caribou jaws in order to extract the animals' tongues. There were also cut marks on the joints of the long bones found at Combe Grenal, indicating butchering. Cut marks Binford noticed on the antler bases of the Combe Grenal reindeer skulls matched those the Nunamiut made on young caribou when they were skinning the animals for winter clothing.

Cut marks that would reflect butchery of the choice cuts of meat were not abundant, however. It may be that the cut marks on mandible and leg bones represent scavenging practices, not hunting behavior. In this reconstruction, cut marks are abundant at Neandertal sites on mandibles and legs because that is where the meat was left on animal carcasses after the carnivores were through with them.

Most human groups are good at planning during times of plenty to ensure food during harder times. Binford suggests that the record at Combe Grenal and other sites shows that Neandertals were not very good at such planning ahead (Binford 1981; and see Fischman 1992). There is no evidence, Binford maintains, for the kind of laying in of food stores commonly practiced by modern people during times when food is abundant to cover needs when food is scarce. As Binford points out, salmon was abundant in the surrounding rivers when Combe Grenal was occupied. Modern people commonly take advantage of the extraordinary abundance of salmon during the fish's annual spawning run, by catching them in large numbers in nets or weirs and then storing the meat for use later on. At Combe Grenal, there is no evidence that the inhabitants did anything of the kind. They probably caught salmon and ate it, Binford asserts, but it was all quite fortuitous, and there was little forethought or planning to take advantage of this cyclically abundant resource. To Binford this suggests an inability on the part of Neandertals to think beyond their immediate needs for food and to plan for their future needs. This bespeaks, according to Binford, a fundamental difference between Neandertals and modern human beings.

Recently, Binford has proposed an even more provocative hypothesis in an attempt to explain the nature of the archaeological record at Combe Grenal (see Fischman 1992). Looking at the spatial distribution of the archaeological remains at the site, Binford identified a peculiar spatial pattern. In the site rock shelters, there is a sequence of accumulations of superimposed ash deposits from hearths, simple stone tools made from rock found in the area immediately surrounding the deposit, and highly fragmented and splintered animal bones, mostly leg and skull fragments. In the area outside the rock shelters or caves, typically from 3 to 10 meters distant, and in the same stratigraphic levels as the cave deposits, excavators found a number of other archaeological deposits, each reflecting a far more sophisticated stone tool assemblage with a variety of specialized, functional tool types often made from lithic raw materials only available a few kilometers distant. Along with the tools, these outlying deposits contained animal bone fragments, some that actually fit together with pieces recovered from the rock shelters, but representing meatier parts of the game animals.

Binford hypothesizes that this interesting pattern implies a distinctive social system. He suggests that women and their children left the ashy deposits with the simple stone tools and splintered animal bones in the caves, while the outlying deposits were left by men. He thinks that such evidence can best be explained as reflecting a remarkable social system where women and children lived lives essentially independent of men. Men, although associated with the home-base rock shelters or "nests," were fundamentally independent and far more mobile, bringing back and sharing with women and children only that meat that they did not immediately eat at their hunting or scavenging locations. Women made their own tools and foraged for themselves and their children, while men, only marginally associated with the female/children social groups, took care of themselves.

Surely, this hypothesis will require quite a bit of testing before we can conclude that the Neandertals practiced such a decidedly nonhuman social system. This is a pattern unlike anything known for modern humans and, if it can be verified, may be an indication of how Neandertal behavior, no less so than their anatomy, differed from that of modern human beings.

## Altruism: Were the Neandertals Their Brothers' Keepers?

That the Neandertals were capable of producing effective tools and of surviving in a rigorous climate is undeniable and reflects their great intelligence and ability. It has also been suggested that in other spheres of behavior they were indistinguishable from modern human beings. Specifically, the Neandertals have been characterized as being altruistic to their comrades, as having engaged in burial ceremonialism, and of having practiced the first religion. Let us consider these cultural activities in turn.

Commonly, the fossil of the "Old Man of La Chapelle-aux-Saints" and the Shanidar I skeleton are cited as evidence that the Neandertals possessed the human quality of altruism by caring for their sick and aged (Constable et al. 1973; Straus and Cave 1957).

The La Chapelle remains are said to be those of an old man who probably suffered from arthritis. This would imply that he could not have contributed much to the subsistence of the group—he was long past the point where he could have hunted or even gathered much in the way of food. He also was missing most of his teeth and, it is often said, may even have needed some help chewing.

A recent reexamination of the "Old Man" has shown that this was not the case (Tappen 1985). In fact, much of the presumed tooth loss in this individual occurred after death, not before. Toward the end of his life, he still had five matching upper and five lower teeth on the left side; he also might have had teeth on the upper right. The only teeth certainly missing were those on the right side of the mandible, where a tumorous growth destroyed the bone, leading to tooth loss. But even this event probably occurred close to the end of this individual's life. In all likelihood, the "Old Man" was perfectly capable of chewing his own food.

Beyond this, we are uncertain how bad his arthritis really was. As stated before, Erik Trinkaus and D. D. Thompson (1987) maintain that the locations of the disease were not those that would have significantly affected locomotion. Characterizing this person as a helpless "cripple" who survived to old age only because of the selfless assistance of his comrades is also wrong.

Finally, it is ironic to note that the so-called "Old Man" who, if not a toothless invalid, at least is evidence for care and nurturing of the elderly, was probably less than 40 when he died (Trinkaus and Thompson 1987), based on tooth wear and cranial suture closure. Trinkaus and Thompson have used this misinterpretation to approach the entire question of Neandertal longevity. Does the evidence here support the scenario of altruistic Neandertals caring for the aged? Is the image of a society very much like our own, where the elderly are nurtured and where they can share the knowledge of their experience with the group, supported by the Neandertal data? Trinkaus and Thompson say no.

In most animal species, they point out, survival beyond the years of reproduction is rare. From an evolutionary perspective, there is little selective pressure for survival beyond the reproductive years for noncultural animals. In humans with our cultural adaptations, however, there are advantages to having older individuals survive. Their greater knowledge, expertise, and experience can greatly improve the chances of group survival and more than make up for whatever burden they might impose if they become physically hampered.

It is therefore significant that in a sample of 246 individual Neandertals, Trinkaus and Thompson found that nearly 40 percent died before reaching adulthood (1987:126). Of the 152 adult Neandertals in the sample, only 8.6 percent show a skeletal age at death of 40 years or more (1987:127). For the Neandertals, death in their twenties was common; in their thirties, it was the rule.

The Shanidar I remains, on the other hand, appear to show compelling evidence of altruism on the part of Neandertals. The skeleton is of an individual who survived some severe injuries that resulted in blindness and the probable paralysis of his right arm (Trinkaus 1983b). It seems likely, at least in this case, that other members of his group cared for this individual during his recuperation, otherwise he would not have survived.

Although the image of compassionate Neandertals caring for their wounded comrade may be compelling, the survival of a wounded individual, as K. A. Dettwyler (1991) maintains, may not mean that much. There is, he points out, an implicit bias in the assumption that simply because an individual was "disabled," he or she was helpless and could survive only through the compassion (pity?) of others in the group. Simply because the Shanidar example had some significant disabilities does not mean that he could not contribute to the survival of the group. As Dettwyler points out, although he may no longer have been able to hunt, he could still have collected plants, processed food, or performed some other useful function. So the archaeological record, although suggestive, does not support an image of compassionate, altruistic Neandertals caring for the sick, the aged, and the disabled. It is just as likely that the survival of such individuals was a result of their own self-determination and, further, made possible because they could still make significant contributions to the survival of the group. The case for Neandertal care and nurturing of the old, as in modern human societies, is simply not supported by the data. The image of altruistic Neandertals is not possible to prove.

## Burial Ceremonialism

The reconstructed scenes are certainly evocative: At Teshik-Tash, in Soviet Asia, a young Neandertal boy, dead in the flower of his youth, was carefully laid out in a shallow grave. Around the grave were placed six pairs of Siberian mountain goat horns as a memorial for the dead child (Movius 1953). At La Chapelle-aux-Saints in France, the "Old Man" had been placed in a shallow trench, surrounded by tools, and even accompanied by a bison leg—perhaps as food thought necessary for use in the afterlife (Bouyssonie et al. 1908). In the Shanidar cave in Iraq, pollen analysis has been used to construct a scenario of a recently deceased young man, placed on a bed of pine boughs and then covered with wild flowers: bachelor's buttons, hollyhock, and grape hyacinth (Solecki 1971). At La Ferrassie in France, six Neandertal burials occur together. A man, a woman, two children, and two infants had been placed in trenches. Five were laid out east to west. The woman was placed in the flexed position (Figure 11.16); the man had a flat stone slab placed over his chest (Heim 1968).

It seems undeniable that Neandertals buried their dead—although, even on this point, there are some skeptics (Gargett 1989). But detailed scenarios are often difficult to assess, and the precise meaning of the burials is even harder to evaluate. Many of the burials were excavated in the late nineteenth and early twentieth centuries. Archaeological methodology was not as advanced as it is today, much information was lost, and the taphonomy of many of the claimed burial sites is impossible to resolve.

Was the bison leg at La Chapelle-aux-Saints intended to be food for the next life, or were the Neandertal and bison bones merely dragged into the cave by carnivores? Is the site at Teshik-Tash evidence of Neandertal ceremonialism or simply carnivore activity? (Actually, only the skull lay within the circle of goat horns; the rest of the bones were dispersed.) Were the flowers at Shanidar intended as symbols of life, were they used for their medicinal qualities, or is the pollen intrusive, brought in later by rodents or, simply, blown in? To some, the meaning of these Neandertal "burials" is clear. They see in them evidence of the origins of belief in an afterlife. That may well be, but the specific meaning is lost to us.

Anthropologist Frank Harrold (1980) has analyzed a sample of presumed Neandertal interments and found thirty-six where the evidence strongly indicated intentional burial. In these, there was clear evidence of the digging of a grave, special positioning of the body (as in, for example, a fetal position), and/or the presence of indisputable grave offerings. These burials had ages of between 75,000 and 35,000 years. When they were compared with ninety-six burials of anatomically mod-

**Figure 11.16** *An undisputed Neandertal burial from La Ferrassie, France. Here, the individual was interred in the flexed position with knees drawn up to the chest.* (Museum of Man, Paris, M. Lucas, photographer)

ern humans dating from 35,000 to 10,000 B.P., some obvious differences became apparent. In those cases where the data could be used, almost 90 percent of the burials of modern humans contained grave goods, including such objects as stone and bone artifacts, mollusc shells, coloring materials, and items of personal adornment such as necklaces (1980:205). On the other hand, only about 40 percent of the Neandertal burials contained grave goods, and these were restricted to objects like stone tools and animal bones.

It seems that the Neandertals indeed buried their dead, although such burials are generally not as elaborate as those of later periods involving anatomically modern humans. Whether Neandertal burials were intended to assure the deceased the necessities for life in the hereafter or were simply part of ceremonies to comfort his or her companions left behind is impossible to determine, although ultimately, perhaps, not so important. Whatever their actual intent, these burials show that the Neandertals treated the dead and death in a ceremonial way, and that is a uniquely human trait. They were conscious of their own mortality, recognized the enormity of that fact, and treated death in a way that reflected that recognition.

### Cave Bears

Neandertals are commonly credited with the worship of a now-extinct species of bear that inhabited the caves of Europe (see Figure 11.9). A closer look at the data, however, does not support the dramatic picture of a prehistoric cave bear "cult."

We know that the European Neandertals used caves. We also know that they competed for such natural shelters with bears that were up to 50 percent larger than the largest living bears, the Alaskan Kodiak. When a Kodiak stands on its back legs, it can be as much as 9 feet tall. When a cave bear stood up, it could surpass 12 feet. Needless to say, people have been fascinated by the suggestion that Neandertals killed such enormous animals and then paid special attention to the remains.

At a cave in Drachenloch, Switzerland, Neandertals are alleged to have made chests of stones more than 3 feet on a side. Inside these chests were several cave bear skulls. Deeper in the cave, six more cave bear skulls had been placed in niches in the cave wall. Other caves supposedly show similar treatment of cave bear remains. For example, Regourdu in France has twenty cached skulls housed in a cubicle topped with an enormous stone slab.

Did Neandertals worship the cave bears? Did they collect their skulls as a part of that worship? Did the Neandertal hunters collect the heads of slain bears and keep them in stone chests much in the way modern trophy hunters collect the heads of animals they have killed and then mount them on their walls? These are all thought-provoking possibilities, but they are unsupported by the data.

Anthropologists Philip Chase and Harold Dibble (1987) have reassessed Neandertal ceremonialism, pointing out that the excavations at Drachenloch and Regourdu were not as carefully conducted as we would have hoped. When original field notes were examined, their descriptions did not always correspond to later, far more dramatic reconstructions. For example, the so-called stone chests at Drachenloch were far less well defined than most people realize; they appear instead to be natural clusters of rock. Beyond this, no butchering marks have been found on the bear bones. One would expect cut marks of some kind if Neandertals had really killed the animals and then removed the bears' heads. The stone slab covering the "cubicle" at Regourdu weighs 850 kilograms and was far more likely the result of a cave-in than any intentional construction by Neandertals or anyone else.

As our understanding of cave taphonomy has become more sophisticated, we have come to recognize that there are many natural processes by which the specific bones of animals may accumulate. It seems that, at least at present, the accumulation of cave bear bones in European caves was the result of natural processes. They do not show that Neandertals worshipped cave bears or practiced a cave bear "cult."

## COULD ARCHAIC *HOMO SAPIENS* TALK?

We saw earlier that examination of the **basicrania** of extinct hominids shows that *Australopithecus* possessed a cranial base comparable to the apes, whereas that of *Homo erectus* was more similar although not identical to modern humans. This implies that while *Australopithecus* likely could not produce human speech, *H. erectus* was at least partially adept at spoken language.

In examining the basicrania of archaic *Homo sapiens*, Jeffery Laitman and R. C. Heimbuch (1984) concluded that specimens like Petralona, Steinheim, and Kabwe (Broken Hill) are essentially modern in form. This implies that the vocal tract anatomy of these fossils dating to more than 250,000 ya was just like ours and their ability to speak was the same as our own.

However, when we come to the basicrania of the Neandertals, the nice, neat progression of vocal tract anatomical evolution appears to have been interrupted or deflected. The base of the Neandertal skull shows a greater degree of flexion than *H. erectus*, but less than that of older archaic *H. sapiens*. It has been suggested that the differences between Neandertal and human vocal tract anatomy, as reconstructed

**basicrania** (sing. **basicranium**): The bones of the base of the skull.

# CONTEMPORARY ISSUE

### Suppose Neandertal Survived

Today there is a single living species of hominid—and, as we will show, a single living subspecies. We are all subsumed under a single taxonomic grouping: *Homo sapiens sapiens*. But as we saw in Chapter 9, a single hominid species has not always been the case. In fact, throughout much of hominid history, there have been multiple contemporary species. *Australopithecus robustus, Australopithecus boisei,* and *Homo habilis* shared the evolutionary stage, overlapping in time and, perhaps, even territory. And, as we will show in Chapter 12, the Neandertals, with differences from anatomically modern human beings and classified in a different subspecies or even a different species, overlapped in time and space with early modern humans.

It is clear that hominid evolution has not been a steady, unbroken progression from the first upright primates to the modern peoples of today. Rather, hominid evolution—like evolution in general—has been a bush with many twigs. It is simply a twist of evolutionary fate that all but one of the hominid twigs is extinct. It needn't have turned out that way.

Evolution follows the principle of historical contingency. The specific nature of each event in evolutionary history is contingent upon—that is, dependent upon—the precise sequence of events that led up to it. If one of those events had been different, all the events that followed would have been different. And, so complex is this series of contingent events, we are not able to predict from knowledge of one event what effects it will have on the future. Had Adolf Hitler, a sickly youth, died at a young age, world history would certainly not have turned out exactly the way it did. But we have no way of knowing *how* it would be different.

The same holds true for biological evolution, even the evolution of the hominids that sometimes seems to us (from our position as the only living hominid) to have been leading in this direction all along. This brings up an interesting and thought-provoking possibility. There are no Neandertals around today. (Their fate is discussed in the next chapter.) But imagine, along with Stephen Jay Gould, what it would be like if the specific events of hominid history had been different and the Neandertals had survived into the present. What would their place be in our world? Would we exploit their great strength, viewing them as expendable draft animals? Would we use them to perform dangerous tasks? "Would we," Gould asks, "have built zoos, established reserves, promoted slavery, committed genocide, or perhaps even practiced kindness?" (1985a:198).

We will, of course, never know what our modern world would have been like had other hominid twigs survived. The prospects of such a scenario, however, are certainly unsettling, considering how poorly we often treat members of our own species and subspecies. Not having been able to work out the difficulties that differences *within* our species present us, we seem hardly prepared to cope with the presence of another *type* of hominid. Perhaps, with this in mind, the Neandertals are better off having become extinct.

from analysis of the basicranium, indicate that Neandertals could not articulate some of the sounds that we can, notably the vowels *a, i,* and *u.* Laitman and Heimbuch, along with Philip Leiberman (1984) and Edmund Crelin (1987) are quick to point out that this still would leave the Neandertals capable of making a wide range of sounds and developing and speaking a complex language. This language may simply have been more restricted than that of modern human beings.

Not all researchers agree with the conclusions reached by these scientists. For example, the form of the recently discovered **hyoid** bone at the Neandertal site of Kebara in Israel has been interpreted by the researchers as being fully modern in appearance (Arensburg et al. 1990). The hyoid bone's location in the throat and its relationship to the larynx, pharynx, basicranium, and mandible indicates to these scientists that Neandertals were capable of fully modern speech.

The question, then, of Neandertal speech capability remains up in the air. Certainly, they could speak, but it is still unclear if they could produce the full range of sounds found in modern human languages.

## THE PLACE OF THE ARCHAICS

We ended Chapter 10 by saying that the appearance of archaic *Homo sapiens* may have been a punctuational event, a sudden surge in evolution. In this chapter, we have shown that the data present a complicated picture. Apart from their brain size, the archaics, including the Neandertals, are a varied lot indeed. Some of the crania look highly advanced in the sense that they are more similar to the modern form than to *Homo erectus.* Others possess a mosaic of traits, some primitive, some modern. The most recent of the archaics and the one about which we possess the most information, the Neandertals, have been shown here to differ in some very significant ways from modern humans.

The false abstraction of evolutionary ladders has not helped our understanding of the place in the human lineage of the Neandertals and the other archaic *H. sapiens.* The "ladder" model of development causes us to interpret fossil species as distinct points on a directional evolutionary continuum. But the archaics do not fit neatly on any particular rung of our evolutionary ladder.

The Neandertals, for example, although more recent than the other specimens of archaic *H. sapiens* discussed in this chapter, appear more primitive in some cranial characteristics, particularly in the size of the face and brow ridges. Their brain size, on the other hand, indicates a great degree of modernity—yet again, it fits no neat continuum because they are even larger than some modern humans.

**hyoid:** The horseshoe-shaped bone in front of throat. Its form and position may provide insights into the ability of members of a species to speak.

**Table 11.3** *The Evolutionary Grades of* Homo sapiens

| | |
|---|---|
| Grade 1: | Arago, Bilzingsleben, Petralona, Vértesszöllös, Bodo, Broken Hill/Kabwe, Ndutu |
| Grade 1/2: | Steinheim, Swanscombe, Omo 2, Laetoli 18, Florisbad |
| Grade 2: | Biache-St-Vaast, La Chaise, Ehringsdorf, Fotechévade, Saccopastore |
| Grade 3: | Jebel Irhoud, Haua Fteah, Neandertal, La-Chapelle-aux-Saints, Monte Circeo, La Ferrassie, Krapina |
| Grade 3/4: | Amud, Tabun |
| Grade 4: | Omo 1, Klasies River Mouth, Border Cave, Cro-Magnon, Jebel Qafzeh, Skhul |

The different grades have no chronological implications and merely convey similarities and differences in various fossils. Grade 1 is the most removed from the anatomically modern human form; Grade 4 is anatomically modern (Brauer 1984; Gamble 1986; Stringer et al. 1979).

The Neandertals and most of the other archaics should be viewed not as rungs on a ladder but as a twig on the human evolutionary bush, parallel to our own. The Neandertals appear more significant than they actually are to human evolution in general because we have the bones of so many of them. But they are so abundant in the archaeological record simply because they lived in caves and buried their dead.

Stringer and colleagues (1979) proposed a series of "grades" of archaic humans, from those most like *H. erectus* to those possessing intermediate appearance to the most modern looking. Günter Brauer (1984) has added to and modified this list of grades (Table 11.3). Importantly, the grades do not represent the gradual evolution of archaic *H. sapiens* after the punctuation that defined them. Although our dating of individual fossils is not as firm as we would like it, it seems clear that some of the specimens in different grades were contemporaries and equally that some of the more modern-looking ones are actually older than some of the less modern. It remains for us to discuss how one of these populations of archaic *sapiens* gave rise to modern humanity (Grade 4).

## SUMMARY

By about 400,000 ya, a new hominid appeared on the evolutionary stage. Called *Homo sapiens*, the creature was so like us that it was given the same biological designation as modern humans. Recognizing that there are physical differences between them and us, however, most scientists designate them as an "archaic" variety of *H. sapiens*, or they identify them as a subspecies different from modern human beings.

The archaics are represented in Europe by fossils like Swanscombe, Steinheim, and Petralona; in Africa by the Kabwe, Ndutu, and Bodo skulls; and in Asia by the remains found at Narmada (India) and Dali and Yingkou (China). Mean cranial capacity for these archaics was about 1220 ml, close to 85 percent of the modern human mean cranial volume.

The best known subset of the archaics were the Neandertals who first appeared about 130,000 ya and lasted, at least in Europe, until just a little more than 30,000 ya. Neandertal or Neandertal-like fossils are best known in Europe but also have been found in Southwest Asia and Africa. The Neandertals possessed large, flat skulls, often exceeding modern human cranial volume, with enormous brow ridges and steeply angled foreheads.

Below their crania, Neandertal bones exhibit features of muscle attachment indicative of great strength, often measurably beyond the modern human range of variation. Although once considered to be sub-human in intellect, we now recognize that the Neandertals were not "brutes," but neither were they exactly like us. They likely were not altruistic people who cared for their sick and aged, buried their dead in elaborate ceremonies, and worshipped cave bears, as was once thought. They were, however, intelligent beings whose role in the evolution of modern humans is still being debated and will be addressed in Chapter 12.

## KEY TERMS

| | |
|---|---|
| postorbital constriction | phalange |
| occipital | tundra |
| parietals | Mousterian |
| Levallois | wear pattern |
| scapula | basicranium |
| humerus | hyoid |

## FOR MORE INFORMATION

For capsule descriptions of many of the fossils discussed in this chapter, see Clark Spencer Larsen and Robert M. Matter's *Human Origins: The Fossil Record* and, especially, Michael H. Day's *Guide to Fossil Man*. Kenneth A. R. Kennedy's *Neanderthal Man* (Constable 1973) provides an excellent discussion of the history of scientific thought on the Neandertals. In the Time-Life *Emergence of Man* series, the volume *The Neanderthals* has some terrific artwork reconstructing the environment of glacial Europe but presents a rather outdated view of the archaics. The February 1992 issue of *Discover* magazine has an informative piece on current thinking about the Neandertals.

# 12

# THE EVOLUTION OF MODERN HUMANITY

In the short story "The Reigate Squires," Sir Arthur Conan Doyle has his great detective Sherlock Holmes characterize the key to successful police work in this way:

> It is of the highest importance in the art of detection to be able to recognize, out of a number of facts, which are incidental and which vital. Otherwise your energy and attention must be dissipated instead of being concentrated. (1981:275)

It is much the same in science. This explains, at least in part, one of the great ironies of scientific investigation: In the journey to understanding a complex issue, we sometimes become *more* confused as more is known about the subject! In a way that is both maddeningly frustrating and, at the same time, intellectually exhilarating, this irony characterizes our understanding of the origin and evolution of anatomically modern human beings.

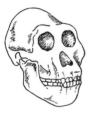

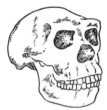

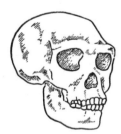

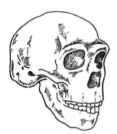

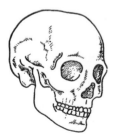

## WHERE DO WE COME FROM: AN EVOLUTIONARY ENIGMA

One would have hoped—and expected—that as we have progressed in our discussion of human antiquity, as we have approached the more recent past, and as the data have become more abundant—more sites, more fossils, more artifacts—the certainty of our constructed evolutionary scenarios would have increased. As will be apparent in this chapter, this, unfortunately, is not the case. To be sure, the "number of facts," as Holmes puts it, increases dramatically. Unfortunately, we are not yet in a position of being able fully to heed Holmes's advice concerning this; we cannot yet distinguish the "incidental" from the "vital." And, perhaps even more lamentably, too often our attention has been dissipated in acrimonious debate between scientists with competing hypotheses.

We cannot provide you with a simple, comprehensive solution to the controversial questions surrounding the origin of anatomically modern human beings: *Homo sapiens sapiens* (Figure 12.1). What we can attempt to do is present you with a synopsis of the evidence presented by the champions of the different explanations.

Two basic models have been proposed to explain the evolution of anatomically modern humans from the archaics: the in-place, or **multiregional, hypothesis** and the **replacement hypothesis** (Figure 12.2).

These competing models have their own cadre of supporters. Most active in advocating the multiregional model has been Milford Wolpoff of the University of Michigan (Thorne and Wolpoff 1992; Wolpoff 1988, 1989; Wolpoff et al. 1984), while speaking most vociferously in favor of the replacement model has been Christopher Stringer of the Natural History Museum in London, England (Stringer 1989, 1990; Stringer and Andrews 1988). Each model also has its own suite of deductive implications—those things that should be true if the hypothesis is true (see Chapter 1 for a brief discussion of the scientific method of reasoning). These deduced "predictions" of what should be found in support of each model are presented in Figure 12.3. We can use these implications to test, at least tentatively, the two models.

### Multiregional Evolution

Multiregional evolution is an explanation that posits the gradual, in-place evolution of regional populations of archaic *Homo sapiens* into modern humanity (see Figure 12.2). In this view, archaic populations

**Figure 12.1** *Comparison of cranial features of* Australopithecus (top), Homo habilis, Homo erectus, *archaic* Homo sapiens, *Neandertal, and anatomically modern* Homo sapiens.

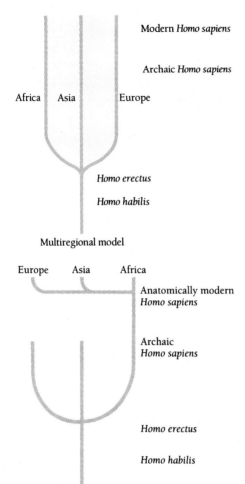

Modern *Homo sapiens*

Archaic *Homo sapiens*

Africa    Asia    Europe

*Homo erectus*

*Homo habilis*

Multiregional model

Europe    Asia    Africa

Anatomically modern
*Homo sapiens*

Archaic
*Homo sapiens*

*Homo erectus*

*Homo habilis*

Replacement model

**Figure 12.2** *The multiregional and replacement models of the evolution of anatomically modern human beings. In the multiregional model, different groups of modern humans have been more or less separate since Homo erectus times. In the replacement model, all modern humans can be derived from a common and relatively recent source.*

throughout the world—the European Neandertals as well as the archaic humans of Africa and Asia—each evolved, more or less separately, into the modern form at about the same time.

As Fred Smith et al. (1989) point out, this explanation presumes that long-term, gradual trends produced modern humans from archaic ones in several areas through the resorting of genetic material and the action of natural selection.

If the multiregional model is correct, the paleontological records of Asia, Africa, and Europe should show parallel changes more or less simultaneously as archaic *H. sapiens* everywhere evolved into modern humans. Within each region, archaic populations would have gradually evolved into moderns, with distinctive regional traits maintained through time within different geographic populations.

**multiregional hypothesis:** The idea that anatomically modern humans evolved independently in a number of different geographic areas.

**replacement hypothesis:** The idea that anatomically modern humans evolved in a limited geographic area and spread from there, replacing indigenous groups of archaics.

|  | Multiregional Model | Replacement Model |
|---|---|---|
| Paleontological evidence necessary | 1. Transitional forms widespread<br>2. Simultaneous worldwide appearance of modern traits<br>3. Regional traits traceable from modern back through ancient forms | 1. Transitional fossils in one or limited areas<br>2. Anatomically modern fossils appear earliest in single region, later elsewhere<br>3. Temporal overlap & contemporaneity of archaic and modern forms outside source area |
| Genetic evidence necessary | 1. High genetic diversity among modern human populations<br>2. Same amount of diversity within each human group | 1. Low genetic diversity among human groups<br>2. Highest genetic diversity among modern humans within source region (where moderns first appeared) |

In other words, regional anatomical traits seen in modern human populations in particular geographic areas today—like the kind discussed in the next chapter—should be traceable through time to the archaic *sapiens* and even earlier *Homo erectus* groups in those same areas. In the multiregional model, human anatomical variation seen in the world today began as much as 1 million years ago (mya). This lengthy period of at least partially separate development should be reflected in substantial amounts of genetic difference between geographically distinct populations of modern humans.

Although it was suggested by one of the earliest advocates of a multiregional model (Coon 1962) that anatomically modern human beings had developed entirely independently from earlier hominids—and at different times—in Europe, Africa, Asia, and Australia, with today's modern "races" representing the endpoints of these separate evolutions, such a scenario is highly unlikely and has virtually no supporters today.

One would have to argue that, among varied groups of archaic humans, the same changes occurred under conditions of very similar selective pressure in areas of the world with strikingly different environments, resulting in interfertile groups of anatomically modern people. Because of the problems presented by this scenario, today's supporters generally maintain that sufficient gene flow occurred across all, or at least most, of the world, biologically linking archaic human groups (Kramer 1991; Wolpoff et al. 1984). Thus, new and highly adaptive biological traits appearing in one corner of the globe would have rapidly moved across the face of the earth through the interbreeding of various archaic human groups, pulling them all along in the evolution toward modern humanity.

The multiregional hypothesis relies on the assumption that enough interbreeding took place among various archaic groups living in small hunting–gathering bands to spread evolving modern characteristics across thousands of miles, over environmental barriers, and through very different climates, all in a remarkably short time period. At the same time, the amount of interbreeding had to be below that necessary to swamp local variation.

## Evolution by Replacement

The replacement hypothesis (see Figure 12.2) proposes that anatomically modern human beings evolved from archaic humans in a single or limited geographic location. These newly evolved modern humans then spread out from this center of origin into areas where only archaic humans lived. Therefore, archaic and anatomically modern humans were, at least for a time, contemporaries and competed for the same territory and resources. As a result of their more highly adaptive traits—perhaps greater intelligence, better ability to communicate, superior hunting abilities, better technology—these modern-looking humans replaced archaic populations wherever they came into contact by actually contributing to the extinction of the archaic groups or perhaps by genetically swamping them through interbreeding.

If this model is correct, then fossils transitional between archaic and modern humans should occur only in the single region where moderns evolved. Elsewhere, there should be evidence of archaics and moderns coexisting in the same regions, once the latter spread out from their initial source area—or their "Eden," as opponents of the replacement model disparagingly characterize it (Smith et al. 1989; Wolpoff 1989). Eventually, the archaic human forms would have become extinct, unable to compete with their anatomically modern cousins. Modern genetic diversity should be small because, in this model, *all* living human groups have descended from a relatively recent, common ancestral group of initial modern *Homo sapiens*—people who evolved in one place and spread out to populate the world while replacing indigenous groups of archaic humans. Anatomical differences visible today among modern humans can have evolved only since the first moderns replaced the archaic forms. Archaic forms in areas outside the source area can have contributed little or nothing to modern human genes. Genetic diversity should be greatest where modern humans first appeared because we have obviously been there the longest.

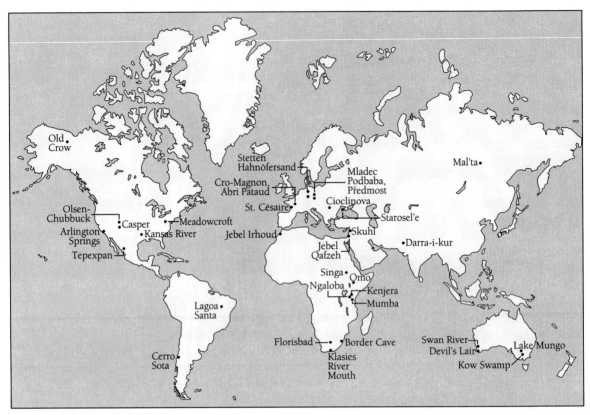

**Figure 12.4** *Locations of the sites of anatomically modern humans.*

## TESTING THE TWO MODELS OF EVOLUTION

To assess the validity of these models, we can first examine the paleontological records of Europe, Asia, and Africa (Figure 12.4).

### Europe

The famous Cro-Magnon fossils of France were discovered in 1868 (Figure 12.5) and are still the oldest examples of anatomically modern humans from western Europe. Although varied, the five individuals found were all clearly modern European in appearance, with long, large skulls; broad, short faces; and narrow noses. Their cranial capacities were quite large (upward of 1600 ml), and their brains were housed in very modern looking skulls with high foreheads, rounded profiles, and small brow ridges. The site dates to after 30,000 years ago (ya)(Stringer et al. 1984).

The site at Abri Pataud, also in France, provides the remains of several more individuals with modern crania and dates to more than 27,000 ya (Stringer et al. 1984).

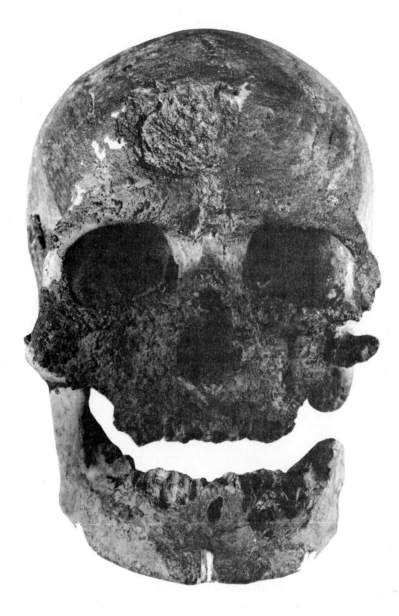

**Figure 12.5** *One of the famous skulls of anatomically modern humans from the cave at Cro-Magnon, France. All the anatomical features of this skull are entirely modern.* (Museum of Man, Paris)

The postcranial skeletons of all of the earliest anatomically modern human fossils from western Europe also show many differences between the first European moderns and the Neandertals. It is potentially quite significant that even though the Neandertals with their short limbs were physically adapted to life in the cold, the earliest European moderns were proportioned more like tropically adapted humans (Trinkaus 1983a). This fact would seem to indicate that they evolved in a warmer climate and had only recently moved into colder regions.

The Cro-Magnons and the other examples from France, therefore, are entirely modern in appearance and quite different from the Neandertals in all of the anatomical features summarized in Chapter 11 (see Figure 12.1). At least here in western Europe, there are *no* fossils that can be interpreted as intermediate in form between Neandertal and these early modern human beings (Smith 1984; Smith et al. 1989). Indeed, here, at least, there seems to be a genuine anatomical gap between the local archaic humans—the Neandertals—and their earliest moderns.

Further east, some other European sites also seem to support replacement. Stetten in Germany, with a radiocarbon date of 36,000 B.P. (Smith 1984), Cioclinova in Romania, and Podbaba and Předmost in Czechoslovakia are only a few examples. All share an entirely modern cranial morphology. None can be interpreted as an intermediate or evolving human. They are all fully modern.

Recent discoveries in western Europe, of Neandertals dating to *after* the initial appearance of modern humans there, seem to further support the replacement hypothesis. At Saint-Césaire in France, a fossil that is clearly Neandertal has been found in a level dated to after 35,000 ya (Stringer et al. 1984). At Hahnöfersand in Germany, a cranial fragment with clear affinities to Neandertal has been dated to 35,000 B.P. (Brauer 1984). These sites date to after the ones just mentioned associated with fully modern human fossils. It is unlikely that the Neandertals were ancestral to modern humans in western Europe if they survived after the appearance of anatomically modern humanity in the same place.

So, the evidence at this point would seem to support a scenario where anatomically modern human beings who had originated someplace else entered into western Europe, coexisted for a while, but then replaced the population of quite different looking, and perhaps quite differently behaving, indigenous Neandertals. So far, so good for the replacement model.

The evidence is not all clear, however, for a distinct break between indigenous Neandertals and the earliest appearance of modern human beings in much of central, southern, or eastern Europe. For example, several robust modern human crania were recovered from the site of Mladeč in Czechoslovakia (Smith 1984). Among the fossils recovered here were the remains of a modern-looking 3-year-old child. The skull is quite different in appearance from that of the 5-year-old Neandertal from Teshik-Tash or the 3-year-old from Gibraltar mentioned in Chapter 11. Nevertheless, some interpret the robust form of the Mladeč crania as representative of a transition between Neandertals and modern humans, with no break or evidence of replacement (Smith et al. 1989).

On the island of Crete, a partial cranium has been found with a uranium series date of 51,000 years (Facchinni and Guisberti 1990). It appears to be modern, but it exhibits anatomical features reminiscent of

Neandertal. Of even greater interest are the eastern European sites of Vindija Cave in Yugoslavia and Kůlna and Sipka Caves in Czechoslovakia. These sites date to between 38,000 to 45,000 ya and have produced fossils, interpreted by some, as morphologically transitional between older Neandertals and more recent, anatomically modern human beings. In particular, their brow ridges are intermediate in size between Neandertals and moderns, and they also seem to be transitional in other aspects of their cranial and facial anatomy (Smith et al. 1989).

So we are left without a clear consensus. In western Europe, there seems to have been a replacement of Neandertals by modern humans, but in eastern Europe (and, possibly, central and southern) there is some evidence supporting continuity.

## Asia

One piece of evidence used by the supporters of the multiregional hypothesis is the apparent continuity through time of specific, regionally distributed physical traits, particularly in Asia. Examples of *Homo erectus*, archaic *Homo sapiens*, and modern humans in the Far East share certain skeletal characteristics that are either rare or absent in populations in Africa and Europe (Wolpoff, et al. 1984). These include shovel-shaped lateral incisor teeth, extra cranial sutures, and a ridge inside the lower jaw. Some examples of traits show continuity in Europe and Africa as well, though such continuity is not nearly as apparent as in the Asian fossils. This evidence is used to support the notion that in the evolution of anatomically modern humans, local populations did not become extinct nor were they replaced by groups from elsewhere. Instead, local groups of archaic humans each evolved into modern humans more or less independently (but always with some amount of gene flow), with local "racial" traits preserved over hundreds of thousands of years.

In a recent, detailed analysis of the Sangiran *H. erectus* specimens (see Chapter 10), Andrew Kramer (1991) compared their lower jaws to those of anatomically modern human beings from Africa and Australia. Kramer deduced that, had the East Asian *erectus* population been replaced by an expanding population of anatomically modern human beings from somewhere else, then the modern mandibles from Australia should not look like those from the *erectus* specimens from Java. The Sangiran and other Javanese hominids would have, in this scenario, contributed nothing to modern human evolution. The modern Australian jaws should look like the modern African jaws because both modern Australians and modern Africans would have shared a relatively recent, common ancestor. In fact, Kramer found that the modern Australian jaws shared many common anatomical features with the San-

**Figure 12.6** *The skulls from Skuhl (top) and Jebel Qafzeh (bottom) from Israel are examples of robust but otherwise anatomically modern crania. Both are dated to more than 90,000 ya. Recently derived dates of up to, and even greater than, 100,000 ya for anatomically modern human skeletons have resulted in a reassessment of the evolution of modern people.* (Skuhl V: Peabody Museum Harvard University, photograph by Hillel Burger. Jebel Qafzeh: Laboratory of Vertebrate and Human Paleontology, Paris. B. Vandermeersch)

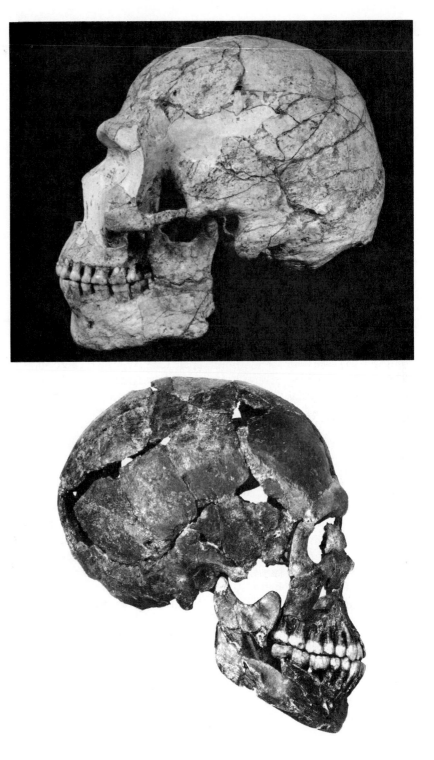

giran mandibles, indicating, to him, genetic continuity supporting the multiregional model.

As Kramer (1991) points out, Australia, in general, poses a real problem for the replacement hypothesis as even its strongest proponents (Stringer and Andrews 1988) admit. The earliest settlement of Australia dates to after 50,000 ya, well after local (to East Asia) *H. erectus* and/or archaic *H. sapiens* would have been replaced by anatomically modern *H. sapiens* who had come from somewhere else. However, some of the early Australian fossil crania—most notably Willandra Lakes Hominid 50—are remarkably robust. These look quite primitive and share many features with older, indigenous (to East Asia) premodern hominids. The question here, ultimately, is, "Do such specimens reflect regional continuity with older, local forms, or did fully modern, gracile humans enter Australia as part of a general wave of replacement of archaics in East Asia and did some evolve a more robust form later on?" This crucial question simply cannot be answered because the dating of the most important crania is uncertain (Habgood 1989; Jones 1989). If the oldest crania in Australia turn out to be the gracile variety, then the replacement model is upheld. If, on the other hand, the robust form turns out to be older, the multiregional model is supported.

Other Asian evidence does not support the multiregional hypothesis. Southwest Asian Neandertals—dating to the early last glacial and including those mentioned in Chapter 11 (Amud, Shanidar, Tabun, and Teshik-Tash)—are all fairly typically Neandertal.

Interestingly different specimens have been excavated in Skhul and Jebel Qafzeh in Israel, and Darra-i-Kur in Afghanistan (Figure 12.6). The skulls are more rounded than those of the Neandertals, with higher foreheads and smaller faces. Where mandibles have been recovered, it is clear that they had chins—a trait exhibited by modern humans but not Neandertals. Nevertheless, these skulls are ruggedly constructed and exhibit, by modern standards, relatively large, distinct brow ridges.

Ostensibly, with their large brow ridges and prognathous profiles, the Skhul and Qafzeh crania could represent "evolved" Neandertals, transitional between the indigenous, far more classically Neandertal hominds from Amud, Tabun, and Shanidar, on the one hand, and anatomically modern human beings with our smaller brows and flat faces, on the other. Most researchers, however, label these rounded crania as anatomically modern.

Beyond this, in the same region, there is the pelvis of the Kebara Neandertal, discussed in Chapter 11, which is fundamentally different from that of modern humans (Rak 1990). Yoel Rak maintains that, in an evolutionary sense, you simply can't readily get from the Kebara to the modern pelvis—they are too different, indicating no continuity between local archaics and moderns.

Finally, for the Skhul and Qafzeh crania to represent transitional forms, they would, of necessity, have to be intermediate in age as well as morphology—younger than the Neandertals from whom they evolved and older than the anatomically modern humans whom they became.

Recent dating does not support such a scenario. Skhul and Qafzeh turn out to be *older* by quite a bit than most of the Neandertal specimens known from the area. Burned flint artifacts associated with the Qafzeh skull have been dated by thermoluminescence (Valladas et al. 1988) to 92,000 B.P. If that date is correct (thermoluminescence dating applied to nonceramic objects is still experimental), then rugged but otherwise anatomically modern human beings would have predated Neandertals in the Middle East by 30,000 years and would have coexisted with them in Eurasia for 60,000 years. This date also means modern humans existed in Southwest Asia almost 60,000 years before they appeared in Europe.

The very similar Skhul specimens have recently been associated with an electron spin resonance date of between 81,000 to 101,000 years (Stringer et al. 1989), and an electron spin resonance date on the Qafzeh materials further verifies a probable age in excess of 90,000 years (Stringer 1988).

These dates on the Southwest Asian material suggest to some a scenario far different than one asserting the transitional position of Skhul and Qafzeh. Stringer (1990; and see Bower 1991) maintains that the evidence indicates that anatomically modern human beings turn up in Southwest Asia sometime *before* the appearance there of the Neandertals. Stringer asserts that the Neandertals may have migrated into the Middle East from Europe only about 70,000 ya. In his view, they shared the region, perhaps intermittently, with modern human beings for 60,000 years, but eventually they became extinct, being completely replaced by anatomically modern human beings.

Some disagree with this view (Smith et al. 1989), interpreting the Shanidar Neandertals and those from another Middle Eastern site, Zuttiyeh, as being ancestral to all Neandertals from that region. In this view, the Neandertals were not European migrants into the area but had evolved in place. In this same model, Shanidar, Amud, Tabun, on the one hand, and the Skhul and Qafzeh specimens, on the other, do not represent two different species but one highly variable species.

Nevertheless, considering the degree of difference, particularly in the pelvis, along with the chronological gap, the Middle Eastern Neandertals do not obviously seem to have been ancestral to modern humans in that region—they are too different and too late. It would seem that there was no transition from Neandertal to modern in the Middle East. The multiregional model cannot be upheld, and the replacement model seems to better fit the data.

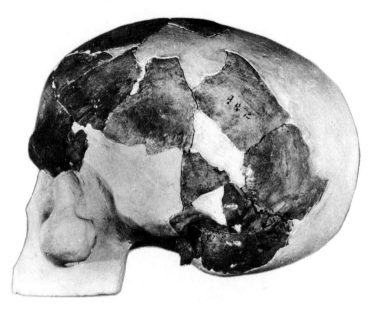

**Figure 12.7** *The Border Cave skull from South Africa may date to more than 100,000 ya. Entirely modern in appearance, it is one of several from sub-Saharan Africa that seem to support the replacement model and point to Africa as the source for modern humanity.* (Photo by A. R. Hughes. Courtesy, Professor P. V. Tobias, University of the Witwatersrand, Johannesburg, South Africa)

## Africa

This brings us back to Africa, where we started the story of human evolution some 4 million years and many pages ago. Several fossil sites in the southern and eastern parts of that continent support the replacement model and ultimately may prove Africa as the source of anatomically modern human beings at a surprisingly early date (Brauer 1984; Rightmire 1984b; Stringer 1989, 1990; Stringer and Andrews 1988).

Klasies River Mouth, Border Cave, Omo (the Omo 1 skull), Kanjera, Mumba, and Singa are all sites in Africa at which the fossils of anatomically modern human beings have been discovered at astonishingly early levels, predating even the early Southwest Asian sites. The specimen from Klasies River Mouth (KRM) is at least 70,000 and perhaps as much as 125,000 years old (Singer and Wymer 1982). The Border Cave remains are at least 50,000 and may be 115,000 years old (Beaumont et al. 1978; Rightmire 1979b; Figure 12.7). As stated earlier, the Omo 1 fossil appears to be pretty firmly dated to 130,000 years, and the Mumba remains (mostly teeth, entirely modern in their appearance) are at least 110,000 years old. Singa and Kanjera appear to be of similar antiquity.

Admittedly, there are problems with some of the specimens (Smith et al. 1989). As luck would have it, the more firmly dated examples like KRM tend to be the more fragmentary, so it is difficult to be certain concerning identification. The more complete specimens like Border Cave and Omo 1, which clearly are anatomically modern, are not as

**Figure 12.8** *The cranium from Jebel Irhoud from Morocco possesses anatomical characteristics intermediate between those of archaic and anatomically modern* Homo sapiens. *Like the Florisband, Ngaloba, and Omo II specimens, it lends support to the hypothesis of in-place evolution of modern from archaic forms in Africa.* (Phototheque Du Musée De L'Homme)

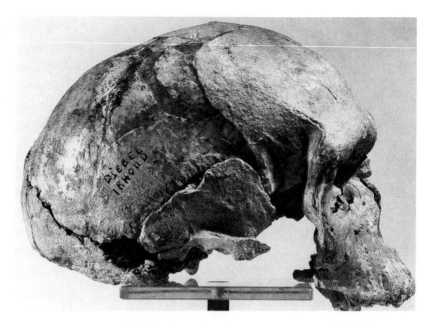

firmly dated. Together, however, these represent a growing group of fossils that cannot be ignored.

Also of significance is the fact that at least some hominid fossils found in Africa appear to represent forms intermediate between archaic and modern humans. For example, the presumably somewhat older fossils from Florisbad, Jebel Irhoud, Omo (Omo 2), and Ngaloba (Laetoli Hominid 18) all exhibit a mixture of archaic and modern traits (Figure 12.8). Smith et al. (1989) label these the "African Transitional Group." These crania are larger, more rounded, and have higher foreheads and smaller brow ridges than older African archaic humans like those mentioned in Chapter 11 from Kabwe, Bodo, or Lake Ndutu. Also, their cranial capacities are larger than other archaic specimens from Africa. At the same time, they have a more modern appearance than some European archaics, although they are not as modern looking as the KRM and other fossils listed earlier.

### The Paleontological Verdict

We began this chapter by warning you that there was no easy solution to the question, "How did modern humanity evolve?" We presume that you will now agree. Nevertheless, although a definitive answer based on the paleontological evidence is yet out of reach, there are some tentative conclusions we can reach. Consider the deductive framework established at the beginning of this chapter and summarized in Figure 12.3. The paleontological evidence needed to support the multiregional hypothesis included the existence of forms intermediate between archaic and modern humans throughout the world. Parallel changes from archaic to modern forms should have been taking place everywhere more or less simultaneously. The evidence presented does not universally support such a scenario.

On the other hand, the replacement model demands that paleontological evidence for modern humans appears in a restricted region at a date preceding their appearance elsewhere. The existence of intermediate forms should similarly be restricted to the source region. Archaic and modern humans should have coexisted for a time outside the source as the moderns spread to other areas. The paleontological evidence as it now stands seems to provide slightly stronger support for this view and points to sub-Saharan Africa as the probable source for all modern human populations.

On the other hand, proponents of the replacement model have to be able to explain the presence of apparently intermediate forms elsewhere, particularly in eastern Europe and perhaps, Australia. It is conceivable here, perhaps, that when modern human beings coexisted with archaics in those regions, there was substantial interbreeding between the two groups. Thus, what appear to some to represent morphologically and chronologically transitional forms are, in reality, the result of the interfertility of the anatomically modern humans and archaics, with offspring exhibiting a mixture of traits.

Thus, although it appears that the paleontological evidence tips the scales a bit toward the replacement hypothesis, it certainly cannot be characterized as definitive. Recent advances in genetic research—a sort of archaeology of our genes—seem, however, to lend support to the replacement hypothesis.

## GENETIC EVIDENCE

We mentioned molecular genetic evidence for evolution in Chapter 8 when discussing the emergence of the hominid lineage. Genetic data from living human populations can also be used to examine the question of modern human origins. Genetic lines of inquiry also lend support to the replacement model and point to an African source for modern humanity.

The multiregional model requires a great deal of genetic variation between different human groups because they evolved more or less separately from archaic to modern forms. Human beings, however, although showing variation in appearance, actually exhibit little genetic variation—in fact, less than that seen within ape species (Stringer and

Andrews 1988:1264). This indicates a relatively recent, common source for all living humans, which is consistent with the replacement hypothesis.

Although genetic variation is low in modern human beings, when some very detailed genetic instructions coded by the DNA contained within our cells (our **nuclear DNA**) are compared across geographic populations, the world's peoples tend to cluster into two groups: those from sub-Saharan Africa and those from everywhere else (Stringer and Andrews 1988:1265). This body of evidence also supports the replacement model and points to an African source for modern humanity because, if people have been evolving in Africa longer than elsewhere, the African population should be distinct from that of Europe and Asia.

A new approach in genetic analysis is now shedding more light on the question of the origin of anatomically modern *Homo sapiens*. This new research involves the analysis of **mitochondrial DNA** (mtDNA). Mitochondria are the energy factories within the cells of plants and animals. They possess their own distinct DNA, which, in complex interaction with the nuclear DNA, codes for the mitochondria's function of producing the biological "fuel" that provides energy for the cell. Each human cell contains hundreds of mitochondria.

At some point in early cellular evolution, the ancestors of mitochondria were separate organisms. Through what may be the first example of **symbiosis**, they became functional elements within larger cells, maintaining their own genetic code. This code is particularly useful for some genetic studies because mtDNA accumulates mutations at a rate five to ten times faster than nuclear DNA, and there is evidence that the mutation rate is fairly constant.

Allan Wilson, Rebecca Cann, and Mark Stoneking are molecular biologists who used mtDNA in an attempt to answer questions concerning human evolution (Cann et al. 1987; Lewin 1987a,b, 1991; Stoneking and Cann 1989; Wilson and Cann 1992). They analyzed the mtDNA of 147 modern human females from New Guinea, Australia, Asia, Europe, and Africa. They chose females because mtDNA is inherited in the female line; although both human eggs and sperm contain mitochondria, sperm do not pass theirs on at fertilization.

If human populations had been geographically separate for a long time, evolving separately into modern humans—as the multiregional model suggests—the mtDNA in each of these geographic subsamples should be quite distinct. Different mutations would have been accumulating in the separate populations during that time.

When the mtDNA of the sample groups was compared, however, the researchers found that it was all quite similar. Compared to chimpanzees, for example, the mtDNA of human beings is extremely homogeneous. In fact, chimp mtDNA commonly exhibits ten times the amount of variation as does human mtDNA (Wilson and Cann 1992:71). From this they inferred that the different geographic groups in the sample could not have evolved separately over a long period. Their mtDNA simply was not different enough to support a hypothesis of ancient separation and separate evolution. This stands in apparent contradiction to the multiregional model of evolution. The mtDNA of women around the world seems to show that their populations all came from the same source at a relatively recent date.

The one geographic group that stood out was the women of sub-Saharan Africa. Just as was the case for nuclear DNA, their mtDNA was relatively distinct from that of the other groups (Figure 12.9). The mtDNA in Africa was also the most internally heterogeneous. Together, these two pieces of evidence suggest that the African mtDNA is older than that of the other groups—it has been independently accumulating mutations longer and therefore has more variation. If the African mtDNA is older, then it would most logically be the source for the mtDNA in the rest of the world's populations. This, in turn, would seem to support the notion that modern human beings evolved first in Africa (and so have been there longer than anywhere else) and that other human populations must be ultimately derived from an African source. This scenario corresponds to the replacement hypothesis.

Beyond this, the researchers were able to suggest a rate for mtDNA mutation accumulation and from this projection construct an mtDNA clock. They used the New Guinea subsample because they could measure two variables in the equation. First, they could measure the amount of mtDNA variation within the New Guinea subsample. Because the aboriginal population of New Guinea probably derives from a small group of original settlers, all the modern mtDNA variation has come about since the initial settlement of the island. Second, we know when that settlement occurred; archaeological evidence indicates that human beings first came to New Guinea about 40,000 ya. Thus, we can calculate how much variation has developed in mtDNA as a result of accumulated mutations over approximately 40,000 years. That enables the calculation of a general rate of mtDNA mutation through time.

The researchers applied this equation to the African subsample. They concluded that the variation of the mtDNA within the African group would have taken five times as long to develop as the variation within New Guinea. In other words, mtDNA in humans has been accumulating mutations in Africa for approximately $5 \times 40,000$ or 200,000 years. This result seems to be in line with the inference drawn from the anatomically modern human fossils found in Africa and dated to more than 100,000 ya. This idea is popularly referred to as the "Eve" hypothesis (see "Contemporary Issue" in this chapter). More results of mtDNA studies will be discussed in Chapter 13.

Recently, parts of this interpretation have been called into question, even by some of its proponents (Barinaga 1992; Hedges et al. 1992). It

**nuclear DNA:** The genetic material in the nucleus of a cell.

**mitochondrial DNA:** DNA from the mitochondria of cells rather than the nucleus.

**symbiosis:** A mutually beneficial relationship between members of two species.

298

**Figure 12.9** *Computer-generated tree showing the lines of descent of the 147 women sampled in the mtDNA study described. Note the cluster of women of African descent at lower right and the proposed ancestor based on the genetic distinctions between African and non-African women. Recent mtDNA studies have generated trees showing very different relationships* (see text). (Allan Wilson, University of California, Berkeley)

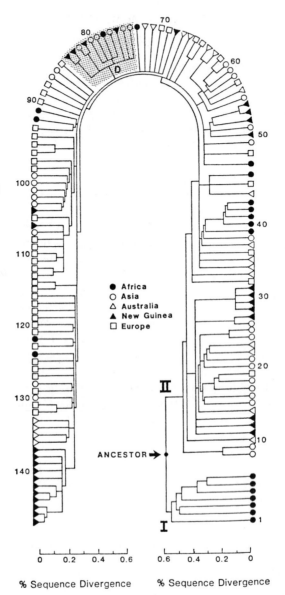

turns out there are far more computer-generated family trees, like the one depicted in Figure 12.9, than previously thought. There may be literally millions of trees that reasonably account for the complex genetic data that are used. These trees show a great deal of variation in terms of the exact relationships of the human groups sampled, and they even vary in which group—African or non-African—is shown to be the ancestral population of modern humans. Indeed, a group of researchers that includes Stoneking, one of the originators of the "Eve" idea, now states that the data, in light of the latest computer analyses, are "insufficient" to resolve the issue of the ancestral population. They do, however, still propose that the data "suggest" an African origin (Hedges et al. 1992:739).

Even though the mtDNA data alone may present problems, however, a recent African origin is still indicated by the fossil evidence, by studies of nuclear DNA, and, as we will see in the next section, to some extent by the archaeological evidence. In addition, it remains unrefuted that the African sample exhibits the greatest variation in mtDNA, and this strongly supports the idea of that population as the oldest among modern *H. sapiens.*

The great antiquity and anatomical modernity of some of the African fossils, the existence of fossils intermediate in appearance between archaic and modern, and the mtDNA research, if supported by further study, may solve the question posed at the beginning of this chapter: Where do we come from? Just as Africa served as the cradle of hominid evolution 4 million ya, it may also have served as the crucible in which modern humanity was forged more than 100,000 ya.

Clearly, however, the issue of modern human origins is confusing. To return to Sherlock Holmes, we cannot yet distinguish the incidental from the vital. Nevertheless, there is currently a plurality of opinion concerning the evolution of anatomically modern *H. sapiens.* Based on the paleontological and genetic evidence, most researchers now support the replacement model and interpret the fossil record in a way similar to that presented in Figure 12.10. Existing evidence supports, if only in part, replacement over continuity, with modern *H. sapiens* appearing first in Africa and then expanding across the surface of the globe (Figure 12.11). As is always the case in science, however, we eagerly await new data that may support or refute the accepted model.

## THE CULTURAL RECORD

There is, of course, another source of data that we may use to assess the two models of modern human origins. If archaic *Homo sapiens* were everywhere replaced by populations of anatomically modern humans expanding out from their source area in Africa, one would expect the archaeological record to show that, where archaics were indigenous, artifacts of the moderns would be superimposed over and replace the artifacts of the archaics.

The artifactual evidence is interesting, although not clearly supportive of either model. It must be said that the stone tool assemblage of the earlier Neandertals of Europe and Southwest Asia simply do not look very different from the toolkits of the early moderns of Africa and Southwest Asia (Wolpoff 1989). Whatever advantage anatomically modern human beings may have had, it does not seem to have been in a more sophisticated material culture. As Alan Thorne and Milford Wolpoff (1992) point out, for example, the artifacts associated with the anatomically modern crania from Skhul and Qafzeh are virtually identical to those recovered from nearby, contemporaneous sites, where they

**Figure 12.10** *Overview of our current understanding of the evolution of modern from archaic Homo sapiens in Africa, showing the early evolution of anatomically modern human beings in Africa and their later appearance in Europe, where they replaced indigenous populations of archaic humans.*

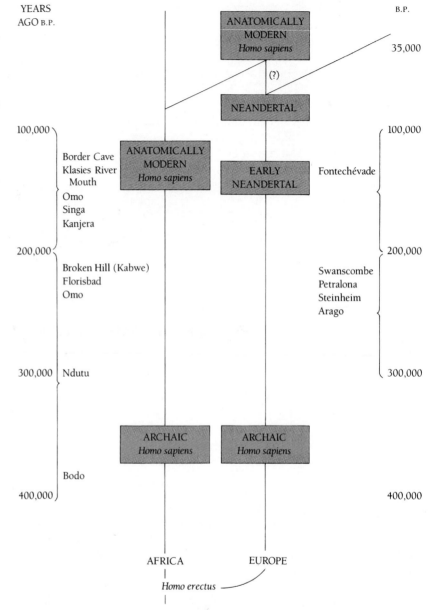

are associated with typically Neandertal crania. There are striking similarities at 100,000 ya and even later, and it is not until fairly recently that the Upper Paleolithic modern human inhabitants of Europe produced the far more sophisticated tools of the Aurignacian tradition, to be discussed later in this chapter.

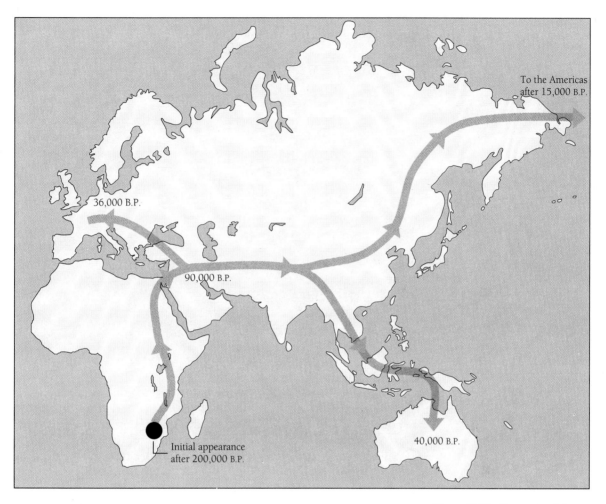

To the Americas
after 15,000 B.P.

36,000 B.P.

90,000 B.P.

Initial appearance
after 200,000 B.P.

40,000 B.P.

**Figure 12.11** *Movement and timing of anatomically modern* Homo sapiens' *appearance in Africa and expansion throughout the world.*

On the other hand, some see elements of replacement in the archaeological sequence. Archaeologist Frank Harrold (1989), for example, compared the older **Mousterian** industry associated with the European Neandertals (discussed in Chapter 11) with a later industry, the **Chăttleperonian**, also associated with the Neandertals. He compared both of these with the **Aurignacian** tool industry of Europe's first anatomically modern humans (see Figure 12.14). The Chăttleperonian possesses more sophisticated tools than the Mousterian, and the Aurignacian, in turn, is more sophisticated than the Chăttleperonian. Harrold suggests that Mousterian wielding Neandertals in Europe developed the more advanced Chăttleperonian after coming into contact with and borrowing some ideas from Aurignacian wielding modern humans who had entered Europe from the south and east: likely from Southwest Asia. Although the Aurignacian and Chăttleperonian share many elements,

**Mousterian:** The culture associated with European Neandertals.

**Chăttleperonian:** The stone tool industry associated with late Neandertals in Europe.

**Aurignacian:** The toolmaking tradition of anatomically modern *Homo sapiens* of the European Upper Paleolithic.

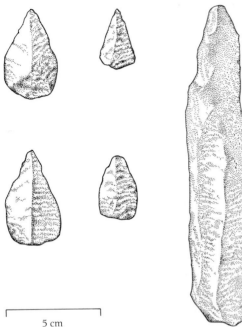

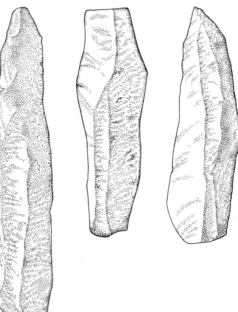

5 cm

**Figure 12.12** *Blade tools from the early anatomically modern* Homo sapiens *site of Klasies River Mouth in South Africa.* (From Singer and Wymer 1982)

Harrold suggests that the modern toolkit was slightly better and provided an advantage to the modern humans who used it. If this is the case, then the artifactual evidence seems to support the replacement hypothesis. But it must be admitted that there is no good evidence in most areas for the wholesale replacement of a primitive tool technology practiced by archaic humans, by an advanced technology practiced by modern humans.

The artifacts recovered at one of the early modern human sites in Africa do show a more sophisticated technology than contemporary tool assemblages in Europe and Asia associated with archaic humans. At Klasies River Mouth (KRM) in southern Africa, there are long, bifacially worked spear points made on stone blades detached from cores by means of a "punch" technique (Singer and Wymer 1982). In this technique, long, narrow flakes called blades are removed from stone core pieces by striking a punch, usually made of antler, with a hammerstone, instead of striking the core directly with the stone hammer. The punch directs the force of the blow precisely, resulting in longer, narrower, thinner flakes of predictable shape and form (Figure 12.12). Such a technique, although more highly developed, occurs much later in Europe.

Although they lived on the coast, the ancient inhabitants of KRM do not appear to have relied very much on fishing (Klein 1982, 1983). They did hunt seal and penguin, and they collected intertidal molluscs.

Of greater importance to their subsistence was the Cape buffalo, an aggressive animal living in large herds and weighing between 700 and 900 kilograms (1500 to 2000 pounds). When threatened, their typical response is not to flee but to charge. They are dangerous to hunt with modern firearms, much less stone-tipped spears.

According to Robert Klein, the faunal assemblage at KRM shows that only very young and very old buffalo were hunted—at least successfully. Adult animals in their prime, providing the most meat but also the most dangerous to attempt to kill, were rarely hunted. In looking at the Klasies River faunal assemblage, Lewis Binford (1984) concludes that scavenging was the dominant mode of subsistence, at least as far as adult animals of large species were concerned.

Klein, on the other hand, believes that the evidence indicates that eland—large (about the same weight as the buffalo) but relatively docile antelope—were hunted in all age categories. The eland response to a threat is to flee, so they are easy to stampede into traps where they can be captured and killed. As a result, Klein thinks, the prehistoric inhabitants of KRM managed to kill many healthy, adult animals.

Having examined the faunal remains at sites associated with the australopithecines, *Homo erectus*, and Neandertal, Binford (1985) suggests that modern humans were in fact the first hominids to develop a hunting mode of subsistence. He believes that this did not occur until sometime between 100,000 and 40,000 ya (1985:20). The evidence at KRM lends some support to his hypothesis.

The KRM data do not justify the conclusion that the inhabitants were full-time "great" hunters. Scavenging probably made a major contribution to their diet. But there is far better evidence for hunting here, among these early anatomically modern humans, than at the sites of previous nonmodern hominids.

## UPPER PALEOLITHIC INNOVATIONS

Although we may no longer view Europe as the initial source for modern human populations, we recognize that once anatomically modern humans showed up on that continent, they developed a remarkable culture adapted to life during the final glacial stage. They hunted the big-game animals that flourished at the end of the Pleistocene with their exquisitely flaked stone spears. Out of the antlers, bone, and ivory of some of the animals they hunted, they manufactured more hunting weapons, such as harpoons and spear points, as well as sewing tools like awls and needles (Figure 12.13).

As mentioned in Europe, ancient modern humans developed a technology of blade tool production known as Aurignacian after a site in

**Figure 12.13** *During the Upper Paleolithic, anatomically modern human beings in Europe developed an impressive bone, antler, and ivory technology. They produced both utilitarian objects, as well as works of probable religious significance.* (American Museum of Natural History, Lee Boltin)

France (Aurignac) where it was initially recognized and defined (Figure 12.14). This technology first shows up in the archaeological record of Europe associated with anatomically modern *H. sapiens* about 35,000 ya.

Although the Mousterian flake industry described in Chapter 11 was more efficient than the previous Acheulian in terms of the number of tools and amount of usable edge produced from the same amount of stone, the Aurignacian technology was more efficient still, producing five times as much length of usable tool edge. In Europe, the practice of making cutting, scraping, piercing, and engraving tools (called **burins**) from blades struck from prepared cores led to some of the most finely flaked works in stone seen anywhere in the world. The burins were used for removing long, sharp slices from antler, bone, or ivory, which, in turn, were made into awls and needles. By about 20,000 ya, the

**Figure 12.14** *Aurignacian flint blades from France. This Upper Paleolithic industry made use of a core and blade technology in which long, thin, extremely sharp stone blades were struck from stone nodules.*

**Figure 12.15** *Bifacially flaked Solutrean spear points of the European Upper Paleolithic are examples of some of the finest stonework the world has ever seen.*

**Solutrean** tradition had emerged in Europe, where true masterpieces in the craft of stoneworking were produced. Some of these bifacially flaked, long, narrow, thin blades are so delicate and so exquisitely flaked that it has been suggested that they were, in fact, works of art not intended for use on the end of spears (Figure 12.15).

**burin:** A stone engraving tool.

**Solutrean:** The Upper Paleolithic culture of France and Spain.

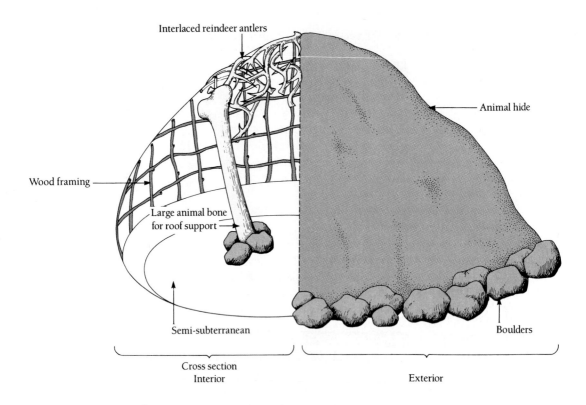

Interlaced reindeer antlers

Animal hide

Wood framing

Large animal bone
for roof support

Semi-subterranean

Boulders

Cross section
Interior

Exterior

**Figure 12.16** *Reconstruction of a hut at the 18,000-year-old site of Mal'ta in south-central Russia. Because wood was not available on the tundra, the bones of woolly mammoth were used as construction materials.*

## Comparing the Middle and Upper Paleolithic

Anthropologist Randall White (1982) has examined some of the major differences between cultures of the European Middle and Upper Paleolithic. He identifies several significant cultural innovations:

1. Increased use of bone, ivory, and antler for making tools
2. Manufacture of nonutilitarian objects, particularly items of personal adornment—indicating, perhaps, a greater sense of self and individuality
3. Broadening of the subsistence base to include fish and birds
4. Larger, perhaps more sedentary, settlements
5. Trade for raw materials across long distances, implying greater social integration of distant and diverse groups

Leslie Freeman (1973) has compared faunal assemblages from seventy-seven levels at twenty Middle and Upper Paleolithic cave sites in northern Spain. He found that the older assemblages showed that a small number of animal species were exploited and few members of each species were represented in archaeological deposits within the caves. He concludes that the Middle Paleolithic inhabitants of this area were "opportunistic" hunters, killing what they could when they could.

Observing a great change in the faunal assemblages dated to the Upper Paleolithic, Freeman identified a consistent increase through time in the number of prey species represented, indicating, perhaps, more efficient hunting strategies. The evidence seems to indicate that the anatomically modern inhabitants of these caves were habitual hunters where their archaic predecessors may not have been.

## Mal'ta

In parts of Eurasia, anatomically modern humans living in the same tundra as their archaic predecessors developed an adaptation of great efficiency. A good example is the site of Mal'ta in south-central Russia near the modern city of Irkutsk (Chard 1974). Occupied as much as 18,000 ya during the end of the final glacial, Mal'ta was a large site covering some 600 square meters with several dwellings. People living in the harsh glacial climate of the area would have needed shelter, but there were no caves like those used by the early anatomically modern humans of Europe. Moreover, during its occupation the site was located in tundra, so trees would have been largely unavailable for construction purposes.

The people at Mal'ta developed an ingenious solution to this problem. They used the leg and rib bones of large animals like woolly mammoth for the structural framework of their dwellings. On the roof, where the weight of such bones would have been too great, they used lighter elements like reindeer antlers. Onto this bone–antler structural skeleton they attached animal hides, held in place on the ground with large boulders (Figure 12.16).

Subsistence at Mal'ta clearly was based on the hunting of the big-game animals that migrated across the tundra in a yearly pattern, especially woolly rhinoceros, woolly mammoth, and reindeer. They almost certainly used the hides from these animals for clothing. They also trapped foxes and other small mammals for their pelts. Interestingly, they buried the remains of the skinned foxes.

Also at Mal'ta we see a tradition of carved artwork, perhaps as part of a religious pattern. These three-dimensional bone and ivory carvings included human female figurines and waterfowl. These people also incised on antler and bone intricate two-dimensional, abstract designs of curved lines and occasional realistic animals like the woolly mammoth.

**Figure 12.17** *Geographical distribution of Upper Paleolithic European cave paintings. Most of the sites are clustered in the area of Franco-Cantabria in southern France and northern Spain.* (After Jochim 1983)

## ART AND IDEAS IN THE UPPER PALEOLITHIC

Clearly, the Upper Paleolithic was a time of great cultural achievement. The broad subsistence base of modern human beings, their manufacture of items of adornment, and long-distance trade are all indications of their sophistication. Probably the most interesting reflection of their adaptation, though, is their artwork.

It was the European moderns who, beginning as much as 35,000 and continuing until about 10,000 ya, produced some of the world's first art. Although groups in other parts of the world also contributed to the growth of artistic expression, it is in the cave paintings and sculptures of Europe that we recognize the development of a unique artistic tradition.

In a 25,000-year period that, as Margaret Conkey (1983) points out, constitutes the first two-thirds of human art history, these Paleolithic Europeans produced a remarkable variety of artwork in numerous media and styles. They carved stone, bone, antler, and ivory; produced bas-reliefs; made ceramic figurines; engraved objects with both natural figures and abstract designs; and painted fantastic friezes on cave walls. Their artwork was rendered in styles ranging from representational to abstract.

The sculptures appear to be older than the paintings. The latter, however, can only be dated accurately when pieces have fallen and been incorporated into an archaeological deposit. Of the sculptures, there are engraved stone blocks from France dated to greater than 32,000 B.P. and ivory animal statuettes from central Europe dated to more than 31,000 B.P. (Conkey 1983:213).

It is largely the cave paintings that so capture the imagination, although only a little more than 200 caves with paintings are known and most of these are clustered in southwest France and northern Spain (the Franco-Cantabrian region; Figure 12.17). In often naturalistic works, the ancient artists painted bison, oxen, horses, deer, mammoth, ibex, rhinoceros, lion, and bear. Though there is a great deal of variation, many of the animals are by no means simplistic, nor are they childishly rendered. They are sophisticated, fluid, and natural.

The artwork is striking indeed, moving even the most objective of scientists to speak in superlatives. Anthropologist Pat Shipman has said, on viewing the paintings for the first time, "I had looked at photographs of Lascaux [one of the best known of the art-bearing caves], of course, so I knew that the paintings were beautiful; but what I did not know was that they would reach across 17,000 years to grab my soul" (1990:62).

Natural pigments were produced by grinding into powder ochre for orange, yellow, and red; iron oxides for brown; and manganese dioxide for black. The powder was then mixed with a binding agent like grease, marrow, or blood. Using fingers, wooden spatulas, and brushes made of twigs or even animal hair, the artists applied the paint to their prehistoric canvases—the cave walls of Lascaux, Roc de Sers, Trois Fréres, and Niaux in France, Altamira and Casares in Spain, and many others.

The painted figures of these caves are not static or two-dimensional. They seem to move across the cave walls with muscles rippling, sinews straining (Figure 12.18). A herd of woolly rhinoceros, extinct for more than 10,000 years, lives again as they march single file across the cave wall at Rouffignac. An extinct bison with tail upraised, poised to flee, is frozen in time in Altamira. Another bison stands motionless, mortally wounded by spears, on the rock face in Niaux. Such paintings offer us a glimpse into an ancient world seldom available to the anthropologist who studies the past. They are a wonderful legacy left by the ancient peoples of Europe (Figure 12.19).

These Upper Paleolithic artists also produced three-dimensional works. For example, carved in limestone or ivory, the so-called **Venus figurines** are faceless women with exaggerated secondary sexual charac-

**Venus figurines:** Sculptures of women with exaggerated secondary sexual characteristics, dating to 32,000 ya.

**Figure 12.18** *A galloping horse frozen in time on the cave wall of Lascaux in France. Note how the left front leg is unconnected to the horse's body, adding to the three dimensional appearance of the figure.* (Mario Ruspoli; Caisse Nationale Des Monuments Historiques et Des Sites)

teristics (large breasts and buttocks) and often swollen stomachs (Figure 12.20). These portable sculptures are more restricted in time than the cave paintings. Most date to a very narrow period between 25,000 and 23,000 ya (Gamble 1983). They are geographically far more widespread than the cave paintings, however, and quite homogeneous with similar examples found in sites up to 2000 kilometers apart (Figure 12.21).

What did the artwork mean? It seems unlikely that cave paintings or sculptures were simply decoration; many of the cave sites where paintings have been found were not occupied by humans. The placement of the paintings is not random. André Leroi-Gourhan (1982) has identified a pattern to the appearance of the animals in the caves. Bison, oxen, and horses generally were accorded a central position within caves as well as within individual groups of paintings. Deer, ibex, and mammoth tend to

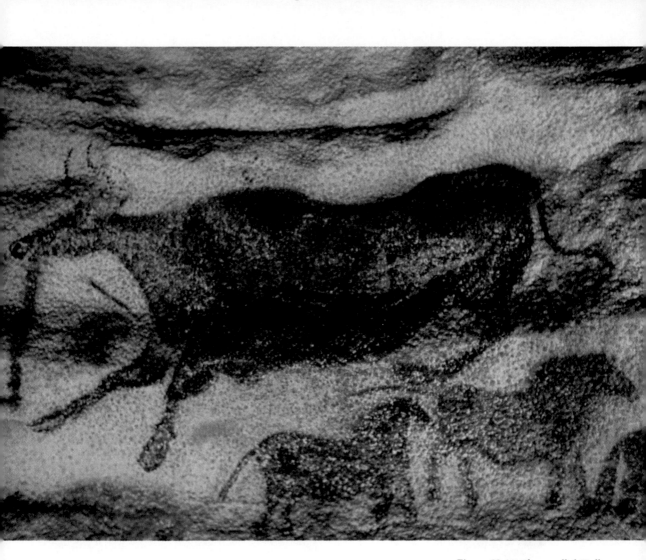

**Figure 12.19** *The so-called "Falling Cow" of Lascaux cave in France. Here again, note the sense of movement the ancient artists imparted in their depiction of the animal. There appears to be a spear thrust into the chest of the animal; the painting has been interpreted as a hunting scene.* (Mario Ruspoli; Caisse Nationale Des Monuments Historiques et Des Sites)

be peripheral. Rhinoceros, bear, and lion are usually far away, often deep in the recesses of caves, as much as a kilometer down narrow, winding, rock-strewn passageways.

Several hypotheses have been advanced to explain the meaning of the cave paintings in particular and Paleolithic art in general. As summarized by Conkey (1983), cave paintings have been explained as

1. The hunter's sympathetic magic
2. Trophyism
3. Expressions of sexual symbolism
4. Components of information/communication systems

Perhaps the early artists were performing sympathetic magic based on the belief that if you can "capture" an animal by painting it, you assure its literal capture in the hunt (Breuil 1952). This might explain

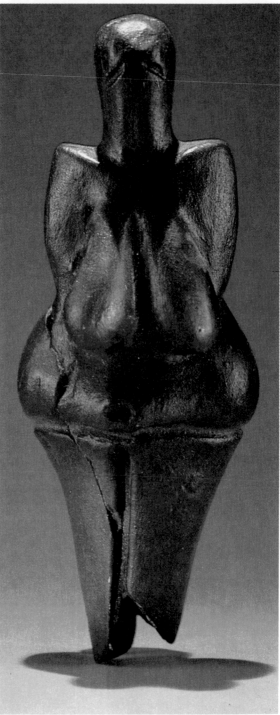

**Figure 12.20** *The precise meaning of the so-called Venus figu-rines is unknown. With their exaggerated secondary sexual fea-tures and pregnant appearance, they may have been fertility sym-bols; they may also have served as symbols of group identity.* (Left) *The famous "Venus of Willendorf."* (Right) *A cast of the Venus from Dolnivestonice, Czechoslovakia.* (American Museum of Nat-ural History, Lee Boltin (*l.*) and Jim Coxe (*r.*))

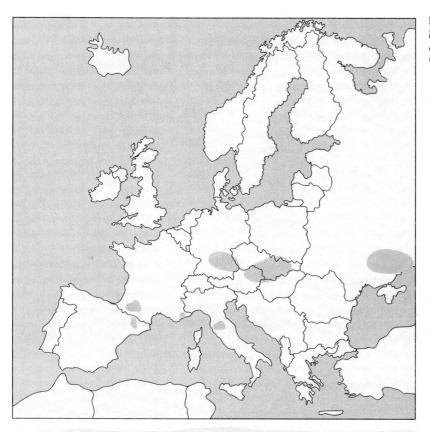

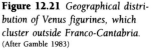

**Figure 12.21** *Geographical distribution of Venus figurines, which cluster outside Franco-Cantabria.* (After Gamble 1983)

the apparent avoidance of realistic depictions of people; maybe painting a person "captures" his or her spirit, soul, or essence.

The hypothesis of trophyism explains the cave paintings as virtual historical records of successful individual hunts (Eaton 1978a,b as cited in Conkey 1983:217). The paintings, in this explanation, are seen as "trophies" much in the way a modern hunter may mount an animal head on a wall.

The idea that the cave paintings reflect sexual symbolism is essentially a psychological explanation and difficult, if not impossible, to test scientifically. Leroi-Gourhan (1968) bases this hypothesis on an analysis of abstract designs on cave walls that he interprets as symbols of masculinity and femininity. In this vein, the Venus figurines may be fertility symbols.

More recent researchers have interpreted what Conkey (1978:74) calls the "explosion of symbolic behavior" in the Upper Paleolithic, as an attempt to transmit information in symbolic ways (Conkey 1980; Gamble 1982, 1983, 1986; Hammond 1974; Jochim 1983). All these researchers propose that as human ecological circumstances changed during the late Pleistocene, social systems changed as well. Art, these writers feel, served the purpose of transmitting socially important information within cultural systems stressed by changes in their ecology.

For example, Michael Jochim notes that most of the art can be dated from the period 25,000 to 10,000 B.P., which corresponds to a glacial maximum. He maintains that parts of Europe became uninhabitable during this period. The Franco-Cantabrian area, where the cave paintings are clustered, would not have been as severely affected, however. Jochim suggests that this would have resulted in population shifts into this area, creating the social problems attendant with different peoples coming into increased contact. He sees art as a way of marking territory, of ritually reinforcing group identity and solidarity.

Anthropologist Patricia Rice and sociologist Ann Paterson have applied a statistical analysis to the cave paintings of two European regions: the Dordogne-Garonne drainage of west-central France (1985) and the Cantabrian region of northern Spain (1986). These researchers found that there was a pattern to how often individual animal species turned up in the paintings. The Paleolithic artists depicted smaller animals like red deer and reindeer in direct proportion to the abundance of their bones in local archaeological sites dating to the period of the paintings. Larger animals, especially horses and bison, were depicted more frequently in the caves than might have been expected from a simple count of their bones at the same sites. Rice and Paterson conclude from this that species frequency in the cave art largely was a function of the economic significance of the animal. Small animals that were hunted with great regularity and large animals that, although hunted less frequently, provided a large amount of meat were the cave artists' favorite subjects. They conclude that the cave art can be explained as "fertility magic, hunting magic, hunting education, and story-telling about hunting" (1985:98).

Interestingly, the Paleolithic cave painters were not so adept at self-portraits. Cave paintings of human subjects are relatively rare and then not nearly as naturalistic as the paintings of animals. Here too, however, such portrayals provide us with a remarkable, if clouded, glimpse into the lives of people who lived more than 15,000 ya. Rice and Paterson (1988) analyzed some thirty-two caves in western Europe where there were a total of 116 human images. Of those images where gender could be identified, 78 percent were male and only 22 percent female. In the paintings, the males tended to be portrayed conducting some specific activity; all cases of running, walking, or dancing figures were males. There were even three paintings of people who appear to have been speared—all males as well.

In the group of paintings Rice and Paterson examined, females were always represented as simply standing or lying down, usually in groups with other females. They were never portrayed in an active mode. Although we cannot be certain of the precise meaning of these paintings and patterns, certainly they reflect on aspects of the differences between the lives of males and females in the Upper Paleolithic.

Conkey (1980) examined 1200 abstractly engraved bones and antlers from twenty-seven sites in the Cantabrian area in Spain. She identified 264 design elements that were engraved according to three structural principles. She then compared the bone and antler assemblages at five cave sites and found that one, Altamira, a cave already mentioned as possessing spectacularly painted walls, was the most diverse. This, she argues, indicates that Altamira was an aggregation spot for Paleolithic populations. Bruce Dickson (1990:215) has gone so far as to state that the larger caves were "ceremonial centers" and the art served as a focal point for ceremonies that took place during such aggregations.

Conkey believes that artifacts like engraved bone and antler contained information that essentially identified and differentiated groups of people living in different areas. These people needed to come together on occasion to exchange environmental information, to trade, and to find mates. Groups congregating at Altamira brought with them their engraved objects, each in their own style. Thus, the assemblage at Altamira is the most diverse because it reflects the styles of a number of different groups.

Clive Gamble (1982, 1983, 1986) has attempted to explain the significance of the Venus figurines. He states that these portable artworks peaked during a glacial maximum. Outside Franco-Cantabria, resources would have been dispersed, and people would have needed similarly to disperse to exploit them. The social problem that resulted was one of maintaining mating networks within cultural systems of low population density. According to Gamble, a common art style associated with ritual would have functioned to keep such a widespread system intact.

The people who produced these spectacular works of art may also have been making simple, though remarkable, advances in science. A more than 30,000-year-old fragment of antler found in a French cave bears a succession of some sixty-nine incised marks. After examining it under a microscope, science writer Alexander Marshack (1972a,b) noted that the marks were made with a number of different tools and that they resembled the succession of lunar phases, the correct order and number for more than two months (Figure 12.22). Marshack believes that this and other artifacts indicate that not only did these people produce the first true art, but they also made the first calendars.

Did people in the Upper Paleolithic practice sympathetic magic, worship a fertility goddess, mark their ritual sites with paintings, engrave antlers with symbols that reflected their membership in distinct hunting bands, and make calendars based on their observation of the sequence of lunar phases? We cannot be certain. As John Halverson (1987) points out, there are great problems posed in testing any of these hypotheses.

**Figure 12.22** *A 32,000-year-old engraved antler plaque from Abri Blanchard, France. Alexander Marshack interprets this as a calendar based on the phases of the moon.* (© Alexander Marshack)

He suggests that perhaps the art had no meaning at all in the sense that no special, and now indecipherable, code was ever attached to it. Maybe, as the title of his article suggests, it was simply "art for art's sake." In his view, Paleolithic painters and sculptors depicted the world around them and produced abstract symbols simply out of a sense of "delight in appearance" (Halverson 1987:68).

It is impossible at present to fully explain the art of the Upper Paleolithic, although the work of Jochim, Conkey, Gamble, and Rice and Paterson has provided great insight into its possible meaning. What is clear is that in viewing the world around them and in translating that reality through a prism of human understanding and belief into engravings, sculptures, and paintings, the people of the European Upper Paleolithic were exhibiting the depth of their intelligence and the degree of their humanity. Whichever hypothesis provides the best explanation for the art of the Upper Paleolithic (and they need not all be mutually exclusive), one thing is clear: In painting cave walls, carving figurines, and engraving bone, ivory, and antler, the people of the Upper Paleolithic in Europe left us an impressive artistic legacy.

## BRAVE NEW WORLDS

Not surprisingly, anatomically modern humans were able to survive in all the environments their archaic predecessors had inhabited before them. But modern humans were also able to thrive under conditions that had previously proved insurmountable and to migrate into areas that were previously unreachable.

## The Arctic

Although archaic *Homo sapiens*, especially the Neandertals, had evolved a highly successful life on the tundra, even they had not penetrated into the ice-covered region of the arctic. It took modern humanity to conquer the earth's coldest places. Perhaps it was their increasingly efficient and effective tool technology. Perhaps it was their ability to clothe and house themselves as protection from the cold. Whatever the reasons, *Homo sapiens sapiens* was first to penetrate and, in fact, thrive in the arctic.

## Australia

Although, as mentioned, some of the fossil crania from Australia are quite robust and reminiscent of earlier, premodern crania from East Asia, they all belonged to anatomically modern human beings. The earliest dated cultural material from Australia, from Swan River in the western part of the country, may be as much as 40,000 years old. Devil's Lair, also in the west, has produced a radiocarbon date of 35,000 B.P. (Wolpoff et al. 1984).

The earliest human fossils from Australia date to a little bit later and are absolutely anatomically modern (Jones 1989). As mentioned, Willandra Lakes Hominid 50 may be more than 34,000 years old, but the dating is a problem. The oldest firmly dated skeletal material is from Lake Mungo (LM III) with a $^{14}$C date of 30,000 years. Other slightly more recent sites where human skeletons were found are Lake Mungo again (LM I, 25,000 B.P.), Lake Tandou (15,000 B.P.), and Kow Swamp (10,000–15,000 B.P.)(Habgood 1985, 1989).

All the skeletal remains are anatomically modern and, in fact, look like the bones of modern aboriginal Australians. What was the probable source of the Australian aboriginal population? Asia is the closest large land mass and had a known prehistoric human population. A recent comparative analysis of anatomically modern fossil crania from Australia, Europe, Asia, and Africa shows that in fact the Australian skulls are most similar to those from Asia (Habgood 1985).

Prehistoric migration into Australia poses an interesting problem. Australia has been separate from the Asian land mass for over 30 million years. Any population movement into the continent after the separation necessarily involved the use of watercraft of some kind. Today this would entail a sea voyage of 1500 kilometers (with a few possible stops in between). At the time of presumed initial migration, sea level was lowered as a result of the freezing of large quantities of the earth's water in land-based glaciers. More of the continental shelves of Asia and Australia would have been exposed, and the voyage would have been substantially shorter, with plenty of island stops on the way (Birdsell 1972). Nevertheless, it was an enormous achievement, and the ability of these first Australians to survive in a new continent with plant and animal life entirely different from their Asian home is a testament to their intelligence and adaptive abilities.

### The Americas

Asia was also the source for human population movements into the New World. Here the trip could have been made entirely by land. Several times during the Pleistocene when a substantial amount of the earth's water was locked up in land-based glaciers, sea level was reduced 125 meters or more. This was sufficient to expose a wide platform of land some 1500 kilometers across, connecting northeast Asia with northwest North America (Figure 12.23). What is now the Bering Sea and Bering Straits (today separating the Chukchi Peninsula in eastern Russia from the Seward Peninsula in Alaska by only about 150 kilometers) was then the Bering Land Bridge, across which animals and people moved. The precise chronology of the exposure and flooding of the land bridge is unknown, but we can be fairly certain that it was intermittently available for human movement between 75,000 and 14,000 ya (Hopkins 1982).

This was no purposeful migration. The earliest migrants could not have known that two continents lay before them. It is likely instead that small groups of migratory hunters and gatherers living in northeast Asia merely expanded their territories, following the movement of large

**Figure 12.23** *When the sea level dropped during the Pleistocene as large quantities of the earth's water became trapped on land as glacial ice, the Bering Land Bridge was exposed. This 1500-km-wide platform connected northeast Asia and northwest North America, allowing Asian populations to migrate into and populate the New World.*

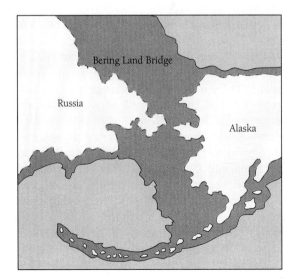

game animals as they moved out onto the newly exposed territory of the land bridge. This journey brought them into the Americas and thrust them, unintentionally, into the role of pioneers with a new world to explore and settle.

The question of when people living in northeast Asia crossed the Bering Land Bridge is still an open one (Owen 1984). A few sites with ages of 200,000 years or more have been proposed. None has convinced the majority of New World archaeologists. It seems unlikely that any preanatomically modern human beings migrated to the New World.

A number of sites in the Old Crow River basin of the Canadian Yukon have produced some interesting material initially presumed to be bone artifacts with radiocarbon dates of approximately 30,000 B.P. Questions have been raised about the artifactual nature of most of the specimens, however. Features of the bone splinters initially thought to be diagnostic of human activity are now known also to be caused by animals chewing. Beyond this, some of the artifacts could have been made on bones that were already old—the $^{14}$C date only refers to the age of the bone, not when someone picked it up and made something out of it. Finally, the specific $^{14}$C technique applied to the Old Crow specimens is now known to result frequently in incorrect old dates.

One of the best possible candidates for a pre-15,000-year-old site in the New World is the Meadowcroft Rockshelter near Pittsburgh, Pennsylvania. Here, in a meticulous excavation that was part of an ambitious, multidisciplinary research project, a deeply stratified deposit with cultural material has produced a layer dated to 19,000 B.P. Unfortunately, the rockshelter is in an area where there is naturally occurring coal. Coal comes from very ancient trees that contain dead carbon—carbon in which all of the $^{14}$C has already decayed away. Water dissolving this coal could have contaminated more recent cultural material and resulted in an incorrectly old $^{14}$C date. Meadowcroft researchers have provided some good arguments in response to this criticism (Adovasio et al. 1983), but the jury is still out on the antiquity of the lower levels of the site.

Though much disagreement exists about these older possible sites, there is no disagreement about the human population explosion that occurred in the New World after 13,000 ya. We call these peoples the **Paleo-Indians**. Whether they were new arrivals or people descended from earlier migrants, they brought with them a hunting–gathering economy with a seasonal emphasis on the big game that flourished in North America at the tail end of the Pleistocene. Using large-bladed spear points somewhat similar to the Solutrean points of Europe of 20,000 ya, with chipped channels or "flutes" on the faces to facilitate hafting, these Paleo-Indians hunted woolly mammoth, bison (a form now extinct), horse, caribou, and other large game animals (Figure 12.24). At sites like Olsen-Chubbuck in Colorado (Wheat 1972) and

**Paleo-Indian:** A New World culture, based on big-game hunting and characterized by fluted points, present from about 12,000 to 10,000 ya.

**Figure 12.24** *Fluted points of the Paleo-Indian settlers of North America. With such weapons, these first inhabitants of the Americas hunted the large game animals that flourished at the end of the Pleistocene.* (Richard Michael Gramly)

Casper in Wyoming (Frison 1974), there is evidence for bison "drives" where hundreds of animals were driven over cliffs in communal hunts. Doubtless they also collected roots, seeds, nuts, and berries where these were available in season.

These people were enormously successful and quickly spread throughout the entire New World. After their initial appearance perhaps 13,000 or 14,000 ya in Alaska, we find sites throughout the American Midwest by 11,500 ya. By 11,000 ya they had reached as far east as Maine, and by 9500 ya we find traces of their presence at the southern tip of South America.

The Paleo-Indians may have been too successful, in fact. It has been suggested that their population grew so quickly and their skill as hunters was so remarkable that they contributed to the extinction of many forms of large animals already strained by the change in climate at the end of the Pleistocene (Martin 1982). Animals like the horse, woolly mammoth, mastodon, bison, and ground sloth, all likely hunted extensively by the Paleo-Indians, became extinct sometime after the Indians' arrival on the scene.

The abundance of their indisputable cultural remains throughout the New World after 13,000 ya is presumed by some to indicate that they were, indeed, the first Americans. At the very least, it is an indication that if people made it to the New World before the Paleo-Indians, they were unsuccessful at conquering this hemisphere.

The earliest fossil remains of the first Americans are even more recent than their initial cultural traces. From Mexico comes Tepexpan Man (probably a female) with a date of 11,000 B.P. (although this date is now questioned). Cerro Sota 2 from Chile is about 11,000 years old. Several individuals from Lagoa Santa in Brazil and a fossil from Arlington Springs, California, are probably 10,000 years old. A recent electron spin resonance analysis performed on human bone found along the Kansas River in Kansas has produced a date of 15,400 B.P. (Bower 1987c). If the date is accurate, this fossil would be the oldest human remain in the New World.

All these fossils are anatomically modern, all resemble modern American Indians, and all share a series of skeletal traits possessed by Asian people. This evidence further supports an Asian source for New World populations.

## LIFE AT THE END OF THE PLEISTOCENE

Toward the end of the Pleistocene, with the last recession of the glaciers and a warming of the world's climate, sites throughout the world show people adapting to the changing conditions in the natural environment. In Europe, tundra-adapted game became regionally extinct as the tundra was replaced by woodland. Local Paleolithic cultures reliant on such game began to shift their subsistence attention to woodland animals like deer and elk.

Sites like Star Carr in England (Clark 1971) provide detailed subsistence data on the so-called Maglemosian culture of the **Mesolithic** (between the Paleolithic and Neolithic periods). Close to 10,000 ya, the inhabitants of Star Carr built a platform of birch and stone to stabilize the swampy surface around their village. From this home base, they hunted red and roe deer, elk, ox, and pig and collected the plants that grew in abundance around their camp. They made tools of flint, and,

**Mesolithic:** The European culture between the Paleolithic and the Neolithic.

using flint burins and chisels, they manufactured barbed spear points from the antlers of the animals they hunted.

In North America, the waning stages of the Pleistocene brought with it extinction of many tundra-adapted large-game species and their replacement with more modern fauna. The so-called Archaic period cultures in North America represent the beginning of regionalization, with cultures settling into different post-Pleistocene environments. Strategies for survival in the northeastern woodlands, southwest desert, northwest coast, and elsewhere were established.

Toward the end of the Pleistocene, in areas not so severely affected by glaciation and deglaciation, we also see the evolution of cultural adaptation. Importantly, in the Middle East we see a number of sites where subsistence emphasis seems to have shifted to plant resources sometime after 18,000 ya. Along the Nile, gazelle, hippopotamus, wild cattle, wart hog, and buffalo were still hunted, but fishing had also become important. At some of the Nile sites, microliths—small stone flakes set in groups into bone, wood, and antler handles—exhibit a characteristic wear pattern that indicates their use in sickles for harvesting plant food (Butzer 1982). The abundance of grinding stones used for processing seeds also points to a focus on plants for food. Finally, the presence of carbonized grains of wild barley, wheat, rye, and oats bears direct witness to the growing importance of plantfoods in the diet.

This shift in subsistence at the end of the Pleistocene and beginning of the modern, or **Holocene**, period led in some places to a radical change in the relationship between people and their environment. It is to this revolution, the Neolithic, that we turn our attention in Chapter 14.


## HUMAN EVOLUTION: GRADUAL OR PUNCTUATED?

We have now brought you from the first steps of our hominid ancestors to the brink of the agricultural revolution. Let us now return to a topic first addressed in Chapter 4 and ask, "To what extent, and at what points, does the process of punctuated equilibrium apply to the evolution of the hominids?"

Some researchers (Eldredge and Tattersall, 1982, for example) believe that each new named species in our evolutionary story (including the Neandertals) represents an episode of punctuation—the fairly sudden appearance of a brand new twig on our evolutionary bush. But the fact that a group of hominids is given a new name does not necessarily mean they were indeed a whole new species. New names are given to a group of fossils because they look different from other groups, but the

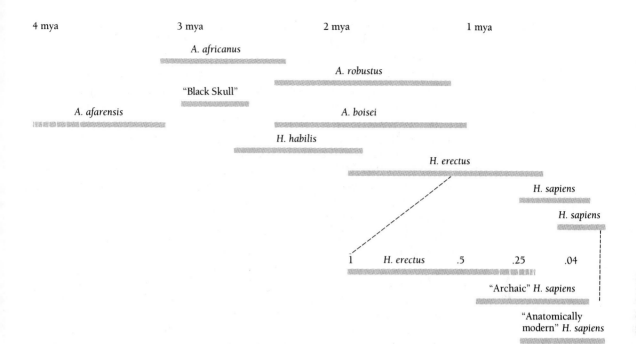

**Figure 12.25** *Summary of the evolutionary chronology of the hominids, from* Australopithecus *to anatomically modern human beings.*

differences can be the result of evolutionary change *within* a single evolving lineage. So the answer to the question hinges on (1) whether a new group appears suddenly or gradually and (2) whether a new group is indeed different on a species level from previous groups, regardless of what we call it for the sake of categorization.

The beginning of the hominid lineage (Chapter 8) is probably an example of a punctuation (Figure 12.25). The bipedalism that is our evolutionary hallmark appears in the fossil record almost fully formed in creatures otherwise apelike. Moreover, there is genetic evidence that some of the differences between humans and apes, including some key facets of bipedalism, may be the results of macromutations of developmental genes; these gave rise to the multiple and extensive phenotypic changes of our neoteny. Macromutations, you recall, are the mechanisms of punctuations. The model of an evolutionary punctuation to bipedality, however, is made problematic by the fact that, for the most important time period in question—3 to 5 mya—the fossil record is quite limited.

A better-supported example of a punctuation is the beginning of the genus *Homo* (Chapter 9). Although in many respects still resembling earlier hominids, *Homo habilis* is defined by its larger brain and its association with stone tool manufacture. These seem to appear suddenly and at the same time as the australopithecine hominid lines are off on their own evolutionary paths.

**Holocene:** The modern geological epoch, beginning about 10,000 ya.

# CONTEMPORARY ISSUE

## The "Eve" Hypothesis

Using mitochondrial DNA differences in modern populations to work backward toward establishing the origin of modern *Homo sapiens* has led to one rather confusing issue. Because mtDNA is only inherited maternally, these studies are actually tracing descent through females. The fact that our species, according to these studies, began fairly recently, coupled with the fact that no modern population differs from any other by even as much as 1 percent of their mtDNA, has led some investigators to conclude that *all* modern mtDNA is derived from a single female who lived in Africa around 200,000 ya. Naturally, it was tempting to dub her "Eve," a metaphorical reference to the creation story in Genesis. It has not helped that some who dispute the replacement model have called the hypothesized source area for modern humanity "Eden."

Obviously, this mitochondrial Eve is *not* the Eve of the Bible. None of the scientific account of evolution is refuted by the mtDNA studies. It was, perhaps, just a poor choice of names, confounded by some very sketchy, sensationalized, and confusing early reports in the media.

The second area of misunderstanding is more technical. Some took the Eve idea to mean that our *entire species* had begun with one African female. First of all, there clearly has to be at least one male involved. (Yes, some media accounts called him "Adam.") But no species (at least no complex, multicellular, sexually reproducing species) begins with a single couple. Anatomically modern *H. sapiens* began with an interbreeding population, genetically different and isolated from its ancestral archaic population.

What the hypothesis says is that all modern *mtDNA* is inherited from a single female. The seeming contradiction is resolved by understanding that although our species began with a number of "Eves," the mitochondrial lines of all but one died out. An analogous phenomenon occurs with family names (Lewin 1991:52–53). You begin with ten couples. Each has a different surname, the surnames are passed down through the males, and each couple has two children. After twenty generations, the chances are very good that only one surname will remain. This is because in each generation one-quarter of the couples, on average, will have two boys who will pass on the name. But one-half will have a boy and a girl, so one of the children will not pass on the name, and one-quarter will have two girls, so the name will die out.

The same thing happens with mtDNA, except, of course, it is inherited through the females, and there is the added factor of different numbers of children born to different women, including, of course, the fact that some women will have *no* children.

So, if the replacement model is correct, all of us living now are descended with nuclear DNA from an African population of "archaic" *H. sapiens* that, for reasons not yet understood, diverged and evolved along its own lines. That we may have all inherited our mtDNA from one female simply serves to indicate that that divergence was a localized event, rather than the widespread event proposed by the multiregional hypothesis.

---

*Homo erectus* (Chapter 10) represents a probable jump in evolutionary change as well. It has a larger body and a larger brain than *Homo habilis*, and the closeness in time of the latest *habilis* and earliest *erectus* fossils argues against a direct, gradual evolution from one form to the other.

There may also have been an evolutionary punctuation from *H. erectus* to archaic *Homo sapiens* (Chapter 11). Although we have seen a mosaic of features in many of the fossils, the apparently rapid jump in brain size after 400,000 B.P. seems to support the punctuation model.

Finally, as we have seen in this chapter, the fossil evidence, as well as some sophisticated and promising new genetic lines of investigation, indicate that anatomically modern *Homo sapiens* appears to be a distinct group, tracing its history to a specific ancestral location at a fairly specific point in time, indeed in the relatively recent past. Whether we are different from archaic *H. sapiens* on a species level remains to be seen, and so we cannot yet determine if our species represents a true punctuational branch or merely a change within a species at one location that then spread throughout the rest of the species replacing older biological characteristics.

Yet, the history of the hominids seems to be largely characterized by the evolution, through fairly sudden punctuations, of new species. And thus the bush model of evolution applies to even the short tenure on earth of the hominids.

## SUMMARY

Although the evidence is far more substantial for this most recent period of hominid evolution, the origin and development of anatomically modern human beings are still points of contention and controversy for paleoanthropologists. Neither of the two major competing models—multiregional or replacement—can be proven absolutely at this time.

Nevertheless, the paleontological, genetic, and archaeological evidence currently available seems to tip the balance in favor of replacement. In this view, anatomically modern human beings evolved in a single place—most likely Africa, south of the Sahara—from a local population of archaic *Homo sapiens*, sometime after 200,000 and before 100,000 ya. From their place of origin, these modern humans spread across the globe, coming into contact with local, indigenous archaics (the Neandertals) in Europe and Southwest Asia and with other archaics and, possibly, even remnant groups of *Homo erectus* in East Asia. Everywhere the moderns came into contact with the archaics, they replaced them as a result of some adaptive advantage.

Once established throughout the world, modern human beings began developing extremely sophisticated cultures—the Upper Paleolithic of Europe with its cave paintings and sculptures is but one remarkable example of the culture of these anatomically modern humans. It was modern human beings, further, who expanded into Australia and the New World, where their populations thrived and their many different cultural adaptations proliferated.

Ultimately, it seems that the evolution of humanity can best be represented as a series of jumps or punctuations: from an apelike creature to the upright *Australopithecus*; then again from the small-brained *Australopithecus* to the larger-brained, tool-using *Homo habilis*; from *H. habilis* to the even larger-brained *Homo erectus* whose cultural abilities allowed its expansion out of Africa; from *H. erectus* to the creature that, although not an exact match to modern humanity, was so similar that it bears our taxonomic name, *Homo sapiens*; then, finally, probably somewhere in southern Africa, a final punctuational event occurred, producing anatomically fully modern human beings who spread across the surface of the earth.

## KEY TERMS

| | | |
|---|---|---|
| multiregional hypothesis | symbiosis | Solutrean |
| replacement hypothesis | Mousterian | Venus figurines |
| nuclear DNA | Chåttleperonian | Paleo-Indian |
| mitochondrial DNA | Aurignacian | Mesolithic |
| | burin | Holocene |

## FOR MORE INFORMATION

For brief descriptions of many of the fossils discussed here, see Michael Day's *Guide to Fossil Man.* Also see Smith (1984), Trinkans (1984), and others in Smith and Spencer (1984).

For presentations of the multiregional hypothesis, see Milford Wolpoff's articles in the *The Emergence of Modern Humans: Biocultural Adaptations in the Later Pleistocene,* and *The Human Revolution: Behavioral and Biological Perspectives in the Origins of Modern Humans.*

For a defense of the replacement hypothesis, see Christopher Stringer's article "The Emergence of Modern Humans," in *Scientific American. Discover* magazine has published a number of articles on this debate; see Jared Diamond's article in their May 1989 issue, James Shreeve's article of August 1990, and Joshua Fischman's February 1992 article.

If you are interested in cave art, there are several splendidly illustrated books. Perhaps the most beautiful now available is Mario Ruspoli's *The Cave of Lascaux: The Final Photographs.* For a detailed summary of the explanations suggested for the cave art, see Bruce Dickson's *The Dawn of Belief: Religion in the Upper Paleolithic of Southwestern Europe.* Also, see Pat Shipman's article about the cave art in the July 1990 issue of *Discover.* On the same topic, John Pfeiffer's book *The Creative Explosion* is another excellent source.

Finally, a series of discussions on the settlement of the Americas, called "The First Americans," has been published in *Natural History* magazine in their November 1986 through October 1987 and January and February 1988 issues.

# 13

# HUMAN VARIATION: THE TIP OF THE TWIG

In Chapter 9 we discussed Stephen Jay Gould's metaphor of evolution as a bush. The modern human species is the single surviving twig on a portion of the evolutionary bush that once had at least three hominid twigs: the two australopithecine lines and the *Homo* line. This bush metaphor accurately depicts the nature of hominid—and, indeed, all—evolution. But our identity as a sole surviving twig leads to two conceptual problems.

First, because we are the only surviving hominids, we easily get the idea that hominid evolution inevitably led to modern humans all along and that the other hominids were just not quite human enough to make it. You should understand now that this is simply not the case. Evolutionary events are not predestined.

Second, because we have no other living hominids with which to compare ourselves, we humans have a tendency to pay close attention to biological and cultural differences among our existing populations. We sometimes overemphasize certain of these differences and endow them with meanings far beyond what is actually warranted. Let's look at the topic of species variation and see how it applies to humans.

## VARIATION WITHIN SPECIES

Because of genetic mutation, recombination, and the random processes of evolution, all species display variation among their members. Some species, however, are more variable than others, and this is based to a great extent on the nature of the species' geographic distribution and the variety of the environments to which its members are adapted.

If a species inhabits a relatively small geographic area and its members are adapted to a highly specific set of ecological circumstances—to a narrow niche—the species will tend to be fairly homogeneous. If its members are adapted to the same conditions, natural selection will select for the same characteristics in all of them. Such a species is said to be **specialized**. A classic example are the koala species that live only in Australia and eat primarily eucalyptus leaves. You wouldn't expect the koala species to show much variation, and they don't.

In species that inhabit a wide geographic range and many different niches, variation may be greater. Selection will promote different versions of the species' basic characteristics in response to the environments found in different parts of the range. Species of this sort are said to be **generalized**. Traits that display variation within a species are called **polymorphisms** (literally, "many forms").

For example, the difference in body size between the Kodiak bear of a group of Alaskan islands and the grizzly of mainland Alaska, Canada, and the United States once led to their classification as separate species. We now understand the Kodiak is merely the largest version of a single species, *Ursus arctos*, spread through North America as well as Europe and Asia. Body size is a polymorphism for this single bear species.

To be a single species, all males and all females of the group must be potentially capable of interbreeding. There must be sufficient gene flow among populations within a species to keep them from becoming so adaptively different that they diverge into separate species. But gene flow is not always even. Populations within a species may be clustered into groups called **demes**. More genes are exchanged within a deme than between demes. This occurs either because some geographic barrier prevents extensive gene flow or because the environmental conditions to which the species is adapted come in clusters, with gaps between that prevent steady genetic exchange (Figure 13.1).

Demes may be thought of as the first stage of speciation. If a deme becomes so isolated that virtually no genes are exchanged, if its environment is different enough to cause selection for distinct characteristics, and if enough time elapses, the deme may eventually become a separate species, unable to interbreed.

If, however, isolation is not complete or has not been complete for a long enough period of time, the demes may represent phenotypically

Species Range

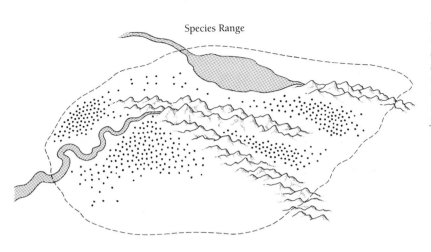

**Figure 13.1** *A species of lowland, nonaquatic animal (dots) is unevenly distributed within its range due to mountain and water boundaries. The separate concentrations of this animal are demes, which may well be physically distinguishable from one another.*

distinguishable populations of the same species. Such species are said to be **polytypic** ("many types"), and such demes referred to as **subspecies**, or **races**.

Reindeer of Europe and Asia and caribou of North America are an example. Although distinguishable physically, they are both members of the same species, *Rangifer tarandus*. Now isolated in separate hemispheres, they were, no doubt, able to interbreed when Alaska and Siberia were connected during the Pleistocene. They have been isolated, then, for only a few thousand years, generally not enough time for speciation to have occurred in a large mammal. Moreover, the environments of the caribou and the reindeer, though different in detail, are generally similar, so natural selection has not taken the two populations in very different adaptive directions.

The North American population of this species is further divided into at least four subspecies, the result of their arrangement into demes living in different environments in Alaska and Canada. These demes, some woodland and some tundra dwellers, differ physically in size, antler shape, and coat color. So even though all caribou and reindeer are members of the same species—all capable of interbreeding—they look different enough in different geographic areas to warrant classification into at least five (one Old World and four New World) distinguishable subspecies or races, (Figure 13.2).

How do these concepts apply to our species? How much variation do we show? What brought it about? Are we divided into demes distinguishable enough to warrant subspecific designations? What about the striking variation in our cultural behaviors? How is that related?

**specialized**: A species adapted to a narrow range of environmental circumstances.

**generalized**: A species adapted to a wide range of environmental circumstances.

**polymorphism**: A trait showing variation within a species.

**deme** A population cluster within a species' range.

**polytypic**: A species with physically distinguishable regional populations.

**subspecies**: A physically distinguishable population within a species.

**race**: Synonym for subspecies.

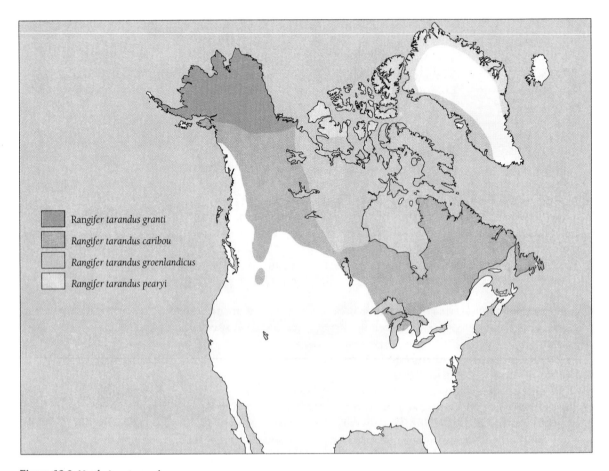

**Figure 13.2** *North American subspecies of the caribou* Rangifer tarandus. *A fifth subspecies is the reindeer of northern Europe and Asia.* (Redrawn from National Geographic Society 1979:340, 343)

Rangifer tarandus granti

Rangifer tarandus caribou

Rangifer tarandus groenlandicus

Rangifer tarandus pearyi

## VARIATION WITHIN THE HUMAN SPECIES

The modern human species inhabits a wide geographic range. Indigenous populations of our species are found on all the continents but Antarctica. Our ancestors were spread throughout the Old World by at least half a million years ago and moved into the New World around 15,000 years ago. We have lived in environments ranging from frigid Arctic tundra to hot, dry deserts; from low-lying, humid tropical rain forests to the cold, thin air of mountains thousands of feet high. One would certainly expect natural selection to have acted on us over these many years and in these many environments to bring about a great deal of adaptive variation.

In addition, such widespread populations must have a degree of isolation from one another. It is unlikely, for example, that indigenous populations of Central Africa exchange genes either directly with peoples in the North American Arctic or in a series of steps through intermediate populations. Moreover, humans add to their reproductive isolation through cultural rules of **endogamy**, which, for purposes of maintaining cultural, religious, or ethnic identity, require people to find mates only within their group. As a result, even human populations living side by side may not exchange genes. Moslems and Jews in the Middle East are an example. Indeed, most societies tend toward endogamy, at least as an ideal rule.

Our wide geographic spread, coupled with our cultural isolation, makes it no surprise that modern humans display a large number of polymorphisms and that certain clusters of these polymorphisms are characteristic of particular geographic areas. The photographs in Figure 13.3 need no captions. You can tell quite accurately where each of these people comes from. Nor can there be any doubt that a good deal of the explanation for human polymorphic traits lies in the process of natural selection, acting on populations as they spread out into their incredible variety of environments.

What is at issue, though, are two concerns: first, the nature and extent of the role of natural selection and the other evolutionary processes in producing our variation, and second, whether our variation is such that we consist of identifiable subspecies, or races.

**Natural Selection and Human Variation**

To determine the role of natural selection in bringing about the variable expressions of a trait, one must first try to link those expressions to particular environmental circumstances. This is a difficult task with humans. For one thing, we have always been a mobile species and, with modern modes of transportation and modern motives for travel, we are becoming more so. As a result, in urban centers or even in the suburbs of populous areas, we can often find a wide cross section of human biological variation. Nearly every corner of the world must be represented by the inhabitants of New York City, for example. We must, then, try to make generalizations about the distributions of our polymorphisms, usually by using only indigenous groups—groups we can assume have been in a certain area for long periods of time with a minimum of genetic exchange.

In addition, as we have shown in previous chapters, culture allows us to adapt to new environmental conditions much more quickly than natural selection can evolve adaptations. Thus, one of our most notable biological traits, our big brain, has actually allowed us, via culture, to buffer ourselves increasingly against some of the action of natural selection.

**endogamy**:  Marriage restricted to those within the same social group. Exogamy is marriage restricted to those outside the social group.

**Figure 13.3** *Variation in modern* Homo sapiens.

Traits that may once have been selectively disadvantageous to humans may now, in the context of our *cultural* adaptations, be fairly meaningless. Biological fitness is a relative concept. The fitness of a trait depends on the environment in which it is found. Recall that the sickle-cell anemia mutation is actually beneficial in areas of high malarial incidence, although maladaptive where no malaria exists. Where a society can correct physical impairments such as visual and hearing defects, certain chemical imbalances, or even problems of major organs, these are no longer a barrier to reproductive success and so, if they have a genetic basis, may be passed on to future generations. Similarly, if a selective agent—some infectious disease, for instance—is cured, then any genes it selected for or against may now vary at random.

As a result, it can be difficult to tell just how important natural selection is in determining the existence and distribution of a human polymorphism. The variation in a trait, if it holds no important adaptive value, may be largely the result of the random processes of evolution. The variation and its distribution may mean little or nothing relative to environmental fitness. It may be hard even to discern some former adaptive value.

For instance, the variation in blood type for the ABO system, a trait controlled by a single gene with three alleles, remained a mystery for some time and is still not entirely solved. All people have one of four phenotypes: A, B, AB, and O (as do chimps and gorillas, by the way). These types appear in markedly different frequencies among populations in different parts of the world (Figure 13.4). Type A, for example, is totally absent among some native South American groups but is found in frequencies of over 50 percent in parts of Europe, native Australia, and native North America. Type O, the most common worldwide, still ranges from 40 percent in parts of Asia to 100 percent among some native South Americans. The distribution once seemed entirely random, lacking any neat correlations with environmental factors or selective agents like those found for sickle cell anemia.

It turned out that the "cultural buffer" was the cause of our difficulty in discerning the explanation for this polymorphism. Studies have indicated that persons with particular blood types have greater susceptibility to such disorders as duodenal ulcer, stomach cancer, forms of anemia, bronchial pneumonia, smallpox, bubonic plague, and typhoid. Type O persons seem more attractive to mosquitoes, that, as we have seen, can be important disease carriers. But the completion of such studies is hindered by two obstacles.

First, because we have gained a good deal of control over many of these diseases, it is difficult to gather data about their links to blood type on a worldwide scale. We are thus forced to look into the past, before such control was gained, and so have to rely on historical records and make inferences based on data that are less than ideal. For example, based on studies of the relatively few modern incidents of the disease, it seems that type O people have a greater susceptibility to plague. Type O tends to be found in its lowest frequencies in areas that historical records indicate have the longest history of plague epidemics.

There is, then, strong evidence that some relationship exists between blood type and disease. But—the second problem—we have yet to es-

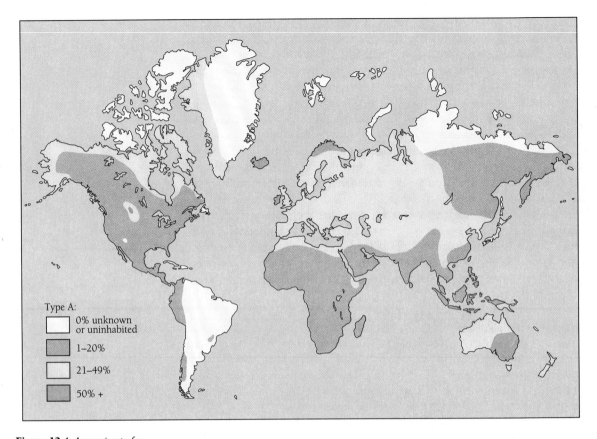

Type A:

| | |
|---|---|
| ☐ | 0% unknown or uninhabited |
| ▨ | 1–20% |
| ☐ | 21–49% |
| ▨ | 50% + |

**Figure 13.4** *Approximate frequency distribution of type A blood group, demonstrating the range of variation among indigenous human populations. The very high frequency in western Canada is among Blackfeet Indians.*

tablish a cause-and-effect connection: What is it *about* certain blood types that make the people who have them more or less susceptible to a disease or to the bite of an insect?

Perhaps phenotypic traits more directly and obviously in contact with outside environmental conditions would be easier to explain adaptively. The human polymorphism of skin color is the classic example. Skin color is determined largely by the amount of the pigment melanin produced in the lowest layer of skin and distributed in the upper layers. This is a genetically controlled trait, though we don't yet know the exact genetic mechanism.

As with many other polymorphisms, we can make some generalizations to describe the distribution of skin color relative to the environment. Looking at indigenous populations, we see that darker skin is found closer to the equator and that skin color gets lighter north and south of that line (Figure 13.5). We know that sunlight is more intense and less affected by seasonal fluctuations at the equator. We also know that too much ultraviolet radiation from the sun can cause sunburn, with accompanying cell destruction, infection, and heat exhaustion. Excessive exposure to the sun has also been shown to cause skin cancer. On the positive side, though, we understand that ultraviolet light is necessary for the synthesis of vitamin D, important for proper bone growth. Simply put, the skin colors of human populations evolved to be dark enough to protect the skin and its underlying tissues from the harmful effects of ultraviolet radiation and light enough to let in sufficient ultraviolet to aid in the synthesis of vitamin D. Dark skin may also protect from the production of too much vitamin D, which can be toxic at high levels.

Because our evolution began in the tropics (some early hominid fossils are found right on the equator), we assume our distant ancestors had dark skin, at least after we evolved our hairless bodies, probably an adaptation to allow sweat to evaporate faster and thus cool the body more efficiently. Populations that stayed in tropical regions retained dark skin. Those that moved away from the tropics gradually underwent selection for lighter skin pigmentation; for them dark skin was a disadvantage in terms of vitamin D synthesis.

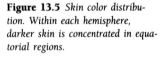

**Figure 13.5** *Skin color distribution. Within each hemisphere, darker skin is concentrated in equatorial regions.*

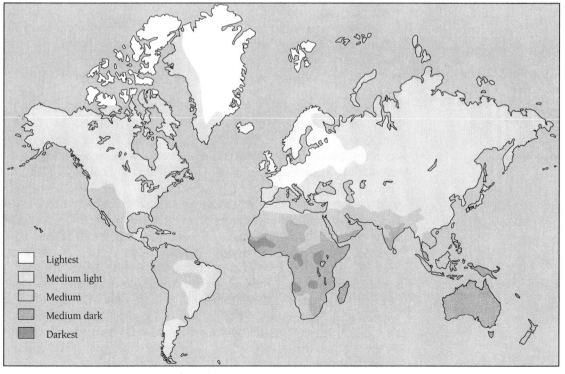

Lightest

Medium light

Medium

Medium dark

Darkest

Although clothing, shelter, more varied diets, and the addition of vitamin D to milk in many northern countries have all but eliminated this selective agent in many areas, it can still be important. Rickets, a bone disease caused by a vitamin D deficiency, was very common among black children in northern U. S. cities only fifty years ago (Molnar 1975). In parts of Russia, winters are long and cloudy enough to warrant exposing children to doses of ultraviolet from quartz lamps to prevent vitamin D deficiency. For skin color then, there is both circumstantial and direct evidence that natural selection has played a role in maintaining and distributing the variation.

There are, in fact, a fair number of human polymorphisms for which selective explanations, of varying strengths, exist. We already discussed sickle cell anemia. Another example is body build, which tends to be linear in hot climates to promote heat loss and, as seen among the Neandertals, stockier in cold climates to preserve heat. This selective factor also applies to more modern populations (Figure 13.6). Noses are long and narrow in cold or dry areas to help warm and moisten the air taken into the lungs, and short and broad in places where air is already warm and moist.

Of course, it is possible that some phenotypic variation is the result not of natural selection to particular environmental circumstances but of one of the random processes of evolution—gene flow and genetic drift (see Chapter 4). This especially may be the case because human groups tend to be temporarily genetically isolated through geography or culture but are generally mobile and prone to genetic exchange. Groups have also, for most of human history, been relatively small. These are, as you recall, the conditions under which gene flow and genetic drift work best.

For example, the high incidence of blood group type A among the Blackfeet Indians might be attributed to a founder effect—the population being originally founded by a small group that, by chance, was uncharacteristically high in type A. Or, in a small ancestral Blackfeet population, allele frequencies may have drifted toward a high percentage of A.

If natural selection is not actively selecting for or against the frequencies of a set of alleles, these random processes are free to operate. Because not all variation is adaptively important all the time, and some variation may not be important at all, gene flow and genetic drift can have major effects on the distribution of alleles. For example, one of us (Park 1979) found a significant degree of variation in inherited features of fingerprints among populations and between generations of the Hutterites, a religious isolate from the western United States and Canada. Because these variables in fingerprints are of no known adaptive significance, this variation could only be the result of gene flow, founder effect, and gamete sampling.

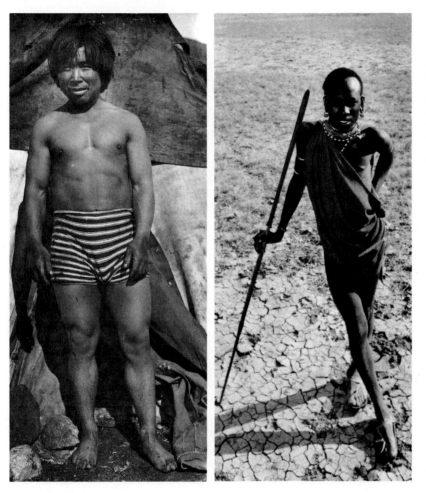

**Figure 13.6** *Body build is in part selected for* (left) *conservation of heat, as in the Eskimo* (Neg. #231604. Courtesy Department of Library Services, American Museum of Natural History) *or* (right) *promotion of heat loss, as in the Masai cattle herder from Kenya.* (Bruce Dale, © 1969 National Geographic Society)

In addition, variation can be the result of environmental effects operating on the genotype–phenotype relationship. Although not clearly understood, we know there is some nongenetic influence on certain aspects of human fingerprints. Skin color is certainly affected by nongenetic factors. So some of the variation in certain phenotypic traits may be caused by complex direct environmental action. For blood type, however, there are no direct environmental influences, so all the variation must be genetic.

We can safely say, then, that logically—from what we know of evolutionary processes, environmental factors, and the extent of human migration—natural selection, in response to differing environmental circumstances, must surely have played some role in our biological variation. The study of specific polymorphisms provides some direct supportive evidence.

We may have come to consider ourselves immune to the effects of the natural environment. We think of ourselves as buffered from it and, indeed, in control of it. But the technology that allows this attitude has been with us—and, even then, not with all of us—for just a few thousand years at most.

### The Question of Human Races

The human species displays numerous variable traits. We can explain some as the results of natural selection to certain environmental contexts. Many of our polymorphisms show regularity in terms of their geographic distribution. Does this all mean that our species consists of identifiable subspecies, or races?

You recall, that four conditions are required for subspecific identity: (1) population isolation, (2) environments different enough to promote adaptive selection in different directions, (3) variation between the populations, and (4) enough time.

The latest evidence (Chapter 12) indicates that modern humans have been around for up to 200,000 years, enough time for even speciation. Since anatomically modern humans arose, however, and while they have been spreading and moving about, no human population has been isolated long enough, or to a complete enough degree, to allow absolutely separate and independent genetic changes to take place. During all that time, humans have in fact become increasingly mobile, and it seems a fair statement to say that we exchange genes at most opportunities.

To be sure, rules of endogamy do exist, and they tend to isolate certain populations genetically at certain times. But such rules are not always fully upheld. Also, rules change, and the populations that are defined by the rules change through time. Endogamy is a temporary condition. Geographic isolation is temporary. Gene flow is the real "rule."

Then there is the matter of culture. Culture is our major adaptive mechanism. Even where natural selection had an effect on certain characteristics—such as blood type or skin color—these adaptive differences were minor compared to the major adaptation of culture. The cultural adaptation was well developed and part of our hominid line long before modern humans arose. Our big brains—the basis for the cultural potential—are shared by all modern humans and are so important and basic that they are unlikely to show much major variation. Further, the products of the cultural ability—social systems, beliefs, technology—act as a buffer against much of the effect of natural selection.

Finally, as recent genetic studies have shown, we are not a very genetically heterogeneous species. About 75 percent of all human genes are monomorphic; that is, all humans are identical for 75 percent of the human genome (Lewontin 1982:120). The genetic variation that does exist is relatively evenly distributed. Richard Lewontin (1982:123) calculates that if some great cataclysm left only Africans alive, that remnant of the human species would still retain 93 percent of the total genetic variation of the former population (although with a darker average skin color).

Our variation, then, is part of ongoing dynamic processes: the "editing" by natural selection of a widespread, highly mobile, generalized, and fairly recent species, combined with the operation of the random processes of evolution on our temporarily isolated but generally highly mobile individual populations. Such a situation simply doesn't allow for the kinds of conditions necessary to produce distinguishable subspecies such as are present within the caribou. Although some human traits or trait clusters tend to be geographically localized (see Figure 13.3), nearly all our features are spread across many populations and geographic areas. Dark skin, for example, is an *equatorial* trait, not only an African one, as many are inclined to consider it.

Further, no real boundaries exist between trait expressions. Although we divided skin color expression into five categories for the sake of diagramming the distribution of this trait (see Figure 13.5), skin color doesn't change abruptly as the map may imply. Actually it changes *gradually* in populations closer to or farther from the equator. Such a distribution, called a **cline**, simply cannot be divided into discrete units because its expressions don't come in neat packages with clear geographic boundaries.

Finally, when we compare the distributions of human polymorphisms, we see "incongruities." The distribution of one trait seldom matches the distribution of any other. Some sort of subspecific division based on one trait will invariably differ from that based on another. Compare the maps (Figures 13.4 and 13.5) for blood type A and skin color, for instance. The variations of these traits are very different in their distributions. Subspecies based on the distribution of one would be very different from those based on the other. The point is, of course, that it would be hard to force either of these traits—or nearly any human trait—into biologically meaningful units in the first place. At the phenotypic level, human variation exists, but human races don't.

Does this mean, however, that the modern human species is one gigantic "stew" of people, with no discernible groups and thus no way to trace the history of our populations? Whereas phenotypic traits only serve to confuse the matter, our increasing knowledge of genetics does allow us to precisely compare living indigenous populations to one another and to begin building a family tree, determining where populations originated and how they spread.

Such an analysis is essentially an extension of that done with mitochondrial DNA, described in Chapter 12. Figure 12.9 (page 298) shows

**cline:** A geographic continuum in the variation of a specific phenotype.

# CONTEMPORARY ISSUE

## Race and Culture

Besides our biological variation, populations of the human species differ in their cultural behaviors. Cultural units are real, and boundaries do exist for these units. They are defined and imposed by the group of people (the society) who practice a particular way of life (a culture).

Most cultures classify other people relative to themselves. Isolated societies with some knowledge that other groups exist will have a very simple classification: us and them. But as knowledge accumulates among more mobile and cosmopolitan populations, the classifications of people become more complex, and the relations among these people more varied. Knowledge about other groups includes such factors as their cultural practices, their relations with your group, and, of course, their physical appearance. This last factor is important because it may be used to classify a person despite his or her cultural behavior.

This is the real definition of "race" for the human species. Race is a set of cultural categories, a folk taxonomy, used by a particular society, at a particular time, for particular culturally based reasons. Every society we know of has a folk taxonomy for race. We in the industrial West are no exception. Our standard categories of race trace their origins to European knowledge and attitudes acquired during the Age of Exploration. Perhaps we would like to think that our racial categories have biological meaning, but, as we have just shown, they don't. They do have

cultural meaning, however, because for much of our history—and still today—a person's place in society is determined at least in part by the racial category to which he or she is defined as belonging.

The concept of racial categories, besides having all manner of social ramifications, can also affect science itself. In the past, when Western scientists took the racial categories of their society to be real and scientifically valid, an important area of inquiry was that of the origins of the races. The belief persisted well into the nineteenth century that the races were virtually, if not actually, separate species. Such theories are called polygenetic. An extreme version had the races of humans descending from different ape species. But although they might have satisfied and supported certain racist social concepts, polygenetic theories ran counter to both the Bible (that said all humans descended from Adam and Eve) and the latest information from evolutionary theory.

For the last century and a half, most investigators have adopted a monogenetic explanation—that all races belong to and originated from a single species. Still, if one maintains that present-day races are distinct entities, then one might logically attempt to seek specific origins for each of those races, a sort of "neopolygenetic" approach.

The best example is the 1962 book by anthro-

a tree indicating the relationships among populations from which mtDNA samples were drawn. A more inclusive study was done by L. L. Cavalli-Sforza and colleagues (summarized in Cavalli-Sforza 1991) that used more than 100 different inherited traits of 3000 individuals taken from 1800 populations. This study compared proteins, the direct products of the genes. A second, although less extensive study, used actual DNA code sequences (see Chapter 4). The data from these two studies agree with one another and with that from the mtDNA study.

pologist Carleton S. Coon titled *The Origin of Races*. Coon claimed that, although modern peoples were highly mixed, races in the past were separate. In fact, he claimed, he could trace modern racial characteristics back to regional varieties of the species *Homo erectus*. That species was divided into five subspecies, each of which evolved separately into *Homo sapiens*, crossing "a critical threshold from a more brutal to a more *sapient state* " (1962:658). This is an extreme example of the multiregional model for the origins of anatomically modern *H. sapiens* discussed in Chapter 12.

Moreover, Coon felt that different races crossed the "sapiens threshold" at different times and that this accounted for some of the differences in cultural level. "If all races had a recent common origin," he asked, "why were the Tasmanians and many of the Australian aborigines still living during the nineteenth century in a manner comparable to that of Europeans of over 100,000 years ago?" (1962:4). It is clear from this statement who Coon thinks crossed the "threshold" first.

Modern scientific knowledge, much of it available in 1962, shows Coon's ideas to be nonsense. We know that human races are not distinct entities and probably never were. Although there is some evidence of regional variations in certain traits among *H. erectus*—the species to which Coon attributes the origin of races—*erectus* is

more characterized by its homogeneity. Anyway, we have clear evidence (see Chapter 11) that the evolution of *H. sapiens* from *H. erectus* was a localized event.

It also goes entirely against evolutionary theory to propose that five subspecies would all evolve *separately* into the same new species, much less that they would do this *at different times*. Moreover, Coon proposes that the differential timing of the "sapiens threshold" crossings accounts for cultural differences among modern human populations. This completely ignores the importance of culture as the major adaptation of our entire species, and the real factors— adaptation, invention, borrowing—that influence cultural differences and the rate of cultural change.

Coon's ideas dramatize the power of our cultural categories, the meanings they hold for us, and the uses to which they can be put. Our perceptions of human differences can influence not only social and political policy but also the very science that seeks to describe and explain those differences. We are still not free from some of these ideas, although the scientific evidence to the contrary is established and well supported.

Viewed from our perspective, at the tip of our evolutionary twig, it seems all the more puzzling and even tragic that this subject is still one of our most poorly understood and frustrating contemporary issues.

Once again, genetic analysis suggests that modern *Homo sapiens* arose in Africa between 100,000 and 200,000 years ago. These new studies also provide evidence for the series of major migrations by which our species populated the planet (see Figure 12.11, page 301). Moreover, it was found that the distribution of genes coincided to a great degree with the distribution of languages. Languages and genetic populations can be correlated because as human populations split and separate, "each fragment evolves linguistic and genetic patterns that

| Genetic Groups | Living Populations | Linguistic Groups |
|---|---|---|
| African | San | Khoisan |
| African | Masai | Nilo-Saharan |
| African | Mbuti | Niger-Congo |
| African | Ethiopian | Afro-Asiatic |
| Caucasoid | Southwestern Asian | Afro-Asiatic |
| Caucasoid | Mediterranean | Indo-European |
| Caucasoid | Northern European | Indo-European |
| Caucasoid | Indian | Indo-European |
| American | North American | Amerind |
| American | Central American | Amerind |
| American | South American | Amerind |
| Arctic | Eskimo | Eskimo-Aleut |
| Arctic | Siberian | Eskimo-Aleut |
| Northeast Asian | Japanese | Altaic |
| Northeast Asian | Korean | Altaic |
| Mainland Island Southeast Asian | Tibetan | Sino-Tibetan |
| Mainland Island Southeast Asian | Southern Chinese | Sino-Tibetan |
| Mainland Island Southeast Asian | Indonesian | Austronesian |
| Pacific Islands | Philippine | Austronesian |
| Pacific Islands | Polynesian | Austronesian |
| Pacific Islands | Melanesian | Indo-Pacific |
| Pacific Islands | New Guinean | Australian |
| Pacific Islands | Australian | Australian |

**Figure 13.7** *The correlation between genetic and language groups within modern humans. The living populations listed are a representative sample. Note that where populations live close to one another under similar conditions, as is the case for Ethiopians and Southwest Asians, they may speak languages of the same group even though they are genetically distinct.* (Data from Cavalli-Sforza 1991)

bear marks of shared branching points" (Cavalli-Sforza 1991:109). In addition, "linguistic differences [and the cultural differences they reflect] may generate or reinforce genetic barriers between populations. Hence, some correlation is inevitable" (1991:109). Figure 13.7 is a simplified diagram of this correlation.

Our species doesn't assort itself into the clear-cut, ancient, and profoundly different racial groups assumed by earlier generations. We are too new, too mobile, too genetically homogeneous, and too culturally adapted for that. But the richness of our genetic, ethnic, and cultural variety is not lost within some worldwide melting pot. And to say that there *are* human populations, identified by several correlated factors, is not to say that such groups are in any way so different as to warrant differential social treatment. We have far more similarities than we do variations. Still, racism and bigotry remain one of our most vexing problems.

## SUMMARY

As members of a widespread, populous, mobile, cultural species, we naturally notice and are fascinated by those things that vary among individuals, populations, and geographic regions. As we struggle with all those things that unite and divide us, our variable traits often provide us with clues to the group identity, behavioral propensities, and mental and physical abilities of a particular individual. These categories then act as cues that can make a complex life a little simpler because then we "know" what to think of people and how to treat them by how they look, where they come from, what language they speak.

So compelling is this seeming benefit, that the perceived fact of such correlations has influenced even science. Anthropology has spent most of its history trying to figure out how many races there are, how to define them, and where and when they originated. This is not a criticism of our discipline, however, because the ultimate result of these endeavors has been to show that, in fact, race in our species is an artifact of culture that has little or no basis in biology.

We are a variable species and our biological variation can be explained by envoking the same processes that produce variation in all living things. As a result, some of that variation is distributed in environmentally meaningful ways; the occurrence of certain traits in certain places makes sense. As a result of *this*, we can often, if not usually, tell the general area of the world of a person's major genetic heritage. The difference is that, given the specific nature of *Homo sapiens*, we simply can't be assorted, on a biological level, into clear-cut, well-defined, stable subgroups. Race is not a valid biological concept for our species.

Still, our 200,000-year history has not been one of random wanderings and genetic exchanges or of completely unstable, ambiguous social groupings. Our populations do have identities and histories, and, as we begin to reconstruct those histories, we see that the journeys from our African homeland out across the planet are those of real populations of real people, with real cultures, and (though insignificant in a relative sense) real genetic variation. And this knowledge, rather than complicating our view of ourselves, should enrich it.

## KEY TERMS

| | | |
|---|---|---|
| specialized | deme | race |
| generalized | polytypic | endogamy |
| polymorphism | subspecies | cline |

## FOR MORE INFORMATION

A nice book on the history of ideas about race is Kenneth A. R. Kennedy's *Human Variation in Space and Time*. On human biological variation, see Stephen Molnar, *Races, Types, and Ethnic Groups: The Problem of Human Variation* and Alice M. Brues, *People and Races*. Carl Jay Bajema has edited a series of articles about *Natural Selection in Human Populations* that includes theoretical works and ones on specific polymorphisms. Perhaps the best collection on the nonexistence of biological races is Ashley Montagu's *The Concept of Race*. The concept of race and the problems it causes is a common theme of Stephen Jay Gould's works. One of his best, in *The Flamingo's Smile*, is called "Human Equality Is a Contingent Fact of History."

For a clear and well-illustrated discussion of the latest evidence from genetics and linguistics, see L. L. Cavalli-Sforza's article, "Genes, Peoples and Languages," in *Scientific American*, November, 1991. Finally, you should at least have a look at Carleton S. Coon's *The Origin of Races*.

# 14

# THE ORIGINS
# OF AGRICULTURE

Over the course of the past chapters of this book, we have recounted the story of human antiquity as we now understand it. The human ancestors we have discussed, whether they belonged to a species different from our own or were entirely modern, were all hunter-gatherers, relying on nature's bounty for their survival.

In fact, for more than 99 percent of hominid history, our ancestors fed themselves by foraging—gathering wild plant foods and hunting and scavenging wild animals. It is difficult to imagine that the subsistence mode that feeds virtually all people on this planet today, and that we so take for granted, developed only in the very recent days of our evolutionary calendar. We are talking about the fundamental subsistence shift from foraging to food *producing*.

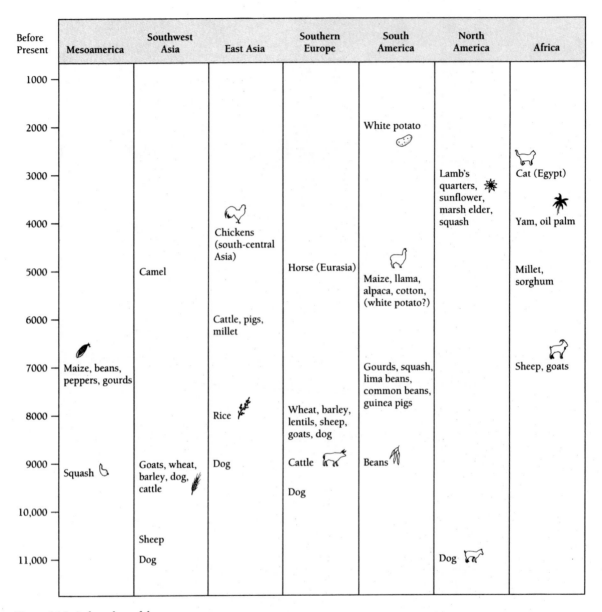

| Before Present | Mesoamerica | Southwest Asia | East Asia | Southern Europe | South America | North America | Africa |
|---|---|---|---|---|---|---|---|
| 1000 | | | | | | | |
| 2000 | | | | | White potato | | |
| 3000 | | | | | | Lamb's quarters, sunflower, marsh elder, squash | Cat (Egypt) |
| 4000 | | | Chickens (south-central Asia) | | | | Yam, oil palm |
| 5000 | | Camel | | Horse (Eurasia) | Maize, llama, alpaca, cotton, (white potato?) | | Millet, sorghum |
| 6000 | | | Cattle, pigs, millet | | | | |
| 7000 | Maize, beans, peppers, gourds | | | | Gourds, squash, lima beans, common beans, guinea pigs | | Sheep, goats |
| 8000 | | | Rice | Wheat, barley, lentils, sheep, goats, dog | | | |
| 9000 | Squash | Goats, wheat, barley, dog, cattle | Dog | Cattle<br>Dog | Beans | | |
| 10,000 | | | | | | | |
| 11,000 | | Sheep<br>Dog | | | | Dog | |

**Figure 14.1** *A chronology of domestication*

## THE FOOD-PRODUCING REVOLUTION

The focus of this chapter is the **Food-Producing Revolution**, or **Agricultural Revolution**. Although its impacts on human life certainly were "revolutionary" in the sense that they were momentous, there was no abrupt change in how people fed themselves. The shift to food produc-

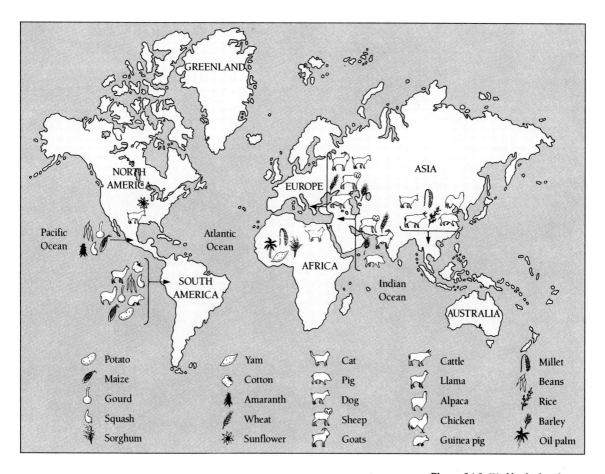

| | | | |
|---|---|---|---|
| Potato | Yam | Cat | Cattle | Millet |
| Maize | Cotton | Pig | Llama | Beans |
| Gourd | Amaranth | Dog | Alpaca | Rice |
| Squash | Wheat | Sheep | Chicken | Barley |
| Sorghum | Sunflower | Goats | Guinea pig | Oil palm |

**Figure 14.2** *Worldwide distribution of apparent hearths of plant and animal domestication.*

tion was a process that transpired over the course of several millennia in a number of different world areas and then spread out from these initial hearths (Figures 14.1 and 14.2).

Archaeologists also call the period when agriculture first became the dominant subsistence mode for some human groups, the **Neolithic**. Neolithic simply means "new stone" and specifically refers to the production, during this period, of a new stone tool type—the polished or ground stone tool, as distinct from the chipped stone tools of the "old stone" age, or Paleolithic. Although we no longer view this shift in tool type as the defining element of this period, the name has stuck.

It is not an exaggeration to say that the kind of life most of the world's people now lead was made possible by this change in subsistence that began only some 12,000 years ago (ya). The shift to food production marks a major break in how people related to their environment. Whereas before they could exploit only what nature already provided, now they could take at least some control over the production of

**Food-Producing Revolution:** The shift from foraging to food production through domestication, beginning after 12,000 ya.

**Agricultural Revolution:** Synonym for Food-Producing Revolution.

**Neolithic:** Literally "new stone age." Now refers to period of the beginning of agriculture.

food. The Neolithic marks a point in time when people began to **domesticate** those plants and animals they previously had relied on for food only in their wild or undomesticated state.

**Domestication** is a process that makes use of **artificial selection** to change the character of a plant or animals species according to a people's own needs or purposes. Artificial selection is analogous to natural selection as Charles Darwin defined it (see Chapter 2). Darwin's hobby

**Figure 14.3** *The many breeds of dogs are all members of the species* Canis familiaris *and are all descended from the wolf,* Canis lupus—*including* (upper left) *the wolflike malamute,* (upper right) *the Dalmatian,* (lower left) *the sheep dog, and* (lower right) *the decidedly nonwolflike poodle.*

as a pigeon breeder, in fact, provided him with crucial insights into how natural selection might work.

In natural selection, the plants or animals that survive and reproduce are those with the characteristics best adapted for survival in a specific environment. In artificial selection the individual members of plant or animals species are *allowed to survive* because they possess certain characteristics deemed desirable by humans. The others are killed off or simply not allowed to reproduce. In essence then, artificial selection is "managed" evolution, and the managers are people.

The social consequences of the shift to a food-producing from a food-gathering existence were enormous. Ultimately, the ability to ensure a constant, reliable, and expanded food supply allowed for an increase in sedentism and population growth, along with the development of new social structures needed to maintain order in these larger settlements. The kinds of social hierarchies made possible by—and sometimes made necessary by—the consequences of food production led to the developments that are the focus of Chapter 15.

## FROM WOLF TO DOG

Although generally not a food species, the dog provides a good example of the process of domestication. Many of us have dogs, and we are all at least passingly familiar with some modern breeds. Although the characteristics selected for were quite different than for those of a food species, the process of selection is essentially the same.

All domesticated dogs are members of the species *Canis familiaris*. Beagles and spaniels, German shepards and chihuahuas, St. Bernards and retrievers, toy poodles and dobermans—these are all members of the same species. And all are ultimately descended from a single wild species, *Canis lupus*—the wolf (Figure 14.3).

Now, as we all know, wolves are pretty fierce creatures, and it is not particularly obvious how a Pekingese can be bred from a wolf. It is, however, all a matter of artificial selection, genetic accidents, and time.

We know that the wolf was one of the first species domesticated by people—though probably not as a source of food. In a scenario suggested by osteologist Stanley Olsen (1985), orphaned wolf pups may have been picked up by local people and brought back to their village as a curiosity. If orphaned early enough in life, the pups would bond with the people raising them, who in turn would tolerate the pups because they were little trouble and very entertaining. As they grew, however, most became dangerous. Because they perceived the people around them as part of their "pack," these wolves would attempt to assert themselves within the pack just as they would in the wild. People would be bitten, children might be seriously hurt, and the wolves would more than likely be killed.

**domesticate:** To change, through selective breeding, a wild form of a plant or animal to a form more useful to humans; also, the end product of this process.

**domestication:** The process of making a plant or animal more useful to humans through selective breeding.

**artificial selection:** The process where humans choose the plant or animal that will live and reproduce, based on its useful characteristics.

There is, however, inherent variation in a wolf population. Although some wolves grow to be quite large, with enormous teeth and aggressive dispositions, others are smaller and more timid. In nature those wolves may be killed by larger wolves or, more likely, simply have a lower status in wolf society, where their characteristics put them at a disadvantage: They may eat only after the more dominant wolves get their fill; if they are males, they may not have much opportunity to mate. Within a human society, however, smaller, timid wolves might be at a tremendous *advantage*. Although their larger, aggressive siblings might be killed off as they presented a danger to their human hosts, the smaller, more compliant wolves might be allowed to live. This would be especially true if they performed valuable services for the humans. Because wolves are social animals that cooperate in nature, it is possible they would do the same when raised by people. They might help in hunting and then, being less aggressive and assertive, would wait to eat what they were given by their human masters. They might also help in protecting the village from animals and even other people.

The point is that by killing off some of the wolves because they have characteristics that make them dangerous and by allowing only those wolves with attractive (from a human standpoint) characteristics to survive, humans are *selecting* which of the animals will live to reproduce. The qualities of small size and nonaggressiveness would tend to be passed down to the next generation, and the selection process would continue, refining the animals to human standards.

As genetic accidents—mutations—occurred, people found even more variation from which to select various desired characteristics like attractive color or extremely small size. Eventually, the wild animal became so changed according to a human "blueprint" that it is no longer considered the same species it originally was.

The same general process of selection is applicable for a plant or animal food species. For example, those individuals of a plant species that possess desired characteristics—they produced bigger seeds or were hardier and easier to harvest—would be allowed to survive, reproduce, and pass down those characteristics. Those with undesirable features would be eliminated. Thus, without knowing anything about genetics, humans have genetically sculpted animal and plant species, in the process of domestication via artificial selection, from the raw material provided by natural species with their inherent variation.

## WHY FOOD PRODUCTION?

Agriculture began just a little after 12,000 ya. By 2000 ya most of the world's people relied on food production for their subsistence. As anthropologist Mark Cohen (1977) has pointed out, 10,000 years is a very small segment of time in the evolutionary history of a lineage that can be traced back more than 4 million years. That in this short time period several different cultures independently developed an agricultural way of life, and that those who didn't quickly borrowed the idea from their neighbors, shows how powerful the forces were that led to this revolution. The goal of the prehistorian is to identify and describe these forces, for in doing so we can explain the Agricultural Revolution.

## Hypotheses

The ancient people ate meat of animals and birds. At the time of Shen Nung, there were so many people that the animals and birds became inadequate for people's wants, and therefore Shen Nung taught the people to cultivate.—from an early Chinese legend about a culture hero, Shen Nung (Chang 1968:79)

It might seem self-evident to us that an agricultural way of life is superior to a hunting and gathering mode of subsistence. But this is not necessarily the case. Studies have shown that a hunting and gathering way of life can be very productive, providing a great deal of security and a lot of free time (Lee 1979). Under most circumstances an agricultural way of life is, in fact, much harder, requiring a good deal more work and quite a bit more risk. If the hunting is bad, after all, it might be relatively easy to pack up and move to where it is better. Agriculture, however, represents a tremendous investment in time and energy devoted to a specific location: to clear fields; prepare the soil for planting; plant, weed, protect the crops from animals; and harvest (Figure 14.4). If, after all that work, the harvest fails, the consequences can be dire. It is also true that although agriculture has the potential of producing enormous quantities of food, reliance on a single or small number of crops can actually result in nutrition levels lower than that of hunter-gatherers (see the discussion later in this chapter). The question remains, then, "Why did different groups of prehistoric people, during a relatively short time span, independently begin the process of domestication and move away from a hunting and gathering way of life?"

Numerous explanations have been proposed. Some cultures, it was suggested, domesticated plants and animals simply because their people were inherently smarter. This sort of nonsense deserves little attention here. We should know that all human groups have equal intellectual capacities.

It was also once common to explain the beginnings of agricultural life as the result of **diffusion**. According to this school of thought, cultures became agricultural because the idea of domestication was introduced to them by other groups—in other words, the process "diffused." This is, in reality, a nonexplanation. Of course, ideas and techniques do

**diffusion:** The geographic movement and sharing of cultural traits.

**Figure 14.4** *Agriculture, whether using plows and draft animals or modern technology, is hard work and clearly did not develop as a strategy for easing the work burden of hunter-gatherers.* (*Top,* Marc Riboud/ Magnum Photos; *bottom,* Cotton Coulson/ Woodfin Camp & Associates)

move from area to area, but this doesn't explain how they got started in the first place or why some groups might accept them when others will not.

We will focus briefly on a number of the more reasonable hypotheses for the origin of agriculture. Then we will present data on the major sequences of prehistoric domestication that archaeologists have developed. Finally, we will assess the hypothesis or hypotheses that best explain the data now in hand. Because each of the hypotheses was introduced and championed by individual scholars, we will present them by researcher. (These hypotheses are summarized in Table 14.1 on page 383.)

### The Oasis Hypothesis

> Food-production—the deliberate cultivation of food-plants, especially cereals, and the taming, breeding, and selection of animals—was an economic revolution—the greatest in human history after the mastery of fire. (Childe 1953:23)

British prehistorian, V. Gordon Childe (1942, 1951, 1953), proposed the "Oasis hypothesis" in the 1920s. Believing that there must have been some reason why agriculture began when and where it did, Childe suggests that certain areas of the world became drier at the end of the Pleistocene. As the European glaciers melted off, weather patterns and attendant storm tracks shifted, and less rain fell in the previously much wetter area of Southwest Asia. Plant life became concentrated in areas that had their own sources of water in the form of underground springs. These were the oases (Figure 14.5). As plant life concentrated in these limited areas, animals too were drawn to the oases, both for the water they contained and the lush stands of plants they supported. Finally, Childe contends, people congregated in such areas to take advantage of the water and food concentrated there.

A previously nomadic people would now have no reason to migrate and, in fact, good reason to stay put—to become **sedentary**. Their concentration in oases resulted in attempts to expand food resources by sowing seeds, weeding, and irrigating. These efforts resulted in artificial selection of seed plants and led to domestication. Animals previously hunted tended to live near the humans who hunted them, for the stubble from the fields of planted crops attracted them even more closely to human settlements. Such close proximity caused humans to become familiar with these animals, perhaps even tending them, and eventually domesticating them through artificial selection. Thus, the shift to food production had an environmental cause in the Oasis hypothesis.

**sedentary:** A settlement pattern where people mostly stay in one place.

**Figure 14.5** *Childe's Oasis hypothesis presumes that the prehistoric inhabitants of Southwest Asia congregated in oases like this one in Jericho as a result of a drying trend at the end of the Pleistocene—setting the stage, Childe believed, for the Agricultural Revolution.* (M. H. Feder)

## The Sedentary Hypothesis

It took man so very long to get around to the invention of agriculture that we may well doubt that the idea came easily or that it came from hunger, as is often supposed. (Sauer 1969:19)

Carl Sauer (1969), a well-known geographer, does not believe that people who were short of food had the time or inclination to experiment actively with domestication. Too much effort devoted to an experiment in basic subsistence where the outcome was uncertain could result in starvation.

Sauer believes instead that the first agriculturalists were well-fed, sedentary people. Nomadic people would not suddenly give up established practices of migration; a migratory people, moreover, are not in one place long enough to make domestication successful. Therefore, domestication began in relatively rich areas where failed experiments in food production would have resulted in nothing more than wasted time and where people could stay in one place long enough to see a crop through from planting to harvesting. Such rich areas, in Sauer's view, also offered these prehistoric experimenters lots of raw material to experiment with. Plant and animal diversity were high, with many different species and abundant variation within each species.

Sauer also thinks that the earliest agriculturalists would not be found along rivers because of the problems of water control, primarily flooding. He believed that woodlands, perhaps in hilly areas, were most amenable to early cultivation, even suggesting that the first domesticates might not be food but rather poisons and fibers. The area of the world that best met his criteria for early domestication, says Sauer, was Southeast Asia.

## The Readiness Hypothesis

> In my opinion there is no need to complicate the story with extraneous "causes." The food producing revolution seems to have occurred as the culmination of the ever increasing cultural differentiation and specialization of human communities. (Braidwood 1960:94)

Robert Braidwood (1960, 1975) is a well-known American prehistorian who has done quite a bit of work on the question of domestication. He does not believe that specific environmental conditions caused domestication to take place. Braidwood ascribes the beginnings of agriculture instead to purely cultural or historical factors. According to Braidwood, people began to domesticate plants as a result of accumulating knowledge of the plants and animals that lived in their territories. As various groups began specializing in their subsistence quests, they became expert in the characteristics of particular plant or animal species, a familiarity that resulted first in domestication and then agriculture. In Braidwood's view, agriculture began where it did because these were areas where the wild ancestors of plants and animals amenable to artificial selection were found.

## The Dump Heap Hypothesis

> It is now becoming increasingly clear that the domestication of weeds and cultivated plants is usually a process rather than an event. (Anderson 1956:766)

Edgar Anderson (1952, 1956) was an eminent plant biologist who was also interested in the beginnings of cultivation. In his "dump heap" hypothesis, Anderson suggests that certain plant species known as "camp followers" establish themselves in the kind of disturbed habitat that human beings produce in and around their villages. Such plants flourish where people dig up the ground, set fires, discard their organic refuse, and so on. As people began to notice the concentrations of these plants around their villages, they began to exploit them. They realized rather quickly that they could further encourage the growth of these plants by purposely creating the disturbances that had previously and accidentally attracted the plants. Because these plants were tended, unconscious artificial selection would have eventually resulted in domestication. Here domestication is viewed as an inevitable by-product of how people alter the landscape.

## The Demographic Hypothesis

> It is more sensible to regard the process of agricultural change in primitive communities as an adaptation to gradually increasing population densities, brought about by changes in the rates of natural population growth or by immigration. (Boserup 1965:117–18)

Ester Boserup (1965) is an agricultural economist. Technically, her hypothesis concerns the evolution of complex agricultural systems, not the origins of domestication. Her explanation, however, can certainly be expanded to cover the Agricultural Revolution as well, and has been used by prehistorians in this way.

Agriculture demands a tremendous investment in terms of time and labor. People would not make such an investment, Boserup contends, unless they had to, unless it was necessary for their survival. Boserup believes that the growth of population forces people to adopt more intensive strategies of subsistence in order to feed a greater number of mouths. New techniques of agriculture are not so difficult to develop, but ordinarily they are not used because they require more work than older, less intensive techniques. Thus, the Agricultural Revolution in this context is seen as having been triggered by demographics, specifically an increase in population.

## The Marginal Habitat Hypothesis

> Change in the demographic structure of a region which brings about the impingement of one group on the territory of another would also upset an established equilibrium system and might serve to increase the population density of a region beyond the carrying capacity of the natural environment. Under these conditions, manipulation of the natural environment in order to increase its productivity would be highly advantageous. (Binford 1968:328)

Lewis Binford (1968), an American archaeologist whose work we have previously discussed, presents a hypothesis that also argues for the beginnings of domestication driven by population increase. In Binford's view just as in Boserup's, agriculture is not so difficult to invent, but it is not terribly attractive because it requires so much work. Because most societies have strategies for maintaining their population below the **carrying capacity** of the natural environment, they remain in equilibrium. In other words, most societies keep their population below the maximum that can be fed in a given environment, and everything goes along quite smoothly.

When climate changed at the end of the Pleistocene, however, certain areas became extremely rich in food resources, leading to increased sedentism and, perhaps, marked population growth. Eventually, in Binford's view, some cultures overshot the carrying capacity of their local environment and were forced to expand into less attractive or marginal areas with lower carrying capacities. Competition with people already living in these areas led to pressure to apply more intensive strategies of subsistence. This led to tending and artificial selection and, ultimately, domestication.

Kent Flannery (1965, 1968, 1973), another American archaeologist, added to Binford's scenario. He suggests that when groups expand into neighboring, less productive areas as a result of population growth, they might bring along with them some of the plant or animal species that were native to their richer home areas. They would do so in a conscious attempt to increase the productivity of their new homes. Because these species were not naturally adapted to these marginal habitats, however, the only way they would survive was with human assistance. Animals might be sheltered and tended, and plants might be planted, weeded, watered, and protected. New selectional pressures, both natural and artificial, would result, and domestication would follow.

Flannery (1968) views this as a process of deviation and amplification. Once a small change occurs in the relationship of people to their food resources, greater changes result. The need to expand the food base by investing increasing amounts of time in tending wild resources can only be satisfied by a greater degree of sedentism; you need to stay in one place for a greater period of time in order to take care of the crops or animals. This results in a greater reliance on tended species because there is no longer as much time to hunt and gather wild foods. Population may increase as a result of greater sedentism through, for example, lower infant mortality. This in turn requires the production of even more food to feed more mouths, which is made possible by an increased investment of time in taking care of the food base, and so on.

Also following Binford, David Harris (1977) suggests that a hunter–gatherer society in equilibrium with its environment could be shifted toward food production as a result of a reduction in the availability of a staple food resource. Such a reduction, he suggests, can lead to an intensification and specialization of the food quest; other food resources, in other words, would be more intensively exploited. Where these alternative food resources were available at fixed points, Harris contends, group mobility would be reduced, and local population would increase. This would lead to a need to further intensify the food quest to feed more mouths, which might result in tending and artificial selection to increase productivity.

## DOMESTICATION: HOW CAN YOU TELL?

Before we test these hypotheses by reference to site data, we need to explain how the early stages of domestication can be recognized archaeologically. Certainly, full-scale agricultural villages look very different from hunter–gatherer villages, and we can recognize this difference in

**carrying capacity:** The number of organisms a given habitat can support.

the ground. But what about the transition, when **settlement patterns** really hadn't yet changed much? Here we have to look at the remains of the plants and animals being exploited to see if any alteration from the wild state has been wrought by human selection. Even this is not a terribly easy identification during early stages of domestication. The changes can be extremely subtle; the vagaries of preservation being what they are, moreover, it is virtually impossible to distinguish absolutely between ancient wild plants and animals and early domesticated species. But a number of features can be examined.

## Recognizing Domesticated Plants

For plant species, domestication serves to alter at least three reasonably recognizable characteristics:

1. *Seed size.* When seeds or fruits are the part of the plant eaten, people will artificially select for those individuals of a species that produce larger seeds. This is done in an obvious attempt to extract a greater amount of food from each plant. Seed size of individual plants may also become more homogeneous as large seeds are regularly selected for.

2. *Seed-dispersal mechanisms.* In nature, plants evolve mechanisms for dispersing seeds to produce the next generation of their species. When ripe, some seeds fall to the ground as a result of wind. Some may be knocked off by passing animals, or they may attach themselves to the fur of animals. Others may be eaten but undigested by animals or birds, to be excreted and, in a sense, planted elsewhere. For any of these mechanisms to work, the seeds have to become readily detachable from the plant at the appropriate time. This, however, poses a problem in human exploitation. Humans wish to harvest the plant and bring the edible part back home. When humans harvest a wild crop, however, at least in some species many if not most of the seeds will fall to the ground; remember, they are designed by nature to do so. This makes harvesting a very inefficient and time-consuming process. In the process of domestication, humans select for those individuals of a plant species that are at a disadvantage in nature because their seeds tend not to fall off when handled roughly. Early evidence for plant domestication includes an alteration in the area of attachment of seeds or fruits to the stem or stalk of the plant. In domestication such areas lose their naturally brittle character and allow for greater adhesion of the seed to the plant.

3. *Geographic distribution.* As Flannery (1965) proposes, when humans expand their territory, perhaps as a result of population growth and attendant dispersion, they often take food resources with them. In this way, wild plants may be introduced into areas where they do not grow naturally. An early sign of domestication is the appearance of a plant species in an area where its wild ancestors are not found.

## Recognizing Domesticated Animals

Some characteristics of early animal domestication can be seen in the archaeological record.

1. *Size selection.* As with seed plants, humans may select animals on the basis of size. Either larger or smaller individuals may be preferred. With the domestication of the wolf, for example, smaller individuals were preferred and selected for. This preference shows up very nicely in the archaeological record of the earliest domesticated dogs, with their smaller jaws but large, wolflike teeth (Olsen 1985). In the process of domesticating cattle, smaller size also was selected for, again probably for the reason of safety. Wild horses, on the other hand, were selected for larger size because their function was to carry loads, pull carts, and transport people. Any sort of ordered change in the size of a species through time, either larger or smaller, may indicate the beginning of domestication.

2. *Geographic distribution.* Just as with plants, one indication of the domestication of animals is their transport by people into habitats where they are not found naturally. As people moved into new territories, they may have brought formerly wild animals with them. Different selection pressures, both natural and artificial, on the species in the new habitat may have resulted in their further alteration.

3. *Population characteristics.* There is a great deal of chance involved in the hunting of wild animals. Animals killed may be male or female, very young, very old, or in the prime of life. Certainly, hunting is not entirely random and hunters may focus their attention on particular animals, but they may not exercise much control over which animal they finally kill. On the other hand, humans have virtually absolute control over domestic animals. The animals are penned or herded together. Most people who keep animals avoid killing females for the obvious reason that they produce more animals; very few males are necessary to maintain a herd, so herders often kill and eat young males and let females survive to an old age. In the case of tended and domesticated animals, we expect to see a recognizable difference from hunted animals in the population statistics of the animals killed.

4. *Osteological changes.* Changes occur in the bones of animals if they are penned and prevented from engaging in their normal activity. Such changes are not genetic; they occur as a result of the difference in lifestyle between the wild and penned individuals in a species. The bones of wild animals tend to be denser and stronger, simply because they need to be and have developed to allow the animals to withstand the rigors of life in the wild. In contrast, penned animals not allowed to roam freely and not forced to escape predators do not develop the denser microscopic architecture of the bones of wild animals. Such osteological changes do not necessarily indicate domestication; they may occur even in wild zoo animals. Such alterations, however, do imply a

**settlement pattern:** The distribution of archaeological sites in relation to each other and to features of the environment.

**Figure 14.6** *The Tehuacan Valley, looking past El Riego Cave on the left. Here Richard MacNeish discovered evidence for a sequence of New World agricultural development.* (R. S. Peabody Foundation for Archaeology, photo by R. S. MacNeish and Paul Mangelsdorf)

change in the relationship between people and the animals on which they subsist, probably indicating, at the very least, the initial stages of the process of animal domestication.

## HEARTHS OF DOMESTICATION

We are now in a position to discuss in some detail archaeological data relevant to the question of the invention of agriculture. We will focus on those areas of the world where domestication seems to have occurred, at least in part, independently. These areas are: Mesoamerica, the Middle East, East Asia, southern Europe, western South America, the North American Midwest, and Africa south of the Sahara (see Figure 14.2).

### Mesoamerica

In the late 1950s and early 1960s, American archaeologist Richard Mac-Neish (1964, 1967) began conducting archaeological surveys in highland Mexico. MacNeish was looking for early evidence of maize—what we commonly call corn. He focused on dry highlands because these regions would have better preservation of ancient organic material and because botanist Paul Mangelsdorf (1958), an expert on maize, had declared that it had originally been a highland grass species.

Searching through several highland valleys with freshwater sources, MacNeish came upon the Tehuacán Valley (Figure 14.6). After scrambling through some thirty-eight caves where organic preservation would have been highest, he was finally successful. A few test pits dug in Coxcatlan Cave produced six of the most primitive-looking maize cobs anyone had ever seen. Radiocarbon dating revealed that the layer in which they were recovered was 5600 years old, making these specimens, at the time, the oldest maize yet found.

This initial find inspired the Tehuacán Valley Project, one of the largest and most ambitious archaeological expeditions ever undertaken. From 1961 to 1964, fifty experts in various fields converged on the valley. Major excavations were conducted on twelve valley sites and hundreds of others were tested (Figure 14.7). What resulted was a nearly continuous stratigraphic sequence of human occupation of the valley from 12,000 B.P. to A.D. 1500. By following this sequence, we can construct a picture of human cultural evolution in the valley—an evolution that included the development of a food-producing economy.

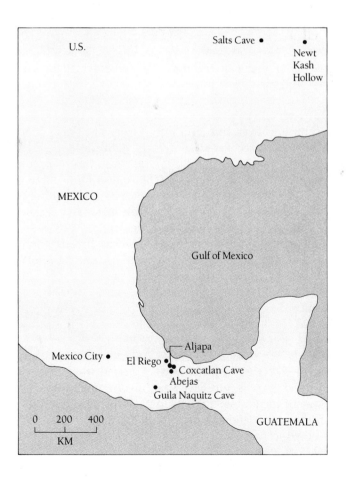

**Figure 14.7** *Map showing the locations of archaeological sites in North and Mesoamerica and mentioned in the text, where evidence of domestication has been recovered.*

Highland cultures in Tehuacán and probably other upland valleys at the end of the Pleistocene depended to a great degree on hunting (Flannery 1967). Of greatest importance at the lowest levels of Coxcatlan Cave were pronghorn antelope and jackrabbit. Such animals can be most easily hunted by groups. Pronghorn travel in herds, and jackrabbits live above ground and can be run into nets in large numbers. As climate changed at the end of the Pleistocene, both these animal species became extinct in the Mexican uplands. They were replaced by whitetail deer and cottontail rabbit, animals that can be hunted most efficiently by solitary hunters or small groups. Deer are solitary animals. Cottontail rabbits live in burrows and cannot be run into nets in large numbers like jackrabbits. It is likely, therefore, that people living in the valley at the end of the Pleistocene found it necessary to broaden their subsistence quest and to spread their numbers out over more territory to exploit these similarly more spread out animal resources. It is possible that, as a result of this change in settlement pattern, the people also intensified their exploitation of the plant species occurring there.

This set the stage, apparently, for an initially minor change in subsistence. At El Riego Cave, at a level radiocarbon dated to 8700 B.P., the then earliest evidence of domestication in the New World was discovered. Here, as at many of the other caves excavated in the project, human **coprolites** had been preserved. A total of 116 were recovered in the project. Their analyses allowed an extremely detailed reconstruction of diet.

In the coprolites from this layer at El Riego, MacNeish's coprologist, E. O. Callen (1967), recovered undigested remains of wild beans, amaranth (a grain), chili peppers, and avocados. Also in the coprolites were the remains of domesticated squash. The squash found here was *not* a primitive or incipient version of a domesticate; it was entirely different from its wild antecedent. So even though this material was close to 9000 years old, the inference was made that the origins of domestication in highland Mexico go back even further. A later investigation, in fact, turned up evidence of the domestication of squash (in Guila Naquitz Cave in Oaxaca, Mexico) more than 9300 ya.

Using the coprolites and other data, MacNeish (1967) has attempted to reconstruct the settlement pattern in the valley. During the initial period, winter occupations were small hunting camps. In the spring, populations coalesced into larger camps along the rivers. During the spring and summer, various wild seeds and cactus pods were important elements of the diet. Wild fruits were exploited when they ripened in the fall. Domesticates would have been incorporated into a still rather nomadic way of life and would have served only as a minor element in the diet in the spring and summer. As the analysis of the food components of the coprolites shows, this was a minor change; domesticates probably constituted no more than 6 percent of the diet at this time.

**Figure 14.8** *Series of maize cobs from Tehuacán, dated, from left, about 7000 years, 6000 years, 5000 years, 3000 years, and 2000 years. The cob on the right is of the modern variety.* (R. S. Peabody Foundation for Archaeology)

If we shift back to Coxcatlan Cave, in a layer dated 7000 to 5400 B.P., we can begin to see another change in subsistence, again based on an analysis of the coprolites. Most of the diet still consisted of wild game and wild plants, but domesticates have increased in frequency to about 14 percent of the diet. Most important here, however, at the 7000 B.P. level, domesticated maize was found.

This is certainly not the "corn" with which we are familiar. Modern maize consists of some 300 different races or varieties, some with enormous ears 12 or more inches long, with many rows and hundreds of kernels. The maize found in this level at Coxcatlan Cave is barely 1 inch long with just a few rows and anywhere from thirty to seventy individual kernels per ear (Figure 14.8). As humble as they appear, these remains nevertheless mark an incredibly important development in the evolution of agriculture.

At another site in the valley, Abejas, we can see the increasing reliance on domesticates. In the period 5400 to 4300 B.P., the coprolite data indicate that fully one-quarter of the diet consisted of domesticated plants. By this time, the domesticates included maize, squash, and beans, the triumvirate that was to become the basis of subsistence for most of the agricultural peoples of the New World before the colonial period.

**coprolite:** A preserved fecal remain.

The sites that date to this period in the valley are beginning to exhibit a size and degree of sedentism previously unknown. MacNeish (1967) has suggested that what had been temporary spring and summer camps along streams were now becoming permanent base camps at which at least some members of the population stayed year round. We are probably seeing a process of **deviation amplification** like that suggested by Flannery (1968), where a small, initial change or deviation in a traditional cultural practice related to subsistence has an enormous ripple effect across the culture, resulting in a fundamental change in a lifeway.

For agriculture to make a significant contribution to the diet, people need to become more sedentary. The more sedentary they become, however, the greater the need to produce food because people cannot roam around as much in the food quest. At the same time, the very old and the very young can make significant contributions to the subsistence quest; they can weed, sort seeds, and perform other light work. In the period we are examining, this very labor in fact may have extended people's life spans and thus increased overall population, which, in turn, would have put pressure on the subsistence system to produce more food. Thus, the original "deviation" from the traditional subsistence practice became "amplified," further necessitating a shift toward food production.

A break occurs in the Tehuacán sequence between 4300 and 3500 B.P. Sites dating to that period have not yet been found. A cave site, Ajalpa, dating to 3500–2900 B.P., picks up the story and again exhibits what

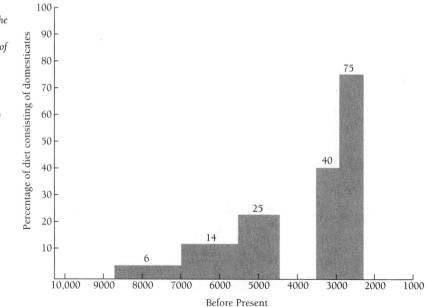

**Figure 14.9** *This graph clearly shows the evolutionary nature of the adoption of agriculture in the Tehuacán Valley. The percentages of various food contributions to the diet as derived from the coprolites demonstrate the long, slow process of the development of an agricultural mode of subsistence.* (Data from Callen 1967 and MacNeish 1967)

Teosinte plant                    Maize plant

**Figure 14.10** *Teosinte* (left), *a wild Mexican grass called "god's corn" by the Aztecs is the most likely candidate for wild maize. It is here compared to maize* (right). (From Beadle in Reed 1977)

appears to be a still very slow evolution toward an agricultural way of life. Domesticates now made up about 40 percent of the diet based on coprolite content. This is a big jump from the Abejas evidence, but still less than half the diet came from agricultural products. The rest was still supplied by hunting wild animals and gathering wild plants. Finally, the Santa Maria site, dating from 2900 to 2200 B.P., exhibits an acceleration in the shift to food production, with more than three-quarters of the diet now provided by agriculture. The Agricultural Revolution, at least as exhibited by the Tehuacán data, is certainly more evolutionary than revolutionary (Figure 14.9).

Though the identification is still uncertain, many researchers believe that the highland grass **teosinte** is, in fact, wild maize (Beadle 1977; Figure 14.10). Teosinte is a wild plant that looks quite a bit like the maize plant; instead of cobs with kernels, however, it produces rows a few inches long of five to ten seeds (technically fruits)(Figure 14.11). A single plant can produce thousands of seeds that fall to the ground when the **rachis**, the membrane between the seeds, becomes brittle and is shattered by any slight movement.

We know that teosinte was used as a prehistoric food source, but quite a bit of work is involved in harvesting and preparing the seeds for eating. The brittleness of the rachis leads to loss of seeds, the individual seeds are very small, and the seed cases are extremely tough. There is variation, however, and mutations do occur. In fact, these characteris-

**deviation amplification:** A small change in one part of a cultural system results in larger changes in the rest of the culture, which cause the original change to become increased.

**teosinte:** The wild ancestor of maize.

**rachis:** The area of attachment between seeds and other seeds or between seeds and other parts of the plant.

**Figure 14.11** *The fruitcase of teosinte (left), with its brittle rachis and tough glumes, can actually be converted to the cob and naked kernels of maize (right) by changes in very few genes.* (From Beadle in Reed 1977)

Teosinte spikelet (left)
and seeds (right)

Maize cob (left)
and kernels (right)

**Figure 14.12** *Map showing the locations of archaeological sites in the Middle East and mentioned in the text, where evidence of domestication has been recovered.*

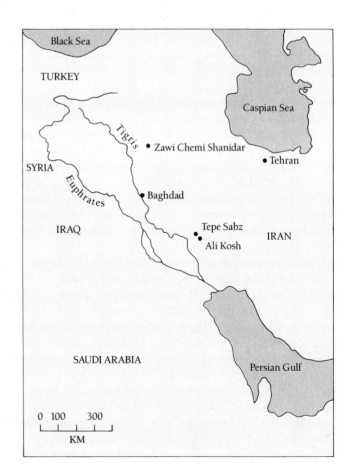

tics are controlled by only a very few genes (Beadle 1977:626). It is likely that during the time teosinte was being exploited, there was selection for those plants with less brittle rachis and naked kernels or seeds. The cob in maize can be accounted for as a mutation of the seed spike in teosinte. Thus, teosinte, called "god's corn" by the Aztecs, appears to have been modified through artificial selection to produce the small, relatively brittle cobbed corn of the Tehuacán valley.

## The Mideast

A series of archaeological sites are known from the area called the Levant, a stretch of uplands across modern Israel, Lebanon, and Syria. The sites all date to the period 12,000–10,000 B.P., about the same time as the earliest occupation of Coxcatlan Cave, and the culture is known as **Natufian.** The sites are mostly in caves, although some open-air camps have been located. The Natufian sites are all nonagricultural; there is no evidence that domestication of any plant or animal species had yet taken place. But the most abundant artifacts recovered as Natufian sites do reflect on the nature of their inhabitants' subsistence and imply a focus on those species that would become part of a food-production strategy just a few thousand years later. Those artifacts are the stone mortars and microliths first seen in African sites about 18,000 ya.

The stone mortars certainly could have been used for grinding plant material, but the evidence from the microliths is even more compelling. These tiny, very sharp stone blades, inset into bone, wood, and antler handles, were used much in the way of modern sickles to harvest wild grains—most probably wheat, barley, and oats. So the Natufians, who lived in an area with the wild ancestors of plant species that were soon to be domesticated, possessed tools that show a reliance on harvesting plants.

Our focus now shifts to the Zagros Mountains of northeastern Iraq, where sites of the Karim Shahir culture have been excavated (Figure 14.12). One of the most important of these sites is Zawi Chemi Shanidar, which dates to 10,600 B.P. (Wright 1971). The site is characterized by round hut floors within a cave. Artifacts included some microliths, grinding and milling stones, beads, rings, pendants, and axes. Most important were the faunal remains, which consisted almost exclusively of the bones of sheep. The bones themselves were not so different from the bones of ordinary wild mountain sheep. What is striking about the assemblage at this site is the population distribution of the animals. Almost all the bones from Zawi Chemi Shanidar are from young animals. As discussed, that kind of consistency almost certainly implies that the people were in control of the population of animals they were feeding on. Such control implies tending, if not incipient domestication.

**Natufian:** A Late Paleolithic, Early Neolithic culture of Southwest Asia, dating from 12,000 to 10,000 ya.

**Figure 14.13** *Excavation of the Bus Mordeh occupation of Tepe Ali Kosh.* (Frank Hole)

In the early to mid-1960s, another multidisciplinary project was undertaken, this time in the Deh Luran Plain of southwestern Iran. The project was directed by archaeologists Frank Hole, Kent Flannery, and James Neely (1969). Their objective was to investigate the nature of early domestication and the development of settled village life in Southwest Asia. Among the sites located in their research were two, Tepe Ali Kosh and Tepe Sabz, that provided data bearing directly on this question.

At Ali Kosh, for the period 9450 to 8700 B.P., the investigators defined the Bus Mordeh Phase of occupation (Figure 14.13). The site was relatively small and so were the individual structures, made from local red clay. The Bus Mordeh people depended for their subsistence, at least in part, on the hunting of wild animals like gazelle, wild ox, boar, and ass. They also fished, as evidenced by the remains of carp and catfish in their trash pits.

The Bus Mordeh people were also pretty clearly at an early stage in the domestication of goats. Just as at Zawi Chemi Shanidar, the remains of the animals themselves differ very little from wild ones. The population distribution of the animals, however, can best be interpreted as indicating tending and an early stage in the process of domestication. Most of the animals killed at Ali Kosh during the Bus Mordeh Phase were young males. Females, it seems, were protected for breeding (Hole et al. 1969:344).

The Bus Mordeh phase also provides evidence for domestication of plants, but just as in Tehuacán it seems that domesticates played a minor role in the diet during this early stage of the evolution of food-producing strategies. Thousands of seeds were recovered in the Bus Mordeh levels at Ali Kosh. Most of these represented wild alfalfa, vetch, goosefoot, and other wild grasses and legumes. The domesticated versions of emmer wheat and two-row barley were also found at this level, but they represent less than 10 percent of the seeds recovered and, certainly made a very small contribution to the diet (Hole et al. 1969:343).

The period of 8700 to 7950 B.P. at Tepe Ali Kosh is called the Ali Kosh Phase. It is unknown whether the site grew larger, but certainly individual structures were larger and more substantial. Here we can see again the rather slow development of a reliance on food production. By this time, Ali Kosh was an agricultural and herding village, but much of the diet still consisted of wild animals and plants as well as fish. In this phase, the osteological evidence shows quite clearly that the goats were no longer wild but domesticated. About 40 percent of the seeds recovered in these levels were from domesticated versions of emmer wheat and two-row barley (Hole et al. 1969:347). Not surprisingly, many small flint blades (for harvesting) as well as grinding stones (for processing) were recovered.

From 7950 to 7550 B.P., the Mohammad Jaffar Phase, the people at Ali Kosh were building larger and more substantial houses, still hunting gazelle and other animals for part of their subsistence, collecting wild plants, planting wheat and barley, and herding goats and increasing numbers of domesticated sheep.

At the Tepe Sabz site, in the period 7450 to 6950 B.P., two significant shifts in food-production strategies occurred. First, there was a change of emphasis from goats to sheep. Second, at least beginning in this phase, these people started to use irrigation to expand the area available to them for agriculture.

After this period, the population of the Deh Luran Plain exploded. There was a greater number of villages, and the villages themselves grew larger and more stable. Here the researchers noted the same feedback pattern we noted with Tehuacán. At first, domesticates were a minor part of the diet. Population was still low, but increased effort in food production resulted in large increases in the amount of food produced, which allowed for increased population, which in turn led to a demand for more agriculture. Eventually, this effect led to the necessity of artificially increasing the amount of cultivatable land through irrigation. This resulted in an even higher output of food, which then allowed for increased population.

The emmer and einkorn wheat that grew wild in the hilly areas of Southwest Asia at the end of the Pleistocene was used by local hunter-gatherers. Modern experiments have shown that large amounts of these

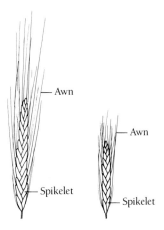

**Figure 14.14** *A comparison of (left) the rachis of wild and (right) domesticated wheat. The brittle rachis of wild wheat allows for the dispersion of seeds; the nonbrittle rachis selected for in domestication allows for ease in human harvesting.*

wild grains can be harvested (Harlan et al. 1966). In fact, the wild wheat kernels are higher in protein than modern domesticated wheat.

There are, however, a number of problems. The rachis of wild wheat, like that of teosinte, becomes quite brittle when the kernels are ripe. In fact, it has been noted that wild emmer wheat and barley growing near some of the older archaeological sites in the region can be harvested only during a very short period because they ripen quickly, their rachis become quite brittle, and the common, strong winds are enough to knock the individual grains off of the plant and onto the ground (Bower 1989b). This renders harvesting wild wheat problematic and provides a rationale for human selection of only those plants with a nonbrittle rachis.

Also, each kernel of wild wheat is encased in a tough rind, or glume. Either you lose a lot of wheat harvesting it because of its brittle attachment, or you must invest a great amount of time picking it up. Even after this, the wheat still needs a good deal of processing to remove the edible kernels from the inedible glumes.

But wild wheat stands have mutants that possess tough rachis and naked glumes. As with teosinte, only a very few genes are involved in determining these characteristics. Under natural conditions, neither a tough rachis nor naked glumes is advantageous because both interfere with seed dispersal and protection. It appears clear, however, that people who were collecting wild wheat in Southwest Asia at the end of the Pleistocene were, in fact, artificially selecting for those very characteristics (Figure 14.14).

Archaeologist Ramona Unger-Hamilton (1989) has conducted an experiment focusing on the tools that may have been used to harvest the wild and early domesticated cereal crops of the Levant. After making 295 stone blades and then using them to harvest a number of locally available wild and domesticated plant species, she compared the wear patterns (see Chapter 7) on these experimental tools with those she found on 761 prehistoric blades from sites in Israel dating from 12,000 to 8000 ya. She found that one-quarter of the blades from Natufian sites (12,000 to 10,000 ya) and three-quarters of the more recent tools had striations, or scratches, that were just like those she experimentally produced when harvesting cereal crops from tilled soil. In her experiment, when harvesting grains from tilled soil, the sickle handle in which the blades were inset invariably would scrape the ground, giving the blades these characteristic scratch marks. Unger-Hamilton interpreted this evidence to indicate that tilling the soil and harvesting the cereals that grew there began as much as 12,000 ya.

Additional evidence of early steps in domestication in the Middle East comes from the 8600-year-old site of Mureybet in northern Syria, where researchers have found the remains of wild wheat and barley. These crops, however, were not native to the region and probably came from a source some 160 kilometers to the north in the Zagros Mountains of Turkey. This is good evidence for human intervention. People, likely from the Zagros Mountains, must have brought these crops with them as they expanded their territory into northern Syria where they planted and tended them. This is an example of one of the sorts of evidence mentioned previously for the early stages of domestication— the appearance of a wild plant or animal species in an area outside its natural habitat. Its movement to and survival in a new territory can be ascribed to human intervention as people expanded their domain.

## The Far East

Much less is known for the sequence of domestication in East Asia (Gorman 1969; Solheim 1972; Figure 14.15). We do know that as much as 15,000 ya in a Southeast Asian culture called Hoabinhian, grinding

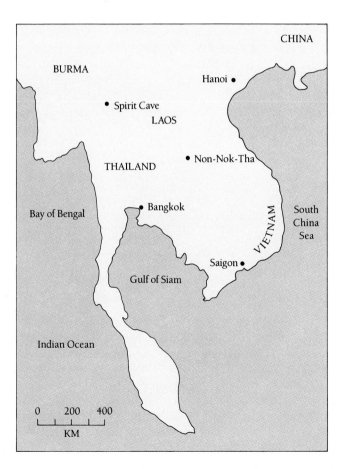

**Figure 14.15** *Map showing the location of archaeological sites in the Far East and mentioned in the text, where evidence of domestication has been recovered.*

stones in the tool assemblage indicate that plant foods played an important role in the diet.

At the Spirit Cave site in northwestern Thailand, excellent preservation allowed researchers to reconstruct much of the diet. As much as 12,000 ya, we can see the utilization of such species as water chestnut, bean, soybean, almond, and cucumber. These plants were probably not yet domesticated at this time. Just as in Mexico and Iran, however, the data shows an early post-Pleistocene adaptation that focused on the local wild antecedents of those species that were to be domesticated shortly afterward and they were to become mainstays of local diet right up to the present time. The data are sparse for the period after this, but we do know that by 6000 B.P. fully agricultural villages had evolved. The site of Non Nok Tha in northeast Thailand, with domesticated rice, cattle, and pigs, is an example (Figure 14.16).

As for the most significant East Asian domesticate, rice, little is known for certain other than it appears to have originated independently in China, Southeast Asia, and India (Ho 1977; Figure 14.17).

**Figure 14.16** *The Non Nok Tha site in Thailand is an early agricultural site in Southeast Asia.* (Wilhelm G. Solheim II)

**Figure 14.17** *Rice cultivation in China, in irrigated rice paddies.*
(Bruno Barbey/Magnum Photos)

Preagricultural people in central China practiced a nomadic way of life, fishing and hunting deer, elephant, and bear. We also know that sometime after 8000 ya, sedentary villages of what is called the **Yang-Shao** culture developed in the Huang-ho River valley in which the domesticated versions of fox-tailed millet, pigs, and dogs were eaten (Chang 1968). Only later did these people begin to plant rice and raise chickens, sheep, horses, and cattle. Here again, though the data are not nearly as detailed as for Mexico and Iran, we do see the slow acceptance of domesticates, for wild plant foods remained important to the Yang-Shao people long after they began using cultivated ones. Full-scale agricultural villages did not appear until the appearance of the **Lung Shan** culture a few thousand years later. Unfortunately, the time period that interests us most in terms of the actual development of domestication is still very poorly known for East Asia.

**Yang-Shao:** An Early Neolithic culture of China, dating to about 8000 ya.

**Lung Shan:** The first fully agricultural group in China, dating to about 6000 ya.

## Europe

In southern Europe at the end of the Pleistocene (Figure 14.18), we see a pattern of big-game hunting, with an emphasis on wild cattle, deer, ass, bison, and mountain goat (Milisauskas 1978; Whittle 1985). A typical site is Franchthi Cave in Greece, where these animals were hunted about 11,000 ya (Figure 14.19). By 9500 B.P., we see a decrease in the size of the animals being hunted and a marked increase in the presence of fish bones and other aquatic resources. This seems to indicate a shift to coastal resources as the coasts were beginning to stabilize after the sea level rise that accompanied glacial meltoff. Although the data are unclear, the emphasis on coastal resources may indicate an increase in sedentism; commonly, coastal areas are rich enough to allow hunter-gatherers to abandon a nomadic way of life. Such a shift, however, may have resulted in a population increase (or at least in an increase in local population densities) sufficient to force some groups to try to intensify

**Figure 14.18** *Map showing the location of archaeological sites in southern Europe and mentioned in the text, where evidence of domestication has been recovered.*

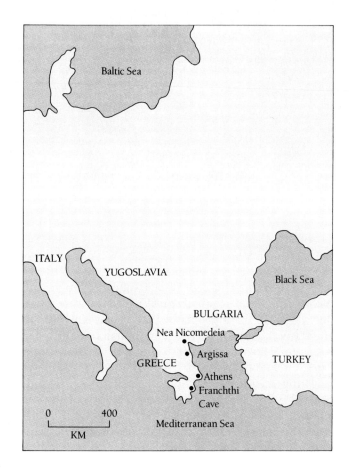

**Figure 14.19** *Franchthi Cave, in Greece, was occupied during the Late Pleistocene and early post-Pleistocene. Wild species of crops that would be later domesticated, such as oats, barley, peas, and lentils, were eaten by the inhabitants more than 8000 ya.* (Thomas W. Jacobsen)

the subsistence quest. Such an intensification may have resulted in the shift from food gathering to food production. At Franchthi Cave, we also see the exploitation of wild oats, barley, peas, and lentils at between 13,000 and 11,000 B.P. (Hansen 1991), showing the use of wild crops that were soon to become important domesticates.

After 8000 B.P. in Europe, the evidence of domestication is clear. Sites become larger and appear to be more permanent. At Franchthi Cave, domesticated wheat appears without antecedents. At the Nea Nicomedeia site on the eastern coast of Greece on the Aegean Sea, the hunting of wild animals such as deer, wild pig, and hare were major components, along with fishing, of the subsistence quest. There is also evidence, however, of the planting of domesticated wheat, barley, and lentils as well as the herding of sheep and goats. All these species were varieties domesticated earlier in Southwest Asia, which probably indicates the diffusion of these domesticates into southern Europe.

Cattle bones recovered at Nea Nicomedeia date to at least 8000 and perhaps 9000 B.P. and may be the oldest domestic specimens in the world. Although the bones themselves are no different from those of wild cattle, the high proportion of young animal bones may indicate that the process of domestication had begun. Another site in Greece, Argissa, shows clearer evidence of domestication, dating to about 8000 B.P., with a decrease in the size of cattle.

The situation in Neolithic Europe may be explained as the result of the complex interplay of environmental change, settlement pattern change, population growth, early domestication, and contact with Southwest Asian agriculturalists. How much of the development of agriculture in Europe was indigenous and how much was a result of contact with Southwest Asia is still unclear.

### South America and North America

Back in the New World, the situation is similar. In both South and North America (Figure 14.20), it is probable that contact with agricul-

**Figure 14.20** *Map showing the location of archaeological sites in South America and mentioned in the text, where evidence of domestication has been recovered.*

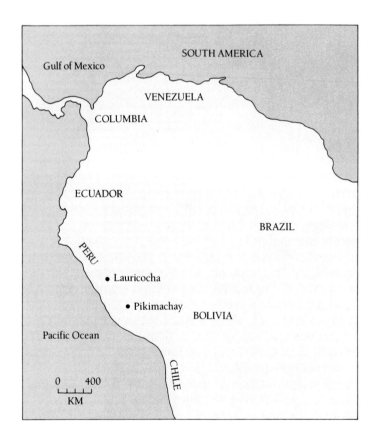

turalists from Mesoamerica together with indigenous experimentation resulted in the development of food-production strategies.

Although hypotheses have been proposed for earlier cultivation of root crops such as manioc in South America, there is no solid evidence to support this notion. It seems that the earliest domesticates used in South America are common beans and lima beans (Patterson 1973). Evidence comes from Guitarrero Cave in the Peruvian highlands, dated to 9500 B.P. (Kaplan et al. 1973; Lynch et al. 1985). By 4950 B.P., maize and other Mesoamerican domesticates were being used in South American agriculture. But other nonMesoamerican crops were also domesticated in South America, including white potatoes, coca, peanuts, lima beans, and cotton (MacNeish 1977).

South America also provides data for the most significant animal domestication in the New World (Kent 1987; Wing 1977). There are four types of camelids in South America: the wild guanaco and vicuña and the domesticated llama and alpaca. The precise relationships among these four types are still unknown—all four are interfertile. Some suggest that the guanaco was domesticated to produce both the llama and the alpaca (Figure 14.21). In any event, the llama is primarily a beast of burden, the alpaca a source of wool, and both are used for food. The llama and alpaca show signs of domestication before 5000 B.P., according to finds in Pikimachay Cave and Lauricocha Cave in Peru (Wing 1977).

In North America, we can also see the adoption of Mesoamerican domesticates, including the all-important triumvirate of maize, beans, and squash as well as the bottle gourd. Because the wild ancestors of these crops do not grow in North America, we are on firm ground when we state that they diffused in. However, there also is evidence of independent domestication perhaps predating the appearance of these Mesoamerican crops (Smith 1989; Yarnell 1971, 1977). (See Figure 14.6.) At Salts Cave in Kentucky, 119 coprolites are associated with a radiocarbon date of 3450 B.P. (Yarnell 1977:864). These coprolites contain an abundance of sunflower and marsh elder (sump weed) seeds, whose large size is indicative of domestication (Figure 14.22). There is also evidence at this site of the use of a domesticated squash. At the Newt Kash Hollow site in Kentucky, there is evidence of marsh elder found outside its wild range and sunflower seeds three times normal wild seed volume, at a date of 2600 B.P. Another native plant that appears to have been domesticated in the American Midwest sometime before 3000 B.P. is lamb's quarters, or pigweed. These local crops, if they, indeed, preceded the introduction of maize, certainly predisposed the local people for an agricultural way of life. Once introduced, maize was such a productive food source that it quickly replaced the indigenous crops.

**Figure 14.21** *Llamas, probably the most important animal domesticated in the New World, were used as beasts of burden and as food. Here, a packtrain of llamas carries firewood in southern Peru.* (Loren McIntyre, © 1973 National Geographic Society)

## Africa

Some of the earliest evidence for domestication in Africa comes from Egypt, where domesticated wheat, barley, sheep, goats, and cattle are present in sites along the Nile dating to more than 7000 ya. Also in North Africa, Haua Fteah Cave in Libya shows early evidence of the use of domesticates. Here the bones of domesticated sheep and goats were found in a level dated to greater than 6800 B.P. (Clark 1976). Domesticated cattle are also known from sites of similar age. Although it cannot

**Figure 14.22** *The sunflower was one of a number of crops domesticated by Native Americans living north of Mexico.* (Marc Banks)

be proven, many believe that these domesticates were introduced from Southwest Asia, where they are older.

The data are very sparse for southern Africa, but there appears to have been a separate hearth of domestication south of the Sahara. At around 5000 B.P., we find evidence of sorghum and at least three varieties of domesticated millet (finger, foxtail, and pearl); these were not Asian or European plants, so it is probable that they were the result of purely local domestication. Each sorghum plant produces a number of stems with clusters of seeds that, in the wild condition, mature at different times. In the process of domestication, plants were selected for that produce seeds maturing all at the same time for ease of harvest (Harlan et al. 1976).

Also, in western Africa, a non-Asian variety of rice was domesticated. Yams were another important crop, but tubers are notoriously difficult to study archaeologically because they do not produce hard parts that might preserve. Sheep, goats, pigs, and cattle came into the area from the north and quickly became significant components in the subsistence of sub-Saharan African agriculturalists. Recent palynological evidence suggests that the oil palm, an important domesticated tree that produces oil used in cooking, wood for construction, leaves for thatching, and fibers for cordage, was probably domesticated at about 2800 B.P. (Sowunmi 1985). It is at about this time in Western Africa that pollen analysis shows a decrease in the percentages of several wild tree species and a dramatic increase in the oil palm.

## THE NUTRITIONAL IMPACTS OF AGRICULTURE

Although a shift to an agricultural mode of subsistence almost always results in increased amounts of food, the diet of agriculturalists is not always nutritionally superior to that of hunter-gatherers. In fact, analysis of the skeletons of some prehistoric agriculturalists shows a marked increase in the incidence of diseases that are related to dietary deficiencies.

A good example of this comes from the work of physical anthropologist George Armelagos and his students (Goodman and Armelagos 1985), who analyzed hundreds of skeletons from the Dickson Mound site in Illinois. The skeletons date to the period A.D. 950 to after 1200—before agriculture made its appearance, during the transition period, and after its acceptance. The skeletons of the site's inhabitants show the effects of dietary emphasis on a single crop, in this case, maize, which, while providing large quantities of food, led to an unvaried diet lacking in some important nutrients. Twice as many of the skeletons after the adoption of agriculture show evidence of anemia and three times as many exhibit the osteological effects of bacterial infections as do those of the earlier hunter-gatherers. Beyond this, the bones of the children of the agriculturalists are narrower and shorter, showing a delayed growth rate in their early years. Among the agriculturalists, there was higher infant mortality and a shortened average life span.

So, it may be, at least in some cases, that the varied diet of hunter-gatherers was more nutritionally complete than that of many early agriculturalists. The health of people often suffered, therefore, in their attempt to produce a greater quantity of food when this resulted in a less varied diet. So, we may infer, there must have been a significant motivation to produce more food.


## CAN AGRICULTURE BE EXPLAINED?

Earlier in this chapter, we presented some hypotheses for explaining the Agricultural Revolution (Table 14.1). Then we presented data on the actual sequences of the evolution of food production in Mesoamerica, Southwest Asia, East Asia, Europe, South and North America, and Africa (see Figure 14.1 for a summary time chart). We are now left with the question of which hypothesis or hypotheses are borne out by the data. In all fairness, the data are too limited even for the most well-known sequences to give a definitive answer. But at the very least we can begin to attempt to isolate the useful aspects of each of the proposed explanations and—to use an appropriate metaphor—winnow out those aspects that do not bear up under scrutiny.

Childe's Oasis hypothesis is probably not correct in positing a significant drying of the environment as a factor. Evidence now shows this long-term climate effect did not occur. Beyond this, the key elements of his hypothesis are not borne out. The idea that only an oasis situation would allow people to become knowledgeable about plants and animals makes no sense. Hunters and gatherers the world over possess detailed knowledge about the plants and animals on which they subsist.

Sauer was correct at least in terms of proposing that a certain degree of sedentism was a significant factor in the development of agriculture. But other aspects of his hypothesis are not supported. Aside from the dog, early domesticates were, in fact, food sources. Also, although the data are meager, Southeast Asia was certainly no earlier and perhaps a bit later in developing an agricultural way of life than was Southwest Asia.

Braidwood may have been correct in assuming that people would not begin the process of domestication without having a great deal of

# CONTEMPORARY ISSUE

### Our Worst Mistake?

We began this chapter by pointing out that the fabric of modern life depends absolutely on the subsistence mode called agriculture. Without a steady, reliable, predictable—not to mention enormous—food supply, modern life with its cities, universities, and, yes, anthropologists simply would not be possible. One might think it obvious, therefore, that agriculture, the invention, which, more than anything else, has made modern life possible, was a good thing. But not everyone agrees. UCLA medical school scientist and writer Jared Diamond (1987) has written a provocative essay in which he characterizes the Food-Producing Revolution as "the worst mistake in the history of the human race."

It is an interesting assertion. Diamond points out that hunter-gatherers, in many instances, led relatively easy lives. In response to the stereotype many of us hold of the short, hard lives and hand-to-mouth existence of hunter-gatherers, it must be said they often have it better than those who rely on agriculture. Their diets frequently are healthier, providing more protein and offering more variety than those of agriculturalists. And, even in those few, relatively poor areas where the last hunter-gatherers were pushed by expanding agriculturalists, they didn't need to work very long for the necessities of existence. Agriculture, with its clearing of land, tilling of soil, planting, weeding, watering, and harvesting, is exceedingly hard work, and farmers typically work far more hours than hunter-gatherers.

While most hunter-gatherers practice a broad-spectrum subsistence strategy where they regularly collect dozens of different kinds of foods, agriculturalists often devote all of their energies to a very small number of crops—generally rice, corn, or wheat. These high-carbohydrate crops are extremely productive and can feed many more people than hunting or gathering, but, because they are lacking in some essential amino

acids, they can lead to a rather poor diet. Also, if a pestilence befalls one of these major crops, the people will starve, having little else to fall back on.

Beyond this, Diamond points out, it was the enormous output potential of agriculture that led to class societies. Where there is the potential for surplus food production, there is the potential for classes of "haves" who control the extra and classes of "have-nots" who may need that food in times of trouble. Eventually, Diamond asserts, this led to class societies where most are poor and work their lives away for those few wealthy individuals who control the food surplus.

Thus, in Diamond's accounting, people at the end of the Pleistocene had two choices: They could maintain their hunting and gathering way of life and invent new ways of keeping population down and thus ensure enough food for their small populations, or they could allow population to grow and intensify the food quest through plant and animal domestication. The irony, in Diamond's view, was that those who made the smart decision—the hunter-gatherers who opted to keep population down and maintain their traditional subsistence mode—were quickly overrun by those who allowed their populations to grow. There was little choice, then, but to adopt a new subsistence mode that would feed far more mouths but lead to the inequality and inequity of modern life.

What are we to make of this? Diamond does have a point, but we are not sure how useful his insight is. Certainly, without agriculture there can be no wealth or classes—or wars to dispute who should have all of that wealth. Equally certainly, however, there could be no anthropologists or UCLA medical school professors. Indeed, agriculture brings with it good and bad. And ultimately, as with nearly all other cultural inventions, the results are up to us.

**Table 14.1** *Summary of Hypotheses Proposed to Explain the Origins of Agriculture*

| Hypothesis | Proponent | Summary |
|---|---|---|
| Oasis | V. Gordon Childe | Post-Pleistocene drying of the environment led to the concentration of people, animals, and plants at permanent water sources, or oases. There, people, in close proximity to wild plants and animals studied them, tended them, and, eventually, domesticated them. |
| Sedentary | Carl Sauer | People living in areas with naturally abundant food would experiment with methods of increasing the abundance of nonfood plants. Eventually, they would apply what they learned through this experimentation to plant foods. |
| Readiness | Robert Braidwood | People had, by the end of the Pleistocene, accumulated knowledge about wild plants and animals in their regions. Where local plants and animals were amenable to domestication, people domesticated them when they were intellectually ready. |
| Dump heap | Edgar Anderson | Human beings disturb the habitat around their settlements as a matter of course. Certain wild plant species grow abundantly in these disturbed habitats. People soon realized that by intentionally disturbing areas they could encourage the growth of such plants, which they then began to tend and, eventually, domesticate. |
| Demographic | Ester Boserup | People had long recognized their ability to manipulate plants and animals through artificial selection. Because of the greatly increased amount of work this entails, however, they did not apply their knowledge of the processes of domestication until population increase and the need to produce more food necessitated it. |
| Marginal habitat | Lewis Binford Kent Flannery David Harris | As population grew at the end of the Pleistocene, human groups expanded into less than optimal habitats. They brought with them wild plants and animals from their source areas. These plants and animals could survive in the new areas only through the care and attention of people. People would begin to select only those individuals among the displaced plants and animals that thrived in the new habitat, thus leading to domestication. |

knowledge about the species they were domesticating, but this really does not explain the timing of the Agricultural Revolution or the fact that it was so widespread. His explanation is really no explanation at all—saying, in essence, agriculture developed when people were ready to develop it. So *why* were they ready?

Anderson's claim that domestication may have been accidentally encouraged by many of the practices of hunter-gatherers is certainly correct. But again, it really does not approach the question of why they would have gone through the extra bother of an agricultural way of life. This, too, is a nonexplanation.

Finally we come to the hypotheses of Boserup and Binford, Flannery, and Harris. These explanations, which are really complementary and not competing, are perhaps the most attractive. Together, they take into account environmental, demographic, and cultural factors. The problem is that the key element of all their explanations—population growth impinging on the carrying capacity of local environments—cannot, at present, be shown to have occurred immediately prior to the beginning of domestication.

Nevertheless, following Binford's model, we can propose a tentative scenario: At the end of the Pleistocene, cultures were forced to adjust their adaptations in response to climatic changes wrought by the melting of the ice sheets. Some groups shifted their subsistence focus to habitats that allowed for a more sedentary existence—the coast, along rivers, and so on. Such sedentism may have produced larger, or at least denser, populations. The rich food resources were localized and group mobility decreased. The old and the lame could make significant contributions to the food quest. Where previously children had been a burden—just more mouths to feed—now they too could become active in the food quest when that quest focused on collecting objects like shellfish, bird eggs, or seeds. The birth rate may have increased as well.

An increase in population, however, may have upset the previously evolved equilibrium between human populations and their environments, causing groups to overshoot the carrying capacity of their territories. This may have resulted in expansion into marginal or less attractive habitats, and subsequent intensification and specialization of the food quest. Historical hunter-gatherers were known to broadcast the seeds of their wild food plants, so it is not difficult to believe that people at the end of the Pleistocene did the same out of the necessity borne of such a "food crisis." We need only assume that in attempting to expand the growth of their wild food plants (or animals) into new habitats or in attempting to intensify their productivity within the same area, the selection for more productive, more easily harvested, more easily processed, or more tractable individuals of a species would have occurred almost as a matter of course. These folks were not stupid. They depended on wild species for their survival. They knew how plants and animals propagated. It would have been a short step for them to assist in propagation and to make the end products more amenable to human utilization through artificial selection.

Whatever the specific case, such decisions made at the end of the Pleistocene forever altered human cultural evolution. They led to the far-reaching developments to be discussed in the next chapter of this book as well as to our current chapter in human history.

## SUMMARY

Beginning sometime after 12,000 ya, human groups in a number of world areas—most notably, Southwest Asia, Southeast Asia, southern Europe, Mesoamerica, coastal South America, central North America, and Sub-Saharan Africa—began to domesticate the plants and animals on which they depended for their subsistence. That is, they began to produce their own food rather than simply gather what nature provided.

Many hypotheses have been proposed for this fundamental change in how people fed themselves. It seems that the best explanation involves the necessity of feeding more mouths as human populations grew in the above-mentioned regions at the end of the Pleistocene. In Southwest Asia, wheat, barley, sheep, and goats were the primary domesticates, whereas in Southeast Asia it was rice, millet, cattle, and pigs; in southern Europe, sheep goats, cattle, wheat, and barley; in Mesoamerica, corn, beans, and squash; in South America, corn, beans, potatoes, llamas, and alpacas; in North America, sunflower; and in Africa, yam, millet, and oil palm.

In a relatively short time—something less than 10,000 years—the vast majority of the world's people had adopted an agricultural mode of subsistence. Agriculture allowed for, in turn, larger, denser populations and necessitated new social structures for controlling and organizing the dense, sedentary settlements that resulted. Ultimately, in some regions, the shift to an agricultural way of life led to the development of cities, civilization, and, eventually, modern life.

## KEY TERMS

Food-Producing
  Revolution
Agricultural
Revolution
  Neolithic
domesticate
domestication
artificial selection
diffusion
sedentary

carrying capacity
settlement pattern
coprolite
deviation
  amplification
teosinte
rachis
Natufian
Yang-Shao
Lung Shan

## FOR MORE INFORMATION

If you are interested in the details of specific hypotheses on the origins of agriculture or if you would like to know more about the development of agriculture in a specific region, any of the works cited in this chapter would be a good place to start. Though a bit out of date, *The First Farmers* volume (Leonard 1973) of the Time/Life series *The Emergence of Man* provides a good general discussion and, as always, the illustrations are terrific. Three compendia of articles on domestication in different world areas are *Prehistoric Agriculture,* ed. Stuart Struever; *The Domestication and Exploitation of Plants and Animals,* eds. Peter Ucko and G. W. Dimbleby; and *Origins of Agriculture*, ed. C. A. Reed. Finally, a monograph by Mark Cohen, *The Food Crisis in Prehistory,* gives a detailed argument for demographically driven hypotheses of the origin of prehistoric agriculture.

# 15

# THE EVOLUTION OF CIVILIZATION

The images are evocative indeed: The sun sets behind the great pyramid of Cheops at Gizeh in Egypt; the dark, humid jungle frames the Temple of the Jaguars at the ancient Mesoamerican city of Tikal; the "skeleton" of urban sprawl that is the ancient Indus Valley city of Mohenjo-daro crawls upslope toward the citadel that marks the political center of the settlement. Although each is unique, these and other images reflect the culmination of what appears to have resulted from a single, unifying process of cultural evolution. For want of a better term, we characterize these great tombs, pyramids, and cities as evidence of civilization. They symbolize and demarcate a way of life far different from any that had preceded it.

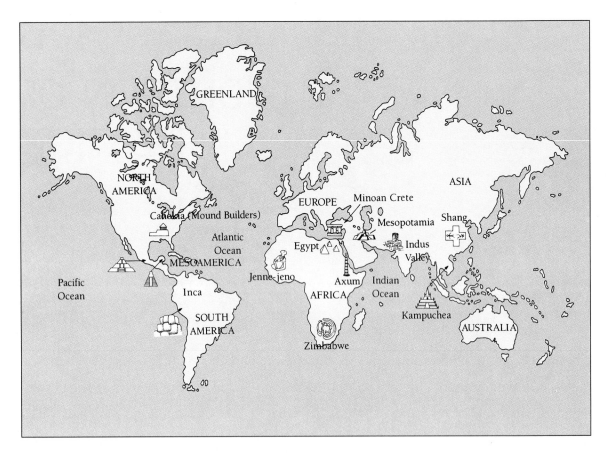

**Figure 15.1** *Locations of the world's earliest civilizations.*

The Food-Producing Revolution set the stage for the development of what we are here calling **civilization**. Perhaps as an inevitable consequence of the shift to an agricultural subsistence mode with the potential for producing enormous surpluses of food—and the attendant potential for the accumulation of wealth and power—beginning close to 6000 years ago (ya), in some world areas (Figure 15.1), the Neolithic pattern of small, largely autonomous farming villages became radically altered. Social and political systems were transformed beyond recognition. The kind of life people led was entirely different from what it had been. We call these developments civilization.

## THE MEANING OF CIVILIZATION

What is civilization? Common usage usually implies a level of social sophistication or gentility. The dictionary definition ordinarily includes reference to a "high level of technological development," being in an "advanced stage in the arts and sciences," and the invention of writing. Confusion over the precise meaning has led some to abandon its use as a scientific term. We will use it here for lack of a better, inclusive expression. Cultures to be categorized as "civilizations" possess the following common features as enumerated by archaeologist V. Gordon Childe (1951):

1. Densely populated settlements
2. Food and labor surplus controlled by an elite
3. Specialization of labor
4. Social stratification
5. Monumental public works
6. A system of record keeping

As we will see, those early civilizations you are probably already familiar with possessed many, if not all, of these qualities.

## Dense Population

With the evolution of civilization comes usually, but not inevitably, the development of the city. Although no absolute line can be drawn between a large village and a small city, we mean the term *city* to indicate a settlement with a large, dense population.

Cities are usually features of civilized life. Dense populations can be more easily ruled than dispersed groups, and large groups of people are needed to support the running of the political entity of civilization, the state.

## Food and Labor Surplus

Food surplus is a requirement for the development of the civilized state. In the beginning of the Neolithic, it is likely that in most societies the great majority of people made contributions to the food quest. Because food output was still relatively low, it was necessary for a large proportion of the population to be directly involved in food production. A very few may have specialized in religious activities or governance, but these people were the exceptions. With the development of higher-yield strains of crops, more efficient methods of agriculture, and the use of animal power, however, the percentage of a given population required to work in the fields certainly dropped.

We can see such a process taking place even in our twentieth-century civilizations. According to census statistics, in 1920 more than 30 percent of the U. S. population lived on farms. By 1950 that figure had dropped to just a little more than 15 percent, and by 1980 less than 3

**civilization:** Cultures with agriculture, dense populations, food and labor surplus, labor specialization, social stratification, public works, and record keeping.

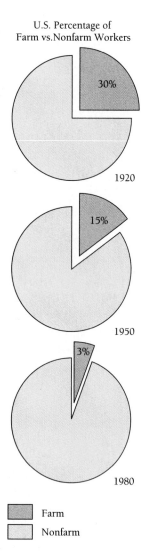

U.S. Percentage of
Farm vs.Nonfarm Workers

30%

1920

15%

1950

3%

1980

Farm

Nonfarm

**Figure 15.2** *Drop in the percentage of U.S. population living on farms, 1920–1980.*

percent lived on farms (Figure 15.2). Looked at another way, before 1920 each American farmer, on the average, supplied food products for about seven people. By the 1940s each American farmer produced enough food to feed almost eleven people. By 1970 that figure jumped to fifty people, and by 1980 the American farmer produced enough food to feed almost eighty people (Kranzberg 1984).

The reason you can be a student—and can go on to become a physician, engineer, social worker, or even an anthropologist—rests on the fact that you are not needed on the farm. For complex civilizations to develop, the same process must have occurred. All of the trappings of civilization—pyramids, temples, great art, science, canals, roads—are possible only when large numbers of people are freed from agricultural activity and available to spend much or even all of their time quarrying stone, building roads, serving in the army, being priests, artisans, builders, merchants, scribes, and so on.

## Labor Specialization

Labor specialization goes hand-in-hand with the foregoing. For great monuments to be constructed, spectacular works of art to be produced, extensive networks of canals to be built, people who are not needed in subsistence activities must specialize. It is unlikely that part-time artists could have painted the Maya murals at Bonampak; it stretches the imagination to believe that part-time sculptors could have produced the carvings at Abu Simbel in Egypt (Figure 15.3). So the ability of civilizations to produce great art, architecture, engineering, crafts, and science depends on specialization, and specialization is permitted only when the farmers produce enough food to feed the people who are engaged in other pursuits.

## Social Stratification

With labor specialization goes **social stratification**. In **egalitarian** societies like those of some hunter-gatherers, people within the same age and sex categories are essentially equal; they have the same rights and privileges, similar responsibilities, and about equal wealth. Although there may be leaders and followers, this comes about as a result of accomplishment and ability. We say that there is *authority* in such societies—earned respect that convinces people to listen to you and follow your lead. There is no force involved, however. If people no longer wish to listen to you, they don't. It is likely that most Paleolithic and many Neolithic societies were egalitarian, or pretty close to being so.

**Figure 15.3** *Monumental architectural or engineering works, along with great works of art, are products of specialist classes of workers, like those who designed and crafted Abu Simbel in Egypt. Such specialization of labor is possible only in civilized state societies.* (M. H. Feder)

Egalitarian societies lack what nonegalitarian societies are characterized by, namely, *power*—the ability to force others by rule or law to do your bidding. Stratified societies are ones that possess layers of power, leadership, or wealth. There is a hierarchy with a great ruler like a king, pharaoh, or emperor on top, his or her family and religious rulers or military leaders next, special workers like craftspeople under them, and perhaps everyone else—farmers, soldiers—below them. And people did not achieve power; they were born into it.

In other words, the creation of an edifice like a pyramid is made possible by a social system shaped like a pyramid. There is a small elite on top with a slightly larger group of specialized workers below them; the great mass of farmers, workers, or peasants make up the base of the social pyramid. (Figure 15.4).

**social stratification**: The presence of acknowledged differences in social status and wealth.

**egalitarian**: A type of society that does not acknowledge differences in social status and wealth.

**Figure 15.4** *The social systems of state societies are pyramidal. The very few who rule, supported by a small class of nobles and specialists, sit atop the social pyramid.*

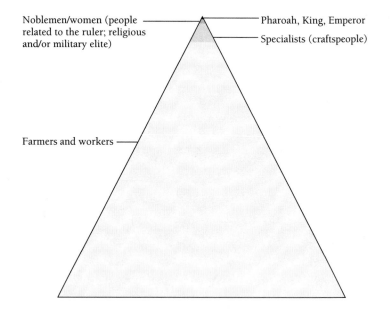

Noblemen/women (people related to the ruler; religious and/or military elite)

Pharoah, King, Emperor

Specialists (craftspeople)

Farmers and workers

## Monumental Works

So if the trappings of civilization require the development of specialization and social stratification, we are left with this question: Why are such works as monumental architecture, great art, and even scientific achievements always associated with civilization and the development of the state? Why are these accomplishments regarded as the hallmarks of civilization?

We can make some rather reasonable guesses. In the next section, we will approach hypotheses about why the civilized state developed in the first place. As for why it developed the *way* it did, however, we can suggest the following.

All civilized societies involve a tradeoff. In return for the protection and security such societies offer, most people end up working harder and giving up some of their freedom and independence. They give up living in an egalitarian society for a stratified system, and most people in a stratified society make up the bottom of the pyramid. Why would anyone consent to this?

Great pyramids, burial chambers, spectacular works of art, great engineering projects, and mysterious astronomical knowledge are all symbols of the power held by the leaders of a given civilization. They are also part of a feedback system that serves to magnify the power of those leaders.

As archaeologist Joseph Tainter points out, rulers in such societies need constantly to reinforce the legitimacy of their leadership. They need, in essence, to continually convince the great mass of people that their position above the masses is reasonable and justifiable. As Tainter points out, until institutions like the army and the police force evolve, enabling rulers to impose their will on people through physical coercion, "sacred legitimization provides a binding framework" (1988:28). Monumental works like pyramids, great tombs, and palaces serve as a sort of "sacred legitimization."

The strategy procedes along the following lines. Pharaoh is the offspring of the gods and therefore deserves our loyalty. Pharaoh decrees that 10,000 of us shall help construct a great pyramid to be his burial chamber. We obey because we believe him to be all-powerful. After a time, the pyramid is complete, and it is indeed spectacular. Only someone with godlike powers could have accomplished such a feat. Any doubts the people may secretly have harbored have been eliminated. The pharaoh's exalted position has been "legitimized" by his ability to produce a spectacular monument to himself. Pharaoh *must* indeed be the offspring of the gods and is absolutely deserving of our loyalty. Pharaoh now decrees that 20,000 of us shall work for him, and, of course, we follow, and on and on.

This is a positive-feedback system, and in this light the great achievements of civilization in the arts and sciences can be seen as being made possible by the nature of civilization. At the same time, they contribute to the creation and further consolidation of such a society. In other words, such cultural achievements are both causes and effects of civilization. A pyramid, the accurate prediction of a solar eclipse, a great wall around a city all are real achievements as well as symbols of the abilities and power of a leader. Such achievements are not usually possible in egalitarian societies.

## A System of Record Keeping

Finally, we come to the necessity of record keeping. We must be careful in this discussion not to equate record keeping with writing because not all records need to be written down.

Record keeping is necessary for a number of reasons. Think of our own civilization. Our government can pay the bills for defense, social programs, and construction only by taxing its citizens. At one time, our nation sustained its military force through a draft, another sort of taxation. Imagine how well these would be carried out if there were no system of record keeping—ways of keeping track in some kind of permanent form of how much wealth each citizen produces, how much tax was paid last year and this year, age, and the like. Without records, it would be virtually impossible to have or make use of this information.

**Figure 15.5** *Examples of early writing:* (top left) *cuneiform from Mesopotamia* (Ashmolean Museum, Oxford); (top right) *Maya hieroglyphs* (University of Pennsylvania Museum, Tikal Project, Neg #58-4-1007); *and* (bottom) *hieroglyphs from Egypt* (M. H. Feder). *A system of record keeping was crucial in the development of early civilizations.*

The same was certainly true for early civilizations. Remember, civilized societies are pyramidal. These early societies depended on a great mass of people providing at least some of their "wealth" in the form of labor, food, and children to support the existence of the elite and the specialists. There had to be some way of keeping track of each citizen's contribution in support of the state. There had to be records to make sure that each farmer provided a certain percentage of his grain to feed those not involved in agriculture. There had to be some way of keeping track of the labor of the citizens as soldiers or monument builders. Without some sort of permanent storage of information, the state could not exist (Figure 15.5).

## EXPLAINING THE EVOLUTION OF CIVILIZATION

We must now address this basic question: Why did civilized states, as we have defined them, develop at all? Interestingly, we see a situation similar to the beginning of domestication. The world's first civilizations appeared in several different areas at about the same time. We expect that this is no coincidence. Such cultures could have evolved only where there was a food surplus, and such a surplus is possible ordinarily only under conditions of intensive agriculture. Because the Food-Producing Revolution occurred almost simultaneously in a number of locations, it is not surprising that civilization later developed in many of these same areas. The fact that it did indicates that under certain conditions civilization may have been almost an inevitable outcome of the Food-Producing Revolution as Jared Diamond asserted in his essay that we discussed in the "Contemporary Issue" section of Chapter 14. It also implies that there were identifiable reasons for these developments.

Just as we did for explanations of the Neolithic Revolution, we will now present some of the hypotheses proposed by various thinkers to explain the emergence of civilization. (See Table 15.1 on page 434 for a summary of these hypotheses.)

### The Explanation of Race

Some hypotheses suggested for the development of civilization in specific locations can be fairly characterized as racist. In the mid-nineteenth century, Gustav Klemm in Germany and Count J. A. de Gobineau in France both argued that race was the key factor in the development of civilization and that each civilization was unique because of biological factors (Harris 1968). Those people who had not attained a level of civilized existence had not because they were biologically unequipped to.

Very often in such racist constructs it could not be admitted that dark-skinned people had attained civilized status, even when the physical evidence argued for it. So American Indian cultures like the Maya, who we clearly recognize as having created a remarkable civilization, were either explained as the result of cultural borrowing or their civilized status was denied entirely. Human history and cultural evolution was reduced to an argument based on biology. As with the Agricultural Revolution, racist explanations are not supported by any data and need not concern us further.

## Environmental Determinism

> Man can apparently live in any region where he can obtain food, but his physical and mental energy and his moral character reach their highest development only in a few strictly limited areas. (Huntington 1924)

Ellsworth Huntington was an early twentieth-century geographer who championed the notion of **environmental determinism**. This approach actually first found favor with the ancient Greeks. In attempting to explain cultural differences and the development of civilized life, Hippocrates suggested that human behavior was the result of the interaction of four bodily "humours," or liquids: yellow bile, black bile, phlegm, and blood. Hippocrates suggested that climate was responsible for the balance of these liquids within the human body. The proportion of these liquids was in turn responsible for the development of the human intellect, health, and personality traits. Thus, climate was a determinant of cultural development.

It is difficult to understand how even into the nineteenth century scholars seriously considered phlegm, bile, and blood as being responsible for culture. Some nevertheless did. Huntington, however, developed a much more complex and reasoned approach to environmental determinism. He felt that climate has a direct impact on human intelligence. In this view, environments that were too easy or too naturally productive would not foster cultural development. If people did not *need* to invent things to survive, if they were not "challenged" by their environment, they would not be obliged to advance, and civilization would not develop. On the other hand, if the climate were too rigorous, people would be too caught up in the necessities of survival to progress beyond mere subsistence. Only those climates lying in between the too generous and the too rigorous would lead to the development of civilized life. Not coincidentally, Western European writers who supported this hypothesis viewed the climate of Europe, particularly Western Europe, as just right for such developments.

Environmental determinism began to fade in importance as a theory because it didn't work. If the European environment was so right for such developments, why did the earliest civilizations evolve elsewhere? Also, the environments in Mesopotamia, Egypt, India, China, lowland Mesoamerica, highland Mesoamerica, and South America were quite different from one another, yet each had early civilizations. Beyond this, even though the climates in these same regions had not changed since the evolution of their civilizations, the cultures had.

As archaeological data were collected, the evidence of early civilizations in very different environments and changes in culture under conditions of static environments showed fairly clearly that environmental determinism could not explain human cultural evolution.

## Unilinear Evolution

It is both a natural and proper desire to learn, if possible, how all these ages upon ages of past time have been expended by mankind; how savages, advancing by slow, almost imperceptible steps, attained the higher condition of barbarians; how barbarians, by similar progressive advancement, finally attained to civilization. (Morgan 1877:5)

Another approach to the question of why civilization developed avoided seeking causes in biology or climate or any factor of influence outside culture itself. This approach sought to explain cultural evolution through cultural explanations. The work of Lewis Henry Morgan (1877), a nineteenth-century lawyer, is of great importance here. Morgan, whom we mentioned briefly in Chapter 2, believed that all cultures developed or evolved through similar phases: "The experience of mankind has run in nearly uniform channels" (1877:15). These general phases Morgan labeled savagery, barbarism, and civilization. Savagery and barbarism could each be broken down into early, middle, and upper (Figure 15.6).

Morgan's view of the development of civilization as a product of cultural evolution was essentially *materialistic*: Culture evolved as successive levels of material achievement were attained. His view was also economically based; Morgan considered advance in subsistence technology to be the most significant aspect of cultural evolution driving people toward civilization. Development was contingent on certain specific inventions and followed a natural sequence. As Morgan put it, "The most advanced portions of the human race were halted, so to express it, at certain stages of progress, until some great invention or discovery, such as the domestication of animals or the smelting of iron ore, gave a new and powerful impulse forward" (1877:40).

Culture, in essence, drove itself forward toward civilized life. But notice that Morgan was circular in his argument while begging the question. Civilization, he said, develops because it does. If great inventions like iron smelting, domestication, and the alphabet were necessary

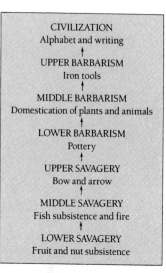

**Figure 15.6** *The cultural evolutionary model of Lewis Henry Morgan. Morgan believed that all cultures passed through these stages of development, although some became "stuck" in a stage.*

**environmental determinism:** The notion that the nature of the environment directly determines the technological level of a culture.

to establish civilization, what in turn caused them? Morgan had no answer to this question. He believed that inventions occurred through ingenuity and spread out from wherever they were invented. Such an approach simply cannot explain why civilization developed where it did and when it did. And these are precisely the questions we are asking.

## Marxism

> Civilization is . . . the stage of development in society at which the division of labor, the exchange between individuals arising from it, and the commodity production which combines them both come to their full growth and revolutionizes the whole of previous society. (Engels 1942:233)

Karl Marx and his benefactor and collaborator Frederich Engels were supporters of Morgan's cultural evolutionary scheme. In a scenario laid out by Engels (1942), the domestication of animals led to specialization in animal herding. Animal domestication also allowed humans to produce far more than was needed for subsistence. Thus, wealth—in the form of meat, milk, hides, and wool—became concentrated in the hands of those groups who possessed animals. With some groups specializing in animal products, there arose a need for regular exchange between the "haves" and the "have-nots." Also, the excess wealth accumulated by the producers had to be defended from those who might want to take it for themselves.

As groups became larger and as the processes of exchange intensified, a class of specialists arose to conduct this new business. These were the first full-time merchants. For the first time, people not involved in subsistence or production were in charge of economic life, and they became rich and powerful at the expense of producers. A class society with rulers, workers, and slaves developed. The trappings of civilization followed, Engels proposed, as the result of the need to formalize and solidify the unequal structure of society. Thus, civilization developed out of a process driven by economics—a sort of economic determinism.

## The Hydraulic Hypothesis

> A large quantity of water can be channeled and kept within bounds only by the use of mass labor; and this mass labor must be coordinated, disciplined, and led. Thus a number of farmers eager to conquer arid lowlands and plains are forced to invoke organizational devices which—on the basis of premachine technology—offer the one chance of success; they must work in cooperation with their fellows and subordinate themselves to a directing authority. (Wittfogel 1957:18)

Karl Wittfogel (1957), a German historian, proposed the Hydraulic hypothesis for the development of ancient civilization. He sees civilization as a logical, though not inevitable, consequence of the need to control water.

To feed an expanding population, more land needs to be brought under cultivation. In some regions, this can be accomplished through the construction of waterworks. The construction of large-scale canals and aqueducts requires a kind of social organization in which people must work together and "subordinate themselves to a directing authority" (Wittfogel 1957:18). Here Wittfogel is proposing a sort of ultimate rationale for the loss of personal independence in the evolution of civilized society. To organize and coordinate a large number of people, a centralized government may develop. There need to be canal designers, supervisors, and workers—thus, specialization in occupation occurs. Mathematics and a recording system can become necessary for planning and designing such projects.

The same social, economic, and political apparatus set in motion by the need to construct canals, Wittfogel suggests, can also be used to build defensive works. Such works become necessary because territory in which so much labor has been expended to increase agricultural production through canal building becomes a tempting target for those who might wish to reap the benefits without investing the labor.

Similarly, the processes of labor organization can be used to construct temples for those important people who are in charge of the canals. Real power and control, and thus wealth, now rest in their hands because they can deny access to water to those who do not follow their lead or heed their commands. The other trappings of civilization all follow as a result of this concentration of power and serve to reinforce that power. Thus, according to Wittfogel, the development of civilization is sparked by a need to increase agricultural production via development and control of water resources.

## The Circumscription Hypothesis

A close examination of history indicates that only a coercive theory can account for the rise of the state. Force, and not enlightened self-interest, is the mechanism by which political evolution has led, step by step, from autonomous villages to the state. (Carneiro 1970:734)

Robert Carneiro (1970), an American anthropologist, does not believe that the civilized state came about through a series of rational choices among the people involved. He maintains that the state developed only through "coercion" or force.

In Carneiro's scenario, civilization developed in areas where resources, especially agricultural lands, were circumscribed—in other words, limited and bounded. Where land is not limited and bounded, people can migrate into new territories as population grows. Where it is circumscribed, however, they cannot move. Mountains, deserts, seas, or other geographic features confine some peoples to a limited area.

Within such a bounded area only a small number of responses are possible if population grows: (1) Restrict population growth through sexual abstinence, contraception, abortion, or infanticide; (2) intensify agriculture through, for example, irrigation; or (3) seize land through warfare against neighboring groups.

In this final option, the territory of the defeated becomes incorporated into the political unit of the victor. In some cases, the members of the defeated group are also integrated into the victorious group, usually as subordinates. Warfare between increasingly larger groups, Carneiro believes, led to larger and larger political entities with progressively larger territories until, finally, entire geographically bounded areas were brought under the domination of a single group. In his opinion, most of the world's early civilizations evolved under conditions of geographic circumscription and developed as a reaction to them.

## HEARTHS OF CIVILIZATION

As we have seen, the world's first civilizations evolved in areas where agriculture also evolved. We must now examine the sequences in a number of these cases to assess the usefulness of the hypotheses presented for explaining the evolution of civilized life. In each instance, our primary question concerns how a pattern of small, sedentary, largely self-sufficient Neolithic farming villages was transformed into one of a dense, socially stratified urban civilization. We will briefly discuss the ancient civilizations of Mesopotamia, Egypt, India/Pakistan, China, Mesoamerica, South America, southern Europe, Africa, North America, and Southeast Asia (see Figure 15.1). Each section begins with a brief image of the civilization at its peak. We will then go on to assess the origins and development of each culture, beginning with their roots in the Neolithic.

### Mesopotamia

At the ancient city of Ur in Mesopotamia (literally "the land between the two rivers," the Tigris and the Euphrates), a massive structure consisting of superimposed platforms was constructed more than 4000 ya. Made of mud brick and faced with fired brick, this **ziggurat** stood 22 meters (70 feet) high and measured over 60 meters (200 feet) long by nearly 46 meters wide (150 feet) at its base (Figure 15.7). Steps led up to each successive platform; at the top was a small temple or shrine where the priests of ancient Ur conducted worship services (Lloyd 1978).

**Figure 15.7** *The ziggurat at Ur, built in stages over a lengthy period, is more than 4000 years old. It stands 22 meters high, with a temple originally on the top platform.* (Comstock/George Gerster)

The cemetery at Ur contains more than 2000 graves, 16 of which were the interments of members of the elite class. These royal tombs were as much as 9 meters (30 feet) deep and 9 meters across. The burials were placed in stone chambers with vaulted roofs—one even possessed a dome. One of the tombs, that of a queen called Pu-abi, is typical of the royal interments at Ur (we know her name because we can read the writing of the ancient Sumerian civilization of which Ur was an important part).

In death Pu-abi wore a headdress of gold and semiprecious stones. Around her were gold and silver containers, an intricately designed harp, a gaming table, and another 250 or so objects. Pu-abi did not have to pass on to the afterlife alone. Like the other royalty at Ur, humans and animals were sacrificed as part of the royal burial ceremony; in Pu-abi's burial chamber were two female attendants. Just outside the royal chamber were ten more women (one with a harp—musical accompaniment for the journey), five soldiers, and two oxen. Beneath Queen Pu-abi's chamber was another tomb—a man's, possibly her husband. This king was accompanied by six soldiers, nineteen females wearing gold head pieces, six oxen, two chariots, a lyre, a gaming table, and an exquisite silver model of a boat.

Such were the death settings of Ur nobility. Their lives were lived in even greater splendor. But how did a pattern of Neolithic farming villages like that described in Chapter 14 give rise to the grandeur of Ur? How did the surplus and social stratification develop that made such monuments as the ziggurat and royal tombs of Ur possible? To answer these questions, we must look back into the Neolithic of Southwest Asia.

**ziggurat:** Large, mud brick structures in Mesopotamia.

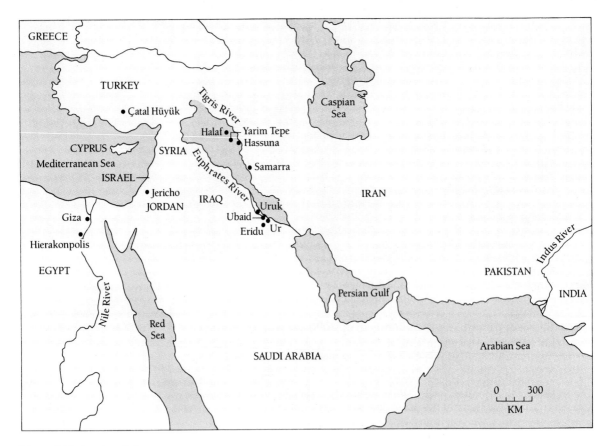

**Figure 15.8** *Location of sites related to the development of civilization and mentioned in the text, in Egypt and the Middle East.*

**The Evolution of Mesopotamian Civilization.**    The modern city of Jericho in Israel is the same town as that mentioned in the Bible (Figure 15.8). But the roots of Jericho go back even further. Excavated by archaeologist Kathleen Kenyon in the 1950s (Kenyon 1954), Jericho is now known to have been occupied more than 9000 ya. At this very early date, Jericho may have been inhabited by more than 3000 people in an area of about ten acres. The entire area was encompassed by what may have been the first example of a large-scale construction project anywhere in the world—an enormous wall (Figure 15.9). This wall ranged from more than 3.5 meters (11 feet) to 7 meters (22 feet) in height and had ramparts more than 9 meters (30 feet) high. The wall was built entirely of dry-laid stone (mortar was not used) and was 2 meters thick at its base.

There is evidence at Jericho of the beginning of a nonegalitarian society, at least as this related to burials. Most of the burials in the earliest levels at Jericho were situated in one area, and all were pretty much the same. A cluster of burials, however, was different. Clay was

**Figure 15.9** *The wall at the ancient city of Jericho, dating back 9000 years, may be the oldest known monumental construction in history.* (Fred Mayer/Magnum)

molded over the faces and shell was positioned over the eyes of the deceased. The significance of this practice is unknown but suggests differences in social status.

Çatal Hüyük is in modern Turkey and postdates Jericho by perhaps 1000 years (Mellaart 1965; Todd 1976). The site covers more than thirty acres and consists of blocks of rooms made of mud brick. In these blocks, there are hundreds of individual rooms. Many were habitation areas, but a large proportion were religious shrines. In these shrines were sculptures of bull heads, bas-reliefs of leopards with female figures riding them, paintings of stylized birds chasing after headless people, and the outlines of human hands.

The population at this site is estimated to have been between 5000 and 10,000. Such a large accumulation of people may have occurred here because of the city's location at the base of the Konya Mountains, a major source of obsidian—volcanic glass used for making sharp-edged tools. It is also located along an historical trade route between Europe and Southwest Asia, and this may have been another important factor in its size and location.

It is to the southeast, however, back in Mesopotamia, that we can construct a sequence for the development of what probably was the world's earliest civilization (Oppenheim 1977). Here, from 8000 to 6500 B.P., we see the beginning of population movement away from the foothills of the Zagros Mountains, mentioned in our discussion of the Neolithic, onto the flood plain between the two rivers.

Interesting developments followed. The site of Halaf, on the Syrian-Turkish border, shows what appear to be the earliest shrines in Mesopotamia. These are circular, beehive-shaped rooms that range from 5 to 10 meters (15 to 30 feet) in diameter at their base. Sites like Hassuna, Yarim Tepe, and Samarra show more evidence for large-scale construction. There are multiroomed houses with courtyards at Yarim Tepe. There are large buildings at Samarra and a buttressed fortification wall. As archaeologists C. C. Lamberg-Karlovsky and Jeremy Sabloff (1979) suggest, it is probable that in the period after 8000 ya economic, social, and political structures were beginning to form at sites like these that would set the stage for later developments.

By 6300 B.P. in southern Mesopotamia, some villages of what is called the Ubaid culture were getting larger, with evidence of specialization in pottery and metallurgy within towns like Uruk, Ur, Ubaid, and Eridu. The population at Eridu is estimated to have exceeded 5000 (Lamberg-Karlovsky and Sabloff 1979:110) even at this early stage. The Ubaidic sites show development of large temple structures that may indicate that these villages functioned as ceremonial centers as they were evolving into urban centers (Wheatly 1971). Temples probably served as granaries, administrative centers, and redistribution points for food. By about 6000 B.P., Ubaidic sites had spread throughout Mesopotamia. And, finally, by 5800 B.P. or so, one of these villages, **Uruk**, had grown to such a size and density that we can confidently proclaim it as the world's first true city. Uruk was not isolated; it appears to have been interconnected in a settlement hierarchy that included, in descending size-order, smaller towns, villages, and hamlets (Crawford 1991). This pattern of large urban centers surrounded by three orders or levels of smaller settlements that owed their political, social, and economic allegiance to the city was to be the rule for Mesopotamian **city-states**.

It is probable that the push toward urbanization in Mesopotamia was encouraged by several factors. First came the need to intensify agriculture through the construction of irrigation networks as a result of population increase. By 5800 B.P., there were 17 villages, three large towns, and maybe one urban center—Uruk—in Mesopotamia; by 4900 B.P., there were 124 villages, twenty towns, and twenty centers of urban populations (Adams and Nissen 1972:18). To expand agricultural production, irrigation was necessary, and canals up to 40 kilometers long were eventually built (Lamberg-Karlovsky and Sabloff 1979:173). The requirement of organizing labor to build canals would have fostered social differentiation, and differential access to irrigation water would have further served to segment and stratify society.

As archaeologist Harriet Crawford (1991) indicates, the need to trade was another important impetus to urbanization. Southern Mesopotamia lacked most resources beyond fertile soil and water. Ores for the production of metals, wood for building and fuel, and stone had to be traded for, and such trade needs to be organized. Just as the necessity of organizing groups to build canals may have fostered social stratification, so too the need to organize people to engage in trading networks may have differentiated classes. Unequal access to trade goods would have served to further distinguish groups of people.

Another likely factor was the presence of nonagricultural, nomadic animal herders on the peripheries of Mesopotamia. From later documentary accounts, we know that settled villagers in Mesopotamia had hostile relations with neighboring nomads. As Lamberg-Karlovsky and Sabloff (1979) point out, however, such nomads probably provided urban dwellers with livestock and, as a result of their greater mobility, may also have assisted in trade and communication. The threat of potentially dangerous nomads, however, may have also forced people out of small, vulnerable outlying villages and into increasingly urban, protected settlements. As wealth became concentrated in such dense settlements and, therefore, was effectively easier to steal, the need grew for protection from these nomads and, as city-states proliferated, from these competing political entities. This may have led to the development of perhaps the earliest monumental works—not pyramids or tombs, but enormous defensive works like walls encompassing the cities. Such projects require a social system unlike that of an egalitarian society.

At the same time, the need to build irrigation canals, the problems in coordinating increasingly dense populations, and the need to construct defensive works led to social stratification. Together, these forces helped transform the village farming culture of Mesopotamia into what is recognized as the world's first civilization.

**Uruk:**  The earliest city in Mesopotamia and, almost certainly, the world, dating to about 5800 ya.

**city-state:**  A large, politically complex society with villages surrounding a central dense population.

**Figure 15.10** *The three great pyramids at Giza. Enormous monuments such as these testify to the power wielded by the rulers of the early Egyptian state.* (M. H. Feder)

## Egypt

The name "Egypt" alone is enough to conjure up potent images in all of us. Great pyramids, the Sphinx, the boy king Tutankhamun, and all-powerful pharaohs are elements of Egyptian civilization that have fascinated people for centuries.

Just consider some of the remarkable accomplishments of the culture of ancient Egypt. For example, at Giza, north of the ancient capital city of Memphis and near modern Cairo, three pyramids rise out of the desert (Figure 15.10). Each one was constructed as the burial chamber and memorial for a different pharaoh; each is a spectacular achievement unto itself. Together they are one of the true wonders of the ancient world.

The two smaller pyramids in the group were actually built later for the pharaohs Cephren and Mycernius (names given to these kings by later Greeks). It was the first and largest, however, built for the pharaoh Khufu (sometimes known by his Greek name, Cheops), that represents one of the largest structures *ever* built by human beings—before or since.

The Great Pyramid at Giza measures over 230 meters (750 feet) on each of the four sides of its base. Rising like an artificial mountain more than 145 meters (almost 500 feet) in height, it was constructed from nearly 2.5 million quarried stone blocks averaging 2270 kilograms

(5000 pounds) each. Some of the larger quarry blocks weigh more than 13,000 kilograms (30,000 pounds).

The pyramid itself was built at a level of accuracy rarely achieved even in modern construction. The smooth blocks making up the surface of the pyramid have joints a mere 0.5 millimeter ($\frac{1}{50}$ inch) in width. The pyramid is aligned almost perfectly to the cardinal compass directions; that this was intentional is clear from the writings of the ancient Egyptians. The margin of error on the north-south sides of the pyramid is 0.09 percent, on the east-west sides 0.03 percent.

But the pyramid of Khufu is not just an enormous, accurately laid pile of limestone blocks. Within the pyramid is a maze of passageways, several connected chambers, and an arched vault that served as the final resting place for the pharaoh and the things intended for his use in the afterlife. It is, indeed, a spectacular achievement. And, though the largest, the Great Pyramid is but one of about seventy large pyramids built by the ancient Egyptians. And pyramids were just one aspect of Egyptian culture.

We are all awed by these spectacular achievements of ancient Egyptian civilization. But we want to go beyond fascination to understanding. How was the magnificence that was ancient Egypt achieved? Where did this civilization come from? How did it develop? To answer these questions, we need to go back to a time before pharaohs and pyramids. We need to examine the Egyptian Neolithic.

**The Evolution of Egyptian Civilization.** The Greek historian Herodotus called Egypt the "gift of the Nile." The Nile River is a narrow ribbon of life winding through a dry, lifeless desert (Figure 15.11). In Egypt a great civilization could have developed only along the banks of the Nile, so our attention must focus there.

Recent excavations led by American archaeologist Michael Hoffman (1979, 1983) at Hierakonpolis have provided a chronology of the early evolution of Egyptian civilization. This site is also significant because it is thought to have been the home of an important figure in Egyptian history, Narmer, who united Egypt for the first time under one ruler.

Located on an embayment adjacent to the Nile, Hierakonpolis consisted of about 100 acres of habitation some 5800 ya. In Egyptian prehistory, this is known as the Amratian period of the Neolithic. Habitation areas consisting of houses of mud brick as well as wattle and daub were surrounded by farmland, and at least 2500 and perhaps as many as 10,000 people lived there.

At Hierakonpolis during this period, we also see the first evidence of impressive tombs. Although by no means comparable to the pyramids, these tombs may be the first step toward their development. The Hierakonpolis tombs were sometimes lined with mud brick; some were

**Figure 15.11** *This photograph of the Nile, taken by astronauts aboard the Space Shuttle, shows how the river literally demarcates the boundaries of life for the inhabitants of Egypt.* (U.S. Geological Survey/NASA)

cut into bedrock. In a practice that was to characterize later Egyptian civilization, these tombs were filled with items to accompany the dead: finely made pottery, baskets, leatherwork, woodwork, and flintwork. The tombs were covered by structures—not yet pyramids, but earth mounds and wood and reed buildings.

But who was buried in the fancy tombs? The town seems to have prospered during the Neolithic on the basis of a booming pottery industry. Enormous kilns and millions of fragments of broken pots have been found here, and pottery manufactured at Hierakonpolis was probably traded to other towns along the Nile for inclusion in their fancy burials.

The largest and most sumptuous of the burials at Hierakonpolis and other Amratian period sites along the Nile were limited to a developing elite class. With increased population density along the Nile came the need to coordinate activity, to enforce rules and law. Although rule by simple authority—where there is consensus, not coercion—was possible in earlier, smaller towns, in a settlement of several thousand it is probable that rule through power was beginning to replace the emphasis on authority. At Hierakonpolis it is possible that a group of leaders evolved simply to maintain order. This elite was in charge of producing pottery, and excess wealth was becoming concentrated in their hands. With wealth came even more power. The production of fancy pottery and the interment of people in impressive tombs may have served as symbols reinforcing the legitimacy of that leadership.

Social and political change began to accelerate by 5500 ya in what is known as the Gerzean period. The local climate seems to have become drier, possibly because of deforestation that resulted from collecting firewood to feed the kilns. This challenge was met at Hierakonpolis and probably elsewhere by the construction of irrigation canals, which allowed for intensification of agriculture even while the local climate was becoming less agreeable for it. As archaeologist Hoffman has pointed out, the power that was already concentrated in the hands of the "pottery barons" probably allowed them to control the construction of irrigation canals. And once the local farmers began to rely on the canals for food production, the former pottery barons became even more powerful, now controlling the water necessary for farming.

For a few hundred years, such developments continued at Hierakonpolis and elsewhere. By 5200 ya, however, local development and expansion began to impinge upon neighboring groups. Warfare among neighbors seems to have been the result. Elites in different towns began to compete among themselves for territory and for the loyalties of the people in these areas.

There appear to have been earlier attempts to unify parts of northern (Lower, as the river runs from south to north) and southern (Upper) Egypt (see Bower 1990), but it was not until about 5100 B.P. that a ruler of Hierakonpolis, whose name has come down to us as *Narmer*, was able to unite all villages up and down the Nile.

Narmer was, indeed, the first ruler of Egypt, if not the first actual pharaoh. On a carved piece of stone found by archaeologists in Hierakonpolis in 1898, Narmer is depicted as uniting the northern and southern halves of Egypt, becoming the ruler of all who dwelled along the Nile (Figure 15.12).

With the growth of villages and then cities along the Nile, the emergence of a powerful elite class, the production of sufficient food surplus to feed this class as well as a class of specialists like the pottery makers, we have all the prerequisites for the evolution of civilization. By 4700 ya, a successor to Narmer, King Djoser, exploited the power that had been concentrated in his hands and caused the construction of the first Egyptian pyramid at a place called Saqqara (Figure 15.13). As kings became pharaohs and as pharaohs became all-powerful, pyramids became larger, construction projects became more ambitious, and the army increased in size. Egyptian civilization flourished.

**Figure 15.12** *Found at Hierakonpolis, this ceremonial macehead depicts the joining of Upper and Lower Egypt. Narmer, a ruler of Hierakonpolis, is credited with bringing all villages along the Nile under the sway of a central authority.* (Ashmolean Museum, Oxford)

## The Indus Valley

That a spectacular early civilization developed in ancient India and Pakistan comes as a surprise to most Americans. Yet a magnificent civilization with two of the ancient world's largest cities did indeed develop and flourish on the Indian subcontinent some 4500 ya (Allchin and Allchin 1982; Fairservis 1975).

Mohenjo-daro was one of those cities. During its peak period—from approximately 4500 to 4000 ya—the religious and political life of the city's 35,000 inhabitants was centered in its citadel. There, on an enormous mound constructed of mud brick, some 450 meters (almost 1500 feet) long, 90 meters (almost 300 feet) wide, and 12 meters (40 feet) high, were built a temple, granary, and bath house (Figure 15.14). Within the great bath house was a bathing pool nearly 12 meters (40 feet) long, 6 meters (20 feet) wide, and 2.5 meters (8 feet) deep. The entire citadel was surrounded by a brick wall reaching 13 meters (over

**Figure 15.13** *The stepped pyramid of King Djoser at Saqqara represented a new stage in the evolution of the pyramid memorial that was to characterize the tombs of later Egyptian pharaohs.* (M. H. Feder)

40 feet) in height in some sections, and marked by square towers and bastions.

To the east of the citadel lay the lower city. Here, spread across 240 acres, lived the vast majority of the residents of Mohenjo-daro. Their streets were laid out in a clearly well-planned fashion. Wide boulevards paralleled each other in a north-south orientation. Other smaller streets ran parallel to the boulevards. Still other streets were neatly perpendicular.

Individual dwellings reflected the wide range in economic, social, and political status of the inhabitants of Mohenjo-daro. There were single-room apartments, houses with many rooms and courtyards, and great houses with dozens of rooms and private wells. Almost all houses had private bathrooms connected by chutes to a citywide network of drains—probably the world's first engineered sewer system.

Mohenjo-daro, like its contemporary sister city on the Indus River, Harappa, was a spectacular achievement of this little-known civilization. But where did this Indus Valley culture come from? How did it develop?

**The Evolution of the Indus Valley Civilization.**   We can trace the roots of this civilization back to a series of Neolithic sites in an area of western Pakistan called Baluchistan (Figure 15.15). The site of Mehrgarh is lo-

**Figure 15.14** *The citadel of Mohenjo-daro, one of the Indus civilization's two great cities. Temples, granaries, and bath houses were located within its walls. Note the brick-covered sewer trench with connections to separate apartments, a testament to city planning some 4500 ya.* (Department of Archaeology and Museums, Karachi)

cated at the foothills of the Baluchistan Mountains. Dated to 7100 B.P., the site is an extensive settlement of mud brick structures. Subsistence was provided by domesticated wheat, barley, and dates along with cattle and water buffalo. The inhabitants of Mehrgarh also participated in a wide-ranging trade network. Conch shell from some 500 kilometers away as well as lapis lazuli and turquoise from similar distances were found at the site.

Another typical site, Kili Ghul Mohammad, was a small agricultural settlement also located in the foothills of the Baluchistan Mountains and dates to 6000 B.P. There is evidence here of domesticated wheat, goats, sheep, and cattle.

Sites like Mehrgarh and Kili Ghul Mohammad grew larger through time, indicating a general population increase. By 5000 ya, settlement was spreading out of the mountain foothills southward along the streams that drained the mountaintops and fed the large Indus River to the southeast.

Sites dating to after 5000 B.P. are included in what is called the Nal culture. Kohtras Buthi is a fairly typical Nal site. It is much larger than sites like Kili Ghul Mohammad, covering some fifteen acres. Significantly, at this site we see some of the earliest evidence for water-control construction. Located on a small river, the inhabitants built a wall surrounding one end of the village, apparently to protect themselves from the intense flooding that characterizes this area in the spring. At other Nal culture sites, we see dams built across small streams for the accumulation of alluvial soils behind the dams, dams on small rivers to impound water, which is then diverted via irrigation canals to fields away from the rivers, and large dams forming reservoirs with impounded water drained away by irrigation canals.

Apparently population kept growing and flood-control technology kept improving. By 4500 B.P., settlement expanded onto the flood plain of the Indus River itself. The Indus is a large, unpredictable river given to violent flooding. It is unlikely that an agricultural people could have survived on its shores without sophisticated flood-control construction. Two sites that typify this period are Kot Diji and Amri. The latter contains a large number of connected mud brick structures, and there is evidence of canal building.

**Figure 15.15** *Location of sites related to the development of civilization and mentioned in the text, in Pakistan, India, and the Far East.*

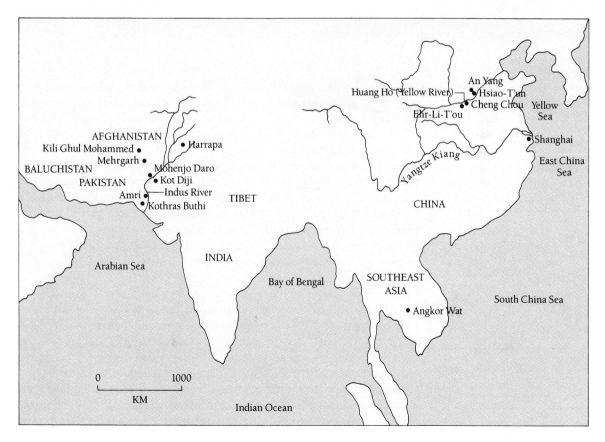

**Figure 15.16** *The excavation at Kot Diji exposed a large village site, predating Mohenjo-daro and Harappa.* (Department of Archaeology and Museums, Karachi)

It is at Kot Diji, however, that we see the earliest evidence for large-scale flood-control construction (Figure 15.16). This site is surrounded by a wall measuring up to 8 meters (26 feet) high and 1.5 meters (about 5 feet) thick. The base of the wall is constructed of cut limestone, and the top is made of mud brick. Such construction implies a certain amount of coordination of the population and may indicate the beginning of social differentiation. After this we see the urban explosion represented by Mohenjo-daro and Harappa. Here again, then, the need to coordinate activities related to the control of water played a major role in the development of civilization.

### China

In northern Honan province of China, on the banks of the Huan River, near the modern city of An-yang, rests the ruins of the ancient city of Yin. Here, in what was the culmination of East Asia's earliest civilization, the Shang, a succession of twelve kings ruled over a period of 273 years beginning about 2400 ya (Chang 1968; Gernet 1987).

In and around An-yang is a series of settlements articulated into what was the center of Shang culture. At Hsiao-t'un were found the royal palaces—large structures with stamped-earth foundations, large stone

**Figure 15.17** *The ancient city of An-yang was the apparent center of the Shang culture of China. Exquisite bronzes were found in elaborate burials of the royalty.* (Courtesy of the Freer Gallery of Art, Smithsonian Institution, Washington, D.C.—36.6 Chinese Bronze: Shang, late An-yang, 11th century B.C., ceremonial vessel/typehuo. 17.2 × 21.2 × 10.6 cm overall)

support pillars, and platform altars. Around the palaces were smaller structures—manufactories for bronze, pottery, stone tools, and bone carvings (Figure 15.17).

At nearby Hsi-pei-kang, there was an extensive cemetery complex containing more than 1200 burials. Eleven large tombs were found, possibly the interments of all but the final of the historically recorded Shang rulers at Yin (the twelfth king is supposed to have died and been consumed in a fire during the destruction of the city). These royal tombs were enormous construction projects with large grave pits up to 40 meters (130 feet) long and 30 meters (nearly 100 feet) wide. Ramps as long as 50 meters (more than 160 feet) led down into the burial pits where the royal personage was interred in a log-lined tomb, accompanied by elaborately manufactured objects of bronze, jade, antler, stone, bone, and shell. Hundreds of people were apparently sacrificed to accompany these kings into their afterlife; their decapitated remains surround the royal tombs (Figure 15.18).

**The Evolution of Chinese Civilization.**   Although once presumed to be the result of outside developments, we now recognize the Shang civilization as having evolved from the Neolithic Lung-shan culture of China (see Figure 15.15). The subsistence base of Shang civilization was essentially the same as that of local Neolithic cultures. Domesticated rice, millet,

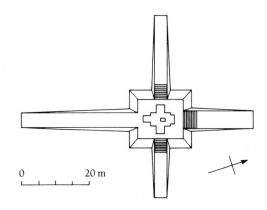

0          20 m

and wheat were the primary agricultural products. Pigs, sheep, cattle, and chickens were raised and eaten. Well into Shang times, this agricultural base was supplemented by hunting (deer and bear) and fishing.

At the Erh-li-t'ou site on the Lo River in Honan province, early manifestations of Shang civilization have been identified. Dating to around 3800 ya, the remains of a large temple or palace were uncovered. Early evidence of bronze metallurgy, characteristic of Chinese civilization, was identified at Erh-li-t'ou.

Also, evidence of social stratification was present in the form of differential burial patterns. Some human remains were rather casually interred in storage or refuse pits with no accompanying grave goods. Other burials were much more elaborate, containing jade carvings, turquoise and shell jewelry, finely made ceramics, and bronze. Finally, some headless human burials bear witness to human sacrifice.

A later site was excavated nearby the modern city of Cheng-chou. The ancient remains at Cheng-chou are clearly urban in character. There are residential areas, industrial zones, elite areas, and a cemetery. Surrounding the central part of the site with its large, upper-class houses and elite burials was a monumental wall more than 7000 meters (more than 22,000 feet) in circumference. It encompasses an area of more than 3 square kilometers, stood close to 10 meters (32 feet) in height, and was more than 35 meters (almost 115 feet) wide at its base. Chinese-American archaeologist K. C. Chang quotes estimates that for construction of the wall alone, 10,000 workers would have been needed for almost two decades for its completion (1968:205). Outside the wall were residential and industrial sectors of the city, with bronze foundries, pottery manufactories, and bone workshops.

Although monumental works in the form of pyramids or ziggurats do not appear at Shang sites, Shang is certainly an early civilization. Large populations were concentrated in urban centers. There is clear evidence of social stratification in the form of differential burials and in variations in house size and construction. There was specialization in various crafts, including bronze metallurgy, ceramics, bone carving, and stone sculpture. Finally, there was writing. More than 100,000 inscribed bones and tortoise shells have been recovered, mostly at Yin. The writing included some 5000 different characters, of which about 1500 have been interpreted (Gernet 1987:47). Translations indicate that most of the writing involved divination and predictions concerning social, political, military, and economic affairs.

### Mesoamerica

The ancient Mexican city of Teotihuacan stands as mute testament to the wondrous achievements of the prehistoric civilizations of Mesoamerica. From 1700 to 1300 ya, Teotihuacan was the most powerful political entity in the Western Hemisphere (Adams, 1991; Lamberg-Karlovsky and Sabloff 1979; Millon et al. 1973; Sabloff 1989; Sanders and Price 1968; Weaver 1972).

At its peak, Teotihuacan was a teaming city covering an area of 20 square kilometers. Its population is estimated between 125,000 and perhaps as many as 150,000 people, living in more than 2000 apartment complexes situated along a patterned grid of streets and avenues (Millon et al. 1973). As many as 1 million people may have been part of what might be considered the nation of which Teotihuacan was the capital.

The center of the city was dominated by two large pyramids connected by a broad boulevard today called the Avenue of the Dead (Figure 15.19). The smaller "Pyramid of the Moon" sits at one end of the boulevard, overlooking a large plaza surrounded by several smaller pyramids and temple complexes. The avenue is lined with temples and palaces. On one side rests the spectacular "Pyramid of the Sun," 210 meters (682 feet) square at its base and rising 64 meters (208 feet) in height. Steps lead to its summit where a small temple once stood. Near the Pyramid of the Sun are compounds, temples, and palaces. Sculpted reliefs of skulls, snakes, birds, jaguars, and mythological creatures adorn walls and ceilings everywhere. When the city was inhabited, the architecture was awash in bright color, with walls and ceilings painted blue, brown, red, green, yellow, white, and black.

In the sixteenth century, when the Spanish *conquistadores* asked the Aztecs, the civilized Mesoamerican inhabitants of that time, who had constructed Teotihuacan, the Aztecs, possessors of a remarkable civilization in their own right, responded that the gods must have built it.

**The Evolution of Mesoamerican Civilization.**    Teotihuacan, of course, did not appear without antecedents (Figure 15.20). Beginning about 3200 B.P., the trajectory of cultural evolution in Mesoamerica changed signifi-

**Figure 15.19** *The Pyramid of the Moon at the ancient city of Teotihuacan in central Mexico. Fifteen hundred years ago, Teotihuacan was a metropolis of more than 125,000 people.* (M. H. Feder)

cantly. We do not see any major change in subsistence technology, nor do we see urbanization. In the uplands and lowlands, people were relying on maize, beans, and squash as their food base. In the lowlands, a form of agriculture called slash-and-burn was practiced. Typical in subtropical and tropical forest lowlands, slash-and-burn involves the cutting of trees, burning to release their nutrients quickly into the soil, planting, harvesting, and then moving on to other areas, allowing the harvested area to return to forest.

After 3200 B.P., we begin to see an interesting phenomenon similar to that seen in the Indus Valley about 4500 B.P.—cultural convergence. In this case, a unique style of art permeates most of Mesoamerica. It consists of stylized jaguar motifs, large sculptures, and the use of jade and shell. The style, called **Olmec**, appears to represent not just a single set of art motifs but a unified ideology.

Along with this converging style and inferred belief system appears a different kind of settlement, concentrated in the lowlands of the Mexican state of Veracruz. Four sites have been discovered—La Venta, San Lorenzo, Tres Zapotes, and Laguna de los Cerros—that appear not to be villages or cities but rather ceremonial centers. Here we find little evidence of habitation, but for the first time in Mesoamerica there are pyramids—albeit constructed of earth and clay. At San Lorenzo, for instance, earth pyramids and flat plazas were built on top of an enormous, artificial earth platform. At La Venta, a single large pyramid 30 meters high was built with long mounds of earth flowing out from it.

Another important and impressive artifact of the Olmec tradition were enormous basalt sculptures of human faces. The largest of these,

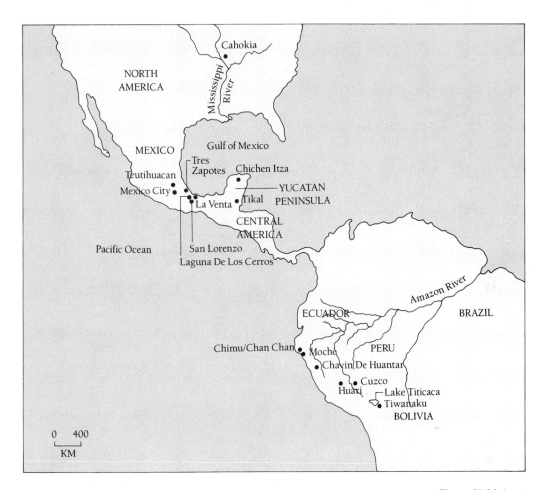

**Figure 15.20** *Location of sites related to the development of civilization and mentioned in the text, in Mesoamerica, South America, and North America.*

standing 3 meters in height and weighing more than 18 tons, was found nearly 130 kilometers from the source of the stone (Figure 15.21).

Archaeologists Linda Schele and David Freidel characterize the Olmec in this way; "They were the people who forged the template of world view and governance" that marked Mesoamerican civilization for more than two millennia (1990:38).

Certainly, we can see in the Olmec artifacts the beginning of the process of state formation in Mesoamerica, but the question remains: *Why* did it happen? Beyond the fact that Olmec appears to be a unifying art style, we do not know what else it signified to the ancient people of Mesoamerica. William Sanders and Barbara Price (1968) suggest that "microgeographical zoning" led to competition among groups in areas that provided different sets of resources. Population grew with the advent of slash-and-burn agriculture in the natural richness of the lowland environment. A single ideology reflected in a panregional art style like

**Olmec:** An artistic and iconographic style in Mesoamerica, starting about 3200 B.P.

**Figure 15.21** *An enormous head carved from a single block of volcanic rock weighing 18 tons. The Olmec civilization of lowland Mesoamerica produced these objects and transported them more than 100 km from the source of the stone.* (Inge Morath/Magnum)

Olmec may have served as a way of unifying disparate groups who needed to trade with each other.

Archaeologist William Rathje (1972) suggests that the Gulf coast of Mesoamerica was poor in salt, obsidian, basalt, and jade. He proposes that the need to organize trade to obtain important, locally unavailable raw materials led to the development of an elite class of traders who became wealthy through their monopoly of trade. The rise of this class fostered social stratification. Thus, the Olmec religion/art may have facilitated trade at the same time that it created an elite to administer the religion that fostered it. This elite, in all likelihood, lived in the ceremonial centers and required specialists to produce the objects necessary for the survival of the system.

Various regional civilizations followed the Olmec in Mesoamerica. The Maya, located in the lowlands of Mexico, Honduras, Belize, and Guatemala, are one of the best known. Their construction of fabulous ceremonial centers and cities like Tikal and Chichén Itzá may have been fostered by trade (Figure 15.22). Rathje also suggests that Maya cities developed as trading centers to attract the salt, obsidian, and jade that were lacking in the lowlands. Population would have grown along with the need for social organization and control. A writing system that is still not fully translated by modern scholars developed, perhaps to keep track of the trade.

It has been through the remarkable and persistent work of many scholars that the Maya are beginning to speak to us in their own voice across the centuries (see Schele and Freidel's splendid book, *A Forest of*

**Figure 15.22** *The Pyramid of the Magician, framed by storm clouds, at the Maya site of Uxmal. The Maya developed a civilization in the tropical lowlands of Mesoamerica.* (Melissa Feder)

**Figure 15.23** *The fortress city of Machu Picchu is located high in the Andes Mountains. Enormous, complex construction projects like this are diagnostic of cultures labeled "civilizations."* (Stuart Franklin/Magnum)

*Kings: The Untold Story of the Ancient Maya* for a discussion of the translation of Maya writing). Their writing tells of a fascinating culture of more than fifty politically independent city-states spread across some 100,000 square kilometers of Mesoamerica. The story of the Maya is one of great achievements in science and engineering, bloody and protracted wars, and an intriguing belief in the cyclicity of time and history. Decipherment of the Maya written language has made enormous strides in recent years. Continued success in this will allow for our more complete understanding of the Maya civilization.

Trade may also have played a role in the development of Teotihuacan (Lamberg-Karlovsky and Sabloff 1979). Because Teotihuacan is situated in an area rich in obsidian, the obsidian trade probably brought great wealth into the hands of the Teotihuacanos. Population may have grown in the surrounding valley as people came in to mine the volcanic glass, making necessary more intensive agricultural practices, including the building of canals, to help feed the workers. This caused even more power and wealth to be concentrated in the hands of those who controlled the obsidian trade. With such a concentration of wealth and power, bigger and more impressive monuments could be constructed, further reinforcing the power of those in control.

### South America

When we think of civilization in South America, the Inca come immediately to mind. The Romans of the New World, the Inca held their far-flung empire together by military might. First fully consolidated in A.D. 1476, at their peak immediately before the Spanish conquest in A.D. 1534, they controlled 2000 miles and millions of people along the South American coast from northern Equador to southern Chile (Obo 1653; Patterson 1973).

The Inca did not achieve control by introducing a new subsistence technology or by imposing their religion. The Inca were, purely and simply, militarists who achieved hegemony through conquest. By using a professional standing army and constructing thousands of kilometers of roads, they were able to control a huge territory (Figure 15.23). They forged bronze tools and made them widely available for the first time in the New World (Figure 15.24). They taxed all under their sway. To be a citizen of the Incan empire meant you had to work for the state—in agriculture, the military, or public works.

Cleverly, the Inca did not depose local deities as they deposed local autonomous rulers. Instead, local gods were incorporated into the Incan pantheon. All living under the Incan state, however, had to learn the language of the Inca, Quechua. Today, this language is still the primary tongue of the central Andes region.

Metallurgists in copper, bronze, silver, and gold, the Inca were also fine stonemasons, and their architecture is a major legacy of this culture. Using neither mortar nor cement, they constructed enormous walls of intricately carved blocks made of volcanic stone. The precision with which individual blocks were fitted together is impressive even from a modern perspective. Gold and silver adorned the walls and temples of the capital city of Cuzco.

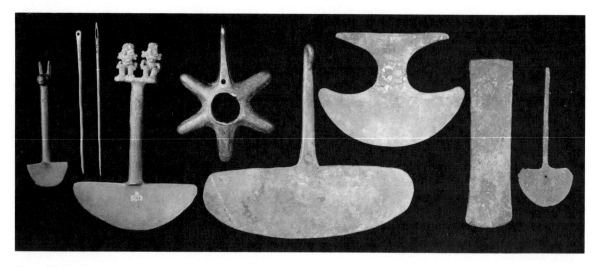

**Figure 15.24** *The Inca were the first New World people to produce bronze tools and to make them widely available.* (American Museum of Natural History, Neg. #36787, Kay C. Lenskjold)

**The Evolution of South American Civilization.** Cultural developments leading to the Inca were greatly affected by environmental features of the western coast of South America. A series of valleys, cut by streams draining the Andes, parallel each other and run westward onto the coastal plain. Resources are similar from valley to valley but differ depending on one's location within an individual valley. Archaeologist Thomas Patterson (1973) maintains that these valleys, each providing a complete mix of resources, appear to have been self-contained cultural units in early South American prehistory. Seasonal movements occurred within the confines of individual valleys, and there was little intervalley contact. By 4000 ya, this general isolation among the inhabitants of different valleys led to distinct cultural differentiation (see Figure 15.20).

At the same time, population was increasing within valleys as agriculture was replacing the hunting and gathering mode of subsistence. Agriculture led to a more sedentary settlement pattern. The patchy nature of resource availability led to differentiation within valleys. In other words, where previously people could get whatever they needed simply by moving within a single valley, they now needed to trade to obtain resources available in other parts of the valley. Some villages, situated where resources were more abundant, became richer at the expense of others. Perhaps as validation of this differentiation, we begin to see the growth of ceremonial centers at this time.

As populations increased and carrying capacities within valleys were approached, the need to trade and cooperate with people in neighboring valleys arose. Then, beginning about 3000 ya, there occurred what archaeologist Richard Burger calls "a decisive change in Central Andean prehistory" that resulted in a "radical restructuring of earlier Andean cultures" (1988:99). A common artistic/iconographic style called **Chavin** quickly spread along natural routes of communication and trade within and across the various, previously entirely autonomous valley cultures. The style consisted of relief and full sculptures of jaguars, caimans (South American alligators), snakes, and eagles as well as humans with jaguarlike features. Along with the images themselves, with Chavin came the spread of technological innovations in textiles and metallurgy, including new methods of manufacturing textiles, the widespread use of gold, methods of alloying gold and silver, soldering, sweat-welding, and the **repoussé** method of decorating gold objects.

The style seems to have been centered at the Chavin de Huantar site in north-central Peru. Here, at about 3000 B.P., a pyramid and temple complex 13 meters (more than 40 feet) high and over 200 meters (650 feet) square was built. Within this complex are many relief sculptures in typical Chavin style and a 4-meter tall carved column of granite representing a standing man with jaguar fangs and snakes for hair (Figure 15.25).

Chavin may have served a function similar to that of the Olmec style in Mesoamerica—a facilitator of trade, communication, and cooperation among people previously alien to each other. Sharing the same art style and, probably more significantly, sharing the same religious belief system with the same gods would have made interaction that much easier. Burger suggests that the spread of a common art style and iconography reflecting a common religious ideology may have resulted from some sort of broad crisis among the people living in their separate Andean river valleys. Chavin, in this interpretation, may have started as a local cult that seemed to many to offer a mystical solution to the crisis.

Whatever the source of Chavin was, it did, for the first time, join the various valley cultures in a set of common cultural practices related to religion. It therefore set the stage for later political amalgamation of the various valley polities into larger, inclusive empires.

At about 1500 ya on the north coast of Peru, we see the Moche site with its 41-meter (more than 130 feet) high stepped pyramid and the spread of its unique pottery style far beyond the confines of its own valley (Conklin and Moseley 1988). By 1400 to 1200 ya, two separate civilized states, Tiwanaku and Huari, came into existence. Again, the respective capitals of these states are marked by monumental architecture, far-flung trading networks, differentiated burials, and a level of artistic skill implying specialization. Art and architectural styles, religious motifs, and burial patterns of the Tiwanaku and Huari civilizations spread over hundreds of square miles through expansion, friendly incorporation, and conquest. As archaeologists William Conklin and Michael Moseley (1988) point out, Tiwanaku and Huari represent the

**Figure 15.25** *The Chavin art style seems to be a South American analogue to the Olmec, serving, perhaps, to draw disparate groups together through its common religious expression.* (Gordon Willey)

**Chavin:** An artistic and iconographic style of Peru starting 3000 ya.

**repoussé:** A method of decorating thin metal where the pattern is beaten up from the underside.

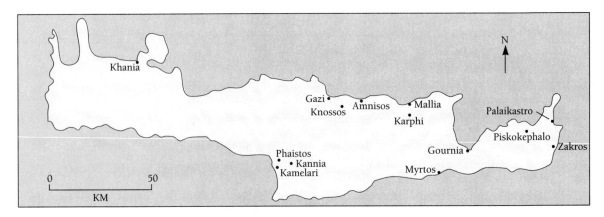

**Figure 15.26** *Major sites of the Minoan civilization on Crete. The site of Knossos with its large palace is the largest and most complex of these sites.*

development of a kind of large-scale "national" Andean unity as the progression of these empires replaced a pattern of small-scale, single river valley political units.

By about 1000 ya, another large state, the Chimu, evolved, with its 6-square mile capital, Chanchan. The Chimu were the precursors of the Inca.

### Southern Europe

The site of Knossos was the center of what certainly was Europe's first literate civilization (Cherry 1987; Warren 1987). Built on the island of Crete close to 4000 ya, it was the nucleus of the **Minoan** civilization whose influence was felt throughout the central Mediterranean (Warren 1975; Figure 15.26). The social and political hub of Knossos was the "Labyrinth," a palace built in 3880 B.P. It covered an enormous area of some 20,000 square meters and may have contained 1000 separate rooms or chambers (Castleden 1990:8; Figure 15.27). It is a remarkable structure made of mud brick, marked with numerous columns tapered from top to bottom, and painted in earth-toned hues of browns and reds. Its interior walls were covered with paintings showing details of Minoan life and belief 3800 ya: Robed priestesses gaze at visitors across the millennia; an athlete-acrobat performs a handstand on the back of an enormous bull in a palace fresco; the images of two animals that appear to be a mythical mixture of dogs and birds flank what seems to be a throne; there is even the beautifully painted rendering of dolphins frolicking among a school of fish.

The palace at Knossos was the center of a civilization that stood at the center of a vast network of trade encompassing the Aegean region of the Mediterranean. This trade, especially for an agricultural product that was cultivated on Crete—olives, particularly valuable for the pro-

**Figure 15.27** *Looking down into one of the rooms of the palace at Knossos on Crete. The columns have been reconstructed and repainted, conveying only an impression of how beautiful it once had been.* (M. H. Feder)

duction of oil—may have been one of the key factors that contributed to the importance of the island, leading to the evolution of a complex political/economic entity to control and coordinate the movement of olives and the oil they produced.

The power of Knossos began to fade after about 3400 ya while the importance of the **Mycenaeans** on the Greek mainland grew at their expense. The Mycenaeans were accomplished traders, although their focus was not in olives but copper and tin. These two metals, when alloyed, produce bronze, a material far more durable and useful than either of the metals from which it was made. It may have been as a result of the need to keep track of trade that the Mycenaeans expanded on the writing system first developed by the Minoans.

The Mycenaeans flourished until a bit after 3200 ya. It was at this time that invasions from the north sapped their strength, leading to the destruction of their civilization. The fall of the Mycenaeans paved the way for the ascendance of the Greek city-states that produced the great architecture, science, and philosophy that contributed so very greatly to the development of Western society. It was in a small colony, founded by the Greeks in 600 B.C. and incorporated into the Roman empire in the 1st century A.D., that the woman whose remains appear on the cover of this book died. She was killed in the spectacular eruption of the volcanic mountain Vesuvius on August 24/25, 79 A.D. along with perhaps hundreds of her neighbors and over 2000 others in the nearby larger Roman city of Pompeii.

**Minoan:** The earliest European civilization, centered on Crete and beginning about 4000 ya.

**Mycenaean:** The civilization of Greece that followed the Minoans and preceded the Greek city-states.

### Africa

The evolution of civilization in Africa presents us with a long, complex, richly detailed story. Once thought to reflect only late reaction to developments in more "civilized" regions, the city, the state, and civilization are now known to have been ancient in Africa and, in some cases, independent from cultural evolution in other areas (Connah 1987; Figure 15.28).

Perhaps the oldest black African civilization is that of Nubia, which dates to 3500 B.P. This culture developed along the Nile, south of the Egyptian civilization, and was influenced by the pyramid builders to the north.

Farther south is the prehistoric city of Axum, in modern Ethiopia. Here the inhabitants built a four-towered "castle" some 2000 ya (Figure 15.29). In Axum and surrounding towns that belonged to the same prehistoric state have been found enormous, narrow towers, each carved from single blocks of stone. The tower at Axum is carved from a block of granite and stands 21 meters (69 feet) tall. False windows and doors have been carved into its four sides, causing it to look not unlike a modern skyscraper.

**Figure 15.28** *Map of sites related to the development of civilization and mentioned in the text, in Africa south of the Sahara.*

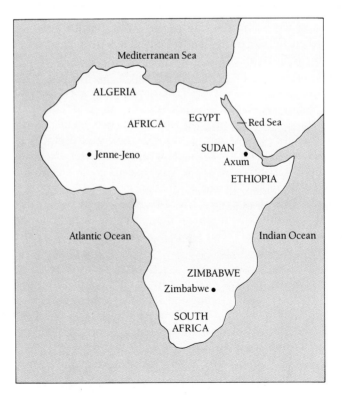

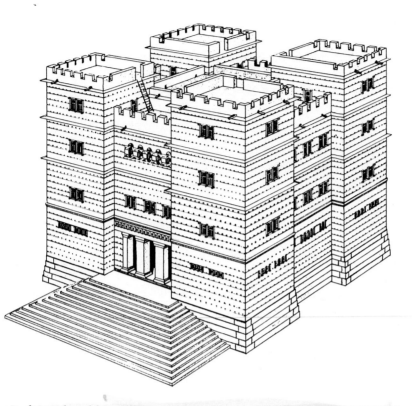

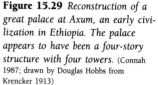

**Figure 15.29** *Reconstruction of a great palace at Axum, an early civilization in Ethiopia. The palace appears to have been a four-story structure with four towers.* (Connah 1987; drawn by Douglas Hobbs from Krencker 1913)

Perhaps the oldest African civilization south of the Sahara is that of Jenne-jeno in Mali (McIntosh and McIntosh 1982). Jenne-jeno was a true city more than 1000 ya, with a population of between 10,000 and 20,000 people. It shows evidence of public works, particularly in the form of its 2-kilometer surrounding wall. Jenne-jeno probably developed before any substantial contact with Arabs living north of the Sahara; so it was truly an indigenous, independent prehistoric black African kingdom. The city may have served as a trading center, bartering its rich agricultural products for salt, iron, and copper—the last being obtained from sources 1000 kilometers distant (McIntosh and McIntosh 1982:414).

In southern Africa, the ruins of Zimbabwe consist of two main groups about a kilometer away from each other: the "Acropolis" and the "Temple" (Figure 15.30). Between the two is an unbroken series of stone walls, enclosures, and foundations—in essence, the heart of an ancient city with an estimated population of about 18,000 (Connah 1987:184). The "Temple" is a large, dry-laid stone ruin surrounded by a huge wall more than 9 meters (30 feet) high, enclosing an area of more than an acre. When the site was "mined" in the late nineteenth century, many artifacts of gold and iron were found. Unfortunately, the site was not professionally investigated until the early twentieth century.

**Figure 15.30** *Ruins of the 1000-year-old Temple of Zimbabwe, an African city of perhaps as many as 18,000 inhabitants.* (Bob Holmes)

The area around Zimbabwe contains more than 300 additional sites that appear to have been inhabited by people bearing the same culture. Dating to sometime after A.D. 1000, Zimbabwe was a black African civilization.

## North America

If Cahokia was not a full-fledged city, it was well on its way to becoming one. Some 200 earthen mounds, platforms, and pyramids were spread across its 7 square miles (Figure 15.31). In the core of the settlement was the largest of the pyramids, covering more than fourteen acres, containing over 50 million cubic meters (60 million cubic yards) of earth, and rising more than 30 meters (100 feet) over the river flood plain. From its summit, one can still gaze out upon a large open plaza encompassed by large mounds: flat-topped pyramids, conical mounds, and low-lying earthworks.

At its peak, Cahokia was an urbanlike settlement of 10,000 and perhaps more inhabitants, including priests, artisans, merchants, farmers, and kings. Its rulers were buried in sumptuous splendor in log-lined tombs with precious artifacts of stone, shell, and copper. One ruler was laid out on a cape made of over 12,000 drilled and sewn shell beads. Around his grave were the remains of more than sixty other people, all killed to accompany the king to the afterlife.

With its food surplus, specialists, stratification, and dense settlement, Cahokia has the appearance of an early stage of a civilization. But

**Figure 15.31** *The tiered earthen pyramid, called "Monk's Mound," at Cahokia once dominated a plaza surrounded by smaller earthworks—the center of a settlement called urban by some archaeologists.*

Cahokia is not in the Indus or Nile valleys. It is not in northern China or Mesoamerica. Cahokia is located on the Illinois side of the Mississippi River, just east of St. Louis. More than 500 ya, Cahokia was the center of an American Indian civilization in its infancy.

## Southeast Asia

In Kampuchea (Cambodia) in Southeast Asia lie the ruins of the spectacular Khmer civilization. There, between A.D. 800 and 1300, seventy-two temples and monuments were constructed of sandstone, laterite (a hard red soil), and brick. Each complex of temples represented the capital of the Khmer state during the reign of successive kings. Angkor Wat, built after A.D. 1100, is the largest and most impressive of these (P. T. White 1982; Figure 15.32).

The temple at Angkor Wat is surrounded by a rectangular outer gallery over 800 meters (0.5 mile) long. The walls of the gallery are covered with bas-relief sculptures depicting important events and personages in Hindu mythology. There are eight huge panels of reliefs, each close to 2 meters (6 feet) in height and from 50 to 100 meters (160 to 300 feet) long. One of the panels depicts the Hindu creation myth; another contains the relief sculptures of 1700 spirit women. There also is an interior rectangular gallery and hallways connecting it to the outer gallery. At the center is the temple of Angkor Wat itself, a hauntingly beautiful building with five intricately carved domes.

**Figure 15.32** *The Khmer civilization constructed a series of magnificent temples from* A.D., *800 to 1300. Angkor Wat, the largest, was built after* A.D. *1100.* (Marc Riboud/Magnum)

Water control seems to have been the key to Khmer civilization. Through a series of enormous reservoirs called *barray* and miles of canals, the Khmer were able to produce two and sometimes three yearly harvests. The Western Barray is, in its way, as monumental and impressive as the temple complex at Angkor Wat. Constructed at ground level with dikes, this reservoir is 8 kilometers (5 miles) long and 2.25 kilometers (1.25 miles) wide.

Khmer civilization fell as a result of warfare with neighboring groups who had previously been under the sway of Khmer rule. Today, modern warfare threatens the remains of this once great civilization.

## WHY DID IT HAPPEN?

The evolution of civilization is difficult to chronicle (Figure 15.33) and even more difficult to explain. There are numerous gaps in the archaeological record, and these translate into gaps in our thinking.

As you read the brief descriptions here, you may have recognized some of the factors mentioned in the hypotheses about the emergence of civilization presented earlier (Table 15.1). As Lamberg-Karlovsky and Sabloff have pointed out, each of the civilizations discussed had its own unique character, but "some strikingly similar developmental patterns characterized the beginnings of agriculture and the later rise of civilizations in both the old and New World localities" (1979:214). Irrigation certainly played an important role in almost all the societies discussed, but it cannot be shown to have occurred first and therefore cannot have been in all places a prime mover. It is certainly the case that circum-scription of resources served as a catalyst in the emergence of the civil-ized state, but a catalyst is not necessarily a cause. Managing trade of highly desirable localized resources seems to have been an important factor in all the examples discussed.

You see the problem here. It becomes a sort of chicken-and-egg argu-ment. We cannot determine which, if any, of those characteristics we have used to define civilization were causes, which were effects, and which were both.

Archaeologist Joseph Tainter (1988:32) has provided a valuable tax-onomy of the hypotheses proposed for the origin of civilization. He categorizes the scientifically based hypotheses we have discussed and the myriad others proposed to explain the development of civilization as follows:

**Figure 15.33** *Summary chart showing the chronology and geogra-phy of the world's ancient civiliza-tions.*

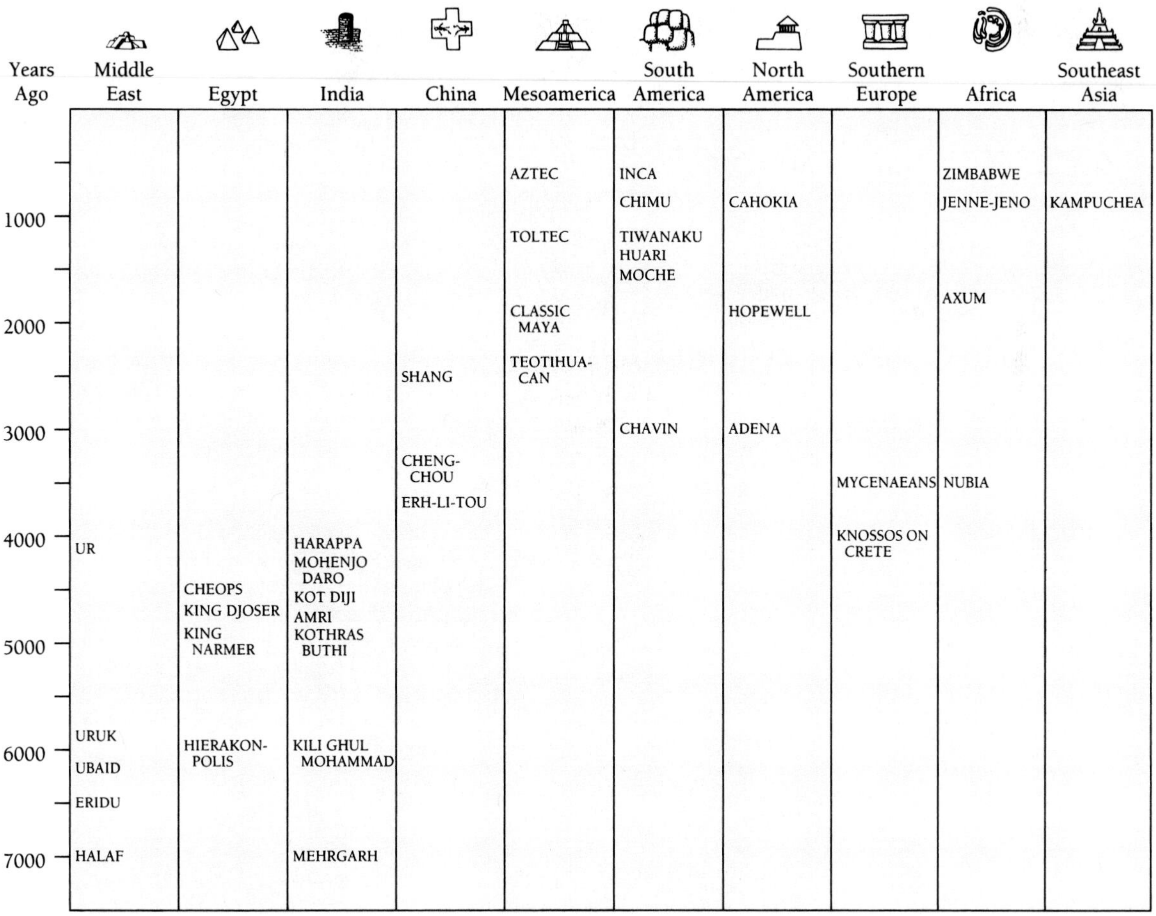

| Years Ago | Middle East | Egypt | India | China | Mesoamerica | South America | North America | Southern Europe | Africa | Southeast Asia |
|---|---|---|---|---|---|---|---|---|---|---|
| | | | | | AZTEC | INCA | | | ZIMBABWE | |
| | | | | | | CHIMU | CAHOKIA | | JENNE-JENO | KAMPUCHEA |
| 1000 | | | | | TOLTEC | TIWANAKU HUARI MOCHE | | | | |
| | | | | | CLASSIC MAYA | | HOPEWELL | | AXUM | |
| 2000 | | | | | TEOTIHUA-CAN | | | | | |
| | | | | SHANG | | | | | | |
| 3000 | | | | | | CHAVIN | ADENA | | | |
| | | | | CHENG-CHOU | | | | MYCENAEANS | NUBIA | |
| | | | | ERH-LI-TOU | | | | | | |
| 4000 | UR | | HARAPPA MOHENJO DARO | | | | | KNOSSOS ON CRETE | | |
| | | CHEOPS KING DJOSER | KOT DIJI AMRI | | | | | | | |
| 5000 | | KING NARMER | KOTHRAS BUTHI | | | | | | | |
| 6000 | URUK UBAID | HIERAKON-POLIS | KILI GHUL MOHAMMAD | | | | | | | |
| | ERIDU | | | | | | | | | |
| 7000 | HALAF | | MEHRGARH | | | | | | | |

**Table 15.1** *Summary of Hypotheses Explaining the Evolution of Civilization*

| Hypothesis | Proponent | Type | Summary |
|---|---|---|---|
| Race | Various | Pseudoscience | A racist explanation that assumed that certain racial or ethnic groups were inherently superior and so evolved civilized societies. |
| Environmental determinism | Ellsworth Huntington | Deterministic | Here it was assumed that human groups became more intelligent and progressed further where the environment was more challenging. |
| Unilinear evolution | Lewis Henry Morgan | Deterministic | Culture, in essence, drives itself forward as specific inventions are made: fire, bow and arrow, pottery, domestication, iron, writing. Without coming upon these successive inventions, cultures became stuck and would not progress. |
| Marxism | Karl Marx Frederich Engels | Internal conflict | The trappings of civilization developed after the invention of private property. Some individuals became wealthy and needed to protect their wealth. Social classes and specialization followed. |
| Hydraulic | Karl Wittfogel | Managerial Integrative | The need to control water for irrigation purposes led to the development of organizations to build and maintain waterworks. To accomplish this, there had to be leaders and followers, and institutions originated for this purpose evolved into the bureaucracy of the state. |
| Circumscription | Robert Carniero | External conflict | Societies that had effectively filled up their territory waged war against their neighbors to obtain their land. The losers in such battles became the lower class in an emerging stratified society that led to the civilized state. |
| Social integration | Jonathan Haas | Synthetic Conflict/integrative | In different combinations, trade, warfare, and irrigation led to the formation of complex social and political structures. This led to social stratification with those at the top of society given differential access to resources. This, in turn, led to their accumulation of wealth and power and the need to symbolically reinforce the legitimacy of their wealth and power through the construction of monumental works. |

1. *Managerial.* Managerial hypotheses essentially maintain that civilization developed in response to a need for more complex forms of political integration. In other words, the need arose in some societies to accomplish some complex task like the construction of irrigation canals or the management of trade for valuable items not locally available. Managerial hierarchies developed to oversee these new, complex tasks, and this led to social stratification and the other trappings associated with civilization. Clearly, the hydraulic hypothesis of Wittfogel fits into this category, as do any of the specific explanations involving trade for the development of civilization in Mesopotamia or Mesoamerica.
2. *Internal conflict.* In this perspective, class conflict is the prime mover behind the rise of civilization. The institutions of the state evolved, in this view, to protect the wealth and power of the privileged few who, by luck and greed, had managed to accumulate more than their neighbors. Marxist theories fit into this category.
3. *External conflict.* In this view, civilization evolved in response to an external threat. The institutions of civilization evolved in order to successfully respond to the external threat and to deal with and administer those groups defeated in warfare. The circumscription hypothesis of Carneiro belongs here.
4. *Synthetic.* Any explanations that combine several interrelated processes belong in this category.

A complementary perspective on such hypotheses is provided by anthropologist Jonathan Haas (1982) who divides the hypotheses of state formation and the development of civilization into "conflict" and "integration" approaches. In the conflict approach, the development of civilization is seen as resulting from competition for access to resources. The hypotheses of Marx and Engels and Carneiro belong to this school of thought.

In the integration approach, civilization is viewed as developing when social groups voluntarily submit to a central power or government to obtain benefits that only such an authority can provide. Wittfogel's hydraulic hypothesis is based on social integration. Hypotheses concerning the necessities of expanded trade networks also belong to this approach.

Haas believes that a combination of both approaches, conflict and integration, has the greatest potential for explaining the evolution of state society and civilization. Haas embeds aspects of the integration explanation within a general model of conflict. Together or separately, and in different combinations in different regions, warfare, trade, and the sociopolitical requirements of irrigation technology led to the development of the state. Processes of social integration are required to maximize the effectiveness of long-distance trade, warfare, or irrigation.

# CONTEMPORARY ISSUE

## The Irony of Civilization

In reading this chapter, you may have become increasingly aware of a terrible irony. This irony has serious implications in terms of human cultural evolution in general and specifically for the future of our own civilization. To recognize it requires only a simple inventory of the world's earliest civilizations, a knowledge of geography, and a familiarity with current events.

Mesopotamian civilization developed in the Tigris–Euphrates area in close proximity to the border between Iran and Iraq. Egyptian civilization evolved in the valley of the Nile. Indus Valley civilization was incubated in the hills of Afghanistan and Pakistan and flowered in the valley of the Indus River in Pakistan. Shang civilization developed in northern China. American Indian civilizations evolved in Mexico, Peru, and North America. Zimbabwe developed in southern Africa, Angkor Wat in Cambodia.

The list itself should make the point clear enough. Today, the areas in which many of the ancient world's civilizations developed are still noteworthy, but not for their level of civilization. These areas that were home to some of the greatest accomplishments of the ancient world are, in the latter half of the twentieth century, characterized by warfare, poverty, hunger, and underdevelopment.

The homeland of the magnificence of Mesopotamian culture, the world's first civilization, is an extreme example. First, there was the eight-year long war between Iran and Iraq, then the short, but deadly Persian Gulf War of 1991. The Egyptian descendants of the builders of the pyramids now live in a poor nation for whom the possibility of yet another war is always present. The inheritors of the wonderful Indus Valley civilization are poor and uneducated. Modern China, though currently at peace, was for years wracked by war and poverty. The modern lands of the Teotihuacanos and the Inca are places of grinding poverty. The American Indian descendants of the builders of Cahokia are an impoverished minority living as outsiders in the wealthiest nation in the world. The modern nation of Zimbabwe, named for the archaeological site, stands in the midst of poverty and possible race war. The ruins of Angkor Wat are surrounded by the larger ruin of the nation of Cambodia, torn by war, poverty, and genocide.

The ancient cultures in these areas reached soaring heights in architecture, science, trade, and agriculture. They flourished over periods of hundreds and even thousands of years. Yet none endured, and some fell to remarkable depths.

This leads to an obvious question: "Is the collapse of civilization inevitable?" It certainly may be the case. Tainter in his book *The Collapse of Complex Societies* (1988) discusses the case histories of all the civilizations mentioned here and many more. In his view, civilizations do not disintegrate because of random or unpredictable factors. He rejects single, serendipitous, fundamental causes like resource depletion, environmental catastrophes, or barbarian invasions. He also rejects claims that civilizations are inherently fragile entities or that the elite classes invariably mismanage things, leading to a revolt by the masses.

Instead, in Tainter's view, civilization and all of its trappings involve increasingly complex and costly investments of time and energy. The development of civilization is seen as an extreme case of a process of deviation amplification; civilization is a runaway train on a track leading to greater political and social complexity. Once the complex social and political structures of "the state" are established, an increasingly greater human investment in terms of time and energy are demanded merely for keeping things going. More and more people are needed to run the bureaucracies that are necessary for the complex social arrays that civilization fosters and depends upon. In essence, for civilizations to survive, the pyramids must continually get bigger, the armies larger, and the food surpluses must increase. But eventually, as greater economic investment is made simply in running the political and social bureaucracies of the civilized state, the economic returns diminish dramatically. As Tainter puts it, "a society invests ever more heavily in a strategy that yields proportionately less" (1988:195).

In Tainter's view, the collapse of a civilization, however, is not a "bad" thing. In his opinion, it is a "rational, economizing process that may well benefit much of the population" (1988:198). While the elite may certainly lose out, the masses may actually see their lives improve as they no longer have to support burdensome, nonutilitarian institutions that had previously served only to maintain the economic, social, and political status quo and that had outlived their ability to effectively manage the society.

Finally, it is little more than conceit on our part to believe that our civilization is immune to the kinds of collapse that befell earlier civilizations.

One major difference is apparent, though. For the first time in human evolution, the collapse of a civilization may come as a result of destruction by our own hand. We can accomplish this through the madness of nuclear annihilation or, perhaps, more likely, environmental destruction. And, unlike the geographically isolated collapses of the world's ancient civilizations, if we go down in a nuclear war or, if we destroy the planetary ecosystem, we will almost certainly bring the rest of humanity with us.

*OZYMANDIAS*

*I MET a traveller from an antique land*
*Who said: Two vast and trunkless legs of stone*
*Stand in the desert . . . Near them, on the sand,*
*Half sunk, a shattered visage lies, whose frown,*
*And wrinkled lip, and sneer of cold command,*
*Tell that its sculptor well those passions read*
*Which yet survive, stamped on these lifeless things,*
*The hand that mocked them, and the heart that fed:*
*And on the pedestal these words appear:*
*'My name is Ozymandias, king of kings:*
*Look on my works, ye Mighty, and despair!'*
*Nothing beside remains. Round the decay*
*Of that colossal wreck, boundless and bare*
*The lone and level sands stretch far away.*
                                    *[1817; publ. 1818]*

*The poem "Ozymandias" by Percy Bysshe Shelley juxtaposed with the ruin that inspired the poem—a colossal statue of the Egyptian pharaoh Rameses II. The message is appropriate for our modern civilization.* (Inge Morath/Magnum)

Such integration leads to social stratification, with those on top of the social pyramid gaining differential access to and control over basic resources. This elite can then accumulate wealth in the form of land, water, or other precious resources that other people in the society need or desire. With differential access based on "control over the *production or procurement* of the resources in question" (Haas 1982:151), the elite also accumulates power which can be used to coerce people to do whatever is required—to fight in wars, be taxed, build pyramids, and so on.

Following Haas's perspective, it likely serves little purpose to look for a single or "prime" cause for the development of any *one* of the civilizations described, much less a single cause that would explain the development of *all* the world's myriad ancient civilizations. Instead, we can generalize that constellations of factors including population growth, warfare, and uneven distribution of resources were involved for all the cultures.

Looked at another way, we can say that post-Pleistocene agricultural societies were living in various states of equilibrium with their environments. Some of these states of equilibrium were "unstable." Archaeologist David Clarke identifies a state of unstable equilibrium as one in which a "small displacement from the equilibrium state gives rise to a cumulatively greater displacement from that specific state" (1978:48).

It is likely that civilization developed where Neolithic cultures were living in unstable equilibrium with their environments. Here, relatively minor perturbations from without or within—population growth, climate change, technological advance, outside threat—may have upset that delicately balanced equilibrium and changed the equation for survival. Decisions were made, challenges met, strategies revised to respond to these changes. Canals may have been built, population density increased, agriculture intensified, or trading networks established. Under conditions of unstable equilibrium, these new approaches, though perhaps solving initial challenges, sometimes produced a ripple effect that greatly transformed other aspects of culture. Patterns of social integration had to change to make such activities possible. Power was invested in emerging elites to build canals or walls, completely altering established social systems. Wars of conquest were initiated, changing the political nature of a region. Certain groups of people obtained differential access to resources by controlling trade. Such changes in turn may have triggered a spiral of change as a new equilibrium was sought but not attained. Changes in subsistence or trade may have required more coordination of individuals and triggered changes in social structure. The maintenance of this new order may have further required symbols in order to perpetuate and justify itself. But this, in turn, would create more power in the hands of the leaders of the new social order. This power would enable even greater accomplishments in architecture and science.

Thus, myriad factors impinging on agricultural groups in the Indus and Nile valleys, in Mesopotamia, highland Mesoamerica, lowland Mesoamerica, China, South America, North America, southern Africa, Southeast Asia, and elsewhere may have set in motion forces whose ultimate impact on these societies was enormous. At least in the broadest sense, we are all living with the consequences of those changes.

## SUMMARY

Beginning sometime after 6000 ya, in several world areas, fundamental changes occurred in the social and political lives of human groups. The food surplus made possible by the Food-Producing Revolution allowed for a dramatic increase in cultural complexity that resulted in what we call "civilization."

Characterized by densely populated settlements, specialization of labor, social stratification, monumental public works, a system of record keeping, along with the aforementioned production of a food surplus, the world's primary civilizations developed in the Middle East in Mesopotamia, in the Nile Valley of Egypt, the Indus Valley of Pakistan, the Huang Ho Valley of China, the highlands and lowlands of Mesoamerica, and the mountain valleys of the Andes in South America. Secondary civilizations (in the sense that they were not independent developments) turn up in southern Europe, Africa south of the Sahara, Kampuchea in Southeast Asia, and the North American Midwest.

The reasons postulated for the development of these societies have been varied: race, environment, invention, class struggle, the need for groups to subordinate themselves to authority, and warfare. It seems that there is no point in suggesting a single cause or prime mover for the development of civilizations in general, or even in individual cases. Civilizations are complex entities with complex explanations. Viable propositions include aspects of both conflict-based and integrative mechanisms. Thus, it is likely that in some world areas, as population grew, complex bureaucratic structures developed to facilitate group projects like the construction of city walls or irrigation network; specialist classes originated to coordinate trade for materials unavailable locally; competition may have led to warfare with defeated groups becoming subordinate classes. As social distinctions developed, monumental projects became common as members of the newly emerged elite classes felt compelled to legitimate in some concrete ways the stratified social system. In this way, civilization, with all of its concomitants, quickly evolved in the world areas discussed in this chapter.

## KEY TERMS

| | | |
|---|---|---|
| civilization | ziggurat | Chavin |
| social stratification | Uruk | repoussé |
| egalitarian | city-state | Minoan |
| environmental determinism | Olmec | Mycenaean |

## FOR MORE INFORMATION

C. C. Lamberg-Karlovsky's and Jeremy A. Sabloff's *Ancient Civilizations: The Near East and Mesoamerica* provides excellent summaries of the various hypotheses presented to explain the development of state society. The book also contains in-depth discussions of the development of civilization in Mesopotamia, Egypt, the Indus Valley, and Mesoamerica. Though the time period discussed is a bit later than that focused on here, John Romer's *Ancient Lives: Daily Life in Egypt of the Pharaohs* provides remarkable insight into life in ancient Egypt. Graham Connah's *African Civilizations* provides the best recent discussion on the development of civilization on that continent. Muriel Porter Weaver's *The Aztecs, Maya, and Their Predecessors: Archaeology of Mesoamerica* is a good source of information about the civilizations of Mesoamerica, as is Jeremy Sabloff's *The Cities of Ancient Mexico: Reconstructing a Lost World*, R. E. W. Adam's *Prehistoric Mesoamerica*, and, especially, Linda Schele and David Freidel's *A Forest of Kings: The Untold Story of the Ancient Maya*. Also see the series "Rediscovering the Maya" in various issues of *Natural History* magazine in 1991 and 1992.

K. C. Chang's *The Archaeology of Ancient China* is a good source of information on the Shang civilization. Thomas Patterson's *America's Past: A New World Archaeology* examines the development of the state in South America. *National Geographic* magazine has published fine articles on the cultures of Cahokia (December 1972 by George Stuart) and Angkor Wat (May 1982 by P. T. White). The *First Cities* volume (Hamblin 1973) of the Time-Life *Emergence of Man* series is still a good source for information about the early civilizations of Southwest Asia and India.

Jonathan Haas's *The Evolution of the Prehistoric State* and Joseph Tainter's *The Collapse of Complex Societies* are especially useful treatments of the birth and death of civilizations.

# 16

# THE ARCHAEOLOGY OF HISTORY

In our chronicle of human antiquity, we have brought you from our earliest hominid ancestors of more than 3 million years ago to the evolution of civilization. You might think our story was largely at an end. After all, throughout most of this book we have relied on the tools and methods of prehistoric archaeology to illuminate the human story.

Much of what we know about ancient Mesopotamia, Egypt, and China, however, comes from the writing of these ancient peoples themselves. The written record after these groups grows increasingly detailed, and one might think that the rest of the saga of human cultural evolution was the exclusive province of historians. After all, why dig in the dirt to learn about a people if we can simply read about them from their own perspective?

Certainly, historians and their analyses of the written record make a major contribution to our understanding of the human historical past. But we should not overestimate the accuracy or inclusiveness of the written record. Perhaps the great satirist Ambrose Bierce said it best in his *Devil's Dictionary* (1911:57) when he defined history as "an account mostly false, of events mostly unimportant, which are brought about by rulers mostly knaves, and soldiers mostly fools." To be fair, we should add that he defined prehistoric as "belonging to an early period—and a museum" (p. 103).

Yet Bierce's point is valid. History, by and large, focuses on "great events" and "great people." As far as the written record is concerned, the bulk of humankind is invisible. In the past especially, most people were illiterate and thus could not write about themselves. Those who could write were usually busy keeping track of the royal granaries, chronicling victories in battle, or considering religious questions. They were too busy and usually simply disinclined to write about the lives of workers, peasants, farmers, or slaves. Yet such people in all periods made up the very great majority of any population.

The material record, however, does not suffer from this sort of bias. It matters little if you were rich or poor. It is of no consequence if you were important or unimportant, singular or common. The process of transforming the material consequences of human lives into the archaeological record is indifferent to our accomplishments, class, wealth, or standing. Whoever we are, we all leave remains, traces of our existence in tools, trash, cherished items, houses, and so on. Those that history forgets or ignores, material remains remember and preserve. That is why our interest in the human past does not and cannot end with the invention of writing.

## VIKING ENGLAND

Located in modern York, England, Jorvik was the capital of an independent Viking kingdom of the same name from A.D. 866 to 954. Excavations in the Coppergate area of York, aimed at preserving information threatened by redevelopment, have brought to light many aspects of the lives of common people in Viking England (Hall 1984).

Much of what we know about the Vikings in general comes from their *sagas*—tales, eventually written down, that were usually embellished and exaggerated of their journeys of exploration, colonization, and conquest. Featured in these sagas, not coincidentally, are the lives of great explorers, colonizers, and conquerors like Eiric the Red and his son Leif.

But now we also know quite a bit about the daily lives of common, anonymous Viking people based on archaeological excavations at Cop-

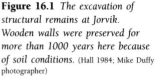

**Figure 16.1** *The excavation of structural remains at Jorvik. Wooden walls were preserved for more than 1000 years here because of soil conditions.* (Hall 1984; Mike Duffy photographer)

pergate (Figure 16.1). We know their diet included meat from cattle, goats, sheep, pigs, and chickens. Shellfish, especially oysters, made an important contribution to the diet, as did freshwater fish, including pike, bream, and perch and sea fish like herring, haddock, and cod. Plant foods also played a role in subsistence; wheat, rye, barley, and oats were important grains for making bread. Remains of apple, plum, blackberry, carrot, and celery were also recovered.

We even know that internal parasites plagued the population of this Viking settlement. Preserved eggs of two types of round worm that inhabit human intestinal tracts were discovered in the excavation of the "cess pits" where human excrement was dumped.

We also have many common objects of everyday Viking life. Antler and bone hair combs and cases, garter hooks, rings, padlocks and keys, pocket knives, and even leather shoes have been recovered at the excavated houses of Jorvik.

Also recovered were items associated with the play and recreational activities of these Viking common folk. Among the Coppergate artifacts were dice made of bone, perhaps used in gambling as they are today. Also found was a fragment of a gameboard not unlike that used in checkers and chess along with game pieces, although the actual game played is unknown.

Fragments of bone-bladed ice skates were also found. These were probably used like skis; the skater propelled him or herself along using wooden poles (history helps us here, as a twelfth-century written account describes the use of these skates). Finally, some simple musical instruments were found, including bone whistles, a lyre, and a panpipe with a five-note scale.

Though much more could be said about the investigation of this Viking site, you can see from this brief description how the archaeology of this historic settlement can help us understand how people lived even when history does not. Archaeology helps us to reconstruct the texture of their lives.

But what about even more recent times, when we are not forced to rely on semilegendary sources such as sagas but have an extensive documentary record? Does our examination of the human past end with the written evidence? Again, the answer is no.

## PARTING WAYS

Cato Howe, Prince Goodwin, Plato Turner, and Quamany were not famous men. They were not wealthy landowners. They did not write the documents that helped forge a new nation. They were not the generals who led brave men into battle to win the independence of this great nation. They were not talented artists who produced timeless works of art. They were not even infamous; they left no legacy of memorable criminality. Although they lived in an historic period, they were not the kind of people whom history exalts. No one wrote books about them—the nature of their lives, their hopes, aspirations, frustrations, or triumphs. They could not even write about themselves, for they were all illiterate. They might be labeled simply "common men," but in a sense they were not even this. Howe, Goodwin, Turner, and Quamany were all black men—freed slaves who lived first in the colony and then in the state of Massachusetts (Deetz 1976, 1977).

We know a little about them from some fragmentary records compiled by archaeologist James Deetz and his students. While slaves, all four served in the Continental Army in the Revolutionary War. Military records indicate, for example, that Quamany was just 17 years old when he enlisted. We also know that Prince Goodwin served for only three months and then deserted. All but Goodwin received their freedom in 1778 in return for their military service. Goodwin was freed in 1783 when Massachusetts emancipated all its slaves.

Beyond their military records, we do have a few other bits of historical evidence of these men's lives. Plymouth, Massachusetts, town records show that in 1792 Cato Howe was granted use of some ninety-four acres of land, where the other three men joined him. Town records again show that this settlement was called "New Guinea," and the men cleared land, built houses, married, and had children.

We even know that Cato Howe applied for a pension. To prove his need, his personal property was inventoried:

Real estate: None
Personal property: 1 cow, 1 pig, 5 chairs, 1 table, 2 kettles, 3 knives and
forks, 3 plates, 2 bowls, ax, hoe.
Total value: 27 dollars. (Deetz 1977:14)

When Howe died in 1824, his property was again inventoried in the town's probate records. By then his estate had swelled to a value of $62.82.

In just these few paragraphs, we have provided very close to the sum total of the written documentation of the lives of four human beings who lived little more than 200 years ago, men who were contemporaries of George Washington, Benjamin Franklin, and Thomas Jefferson, about whom dozens of books have been written. But this "history" of the famous tells us next to nothing about the lives of these other men. What was it like to be a freed slave in the North in the latter half of the eighteenth century? How did these people survive? How were they treated? How did they fit in as newly freed black Americans? For all that history tells us, their story might as well be prehistoric. What history has forgotten, however, the material record has remembered. The lives of Cato Howe, Prince Goodwin, Plato Turner, and Quamany may not have been "important" enough to rate historical mention, but their lives left a material record. Although their personal histories have been lost, the texture of their lives has been preserved.

In 1975, at a place today called Parting Ways—in 1783 called New Guinea—archaeologist Deetz initiated an investigation of the lives of these unexamined men. He found and excavated the house of Plato Turner.

The original Turner house, today just a cellar hole, was a small structure, just 12 feet square (Figure 16.2). Turner's grandson apparently added on another 12-foot section. Another cellar hole at Parting Ways also conforms to the 12-foot square pattern. This seemingly trivial fact—the size and shape of the house sections—is actually significant. Colonial houses tended to conform to a 16-foot standard. The Turner house, however, and the other cellar holes at Parting Ways, seem to indicate adherence to a 12-foot standard. As Deetz points out, this standard was common not to European colonial architecture but to houses built in West Africa, where many American slaves originated.

A great number of pottery fragments were recovered in the excavation. Remember, even though these men had been granted their freedom by the state of Massachusetts, they had not been guaranteed jobs or money. Ironically, slaves were often freed of legal servitude only to suffer the bondage of poverty. These men were no exception.

Much of the pottery found at Parting Ways, however, was of high quality and expensive. Deetz suggests that in all likelihood the people at Parting Ways were given crockery by the white inhabitants of Plymouth. The fine pottery at Parting Ways was too good for common whites

**Figure 16.2** *The foundation of Plato Turner's house at Parting Ways. The dimensions of the house are similar to West African structures of the same period.* (Courtesy Parting Ways and Plimoth Plantation; Ted Avery, photographer)

to have owned, so wealthy folks must have donated the pottery to the freed slaves. And the wealthy of Plymouth are probably the same people who had previously kept slaves. It is even possible that the white owners of these very slaves were the providers of the ceramics.

Beyond this, the settlement pattern at the site is instructive. Where colonial farmhouses were spread out, the homes at Parting Ways were clustered together. Although the ninety-four acres of the community were apportioned between the four men, their houses were built adjacent to one another. Here again, this pattern may be indicative of a continuing African cultural tradition. Instead of following a European pattern of private ownership of land, the people at Parting Ways may have been following an African tradition of corporate-communal land use. Thus, instead of being located separately on the plots that each man individually "owned," the houses were placed together in the middle of the land they all "owned" together.

Other aspects of the material culture, including earthenware pottery and some of the food remains, bear out these patterns of a West African cultural tradition. The persistence of African culture in people forcibly removed from their homeland is not something history cared to remember. But as Deetz says,

> It would be the height of ethnocentric arrogance to assume that people recently a part of a very different culture would, upon coming to America, immediately adopt an Anglo-American set of values, of ways of doing things, and of organizing their existence. (1977:148)

These facts and these lives have been victims of official indifference and cultural amnesia. Historical archaeology allows us to remember.

## THE LIGHTHOUSE

The lives of the people of the Lighthouse are remembered in legend and poetry:

> Where now grow the birch and alder,
> Hardy maple, oak, and walnut,
> Graceful hemlocks, lofty pine trees,
> Spreading up the shady hill-side,
> Hill-side stony, steep, and rocky,
> Was a ragged group of cabins,
> Dwelt in by a people blended,
> Partly white and partly Indian,
> Partly from the early settlers,
> And the vagabonds of travel . . .

**Figure 16.3** *Looking north along the Farmington River, we can see to the east the wooded hill where the hamlet called the Lighthouse was located.*

These words are from a lengthy poem published in 1952 by Lewis Sprague Mills, a well-known Connecticut educator, in the manner of Longfellow's *Hiawatha*. In it, Mills tells the legend of the Lighthouse, which ran as follows: In 1740 Molly Barber, a strong-willed young woman living in Wethersfield, Connecticut, rebeled against her father's command forbidding her marriage to a young suitor. To punish and embarrass her father, Molly eloped with another man, James Chaugham. As if the scandal of elopement were not enough, Chaugham was a Narragansett Indian, born on Block Island off the coast of Rhode Island.

Fearful of her father's reaction, the two ran off to the densely forested northwestern hills of Connecticut. There they settled on the west side of Ragged Mountain, on a terrace above the Farmington River in the modern town of Barkhamsted (Figure 16.3). According to the legend, they raised a large family of eight children in their wooded hideaway. Other displaced people, white and Indian as well as black, settled in their little village. As many as forty cabins or wigwams are supposed to have dotted the hillside as the village flourished.

In the early nineteenth century, a road was built within sight of the settlement as part of the turnpike from Albany, New York, to Hartford, Connecticut. Stagecoach drivers traveling from Albany to Hartford had to pass through miles of uninhabited forest; when they saw the hearth fires of the Chaugham settlement through the chinks in the walls of the roughly constructed houses, they knew they were just 5 miles from their resting stop, the small town of New Hartford, Connecticut. It was apparently these drivers who called the hamlet the "Lighthouse," and the name stuck.

Most of what we know about the Lighthouse settlement and the lives of its residents has been handed down in legend and oral history. The people who lived there were by and large outcasts and not the sort upon whom history focuses its attention.

According to the legend, for a time the settlement thrived. Several of Molly and James's children remained in the Lighthouse village, marrying and having children of their own. The inhabitants, as the story goes, hunted in the forest and fished in the river following the old Indian ways. They also raised crops and made baskets to sell to the ever-increasing number of white settlers moving into northwestern Connecticut in the nineteenth century. They buried their dead on a small knoll just south of the village; about fifty are supposed to be interred in the Lighthouse cemetery. James Chaugham died in about 1800. Molly lived to be 105 years old, dying in 1820. Both, says the legend, are buried on that knoll.

Molly Chaugham's strong personality seems to have been the glue that kept the settlement together. After her death, the village began to fall into decline, though it was inhabited for some time after. In 1854 an article appeared in a small local newspaper, the *Mountain County Herald*, concerning what was left of the Lighthouse village. The writer visited the spot and reported that just four or five crude shelters remained and only a handful of destitute people lived there, the last of the Lighthouse "tribe."

When the *Hartford Courant* carried an article about the fate of the Lighthouse in 1900, the writer commented on the lack of information about the actual history of the settlement and its people. He concluded: "Inquiries into its history, when they were made by curious eyes, came too late; the true story of one of the last Indian resorts in the State will, perhaps, never be unearthed."

"Unearthed" was an extremely appropriate term. For though there was little written about the Lighthouse during its existence and much of what we presume to know about it is legend, the Lighthouse village does survive as an archaeological site, providing a wonderful opportunity to investigate the lives of individuals whose histories were not written. How did this fascinating mixture of Indian, white, and black survive in the hills of northwestern Connecticut? How did the cultures of

**Figure 16.4** *Stone foundations are all that remain of the forty cabins that, legend says, made up the Lighthouse village.*

New England Indians, white European settlers, and former black African slaves mesh to produce a thriving settlement? What foods did they eat? What did their houses look like? What sort of religion did they practice? What was the nature of their relationship to others—both white and Indian—who lived in the northwestern hills of Connecticut? Legend focuses on the romantic aspects of Molly and James's elopement and is silent on these other points. For these reasons one of the authors (Feder 1988) has initiated an investigation to literally "unearth" the facts about the Lighthouse.

The actual site of the settlement was never forgotten; in fact, the Daughters of the American Revolution erected a plaque nearby in memory of the villagers. In the field seasons of 1990 and 1991 we conducted extensive excavations at the site. We have so far identified seven houses in the village. These structures had stone foundations and were relatively easy to find (Figure 16.4). Many of the other houses probably did not have durable foundations and so have left no obvious surface indications. Future excavation should result in the location of these other houses, if they did, in fact, exist.

We have also located an area with a number of upright unmarked fieldstones. This is likely to have been the cemetery mentioned in the legend; at least fifty and possibly more stones thought to be grave markers remain. To this day, on Memorial Day people still place American flags on these supposed graves.

The artifacts and features identified at this very early stage in the research are interesting, especially because they appear to reflect a mixture of Indian and European cultures. Artifacts recovered include an

English-style gunflint used in muskets, European whiteware crockery, and metal nails, along with typically Indian cutting and scraping tools of stone (Figure 16.5). Also, a large Indian mortar for grinding seeds into flour was discovered at the site.

The house remains are clearly a mixture of European colonial and native Indian architecture. Stone foundations are typical of European houses; but here the stonework is quite crude, and the size is very atypical. Remember the 16-foot standard size of colonial houses mentioned in our discussion of the Parting Ways settlement? Here again the foundations are smaller, ranging from 9 to 14 feet in their dimensions.

Interestingly, house foundations comparable in size and construction have been found on the other side of Connecticut on the Pequot Indian reservation. These also date to the eighteenth and nineteenth centuries. This evidence suggests that Indians may have been *adopting* European architectural patterns but *adapting* them to their own needs.

## HISTORICAL ARCHAEOLOGY AS ANTHROPOLOGY

It is undeniable that historic sites archaeology is in some ways different from prehistoric archaeology. In the former, we can attain a level of detail impossible in prehistory. We can know people's names. We may

**Figure 16.5** *Sample of artifacts from the Lighthouse site.* Top row, from left to right: *Large fragment of stoneware jug; kaolin clay pipe bowl fragment; kaolin clay pipe bowl and stem fragment.* Bottom row, from left to right: *Fragment of pewter tableware; three brass buttons; kaolin clay pipe bowl fragment.*

be able to obtain records of their lives. It is sometimes even possible to speak to living individuals who are old enough to remember life in what is now an archaeological site.

This merely means that the raw data of the historic sites archaeologist are a bit different from those of the prehistorian. It does not, however, make their anthropological research goals any different. The study of village life at Jorvik, the examination of the interplay of two cultures in contact and minority group cultural survival at Parting Ways, and the analysis of culture contact and the survival of outcast groups within a broader cultural pattern at the Lighthouse are all clearly part of anthropology. The fact that these sites are not truly "ancient" and were occupied by people living in literate cultures does not diminish our interest in them. Our anthropological scrutiny of the human story does not end at any chronological or cultural boundary.

## SUMMARY

Our interest in the human past does not end with the beginning of recent history. Historical archaeology focuses on sites from the recent human past. The historical record, although it can be quite detailed, does not necessarily tell the entire story. The material, archaeological record allows us to fill in gaps in our knowledge and to test the known historical record. This is especially useful when we are investigating the lives of common people who could not write and whose lives were deemed of insufficient interest to chronicle by those who could. The freed slaves of Parting Ways and the culturally and ethnically mixed population of the Lighthouse are examples. Analysis of the material record provides an avenue for the study of people in the recent past for whom history provides no voice.

## FOR MORE INFORMATION

For a detailed discussion of the excavations at Jorvik, see R. Hall's *The Excavations at York: The Viking Dig*. For more on Parting Ways in particular, as well as historical sites archaeology in general, James Deetz's *In Small Things Forgotten: The Archaeology of Early American Life* is the best source. Ivor Noël Hume's *Historical Archaeology* provides a useful introduction to the methods of the archaeology of the historical past. A fascinating account of the discovery and excavation of a colonial settlement can be found in Hume's *Martin's Hundred: The Discovery of a Lost Colonial Virginia Settlement*. The book *The Lighthouse: An Archaeological and Documentary Investigation of a Legend*, by Kenneth L. Feder, is currently in press.

# AN EVOLUTIONARY AFTERWORLD

*Lately it's occurred to me*
*What a long, strange trip it's been.*
*—The Grateful Dead*

We have depicted the evolution of all life on earth as a bush—enormous and incredibly complex. Stephen Gould's bush image captures perfectly the way we now think evolution occurs: by the production of countless adaptive experiments we call species, the twigs on the bush. Most are short-lived, but a few possess enough longevity to divide and give rise to still newer species, to sprout more twigs. In this book, we have focused on the story of the few twigs that make up our part of the evolutionary bush.

Life, and the earth on which it evolved, can be seen as an integrated whole, just as a bush is intimately and inextricably part of the environment in which it is rooted. Species of organisms, past and present, and the environments in which they live make up a truly living planet, on which each form of life depends for its survival on its adaptation to other forms of life and to the natural features of its environment. Although most of the species that have ever existed are now extinct, they are still part of that integrated whole. The evolutionary bush and our planet are as they are because these species once existed, just as the whole form of a bush depends on the specific pattern of its branching as it grows.

As you have seen, the hominids have been part of the evolutionary bush for a relatively short time. But one hominid, *Homo sapiens*, is now, in many ways, the dominant twig on the bush. Our twig is swollen far out of proportion to the others on the plant: There are nearly 6 billion of us. We live in every conceivable place on earth. We change the very face of the planet to suit our needs. And this success—if success it proves to be—is largely the result of an accident of evolution that has given us enormous and complex brains with their abilities to store massive amounts of information and to use that information to think and reason.

Many see this "gift" of conscious thought as an indication that humans are superior to the other forms of life on this planet. What more advanced adaptation could there be, they say, than the ability to think about things, including one's own origins? Such a philosophy creates an unbridgeable gulf between humans and other living things, a difference between "us" and "them" of kind rather than degree.

Such attitudes arise, of course, where a group of people have come to rely heavily on their ability to control natural resources in agricultural and civilized state societies. These attitudes also serve to justify the manipulation and exploitation of nature that is necessitated by such cultural systems. This sense of human superiority is seldom found among hunter-gatherers, who see themselves as part of, rather than above and in control of, the natural world.

A belief in the superiority of our species is often incorporated into a society's religious system, where it is seen as having been bestowed on us by a higher authority and where it then easily influences, if not determines, the behavior of future generations. In the Judeo-Christian tradition of Western agricultural societies, God clearly tells Noah and his sons that all the beasts of the earth, sea, and air are "delivered" into their hands and that "every moving thing that liveth shall be meat for you" (Genesis 9:2,3). So much did Europe, in fact, rely on animals for food and labor that extensions of this attitude moved into philosophical-scientific areas. The famous French thinker René Descartes held that animals were mere machines, incapable of thought or even sensation.

We now have sufficient scientific information to understand that these ideas have no basis in fact and indeed are, to say the least, counterproductive. Our modern view of evolution as a bush shows us clearly that we are in no way the inevitable culmination of evolution. Evolution could have happened in countless thousands of other ways. Our physical and genetic closeness to the other primates tells us that the differences between us and them are differences of degree, not kind. We must see our major adaptation—our brain—in the same light as we see the major adaptations of any living thing. The cheetah's swiftness, the eagle's visual acuity, the peppered moth's camouflage, and our complex brain are all no more and no less than means to survival that the processes of evolution have provided our respective species.

Moreover, we also now understand the interrelated nature of all life on earth. The evolutionary bush persists because its twigs support one another according to the principles of ecological relationships. We may have the ability to understand and control many aspects of the natural world, but we must not forget that we arose from that world and are still, despite our sense of superiority, a part of that world, dependent ultimately on its resources and thus on its continuation.

In this regard, we believe, as do many, that evolution has placed on our shoulders not only a large brain but along with it a responsibility of guardianship over our planet. Our ability to exploit and control nature doesn't give us the right to do so without limits or moral considerations. Nor are such activities justified because they happen to fill our needs at the moment. Ironically, though, the growing recognition of this responsibility has come about at the very time we are accelerating our destruction of the earth and of many twigs on the evolutionary bush.

The list of species we have hunted to extinction is depressingly long. Not long after our species first arrived in the New World, hunting contributed to the complete demise of some thirty-five genera of American mammals. More recently, the dodo of Mauritius, the passenger pigeon of North America, and the Tasmanian wolf, to name but a few, have all been hunted to extinction. And the list of species still living but currently endangered by human predation is even longer. It includes many of the African big-game animals, species we thought so numerous as to be eternal.

Yet hunting is not nearly the most significant impact we have. Much more important is habitat destruction. If you think back over the story of our past, you see a clear trend. As we evolved bigger brains and greater intelligence, our cultures became more complex and our populations grew. We made greater demands on our environments. At first, we manipulated those environments simply. Our earliest ancestors knocked a few flakes off a rock, creating an edge sharper and more durable than the teeth and nails biological evolution provided us. Such tools allowed us to procure more efficiently the plants and animals we used for food and as raw materials for various artifacts.

Our manipulation and exploitation of the environment took a great leap forward when later ancestors began to build shelters and control fire. More resources were required from the environment. Fire, along with better tools, allowed us to kill larger numbers of animals. Later still the shift from food gathering to food production literally began reshaping the landscape to human specifications.

Finally, in the development of civilization and the state, new patterns of social and political integration allowed for dense population aggregations and communal works like irrigation and road building, with associated environmental impacts never before even possible. The history of culture has thus been one of increasing control, of the ever-greater human ability to rework and shape the world to fit our needs, real and perceived.

But the effects of these environmental impacts, even in ancient times, have been two-sided. For example, irrigation played a significant role in the development of Mesopotamian civilization, but resulting salinization of the soil rendered much of the land useless for agriculture.

More recently, short-term benefits have been derived from clearing tropical forests to create farmland, damming rivers to produce reservoirs or rerouting them for irrigation, or carving up large sections of the earth to extract resources. But these activities can have dire results, including the extinction of other species. In the United States alone, some 300,000 acres per year of freshwater wetlands are drained for farming and building. Overall, 1 million acres of wildlife habitats are lost every year to development. Because we have no precise idea how many species of living things exist, estimates vary on the number of species becoming extinct, but they range from one species of plant or animal per day to the incredible figure of one species per hour. Indeed, the human twig on the evolutionary bush has become the dominant one at least in part through our destruction and replacement of other living things with which we once shared the earth.

The ultimate irony is that our understanding and control over nature may now lead to our directly bringing about the end of 4 billion years of evolution. Within the last century, we have come to understand the basic forces of the universe contained within the nucleus of the atom. We have tapped into those forces to generate electrical energy, diagnose and treat illnesses, and, tragically, to create weapons of terrifying destructive power. In a matter of minutes, we can destroy what evolution took billions of years to produce.

One of the major conclusions to be drawn from the study of the past is that no species is permanent. All species undergo change, and all ultimately become extinct. The human species is no exception. We were not destined to evolve, and we are not destined to last forever. We share that fate with all other living things, past, present, and future.

That accident of evolution, our big brain, however, makes us capable of understanding our world to a degree far greater than any other species. We use our brain to exploit and manipulate nature, but we also have an obligation to use it to devise ways we can survive—as we have a right to—and yet still protect our planet and share it with our fellow species.

We humans—the tip of a short twig—must live with the awesome knowledge that we have in our power the ability, with our conscious consent, to uproot the rest of the bush of evolution that supports us. Only by fully understanding our world, as it is now and as it was in the past, can we hope to prevent that. Toward that hope, we have addressed this book.

## FOR MORE INFORMATION

Only when a majority of the world's almost 6 billion people change their attitudes toward the issues addressed in this afterword will the earth and *all* its inhabitants be able to live without the threat of the accelerated destruction of the environment and extinction of organisms that our species has brought about.

How (and if) that change in attitude may happen remains to be seen. There are, though, a number of organizations committed to educating the public and to directly dealing with some of the threats we humans have posed to our world, and thus to ourselves. Some of the most successful are:

- The World Wildlife Fund (1250 Twenty-Fourth Street, NW, Washington, D. C. 20037), focusing on the protection of living creatures and their environments worldwide.
- Greenpeace USA (1436 U Street, NW, Washington, D. C. 20009), aimed at protecting the environment, especially the oceans and marine animals.
- The National Audubon Society (950 Third Avenue, New York, NY 10022), one of the nation's oldest conservation organizations, dedicated to the protection of America's wildlife.
- People for the Ethical Treatment of Animals (P.O. Box 42516, Washington, D. C. 20015), fighting any form of cruelty to animals and advocating the idea that our fellow creatures share our basic rights.
- Survival International (2121 Decatur Place, NW, Washington, D. C. 20008), an organization dedicated to the protection of the world's tribal people and their ways of life.
- Amnesty International (322 Eighth Avenue, New York, NY 10001), working to promote human rights for all the world's people.
- The Jane Goodall Institute for Wildlife Research, Education and Conservation (P.O. Box 26846, Tucson, AR 85726), headed by the famous chimpanzee behaviorist and working to promote those things indicated in its title.
- The Sierra Club (330 Pennsylvania Ave. SE, Washington, D. C. 20003), a broad-based organization that promotes the preservation and appreciation of wilderness.
- The Archaeological Conservancy (415 Orchard Drive, Sante Fe, NM 87501), a group committed to the preservation of America's past through the novel approach of buying land with significant archaeological resources in order to preserve them.

There are many more organizations with similar goals. For more information on the work of any of the groups we have listed here, simply write to the addresses provided. Certainly, if evolution has provided us with the capability to destroy our planet, we also are endowed with the intelligence to preserve it. These organizations are a testament to that hope.

# GLOSSARY OF HUMAN AND NONHUMAN PRIMATES

*Adapidae* (ah-dá-pi-day)  Group of early primates from the then-connected landmass of North America and Europe, dating to more than 50 mya and thought to be ancestral to lemurs and lorises.

*Aegyptopithecus* (ee-gyp'-tah-pith'-ah-cuss)  Fossil species of an extinct monkey with several ape-like characteristics. Discovered in Egypt, *Aegyptopithecus* dates to more than 25 mya and may represent a form of primate ancestral to Old World monkeys and apes.

*Anthropoidea* (an-throw-poid'-ee-ah)  One of the two suborders of the order *Primates* (the other suborder is *Prosimii*). *Anthropoidea* means "humanlike" and includes monkeys, apes, and humans.

*Australopithecus afarensis* (os-trail-oh-pith'-ah-cuss af-far-en'-sis)  Fossil species from East Africa presumed by many to be the oldest known fossil in the human line. Dating to more than 3.5 mya, *afarensis* had a small, chimplike brain of around 440 ml but walked almost fully upright.

*Australopithecus africanus* (os-trail-oh-pith'-ah-cuss af-frih-can'-us)  A bipedal fossil species of *Australopithecus* more recent than *afarensis*. With its mean brain size of about 450 ml, *africanus* first appeared about 3 mya and seems to represent one of three possible lines that descended from *Australopithecus afarensis*. *Africanus* became extinct about 2.3 mya.

*Australopithecus boisei* (os-trail-oh-pith'-ah-cuss boys'-ee-eye)  The East African robust form of *Australopithecus, boisei* lived from about 2 to 1 mya. It possessed huge molars and a sagittal crest, both indicative of a powerful chewing ability. This, in turn, may indicate a diet focused on tough materials like seeds. It was fully bipedal and its mean brain size was 515 ml.

*Australopithecus robustus* (os-trail-oh-pith'-ah-cuss row-bust'-us)  The southern African robust form of *Australopithecus* dating from 2.2 to about 1.5 mya. Its large teeth and sagittal crest probably indicate a diet composed of tough items like seeds. Like the other Australopithecines, it was bipedal. Its mean brain size was 520 ml.

*Catarrhini* (cat-ah-rhine'-eye)  One of two infraorders of the suborder *Anthropoidea* (the other infraorder is *Platyrrhini*). *Catarrhini* is the infraorder of the Old World monkeys, apes, and hominids. Along with this geographic distinction, members of *Catarrhini* can be distinguished from *Platyrrhini* by nose shape, tooth patterns, and for some, tail function.

*Cercopithecidae* (sir-co-pith'-ah-sigh'-day)  The taxonomic family of all monkeys of Europe, Africa, and Asia.

*Cercopithecoidea* (sir-co-pith'-ah-coy'-dee-ah)  The taxonomic superfamily of all monkeys of Europe, Africa, and Asia.

*Dryopithecus* (dry-oh-pith'-ah-cuss)  Name given to a group of fossil apes that appear to have been adapted to forested areas of Europe and Africa between 10 and 15 mya. Though physically different in many respects from modern apes, the dryopithecines have teeth that exhibit detailed similarities to those of modern apes.

*Eoanthropus* (ee-oh-an'-throw-pus)  The "Dawn Man." Taxonomic genus of the Piltdown fossil "discovered" in 1912. *Eoanthropus* had a very humanlike cranium but an apelike jaw, fulfilling the expectations of many in the early part of this century concerning the appearance of early humans. It was later proven to be a fraud— an amalgamation of a modern human skull and an actual ape jaw. The name is no longer valid.

*Gigantopithecus* (ji-gan-toh-píth-ah-cuss)  Genus name for fossil apes, from 12 to perhaps 1 mya, probably a ramapithecine, that reached a height of 12 feet and weight of 1200 pounds.

*Hominidae* (hom-in'-ah-day)  The taxonomic family of modern and fossil human beings, including forms now extinct. Members of the family *Hominidae* are called hominids.

*Hominoidea* (hom-in-oy'-dee-ah)  The taxonomic superfamily that includes the large, tailless primates: apes and humans.

*Homo erectus* (ho'-mow ee-wreck'-tuss)  Fossil hominid species dating from about 1.8 million to as late as 250,000 years ago. First appearing in Africa, *erectus* seems to have been the first hominid species to expand its population beyond Africa. Members of this species possessed a mean brain size of 1000 ml—about two-thirds that of modern humans—made great advances in stone tool technology, and probably were able to control fire toward the end of their evolutionary existence.

*Homo habilis* (ho'-mow ha'-bill-us)  Fossil hominid species dating from about 2.5 to 1.5 mya. Fully bipedal, and with a mean brain size of 680 ml, about half that of modern humans, *habilis* was the first confirmed hominid who made and used stone tools. *Homo habilis* and the Australopithecines represented by *africanus, robustus,* and *boisei* probably represent distinct but temporally overlapping branches on the evolutionary bush. *Australopithecus afarensis* is the most likely common ancestor.

*Homo neanderthalensis* (ho'-mow knee-an'-dir-tall-en'-sis)  Taxonomic label once applied to the Neandertal fossils. This placed the Neandertals in a different species from modern humans, an exaggeration of some of the then recognized differences between the Neandertals and modern people. Based on very recent research, however, some have suggested reinstituting this name, indicating that previous scholars may have been right about the level of difference between the Neandertals and modern humans, though for the wrong reasons.

*Homo sapiens* (ho'-mow say'-pee-ens)  Genus and species of human beings. Includes archaic and anatomically modern forms (see *Homo sapiens, archaic* and *Homo sapiens sapiens*).

*Homo sapiens,* **archaic** (ho'-mow say'-pee-ens)  Fossil hominid species dating from as much as 400,000 to about 35,000 ya. Their mean brain size of 1200 ml falls within the modern human range, though at the low end. Known primarily from a number of skulls, archaic *Homo sapiens* possessed a larger, more rounded skull than *erectus* but retained a number of primitive traits, including large brow ridges and generally thick cranial bones.

*Homo sapiens neanderthalensis* (ho'-mow say'-pee-ens knee-an'-dir-tall-en'-sis)  An archaic form of *Homo sapiens* dating from about 125,000 to as late as 35,000 ya. They have been found primarily in Europe and Southwest Asia, though Neandertal-like specimens are known from Africa. Physically adapted to cold conditions, *Homo sapiens neanderthalensis,* with a mean brain size of about 1500 ml, larger than modern humans, seems to represent an extinct side branch of the human evolutionary bush, having been replaced by coexisting anatomically modern human beings who evolved in Africa and spread out from there.

*Homo sapiens sapiens* (ho'-mow say'-pee-ens say'-pee-ens) Anatomically modern human beings. Though great physical variation exists, all modern human beings belong under this heading. *Homo sapiens sapiens* seems now to have first appeared more than 100,000 ya. From its first appearance in Africa, it spread, replacing archaic groups of *Homo sapiens* in Europe and Asia. The mean brain size of modern humans is about 1400 ml, with a very broad range of 1000 to 2200 ml for normal adults.

*Hylobatidae* (high-low-bat'-ah-day) Taxonomic family that includes the gibbons and siamangs, the arboreal, so-called lesser apes of Southeast Asia. They are highly efficient brachiators.

*Macaca* (mah-cah'-cah) A highly successful genus within the family *Cercopithecoidea* (Old World monkeys), with representatives found from North Africa to Europe, to Japan.

*Omomyidae* (oh-mow-me'-ah-day) One group of early primates that lived in the then-connected landmass of North America and Europe. Dating to more than 50 mya, they are ancestral to tarsiers and may have been ancestral to *Anthropoidea*: monkeys, apes, and humans.

*Papio* (pay'-pee-oh) A genus within the superfamily *Cercopithecoidea* (the Old World monkeys). They are the baboons, large monkeys living in substantial social groups on the African savannas.

*Paranthropus* (par-án-throw-puss) Alternative genus name for the robust australopithecines, *Australopithecus robustus* and *Australopithecus boisei.*

*Pithecanthropus erectus* (pith-ah-can'-throw-pus ee-wreck'-tus) Literally, "upright ape-man." This was the original designation given to fossils found in Java (Java Man) and China (Peking Man) now labeled *Homo erectus.*

*Platyrrhini* (plat-ah-rhine'-eye) One of two infraorders of the suborder *Anthropoidea* (the other infraorder is *Catarrhini*). *Platyrrhini* is the infraorder of New World monkeys. Along with this geographic distinction, members of *Platyrrhini* can be distinguished from *Catarrhini* by the presence of prehensile tails in some groups, nose shape, and tooth patterns.

*Pongidae* (pon'-jih-day) Taxonomic family of the so-called great apes. Members of this family include chimpanzees, gorillas, and orangutans. They are all large, highly intelligent creatures.

*Primates* (pry-mate'-ees) Order within class *Mammalia.* Large-brained arboreal mammals with stereoscopic color vision and grasping hands and feet.

*Prosimii* (pro-sim'-ee-eye) One of two suborders of the order *Primates* (the other suborder is *Anthropoidea*). Prosimians are the more primitive of the two suborders in the sense that they retain features of some of the oldest fossil primates of more than 50 mya. The first primates, therefore, were prosimians.

*Ramapithecus* (ram-ah-pith'-ah-cuss) Fossil species known from Africa, southeastern Europe, and western Asia dating from 10 to 15 mya. Although at one time thought to have been a hominid ancestral to the *Australopithecus* line, we now know that *Ramapithecus* was a ground-dwelling form of ape that may have given rise to the living forms of the great apes.

*Sivapithecus* (she'-vah-pith-ah-cuss) The name now given to *Ramapithecus*-like fossils from India and Pakistan. It has been suggested that *Sivapithecus* is ancestral to the modern orangutan.

# GLOSSARY OF TERMS

**absolute dating** Any dating technique in which a specific age, year, or range of years can be assigned to an object or site. See *relative chronological sequence*.

**Acheulian** A toolmaking tradition of *Homo erectus* in Europe and Africa. Includes hand axes, cleavers, and flake tools.

**adaptation** The adjustment of an organism to a particular set of environmental circumstances.

**adapted** See *adaptation*.

**aerial photography** Low- and high-altitude photography in an archaeological site survey. Especially useful when topographic or subtle vegetational changes have resulted from the presence of archaeological features.

**Agricultural Revolution** See *Food-Producing Revolution*.

**allele** A variant of a genetic **locus**. Most loci possess more than one allele, the different alleles conveying different instructions for the development of a certain phenotype (for example, blue eyes versus brown eyes and type O versus type A versus type B blood).

**allele frequency** The percentage of times a certain allele appears in a population relative to the other possible alleles at the same genetic **locus**.

**amino acid** The chief component of proteins; the building block of all life.

**analogy** In evolution, a trait that is similar in function in two or more species but that is unrelated evolutionarily. See *homology*.

**anthropological linguistic** The anthropological study of language and languages.

**anthropology** The holistic and integrative study of people. Anthropology includes the study of human biology, human physical evolution, human cultural evolution, and human adaptation.

**arboreal** Living in or adapted to life in trees.

**archaeology** A branch of anthropology focusing on human cultural evolution through the study of the material remains of past societies.

**artifact** Any object, usually found at an archaeological site, that was made by humans.

**artificial selection** The process in which human beings choose those members of a plant or animal species that will live and reproduce and those that will not. Animals or plants are "selected" that possess characteristics desirable to humans.

**association** Objects found together in the same archaeological or geological stratum in proximity to one another are said to be in association.

**Aurignacian**  A toolmaking tradition of anatomically modern *Homo sapiens* of the European Upper **Paleolithic**. Includes stone and bone spear points.

**australopithecines**  A small-brained **hominid** from 4 to 1 mya that represents the ancestors of all later hominids and several extinct hominid branches.

**basicrania**  The bones of the base of the skull.

**biological anthropology**  See *physical anthropology*.

**bipedal**  The ability to walk on two feet.

**brachiate**  The ability to swing through trees, using arms and hands.

**breeding population**  A population within a species with some degree of genetic isolation from other populations of that species.

**Bronze Age**  The period in European prehistory when people began making bronze tools.

**burin**  A chisellike stone tool used in engraving bone, ivory, or antler.

**carbon dating**  A **radiometric dating** technique using the decay rate of a **radioactive isotope** of carbon found in organic remains.

**carrying capacity**  The number of organisms a given habitat or region can support.

**catastrophist**  Adherent to the hypothesis of catastrophism—that the world was produced through a series of catastrophic events, usually including Noah's flood.

**Chavin**  An art and iconographic style that appeared about 3000 ya and spread across previously culturally separate groups living in a series of river valleys in the western Andes in Peru. Chavin apparently set the stage for the development of larger, politically united entities in western South America.

**Châttleperonian**  A stone tool industry associated with late Neandertals in Europe. It appears to reflect an amalgam of the older Neandertal **Mousterian** industry and the **Aurignacian** of anatomically modern humans.

**chromosome**  A strand of **DNA** in the nucleus of a cell that carries genetic information passed down to subsequent generations.

**city-state**  A large, politically complex entity, including a central dense population with surrounding villages owing allegiance to the city. The early civilization of Mesopotamia was characterized by the presence of city-states.

**civilization**  Here, used to label cultures with an ag-ricultural surplus, social stratification, labor specialization, rule by power, monumental construction projects, and a system of record keeping. Cultures evolved into early civilizations in a number of world areas from local **Neolithic** adaptations.

**cline**  A geographic continuum in the variation of a specific phenotype.

**codominance**  When neither allele of a gene pair is dominant and both are expressed in the organism.

**codon**  A section of the **DNA** molecule that codes for a particular **amino acid**.

**comparative biology**  The study of the similarities and differences among animal and plant species.

**comparative collection**  A bone library. A collection of animal bones with which archaeological specimens can be compared to determine species, six, age at death, and health status.

**comparative osteology**  Comparing the bones of different animal species. A comparative osteological collection is a library of bones used in the identification of bone remains recovered at archaeological or paleontological sites.

**coprolite**  Ancient preserved fecal remains.

**coprology**  The study of coprolites. Useful in the reconstruction of ancient diets.

**core**  A stone nucleus that can be shaped into a tool or can serve as a source of stone flakes capable of being used either unaltered or modified for specific functions.

**creation myth**  Story that accounts for the origin, early history, and world view of a society.

**creationist**  Anyone who believes that a supernatural power was directly or indirectly responsible for the origin of the universe, the earth, and, especially, living things.

**cultural anthropology**  The branch of anthropology that focuses on culture. **Archaeology, ethnography,** and **anthropological linguistics** are included in cultural anthropology.

**cultural evolution**  Changes in cultural patterns through time.

**cultural technique**  A dating method that is based on cultural comparisons and the processes of culture change. A site may be dated based on the degree of similarity between the artifacts found there and those from other sites where absolute dates have been derived. Cultural dating techniques also include **seriation**.

**culture** Nongenetic means of adaptation. The sum total of those things people invent or develop and then pass down, including political, social, technological, economic, and ideological systems.

**deduction** A step in the scientific method. After developing a *general* explanation (called a **hypothesis**) from *specific* observations (the process of **induction**), those things that must be true (new data) if the hypothesis is valid are suggested and tested for. This final step is called deduction.

**deme** A genetically isolated population within a species; generally, the same as a **breeding population** and often physically distinguishable. See *breeding population, polytypic, race, subspecies.*

**dendrochronology** A dating technique based on the unique, nonrepeating sequence of tree-ring widths.

**deviation amplification** A small change in one part of a cultural system results in larger changes in the rest of the culture, which cause the original change to become increased. The development of agriculture and civilization are deviation amplification processes.

**diaphysis** The shaft of a long bone—for example, femur, humerus, tibia (pl. *diaphyses*).

**differential reproduction** When some individuals of a species are more successful than others at surviving, attracting mates, producing offspring, and hence passing down their characteristics. See *natural selection.*

**diffusion** The geographic movement of cultural traits or ideas; the sharing of these traits among societies.

**DNA** Deoxyribonucleic acid. The molecule that contains the genetic code.

**DNA hybridization** A method for establishing the biological distance between species based on the ability of strands of DNA from each species to bond to one another.

**domesticate** To domesticate a plant or animal is to change, through **artificial selection**, its wild form to a form more useful to humans. The end-product species is also called a domesticate.

**domestication** The process of making a plant or animal more useful to humans through **artificial selection**.

**dominance hierarchy** A social pattern seen in animal species in which certain individuals have preferential access to food, mates, and social activities.

**dominant** Of a pair of alleles, the one that is expressed in the **heterozygous** condition.

**ecofact** Item found at an archaeological site that shows evidence of human activity but not manufacture. A deer bone showing tool-cut marks, seeds stored in a clay vessel, and wood intentionally burned in a fireplace are examples of ecofacts.

**egalitarian** Societies in which, within the same age–sex categories, all people are more or less equal in terms of wealth, social standing, and authority.

**electrical resistivity survey** A noninvasive procedure used in archaeological survey where an electrical current is passed through the ground. Variations in soil resistance to the current are used to pinpoint the location of archaeological artifacts or features.

**endocast** A natural or artificially made cast or model of the interior of a fossil skull. In nature, loose material may fill a skull and harden, producing a model of the surface of the brain the skull housed. In the lab, latex or similar material can be poured into the skull or painted onto the interior surface, again producing a model of the surface of the brain.

**endogamy** Marriage restricted to those within the same social group. Exogamy is marriage restricted to those outside the social group.

**environmental determinism** The notion, popular in the nineteenth century, that the nature of the environment directly determines the technological level a culture will attain. Determinists assumed that more challenging environments would produce more developed cultures.

**enzyme** A **protein** in the body that causes and in part controls chemical processes.

**epiphyseal union** The fusion during growth of the ends of long bones (**epiphyses**) to the shafts (**diaphyses**).

**epiphysis** The end or cap of a long bone. Long bones have two epiphyses.

**estrus** The period during which a female is fertile. The signals indicating this condition to males of the species.

**ethnoarchaeology** Conducting ethnographic research among a living people from the perspective of an archaeologist, focusing on the processes by which people's behavior becomes translated into the archaeological record.

**ethnocentric** Judging another society's values in terms of one's own social values.

**ethnography** A subfield within **cultural anthropology** that involves the intensive study of a group of people. The ethnographer lives with a group of people, often for a number of years. Ethnography is also the term applied to the written work produced by an ethnographer.

**ethology** The study of the natural behavior of organisms under natural conditions.

**evolution** Systematic change through time, especially with reference to biological change among organisms and cultural change among social systems.

**faunal analysis** The examination of animal remains from archaeological sites. Faunal analysis is helpful in the reconstruction of diet, seasonality, and subsistence technology.

**feature** An element of an archaeological site, generally composed of **artifacts** and/or **ecofacts**. Features reflect an activity or set of activities. Trash pits, fireplaces, graves, and stone tool manufacturing stations are all examples of features.

**field survey** The process whereby archaeological sites are discovered in the field. Surface walkovers, **test pits**, and **aerial photography** are important aspects of field survey.

**fission** The division, or splitting up, of a **breeding population**.

**flake** Stone fragment removed from a **core**. Flakes with sharp points or edges may be used as tools without modification or can be further shaped and/or sharpened for use.

**flotation** Technique of archaeological analysis in which organic and nonorganic remains are separated from their surrounding soil by placing the recovered remains in a liquid.

**Food-Producing Revolution** The same as the **Agricultural Revolution**. The slow change, beginning after 12,000 ya, of a shift from foraging to food production among human groups, through the process of **domestication**.

**forager** See *hunter-gatherer*.

**foraminifera** Microscopic marine organisms whose exoskeletons are used in the analysis of the oxygen isotope ratio in seawater. This ratio varies in proportion to the amount of the earth's water that is contained in land-based **glaciers**.

**founder effect** Differences in an isolated population of a species caused by the characteristics of those individuals who randomly established the isolate.

**gamete sampling** The form of **genetic drift** that operates when genes are passed on to offspring in proportions not like those of the parental population.

**gamete** The cells of sexual reproduction, for example, sperm and eggs.

**gene** Generally, the portion of the DNA molecule that codes for a specific trait. **Locus** is now the preferred term.

**gene flow** The exchange of genes among populations of a species through interbreeding.

**gene pool** All alleles within a population.

**generalized** Refers to a species that is adapted to a wide range of environmental niches. See *specialized*.

**genetic drift** The change in **allele frequencies** caused by random fluctuations within a population through time.

**genetic engineering** Any intentional human manipulation of the mechanism of inheritance of some organism, especially of human beings.

**genetics** The study of the mechanism of inheritance and the physical results of that mechanism.

**genome** The total genetic endowment of a species.

**genotype** The alleles possessed by an organism.

**glacial** See *glacial period*.

**glacial period** Phases of the **Pleistocene Epoch** during which worldwide temperature dropped and substantial, long-term glacial expansion occurred. There have been as many as eighteen separate glacial periods during the last 1.6 million years, each lasting thousands of years. See *interglacial*.

**glacier** A massive body of ice that, through a number of processes, can expand and move.

**gradualism** The approach in evolution that views change as slow and cumulative. See *punctuated equilibrium*.

**grooming** The practice among social primates in which one animal cleans the fur of another; helps promote social cohesion.

**half-life**   The amount of time it takes for half of a **radioactive isotope** to decay to a stable one.

**hammerstone**   A stone used to strike a stone core or nucleus in order either to shape the core into a tool or remove flakes, which can then serve as tools.

**hand axe**   A bifacial, all-purpose stone tool produced by *Homo erectus,* axelike in shape.

**Hardy–Weinberg equilibrium**   The formula that shows genotypic percentages within a population under hypothetical conditions of no evolutionary change.

**heterozygous**   Possessing two different alleles in a gene pair.

**holistic**   In anthropology, viewing a culture as an interconnected whole rather than as a group of distinct, disconnected behaviors.

**Holocene**   The modern geological epoch. The Holocene began about 10,000 ya with the end of the **Pleistocene.**

**hominid**   Any member of the taxonomic family *Hominidae.* Anatomically modern human beings and our ancestors. The bipedal primate.

**hominid radiation**   The expansion of the hominids out of Africa, where they initially evolved, into Europe and Asia close to 1 mya.

**homology**   In evolution, a trait shared by two or more species through inheritance from a common ancestor. See *analogy.*

**homozygous**   Possessing two of the same allele in a gene pair.

**humerus**   Upper-arm bone (pl. *humeri*).

**hunter-gatherer**   A society that relies on naturally occurring sources of food.

**hyoid**   Horseshoe-shaped bone in the front of throat. Its form and position may provide insights into the ability of members of a species to speak.

**hypothesis**   In the scientific method, an educated guess to explain a natural phenomenon that subsequently undergoes testing. See *theory.*

**induction**   A step in the scientific method. The process of developing a *general* explanation (called a **hypothesis**) from *specific* observations.

**inheritance of acquired characteristics**   Now discredited idea that traits acquired during the lifetime of an individual organism could be passed on to its offspring. This idea was once proposed as a mechanism for biological adaptive evolution.

*in situ*   In place. An **artifact, ecofact,** or **feature** that remains in its exact place of discovery is said to be *in situ.*

**intelligence**   The relative ability of an organism to take in, store, process, and utilize information from the environment.

**interglacial**   Long-term phases during the **Pleistocene** between glacial periods, when glacial ice receded and worldwide temperature increased.

**interstadial**   Short-term, relatively minor periods of glacial retreat during longer phases of general glacial advance (**glacial periods**).

**K/Ar dating**   Potassium/argon dating. Absolute dating technique based on the decay of a **radioactive isotope** of potassium into argon. Often used to date volcanic rock that can be stratigraphically related to archaeological materials. The long **half-life** of the radioactive isotope of potassium renders the technique useful generally only for materials more than 100,000 years old. It is often applied to fossil hominid sites.

**Laurasia**   Former northern landmass made up of present-day North American and Eurasia. Where primates first evolved 65 mya.

**law of superposition**   Stratigraphic law that the more recent layers are superimposed over the older ones.

**Levallois**   Tool technology involving striking uniform flakes from a prepared stone core. Began about 200,000 ya.

**living floor**   Generally uncovered through excavation, the living floor represents the actual surface lived on by the prehistoric inhabitants of the site.

**locus**   The location on a chromosome of the genetic code for a specific trait (pl. *loci*).

**Lower Paleolithic**   See *Paleolithic.*

**Lower Pleistocene**   The first part of the **Pleistocene** Epoch from 1.5 mya to 780,000 ya.

**Lung Shan**   The name given to the first fully agricultural group in China, dating to about 6000 ya.

**macromutation**   Change in a large number of genes, or in a small number of important genes, with extensive physical results. See *mutation.*

**magnetic probe**   A noninvasive procedure in archaeological site survey involving the search for subsurface magnetic anomalies resulting from buried archaeological objects.

**manuport**   An object, usually stone, which, although

unmodified by humans or human ancestors, is assumed to have been used by hominids because it has been found at an archaeological site, removed from its natural source.

**matrilocal** A type of society where a married couple lives with the wife's family.

**meiosis** The process of cell division in which **gametes** are produced, each with half the normal number of chromosomes for that species.

**Mesolithic** Designation of cultures in Europe at the end of the **Pleistocene** and before the **Agricultural Revolution**. Adaptations of the Mesolithic usually reflect a change from those of the **Paleolithic** as plant and animal communities changed with the waning of the glaciers.

**messenger ribonucleic acid (mRNA)** The form of ribonucleic acid that carries that genetic code out of the cell nucleus and into the cytoplasm where it is translated into proteins.

**Middle Paleolithic** See *Paleolithic.*

**Middle Pleistocene** The second phase of the **Pleistocene Epoch** from 780,000 to 200,000 ya.

**Minoan** Name of the earliest civilization in Europe. Centered on the island of Crete and beginning about 3900 ya, it appears to have been a **city-state** with Knossos as its capital.

**mitochondrial DNA** Genetic material contained in the mitochondria of cells. This DNA does not play a role in inheritance. Analysis of mitochrondrial DNA (mtDNA) of modern humans has provided researchers with an estimate for the age of anatomically modern *Homo sapiens.*

**mitosis** The process of cell division that produces exact copies of the original cell.

**monogenic** A trait coded for by a single locus.

**Mousterian** The **Middle Paleolithic** culture associated with the European Neandertals that included a unifacial flake tool technology.

**multiregional hypothesis** The hypothesis that anatomically modern human beings evolved more or less independently in a number of different geographic areas. See *replacement hypothesis.*

**mutation** Any change in an organism's genetic material.

**Mycenaean** Refers to the civilization in Greece that followed that of the Minoans and preceded that of the Greek city-states.

**myth** A story, usually invoking the supernatural, to account for a society's origin and early history.

**Natufian** The Upper **Paleolithic**, Early **Neolithic** culture of Southwest Asia, dating from 12,000 to 10,000 ya.

**natural selection** Evolution based on the relative reproductive success of individuals within a species, the degree of success determined by the individual's adaptive fitness. See *differential reproduction.*

**neocortex** The part of the brain of complex organisms responsible for memory and thought, in other words, for **intelligence**.

**Neolithic** The "New Stone Age," characterized by **domestication** of plants and animals.

**neoteny** Literally, "holding onto youth." The retention, in adults of one species, of the juvenile features of an evolutionarily related species.

**niche** Often referred to as the "ecological address" of an organism, this is the actual space inhabited by an organism as well as its functional place in a community of organisms—where it lives as well as what it does to make a living.

**notochord** A long cartilaginous rod that supports the body and protects the dorsal nerve. The evolutionary precursor of the vertebral column.

**nuclear DNA** The genetic material contained in the nucleus of a cell. See *DNA.*

**nuclear family** The family unit made up of parents and their offspring.

**occipital** The bone of the rear of the skull. The occiput tends to be rounded and smooth in anatomically modern human beings, angled and rough in nonmodern hominids.

**occupation floor** See *living floor.*

**Oldowan** Tool technology associated with *Homo habilis* approximately 2 mya. Involved striking off a few flakes from a stone core to produce a sharp edge.

**Olmec** A common artistic and iconographic style that spread throughout parts of Mesoamerica beginning about 3200 ya. Olmec, with its four major ceremonial centers, appears to have been the first civilization in Mesoamerica.

**opposability** The ability of the thumb to touch (oppose) the tips of the other digits.

**organelle** A structure in the cytoplasm of cells that performs various cellular functions.

**paleoanthropologist** Biological anthropologist specializing in the analysis of human fossil remains.

**paleoclimatologist** A specialist in ancient climatic conditions.

**paleoethnography** In essence, performing an **ethnography** of an archaeological culture. Ethnographers study a group by living among them and studying their lifeways. Paleoethnographers study a people by excavating their material remains and by attempting to reconstruct their life way based upon these remains.

**Paleo-Indian** New World cultures, based on big-game hunting and characterized by fluted points, present from about 12,000 to 10,000 ya.

**Paleolithic** The Old Stone Age. Time for which our most abundant archaeological artifactual evidence is stone tools. Generally divided into a Lower, Middle, and Upper Paleolithic. The Lower Paleolithic includes the stone tool industries of *Homo habilis* and *Homo erectus* from 2 mya to 250,000 ya. The Middle Paleolithic includes the stone tool industries of the archaic *Homo sapiens* from about 250,000 to 40,000 ya. The Upper Paleolithic includes the stone tool industries of anatomically modern *Homo sapiens* from about 40,000 to 10,000 ya.

**paleopathology** The study of disease and nutritional deficiency in prehistoric populations, usually with reference to the study of their skeletons.

**palynology** The identification of plants through the remains of their pollen grains.

**Pangea** The supercontinent that included parts of all present-day landmasses. Began to break up about 138 mya.

**parent material** Term used to indicate the source material of a particular soil. The parent material is often local bedrock that, through various processes of erosion, becomes soil.

**parietals** The bones of the sides and top of the skull.

**particulate** In the study of heredity, the idea that **traits** are controlled separately by individual particles rather than all together by a single agent. The genetic theory of heredity.

**patrilocal** A type of society where a married couple lives with the husband's family.

**phalanges** Bones of the fingers and toes.

**phenotype** Any physical or chemical trait that can be observed or measured. The expression of the genetic code.

**physical anthropology** The focus of the discipline that studies humans as a biological species.

**plate tectonics** The well-supported theory of the earth's composition that states that the surface of our planet consists of a number of moving plates. The movement of these plates causes continents to drift.

**Pleistocene Epoch** The geological time period, from about 1.5 mya to 10,000 ya, characterized by a series of glacial advances and retreats.

**point mutation** A mutation of a single **codon**.

**polygenic** A trait coded for by more than one **locus**.

**polymorphism** A trait showing variation within a species.

**polytypic** A species with physically distinguishable regional populations.

*Popol Vuh* Book relating the creation story of the Maya of Mesoamerica.

**population** Any reproductive unit within a species. May be the species itself.

**postnatal dependency** The period after birth when a young animal is dependent on adults for survival.

**postorbital constriction** A narrowing of the skull behind the eyes, as viewed from above.

**potassium/argon dating** See *K/Ar dating*.

**preadapted** Refers to an adaptive trait that originally evolved under different environmental circumstances.

**prehensile** Grasping, with particular reference to the hands and feet of primates. A few New World monkeys possess prehensile tails.

**primate** Large-brained, arboreal mammal with stereoscopic color vision and grasping hands and (often) feet.

**prognathism** Protrusion of the lower portion of the face.

**progressive evolution** The now-outmoded idea that evolution is always producing organisms that are "better" by our cultural standards of size, complexity, and the like. In fact, the only direction toward which evolution operates is that of better adaptation, and that only when possible.

**prosimian** A member of the group of primates with the most primitive features, that is, that most resemble the earliest primates.

**protein**   One of a family of molecules that are the main constituent of cells and that carry out cellular functions. See *amino acid.*

**protein synthesis**   The process by which the genetic code puts together **proteins** in the cell.

**provenience**   The precise location of something; here, of archaeological artifacts.

**punctuated equilibrium**   The theory that species remain stable for most of their history and that new species arise fairly suddenly as the result of mutations. See *gradualism, macromutation.*

**quadrupedal**   The ability to walk on four legs.

**race**   A physically distinguishable population within a species. See *deme, polytypic, subspecies.*

**rachis**   Area of attachment between seeds and other seeds or between seeds and other parts of a plant. A brittle rachis is an adaptive advantage in nature but is selected against by humans in artificial selection.

**radar imaging**   A procedure in archaeological site survey using radar images in the search for sites.

**radioactive isotope**   An unstable form of an element that decays to a stable form by giving off particles, or rays.

**radiometric dating**   A dating technique that uses the known rate of decay of radioactive substances found either in or in association with the item to be dated.

**recessive**   Of an allele pair, the one that is not expressed when combined in the heterozygous state with a dominant allele. See *dominant.*

**recombination**   The reconstitution of allele pairs at fertilization from single alleles produced when the pairs of each parent are broken up during the production of the gametes. See *segregation.*

**relative chronological sequence**   A sequence of sites, events, or artifacts arranged in older-younger relationships, usually without absolute dates. See *absolute dating.*

**remote sensing**   A procedure in archaeological site survey where sites are searched for and examined once discovered through noninvasive techniques where no soil is moved.

**replacement hypothesis**   The hypothesis that anatomically modern human beings evolved in a limited geographic area and spread out from there, replacing indigenous groups of archaic *Homo sapiens.*

**repoussé**   A method of decorating thin metal, including gold, where the pattern is beaten up from the underside.

**savanna**   Tropical grassland with trees scattered throughout. It is probably on the African savanna that the hominid adaptation of bipedal locomotion first developed.

**scapula**   The shoulder blade (pl. *scapulae*).

**science**   See *scientific method.*

**scientific method**   The method of inquiry that requires the generation, testing, and subsequent acceptance or rejection of **hypotheses.**

**sedentary**   Human settlement pattern where people largely stay in one place or settlement year-round, although some members of the population may still be mobile in the search for food and raw materials.

**segregation**   The breaking up of allele pairs during the production of **gametes.** See *recombination.*

**seriation**   A process of establishing a **relative chronological sequence** based on the pattern of replacement of styles of a type of artifact.

**settlement patterns**   The distribution of archaeological sites and analysis of their functions in relation to one another and features of the environment.

**sexual dimorphism**   When the sexes of a species can be distinguished by physical appearances.

**sexual selection**   Form of selection where mating partners are actively, rather than randomly, chosen by individuals within a population. The choice is based on such things as appearance, presence of a nest site, and successful competition with other potential mates.

**site**   Any place that contains evidence of human presence.

**social stratification**   The presence of acknowledged differences in social status and/or wealth among the people within a society.

**Solutrean**   An Upper **Paleolithic** culture of France and Spain, dating to about 20,000 ya, that included the manufacture of leaf-shaped, bifacial spear points.

**spatial context**   Where and with what an **artifact, ecofact,** or **feature** was found at an archaeological site. Precisely where something is found and with what can provide information concerning how it was made, what it was used for, and/or how it was discarded.

**specialized**   Refers to a species adapted to a narrow range of environmental circumstances. See *generalized*.

**speciation**   The evolution of new species from existing species.

**species**   A group of organisms that can produce fertile offspring among themselves but not with any other group. A closed genetic population, usually physically distinguishable from other populations and with a unique **gene pool**.

**stadial**   A short-term period of extreme cold and rapid glacial advance during a longer-term period of general, slow glacial expansion.

**stereoscopic vision**   The ability to see in three dimensions; depth perception.

**strata**   Layers; here, layers of different rock and soil types under the surface of the earth (sing. *stratum*).

**stratigraphy**   The study of the earth's **strata**.

**subspecies**   A physically distinguishable population within a species. See *deme, polytypic, race*.

**suture**   A cranial suture is the line of contact between the bones that make up the skull. Analysis of the state of sutures can be used to provide an estimate for the age at death of an individual.

**taphonomy**   The analysis of how organisms become part of the archaeological or paleontological record.

**taxonomy**   A systematic classification based on similarities and differences among the things being classified.

**teosinte**   Called "God's corn" by the Aztecs, teosinte is a good candidate for wild maize.

**test boring**   See *test pit*.

**test pit**   An exploratory, usually small excavation, made to establish the presence or absence of an archaeological site.

**theory**   After developing a *general* explanation (called a **hypothesis**) from *specific* observations (the process of **induction**), those things that must be true (new data) if the hypothesis is valid are suggested and tested for. This step is called **deduction**. A hypothesis that has been tested repeatedly and has been consistently validated is elevated to the status of theory.

**torus**   A continuous ridge of bone.

**trace element analysis**   A process in which the geographic source of a raw material can be determined through the analysis of small or trace amounts of impurities.

**trait**   A measurable, observable chemical or physical feature of an organism.

**transect**   A line or grid of systematically located test pits.

**transfer ribonucleic acid (tRNA)**   The form of ribonucleic acid that lines up **amino acids** in their proper sequence along the **messenger RNA** to make proteins.

**trephining**   Cutting a hole in the skull, presumably to treat some illness. Generally practiced in societies with prescientific medical knowledge.

**tundra**   A treeless expanse with low-growing vegetation and permanently frozen ground. Usually located in the Arctic, but during the **Pleistocene**, tundra conditions were found in the vicinity of glaciers in regions far to the south.

**uniformitarianism**   The concept that biological and geological processes that affected the earth in the past are still in operation today, and vice-versa.

**Upper Paleolithic**   See *Paleolithic*.

**Upper Pleistocene**   The final phase of the **Pleistocene Epoch** from 200,000 to 10,000 ya.

**Uruk**   The earliest city in Mesopotamia and, almost certainly, the world. It dates to about 5800 ya.

**Venus figurines**   Among the first sculptures produced by humanity, the oldest date to 32,000 ya. These figurines in stone, ivory, antler, and clay depict women, usually with exaggerated secondary sexual characteristics.

**wear pattern**   The mark left on stone tools as a result of their use. Such marks include polish, striations, chipping, and scarring. Analysis of wear patterns can provide information concerning how a tool was used and on what raw material.

**Yang-Shao**   The early **Neolithic** culture of China, dating to about 8000 ya.

**ziggurat**   Large mud brick structures built in Mesopotamia. Among the earliest examples of monumental architectures in the world's earliest civilization.

**zygote**   A fertilized egg before cell division begins.

# BIBLIOGRAPHY

Adams, R. E. W. 1991. *Prehistoric Mesoamerica.* Norman: University of Oklahoma.

Adams, R. McC. and H. Nissen. 1972. *The Uruk Countryside.* Chicago: University of Chicago Press.

Adovasio, J. M., J. Donahue, K. Cushman, R. C. Carlisle, R. Stuckenrath, J. D. Gun, and W. C. Johnson. 1983. Evidence from Meadowcroft Rockshelter. In *Early Man in the New World,* ed. R. Shutler, Jr., pp. 163–89. Beverly Hills, Calif.: Sage.

Allchin, B. and R. Allchin. 1982. *The Rise of Civilization in India and Pakistan.* Cambridge, Mass.: Cambridge University Press.

Anderson. E. 1952. *Plants, Life and Man.* Boston: Little, Brown.

———. 1956. Man as a maker of new plants and new plant communities. In *Man's Role in Changing the Face of the Earth,* Vol. 2, ed. W. L. Thomas, Jr., pp. 767–77. Chicago: University of Chicago Press.

Appleman, P. (ed.) 1970. *Darwin.* New York: Norton.

Arensburg, B., L. A. Schepartz, A. M. Tiller, B. Vandermeersch, and Y. Rak 1990. A reappraisal of the anatomical basis for speech in Middle Paleolithic hominids. *American Journal of Physical Anthropology* 83: 137–46.

Asimov, I. 1969. Asimov's *Guide to the Bible.* New York: Avenel Books.

Attenborough, D. 1979. *Life on Earth.* Boston: Little, Brown.

Bajema, C. J. (ed.) 1971. *Natural Selection in Human Populations.* New York: J. Wiley.

Barinaga, M. 1992. "African Eve" backers beat a retreat. *Science* 255: 686–87.

Bartstra, G. J., S. Soegondho, and A. V. D. Wijk. 1988. Ngandong man: Age and artifacts. *Journal of Human Evolution* 17: 325–37.

Bass, W. 1971. *Human Osteology: A Laboratory and Field Manual of the Human Skeleton.* Columbia: Missouri Archaeological Society.

Beadle, G. 1977. The origin of *Zea Mays.* In *Origins of Agriculture,* ed. C. A. Reed, pp. 615–36. The Hague: Mouton.

Beaumont, P., H. deVilliers, and J. C. Vogel. 1978. Modern man in sub-Saharan Africa prior to 49,000 years B.P.: A review and evaluation with particular reference to Border Cave. *South African Journal of Science* 74: 409–19.

Begley, S. and F. Gleizes. 1989. My grandad, Neandertal? *Newsweek,* October 16, pp. 70–71.

Ben-Itzhak, S., P. Smith and R. A. Bloom. 1988. Radiographic study of the humerus in Neandertals and *Homo sapiens sapiens. American Journal of Physical Anthropology* 77: 231–42.

Berreman, G. D. 1991. The incredible "Tasaday": Deconstructing the myth of a "stone-age" people. *Cultural Survival Quarterly* 51(1): 3–45.

Bierce, A. 1911. *The Devil's Dictionary.* 1958 ed. New York: Dover.

Binford, L. 1968. Post-Pleistocene adaptations. In *New Perspectives in Archaeology,* eds. L. Binford and S. Binford, pp. 313–41. Chicago: Aldine.

———. 1978. *Nunamiut Ethnoarchaeology.* New York: Academic Press.

———. 1984. *Faunal Remains from Klasies River Mouth.* New York: Academic Press.

———. 1985. Ancestral life ways: The faunal record. *Anthroquest* 32: 1, 15–20.

———. 1987. *Bones: Ancient Men and Modern Myths.* New York: Academic Press.

Binford, L. and S. Binford. 1966. A preliminary analysis of functional variability in the Mousterian of Levallois facies. *American Anthropologist* 68: 239–95.

Binford, L. and K. Chuan. 1985. Taphonomy at a distance: Zhoukoudian, "The Cave Home of Beijing Man." *Current Anthropology* 26: 413–43.

Binford, L. and N. M. Stone. 1986. Zhoukoudian: A closer look. *Current Anthropology* 27: 453–76.

Binford, S. 1968. Variability and change in the Near Eastern Mousterian of Levallois facies. In *New Perspectives in Archaeology,* eds. L. Binford and S. Binford, pp. 49–60. Chicago: Aldine.

Birdsell, J. 1972. *Human Evolution.* Boston: Houghton Mifflin.

Blinderman, C. 1986. *The Piltdown Inquest.* Buffalo: Prometheus Books.

Blumenschine, C. 1986. Chased or found: How did our ancestors acquire animal foods? *Anthroquest* 32: 10–11.

Boas, N. T. 1988. Status of *Australopithecus afarensis. Yearbook of Physical Anthropology* 31: 85–113.

Boesch, C. and H. Boesch-Achermann. September 1991. Dim forest, bright chimps. *Natural History,* pp. 50–57.

Bordaz, J. 1970. *Tools of the Old and New Stone Age.* New York: Natural History Press.

Bordes, F. 1972. *A Tale of Two Caves.* New York: Harper & Row.

Boserup, E. 1965. *The Conditions of Agricultural Growth: The Economics of Agrarian Change Under Population Pressure.* Chicago: Aldine.

Boule, M. and H. V. Vallois. 1923. *Fossil Men.* 1957 ed. New York: Dryden Press.

Bouyssonie, A., J. Bouyssonie, and L. Bardon. 1908. Découverte d'un squelette humain mousterian à la Bouffia de la Chapelles-aux-Saints (Correze). *L'Anthropologie* 19: 513–18.

Bowen, D. Q. 1978. *Quarternary Geology.* New York: Pergamon Press.

———. 1979. Quarternary correlations. *Nature* 277: 171–72.

Bower, B. 1987a. Uncovering life by an ancient lake. *Science News* 131: 264.

———. 1987b. Stone age site gets pushed back in time. *Science News* 132: 199.

———. 1987c. Skeletal aging of New World settlers. *Science News* 133: 215.

———. 1988a. Pelvic angle to Neandertal dispute. *Science News* 133: 232.

———. 1988b. Retooled ancestors. *Science News* 133: 344–45.

———. 1989a. Ritual clues flow from prehistoric blood. *Science News* 136: 405.

———. 1989b. Stone blades yield early cultivation clues. *Science News* 135: 101.

———. 1989c. Talk of ages. *Science News* 136: 24–26.

———. 1990. Civilization and its discontents. *Science News* 137: 136–39.

———. 1991. Neandertals' disappearing act. *Science News* 139: 360–63.

Brace, C. L. 1964. A nonracial approach towards the understanding of human diversity. In *The Concept of Race,* ed. A. Montagu, pp. 103–52. New York: Collier.

Bradley, R. S. 1985. *Quarternary Paleoclimatology: Methods of Paleoclimatological Reconstruction.* Boston: Allen and Unwin.

Braidwood, R. 1960. The agricultural revolution. *Scientific American* 203: 130–48.

———. 1975. *Prehistoric Men.* Glenview, Ill.: Scott, Foresman.

Brauer, G. 1984. A craniological approach to the origin of anatomically modern *Homo sapiens.* In

*The Origins of Modern Humans: A World Survey of the Fossil Evidence,* eds. F. H. Smith and F. Spencer, pp. 327–410. New York: Liss.

Breuil, H. 1952. *Four Hundred Centuries of Cave Art.* Montignac, France: Centre D'études et de Documentation Prehistorique.

Brown, F., J. Harris, R. Leakey, and A. Walker. 1985. Early *Homo erectus* skeleton from West Lake Turkana. *Nature* 316: 788–92.

Brues, A. M. 1977. *People and Races.* New York: Macmillan.

Burger, R. L. 1988. Unity and heterogeneity within the Chavin Horizon. In *Peruvian Prehistory,* ed. R. W. Keatinge, pp. 99–144. Cambridge, Eng.: Cambridge University.

Buttrick, G. A. (ed.) 1952. *Interpreter's Bible.* New York: Abingdon Press.

Butzer, K. 1971. *Environmental Archaeology: An Ecological Approach to Prehistory.* New York: Aldine-Atherton.

———. 1976. *Early Hydraulic Civilization in Egypt: A Study in Cultural Ecology.* Chicago: University of Chicago Press.

———. 1982. *Archaeology as Human Ecology.* Cambridge, Mass.: Cambridge University Press.

Byrne, R. W. and J. M. Byrne. 1988. Leopard killers of Mahale. *Natural History* 97(3): 22–26.

Calder, N. 1983. *Timescale.* New York: Viking Press.

Callen, E. O. 1967. Analysis of the Tehuacán coprolites. In *The Prehistory of the Tehuacán Valley: Volume One—Environment and Subsistence,* ed. D. Byers, pp. 261–89. Austin: University of Texas Press.

Campbell, B. 1983. *Human Ecology.* New York: Aldine.

Cann, R. L., M. Stoneking and A. C. Wilson. 1987. Mitochondrial DNA and human evolution. *Nature* 325: 31–36.

Carniero, R. 1970. A theory of the origin of the state. *Science* 169: 733–38.

Cartmill, M. 1983. "Four legs good, two legs bad." *Natural History* 92(11): 64–79.

Castleden, R. 1990. *The Knossos Labyrinth.* London: Routledge.

Cavalli-Sforza, L. L. 1991. Genes, peoples and languages. *Scientific American* 265: 104–10.

Cavallo, J. A. 1990. Cat in the human cradle. *Natural History* 99(2): 53–60.

Chagnon, N. 1977. *Yąnomamö: The Fierce People,* 2nd ed. New York: Holt, Rinehart & Winston.

Chang, K. C. 1968. *The Archaeology of Ancient China.* New Haven, Conn.: Yale University Press.

Chard, C. 1974. *Northeast Asia in Prehistory.* Madison: University of Wisconsin Press.

Chase, P. and H. Dibble. 1987. Middle Paleolithic symbolism: A review of current evidence and interpretations. *Journal of Anthropological Archaeology* 6: 263–96.

Cherry, J. F. 1987. Island origins: The early prehistoric Cyclades. In *Origins: The Roots of European Civilisation,* ed. B. Cunliffe, pp. 16–29. Chicago: Dorsey Press.

Childe, V. G. 1942. *What Happened in History.* Baltimore: Pelican Books.

———. 1951. *Man Makes Himself.* New York: Mentor Books.

———. 1953. *New Light on the Most Ancient East.* New York: Norton.

Churchill, S. and E. Trinkaus. 1990. Neandertal scapular glenoid morphology. *American Journal of Physical Anthropology* 83: 147–60.

Clark, J. D. 1976. Prehistoric population pressures favoring plant domestication in Africa. In *Origins of African Plant Domestication,* eds. J. R. Harlan, J. M. J. De Wet, and A. B. L. Stemler, pp. 67–106. The Hague: Mouton.

Clark, J. G. D. 1971. *Excavation at Star Carr.* Cambridge, Mass.: Cambridge University Press.

Clarke, D. 1978. *Analytical Archaeology.* New York: Columbia University Press.

Cobo, B. 1653. *History of the Inca Empire* (R. Hamilton, trans.). 1979 ed. Austin: University of Texas.

Cohen, M. 1977. *The Food Crisis in Prehistory.* New Haven, Conn.: Yale University Press.

Coltorti, M., M. Cremaschi, M. C. Delitala, D. Esu, M. Fornaseri, A. McPherron, M. Nicoletti, R. van Otterloo, C. Peretto, B. Sala, V. Schmidt, and J. Sevink. 1982. Reversed magnetic polarity in an early Lower Paleolithic site in central Italy. *Nature* 300: 173–76.

Conkey, M. 1978. Style and information in cultural evolution: Toward a predictive model for the Paleolithic. In *Social Archaeology: Beyond Subsistence and Dating,* eds. C. Redman, M. J. Berman, E. V. Curtin, W. T. Langhorne, N. M. Versaggi, and J. C. Wanser, pp. 61–85. New York: Academic Press.

———. 1980. The identification of prehistoric hunter–gatherer aggregation sites: The case of Altamira. *Current Anthropology* 21: 609–39.

———. 1983. On the origins of Paleolithic art: A review and some critical thoughts. In *Mousterian Legacy,* ed. E. Trinkaus, pp. 201–27. Oxford, Eng.: British Archaeological Reports, International Series, 164.

Conklin, W. J. and M. E. Moseley. 1988. The patterns of art and power in the Early Intermediate period. In *Peruvian Prehistory,* ed. R. W. Keatinge, pp. 145–63. Cambridge, Engl.: Cambridge University.

Connah, G. 1987. *African Civilizations.* Cambridge, Mass.: Cambridge University Press.

Constable, G. and the Editors of Time-Life. 1973. *The Neanderthals.* New York: Time-Life Books.

Cook, J., C. B. Stringer, A. P. Current, H. P. Schwarcz, and A. G. Wintle. 1982. A review of the chronology of the European Middle Pleistocene hominid record. *Yearbook of Physical Anthropology* 25: 19–65.

Coon, C. S. 1962. *The Origin of Races.* New York: Knopf.

Crawford, H. 1991. *Sumer and the Sumerians.* Cambridge, Engl.: Cambridge University.

Crelin, E. S. 1987. *The Human Vocal Tract: Anatomy, Function, Development, and Evolution.* New York: Vantage Press.

Cronin, J. E., N. T. Boaz, C. B. Stringer, and Y. Rak. 1981. Tempo and mode in hominid evolution. *Nature* 292: 113–22.

Dahlberg, F. 1981. *Woman the Gatherer.* New Haven, Conn.: Yale University Press.

Darwin, C. R. 1898. *On the Origin of Species by Means of Natural Selection,* 6th ed., 1872. New York: Appleton.

Davern, C. F. (ed.) 1981. *Genetics: Readings from Scientific American.* San Francisco: Freeman.

Day, M. H. 1971. Postcranial remains of *Homo erectus* from bed IV Olduvai Gorge, Tanzania. *Nature* 232: 283–87.

———. 1988. *Guide to Fossil Man,* 4th ed. Chicago: University of Chicago Press.

Deagan, K. 1991. Historical archaeology's contribution to our understanding of early America. In *Historical Archaeology in Global Perspective,* ed. L. Falk, pp. 97–112. Washington, D.C.: Smithsonian Institution Press.

Dean, M. C., C. B. Stringer, and T. G. Bromage. 1986. Age at death of the Neandertal child from Devil's Tower, Gibraltar and the implications for students of general growth and development in Neandertals. *American Journal of Physical Anthropology* 70: 301–309.

Deetz, J. 1965. *The Dynamics of Stylistic Change in Arikara Ceramics.* Urbana: University of Illinois Series in Anthropology, No. 4.

———. 1976. Black settlement at Plymouth. *Archaeology* 29: 207.

———. 1977. *In Small Things Forgotten: The Archaeology of Early American Life.* Garden City, N.Y.: Anchor Books.

de Lumley, H. 1969. A Paleolithic camp at Nice. *Scientific American* 220(5): 42–50.

———. 1975. Cultural evolution in France in its Paleolithic setting during the Middle Pleistocene. In *After the Ausralopithecines: Stratigraphy, Ecology and Culture Change in the Middle Pleistocene,* eds. K. Butzer and G. Issac, pp. 745–807. The Hague: Mouton.

Dettwyler, K. A. 1991. Can paleopathology provide evidence for "compassion"? *American Journal of Physical Anthropology,* 84: 375–84.

Diamond, J. 1987. The worst mistake in the history of the human race. *Discover* 8(5): 64–66.

———. 1989. The great leap forward. *Discover* 10(5): 50–60.

Dibble, H. 1987. The interpretation of Middle Paleolithic scraper morphology. *American Antiquity* 52: 108–18.

Dickson, D. B. 1990. *The Dawn of Belief: Religion in the Upper Paleolithic of Southwestern Europe.* Tucson: University of Arizona Press.

Doyle, A. C. 1981. *The Celebrated Cases of Sherlock Holmes.* London: Octopus Books.

Editors of Time-Life. 1973. *The First Men.* New York: Time-Life Books.

Eldredge, N. and S. J. Gould. 1972. Punctuated equilibria: An alternative to phyletic gradualism. In *Models in Paleobiology,* ed. T. S. Schopf, pp. 82–115. San Francisco: Freeman, Cooper.

Eldredge, N. and I. Tattersall. 1982. *The Myths of Human Evolution.* New York: Columbia University Press.

Engels, F. 1942. *The Origin of the Family, Private Property and the State.* 1972 ed. Chicago: Kerr.

Facchini, A. and G. Guisberti. 1990. *Homo sapiens*

*sapiens* remains from the island of Crete. In *Continuity or Replacement: Controversies in* Homo Sapiens *Evolution,* eds. G. Bräuer and F. H. Smith. Rotterdam: Balkema.

Fagan, B. 1988. *In the Beginning: An Introduction to Archaeology.* Boston: Little, Brown.

Fairservis, W. A. 1975. *The Roots of India.* Chicago: University of Chicago Press.

Farnsworth, P., J. Brady, M. DeNiro, and R. S. MacNeish. 1985. A re-evaluation of the isotopic and archaeological reconstructions of diet in the Tehuacán Valley. *American Antiquity* 50: 102–16.

Feder, K. L. 1988. *The Beaver Meadow Complex Prehistoric Archaeological District.* National Register of Historic Places—Nomination Form. Unpublished manuscript on file at the Connecticut Historical Commission.

———. 1990. *Frauds, Myths, and Mysteries: Science and Pseudoscience in Archaeology.* Mountain View, Calif.: Mayfield.

———. In press. *The Lighthouse: An Archaeological and Documentary Investigation of a Legend.* Mountain View, Calif.: Mayfield.

Fedigan, L. M. and L. Fedigan. 1988. Gender and the study of primates. *Curricular Module for the Project on Gender and Curriculum.* Washington, D.C.: American Anthropological Association.

Feibel, C. S., F. H. Brown, and I. McDougal. 1989. Stratigraphic context of fossil hominids from the Omo Group deposits: Northern Turkan basin, Kenya and Ethiopia. *American Journal of Physical Anthropology* 78: 595–622.

Fischman, J. 1992. Hard Evidence. *Discover* 13(2): 44–51.

Flannery, K. 1965. The ecology of early food production in Mesopotamia. *Science* 147: 1247–56.

———. 1967. Vertebrate fauna and hunting patterns. In *The Prehistory of the Tehuacán Valley: Volume One—Environment and Subsistence,* ed. D. Byers, pp. 132–77. Austin: University of Texas Press.

———. 1968. Archaeological systems theory in early Mesoamerica. In *Anthropological Archaeology in the Americas,* ed. B. J. Meggers. Washington, D.C.: Anthropological Society of Washington.

———. 1973. The origins of agriculture. *Annual Review of Anthropology* 2: 271–310.

Flint, R. F. 1971. *Glacial and Quarternary Geology.* New York: Wiley.

Fossey, D. 1983. *Gorillas in the Mist.* Boston: Houghton Mifflin.

Franciscus, R. G. and E. Trinkaus. 1988. Nasal morphology and the emergence of *Homo erectus.* *American Journal of Physical Anthropology* 75: 517–27.

Freeman, L. G. 1973. The significance of mammalian faunas from Paleolithic occupations in Cantabrian Spain. *American Antiquity* 38: 3–44.

Frison, G. B. (ed.) 1974. *The Casper Site.* New York: Academic Press.

Galdikas, B. M. F. 1980. Living with the great orange apes. *National Geographic* 157(6): 830–53.

Gamble, C. 1982. Interaction and alliance in Paleolithic society. *Man* 17: 92–107.

———. 1983. Culture and society in the Upper Paleolithic of Europe. In *Hunter–Gatherer Economy in Prehistory: A European Perspective,* ed. G. Bailey, pp. 210–11. Cambridge, Mass.: Cambridge University Press.

———. 1986. *The Paleolithic Settlement of Europe.* Cambridge, Mass.: Cambridge University Press.

Gargett, R. H. 1989. Grave shortcomings: Evidence for Neandertal burial. *Current Anthropology* 30: 157–90.

Gernet, J. 1987. A *History of Chinese Civilization.* Cambridge, Mass.: Cambridge University Press.

Goodall, J. 1971. *In the Shadow of Man.* Boston: Houghton Mifflin.

———. 1986. *The Chimpanzees of Gombe: Patterns of Behavior.* Cambridge, Mass.: Belknap Press.

———. 1990. *Through a Window: My Thirty Years with the Chimpanzees of Gombe.* Boston: Houghton Mifflin.

Goodman, A. H. and G. Armelagos. 1985. Disease and death at Dr. Dickson's mound. *Natural History* 94(9): 12–18.

Gorman, C. 1969. Hoabinhian: A pebble-tool complex with early plant associations in Southeast Asia. *Science* 163: 671–73.

Gould, S. J. 1977. *Ever Since Darwin.* New York: Norton.

———. 1980. *The Panda's Thumb.* New York: Norton.

———. 1981. *The Mismeasure of Man.* New York: Norton.

———. 1983. Part 4: Teilhard and Piltdown. In *Hen's Teeth and Horse's Toes.* New York: Norton.

———. 1985a. Human equality is a contingent fact of history. In *The Flamingo's Smile.* New York: Norton.

———. 1985b. Darwin at sea—and the virtues of port. In *The Flamingo's Smile.* New York: Norton.

———. 1987a. Life's little joke. *Natural History* 96(4): 16–25.

———. 1987b. Empire of the apes. *Natural History* 96(5): 20–25.

———. 1987c. Bushes all the way down. *Natural History* 96(6): 12–19.

———. 1988. A novel notion of Neanderthal. *Natural History* 97(6): 16–21.

———. 1991. *Bully for Brontosaurus.* New York: Norton.

Greene, J. C. 1959. *The Death of Adam: Evolution and Its Impact on Western Thought.* Ames: Iowa State University Press.

Grine, F. E. (ed.) 1988a. *Evolutionary History of the "Robust" Australopithecines.* New York: Aldine de Gruyter.

———. (ed.) 1988b. Evolutionary history of the "robust australopithecines: A summary and historical perspective. In *Evolutionary History of the "Robust" Australopithecines,* pp. 509–20. New York: Aldine de Gruyter.

Haas, J. 1982. *The Evolution of the Prehistoric State.* New York: New York University Press.

Habgood, P. J. 1985. The origin of Australian Aborigines: An alternative approach and view. In *Hominid Evolution: Past, Present, and Future,* ed. P. V. Tobias, pp. 367–80. New York: Liss.

———. 1989. The origin of anatomically modern humans in Australasia. In *The Human Revolution: Behavioural and Biological Perspectives in the Origins of Modern Humans,* eds. P. Mellars and C. Stringer, pp. 245–73. Princeton, N.J.: Princeton University Press.

Hall, R. 1984. *The Excavations at York: The Viking Dig.* Oxford, Eng.: Bodley Head.

Halvorson, J. 1987. Art for art's sake in the Paleolithic. *Current Anthropology* 28: 63–71.

Hamblin, D. J. and the Editors of Time-Life. 1973. *The First Cities.* New York: Time-Life Books.

Hammond, N. 1974. Paleolithic mammalian faunas and parietal art in Cantabria: A comment on Freeman. *American Antiquity* 39: 618–19.

Hansen, J. M. 1991. *The Paleoethnobotany of Franchthi Cave, Greece.* Bloomington: Indiana University Press.

Harlan, J. R., J. M. J. De Wet, and A. Stemler. (eds.)

1976. Plant domestication and indigenous African agriculture. In *Origins of African Plant Domestication,* pp. 3–22. The Hague: Mouton.

Harlan, J. R., J. M. J. De Wet, A Stemler, and D. Zohary. 1966. Distribution of wild wheats and barley. *Science* 153: 1074–80.

Harmon, R., J. Glaze, and K. Nowak. 1980. $^{230}$Th/$^{234}$U dating of travertines from the Bilzingsleben archaeological site. *Natue* 284: 132–35.

Harris, C. L. (ed.) 1981. *Evolution: Genesis and Revelations.* Albany: State University of New York Press.

Harris, D. 1977. Alternative strategies toward agriculture. In *Origins of Agriculture,* ed. C. A. Reed, pp. 179–243. The Hague: Mouton.

Harris, M. 1968. *The Rise of Anthropological Theory.* New York: Cromwell.

Harrold, F. B. 1980. A comparative analysis of Eurasian Paleolithic burials. *World Archaeology* 12: 195–211.

———. 1989. Mousterian, Châtelperronian and early Aurignacia in Western Europe: Continuity or Discontinuity. In *The Human Revolution: Behavioural and Biological Perspectives in the Origin of Modern Humans,* eds. P. Mellars and C. Stringer, pp. 677–713. Princeton, N.J.: Princeton University Press.

Hartl, D. L. 1977. *Our Uncertain Heritage: Genetics and Human Diversity.* New York: Lippincott.

Hedges, S. B., S. Kumar, K. Tamura, and M. Stoneking. 1992. Technical comments. *Science* 255: 737–39.

Heim, J. L. 1968. Les restes Neandertaliens de La Ferassie 1: Nouvelles données sur la stratigraphie et inventure de squelettes. *Computes Reneud de l'Academie del Sciences,* Series D, 266: 576–78.

Henning, G. J., W. Herr, E. Weber, and N. I. Xirotiris. 1981. ESR-dating of the fossil huminid cranium from Petralona Cave, Greece. *Nature* 292: 533–36.

Hill, A. and S. Ward. 1988. Origin of the *Hominidae:* The record of African large hominoid evolution between 14 my and 4 my. *Yearbook of Physical Anthropology* 31: 49–83.

Ho, P. 1977. The indigenous origins of Chinese agriculture. In *Origins of Agriculture,* ed. C. A. Reed, pp. 413–84. The Hague: Mouton.

Hoffman, M. 1979. *Egypt Before the Pharoahs*. New York: Knopf.

———. 1983. Where nations began. *Science 83* 4(8): 42–51.

Hole, F., K. Flannery, and J. A. Neely. 1969. *Prehistory and Human Ecology of the Deh Luran Plain: An Early Village Sequence from Khuzistan, Iran.* Ann Arbor: University of Michigan Press.

Holloway, R. 1980. Indonesian "Solo" (Ngandong) endocranial reconstructions: Preliminary observations and comparisons with Neandertal and *Homo erectus* groups. *American Journal of Physical Anthropology* 53: 285–95.

———. 1981. The Indonesian *Homo erectus* brain endocasts revisited. *American Journal of Physical Anthropology* 55: 503–21.

Hopkins, D. 1982. Aspects of the paleogeography of Beringia during the late Pleistocene. In *The Paleoecology of Beringia,* eds. D. Hopkins, J. Matthews, C. Schweger, and S. Young, pp. 3–28. New York: Academic Press.

Howard, R. W. 1975. *The Dawn Seekers: The First History of American Paleontology.* New York: Harcourt Brace Jovanovich.

Howell, F. C. 1960. European and northwest African Middle Pleistocene hominids. *Current Anthropology* 1: 195–232.

———. 1966. Observations on the earlier phases of the European Lower Paleolithic. Special publication of *American Antropologist* 68: 88–201.

Howells, W. W. 1980. *Homo erectus*—who, when, and where: A survey. *Yearbook of Physical Anthropology* 23: 1–23.

Huddleston, L. E. 1967. *Origins of the American Indians: European Concepts 1492–1729.* Austin: University of Texas Press.

Huntington, E. 1924. *Civilization and Climate.* New Haven, Conn.: Yale University Press.

Ikeya, M. 1982. Petralona Cave dating controversy: Response to Henning et al. *Nature* 299: 281.

Isaac, G. 1977. *Olorgesailie: Archaeological Studies of a Middle Pleistocene Lake Basin in Kenya.* Chicago: University of Chicago Press.

James, S. 1989. Hominid use of fire in the Lower and Middle Pleistocene. *Current Anthropology* 30: 1–11.

Janus, C. 1975. *The Search for Peking Man.* New York: Macmillan.

Jochim, M. 1983. Paleolithic cave art in ecological perspective. In *Hunter–Gatherer Economy in Prehistory: A European Perspective,* ed. G. Bailey, pp. 212–19. Cambridge, Mass.: Cambridge University Press.

Johanson, D. and M. Edey. 1981. *Lucy: The Beginnings of Humankind.* New York: Simon & Schuster.

Johanson, D., F. T. Masao, G. G. Eck, T. D. White, R. C. Walter, W. H. Kimbel, B. Asfaw, P. Manega, P. Ndessokia, and G. Suwa. 1987. New partial skeleton of *Homo habilis* from Olduvai Gorge, Tanzania. *Nature* 327: 205–209.

Johanson, D. and J. Shreeve. 1989. *Lucy's Child: The Discovery of a Human Ancestor.* New York: Morrow.

Johanson, D. C., and T. D. White. 1979. A systematic assessment of early African hominids. *Science* 203: 321–30.

Jones, R. 1989. East of Wallace's Line: Issues and problems in the colonization of the Australian continent. In *The Human Revolution: Behavioural and Biological Perspectives in the Origins of Modern Humans,* eds. P. Mellars and C. Stringer, pp. 743–82. Princeton, N.J.: Princeton University Press.

Kano, T. November 1990. The bonobos' peaceable kingdom. *Natural History,* pp. 62–71.

Kaplan, L., T. F. Lynch, and C. E. S. Smith, Jr. 1973. Early cultivated beans (*Phaseolus vulgaris*) from an intermontaine Peruvian valley. *Science* 179: 76–77.

Keeley, L. H. 1980. *Experimental Determination of Stone Tool Use: A Microwear Analysis.* Chicago: University of Chicago Press.

Kennedy, K. A. R. 1975. *Neanderthal Man.* Minneapolis: Burgess Press.

———. 1976. *Human Variation in Space and Time.* Dubuque, Iowa: Brown.

Kennedy, K. A. R., A. Sonakia, J. Chimet, and K. K. Verma. 1991. Is the Narmada hominid an Indian *Homo erectus? American Journal of Physical Anthropology* 86: 475–96.

Kent, J. 1987. The most ancient south: A review of the domestication of the Andean camelids. In *Studies in the Neolithic and Urban Revolutions,* ed. L. Manzanilla, pp. 169–84. Oxford, Eng.: British Archaeological Review.

Kenyon, K. 1954. Ancient Jericho. *Scientific American* 190: 76–82.

Kimbel, W. H., T. D. White, and D. C. Johanson. 1988. Implications for KNM-WT 17000 for the evolution of "robust" australopithecines. In *Evolutionary History of the "Robust" Australopithecines,* ed. F. E. Grine, New York: Aldine de Gruyter.

Klein, R. G. 1982. Age (mortality) profiles as a means of distinguishing hunted species from scavenged ones in Stone Age archaeological sites. *Paleobiology* 8: 151–58.

———. 1983. The Stone Age prehistory of southern Africa. *Annual Review of Anthropology* 12: 25–48.

Kramer, A. 1991. Modern human origins in Australasia: Replacement or evolution. *American Journal of Physical Anthropology* 86: 455–73.

Kranzberg, M. 1984. Technological revolutions. *National Forum: The Phi Kappa Phi Journal* 64(3): 6–10.

Kurtén, B. 1968. *The Pleistocene Mammals of Europe.* London: Weiderfield and Nicholson.

Laitman, J., R. C. Heimbuch. 1984. The basicranium and upper respiratory system of African *Homo erectus* and early *Homo sapiens. American Journal of Physical Anthropology* 63: 180.

Lamberg-Karlovsky, C. C. and J. Sabloff. 1979. *Ancient Civilizations: The Near East and Mesoamerica.* Prospect Heights, Ill.: Waveland Press.

Landau, M. 1991. *Narratives of Human Evolution.* New Haven, Conn.: Yale University Press.

Larsen, C. S. and R. M. Matter. 1985. *Human Origins: The Fossil Record.* Prospect Heights, Ill.: Waveland Press.

Leakey, M. D. 1971. *Olduvai Gorge,* Vol. 3. Cambridge, Mass.: Cambridge University Press.

Leakey, R. E. F. and A. Walker. 1980. On the status of *Australopithecus afarensis. Science* 207: 1103.

———. 1985a. A fossil skeleton 1,600,000 years old: *Homo erectus* unearthed. *National Geographic* 168(5): 624–29.

———. 1985b. Further hominids from the Plio-Pleistocene of Koobi Fora, Kenya. *American Journal of Physical Anthropology* 67: 135–63.

Lee, R. 1979. *The !Kung San: Men, Women, and Work in a Foraging Society.* Cambridge, Mass.: Cambridge University Press.

Lee, R. B. and I. DeVore. 1968. *Man the Hunter.* Chicago: Aldine.

Leiberman, P. 1984. *The Biology and Evolution of Language.* Cambridge, Mass.: Harvard University Press.

Leigh, S. 1992. Cranial capacity evolution in *Homo erectus* and early *Homo sapiens. American Journal of Physical Anthropology* 87: 1–13.

Leonard, J. N. and the Editors of Time-Life Books. 1973. *The First Farmers.* New York: Time-Life Books.

Leroi-Gourhan, A. 1968. The evolution of Paleolithic art. *Scientific American* 218: 58–70.

———. 1982. *The Dawn of European Art: An Introduction to Paleolithic Cave Painting.* Cambridge, Mass.: Cambridge University Press.

Lewin, R. 1982. *Thread of Life: The Smithsonian Looks at Evolution.* Washington, D.C.: Smithsonian Books.

———. 1984. Unexpected anatomy of *Homo erectus. Science* 226: 529.

———. 1987a. Africa: Cradle of modern humans. *Science* 237: 1292–95.

———. 1987b. The unmasking of mitochondrial Eve. *Science* 238: 24–26.

———. 1987c. *Bones of Contention: Controversies in the Search for Human Origins.* New York: Simon & Schuster.

———. 1988. Modern human origins under close scrutiny. *Science* 239: 1240–41.

———. 1989. *In the Age of Mankind: A Smithsonian Book of Human Evolution.* Washington, D.C.: Smithsonian Institution Press.

———. 1991. The biochemical ? to human origins. *Mosaic* 22(3): 46–55.

Lewontin, R. 1982. *Human Diversity.* New York: Scientific American Library.

Lloyd, S. 1978. *The Archaeology of Mesopotamia.* London: Thames and Hudson.

Lovejoy, C. O. 1984. The natural detective. *Natural History* 93(10): 24–28.

Lovejoy, C. O. and E. Trinkaus. 1980. Strength and robusticity of the Neandertal tibia. *American Journal of Physical Anthropology* 53: 465–70.

Lu Zun'e. 1987. Cracking the evolutionary puzzle: Jinniushan Man. *China Pictorial* 4: 34–45.

Lyell, C. 1873. *The Geological Evidences of the Antiquity of Man.* London: Murray.

Lynch, T. F., R. Gillespie, J. A. J. Gowlett, and R. E. M. Hedges. 1985. Chronology of Guitarrero Cave, Peru. *Science* 229: 864–67.

MacNeish, R. S. 1964. Ancient Mesoamerican civilization. *Science* 143: 531–37.

———. 1967. An interdisciplinary approach to an archaeological problem. In *The Prehistory of the Tehuacán Valley: Volume One—Environment and Subsistence,* ed. D. Byers, pp. 14–23. Austin: University of Texas Press.

———. 1977. The beginnings of agriculture in central Peru. In *Origins of Agriculture,* ed. C. A. Reed, pp. 753–801. The Hague: Mouton.

Manglesdorf, P. 1958. Reconstructing the ancestor of corn. *Proceedings of the American Philosophical Society* 102: 454–63.

Manglesdorf, P., R. S. MacNeish, and W. C. Gallinat. 1967. Prehistoric wild and cultivated maize. In *The Prehistory of the Tehuacán Valley: Volume One—Environment and Subsistence,* ed. D. Byers, pp. 178–200. Austin: University of Texas Press.

Marks, J. 1991. What's old and new in molecular phylogeny. *American Journal of Physical Anthropology* 85: 207–19.

Marshak, A. 1972a. *The Roots of Civilization.* New York: McGraw-Hill.

———. 1972b. Cognitive aspects of Upper Paleolithic engraving. *Current Anthropology* 13:445–77.

Martin, P. S. 1982. The pattern of meaning of Holarctic mammoth extinction. In *Paleoecology of Beringia,* eds. D. Hopkins, J. Matthews, C. Schweger, and S. Young, pp. 399–408. New York: Academic Press.

Martin, R. D. 1990. *Primate Origins and Evolution: A Phylogenetic Reconstruction.* Princeton, N.J.: Princeton University Press.

McConnell, J. B. 1988. Whence we've come, where we're going, how we're going to get there. In *Biotechnology and the Human Genome,* eds. A. D. Woodhead and B. J. Barnhart. New York: Plenum.

McCrone, J. 1991. *The Ape That Spoke: Language and the Evolution of the Mind.* New York: Avon Books.

McHenry, H. M. 1988. New estimates of body weight in early hominids and their significance to encephalization and megadontia in "robust" australopithecines. In *Evolutionary History of the "Robust" Australopithecines,* ed. F. E. Grine, New York: Aldine de Gruyter.

McIntosh, S. and R. McIntosh. 1982. Finding West Africa's oldest city. *National Geographic* 162(3): 396–418.

Mellaart, J. 1965. *Earliest Civilizations of the Near East.* London: Thames and Hudson.

Milisauskas, S. 1978. *European Prehistory.* New York: Academic Press.

Miller, D. A. 1977. Evolution of primate chromosomes. *Science* 198: 1116–24.

Miller, J. M. 1991. Does brain size variability provide evidence of multiple species in *Homo habilis*? *American Journal of Physical Anthropology* 84: 385–98.

Million, R., B. Drewit, and G. Cowgill. 1973. *The Teotihuacan Map: Urbanization at Teotihuacan,* Vol. 1. Austin: University of Texas Press.

Mills, L. S. 1952. *The Legend of the Barkhamsted Lighthouse.* Hartford, Conn.: Author.

Molnar, S. 1975. *Races, Types, and Ethnic Groups: The Problem of Human Variation.* Englewood Cliffs, N.J.: Prentice-Hall.

Monastersky, R. 1991. Tales from ice time: Two holes through Greenland offer a glimpse of climates past and future. *Science News* 140: 161–76.

———. 1992. New date resets geologic clocks. *Science News* 141: 14.

Montague, A. (ed.) 1964. *The Concept of Race.* New York: Collier.

Morgan, L. H. 1877. *Ancient Society.* 1964 ed. Cambridge, Mass.: Belknap Press.

Morse, D. 1969. *Ancient Disease in the Midwest.* Springfield: Illinois State Museum.

Morse, D., J. Duncan, J. Stoutamire (eds.) 1983. *Handbook of Forensic Archaeology and Anthropology.* Tallahassee, Fla.: Published by the editors, distributed by Bill's Bookstore.

Movius, H. 1953. The Mousterian cave of Teshik-Tash, south-central Uzbekistan, Central Asia. *Bulletin of the American School of Prehistorical Research* 17:11–71.

Mowat, F. 1987. *Woman in the Mists.* New York: Warner Books.

Napier, J. 1967. The antiquity of human walking. In *Human Ancestors: Readings from Scientific American,* eds. G. Isaac and R. E. F. Leakey. San Francisco: Freeman.

Napier, J. R. and P. H. Napier. 1967. *A Handbook of Living Primates.* New York: Academic Press.

National Geographic Society. 1979. *Wild Animals of North America.* Washington, D.C.: Author.

Natural History. 1986–1988. The first Americans. *Natural History.*

Natural History. 1991–1992. Rediscovering the Maya. *Natural History.*

Newcomer, M. 1971. Some quantitative experiments in handaxe manufacture. *World Archaeology* 3: 85–94.

Noël Hume, I. 1974. *Historical Archaeology.* New York: Knopf.

———. 1982. *Martin's Hundred: The Discovery of a Lost Colonial Virginia Settlement.* New York: Delta Books.

O'Brien, E. M. 1984. What was the Acheulean hand ax? *Natural History* 93(7): 20–23.

Olsen, S. J. 1985. *Origins of the Domestic Dog.* Tucson: University of Arizona Press.

Oppenheim, L. 1977. *Ancient Mesopotamia: Portrait of a Dead Civilization.* Chicago: University of Chicago Press.

Ortner, D. J. and W. G. J. Putschar. 1985. *Identification of Pathological Conditions in Human Skeletal Remains.* Washington, D.C.: Smithsonian Institution Press.

Ovey, C. (ed.) 1964. *The Swanscombe Skull: A Survey of Research on a Pleistocene Site.* Royal Anthropological Institute of Great Britain and Ireland, Occasional Paper 20.

Owen, R. 1984. The Americas: The case against an Ice-Age human population. In *The Origins of Modern Humans: A World Survey of the Fossil Evidence,* eds. F. H. Smith and F. Spencer, pp. 517–64. New York: Liss.

Park, M. A. 1979. *Dermatoglyphics as a Tool for Population Studies: An Example.* Unpublished doctoral dissertation. Bloomington: Indiana University Department of Anthropology.

Passingham, R. E. 1982. *The Human Primate.* Oxford, Eng.: Freeman.

Patterson, T. 1973. *America's Past: A New World Archaeology.* Glenview, Ill.: Scott, Foresman.

Pfeiffer, J. E. 1969. *The Emergence of Man.* New York: Harper & Row.

———. 1982. *The Creative Explosion: An Inquiry into the Origins of Art and Religion.* New York: Harper & Row.

Pilbeam, D. 1984. The descent of the hominoids and hominids. *Scientific American* 250: 84–96.

———. 1986. Human origins. *David Skomp Distinguished Lecture in Anthropology.* Bloomington: Indiana University.

Pope, G. G. 1988. Recent advances in Far Eastern paleoanthropology. *Annual Reviews in Anthropology* 17: 43–77.

Potts, R. 1984. Home bases and early hominids. *American Scientist* 72: 338–47.

Poulianos, A. N. 1971–72. Petralona: A Middle Pleistocene cave in Greece. *Archaeology* 24/25: 6–11.

Radner, D. and M. Radner. 1982. *Science and Unreason.* Belmont, Calif.: Wadsworth.

Rak, Y. 1990. On the differences between two pelvises of Mousterian context from the Qafzeh and Kebara Caves, Israel. *American Journal of Physical Anthropology* 81: 323–332.

Rak, Y. and B. Arensberg. 1987. Kebara 2 Neandertal pelvis: First look at a complete inlet. *American Journal of Physical Anthropology* 73: 227–31.

Rathje, W. 1972. Praise the gods and pass the metates: A hypothesis of the development of lowland rain forest civilization in Mesoamerica. In *Contemporary Archaeology,* ed. M. Leon, pp. 365–92. Carbondale: University of Illinois Press.

Read-Martin, C. E. and D. W. Read. 1975. *Australopithecus* scavenging and human evolution: Approach from fauna analysis. *Current Anthropology* 16: 359–68.

Reed, C. A. (ed.) 1977. *Origins of Agriculture.* The Hague: Mouton.

Rensberger, B. 1981. Facing the past. *Science 81* 2(8): 40–51.

Rice, P. and Paterson, A. 1985. Cave art and bones: Exploring the interrelationships. *American Anthropologist* 87: 94–100.

———. 1986. Validating the cave art-archaeofaunal relationship in Cantabrian Spain. *American Anthropologist* 88: 658–67.

———. 1988. Anthropomorphs in cave art: An empirical assessment. *American Anthropologist* 90: 664–74.

Richard, A. F. 1985. *Primates in Nature.* New York: Freeman.

Rightmire, G. P. 1979a. Cranial remains of *Homo erectus* from Beds II and IV, Olduvai Gorge, Tanzania. *American Journal of Physical Anthropology* 51: 99–116.

———. 1979b. Implications of the Border Cave skeletal remains for Later Pleistocene human evolution. *Current Anthropology* 20: 23–35.

———. 1981. Patterns in the evolution of *Homo erectus*. *Paleobiology* 7: 241–46.

———. 1984. *Homo sapiens* in sub-Saharan Africa. In *The Origins of Modern Humans: A World Survey of the Fossil Evidence,* eds. F. H. Smith and F. Spencer, pp. 295–326. New York: Liss.

———. 1985. The tempo of change in the evolution of Mid-Pleistocene *Homo*. In *Ancestors: The Hard Evidence,* ed. E. Delson, pp. 255–64. New York: Liss.

———. 1990. *The Evolution of* Homo erectus: *Comparative Anatomical Studies of an Extinct Human Species.* New York: Cambridge University Press.

Romer, J. 1984. *Ancient Lives: Daily Life in Egypt of the Pharoahs.* New York: Holt, Rinehart and Winston.

———. 1988. *Testament: The Bible and History.* New York: Holt.

Ruspoli, M. 1986. *The Cave of Lascaux: The Final Photographs.* New York: Abrams.

Sabloff, J. 1989. *The Cities of Ancient Mexico: Reconstructing a Lost World.* New York: Thames and Hudson.

Sagan, C. 1980. *Cosmos.* New York: Random House.

Sanders, W. and B. Price. 1968. *Mesoamerica: The Evolution of a Civilization.* New York: Random House.

Sarich, V. 1971. A molecular approach to the question of human origins. In *Background for Man,* eds. P. Dolhinhow and V. M. Sarich. Boston: Little, Brown.

Sauer, C. 1969. *Seeds, Spades, Hearths, and Herds: The Domestication of Animals and Foodstuffs.* Cambridge, Mass.: MIT Press.

Savaria. 1965. *The Popol Wuh.* Guatemala: Publicaciones Turisticas.

Schele, L. and D. Freidel. 1990. *A Forest of Kings: The Untold Story of the Ancient Maya.* New York: Morrow.

Scott, D., R. Fox, Jr., and M. Conner. 1989. *Archaeological Perspectives on the Battle of the Little Big Horn.* Norman: University of Oklahoma.

Shackleton, N. J. and N. D. Opdyke. 1973. Oxygen isotope and paleomagnetic stratigraphy of equatorial Pacific core V28-238: Oxygen isotope temperatures and ice volumes on a $10^5$ and $10^6$ year scale. *Quaternary Research* 3: 39–55.

Shapiro, H. L. 1974. *Peking Man.* New York: Simon & Schuster.

Sharer, R. and W. Ashmore. 1987. *Archaeology: Discovering Our Past.* Mountain View, Calif.: Mayfield.

Shea, B. T. 1989. Heterochrony in human evolution: The case for neoteny reconsidered. *Yearbook of Physical Anthropology* 32: 69–101.

Shea, J. 1989. A functional study of the lithic industries associated with hominid fossils in Kebara and Qafzeh Caves, Israel. In *The Human Revolution: Behavioural and Biological Perspectives in the Origins of Modern Humans,* eds. P. Mellars and C. Stringer, pp. 611–25. Princeton, N.J.: Princeton University Press.

Shipman, P. 1984. Scavenger hunt. *Natural History* 93(4): 20–27.

———. 1986. Scavenging or hunting in early hominid: Theoretical frameworks and tests. *American Anthropologist* 88: 27–43.

———. 1990. Old masters. *Discover* 11(7): 60–65.

Shipman, P. and J. Rose. 1983. Evidence of butchery and hominid activities at Torralba and Ambrona: An evaluation using microscopic techniques. *Journal of Archaeological Science* 10: 465–74.

Shreve, J. 1990. Argument over a woman: Science searches for the mother of us all. *Discover* 11(8): 52–59.

Sillen, A. and C. K. Brain. April 1990. Old flame: Burned bones provide evidence of an early use of fire. *Natural History,* pp. 6–10.

Singer, R. and J. Wymer. 1982. *The Middle Stone Age at Klasies River Mouth in South Africa.* Chicago: University of Chicago Press.

Skelton, R. R., H. M. McHenry, and G. M. Drawhorn. 1986. Phylogenetic analysis of early hominids. *Current Anthropology* 27: 21–43.

Smith, B. 1989. Origins of agriculture in Eastern North America. *Science* 246: 1566–70.

Smith, F. H. 1984. Fossil hominid from the Upper Pleistocene of central Europe and the origins of modern Europeans. In *The Origins of Modern Humans: A World Survey of the Fossil Evidence,* eds. F. H. Smith and F. Spencer, pp. 137–210. New York: Liss.

Smith, F. H. and F. Spencer (eds.) 1984. *The Origins*

*of Modern Humans: A World Survey of the Fossil Evidence.* New York: Liss.

Smith, F. H., A. B. Falsetti, and S. M. Donnelly. 1989. Modern human origins. *Yearbook of Physical Anthropology* 32: 35–68.

Smith, J. M. 1984. Science and myth. *Natural History* 93(11): 10–24.

Smuts, B. 1985. *Sex and Friendship in Baboons.* Hawthorne, N.Y.: Aldine de Gruyter.

Solecki, R. S. 1971. *Shanidar: The First Flower People.* New York: Knopf.

Solheim, W. 1972. An earlier agricultural revolution. *Scientific American* 226: 34–41.

Sowunmi, M. A. 1985. The beginnings of agriculture in West Africa: Botanical evidence. *Current Anthropology* 26: 127–29.

Spencer, F. 1990. *Piltdown: A Scientific Forgery.* New York: Oxford University Press.

Stebbins, G. L. 1982. *Darwin to DNA: Molecules to Humanity.* San Francisco: Freeman.

Stoneking, M. and R. L. Cann. 1989. African origin of human mitochondrial DNA. In *The Human Revolution: Behavioural and Biological Perspectives in the Origins of Modern Humans,* eds. P. Mellars and C. Stringer, pp. 17–30. Princeton, N.J.: Princeton University Press.

Straus, W. L. and A. J. E. Cave. 1957. Pathology and the posture of Neandertal Man. *Quarterly Review of Biology* 32: 348–63.

Stringer, C. B. 1974. A multivariate study of the Petralona skull. *Journal of Human Evolution* 3: 397–404.

———. 1988. The dates of Eden. *Nature* 331: 565–66.

———. 1989. The origin of early modern humans: A comparison of the European and non-European evidence. In *The Human Revolution: Behavioural and Biological Perspectives in the Origins of Modern Humans,* eds. P. Mellars and C. Stringer, pp. 232–44. Princeton, N.J.: Princeton University Press.

———. 1990. The emergence of modern humans. *Scientific American* 263: 98–104.

Stringer, C. B. and P. Andrews. 1988. Genetic and fossil evidence for the origin of modern humans. *Science* 239: 1263–68.

Stringer, C. B., F. C. Howell, and J. K. Melentis. 1979. The significance of the fossil hominid skull from Petralona, Greece. *Journal of Archaeological Science* 6: 235–253.

Stringer, C. B., R. Grün, H. P. Schwarcz, and P. Goldberg. 1989. ESR dates for the hominid burial site of Es Skhul in Israel. *Nature* 338: 756–58.

Stringer, C. B., J. J. Hublin, and B. Vandermeersch. 1984. The origin of anatomically modern humans in western Europe. In *The Origins of Modern Humans: A World Survey of the Fossil Evidence,* eds. F. H. Smith and F. Spencer, pp. 51–136. New York: Liss.

Struever, S. (ed.) 1971. *Prehistoric Agriculture.* New York: Natural History Press.

Strum, S. 1987. *Almost Human.* New York: Random House.

Stuart, G. E. 1972. Who were the "mound builders"? *National Geographic* 142(6): 783–801.

Susman, R. 1988. New postcranial remains from Swartkrans and their bearing on the functional morphology and behavior of *Paranthropus robustus.* In *Evolutionary History of the "Robust" Australopithecines,* ed. F. E. Grine, New York: Aldine de Gruyter.

Szabo, B. and D. Collins. 1975. Ages of fossil bones from British interglacial sites. *Nature* 254: 680–682.

Szalay, F. S. and E. Delson. 1979. *Evolutionary History of the Primates.* New York: Academic Press.

Tainter, J. A. 1988. *The Collapse of Complex Societies.* Cambridge, Eng.: Cambridge University.

Tanner, N. M. 1981. *On Becoming Human.* Cambridge, Mass.: Cambridge University Press.

Tappen, N. C. 1985. The dentition of the "Old Man" of La Chapelle-aux-Saints and inferences concerning Neandertal behavior. *American Journal of Physical Anthropology* 67: 43–50.

Taylour, L. W. 1983. *The Mycenaeans.* London: Thames and Hudson.

Thomas, D. H. 1979. *Archaeology.* New York: Holt, Rinehart & Winston.

Thorne, A. G. and M. H. Wolpoff. April 1992. The multiregional evolution of humans. *Scientific American,* pp. 76–83.

Tobias, P. V. 1980. *Australopithecus afarensis* and *A. africanus.* Critique and an alternative hypothesis. *Palaeontologica Africana* 23: 1–17.

———. 1987. The brain of *Homo habilis:* A new level of organization in cerebral evolution. *Journal of Human Evolution* 16: 741–61.

Todd, I. A. 1976. *Çatal Hüyük in Perspective.* Menlo Park, Calif.: Benjamin/Cummings.

Trinkaus, E. (ed.) 1983a. Neanderthal postcrania and the adaptive shift to modern humans. In *The Mousterian Legacy,* pp. 165–200. Oxford: British Archaeological Reports, International Series, 164.

———. 1983b. *The Shanidar Neandertals.* New York: Academic Press.

———. 1984a. Western Asia. In *The Origins of Modern Humans: A World Survey of the Fossil Evidence,* eds. F. H. Smith and F. Spencer, pp. 251–94. New York: Liss.

———. 1984b. Neanderthal pubic morphology and gestation length. *Current Anthropology* 25:509–14.

———. 1985. Pathology and the posture of the La Chapelle-aux-Saints Neandertal. *American Journal of Physical Anthropology* 67: 19–41.

———. 1986. The Neandertals and modern human origins. *Annual Review of Anthropology* 15: 193–218.

———. (ed.) 1988. The Upper Pleistocene transition. In *The Emergence of Modern Humans: Biocultural Adaptations in the Later Pleistocene,* pp. 42–66. New York: Cambridge University Press.

Trinkaus, E. and D. D. Thompson. 1987. Femoral diaphyseal histophometric age determinators for the Shanidar 3, 4, 5 and 6 Neandertals and Neandertal longevity. *American Journal of Physical Anthropology* 72: 123–29.

Trinkaus, E. and I. Villemeur. 1991. Mechanical advantages of the Neandertal thumb in flexion: A test of an hypothesis. *American Journal of Physical Anthropology* 84: 249–260.

Tyler, E. B. 1871. *Primitive Culture: Part I—The Origins of Culture.* 1958 ed. New York: Harper and Brothers.

Ucko, P. and G. W. Dimbleby. 1969. *The Domestication and Exploitation of Plants and Animals.* Chicago: Aldine.

Unger-Hamilton, R. 1989. The epi-Paleolithic southern Levant and the origins of cultivation. *Current Anthropology* 30: 88–103.

Valladas, H., J. L. Reyss, J. L. Joron, G. Valladas, O. Bar-Yosef, and B. Vadermeersch. 1988. Thermoluminescence dating of Mousterian "Proto-Cro-Magnon" remains from Israel and the origin of modern man. *Nature* 331: 614–16.

Villa, P. 1982. Conjoinable pieces and site formation processes. *American Antiquity* 47: 276–90.

Vrba, E. S. 1988. Late Pleistocene climatic events and hominid evolution. In *Evolutionary History of the "Robust" Australopithecines,* ed. F. E. Grine, New York: Aldine de Gruyter.

Walker, A. C. and R. E. Leakey. 1978. The East Turkana hominids. *Scientific American* 239: 54–66.

Walker, A., R. E. Leakey, J. M. Harris, and F. H. Brown. 1986. 2.5 million year old *Australopithecus boisei* from west of Lake Turkana, Kenya. *Nature* 322: 517–22.

Warren, P. 1975. *The Aegean Civilizations.* Oxford, Eng.: Elsevier Phaidon.

———. 1987. Crete: The Minoans and their gods. In *Origins: The Roots of European Civilisation,* ed. B. Cunliffe, pp. 30–41. Chicago: Dorsey Press.

Watson, J. D. 1968. *The Double Helix.* New York: Athenaeum.

Weaver, K. 1985. The search for our ancestors. *National Geographic* 168(5): 560–623.

Weaver, M. P. 1972. *The Aztecs, the Maya, and Their Predecessors: Archaeology of Mesoamerica.* New York: Seminar Press.

Weaver, R. F. 1984. Changing life's genetic blueprint. *National Geographic* 166(6): 818–47.

Weiner, J. S. 1955. *The Piltdown Forgery.* London: Oxford Press.

Weiner, J. S. and B. G. Campbell. 1964. The taxonomic status of the Swanscombe skull. In *The Swanscombe Skull: A Survey of Research on a Pleistocene Site,* ed. C. Ovey, pp. 175–209. Royal Institute of Great Britain and Ireland, Occasional Paper 20.

Wheat, J. B. 1972. *The Olsen–Chubbuck Site: A Paleo-Indian Bison Kill.* Salt Lake City: Memoirs of the Society for American Archaeology, No. 26.

Wheatly, P. 1971. *The Pivot of the Four Quarters.* Chicago: Aldine.

White, P. T. 1982. The temples of Angkor: Ancient glory in stone. *National Geographic* 161(5): 552–89.

White, R. 1982. Rethinking the Middle-Upper Paleolithic transition. *Current Anthropology* 23(2): 169–92.

White, T. 1986. Cut marks on the Bodo cranium: A case of prehistoric defleshing. *American Journal of Physical Anthropology* 69: 503–509.

White, T. D. and P. A. Folkens. 1991. *Human Osteology.* San Diego: Academic Press.

Whittle, A. 1985. *Neolithic Europe: A Survey.* Cambridge, Mass.: Cambridge University Press.

Wilmsen, E. 1974. *Lindenmeier: A Pleistocene Hunting Society.* New York: Harper & Row.

Wilson, A. C. and R. L. Cann. April 1992. The recent African genesis of humans. *Scientific American,* pp. 68–73.

Wing, E. 1977. Animal domestication in the Andes. In *Origins of Agriculture,* ed. C. A. Reed, pp. 837–60. The Hague: Mouton.

Wittfogel, K. 1957. *Oriental Despotism: A Comparative Study of Total Power.* New Haven, Conn.: Yale University Press.

Wolpoff, M. 1980a. *Paleoanthropology.* New York: Knopf.

———. 1980b. Cultural remains of Middle Pleistocene hominids. *Journal of Human Evolution* 9: 339–58.

———. 1984. Evolution in *Homo erectus:* The question of stasis. *Paleobiology* 10: 389–406.

———. 1988. The place of the Neandertals in human evolution. In *The Emergence of Modern Humans: Biocultural Adaptations in the Later Pleistocene,* ed. E. Trinkaus, pp. 97–141. New York: Cambridge University Press.

———. 1989. Multiregional evolution: The fossil alternative to Eden. *The Human Revolution: Behavioural and Biological Perspectives in the Origins of Modern Humans,* eds. P. Mellars and C. Stringer, pp. 62–108. Princeton, N.J.: Princeton University Press.

Wolpoff, M., X. Z. Wu, and A. G. Thorpe. 1984. Modern *Homo sapiens* origins: A general theory of hominid evolution involving the fossil evidence from East Asia. In *The Origins of Modern Humans: A World Survey of the Fossil Evidence,* eds. F. H. Smith and F. Spencer, pp. 411–84. New York: Liss.

Woo Ju-Kang (Wu Rukang). 1966. The skull of Lantian Man. *Current Anthropology* 7: 83–86.

Wood, B. A. 1984. The origin of *Homo erectus. Courier Forschungsinstitut Seckenberg* 69: 99–111.

Woodhead, A. D. and B. J. Barnhart. 1988. *Biotechnology and the Human Genome.* New York: Plenum.

Wright, G. 1971. Origins of food production in Southwestern Asia: A survey of ideas. *Current Anthropology* 12: 447–77.

Wu Rukang (Woo Ju-kang). 1985. New Chinese *Homo erectus* and recent work at Zhoukoudian. In *Ancestors: The Hard Evidence,* ed. E. Delson, pp. 245–48. New York: Liss.

Wu Rukang (Woo Ju-kang) and S. Lin. 1983. Peking Man. *Scientific American* 248: 86–94.

Yarnell, R. 1971. Early woodland plant remains and the question of cultivation. In *Prehistoric Agriculture,* ed. S. Struever, pp. 550–56. New York: Natural History Press.

———. 1977. Native plant husbandry north of Mexico. In *Origins of Agriculture,* ed. C. A. Reed, pp. 861–78. The Hague: Mouton.

Zihlman, A. 1979. Gathering and the hominid adaptation. In *Female Hierarchies,* eds. L. Tiger and H. M. Fowler. Chicago: Beresford Book Service.

# INDEX